W9-CTY-819

Israel in the Middle East

THE TAUBER INSTITUTE FOR THE STUDY OF EUROPEAN JEWRY SERIES

Jehuda Reinharz, General Editor
Sylvia Fuks Fried, Associate Editor

The Tauber Institute Series is dedicated to publishing compelling and innovative approaches to the study of modern European Jewish history, thought, culture, and society. The series has a special interest in original works related to the Holocaust and its aftermath, as well as studies of Zionism and the history, society, and culture of the State of Israel. The series is published by the Tauber Institute for the Study of European Jewry—established by a gift to Brandeis University from Dr. Laszlo N. Tauber—and the Jacob and Libby Goodman Institute for the Study of Zionism and Israel, and is supported, in part, by the Tauber Foundation.

For the complete list of books in this series, please see www.upne.com and www.upne.com/series/TAUB.html

Itamar Rabinovich and Jehuda Reinharz, editors
Israel in the Middle East: Documents and Readings on Society, Politics, and Foreign Relations, Pre-1948 to the Present

Christian Wiese
The Life and Thought of Hans Jonas: Jewish Dimensions

Eugene R. Sheppard
Leo Strauss and the Politics of Exile: The Making of a Political Philosopher

Samuel Moyn
A Holocaust Controversy: The Treblinka Affair in Postwar France

Margalit Shilo
Princess or Prisoner? Jewish Women in Jerusalem, 1840–1914

Haim Be'er
Feathers

Immanuel Etkes
The Besht: Magician, Mystic, and Leader

Avraham Grossman
Pious and Rebellious: Jewish Women in Medieval Europe

Ivan Davidson Kalmar and Derek J. Penslar, editors
Orientalism and the Jews

Iris Parush
Reading Jewish Women: Marginality and Modernization in Nineteenth-Century Eastern European Jewish Society

Thomas C. Hubka
Resplendent Synagogue: Architecture and Worship in an Eighteenth-Century Polish Community

Uzi Rebhun and Chaim I. Waxman, editors
Jews in Israel: Contemporary Social and Cultural Patterns

Gideon Shimoni
Community and Conscience: The Jews in Apartheid South Africa

Haim Be'er
The Pure Element of Time

ChaeRan Y. Freeze
Jewish Marriage and Divorce in Imperial Russia

Yehudit Hendel
Small Change: A Collection of Stories

Ezra Mendelsohn
Painting a People: Maurycy Gottlieb and Jewish Art

Alan Mintz, editor
Reading Hebrew Literature: Critical Discussions of Six Modern Texts

Mark A. Raider and Miriam B. Raider-Roth, editors
The Plough Woman: Records of the Pioneer Women of Palestine

Walter Laqueur
Generation Exodus: The Fate of Young Jewish Refugees from Nazi Germany

Renée Poznanski
Jews in France during World War II

Jehuda Reinharz
Chaim Weizmann: The Making of a Zionist Leader

Jehuda Reinharz
Chaim Weizmann: The Making of a Statesman

Israel in the Middle East

DOCUMENTS AND READINGS ON SOCIETY, POLITICS, AND FOREIGN RELATIONS, PRE-1948 TO THE PRESENT

SECOND EDITION

Edited by
Itamar Rabinovich and Jehuda Reinharz

Brandeis University Press
Waltham, Massachusetts

PUBLISHED BY UNIVERSITY PRESS OF NEW ENGLAND
HANOVER AND LONDON

Brandeis University Press
Published by University Press of New England,
One Court Street, Lebanon, NH 03766
www.upne.com
© 2008 by Brandeis University Press
Printed in the United States of America

5 4 3 2 1

All rights reserved. No part of this book may be reproduced in any form or by any electronic or mechanical means, including storage and retrieval systems, without permission in writing from the publisher, except by a reviewer, who may quote brief passages in a review. Members of educational institutions and organizations wishing to photocopy any of the work for classroom use, or authors and publishers who would like to obtain permission for any of the material in the work, should contact Permissions, University Press of New England, One Court Street, Lebanon, NH 03766.

LIBRARY OF CONGRESS CATALOGING-IN-PUBLICATION DATA
Israel in the Middle East : documents and readings on society, politics, and foreign relations, pre-1948 to the present / [edited] by Itamar Rabinovich, Jehuda Reinharz.—2nd ed.
p. cm.—(Tauber Institute for the Study of European Jewry series)
ISBN-13: 978–0–87451–962–4 (paperback : alk. paper)
ISBN-10: 0–87451–962–4 (pbk. : alk. paper)
1. Israel—History—Sources.
I. Rabinovich, Itamar, 1942– II. Reinharz, Jehuda.
DS126.5.I784 2007
956.94—dc22 2007034270

University Press of New England is a member of the Green Press Initiative.
The paper used in this book meets their minimum requirement for recycled paper.

This publication has been made possible
through the generous support of
S. Daniel Abraham
and
Arnon Adar

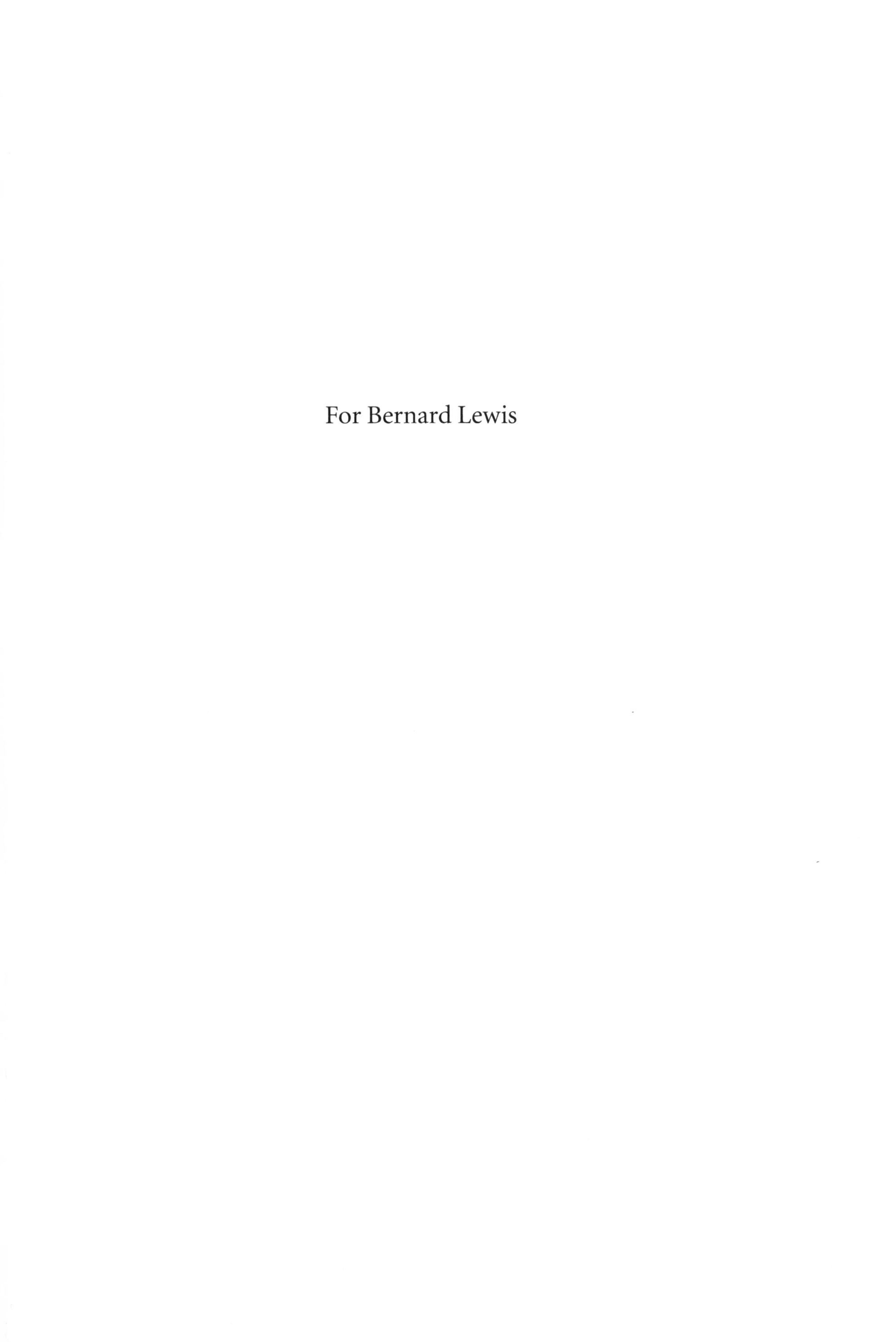

For Bernard Lewis

Contents

Maps

Preface

The purpose of this volume is to provide the English-reading public with convenient access to the most significant documents relating to the State of Israel, from the Zionist movement through Israel's domestic politics and foreign policies up to 2006.

The first edition of this collection was published in 1984. We believed then that a collection of primary sources is essential in a field that engendered so many diverse, and at times adverse, perspectives. What was needed in the early 1980s is in even greater demand today. In the wake of the recent round of Israeli-Palestinian and Israeli-Hezbollah violence academics are called to offer a comprehensive picture of a complicated reality in a field mired with debate and high emotion. It is our hope that this collection will make the task easier.

This second edition not only updates the 1984 book but also addresses the renewed interest in issues relating to Israel's inception. We added a new chapter that covers the pre-state period, beginning with the early days of modern Zionism in the 1880s until Israel's establishment in 1948. We further added a number of documents that reflect the Palestinian perspective in other chapters and eras.

The second edition reflects a broader understanding of modern Israel. Voices that were hardly recognized when the first edition was published, such as a gendered perspective, are now fully present in the academic comprehension of Israel and are duly covered in this collection.

Several criteria determined our selection of materials. Whenever possible we chose a primary source, such as memoirs, treaties, legal texts, exchanges of letters, parliamentary debates, diaries, speeches, and the like. For a number of issues a single primary source could not by itself illuminate the matter under consideration. In such cases a secondary source—scholarly or journalistic—was chosen. A special effort was made to diversify the nature and scope of the sources. These materials were selected from Israeli, Arab, and American records, including government archives, as well as journalistic accounts. The range of materials has not been limited to political and diplomatic history but includes economic, cultural, legal, and social material as well.

The volume consists of eight chronological divisions, 1882 to 2006; maps; appendices that include population and political data; and a glossary of names and organizations referred to with some frequency in the text. Each document is preceded by an explanatory headnote and is annotated as necessary. Major figures, events, and organizations are usually identified at first mention or in the glossary. Documents are cross-referenced. Our interpolations in the documents appear in brackets; all interpolations appearing in the original documents are in parentheses. Italics appearing in original documents are preserved. Transliterations of Hebrew and Arabic names and terms have been standardized throughout; where events such as wars are known by several names, we have sought to standardize them as well. Some of the documents were originally written in English; others were translated from Hebrew and Arabic especially for this volume.

Many of our colleagues and friends in academic and public life generously gave their permission to reprint articles or chapters from their books. In some instances, as no written material was available, they prepared original contributions for this book. All of these individuals are acknowledged in source notes.

This new edition would not have been possible without the assistance and expertise of many individuals. Kenneth Stein contributed significantly to the effort to develop an expanded edition. David Myers, Derek Penslar, and S. Ilan Troen offered valuable suggestions on the kinds of documents that would prove useful to students and professors alike. We wish to acknowledge our research assistants, Efrat Harel, Gili Gurel, Amaryah Orenstein, and Rachel Fish, for diligently assembling documents and assisting with the scholarly apparatus. We particularly appreciate the dedication and excellent work of Ehud Eiran whose depth of knowledge of the subject made him an ideal assistant editor. Adele Sage and Meechal Hoffman thoughtfully read an early draft of the manuscript and helped us avoid numerous errors, while Jennifer Kachel, Dorit Ingber, Adam Curley, and Sophie Azeroual made sure we had enough copies of the manuscript to go around. Miriam Hoffman, Senior Program Administrator of the Tauber Institute for the Study of European Jewry at Brandeis University, skillfully and resourcefully secured permissions and kept track of the various versions of the manuscript. Robert Grogg shaped a most helpful glossary of names and organizations, and followed Israeli news to be sure all the facts were up-to-date. Ann Hofstra Grogg, who copyedited the first edition many years ago, proved once again to be a masterful editor. Her meticulous treatment of every document and her creative input are reflected throughout the work. Sylvia Fuks Fried, Associate Editor of the Tauber Series, managed this enormous undertaking and was attentive to every detail even as she helped shape its broad sweep. We express our thanks also to the editors and staff of the University Press of New England and to Dr. John Hose, governor of Brandeis University Press, for their steadfast commitment to this project.

The efforts of all these individuals were supported through funds provided by Brandeis University and Tel Aviv University. Arnon Adar stepped in at an early stage to provide generous funding to enable us to include more rather than fewer documents. Danny Abraham recognized the need in American college and university classrooms for an affordable textbook that offered a comprehensive view of a complex reality. His generous and timely support made our effort to meet that goal possible. We hope this book meets their expectations.

I. R. & J. R.

Introduction

Scholars characteristically demarcate Israel's history by its wars. These wars are turning points not only in Israel's foreign policy but also in the country's internal development. Following this practice, the chronological framework of this book's treatment of Israel's domestic and foreign issues is based on a division into seven chapters with a postscript.

1882–1948

The 1881 pogroms in Russia and antisemitism in Western Europe solidified the rise of Zionism, a modern Jewish national movement, in the last two decades of the nineteenth century. Zionism was further politicized through the debates within European Jewish communities regarding the most effective solutions to the challenges facing Jews and Judaism.

By the early years of the twentieth century, the young movement had an institutional framework to support the establishment of a national territorial home for Jews in Palestine (though other locations were considered at first). The political effort culminated with international acceptance of Zionist aspirations following the First World War. First the British, who were entrusted with the Mandate for Palestine following the demise of the Ottoman Empire, and then the League of Nations agreed to make Palestine a "Jewish National Home."

Alongside the political efforts on the international arena, the emergence of a modern Jewish national movement inspired waves of Jewish immigrants to Palestine beginning in 1882. As opposed to past movements of Jews to Palestine, the Zionist immigrants established new settlements, and once the British gained control over the land, created a set of Jewish political institutions.

The indigenous population grew increasingly concerned with these developments and turned to violence in 1920, 1929, and 1936. Arab resistance and British political calculations curtailed British support for a future independent Jewish state, and the British government placed restrictions on Jewish immigration. Following the Second World War and growing tensions regarding the future of Palestine, the United Nations reaffirmed the international commitment to the creation of a Jewish state in Palestine. The U.N. also called for the establishment of a Palestinian state. Nevertheless, the Arab world and the local Palestinian population rejected the U.N.'s two-state resolution, and in late 1947 hostilities resumed between Jews and Arabs.

1948–1956

This phase began with the first full-scale Arab-Israeli war (the War of Independence, from Israel's perspective) and ended with the Sinai Campaign of 1956. During these years the State of Israel was proclaimed, established, and recognized, the institutions of the state and a governmental structure were formed or transformed from their pre-state versions, social and economic patterns were set, and great numbers of immigrants from Europe and the Islamic world arrived and settled. The enormity and pace of these changes made the early years of Israel's statehood highly turbulent. In addition, the period was characterized by debates over the nature of the political system, the relation of state and religion, the need for a constitution, the question of reparations from Germany, and other issues.

Israel's international position during this period, as in later years, was determined primarily by the severity and salience of the Arab-Israeli conflict. This relation was not immediately apparent. The War of Independence ended with armistice agreements and attempts at reconciliation and peacemaking. But by 1950 it became clear that the conflict between the Arabs and the Israelis was deep and complex and intertwined with numerous regional and international political issues.

During this period Israel gradually drew away from the Soviet Union and became increasingly tied to and dependent on the West. The Western powers, however, were interested in tying the Arab world to a pro-Western alliance, and Israel found itself in the early 1950s at the height of its international isolation. This isolation diminished in 1955 with the emergence of the French-Israeli alliance. The rise of Nasserism, the radicalization of Arab politics, and the Soviet-Western rivalry all exacerbated the Arab-Israeli conflict, which culminated in the second Arab-Israeli war, the Sinai Campaign of 1956.

1956–1967

Following the Sinai Campaign there was a gradual improvement in the economic condition and standard of living in Israel. The austerity regimen of the early 1950s ended, and a variety of development schemes were inaugurated. The years of sound economic growth and relative prosperity ended with the recession of 1965–67.

In the country's domestic politics the most important development of the period was the demise of David Ben-Gurion's leadership. Ben-Gurion had dominated the Jewish community in Palestine since the late 1920s, but his power and influence began to decline in the mid-1950s. He retired in 1963 but continued to affect the politics of the state and his party under his successor, Levi Eshkol. Ben-Gurion's conflict with his own party's leadership reflected a changing of the guard in Mapai, the major political force in Israel. The changes within Mapai and the Labor movement were, in turn, related to a diminution of the chief dichotomy of Israeli public life: the Labor movement and Mapai on the one hand, and the nationalist Right, led by the Herut movement, on the other.

The social and economic stabilization within Israel during these years was matched by the consolidation of Israel's regional and international position. First, the international isolation that characterized the early 1950s gave way to a virtual alliance with France and improved relations with Britain and the United States. This development, however, came at the cost of growing friction in Israel's relationship with the Soviet Union. Second, while Israel's cooperation with Britain and France in the Sinai Campaign damaged its relationship with the Third World, it also endowed it with a new stature. Ben-Gurion was able to convert this prestige into an improved regional position through the development of the "periphery orientation"—a semialliance with other non-Arab, anti-Soviet states such as Iran, Turkey, and Ethiopia. Finally, Israel's military success in the Sinai Campaign and the security arrangements made in its aftermath served as a deterrent and helped stabilize Arab-Israeli relations for approximately ten years.

This stability diminished in the mid-1960s as the Arab-Israeli conflict and the international conflict in the region were once more exacerbated. Among the issues at stake were the waters of the

Jordan, the reemergence of an autonomous Palestinian national movement, border clashes with Syria, and conflicts between moderate and radical Arab states and their respective superpower patrons. These culminated in the crisis of May 1967 and the next month in the Six-Day War.

1967–1973

The events of May–June 1967—the May crisis, the decisive military victory, the capture of territories from Syria, Jordan, and Egypt—constitute a watershed in the domestic and external history of Israel.

Domestically, the formation of the National Unity government as a result of the May crisis brought the Herut movement for the first time into national leadership and power. Previously Ben-Gurion had deliberately and successfully kept the Herut movement on the outside. The movement's participation in the government (June 1967–August 1970) was an important aspect of the process that enhanced the nationalist Right's power, legitimacy, and respectability and culminated in its electoral victory ten years later.

Israel's postwar control over all of Palestine west of the Jordan, all of the Sinai, and a major portion of the Golan Heights turned the debate over the future of these territories and Jerusalem into the major issue of Israel's domestic and foreign politics. The debate has not been confined to the narrower questions of control and final disposition of these territories but addresses a variety of related issues such as the essence of Zionism, the allocation of resources, and the transformation of religious Zionism.

The Six-Day War terminated the economic recession of the mid-1960s and ushered in a boom period marked by an accelerated inflationary pace and growing political tensions among ethnic, social, and economic groups. The partial overlapping of socioeconomic disparities and communal ethnic differences led to occasional outbursts of frustration, particularly by Israelis of North African descent. In the 1970s such tensions were aggravated by the increased immigration from the Soviet Union. The special privileges extended to this group as well as to new immigrants from other countries who came in the 1970s irritated underprivileged groups who had arrived in the 1950s and were absorbed in the austere conditions of those years.

Externally, the Arab-Israeli conflict came to assume a progressively central place in Israel's policies. In the early 1960s the development of Israel's relations with Africa and Latin America was an important concern of Israel's foreign policy. After 1967 these interests were submerged by the special considerations arising as a consequence of the Six-Day War. The Israeli government sought to use its military victory and control of former Arab territories to achieve a settlement of the Arab-Israeli conflict. Over time an interest in retaining at least some of these territories developed. The Arab states, as a rule, sought to regain the lost territories without giving up their pre-1967 stance in the conflict. All Arab efforts to dislodge Israel from the territories, first through the United Nations and then through the War of Attrition, proved futile, and a stalemate ensued until 1973.

With this stalemate Israel found it increasingly difficult to obtain international support for its position. The Soviet Union and the Eastern bloc countries severed diplomatic relations with Israel immediately after the Six-Day War. Later the Arab and particularly Palestinian position received increasing support in Third World and then Western countries. The initially favorable reception accorded to Israel's benign rule in the West Bank and Gaza was gradually replaced by criticism of what was termed Israel's intransigence and suppression of a Palestinian national movement.

Israel's ability to withstand Arab and Soviet pressures during this period can be explained largely by the backing and support of the United States. The United States did not agree with all aspects of Israeli policy but accepted its fundamental premise, that—unlike the situation following the Sinai Campaign—Israel should not relinquish the captured territories without a solid and proper settlement of the Arab-Israeli conflict. In addition, as Soviet-U.S. rivalry in the Middle East stiffened in the late 1960s, Israel played an important role as a powerful and reliable American ally.

The sense of American-Israeli partnership was particularly strong in the years 1970–73 following the two countries' successful cooperation during the Jordanian crisis of September 1970. But by 1973 a reassessment of U.S. policies in the Middle East was under way. Egypt's turn toward the West in 1972 and the oil crisis—of both supply and cost—created new opportunities and new constraints for the United States, but their full impact was felt only after the Yom Kippur War in October 1973.

1973–1982

The Yom Kippur War ended ambiguously. A cease-fire was imposed by the United States as Israel was about to defeat the Egyptian army, yet Egypt controlled most of the Suez Canal. The Egyptians and Syrians had enjoyed military success at the outset of the surprise war. Israel had suffered heavy casualties and loss of matériel and had to resort to an American airlift.

These failures expedited the Labor movement's decline, and in the elections of 1977 Menahem Begin, the leader of the Likud alignment, was elected prime minister. Less than two years later Begin was the first Israeli prime minister to sign a peace treaty with an Arab country, Egypt. Paradoxically, though, the peace treaty—the chief goal of Israeli policy since independence—met with little enthusiasm, internationally or regionally, and produced domestic difficulties in both Israel and Egypt.

In 1981, Likud won a second victory and a year later led Israel to a war in Lebanon, where Israeli forces would remain until 2000. Initially Israel sought to solve its security problem in southern Lebanon. But the government, moved primarily by Defense Minister Ariel Sharon, tried at the same time to bring about a whole other set of outcomes, most of all regime change in Beirut. These proved too ambitious. Israeli fatalities and the loss of internal legitimacy for the war, as well as Syria's ability to curtail Israel's strategy, finally led to an Israeli partial withdrawal in 1985.

One significant outcome of the war was the PLO's forced evacuation of Beirut. Combined with Syria's attempts to bring the organization under its firm authority, this evacuation resulted in a serious decline in the PLO's standing. By 1983 Begin resigned, and a third Likud government was formed by Yitzhak Shamir.

1982–1991

Ironically, the Begin government's debacle in Lebanon and its aftermath—Menahem Begin's resignation, Ariel Sharon's removal, and the beginning of the War of Attrition in Lebanon—failed to produce a shift of power in Israeli politics. The Israeli public's disenchantment with the Likud did not lead to a renewal of support for Labor. The result was the deadlocked elections of 1984 (with a small edge for Labor and its allies) and in 1988 (with a small edge for Likud and its partners). Two National Unity governments were formed. The first was predicated on "rotation" with Shimon Peres serving as prime minister for the first two years and Yitzhak Shamir in the second two. In 1988 the rotation arrangement was not repeated. Shamir became prime minister, and Labor joined the coalition, with Yitzhak Rabin holding the post of defense minister and Peres becoming finance minister. The partnership broke down in 1990, and Israel was governed by a right-wing coalition for the next two years.

National Unity provided stability and effective governance. As prime minister, Peres was able to defeat a spiraling inflation and to withdraw troops from the Beirut area to southern Lebanon. But consensus also meant an inability to move forward in the Israeli-Arab peace process. Israeli foreign and national security policies during the rest of the decade revolved around three issues.

First, in Lebanon the Israeli-Palestinian conflict was replaced by conflict with the newly mobilized Shiite community. Lebanon's Shi'is were led by Amal (essentially a pro-Syrian militia) and subsequently by Hezbollah (practically an arm of the Iranian regime). With the Shiite community's mobilization, a new weapon was introduced to the Middle Eastern arena—suicide bombing.

Second, the war in Lebanon resulted in a major defeat for Yasir Arafat and the PLO, who were banished to Tunis. But it took less than five years for a more significant turning point to occur—the outbreak of an *intifada* in December 1987. It was a spontaneous development, but the first manifestation of massive popular resistance to Israel confronted the Israeli public and political system with the need to make the fundamental choices it had evaded for the previous twenty years.

Third, in the region's eastern flank a seven-years hiatus was provided by the Iran-Iraq War (1980–1988), but the war's end and Iraq's victory placed Saddam Hussein in a position to use the military machine he had built in order to project power beyond Iraq's borders. He decided to occupy Kuwait and threaten Saudi Arabia, thus bringing about the Gulf crisis and the first Persian Gulf War in 1991.

Israel was attacked by Iraqi scud missiles. Despite the damage to its deterrence, it chose not to respond and not to play into Saddam Hussein's hands by adding an Arab-Israeli dimension to a war defined by Iraqi, inter-Arab, and international issues. Israel's patience was handsomely rewarded by the destruction of Saddam's military machine and by the decline in the fortunes of the PLO and Arafat, who had allied himself with Iraq. The PLO's weakness facilitated the George H. W. Bush administration's decision to launch in the aftermath of the Gulf War a new Israeli-Arab peace process. The PLO was denied an independent position and had to settle on the formation of a unified Jordanian-Palestinian delegation. This arrangement was but one of the successes of U.S. Secretary of State James Baker, who put together the Middle East Peace Conference. Meeting in Madrid in October 1991, the conference launched the single most ambitious effort to resolve the Arab-Israeli conflict.

1991–2000

The Madrid Process, as it came to be known, was predicated on a two-pronged strategy—three tracks of bilateral negotiations (between Israeli and Syrian, Lebanese, and Jordanian-Palestinian delegations) and five multilateral working groups dealing with such final status issues as refugees, water, and the environment. But after a festive opening session in Madrid and several rounds of negotiations, by mid-1992 it became clear that the new process was growing stale. It took Yitzhak Rabin's election as Israel's new prime minister to introduce new life into the Madrid Process.

Rabin's return to power fifteen years after his resignation unfolded through two phases. In February 1992 the Labor Party's membership decided that a centrist candidate with distinctive security credentials stood a better chance of defeating Likud and chose Rabin over Peres. The decision was, indeed, vindicated. A few months later when Rabin won the national election, albeit by a small margin, he had persuaded the Israeli electorate that he was more likely to provide an effective response to the lingering crisis with the Palestinians and to better manage Israel's relationship with the United States.

Prime Minister Rabin was determined to change Israel's order of priorities—to effect a breakthrough in the peace process and to channel resources away from the settlement project in the West Bank and Gaza into Israel proper. For about a year he sought a breakthrough on either the Syrian or Palestinian track of the negotiations. In August 1993 he chose to endorse the Oslo Agreement with the PLO over the ambiguous prospect of an agreement with Hafez al-Assad. The Oslo Accords and

Washington Accords created a framework for resolving the Israeli-Palestinian conflict, provided for mutual recognition, and laid the groundwork for the establishment of a provisional Palestinian Authority in much of the West Bank and the Gaza Strip. This breakthrough led the way for the scintillating events of the next two years: a peace agreement between Israel and Jordan, semidiplomatic relations with several Arab states, and a significant degree of Israeli-Arab normalization.

But there was also a dark side to the Madrid (or Oslo) Process—radical Islamic terrorism, radical right-wing Israeli terrorism, failure to make peace with Syria and ongoing violence in southern Lebanon, Arab state unhappiness with Israel's new position in the region, and continuing competition and conflict between Israel and the PLO. By the end of 1995 the dark side had triumphed with Rabin's assassination.

Rabin was succeeded by Peres, who staked his prestige (and the 1996 election) on a swift negotiation with Syria. The negotiation collapsed in March 1996 and Peres was dealt a still deadlier blow by a surge of Palestinian terrorism. Peres lost the 1996 election to the Likud's young leader, Benjamin Netanyahu, the first Israeli prime minister chosen in a direct election.

Netanyahu won on a complex platform. He was a right-wing critic of the Oslo Accords but sought the support of centrist voters by promising to keep them. During a tenure of nearly three years he vacillated between acting and agitating against Yasir Arafat and the Palestinian Authority and a more pragmatic policy of implementing the Oslo Accords. It was the signing of the Wye River Memorandum in October 1998 that led the radical right wing to remove its support from Netanyahu and put an end to his turbulent tenure.

In May 1999 Israel's second and last direct election was won by Ehud Barak. His tenure lasted less than two years and was marked primarily by the collapse of the peace process. In March 2000 an abortive meeting between President Bill Clinton and Hafez al-Assad in Geneva ended a ten-month effort to revive and conclude the Israeli-Syrian negotiations. Barak, who had preferred a "Syria First" policy, shifted his efforts to an accelerated negotiation with the Palestinians. By the summer of 2000 he adopted an "end game" strategy and persuaded President Clinton to convene a summit at Camp David in order to seek a final status agreement.

The failure of the Camp David conference is and will probably remain a controversial issue, but there is no denying the fact that Barak broke the Israeli consensus and offered far-reaching concessions and that Yasir Arafat was not willing to sign a final status agreement on those terms or on the terms offered in Clinton's "bridging proposals" in December.

In September 2000 the Palestinian-Israeli War of Attrition, known as the Second Intifada, broke out. In early October its impact was magnified by massive collisions between Israel's police and a large group of Israeli Arab demonstrators and rioters. These riots dealt the final blow to Barak's government and pushed the center-left and left segments of the Israeli political spectrum into a profound crisis. In the elections of 2001 Ariel Sharon, the leader of Israel's activist right wing, was elected as prime minister by a landslide.

After 2000

Sharon's election signified a reversal of several trends. The direct election was abolished. After the failure of two younger prime ministers, a member of the 1948 generation took the helm again. The peace process of the 1990s was suspended, and Israelis and Palestinians were once again engulfed in war. Years of fighting left thousands of Israelis and Palestinians dead. This round of Israeli-Palestinian conflict demonstrated Israel's massive military superiority but also showed that Israel is unable to impose a military solution to the conflict.

In 2003 the right-wing Sharon was elected again as prime minister, but he quickly moved to adopt part of Labor's platform when he initiated the relocation of all Israeli settlers from the Gaza Strip and four communities in the West Bank by the summer of 2005. Sharon established his leadership in Israel by taking strong measures to quell the "Second Intifada." But he had come to understand that there was no military solution to the Israeli-Palestinian conflict. Still distrustful of the Palestinian leadership, he adopted the concept of unilateralism.

In the summer of 2005 Sharon led a dramatic unilateral disengagement from the Gaza Strip, dismantling the Israeli settlements and forcing the settlers to evacuate. Shortly thereafter, Sharon broke with his own party, the Likud, and formed a new party, Kadima, with a clear platform—to continue the unilateral approach to resolving the Israeli-Palestinian conflict by applying it to the West Bank. In early 2006 Sharon was incapacitated by a stroke and Kadima was led in the elections by Ehud Olmert.

Kadima won the elections but instead of the forty seats predicted during Sharon's leadership, Olmert received twenty-nine seats in the Knesset. He formed a coalition with the Labor Party led by Amir Peretz, who was given the defense portfolio. The program of Olmert's government reflected Sharon's legacy—unilateralism for the West Bank was termed "Convergence" or "Realignment." This policy soon met with two challenges—a Hamas victory in the Palestinian elections and the renewal of Kassam-rocket attacks from the Gaza Strip, and the outbreak and course of the second Lebanon War in the summer of 2006.

These developments inflicted a severe blow to the whole idea of unilateralism and weakened Olmert's government to the point where he became preoccupied with survival rather than with a national agenda. The second Lebanon War also underscored the significance of Iran's emergence as the new existential threat facing Israel.

CHAPTER 1

Zionism and the Mandate, 1882–1948

1882
Bilu is founded in Kharkov

First Aliyah begins, as immigrants, mainly refugees from Russian pogroms, start arriving in Palestine

1884
Founding conference of Hibbat Zion meets at Kattowitz

1896
Theodor Herzl publishes *The Jewish State*

1897
First Zionist Congress, in Basle, Switzerland, establishes the Zionist Organization

1904
Second Aliyah begins

1914–1918
World War I

1916
Sykes-Picot Agreement signed between Britain and France

1917
Balfour Declaration commits Britain to a favorable view of a Jewish National Home in Palestine

1919
Third Aliyah begins

1920–1921
Arab riots

1922
Churchill White Paper establishes the principle of "double obligation" to Jews and Arabs in Palestine

British Mandate for Palestine establishes British rights and duties related to the administration of Palestine

1924
Fourth Aliyah begins

1929
Fifth Aliyah begins

1937
Peel Commission Report proposes a partition of Palestine between Jews and Arabs

1936–1939
Arab Revolt

1939
London Conference

MacDonald White Paper limits future Jewish immigration and leads to limitations on Jewish land purchases

1939–1945
World War II

1945
League of Arab States is established

1947
United Nations Resolution 181 calls for the partition of Palestine

Arab paramilitaries launch guerrilla and terror war

War of Independence begins

1

Bilu

Manifesto

Summer 1882

The Bilu was an organization of young Russian Jews, mostly students, who were part of the First Aliyah (wave of immigration) to Palestine and spearheaded the national-secular effort that would eventually dominate later waves of immigration. The group was established on January 30, 1882, in Kharkov, Russia (current Ukraine) in response to the 1881 pogroms—the organized, often officially encouraged, massacre or persecution of Jews in Russia. The name Bilu is the Hebrew acronym of the biblical calling "Beit Yisrael Lechu Venelcha" (House of Jacob, come, let us go) (Isaiah 2:5), and it reflects the movement's transformation in focus from advocating emigration to calling on its members to make a personal commitment. Partly influenced by Russian revolutionaries, the movement saw itself as a vanguard that would stimulate the larger masses. The Bilu movement spread quickly in Russia and Rumania and even registered some support in the United States.

Fifteen members of the Bilu arrived in Palestine, on July 6, 1882. At first, they worked on an agricultural farm, Mikve Israel, and in December 1884 nine of them established Gedera, in south-central Palestine. Other Biluim joined agricultural communities, such as Rishon Letzion, or old, established communities such as Jerusalem.

The movement's early promise was not fulfilled, however, as it lacked strong leadership and a clearly defined policy. Its members were also disenchanted by conditions in Palestine. Some left for the United States, Egypt, France, and Australia; others returned to Russia.

Though the Bilu faced many challenges and disappointments and did not achieve its high ideals, its model of radical, secular communitarianism and personal commitment was an inspiration for subsequent waves of immigration.

The manifesto that follows was issued by members of the Bilu in Constantinople (current Istanbul, in Turkey) en route to Palestine in the summer of 1882.

To Our Brethren and Sisters in the Exile, Peace Be with You!

"If I help not myself, who will help me?"
(Hillel)[1]

Nearly two thousand years have elapsed since, in an evil hour, after an heroic struggle, the glory of our Temple vanished in fire and our Kings and chieftains changed their crown and diadems for the chains of exile. We lost our country, where dwelt our beloved sires. Into the Exile we took with us, of all our glories only a spark of fire, by which our Temple, the abode of our Great One, was engirdled, and this little spark kept us alive while the towers of our enemies crumbled to dust, and this spark

Source: Nahum Sokolow, *History of Zionism* (London: Longmans, Green & Co., 1919), 2:332–33. Reprinted in *The Jew in the Modern World*, ed. Paul R. Mendes-Flohr and Jehuda Reinharz (New York: Oxford University Press, 1980), pp. 421–22. Annotations adapted and used by permission.

leapt into celestial flame and shed light upon the faces of the heroes of our race and inspired them to endure the horrors of the Dance of Death and the tortures of the autos-da-fe. And this spark is now again kindling and will shine for us, a true pillar of fire going before us on the road to Zion, while behind us is a pillar of cloud, the pillar of oppression threatening to destroy us. Sleepest thou, O our nation? What hast thou been doing till 1882? Sleeping and dreaming the false dream of Assimilation. Now, thank God, thou are awakened from thy slothful slumber. The pogroms have awakened thee from thy charmed sleep. Thine eyes are open to recognize the cloudy structure of delusive hopes. Canst thou listen silently to the flaunts and the mockery of thine enemies? Where is thine ancient pride, thine olden spirit? Remember that thou wast a nation possessing a wise religion, a law, a constitution, a celestial Temple, whose wall[2] is still a silent witness to the glories of the Past, that thy sons dwelt in Palaces and towers, and thy cities flourished in the splendour of civilization, while these enemies of thine dwelt like beasts in the muddy marshes of their dark woods. While thy children were clad in purple and linen, they wore the rough skins of the wolf and the bear. Art thou not ashamed to submit to them?

Hopeless is your state in the West; the star of your future is gleaming in the East. Deeply conscious of all of this, and inspired by the true teaching of our great master Hillel: "If I help not myself, who will help me?" we propose to build the following society for national ends: (1) The Society will be named Bilu, according to the motto: "House of Jacob, come, let us go!" It will be divided into local branches according to the number of members. (2) The seat of the Committee shall be Jerusalem. (3) Donations and contributions shall be unfixed and unlimited.

What we want: (1) A Home in our country. It was given to us by the mercy of God, it is ours as registered in the archives of history. (2) To beget it of the Sultan himself,[3] and if it be impossible to obtain this, to beg that at least we may be allowed to possess it as a state within a larger state; the internal administration to be ours, to have our civil and political rights, and to act within the Turkish Empire only in foreign affairs, so as to help our brother Ishmael in his time of need.

We hope that the interest in our glorious nation will rouse the national spirit in rich and powerful men, and that everyone, rich or poor, will give his best labors to the holy cause.

Greetings, dear brethren and sisters.

Hear, O Israel, the Lord our God, the Lord is one, and our Land, Zion is our one hope.

God be with us!

NOTES

1. Hillel was a first-century rabbinic authority.
2. The reference is to the Western or Wailing Wall.
3. The Sultan Abdul Hamid II (1842–1918) was ruler of the Ottoman Empire (1876–1909), which had controlled Palestine since 1517. During his reign the Ottoman authorities placed restrictions on Jewish immigration and Jewish land purchases in Palestine. The Biluim sought to end the restriction through the intervention of a pro-Zionist Englishman, Sir Laurence Oliphant, who lobbied the Ottoman authorities in Constantinople to grant Jews land rights in Palestine.

2

Leon Pinsker

Auto-Emancipation

October 17, 1882

Auto-Emancipation *is widely acknowledged as the first modern articulation of political Zionism as a solution to the so-called Jewish Problem. It was written (but published anonymously) by Judah Leib (Leon) Pinsker (1821–1891), a Russian Polish Jewish physician, in response to the 1881 pogroms. The pamphlet analyzes antisemitism, arguing that it is a modern phenomenon and thus not able to be solved through earlier strategies such as the Haskalah movement, which encouraged Jews in Western Europe to be open and to integrate into the European communities in which they lived. Pinsker's analysis reflects the pragmatic roots of political Zionism, seeing Zionism as responding to the need for a solution to the problem faced by Jews in Europe rather than the ancient religious plea to return to the Jewish ancestral land. Pinsker, himself a disappointed former supporter of the Haskalah, went on to take a leading role in the early efforts of organizing political Zionists. In 1884 he was one of the architects of the Kattowitz Conference, which founded the Hibbat Zion movement on a national level. Hibbat Zion (Love of Zion) promoted Jewish settlement and a Jewish national revival in Palestine. Pinsker served as the head of the Hibbat Zion movement until 1889, and again from 1890 until his death.*

This is the kernel of the problem, as we see it: *the Jews comprise a distinctive element among the nations under which they dwell, and as such can neither assimilate nor be readily digested by any nation.*

Hence the solution lies in finding a means of so readjusting this exclusive element to the family of nations, that the basis of the Jewish question will be permanently removed. . . .

But the greatest impediment in the path of the Jews to an independent national existence is that they do not feel its need. Not only that, but they go so far as to deny its authenticity.

In the case of a sick man, the absence of desire for food is a very serious symptom. It is not always possible to cure him of this ominous loss of appetite. And even if his appetite is restored, it is still a question whether he will be able to digest food, even though he desires it.

The Jews are in the unhappy condition of such a patient. We must discuss this most important point with all possible precision. We must prove that the misfortunes of the Jews are due, above all, to their lack of desire for national independence; and that this desire must be awakened and maintained in time if they do not wish to be subjected forever to disgraceful existence—in a word, we must prove that *they must become a nation.*

In the seemingly irrelevant circumstances, that the Jews are not regarded as an independent nation by other nations, rests in part the secret of their abnormal position and of their endless misery. Merely to belong to this people is to be indelibly stigmatized, a mark repellent to non-Jews and painful to the Jews themselves. However, this phenomenon is rooted deeply in human nature.

Source: L. S. Pinsker, *Auto-Emancipation* (Washington, D.C.: Zionist Organization of America, 1944). Translated from the German by Dr. D. S. Blondheim.

Among the living nations of the earth the Jews are as a nation long since dead.

With the loss of their country, the Jewish people lost their independence, and fell into a decay which is not compatible with existence as a whole vital organism. The state was crushed before the eyes of the nations. But after the Jewish people had ceased to exist as an actual state, as a political entity, they could nevertheless not submit to total annihilation—they lived on spiritually as a nation. The world saw in this people the uncanny form of one of the dead walking among the living. The Ghostlike apparition of a living corpse, of a people without unity or organization, without land or other bonds of unity, no longer alive, and yet walking among the living—this spectral form without precedence in history, unlike anything that preceded or followed it, could but strangely affect the imagination of the nations. And if the fear of ghosts is something inborn, and has a certain justification in the psychic life of mankind, why be surprised at the effect produced by this dead but still living nation.

A fear of the Jewish ghost has passed down the generations and the centuries. First a breeder of prejudice, later in conjunction with other forces we are about to discuss, it culminated in Judeophobia.

Judeophobia, together with other symbols, superstitions and idiosyncrasies, has acquired legitimacy among all the peoples of the earth with whom the Jews had intercourse. Judeophobia is a variety of demonopathy with the distinction that it is not peculiar to particular races but is common to the whole of mankind, and that this ghost is not disembodied like other ghosts but partakes of flesh and blood, must endure pain inflicted by the fearful mob who imagines itself endangered.

Judeophobia is a psychic aberration. As a psychic aberration it is hereditary, and as a disease transmitted for two thousand years it is incurable.

It is this fear of ghosts, the mother of Judeophobia, that has evoked this abstract, I might say Platonic hatred, thanks to which the whole Jewish nation is wont to be held responsible for the real or supposed misdeeds of its individual members, and to be libeled in so many ways, to be buffeted about so shamefully. . . .

Since the Jew is nowhere at home, nowhere regarded as a native, he remains an alien everywhere. That he himself and his ancestors as well are born in the country does not alter this fact in the least.

In the great majority of cases, he is treated as a stepchild, as a Cinderella; in the most favorable cases he is regarded as an adopted child whose rights may be questioned; *never* is he considered a legitimate child of the fatherland.

The German proud of his Teutonism, the Slav, the Celt, not one of them admits that the Semitic Jew is his equal by birth; and even if he be ready, as a man of culture, to admit him to all civil rights, he will never quite forget that his fellow-citizen is a Jew. The *legal emancipation* of the Jews is the culminating achievement of our century. But *legal* emancipation is not *social* emancipation, and with the proclamation of the former the Jews are still far from being emancipated from their exceptional *social position.*

The emancipation of the Jews is required as a postulate of *logic,* of *law,* and of *enlightened national interest,* but it can never be a spontaneous expression of human *feeling.* Far from owing its origin to spontaneous *feeling,* it is *never a matter of course*; and it has never yet taken root so deeply that further discussion of it becomes unnecessary. In any event, whether emancipation was undertaken from spontaneous impulse or from conscious motives, it remains a rich gift, a splendid alms, willingly or unwillingly flung to the poor, humble beggars whom no one, however, cares to shelter, because a homeless, wandering beggar wins confidence or sympathy from none. The Jew is not permitted to forget that the daily bread of civil rights must be given him. . . .

Our tragedy is that we can neither live nor die. We cannot die despite the blows of our enemies, and we do not wish to die by our own hand through apostasy or self-destruction. Neither can we live; our enemies have taken care of that. We will not recommence life as a nation, live like the other peoples, thanks to those overzealous patriots, who think it is necessary to sacrifice every claim upon independent national life to their loyalty as citizens—which should be a matter of course. Such fanatical patriots deny their ancient national character for the sake of any other nationality, whatever it may be, of high rank or low. But they deceive no one. They do not see how glad one is to decline Jewish companionship.

Thus for eighteen centuries we have lived in disgrace, without a single earnest attempt to shake it off! . . .

Moreover, the belief in a Messiah, in the intervention of a higher power to bring about our political resurrection, and the religious assumption that we must bear patiently divine punishment, caused us to abandon every thought of our national liberation, unity and independence. Consequently, we have renounced the idea of a nationhood and did so the more readily since we were preoccupied with our immediate needs. Thus we sank lower and lower. The people *without a country forgot their country*. Is it not high time to perceive the disgrace of it all?

Happily, matters stand somewhat differently now. The events of the last few years in *enlightened* Germany, in Roumania, in Hungary, and especially in Russia, have effected what the far bloodiest persecutions of the Middle Ages could not. The national consciousness which until then had lain dormant in sterile martyrdom awoke the masses of the Russian and Roumanian Jews and took form in an irresistible movement toward Palestine. Mistaken as this movement has proved to be by its results, it was, nevertheless, a right instinct to strike out for home. The severe trials which they have endured have now provoked a reaction quite different from the fatalistic submission to a divine punishment. Even the unenlightened masses of the Russian Jews have not entirely escaped the influences of the principles of modern culture. Without renouncing Judaism and their faith, they revolted against undeserved ill-treatment which could be inflicted with impunity only because the Russian Government regards the Jews as aliens. And the other European Governments—why should they concern themselves with the citizens of a state in whose internal affairs they have no right to interfere?

Today, when our kinsmen in a small part of the earth are allowed to breathe freely and can feel more deeply for the sufferings of their brothers; today, when a number of other subject and oppressed nationalities have been allowed to regain their independence, we, too, must not sit a moment longer with folded hands; we must not consent to play forever the hopeless role of the "Wandering Jew." It is a truly hopeless one, leading to despair. . . .

If other national movements which have risen before our eyes were their own justification, can it still be questioned whether the Jews have a similar right? They play a larger part in the life of the civilized nations, and they have rendered greater service to humanity; they have a greater past and history, a common, unmixed descent, an indestructible vigor, an unshakable faith, and an unexampled martyrology; the peoples have sinned against them more grievously than against any other nation. Is not that enough to make them capable and worthy of possessing a fatherland? The struggle of the Jews for national unity and independence as an established nation not only possesses the inherent justification that belongs to the struggle of every oppressed people, but it is also calculated to win the support of the people by whom we are now unwanted. This struggle must become an irresistible factor of contemporary international politics and destined for future greatness. . . .

If we would have a secure home, give up our endless life of wandering and rise to the dignity of a nation in our own eyes and in the eyes of the world, we must, above all, not dream of restoring ancient Judea. We must not attach ourselves to the place where our political life was once violently interrupted and destroyed. The goal of our present endeavors must be not the "Holy Land," but a land of our own. We need nothing but a large tract of land for our poor brothers, which shall remain our property and from which no foreign power can expel us. There we shall take with us the most sacred possessions which we have saved from the shipwreck of our former country, the *God-idea* and the *Bible*. It is these alone which have made our old fatherland the Holy Land, and not Jerusalem or the Jordan. Perhaps the Holy Land will again become ours. If so, all the better, but *first of all,* we must determine—and this is the crucial point—what country is accessible to us, and at the same time adapted to offer the Jews of all lands who must leave their homes a secure and indisputed refuge, capable of productivization. We do not overlook the enormous external and internal difficulties involved in this, which is to be the life-long endeavor of our people. But most difficult of all will be the attainment of the first and most necessary prerequisite, the *national resolution*; for we are, to our sorrow, a stiff-necked people. How readily could conservative opposition, of which our history has so much to tell, nip such a resolution in the bud! If it should, then woe to our entire future! . . .

But what are we to do next, how should we begin? We believe that a nucleus for this beginning already lies at hand *in the existing societies*. It is incumbent upon them, they are called and in duty bound, to lay the foundation of the lighthouse to which our eyes will turn. If they are to be equal to their new task, these societies must, of course, be completely transformed. They must convoke a *national congress*; of which they are to form the centre. If they decline that function, however, and refuse to go beyond the limits of their present activity, they must at least depute some of their numbers as a national board, let us say a *directorate,* which will have to establish that unity which we now lack and without which the success of our endeavors is unthinkable. To represent our national interests this institute must comprise the leaders of our people, and it must energetically take in hand the direction of our general, national affairs. Our greatest and ablest forces—men of finance, of science, and of affairs, statesmen and publicists—must join hands with one accord in steering toward the common destination. They would aim chiefly and especially at creating a secure and inviolable home for the *surplus* of those Jews who live as proletarians in the different countries and are a burden to the native citizens. . . .

The first task of this national institute, which we miss so much and must unconditionally call into existence, would have to find a territory adapted to our purpose, as far as possible continuous in extent and of uniform character. In this respect, two countries, lying at opposite points of the globe, which have lately vied with each other for first place and created two opposite currents of Jewish emigration, present themselves. This division caused the failure of the entire movement. . . .

Whether this act of national self-help on our part might turn out profitably or otherwise, however, is of little consequence as compared with the great significance which such an undertaking would have for the future of our unsettled people; for our future will remain insecure and precarious unless a radical change in our position is made. This change cannot be brought about by the civil emancipation of the Jews in this or that state, but only by the auto-emancipation of the Jewish people as a nation, the foundation of a colonial community belonging to the Jews, which some day is to become our inalienable home, our country. . . .

Of course, the establishment of a Jewish refuge cannot come about without the support of the governments. In order to obtain the latter and to insure the perpetual existence of a refuge, the molders of our national regeneration must proceed with caution and perseverance.

What we seek is at bottom neither new nor dangerous to anyone. Instead of the many *refuges* which we have always been accustomed to seek, we would fain have *one single refuge,* the existence of which, however, would have to be politically assured.

Let "Now or never" be our watchword. Woe to our descendants, woe to the memory of our Jewish contemporaries, if we let this moment pass by!

The Jews are not a living nation; they are everywhere aliens; therefore they are despised.

The civil and political emancipation of the Jews is not sufficient to raise them in the estimation of the peoples.

The proper, the only solution, is in the creation of a Jewish nationality, of a people living upon its own soil, the auto-emancipation of the Jews; their return to the ranks of the nations by the acquisition of a Jewish homeland.

We must not persuade ourselves that humanity and enlightenment alone can cure the malady of our people.

The lack of national self-respect and self-confidence of political initiative and of unity, are the enemies of our national renaissance.

That we may not be compelled to wander from one exile to another, we must have an extensive, productive land of refuge, a *center* which is our own. The present moment is the most favorable for this plan.

The international Jewish question must have a national solution. Of course, our national regeneration can only proceed slowly. *We* must take the first step. Our *descendants* must follow us at a measured and not over-precipitant speed.

The national regeneration of the Jews must be initiated by a congress of Jewish notables. No sacrifice should be too great for this enterprise which will assure our people's future, everywhere endangered.

The financial execution of the undertaking does not present insurmountable difficulties.

Help yourselves and God will help you!

3
Theodor Herzl
A Solution of the Jewish Question
January 17, 1896

Theodor Herzl (1860–1904) was the father of political Zionism and founder of the Zionist Organization. An assimilated Jew of minimal Jewish commitment, he was aroused by the growing antisemitism he witnessed as the Paris correspondent for the Neue Freie Presse *of Vienna from 1890 to 1895. He concluded that the only feasible solution to the Jewish Problem was a mass exodus of the Jews from the countries of their birth and a resettlement in the Land of Israel, and he devoted the rest of his life to realizing this idea. His book,* The Jewish State: An Attempt at a Modern Solution of the Jewish Question *(1896), set forth his basic ideas and program.*

Source: Theodor Herzl, "A Solution of the Jewish Question," *Jewish Chronicle,* January 17, 1896, pp. 12–13. Reprinted in *The Jew in the Modern World,* ed. Paul R. Mendes-Flohr and Jehuda Reinharz (New York: Oxford University Press, 1980), pp. 422–27. Annotations adapted and used by permission.

I have been asked to lay my scheme in a few words before the readers of the *Jewish Chronicle*.[1] This I will endeavor to do, although in this brief and rapid account, I run the risk of being misunderstood. My first and incomplete exposition will probably be scoffed at by Jews. The bad and foolish way we ridicule one another is a survival of slavish habits contracted by us during centuries of oppression. A free man sees nothing to laugh at in himself, and allows no one to laugh at him.

I therefore address my first words to those Jews who are strong and free of spirit. They shall form my earliest audience, and they will one day, I hope, become my friends. I am introducing no new idea; on the contrary, it is a very old one. It is a universal idea and therein lies its power—old as the people, which never, even in the time of bitterest calamity, ceased to cherish it. This is the restoration of the Jewish State.

It is remarkable that we Jews should have dreamt this kingly dream all through the long night of our history. Now day is dawning. We need only rub the sleep out of our eyes, stretch our limbs, and convert the dream into a reality. Though neither prophet nor visionary, I confess I cherish the hope and belief that the Jewish people will one day be fired by a splendid enthusiasm. For the present, however, I would appeal in calm words to the common sense of men of practical judgment and of modern culture. A subsequent task will be to seek out the less favored, to teach and to inspire them. This latter task I cannot undertake alone. I shall take my part in it, in the ranks of those friends and fellow workers whom I am endeavoring to arouse and unite for a common cause. I do not say "my adherents," for that would be making the movement a personal one, and consequently absurd and contemptible from the outset. No, it is a national movement, and it will be a glorious one, if kept unsullied by the taint of personal desires, though these desires took no other form than political ambition. We, who are the first to inaugurate this movement, will scarcely live to see its glorious close; but the inauguration of it is enough to bring a noble kind of happiness into our lives. We shall plant for our children in the same way as our fathers preserved the tradition for us. Our lives represent but a moment in the permanent duration of our people. The moment has its duties.

Two phenomena arrest our attention by reason of the consequences with which they are fraught. One, the higher culture; the other, the profound barbarism of our day. I have intentionally put this statement in the form of a paradox. By high culture, I mean the marvelous development of all mechanical contrivances for making the forces of nature serve man's purposes. By profound barbarism, I mean antisemitism. . . .

The Jewish Question still exists. It would be foolish to deny it. It exists wherever Jews live in perceptible numbers. Where it does not yet exist, it will be brought by Jews in the course of their migrations. We naturally move to those places where we are not persecuted, and there our presence soon produces persecution. This is true in every country, and will remain true even in those most highly civilized. France itself is no exception till the Jewish Question finds a solution on a political basis. I believe that I understand antisemitism, which is in reality a highly complex movement. I consider it from a Jewish standpoint, yet without fear or hatred. I believe that I can see what elements there are in it of vulgar sport, of common trade, of jealousy, of inherited prejudice, of religious intolerance, and also of legitimate self-defense.

Only an ignorant man would mistake modern antisemitism for an exact repetition of the Jew-baiting of the past. The two may have a few points of resemblance, but the main current of the movement has now changed. In the principal countries where antisemitism prevails, it does so as the result of the emancipation of the Jews. When civilized nations awoke to the inhumanity of exclusive legislation, and enfranchised us, our enfranchisement came too late. For we had, curiously enough, developed while in the Ghetto into bourgeois people, and we stepped out of it only to enter into fierce competition with the middle classes. Historical circumstances make us take to finance, for which, as every educated man knows, we had, as a nation, no original bent. One of the most important of these circumstances was the relation of the Catholic Church to "anatocism."[2] In the Ghetto we had become somewhat unaccustomed to bodily labour and we produced in the main but a large number of mediocre intellects. Hence, our emancipation set us suddenly within the circle of the middle classes, where we have to sustain a double pressure, from within and from without. The Christian bourgeoisie would not be unwilling to cast us as a sacrifice to Socialism, though that would naturally not improve matters much. But the Jewish Question is no more a social than a religious one, notwithstanding that it sometimes takes on these and other forms. It is a national question which can only be solved by making it a political world-question to be discussed and controlled by the nations of the civilised world in council.

We are one people—One People. We have honestly striven everywhere to merge ourselves in the social life of surrounding communities, and to preserve only the faith of our fathers. It has not been permitted to us. In vain we are loyal patriots, in some places our loyalty running to extremes; in vain do we make the same sacrifices of life and property as our fellow-citizens; in vain do we strive to increase the fame of our native land in science and art, or her wealth by trade and commerce. In countries where we have lived for centuries we are still cried down as strangers; and often by those whose ancestors were not yet domiciled in the land where Jews had already made experience of suffering. Yet, in spite of all, we are loyal subject, loyal as the Huguenots, who were forced to emigrate. If we could only be left in peace.[3] . . .

We are one people—our enemies have made us one in our despite, as repeatedly happens in history. Distress binds us together, and thus united, we suddenly discover our strength. Yes, we are strong enough to form a state, and a model state. We possess all human and material resources necessary for the purpose. . . . The whole matter is in essence perfectly simple, as it must necessarily be, if it is to come within the comprehension of all.

Let the sovereignty be granted us over a portion of the globe large enough to satisfy the requirements of the nation, the rest we shall manage for ourselves. Of course, I fully expect that each word of this sentence, and each letter of each word, will be torn to tatters by scoffers and doubters. I advise them to do the thing cautiously, if they are themselves sensitive to ridicule. The creation of a new state has in it nothing ridiculous or impossible. We have, in our day, witnessed the process in connection with nations which were not in the bulk of the middle class, but poor, less educated, and therefore weaker than ourselves. The governments of all countries, scourged by antisemitism, will serve their own interests, in assisting us to obtain the sovereignty we want. These governments will be all the more willing to meet us half-way, seeing that the movement I suggest is not likely to bring about any economic crisis. Such crises, as must follow everywhere as a natural consequence of Jew-baiting, will rather be prevented by the carrying out of my plan. For I propose an inner migration of Christians into the parts slowly and systematically evacuated by Jews. If we are not merely suffered to do what I ask, but are actually helped, we shall be able to effect a transfer of property from Jews to Christians in a manner so peaceable and on so extensive a scale as has never been known in the annals of history.

Everything must be carried out with due consideration for acquired rights and with absolute conformity to law, without compulsion, openly and by light of day, under the supervision of authority and the control of public opinion. . . .

Our clergy, on whom I most especially call, will devote their energies to the service of this idea. They must, however, clearly understand from the outset, that we do not mean to found a theocracy, but a tolerant modern civil state. We shall, however, rebuild the Temple in glorious remembrance of the faith of our fathers. We shall unroll the new banner of Judaism—a banner bearing seven stars on a white field. The white field symbolizes our pure new life, the seven stars, the seven golden hours of a working-day. For we shall march into the Promised Land carrying the badge of labour. . . .

Let all of you who will join us fall in behind our flag [and] fight for our cause with voice and pen and deed. I count on all our ambitious young men, who are now debarred from making progress elsewhere. . . .

Thus we also need a "gestor" [manager] to direct this Jewish political cause. The Jewish people are as yet prevented by the Diaspora from undertaking the management of their business for themselves. At the same time they are in a condition of more or less severe distress in many parts of the world. They need a "gestor." A first essential will therefore be the creation of such.

This "gestor" cannot, of course, be a single individual, for an individual who would undertake this giant work alone would probably be either a madman or an imposter. It is therefore indispensable to the integrity of the idea and the vigour of its execution that the work should be impersonal. The "gestor" of the Jews must be a union of several persons for the purpose, a body corporate. This body corporate or corporation, I suggest, shall be formed in the first instance from among those energetic English Jews to whom I imparted my scheme in London. Let that body be called "the Society of Jews," and be entirely distinct from the Jewish Company[4] previously referred to. The Society of Jews is the point of departure for the whole Jewish movement about to begin. It will have work to do in the domains of science and politics, for the founding of the Jewish state, as I conceive it, presupposes the application of scientific methods. We cannot journey out of Mizraim [Egypt] today, in the primitive fashion of ancient times. We must previously obtain an accurate account of our number and strength.

My pamphlet [*The Jewish State*] will open a general discussion on the Jewish Question. Friends and enemies will take part in it, but it will no longer, I hope, take the form either of violent abuse or of sentimental vindication, but of a debate, practical, large, earnest, and political. The Society of Jews will gather all available information from statesmen, parliaments, Jewish communities and societies, from speeches, letters and meetings, from newspapers and books. It will thus find out for the first time whether Jews really wish to go to the Promised Land, and whether they ought to go there. Every Jewish community in the world will send contributions to the Society towards a comprehensive collection of Jewish statistics. Further tasks, such as investigation by experts of the new country and its natural resources, planning of joint migration and settlement, preliminary work for legislation and administration, etc., must be judiciously evolved out of the original scheme. In short, the Society of Jews will be the nucleus of our public organizations. . . .

Shall we choose [the] Argentine [Republic] or Palestine? Will we take what is given us and what is selected by Jewish public opinion? Argentina is one of the most fertile countries in the world, extends over a vast area, and has a sparse population. The Argentine Republic would derive considerable profit from the cession of a portion of its territory to us. The present infiltration of Jews has certainly produced some friction, and it would be necessary to enlighten the Republic on the intrinsic differences of our new movement.

Palestine is our ever-memorable historic home. The very name of Palestine would attract our people with a force of extraordinary potency. Supposing His Majesty the Sultan were to give us Palestine, we could in return pledge ourselves to regulate the whole finances of Turkey. There we should also form a portion of the rampart of Europe against Asia, an outpost of civilization as opposed to barbarism.[5] We should remain a neutral state in intimate connection with the whole of Europe, which would guarantee our continued existence. The sanctuaries of Christendom would be safeguarded by assigning to them an extra-territorial status, such as is well known to the law of nations. We should form a guard of honor about these sanctuaries, answering for the fulfillment of this duty with our existence. This guard of honor would be the great symbol of the solution of the Jewish Question after nearly nineteen centuries of Jewish suffering. . . .

I know full well that in bringing forward a very old idea in a new form, I am laying myself open to derision and to every kind of attack. Gentler spirits will call my idea Utopian. But what is the difference between a Utopian scheme and a possible one? A Utopian scheme may be a piece of cleverly combined mechanism, lacking only the requisite force to set it in motion; a possible scheme on the other hand rests on a known and existent propelling force.

The force we need is created in us by antisemitism. Some people will say that what I am doing is to kindle antisemitism afresh. This is not true, for antisemitism would continue to increase, irrespective of my project, so long as the causes of its growth are not removed. Others will tremble for their goods and chattels, and professional business interests. . . .

What form of constitution shall we have? I am inclined to an aristocratic republic, although I am an ardent monarchist in my own country. Our history has been too long interrupted for us to attempt direct continuity of the ancient constitutional forms without exposing ourselves to the charge of absurdity.

What language shall we speak? Every man can preserve the language in which his thoughts are at home. Switzerland offers us an example of the possibility of a federation of tongues. We shall remain there in the new country what we now are here, and shall never cease to cherish the memory of the native land out of which we have been driven.

People will say that I am furnishing our enemies with weapons. This is also untrue, for my proposal can only be carried out with the free consent of a majority of Jews. Individuals, or even powerful bodies of Jews, might be attacked, but governments will take no action against the collective nation. The equal right of Jews before the law cannot be withdrawn where they have once been conceded, for their withdrawal would immediately drive all Jews, rich and poor alike, into the ranks of the revolutionary party. Even under present conditions the first official violation of Jewish liberties invariably brings about an economic crisis. The weapons used against us cut the hands that wield them. Meantime, hatred grows apace.

Again, it will be said that our enterprise is hopeless, because, even if we obtain the land with the supremacy over it, the poorest Jews only will go there. But it is precisely the poorest whom we need at first. Only desperados make good conquerors. The rich and well-to-do will follow later, when they will find the new country as pleasant as the old, or ever pleasanter. . . .

But we can do nothing without the enthusiasm of our own nation. The idea must make its way into the most distant miserable holes where our people dwell. They will awaken from gloomy brooding, for into their lives will come a new significance. Let each of them but think of himself, and what vast proportions the movement must assume! And what glory awaits those who fight unselfishly for the cause! A wondrous generation of Jews will spring into existence. The Maccabeans will rise again.

And so it will be: It is the poor and the simple who do not know what power man already exercises over the forces of nature, it is just these who will have the firmest faith in the new message. For these have never lost the hope of the Promised Land. This is my message, fellow Jews! Neither fable nor fraud! Every man may test its truth for himself, for every man will carry with him a portion of the Promised Land—one in his head, another in his arms, another in his acquired possessions. We shall live at last as free men, on our own soil, and die peacefully in our own home.

NOTES

1. Herzl arrived in London on November 21, 1895. Through Max Nordau he met Israel Zangwill, who obtained for him an invitation to a banquet of the Maccabaeans Club, where Herzl expounded his ideas and established important contacts. There Herzl met Asher Myers of the *Jewish Chronicle*, who asked Herzl for an article. Consequently, the *Jewish Chronicle* article preceded *The Jewish State* by four weeks in its publication of Herzl's views.
2. "Anatocism" is the principle of charging compound interest.
3. This paragraph appears to have been taken verbatim from *The Jewish State*.
4. According to Herzl's plan, the Jewish Company was to be entrusted with the execution of the transfer of the Jews to their own state. The society that Herzl proposed was later to be called the Zionist Organization (after 1960, the World Zionist Organization).
5. This passage, which also appears in *The Jewish State*, is frequently cited as proof of the colonial, imperialist intentions of Zionism. It must be viewed, however, in light of Herzl's vision of the Zionist homeland as an ally of the colonized people in their struggle for liberation and restored dignity. In his novel *Old-New Land* (1902), for example, Herzl presents a romantic vision that encompasses the restoration of slaves to Africa as a solution to the so-called Negro Problem.

4
First Zionist Congress
The Basle Program
August 31, 1897

The First Zionist Congress, convened by Theodor Herzl in the summer of 1897 in Basle, Switzerland, founded the Zionist Organization and adopted the following official statement of Zionist purpose. While taking into consideration the agricultural achievements of such groups as the Bilu (see doc. 1) and Hibbat Zion (see doc. 2), the congress endorsed, in this statement, Herzl's political Zionism. According to Herzl, the Jewish Problem could be solved only by large-scale migration and settlement of Palestine, which could be attained only through the political assistance and consent of the community of nations. The solution to the Jewish Problem would thus be politically and internationally guaranteed by a charter granting the Jewish people (through the Zionist Organization) the right to reestablish an autonomous homeland in Palestine.

The aim of Zionism is to create for the Jewish people a home in Palestine secured by public law.

The Congress contemplates the following means to the attainment of this end:

1. The promotion, on suitable lines, of the colonization of Palestine by Jewish agricultural and industrial workers.
2. The organization and binding together of the whole Jewry by means of appropriate institutions, local and international in accordance with the laws of each country.
3. The strengthening and fostering of Jewish national sentiment and consciousness.
4. Preparatory steps toward obtaining government consent, where necessary, to the attainment of the aim of Zionism.

Source: Jewish Chronicle, September 3, 1897, p. 13. Reprinted in *The Jew in the Modern World,* ed. Paul R. Mendes-Flohr and Jehuda Reinharz (New York: Oxford University Press, 1980), p. 429. Annotations adapted and used by permission.

5

Ahad Ha'am

The First Zionist Congress

August–September 1897

Ahad Ha'am was the pen name of Asher Hirsh Ginsberg (1856–1927)—Russian Jew, Hebrew essayist, and a dominant figure in the Hibbat Zion movement (see doc. 2). Ahad Ha'am was critical of both political and practical Zionism, the latter because he felt that the mass resettlement of Jewry in Palestine was not feasible, the former because he did not believe its diplomatic program would work and found its neglect of Jewish cultural reconstruction disabling. Properly considered, Ahad Ha'am maintained, Zionism could not solve the "problem of the Jews"—their economic, social, and political plight—but it could solve "the problem of Judaism," that is, assimilation. With the eclipse of religion in the modern period, he observed, Jews were increasingly defecting to non-Jewish secular cultures. Zionist settlement in Palestine should therefore concentrate on fostering a secular Jewish culture based on Jewish national consciousness and the renewal of Hebrew as a means of ensuring the continuity of Jewish creativity. Palestine Jewry would thereby serve as a "spiritual center" nourishing Jewish life in the Diaspora, where most of the Jewish people would undoubtedly continue to live.

"The Congress of the Zionists"—the struggle over which filled the vacuum of our small world during the past months—is now past history.

Approximately two hundred members of the House of Israel from all lands and all countries gathered together in Basle.[1] For three days, from morning to evening, they conducted public proceedings before all the nations concerning the establishment of a secure home for the Jewish people in the land of their fathers.

The *national* response to the Jewish question thus broke the barriers of "modesty" and entered into the public realm. With a loud voice, clear language and proud bearing, a message whose like had not been heard since the time of Israel's exile from its land was proclaimed to all the world.

And that was all. This assembly *could* have done no more, and *should* have done no more.

For—why should we delude ourselves?—of all the great aims to which *Hibbat Zion* (or, as they say now, "Zionism") aspires, for the time being it is within our powers to draw near in a truly fitting manner to only one of them, namely the *moral* aim. We must liberate ourselves from the *inner* slavery, from the degradation of the spirit caused by assimilation, and we must strengthen our national unity until we become capable and worthy of a future life of honor and freedom. All other aims are still part of the world of ideas and fantasies. The opponents of the Jewish state doubt whether it will be possible to obtain the consent of the nations, especially Turkey, to the establishment of this state. It appears to me, however, that there is an

Source: Hashiloah 2, no. 6 (Elul 5647; August–September 1897): 568–70. Translated by S. Weinstein. Reprinted in *The Jew in the Modern World*, ed. Paul R. Mendes-Flohr and Jehuda Reinharz (New York: Oxford University Press, 1980), pp. 430–32. Annotations adapted and used by permission.

even more serious question [that must be asked]. Were this consent to be given would we, in our present moral condition, be capable of seizing the opportunity? Moreover, is it also possible to question the very nature of the proposal for a Jewish state? In light of the prevailing situation of the world in general, would the establishment of the Jewish state in our times, even in the most complete form imaginable, permit us to say that "our question" has been solved in its entirety and that the national ideal has been attained? "According to the suffering—the reward." After thousands of years of unfathomable calamity and misfortune, it would be impossible for the Jewish people to be happy with their lot if in the end they would reach [merely] the level of a small and humble people, whose state is a play-thing in the hands of its mighty neighbors and exists only by means of diplomatic machinations and perpetual submission to whomever fate is smiling upon. It would be impossible for an ancient people, one that was a light unto the nations, to be satisfied with such an insignificant recompense for all their hardships. Many other peoples, lacking both name and culture, have been able to attain the same thing within a brief period of time without having had to suffer even the smallest part of what the Jews have suffered. It was not in vain that the prophets rose to the aid of Israel, envisioning the reign of *justice* in the world at the end of days. Their *nationalism*, their love for their people and for their land, led them to this. For even in biblical times the Jewish state was caught between two lions—Assyria or Babylonia on the one side and Egypt on the other—so that it had no hope to dwell in tranquility and develop in a suitable fashion. Accordingly, "Zionism" developed in the hearts of the prophets, giving rise to the great vision of the end of days when "the wolf shall dwell with the lamb and nation shall not lift up sword against nation"[2]—and when Israel shall once again safely dwell in its own land. Hence, this *human* ideal was and perforce always will be an integral part of the *national* ideal of the Jewish people. The Jewish state can only find peace when universal justice will ascend to the throne and rule the lives of the peoples and the states.

And so, we did not come to Basle to found the Jewish state today or tomorrow. Rather, we came to issue a great proclamation to all the world: the Jewish people is still alive and full of the will to live. We must repeat this proclamation day and night, not so that the world will hear and give us what we desire, but above all, in order that we ourselves will hear the echo of our voice in the depths of our soul. Perhaps in this way our soul will awaken and cleanse itself of its degradation. . . .

This indeed is what the Basle assembly accomplished at its beginning in a sublime fashion. And for this it would have deserved to have been inscribed in golden letters as a testimony to the generations, were it not for its desire to accomplish even more.

Here, too, rashness—this curse which lies over us and sabotages all our action—appeared in full force. Had the initiators of the assembly armed themselves with patience and explicitly declared from the beginning that the traces of the Messiah are not yet visible and that for the time being our strength lies only in our mouths and hearts—to revive our national spirit and spread the tidings of this renewal among the public at large—then without doubt the list of delegates would have been much smaller. Instead of three days the assembly could have finished its work in one day, but this day would have been the equivalent of entire generations. Those delegates, the elect of our people—for only the elect would have been attracted to an assembly of this kind—would then return, each to his own country, with hearts full of life, will and new energy, to instill this life and energy into the hearts of all the people.

But now . . .

The initiators of this movement are "Europeans." They are expert in the rules of diplomacy and in the customs of the political sects of our day, and they are bringing these rules and customs with them to the "Jewish state." . . .

Emissaries were dispatched prior to the assembly and various "hints" were distributed orally and in writing in order to awaken among the masses an exaggerated hope for imminent salvation. Hearts were inflamed by an idolatrous fire, a febrile passion, which brought to the Basle assembly a motley crowd of youths, immature both in years and in wisdom. This mob robbed the assembly of its splendor and through their great foolishness turned it into a laughing stock.

Large and small committees, endless commissions, a multitude of imaginary "proposals" concerning the "national treasury" and the rest of the "exalted politics" of the Jewish state—these are the "practical" results of the assembly. How could it have been otherwise? The majority of the delegates, the emissaries of the wretched members of our people waiting for redemption, were sent solely for the purpose of bringing redemption with them upon their return. How, then, could they return home without bearing the tidings that the administration of the "state" in all its various branches, had been placed in trustworthy hands, and that all the important questions concerning the "state" had been examined and solved?

The delegates will return [from Basle] with the message that redeemers have arisen in Israel and that all we have to do is wait for "diplomacy" to finish its task. [But] the eyes of the people will quickly be opened and they will realize that they have been led astray. The sudden fire which ignited hope in their hearts will once again be extinguished, perhaps even to the final spark. . . .

If I could only enter into a pact with the angel of oblivion I would make him vow to obliterate from the hearts of the delegates all traces of what they saw and heard at Basle, leaving them with only one memory. [I am referring to] the memory of that great and sacred hour when they all stood together as brothers—these forlorn men of Israel who came from all corners of the earth—their hearts full of feelings of holiness and their eyes lovingly and proudly directed to their noble brother standing on the platform preaching wonders to his people, like one of the prophets of days of yore. The memory of this hour, had it not been followed by many other hours which deprived the first impression of its purity, could have turned this assembly into one of the most distinguished events in the history of our people.

The deliverance of Israel will come at the hands of "prophets," not at the hands of "diplomats."

NOTES

1. The First Zionist Congress was held in Basle, August 29–31, 1897.
2. The quotation is from Isaiah 11:6, 2:4.

6

Manya Shochat

The Collective

1904–1909: Memoir

Manya Shochat (1879–1961) was a legendary figure among the early pioneers in Palestine. A committed Russian socialist revolutionary, Shochat became a Zionist following her visit to Palestine in 1904. She played important roles in the establishment of the Jewish self-defense organizations Bar Giora (1907) and Hashomer (1909) as well as radical socialist collectives in Sejera and Gdud Haavoda (Battalion of Work). Her efforts paved the way for the kibbutz movement, and she herself joined Kibbutz Kfar Giladi. The following is an account of her efforts to demonstrate the feasibility of collective settlements.

In the spring of 1904 I became acquainted with [Yehoshua] Hankin's *kvuzah* [group] in Rehovot. I had by that time determined to find out what it was that the country meant to me, as an individual. My plan was to make a tour of the Jewish colonies and to get together such statistics as were available. The task took up a year of my time. I worked out a questionnaire that covered the economic side of colony life. I asked in particular for details of income, and the employment of Arab workers. Few indeed were the colonists who at that time kept statistics of their own. But I became acquainted with the character of our First Aliyah, and I came to a definite conclusion. My *haverim*—the workers—were completely mad! *The way they were working there was absolutely no hope of creating in Eretz Israel a Jewish agricultural proletariat!*

The Jewish workers in the colony of Petah Tikvah had accepted the same conditions as the Arabs: their pay was 5 *piastres* [25 cents] a day. They believed that as Zionists they simply had not the right to ask for more. They lived eight in a room—a small room—and their beds were mattresses on the floor. When I told them that they ought to demand houses and public buildings from the colony, they answered proudly that this would be philanthropy. . . . They would ask for no help from these sources: it would only be a renewal of the immemorial evil of the *halukah* [allowance].

Finally, the Jewish workers of Petah Tikvah were driven by sheer need to live in a commune. There was no other way out for them. Their commune was the second in Eretz Israel, and the first was Hankin's commune in Rehovot.

I had already had some experience with a commune—in Minsk. A group of us wanted to organize the workers without the help of the intelligentsia, and to that end we started a workers' commune. The life was harsh and meager, and the budget was between three and five *kopeks* [a *kopek* was half a cent] per day per person. All earnings were turned in to the common fund. It was while living with this commune that I learned an important principle: the commune provides the proletariat with the means for its struggle. The Minsk commune[1] prepared me for the collective lifestyle in Eretz Israel.

Source: *The Plough Woman: Records of the Pioneer Women of Palestine,* ed. Mark A. Raider and Miriam Raider Roth (Hanover and London: University Press of New England, 2002), pp. 6–12.

I began on my arrival in Eretz Israel with an urban cooperative, for I was more accustomed to city conditions. In Russia, I had learned carpentry in the factory of my brother, Gedaliah Wilbushevitz. I raised a loan in order to start a carpenters' cooperative in Jaffa, and I worked out its rules on the basis of the Russian *artels,*[2] which had a communist background. The cooperative existed for three months. When I left for Galilee, internal dissensions broke out and the cooperative fell to pieces.

In the year 1905, Yehoshua Hankin spoke to me about the possibility of buying up the Jezreel Valley[3] [hereafter, *emek*], and it was clear to me that only through such a purchase could a Jewish agricultural class be established in Eretz Israel. I was anxious to help Hankin, and I placed before him my plans for collectivist colonization. Meanwhile, Jewish immigration into Eretz Israel kept growing.

I then made up my mind to go to Paris and approach the Jewish Colonization Association, founded by Baron Hirsch[4]—to buy land in the *emek* for workers' colonization. I also wanted to do some research in Paris on various attempts that have been made at collectivist colonization. There I came across a cousin of mine, Ivan Wilbushevitz, who was editing the government organ for the French colonies. Through him, I obtained access to the material of the government departments on the colonization in Tunis and Algeria.

I realized soon enough that what I had in mind was not to be found anywhere. Indeed, the experts considered agricultural collectivism ridiculous, and were ready to prove that the agricultural commune had never been able to succeed.

At about that time a Jewish comrade of mine, arriving from Russia, asked me to help him raise money for the Jewish self-defense in that country. I collected two hundred thousand francs for that purpose—fifty thousand of it coming from Baron Edmond de Rothschild[5]—and helped him, further, to smuggle arms into Russia.

I re-entered Russia illegally. During the *pogrom* in Shedliz [1906],[6] I took an active part in the Jewish self-defense. Later, I organized a national group to exact vengeance from the leaders of Russian antisemitism. One of the comrades in the group was Pinhas Dashevsky, who shot the famous antisemite [Pavolaki] Krushevan. The entire group was arrested—with the exception of Dashevsky. Again the traitor was Azeff, who got his information through two socialist revolutionaries who worked with us. The police looked for me in Saint Petersburg. I changed my lodgings every day, never sleeping twice in the same place. With clockwork regularity the police always searched, too late, the place I had slept in the night before. My name was unknown to them.

I worked for three months with "The Group of Vengeance." The only Jewish party which supported us were the Territorialists (S.S.).[7] Later, toward the end of 1906, I returned to Eretz Israel via Constantinople.

Once again, I turned to my *haverim* with the old idea of a collective. I wanted to go to America to raise money for collective colonization in Transjordania and in the Hauran. I also planned to visit the American collectivist colonies.[8]

Early in 1907, I arrived in America and spent nearly half a year there. I became acquainted with Dr. Judah L. Magnes and with Henrietta Szold.[9] I visited South America, too, taking in the collectivist colonies,[10] and convinced myself at first hand that the agricultural commune could succeed. What we needed was a substitute for the religious enthusiasm that had made these settlements possible, and for this substitute I looked to socialism.

In August 1907, I returned to Eretz Israel via Paris. I had one ideal now: the realization of agricultural collectivism. During my absence, the idea had taken somewhat deeper root in Eretz Israel. In the colonies of Lower Galilee the Jewish workers lived wretched, disorganized lives. They were housed in stables. Some of them had already lost all faith in the burning ideal of *kibush haavodah.*[11] They could not become individualist farmers, planters, exploiters of others; their socialist principles forbade it. And they could not continue their competition with Arab labor, for no European can long subsist on five *piastres* a day. I for my part, had never believed in *kibush haavodah* through adaptation to the Arab standard of life. At that time, the Jewish National Fund had begun to purchase land as the inalienable property of the Jewish people. The ideal of national territory of this kind had always been close to my heart, for I saw in it the foundation of collectivist colonization. Eliezer Shochat[12] was against my plan. His argument was: "We dare not assume this responsibility. If the particular plan that we adopt for collectivist colonization fails, we shall lose faith in the ideal of colonization as such. The first thing we must learn is to become land workers."

In the farm of the [Jewish Colonization Association] at Sejera, there were *haverim* of ours working under the direction of the agronomist Krause.[13] Every year this farm showed a deficit. I said: "Give us a chance to work here on our own responsibility, and we'll manage without a deficit."

The opportunity was given to us. At Sejera, I worked half-days on the books and the other half-days in the cow shed. I told Krause that he ought to admit women to the work, and the first three women workers there were the Shturman sisters: Sarah (Krigser), Shifra (Bezer), and Esther (Becker). They were all very young, and they followed the plough like real peasants.

When we founded the collective, we were eighteen in all who had drifted together gradually toward Sejera. The contract with the agronomist Krause turned over to us the field and dairy work on the same terms as were demanded of an Arab lessee. The owners gave us all the dead and live stock, the inventory, and the seed. In return, we had to turn over one-fifth of the harvest. We were also given sleeping quarters—and very poor ones they were—and a sum of money to carry us through the season. When there was not enough work on the farm to go round, the management would employ some of us in the afforestation work.

We worked on our own responsibility. We arranged our own division of labor. Only once a week, when the program was planned, we would have Krause in for a consultation. We also asked him to give regular lectures on agriculture, and no one who lived with us through that time has forgotten those clear and practical expositions.

The workers on the farm did not have a kitchen of their own, and until the coming of the collective they used to eat at a private inn. We organized a communal kitchen, and later on we were even able to feed workers not belonging to our commune.

The name we gave ourselves was, simply, "The Collective." The relations between us and the other workers on the farm were excellent. But they had no faith in our plan and did not believe we would come out without a deficit.

The Sejera collective lasted a year and a half. It ended its work successfully, paid the farm its fifth of the harvest, returned in full the money that had been advanced, and demonstrated once for all that a collective economy was a possibility.

NOTES

1. The Minsk commune, lasting half a year, prized equality and revolutionary activity. At the time, Minsk, the current capital of Belorussia, had a large Jewish population and was a hotbed of Jewish political radicalism.
2. *Artels* were groups of laborers or craftsmen in Russia organized on a cooperative and often egalitarian basis.
3. The Jezreel Valley, with its critical mass of agricultural and pioneering activity, attained a near-mythic status in Zionist circles and was referred to simply as the *emek*, Hebrew for "valley."
4. Baron Maurice de Hirsch (1831–1896), a German Jewish banker and rail developer, was a major benefactor of a variety of Jewish agencies including the Alliance Israélite Universelle, the French Jewish aid society; the Baron de Hirsch Fund, established to assist Jewish immigrants in New York City; and the Jewish Colonization Association, established in 1891 to support and coordinate the mass emigration of Russian Jews and to encourage their resettlement in agricultural colonies, particularly in Argentina and Brazil.

5. Edmond de Rothschild (1845–1934), a French Jewish businessman who supported the Zionist movement, played a critical role in financing the First Aliyah.

6. Shedliz (Siedlce), a city in eastern Poland with a large Jewish population.

7. The reference here is to the Sionistsko-sotsialisticheskiaia Rabochaia Partiia (Zionist Socialist Labor Party), one of the first Russian Jewish revolutionary parties, usually known as the "S.S."

8. The era of mass Eastern European Jewish immigration to the United States witnessed the advent of Jewish agricultural colonies in many regions of the country. The Am Olam (Eternal People) movement, founded in Odessa in 1881, promoted the settlement of Jews in the United States in agrarian communes guided by socialist ideals. Several Am Olan communes were established in 1882 in Louisiana, South Dakota, and Oregon, but they soon disbanded due to debt and other hardships. In subsequent years, the Jewish Agricultural and Industrial Aid Society undertook to create small agricultural settlements in different parts of the country. With the support of the Baron de Hirsch Fund, it provided support and administrative guidance to thousands of Yiddish-speaking immigrants, primarily in the northeast and southern New Jersey. Though numerically insignificant, the colonies served as a training ground for many of the leaders of the American Jewish labor movement.

9. Henrietta Szold (1860–1945), an American educator and social worker, was one of the outstanding leaders of American Zionism. In 1912, she founded Hadassah, the Women's Zionist Organization of America. She settled in Palestine in 1920, where she directed many projects on behalf of Hadassah. With Adolf Hitler's rise to power, she also devoted herself to Youth Aliyah, which sought to facilitate the passage of children and youth from Europe and their resettlement in Palestine.

10. Jewish agricultural colonization in South America was largely confined to Argentina. Starting in 1891, the Jewish Colonization Association of Paris, of which Baron Maurice de Hirsch was virtually the sole stockholder, purchased large tracts of land in various parts of the Argentine Republic. By 1905, more than 17 million acres had been acquired, mostly in the provinces of Buenos Aires and Santa Fé.

11. The idea of *kibush haavodah* (conquest of labor) derives from the philosophy and writings of Aharon David Gordon. This voluntaristic notion, with its layers of unfolding meaning—*avodah*, the Hebrew word for "labor," is also the classical term for worship—tapped an idealistic vein in the radical Zionist milieu of the period. *Kibush haavodah* symbolized the complete transformation of Jewish life.

12. Eliezer Shochat (1874–1971) was one of the first members of Poalei Zion in his home region of Grodno, Russia. After arriving in Petah Tikvah in 1904, he worked in agriculture and helped to establish Hapoel Hazair (Young Worker). A devoted organizer of workers in the Jewish colonies, he was a founder of Hahoresh (Plowman), the union of Jewish agricultural workers in the Galilee, and served as a delegate to the Eighth and Ninth Zionist Congresses. He was also one of the first settlers in Merhavyah.

13. Eliyahu Krause (1876–1962) emigrated to Palestine from his native Russia in 1892. An agronomist, he was employed by the Jewish Colonization Association and helped to create an agricultural school near Izmir, Turkey. Without his cooperation, Manya Shochat and her comrades could not have realized their program to establish a collective at Sejera. In 1915, Krause became director of the Mikveh Israel Agricultural School, a position he held until his retirement in 1954.

7

Lord Balfour, for the British Cabinet

Balfour Declaration

November 2, 1917

The first major political achievement of Zionism in the international arena, this official declaration committed Britain to a favorable stance toward Jewish aspirations for sovereignty in Palestine. The declaration, which was approved by the British cabinet, was sent as a letter from the foreign secretary, Lord Balfour, to the honorary president of the Zionist Federation in Britain, Lord Rothschild.

The final text, presented below, is a diluted form of an earlier draft that was submitted in July to the British government. The earlier version, which had been drafted by a small group of Zionist activists, used stronger language regarding the Jewish right to the land, committed the British in a more serious manner to support the Zionist project, and named the Zionist Organization as the counterpart the British should consult about the methods and means to be used.

The Balfour Declaration reflected the Zionist choice to focus on Britain as its primary political patron, and it secured the leadership of the Zionist movement to Chaim Weizmann, who led this approach from 1914 on and was the driving force behind the declaration.

Foreign Office
November 2nd, 1917

Dear Lord Rothschild,[1]

I have much pleasure in conveying to you, on behalf of His Majesty's Government, the following declaration of sympathy with Jewish Zionist aspirations which has been submitted to, and approved by, the Cabinet.

His Majesty's Government view with favour the establishment in Palestine of a national home for the Jewish people, and will use their best endeavours to facilitate the achievement of this object, it being clearly understood that nothing shall be done which may prejudice the civil and religious rights of existing non-Jewish communities in Palestine, or the rights and political status enjoyed by Jews in any other country.

I should be grateful if you would bring this declaration to the knowledge of the Zionist Federation.

Yours,

James Balfour

NOTE

1. Lionel Walter Rothschild, the second Baron Rothschild (1868–1937), honorary president of the Zionist Federation of Great Britain and Ireland at the time of the Balfour Declaration. It was Baron Rothschild who forwarded the Zionist draft to the British cabinet in the summer of 1917.

Source: "Book of Documents," submitted to the General Assembly of the United Nations by the Jewish Agency for Palestine (New York: Jewish Agency for Palestine, 1947), p. 1. Reprinted in *The Jew in the Modern World,* ed. Paul R. Mendes-Flohr and Jehuda Reinharz (New York: Oxford University Press, 1980), p. 458. Annotations adapted and used by permission.

8

London Bureau of the Zionist Organization

Zionist Manifesto

December 21, 1917

Despite reservations held by Jews and non-Jews alike because of its ambiguous formulation, the Balfour Declaration was received with enthusiasm in Zionist circles. This assessment by the London Bureau was published about six weeks after the declaration by Nahum Sokolow, Yehiel Tschlenow, and Chaim Weizmann, three talented leaders of the Zionist movement in London.

Sokolow (1860–1936) was one of the most important figures of post-Herzlian Zionism. He was associated with Weizmann in the negotiations leading to and following the Balfour Declaration, in connection with which he undertook missions to the French and Italian governments and to the Papal Curia. He was president of the Jewish Agency for Palestine and the Zionist Organization from 1931 to 1935. Yehiel Tschlenow (1863–1918) was a leading figure in Russian and world Zionism. Chaim Weizmann (1874–1952) was the most prominent figure in the Zionist movement following the Balfour Declaration. He was president of the Zionist Organization from 1920 to 1931 and from 1935 to 1946, and the first president of the state of Israel from 1949 until his death.

To the Jewish People:

The second of November, 1917, is an important milestone on the road to our national future; it marks the end of an epoch, and it opens up the beginning of a new era. The Jewish people has but one other such day in its annals: the twenty-eighth of August, 1897, the birthday of the New Zionist Organization at the first Basle Congress. But the analogy is incomplete, because the period which then began was Expectation, whereas the period which now begins is Fulfillment.

From then till now, for over twenty years, the Jewish people has been trying to find itself, to achieve a national resurrection. The advance-guard was the organized Zionist party, which in 1897 by its programme demanded a home for the Jewish people in Palestine secured by public law. A great deal was written, spoken, and done to get this demand recognized. The work was carried out by the Zionist Organization on a much greater scale and in a more systematic manner than had been possible for the Hovevei Zion,[1] the first herald of the national ideal, who had tried to give practical shape to the yearning which had burnt like a light in the Jewish spirit during two thousand years of exile and had flamed out at various periods in various forms. The Hovevei Zion had the greatest share in the practical colonization. The Zionist movement wrestled with its opponents and with itself. It collected means outside Palestine, and laboured with all its strength in Palestine. It founded institutions of all kinds for colonization in

---

Source: Jewish Chronicle, December 21, 1917, p. 16. Reprinted in *The Jew in the Modern World,* ed. Paul R. Mendes-Flohr and Jehuda Reinharz (New York: Oxford University Press, 1980), pp. 458–60. Annotations adapted and used by permission.

Palestine. There was a preface, full of hope and faith, full of experiments and illusion, inspired by a sacred and elevating ideal, and productive of many valuable and enduring results.

The time has come to cast the balance of the account. That chapter of propaganda and experiments is complete, and the glory of immortality rests upon it. But we must go further. To look back is the function of the historian; life looks forwards.

The turning point is the Declaration of the British Government that they "view with favour the establishment in Palestine of a National Home for the Jewish people, and will use their best endeavours to facilitate the achievement of this object."

The progress which our idea has made is so colossal and so obvious that it is scarcely necessary to describe it in words. Nonetheless, a few words must be addressed to the Jewish people, not so much by way of explanation, as to demand the new and greater efforts which are imperative.

The outstanding feature of the Declaration is, that which has been a beautiful ideal—and according to our opponents an empty dream—has now been given the possibility of becoming a reality. The aspirations of 1897 now find solid ground in the British Government's official Declaration of the second of November, 1917. That in itself is a gigantic step forward. The world's history, and particularly Jewish history, will not fail to inscribe in golden letters upon its bronze tablets that Great Britain, the shield of civilization, the country which is preeminent in colonization, the school of constitutionalism and freedom, has given us an official promise of support and help in the realization of our ideal of liberty in Palestine. And Great Britain will certainly carry with her the whole political world.

The Declaration of His Majesty's Government coincides with the triumphant march of the British Army in Palestine. The flag of Great Britain waves over Jerusalem and all Judea. It is at such a moment, while the army of Great Britain is taking possession of Palestine, that Mr. Balfour assures us that Great Britain will help us in the establishment of a National Home in Palestine. This is the beginning of the fulfillment.

To appreciate and to understand accurately is the first essential, but it is not all. It is necessary to go further, to determine what is the next step. This must be set forth in plain words.

The Declaration puts in the hands of the Jewish people the key to a new freedom and happiness. All depends on you, the Jewish people, and on you only. The Declaration is the threshold, from which you can place your foot upon holy ground. After eighteen hundred years of suffering your recompense is offered to you. You can come to your haven and your heritage, you can show that the noble blood of your race is still fresh in your veins. But to do that you must begin work anew, with new power and with new means—the ideas and the phrases and the methods of the first period no longer suffice. That would be an anachronism. We need new conceptions, new words, new acts. The methods of the period of realization cannot be the methods of the time of expectation.

In the first place, the whole Jewish people must now unite. Now that fulfillment is displacing expectation, that which was potential in the will of the Jewish people must become actual and reveal itself in strenuous labour. The whole Jewish people must come into the Zionist Organization.

Secondly, a word to our brothers in Palestine. The moment has come to lay the foundations of a National Home. You are now under the protection of the British military authorities, who will guard your lives, your property, your freedom. Be worthy of that protection, and begin immediately to build the Jewish National Home upon sound foundations, thoroughly Hebrew, thoroughly national, thoroughly free and democratic. The beginning may decide all that follows.

Thirdly, our loyal acknowledgement of the support of Great Britain must be spontaneous and unmeasured. But it must be the acknowledgement of free men to a country which breeds and loves free men. We must show that what Great Britain has given us through her generosity, is ours by virtue of our intelligence, skill, and courage.

Fourthly, we must have ample means. The means of yesterday are ridiculously small compared with the needs of today. Propaganda, the study of practical problems, expeditions, the founding of new offices and commissions, negotiations, preparations for settlement, relief and reconstruction in Palestine for all these, and other indispensable tasks, colossal material means are necessary, and necessary forthwith. Small and great, poor and rich, must rise to answer the call of this hour with the necessary personal sacrifice.

Fifthly, we need discipline and unity. This is no time for hair-splitting controversy. It is a time for action. We ask for confidence. Be united and tenacious, be quick but not impatient, be free men, but well-disciplined, firm as steel. From now onwards every gathering of Jews must have a practical aim, every speech must deal with a project, every thought must be a brick with which to build the National Home.

These are the directions for your work today.

Worn and weary through your two thousand years of wandering over the desert and ocean, driven by every storm and carried on every wave, outcasts and refugees, you may now pass from the misery of exile to a secure home; a home where the Jewish spirit and the old Hebrew genius, which so long have hovered broken-winged over strange nests, can also find healing and be quickened into new life.

N. Sokolow, E. W. Tschlenow, and
Ch. Weizmann

NOTE

1. Hovevei Zion were the members of Hibbat Zion.

9

Winston Churchill, for the British Government

Palestine White Paper

June 3, 1922

This policy paper, published in June 1922 by the British secretary of state for the colonies, Winston Churchill, included an interpretation of the text of the mandate for Palestine, soon to be approved by the League of Nations. The paper included nine letters concerning the political future of Palestine, exchanged between the British Colonial Office and the Zionist Organization and an Arab delegation then visiting London. The central document was a statement that came as an enclosure to the fifth letter. Although sent in Churchill's name, this document was elaborated and promoted by the high commissioner for Palestine, Herbert Samuel.

The white paper addressed the Arab concerns that had caused the 1920–21 riots through a profound revision of the 1917 Balfour Declaration. Establishing the principle of "double obligation" of the British regarding Jews and Arabs in Palestine, the paper stated that the civil, religious, and cultural rights of all inhabitants

Source: *British White Paper,* June 3, 1922, Cmd. 1700.

would be equally respected and that the Jews were in, and immigrating to, Palestine "as of right and not on sufferance." The document envisioned the development of the country through collaboration among British, Arabs, and Jews as well as a degree of Jewish and Arab participation in the government. The Palestine statement was accepted, though grudgingly, by the Zionists but rejected by the Arabs.

The Secretary of State for the Colonies has given renewed consideration to the existing political situation in Palestine, with a very earnest desire to arrive at a settlement of the outstanding questions which have given rise to uncertainty and unrest among certain sections of the population. After consultation with the High Commissioner for Palestine, the following statement has been drawn up. . . .

The tension which has prevailed from time to time in Palestine is mainly due to apprehensions, which are entertained both by sections of the Arab and by sections of the Jewish population. These apprehensions, so far as the Arabs are concerned, are partly based upon exaggerated interpretations of the meaning of the Declaration favoring the establishment of a Jewish National Home in Palestine, made on behalf of His Majesty's Government on 2 November 1917 [doc. 7]. Unauthorized statements have been made to the effect that the purpose in view is to create a wholly Jewish Palestine. Phrases have been used such as that Palestine is to become "as Jewish as England is English." His Majesty's Government regard any such expectation as impracticable and have no such aim in view. Nor have they at any time contemplated, as appears to be feared by the Arab Delegation, the disappearance or the subordination of the Arabic population, language or culture in Palestine. They would draw attention to the fact that the terms of the Declaration referred to do not contemplate that Palestine as a whole should be converted into a Jewish National Home, but that such a Home should be founded *in Palestine*. In this connection, it has been observed with satisfaction that at the meeting of the Zionist Congress, the supreme governing body of the Zionist Organization, held at Carlsbad in September 1921, a resolution was passed expressing as the official statement of Zionist aims, "the determination of the Jewish people to live with the Arab people on terms of unity and mutual respect, and together with them to make the common home into a flourishing community, the up-building of which may assure to each of its peoples an undisturbed national development."

It is also necessary to point out that the Zionist Commission in Palestine, now termed the Palestine Zionist Executive, has not desired to possess, and does not possess, any share in the general administration of the country. Nor does the special position assigned to the Zionist Organization in Article IV of the Draft Mandate for Palestine imply any such functions. That special position relates to the measures to be taken in Palestine affecting the Jewish population, and contemplates that the Organization may assist in the general development of the country, but does not entitle it to share in any degree in its Government.

Further, it is contemplated that the status of all citizens of Palestine in the eyes of the law shall be Palestinian, and it has never been intended that they, or any section of them, should possess any other juridical status. So far as the Jewish population of Palestine are concerned, it appears that some among them are apprehensive that His Majesty's Government may depart from the policy embodied in the Declaration of 1917. It is necessary, therefore, once more to affirm that these fears are unfounded, and that Declaration, reaffirmed by the Conference of the Principal Allied Powers at San Remo and again in the Treaty of Sevres, is not susceptible of change.

During the last two or three generations, the Jews have recreated in Palestine a community, now numbering 80,000, of whom about one-fourth are farmers or workers upon the land. This community has its own political organs; an elected assembly for the direction of its domestic concerns; elected councils in the towns; and an organization for the control of its schools. It has its elected Chief Rabbinate and Rabbinical council for the direction of its religious affairs. Its business is conducted in Hebrew as a vernacular language, and a Hebrew Press serves its needs. It has its distinctive intellectual life and displays considerable economic activity. This community, then, with its town and country population, its political, religious and social organizations, its own language, its own customs, its own life, has in fact "national" characteristics. When it is asked what is meant by the development of the Jewish National Home in Palestine, it may be answered that it is not the impression of a Jewish nationality upon the inhabitants of Palestine as a whole, but the further development of the existing Jewish community, with the assistance of Jews in other parts of the world, in order that it may become a center in which the Jewish people as a whole may take, on grounds of religion and race, an interest and a pride. But in order that this community should have the best prospect of free development and provide a full opportunity for the Jewish people to display its capacities, it is essential that it should know that it is in Palestine as of right and not on sufferance. That is the reason why it is necessary that the existence of a Jewish National Home in Palestine should be internationally guaranteed, and that it should be formally recognized to rest upon ancient historic connection.

This, then, is the interpretation which His Majesty's Government place upon the Declaration of 1917, and, so understood, the Secretary of State is of the opinion that it does not contain or imply anything which need cause alarm to the Arab population of Palestine or disappointment to the Jews. For the fulfillment of this policy, it is necessary that the Jewish community in Palestine should be able to increase its numbers by immigration. This immigration cannot be so great in volume as to exceed whatever may be the economic capacity of the country at the time to absorb new arrivals. It is essential to ensure that the immigrants should not be a burden upon the people of Palestine as a whole, and that they should deprive any section of the present population of their employment. Hitherto, the immigration has fulfilled these conditions. The number of immigrants since the British occupation has been almost 25,000.

Nevertheless, it is the intention of His Majesty's Government to foster the establishment of a full measure of self-government in Palestine. But they are of opinion that, in the special circumstances of that country, this should be accomplished by gradual stages and not suddenly. The first step was taken when, on the institution of a civil Administration, the nominated Advisory Council, which now exists, was established. It was stated at the time by the High Commissioner that this was the first step in the development of self-governing institutions, and it is now proposed to take a second step by the establishment of a Legislative Council containing a large proportion of members elected on a wide franchise. It was proposed in the published draft that three of the members of this Council should be non-official persons nominated by the High Commissioner, but representations having been made in opposition to this provision, based on cogent considerations, the Secretary of State is prepared to omit it. The Legislative Council would then consist of the High Commissioner as President and twelve elected and ten official members. The Secretary of State is of the opinion that before a further measure of self-government is extended to Palestine and the Assembly placed in control over the Executive, it would be wise to allow some time to elapse. During this period, the institutions of the country will have become well established; its financial credit will be based on firm foundations; and the Palestinian officials will have been enabled to gain experience of sound methods of government. After a few years, the situation will be again reviewed, and if the experience of the working of the Constitution now to be established so warranted, a larger share of authority would then be extended to the elected representatives of the people.

10

Council of the League of Nations

Mandate for Palestine

July 24, 1922

On July 24, 1922, the Council of the League of Nations approved the draft of the British Mandate for Palestine, and it was ratified. Suzerainty over the country remained in the hands of the League of Nations, but Great Britain received a broad latitude for its presence in Palestine and for the rights and duties related to the administration of the country. While the Arabs were barely mentioned, the development of the Jewish National Home was specifically mentioned in several articles as one of the goals of the British Mandate. A Jewish public body, the Jewish Agency, representing the Zionist organizations and "all Jews" was recognized as the institution that should cooperate with the British administration for the establishment of the Jewish National Home. Recognizing the asymmetry between Jews and Arabs in the draft of the Mandate for Palestine, the British approved at the same time the Churchill memorandum included in the Palestine White Paper of June 1922 (doc. 9).

A note appended to the text of the mandate, approved by the Council of the League of Nations in September 1922, established that the articles dealing with the development of a Jewish National Home in Palestine did not apply to the "territory known as Trans-Jordan."

The Council of the League of Nations:

Whereas the Principal Allied Powers[1] have agreed, for the purpose of giving effect to the provisions of Article 22[2] of the Covenant of the League of Nations to entrust to a Mandatory selected by the said Powers the administration of the territory of Palestine, which formerly belonged to the Turkish Empire, within such boundaries as may be fixed by them; and

Whereas the Principal Allied Powers have also agreed that the Mandatory should be responsible for putting into effect the declaration originally made on November 2, 1917, by the Government of His Britannic Majesty,[3] and adopted by the said Powers,[4] in favour of the establishment in Palestine of a National Home for the Jewish people, it being clearly understood that nothing should be done which might prejudice the civil and religious rights of existing

---

Source: *British White Paper*, Cmd. 1785, in British Foreign Office, *The Constitutions of All Countries* (London: British Empire, 1938), 1:539–45. Reprinted in *The Jew in the Modern World*, ed. Paul R. Mendes-Flohr and Jehuda Reinharz (New York: Oxford University Press, 1980), pp. 461–62. Annotations adapted and used by permission.

non-Jewish communities in Palestine, or the rights and political status enjoyed by Jews in any other country; and

Whereas recognition has thereby been given to the historical connection of the Jewish people with Palestine and to the grounds for reconstituting their National Home in that country; and

Whereas the Principal Allied Powers have selected His Britannic Majesty as the Mandatory for Palestine; and

Whereas the Mandate in respect of Palestine has been formulated in the following terms and submitted to the Council of the League for approval; and

Whereas His Britannic Majesty has accepted the Mandate in respect of Palestine and undertaken to exercise it on behalf of the League of Nations in conformity with the following provisions; and

Whereas by the aforementioned Article 22 (paragraph 8), it is provided that the degree of authority, control or administration to be exercised by the Mandatory, not having been previously agreed upon by the Members of the League, shall be explicitly defined by the Council of the League of Nations;

Confirming the said Mandate, defines its terms as follows:

Article 1. The Mandatory shall have full powers of legislation and of administration, save as they may be limited by the terms of this Mandate.

Article 2. The Mandatory shall be responsible for placing the country under such political, administrative and economic conditions as will secure the establishment of the Jewish National Home, as laid down in the preamble, and the development of self-governing institutions, and also for safeguarding the civil and religious rights of all the inhabitants of Palestine, irrespective of race and religion.

Article 3. The Mandatory shall, so far as circumstances permit, encourage local autonomy.

Article 4. An appropriate Jewish Agency shall be recognized as a public body for the purpose of advising and cooperating with the Administration of Palestine in such economic, social and other matters as may affect the establishment of the Jewish National Home and the interests of the Jewish population in Palestine, and, subject always to the control of the Administration, to assist and take part in the development of the country.

The Zionist organization, so long as its organization and constitution are in the opinion of the Mandatory appropriate, shall be recognized as such agency. It shall take steps in consultation with His Britannic Majesty's Government to secure the cooperation of all Jews who are willing to assist in the establishment of the Jewish National Home.

Article 5. The Mandatory shall be responsible for seeing that no Palestine territory shall be ceded or leased to, or in any way placed under the control of, the Government of any foreign Power.

Article 6. The Administration of Palestine, while ensuring that the rights and position of other sections of the population are not prejudiced, shall facilitate a Jewish immigration under suitable conditions and shall encourage, in cooperation with the Jewish Agency referred to in Article 4, close settlement by Jews on the land, including State lands and waste lands not required for public purposes.

Article 7. The Administration of Palestine shall be responsible for enacting a nationality law. There shall be included in this law provisions framed so as to facilitate the acquisition of Palestinian citizenship by Jews who take up their permanent residence in Palestine.

Article 8. The privileges and immunities of foreigners, including the benefits of consular jurisdiction and protection as formerly enjoyed by Capitulation or usage in the Ottoman Empire, shall not be applicable in Palestine.

Unless the Powers whose nationals enjoyed the aforementioned privileges and immunities on August 1, 1914, shall have previously renounced the right to their reestablishment, or shall have agreed to their non-application for a specified period, these privileges and immunities shall, at the expiration of the Mandate, be immediately reestablished in their entirety or with such modifications as may have been agreed upon between the Powers concerned.

Article 9. The Mandatory shall be responsible for seeing that the judicial system established in Palestine shall assure to foreigners, as well as to natives, a complete guarantee of their rights.

Respect for the personal status of the various peoples and communities and for their religious interests shall be fully guaranteed. In particular, the control and administration of *waqfs*[5] shall be exercised in accordance with religious law and the dispositions of the founders.

Article 10. Pending the making of special extradition agreements relating to Palestine, the extradition treaties in force between the Mandatory and other foreign Powers shall apply to Palestine.

Article 11. The Administration of Palestine shall take all necessary measures to safeguard the interests of the community in connection with the development of the country, and, subject to any international obligations accepted by the Mandatory, shall have full power to provide for public ownership or control of any of the natural resources of the country or of the public works, service and utilities established or to be established therein. It shall introduce a land system appropriate to the needs of the country, having regard, among other things, to the desirability of promoting the close settlement and intensive cultivation of the land.

The Administration may arrange with the Jewish Agency mentioned in Article 4 to construct or operate, upon fair and equitable terms, any public works, services and utilities, and to develop any of the natural resources of the country, in so far as these matters are not directly undertaken by the Administration. Any such arrangements shall provide that no profits distributed by such Agency, directly or indirectly, shall exceed a reasonable rate of interest on the capital, and any further profits shall be utilized by it for the benefit of the country in a manner approved by the Administration.

Article 12. The Mandatory shall be entrusted with the control of the foreign relations of Palestine and the right to issue *exequaturs*[6] to consuls appointed by foreign Powers. He shall also be entitled to afford diplomatic and consular protection to citizens of Palestine when outside its territorial limits.

Article 13. All responsibility in connection with the Holy Places and religious buildings or sites in Palestine, including that of preserving rights existing and of securing free access to the Holy Places, religious buildings, and sites, and the free exercise of worship, while ensuring the requirements of public order and decorum, is assumed by the Mandatory, who shall be responsible solely to the League of Nations in all matters connected herewith, provided that nothing in this Article shall prevent the Mandatory from entering into such arrangements as he may deem reasonable with the Administration for the purpose of carrying the provisions of this Article into effect; and provided also that nothing in this Mandate shall be construed as conferring upon the Mandatory authority to interfere with the fabric or the management of purely Moslem sacred shrines, the immunities of which are guaranteed.

Article 14. A special Commission shall be appointed by the Mandatory to study, define and determine the rights and claims in connection with the Holy Places and the rights and claims relating to the different religious communities in Palestine. The method of nomination, the composition and the functions of this Commission shall be submitted to the Council of the League for its approval, and the Commission shall not be appointed or enter upon its functions without the approval of the Council.

Article 15. The Mandatory shall see that complete freedom of conscience and the free exercise of all forms of worship, subject only to the maintenance of public order and morals, are ensured to all. No discrimination of any kind shall be made between the inhabitants of Palestine on the ground of race, religion or language. No person shall be excluded from Palestine on the sole ground of his religious belief.

The right of each community to maintain its own schools for the education of its own members in its own language, while conforming to such educational requirements of a general nature as the Administration may impose, shall not be denied or impaired.

Article 16. The Mandatory shall be responsible for exercising such supervision over religious or eleemosynary bodies of all faiths in Palestine as may be required for the maintenance of public order and good government. Subject to such supervision, no measures shall be taken in Palestine to obstruct or interfere with the enterprise of such bodies or to discriminate against any representative or member of them on the ground of his religion or nationality.

Article 17. The Administration of Palestine may organize on a voluntary basis the forces necessary for the preservation of peace and order, and also for the defense of the country, subject, however, to the supervision of the Mandatory, but shall not use them for the purposes other than those above specified save with the consent of the Mandatory. Except for such purposes, no military, naval or air forces shall be raised or maintained by the Administration of Palestine.

Nothing in this Article shall preclude the Administration of Palestine from contributing to the cost of the maintenance of the force of the Mandatory in Palestine.

The Mandatory shall be entitled at all times to use the roads, railways and ports of Palestine for the movement of armed forces and the carriage of fuel and supplies.

Article 18. The Mandatory shall see that there is no discrimination in Palestine against the nationals of any State Member of the League of Nations (including companies incorporated under its laws) as compared with those of the Mandatory or of any foreign State in matters concerning taxation, commerce, or navigation, the exercise of industries or professions, or in the treatment of merchant vessels or civil aircraft. Similarly, there shall be no discrimination in Palestine against goods originating in or destined for any of the said States, and there shall be freedom of transit under equitable conditions across the Mandated area.

Subject as aforesaid and to the other provisions of this Mandate, the Administration of Palestine may, on the advice of the Mandatory, impose such taxes and Customs duties as it may consider necessary, and take such steps as it may think best to promote the development of the natural resources of the country and to safeguard the interests of the population. It may also, on the advice of the Mandatory, conclude a special Customs agreement with any State the territory of which in 1914 was wholly included in Asiatic Turkey or Arabia.

Article 19. The Mandatory shall adhere on behalf of the Administration of Palestine to any general international conventions already existing, or which may be concluded hereafter with the approval of the League of Nations, respecting the slave traffic, the traffic in arms and ammunition, or the traffic in drugs, or relating to commercial equality, freedom of transit and navigation, aerial navigation and postal, telegraphic and wireless communication or literary, artistic or industrial property.

Article 20. The Mandatory shall cooperate on behalf of the Administration of Palestine, so far as religious, social and other conditions may permit, in the execution of any common policy adopted by the League of Nations for preventing and combating disease, including diseases of plants and animals.

Article 21. The Mandatory shall secure the enactment within twelve months from this date, and shall ensure the execution of a law of antiquities based on the following rules. The law shall ensure equality of treatment in the matter of excavations and archaeological research to the nations of all States Members of the League of Nations.

1. "Antiquity" means any construction or any product of human activity earlier than the year A.D. 1700.
2. The law for the protection of antiquities shall proceed by encouragement rather than by threat.

   Any person who, having discovered an antiquity without being furnished with the authorization referred to in paragraph 5, reports the same to an official of the competent Department, shall be rewarded according to the value of the discovery.
3. No antiquity may be disposed of except to the competent Department, unless this Department renounces the acquisition of any such antiquity.

   No antiquity may leave the country without an export licence from the said Department.
4. Any person who maliciously or negligently destroys or damages an antiquity shall be liable to a penalty to be fixed.
5. No clearing of ground or digging with the object of finding antiquities shall be permitted, under penalty of fine, except to persons authorized by the competent Department.
6. Equitable terms shall be fixed for expropriation, temporary or permanent, of lands which might be of historical or archaeological interest.
7. Authorization to excavate shall only be granted to persons who show sufficient guarantees of archaeological experience. The Administration of Palestine shall not, in granting these authorizations, act in such a way as to exclude scholars of any nation without good grounds.
8. The proceeds of excavations may be divided between the excavator and the competent Department in a proportion fixed by that Department. If division seems impossible for scientific reasons, the excavator shall receive a fair indemnity in lieu of a part of the find.

Article 22. English, Arabic and Hebrew shall be the official languages of Palestine. Any statement or inscription in Arabic on stamp or money in Palestine shall be repeated in Hebrew, and any statement or inscription in Hebrew shall be repeated in Arabic.

Article 23. The Administration of Palestine shall recognize the holy days of the respective communities in Palestine as legal days of rest for the members of such communities.

Article 24. The Mandatory shall make to the Council of the League of Nations an annual report to the satisfaction of the Council as to the measures taken during the year to carry out the provisions of the Mandate. Copies of all laws and regulations promulgated or issued during the year shall be communicated with the report.

Article 25. In the territories lying between the Jordan and the eastern boundary of Palestine as ultimately determined, the Mandatory shall be entitled, with the consent of the Council of the League of Nations, to postpone or withhold application of such provisions of this Mandate as he may consider inapplicable to the existing local conditions, and to make such provision for the administration of the territories as he may consider suitable to those conditions, provided that no action shall be taken which is inconsistent with the provisions of Articles 15, 16 and 18.

Article 26. The Mandatory agrees that if any dispute whatever should arise between the Mandatory and another Member of the League of Nations relating to the interpretation or the application of the provisions of the Mandate, such dispute, if it cannot be settled by negotiation, shall be submitted to the Permanent Court of International Justice provided for by Article 14[7] of the Covenant of the League of Nations.

Article 27. The consent of the Council of the League of Nations is required for any modification of the terms of this Mandate.

Article 28. In the event of the termination of the Mandate hereby conferred upon the Mandatory, the Council of the League of Nations shall make such arrangements as may be deemed necessary for safeguarding in perpetuity, under guarantee of the League, the rights secured by Articles 13[8] and 14, and shall use its influence for securing, under the guarantee of the League, that the Government of Palestine will fully honour the financial obligations legitimately incurred by the Administration of Palestine during the period of the Mandate, including the rights of public servants to pensions or gratuities.

The present instrument shall be deposited in original in the archives of the League of Nations and certified copies shall be forwarded by the Secretary-General of the League of Nations to all Members of the League.

Done at London the twenty-fourth day of July, one thousand nine hundred and twenty-two.

NOTES

1. The Principal Allied Powers were Britain, France, Italy, and Japan.
2. Article 22 of the Covenant of the League of Nations reads as follows:

> To those colonies and territories which as a consequence of the late war have ceased to be under the sovereignty of the States which formerly governed them and which are inhabited by peoples not yet able to stand by themselves under the strenuous conditions of the modern world, there should be applied the principle that the well-being and development of such peoples form a sacred trust of civilisation and that securities for the performance of this trust should be embodied in this Covenant.
>
> The best method of giving practical effect to this principle is that the tutelage of such peoples should be entrusted to advanced nations who by reason of their resources, their experience or their geographical position can best undertake this responsibility, and who are willing to accept it, and that this tutelage should be exercised by them as Mandatories on behalf of the League.
>
> The character of the mandate must differ according to the stage of the development of the people, the geographical situation of the territory, its economic conditions and other similar circumstances.
>
> Certain communities formerly belonging to the Turkish Empire have reached a stage of development where their existence as independent nations can be provisionally recognized subject to the rendering of administrative advice and assistance by a Mandatory until such time as they are able to stand alone. The wishes of these communities must be a principal consideration in the selection of the Mandatory.
>
> Other peoples, especially those of Central Africa, are at such a stage that the Mandatory must be responsible for the administration of the territory under conditions which will guarantee freedom of conscience and religion, subject only to the maintenance of public order and morals, the prohibition of abuses such as the slave trade, the arms traffic and the liquor traffic, and the prevention of the establishment of fortifications or military and naval bases and of military training of the natives for other than police purposes and the defense of territory, and will also secure equal opportunities for the trade and commerce of other Members of the League. There are territories, such as South-West Africa and certain of the South Pacific Islands, which, owing to the sparseness of their population, or their small size, or their remoteness from the centres of civilisation, or their geographical contiguity to the territory of the Mandatory, and other circumstances, can be best administered under the laws of the Mandatory as integral portions of its territory, subject to the safeguards above mentioned in the interests of the indigenous population.
>
> In every case of mandate, the Mandatory shall render to the Council an annual report in reference to the territory committed to its charge.
>
> The degree of authority, control, or administration to be exercised by the Mandatory shall, if not previously agreed upon by the Members of the League, be explicitly defined in each case by the Council.
>
> A permanent Commission shall be constituted to receive and examine the annual reports of the Mandatories and to advise the Council on all matters relating to the observance of the mandates.

3. The reference is to the Balfour Declaration (doc. 7).
4. The Principal Allied Powers adopted the Balfour Declaration at the San Remo Peace Conference on April 25, 1920.
5. *Waqfs* are religious endowments.
6. *Exequatur* is an authorization from a receiving state that a head of a consular post of another state is admitted to exercise his functions.
7. Article 14 of the Covenant of the League of Nations reads as follows:

> The Council shall formulate and submit to the Members of the League for adoption plans for the establishment of a Permanent Court of International Justice.

The Court shall be competent to hear and determine any dispute of an international character which the parties thereto submit to it. The Court may also give an advisory opinion upon any dispute or question referred to it by the Council or by the Assembly.

8. Article 13 of the Covenant of the League of Nations reads as follows:

The Members of the League agree that whenever any dispute shall arise between them which they recognize to be suitable for submission to arbitration or judicial settlement and which cannot be satisfactorily settled by diplomacy, they will submit the whole subject-matter to arbitration or judicial settlement.

Disputes as to the interpretation of a treaty, as to any question of international law, as to the existence of any fact which if established would constitute a breach of any international obligation, or as to the extent and nature of the reparation to be made for any such breach, are declared to be among those which are generally suitable for submission to arbitration or judicial settlement.

For the consideration of any such dispute, the court to which the case is referred shall be the Permanent Court of International Justice, established in accordance with Article 14, or any tribunal agreed on by the parties to the dispute or stipulated in any convention existing between them.

The Members of the League agree that they will carry out in full good faith any award or decision that may be rendered, and that they will not resort to war against a Member of the League which complies therewith. In the event of any failure to carry out such an award or decision, the Council shall propose what steps should be taken to give effect thereto.

11

Vladimir (Zeev) Jabotinsky

The Iron Wall

November 4, 1923

Vladimir (Zeev) Jabotinsky (1880–1940) was a thinker, journalist, author, and founder and leader of Revisionist Zionism. An activist in the Zionist movement and a leader in a number of Jewish self-defense efforts in Russia and Palestine, Jabotinsky played a crucial role in establishing a Jewish unit in the British Armed Forces in the First World War. During the 1920s he emerged as an opposition voice to Zionist leadership, first to Chaim Weizmann and later to David Ben-Gurion. Jabotinsky objected to the political pragmatism of the Zionist movement, with policies such as cooperation with the British, and in 1935 led his faction, the Union of Revisionist Zionists, out of the Zionist Organization and established the New Zionist Organization. Jabotinsky died in 1940, but the ideological framework he created lasted well into the late twentieth century in Israel's main right-wing party Herut (later, Likud).

The following article, written by Jabotinsky in 1923, formulated what had become the basic attitude of the Revisionist movement to the Arab Question. The Arabs, he stated, were unable to accept the idea that in the course of time the Jews might constitute a majority in Eretz Israel. His conclusion was that the Zionist effort could only be implemented behind "an Iron Wall" to be built by the Zionists in cooperation with Britain. The term "Iron Wall" meant the imposition, even by force, of a series of political conditions that would prevent the Arabs from interfering with the Zionist enterprise.

Source: Zeev Jabotinsky, *Baderech Lamedina* [On the Way to a State] (Jerusalem, 1953). English translation from *Jewish Herald* (South Africa), November 26, 1937.

I must begin this essay by deviating from the attractive rule—that essays should begin with the subject matter itself—and start with an introduction, a personal one. The present writer is considered an enemy of the Arabs, a person who wishes to push them out of Palestine, etc. This is not true. My emotional attitude to the Arabs is identical to my attitude toward all other nations: polite indifference. My political attitude toward them is determined by two principles: First, I regard the Arabs' removal from Palestine as absolutely unacceptable. Palestine has always been inhabited by two peoples. Second, I am proud of being part of the group that had drafted the Helsingfors Plan,[1] the plan offering national rights to all peoples living in one state. In formulating this plan, we were thinking not only of the Jews but of all peoples, wherever they may reside. The plan is predicated on absolute equality of rights. I am willing to take an oath in our name and in the name of our descendants that we will never challenge this equality of rights and will never try to dispossess anyone. As the reader can see, this is a purely peaceful credo.

But there is another question, couched in very different terms, as to whether the objective of peace can be always reached through peaceful means. The answer to that question depends purely on the Arab attitude towards us and towards Zionism and not on our attitude to the Arabs.

In the aftermath of this introduction, we can move to the actual issue.

It is impossible to dream, now and in the foreseeable future, of a voluntary agreement between Jews and the Palestinian Arabs. I am resorting to their short formulation not because I wish to aggravate the moderate section of the Zionist camp, but simply because this will not inflict on them any aggravation. Apart from those who were born blind, all moderate Zionists had understood that there can be no hope—not a glimmer of it—to obtain the consent of the Palestinian Arabs to the idea of turning "Palestine" into a country with a Jewish majority.

Every reader knows something about the history of settlement in other countries of settlement. I ask him to recall all the examples he is familiar with and to find at least one instance of a country settled with the consent of the indigenous population. There is no such example. . . . Any indigenous nation, civilized or backward, views its country as its "national home" where it wants to be and remain forever the only landlord. And such a nation will not willingly agree to new landlords or even to partners.

This principle applies also to the Arabs. The trumpeters of peace among us are trying to persuade us that the Arabs are either fools who can be deceived by a softened interpretation of our objective or that they are an avaricious lot, ready to surrender its title in exchange for cultural or economic advantages. I totally reject this explanation of the Arab character. Their cultural level is low and they do not possess our perseverance and will power. But they are subtle psychologists exactly like us, and like us have been educated for centuries to split hairs and sharpen their brain. We can tell them at length about the nature of our aspirations, but they understand precisely like us what is not to their advantage. . . . Individual Arabs can certainly be bribed but this does not mean that Palestine's Arabs as a whole are willing to sell it. . . .

Some of us thought that a misunderstanding has occurred, that the Arabs failed to understand our true will, and that it is only due to this that they are against us; if we could only make it clear to them how modest and limited our true ambitions are, they would immediately offer their hand in peace. But this too is a mistake that has been demonstrated innumerable times. . . .

Many Zionists are attracted by the following plan. If Zionism cannot obtain a stamp of approval from the Palestinian Arabs, it should be obtained from other Arabs—the Arabs of Syria, Mesopotamia, Hidjaz and maybe even Egypt. But even if such an idea were feasible, it would fail to transform the situation; in Palestine itself the Arabs' attitude toward us wouldn't change . . . it would remain necessary to conduct the settlement project without the consent of the Palestinian Arabs.

But an agreement with the Arabs outside Palestine is also a delusion. . . .

. . . And the conclusion: we cannot offer an "exchange" to the Arabs in or outside Palestine. A voluntary agreement is impossible. Therefore, those who regard an agreement with the Arabs as a *sine qua non* of Zionism can tell themselves right now that this condition is impossible to obtain and Zionism should be given up. Our settlement should either be stopped or be continued regardless of the indigenous population's attitude. Or, the settlement project can continue under the protection of a power independent of the indigenous population, behind an iron wall that the indigenous population could not break.

This is the content of our policy towards the Arab question. Not only must it be its contents, but whether we admit it or not, our policy is predicated on it. What is the value of the Balfour Declaration for us? What is the value of the Mandate? Their significance for us is that an external force has undertaken to establish in the country such terms of administration and security so as to prevent the local population from any attempt to interfere with our effort should they decide to do so. And all of us, without exception, keep demanding of the external force to meet this obligation strictly. In this regard there is no distinction between our "militants" and our "vegetarians." . . . We all want the iron wall. But we cause damage to ourselves if we chant of agreement and enter into the hands of the Mandatory Powers' leaders that think the essential thing is not the iron wall but uninterrupted discussion. This resolution can do harm to our camp. Therefore, it is not merely a pleasure but a holy duty to discredit the empty phrase, to prove that it is a pipe dream, to point out the double standard.

I do not intend to state that no agreement with the Palestinian Arabs is possible. Only a voluntary agreement is impossible. As long as the Arabs harbor even a glimmer of hope that they could get rid of us, no sweet talk or enticing promises will motivate the Arabs to abandon this hope, precisely because they are not a mob but a living nation. A living nation is ready for concessions in such fateful issues only when all hope for "getting rid" is lost; when all holes are sealed in the iron wall. Only then do the extreme factions testing the hammer of "never" lose their influence, and influence shifts to more moderate quarters. The moderates then emerge with offers of mutual concessions. Only then will they begin to bargain with us over such practical issues as guarantees against displacing the Arabs, and civic and national equality. It is my hope and belief that we will offer them satisfactory guarantees and that both people could live in peace like good neighbors. But the only path leading to such an agreement is the iron wall, namely the existence in Palestine of a power that will not be affected by the Arabs' pressure. In other words, the only way to obtain an agreement in the future is total abdication of all attempts at agreement at the present.

NOTE

1. The Helsingfors Plan was adopted in the third conference of Russian Zionists held December 4–10, 1906, in Helsingfors (Helsinki), in the Grand Duchy of Finland. The plan offered a dual vision of a future national revival in Palestine alongside interim measures for Russian Jews that included autonomous rights, for all non-Russian minorities, under a democratic regime. By referring to the plan in "The Iron Wall," Jabotinsky affirmed his commitment to awarding minority rights for Arabs in Palestine, as they flow from the same principle that was suppose to apply for Jews under the Helsingfors Plan.

12

Peel Commission

Report Conclusions

July 7, 1937

Arab resistance to the creation of a Jewish National Home in Palestine brought the proclamation of a general Arab strike in the spring of 1936, accompanied by first acts of violence. In August 1936 a royal commission, headed by Lord Peel, was charged to ascertain the underlying causes of the disturbances, to inquire how the terms of the Mandate for Palestine (doc. 10) were being implemented, to examine the grievances of Arabs and Jews, and to recommend ways to improve the public situation in Palestine.

The commission arrived at far-reaching conclusions, printed here, that changed the basic assumption of the British administration in Palestine: to partition most of Palestine between Arabs and Jews, toward the establishment of two independent states. The proposal was elaborated by commission member Reginald Coupland, professor of colonial history at Oxford University. The leading idea was that no common public ground had developed between Arabs and Jews and that "neither Arab nor Jew has any sense of service to a single state."

Although the British cabinet endorsed partition, soon second thoughts arose in government circles, and toward the end of 1937 the Partition Plan was quietly rejected. This change in British policy was due largely to a belief, especially in the Foreign Office, that in the worsening conflict between Arabs and Jews in Palestine, British interests in the region and in the Middle East were better served by larger support for the demands of the Arab side.

The Zionist movement considered the plan at the Twentieth Zionist Congress in August 1937. While rejecting the specific proposals of the Peel Commission, the congress expressed readiness, in principle, to consider a better partition proposal.

The Arabs rejected the Partition Plan and in the fall of 1937 their armed revolt against the British and the Jews took on serious dimensions. Only toward the end of 1938 was the revolt brought under control.

"Half a loaf is better than no bread" is a peculiarly English proverb; and, considering the attitude which both the Arab and Jewish representatives adopted in giving evidence before us, we think it improbable that either party will be satisfied at first sight with the proposals we have submitted for the adjustment of their rival claims. For Partition means that neither will get what it wants. It means that the Arabs must acquiesce in the exclusion from their sovereignty of a piece of territory, long occupied and once ruled by them. It means that the Jews must be content with less than the Land of Israel they once ruled and have hoped to rule again. But it seems to us possible that on reflection both parties will come to realize that the drawbacks of Partition are outweighed by its advantages. For, if it offers neither party all it wants, it offers each what it wants most, namely, freedom and security.

The advantages to the Arabs of Partition on the lines we have proposed may be summarized as follows:

Source: Report, July 7, 1937, Cmd. 5479, pp. 394–96.

a. They obtain their national independence and can cooperate on an equal footing with the Arabs of the neighboring countries in the cause of Arab unity and progress.
b. They are finally delivered from the fear of being "swamped" by the Jews and from the possibility of ultimate subjection to Jewish rule.
c. In particular, the final limitation of the Jewish National Home within a fixed frontier and the enactment of a new Mandate for the protection of the Holy Places solemnly guaranteed by the League of Nations removes all anxiety lest the Holy Places should ever come under Jewish control.
d. As a set-off to the loss of territory the Arabs regard as theirs, the Arab State will receive a subvention from the Jewish State. It will also, in view of the backwardness of Transjordan, obtain a grant of £2,000,000 from the British Treasury and, if an arrangement can be made for the exchange of land and population, a further grant will be made for the conversion, as far as may prove possible, of uncultivable land in the Arab State into productive land from which the cultivators and the State alike will profit.

The advantages of Partition to the Jews may be summarized as follows:

a. Partition secures the establishment of the Jewish National Home and relieves it from the possibility of its being subjected in the future to Arab rule.
b. Partition enables the Jews in the fullest sense to call their National Home their own: for it converts it into a Jewish State. Its citizens will be able to admit as many Jews into it as they themselves believe can be absorbed. They will attain the primary objective of Zionism—a Jewish nation, planted in Palestine, giving its nationals the same status in the world as other nations give theirs. They will cease at last to live a "minority life."

To both Arabs and Jews, Partition offers a prospect—and we see no such prospect in any other policy—of obtaining the inestimable boon of peace. It is surely worth some sacrifice on both sides if the quarrel which the Mandate started could be ended with its termination. It is not a natural or old-standing feud. An able Arab exponent of the Arab case told us that the Arabs throughout their history have not only been free from anti-Jewish sentiment but have also shown that the spirit of compromise is deeply rooted in their life. And he went on to express his sympathy with the fate of the Jews in Europe. "There is no decent-minded person," he said, "who would not want to do everything humanly possible to relieve the distress of those persons," provided that it was "not at the cost of inflicting a corresponding distress on another people." Considering what the possibility of finding a refuge in Palestine means to many thousands of suffering Jews, we cannot believe that the "distress" occasioned by Partition, great as it would be, is more than Arab generosity can bear. And in this, as in so much else connected with Palestine, it is not only the peoples of that country that have to be considered. The Jewish Problem is not the least of the many problems which are disturbing international relations at this critical time and obstructing the path to peace and prosperity. If the Arabs, at some sacrifice, could help to solve that problem, they would earn the gratitude, not of the Jews alone, but of all the Western World.

There was a time when Arab statesmen were willing to concede little Palestine to the Jews, provided that the rest of Arab Asia were free. That condition was not fulfilled then, but it is on the eve of fulfillment now. In less than three years' time, all the wide Arab area outside Palestine between the Mediterranean and the Indian Ocean will be independent, and, if partition is adopted, the greater part of Palestine will be independent too.

There is no need to stress the advantage to the British people of a settlement in Palestine.

We are bound to honor to the utmost of our power the obligations we undertook in the exigencies of war towards the Arabs and the Jews. When those obligations were incorporated in the Mandate, we did not fully realize the difficulties of the task it laid on us. We have tried to overcome them, not always with success. They have steadily become greater till now they seem almost insuperable. Partition offers a possibility of finding a way through them, a possibility of obtaining a final solution of the problem which does justice to the rights and aspirations of both the Arabs and the Jews and discharged the obligations we undertook towards them twenty years ago to the fullest extent that is practicable in the circumstances of the present time.

13
George Antonius
The Arab Awakening
1938

Published in 1938, The Arab Awakening: The Story of the Arab National Movement, *was one of the earliest manifestations of a historical narrative of the Arab national movement. The book critiqued British policy in Palestine as supportive to Zionism and argued that a two-state solution would never materialize there. An excerpt appears below. The author was George Antonius (1891–1941), a scholar and former civil servant in the British colonial bureaucracy in Egypt and Palestine who turned to Arab political activism later in his life. In February 1939 he participated in the London Conference as a member of the Palestinian delegation.*

Antonius's biography offers a key to the origins of his argument and how it transcended traditional religious and local notions of identity. Antonius lived in a number of different Arab centers such as Cairo, Jerusalem, and Beirut. He was a Greek Orthodox in a largely Muslim world. He was also a member of the small Arab elite educated in the West, taking his undergraduate degree at Cambridge University. For many years he was supported by the New York-based Institute for Current World Affairs.

Perhaps the best approach to the problem is to begin with a review of the rights, claims and motives of each of the three parties concerned, as they stood at the end of the War.

The rights of the Arabs are derived from actual and longstanding possession, and rest upon the strongest human foundation. Their connection with Palestine goes back uninterruptedly to the earliest historic times, for the term "Arab" denotes nowadays not merely the incomers from the Arabian Peninsula who occupied the country in the seventh century, but also the older populations who intermarried with their conquerors, acquired their speech, customs and ways of thought and became permanently arabised. The traditions of the present inhabitants are as deeply rooted in their geographical surroundings as in their adoptive

Source: George Antonius, *The Arab Awakening: The Story of the Arab National Movement* (Beirut: Librairie de Liban, 1969).

culture, and it is a fallacy to imagine that they could be induced to transplant themselves, even to other Arab surroundings, any more than the farmers of Kent or Yorkshire could be induced to go and settle in Ireland. It may seem superfluous to point this out, but the fallacy is one on which the Palestine Royal Commission [see doc. 12] have raised a new edifice of false hopes; and the fact needs stressing, therefore, that any solution based on the forcible expulsion of the peasantry from the countryside in which they have their homesteads and their trees, their shrines and graveyards, and all the memories and affections that go with life on the soil, is bound to be forcibly resisted.

In addition to those natural rights, the Arabs had acquired specific political rights derived from the Sharif Husain's[1] compact with Great Britain and the help they gave her, in Palestine amongst other theatres. The thesis that Palestine west of the Jordan was excluded from the British pledges can no longer be maintained. The texts now available show that the Sharif Husain was given a general promise relating to its independence in the McMahon Correspondence[2] and a specific promise securing the political and economic freedom of its Arab population in the message conveyed to him by the late Commander Hogarth.[3] There is also the pledge contained in the Declaration to the Seven.[4] Taken together, these undertakings amount to a binding recognition of Arab political rights; but, here again, the real position has become obscured by a mass of contentious literature and utterances, abetted by official concealment. In spite of its circulation in the Arab countries, the McMahon Correspondence has remained hidden from public knowledge in England and in the Western world at large. As for Hogarth's message and the Declaration to the Seven, they lie buried in Whitehall in a sea of oblivion. The Report of the Royal Commission does not mention either; and it is obvious that important decisions of the British Government have been taken in the last eighteen years without reference to their contents. The point needs stressing not only because of its historical interest but for its practical bearing on the solution of the Palestine problem. It would be vain to seek a solution that does not take into account the significance of those undertakings and the importance which is attached to them in the Arab world as evidence of the validity of Arab political rights.

In other words, the Arab claims rest on two distinct foundations: the natural right of a settled population, in great majority agricultural, to remain in possession of the land of its birthright; and the acquired political rights which followed from the disappearance of Turkish sovereignty and from the Arab share in its overthrow, and which Great Britain is under a contractual obligation to recognise and uphold. . . .

The rights of the Jews are of a different order. In the minds of many people in the West, and more particularly in the Protestant countries, Zionism appears as a new embodiment of the old Jewish yearning for the Holy Land, and one that is destined to bring about the fulfilment of the Biblical prophecies. That is only one more of the prevalent misconceptions. There does exist a school of "spiritual" Zionists, sponsored by some of the most eminent names in Jewry, whose aims are primarily cultural and whose mainsprings are to be found in the idealistic and religious sentiments which had hitherto inspired Judaism in its affection for Palestine. But their influence in international politics has become relatively insignificant. The real power is wielded by the exponents of "political" Zionism which is not a religious but a nationalist movement aiming at the establishment of a Jewish state in Palestine on a basis of temporal power backed by the usual attributes of possession and sovereignty. It is against that school of Zionism that the Arab resistance in Palestine is directed.

The motives animating Zionism sprang from a humane concern over the precarious position of the Jews in certain countries in Europe. It had come into being as a reaction against antisemitism, in the last quarter of the nineteenth century, with the specific object of providing a remedy through the creation of a national state to which Jews might migrate and in which they could live in peace, freedom and the dignity of self-government. The motive was altogether humanitarian and generous, but whether the remedy proposed was a wise one is open to question. It rested on the theory that the Jews of the world formed one race and so could become one nation; and, in the eyes of many thoughtful Jews, it carried, in addition to the defects inherent in all racial nationalisms, the drawback that it implied a challenge to the position and the citizenship acquired by Jews in the countries of their adoption. But the crucial point in the Zionist programme is that it looks to Palestine as the only acceptable home of the proposed Jewish state. Such had not been the original intention of Theodor Herzl, the founder of Zionism; but when, in 1903, the British Government offered to make Uganda available for Jewish colonisation, a majority of Zionist pioneers overruled Herzl, rejected the offer and carried the vote in favour of a Palestinian state.

NOTES

1. Sharif Husain (Sharif Hussein, also known as Husain Ben-Ali) (1853–1931) was a descendant of the Hashemite dynasty that ruled the Islamic holy cities of Mecca and Medina under the Turkish Empire (1909–1917). Hussein allied himself with the British during the First World War.
2. The McMahon Correspondence was an exchange of letters between Sharif Hussein and Sir Henry McMahon (1862–1949), British high commissioner in Cairo in 1915–16. In the exchange the British promised Hussein support for an "Arab Kingdom" under his leadership in return for his support against the Turks.
3. David George Hogarth (1862–1927) was a British archaeologist and diplomat who was sent in January 1918 to assuage Sharif Hussein following the Balfour Declaration. In the meetings, Hogarth assured Hussein that the British government supported the aspiration of the Jews to return to Palestine as long as it did not intrude on the political and economic rights of the local Palestinian population.
4. This British statement, June 16, 1918, was intended to address Arab concerns following the Balfour Declaration and the Sykes-Picot Agreement. Read to seven Arab leaders who resided in Cairo at the time, at the British "Arab Bureau" there, the statement committed the British to promote the "complete and sovereign independence of the Arabs" in the Arabian Peninsula and laid down some principles for the future of other parts of the Arab world.

14

Malcolm MacDonald, for the British Government

White Paper

May 17, 1939

The London Conference's failure to reach an agreement between Jews and Arabs about the future administration of Palestine led British Colonial Secretary Malcolm MacDonald to announce a policy that returned to the principle of Palestine as an undivided country. The white paper stated that a Jewish National Home had been

Source: *British White Paper*, Cmd. 6019. Reprinted in *The Jew in the Modern World*, ed. Paul R. Mendes-Flohr and Jehuda Reinharz (New York: Oxford University Press, 1980), pp. 466–69. Annotations adapted and used by permission.

established in the country, thus fulfilling the British promises and the terms of the Mandate for Palestine (doc. 10). The document declared that Palestine should become, internal conditions permitting, an independent state in ten years. Jewish immigration was to be reduced to a total of 75,000 over a period of five years; further Jewish immigration should be dependent on Arab consent. Finally, further acquisition of Arab land by Jews was severely limited.

The Jewish Agency rejected the white paper, declaring that it was a violation of the terms of the Mandate and that it condemned the Jewish community in Palestine to a minority status in what would become a hostile, Arab-dominated state.

Further steps against the white paper had to be postponed because of the outbreak of World War II, during which the Zionists found themselves fighting on the side of the British against Nazi Germany.

In the Statement on Palestine, issued on 9 November 1938,[1] His Majesty's Government announced their intention to invite representatives of the Arabs of Palestine, of certain neighbouring countries, and of the Jewish Agency to confer with them in London regarding future policy. It was their sincere hope that, as a result of full, free and frank discussion, some understanding might be reached. Conferences recently took place with Arab and Jewish Delegations lasting for a period of several weeks, and served the purpose of a complete exchange of views between British Ministers and the Arab and Jewish representatives. In the light of the discussions as well as of the situation in Palestine and of the Reports of the Royal Commission[2] and the Partition Commission,[3] certain proposals were formulated by His Majesty's Government and were laid before the Arab and Jewish Delegations as the basis of an agreed settlement. Neither the Arab nor the Jewish Delegations felt able to accept these proposals, and the Conferences, therefore, did not result in an agreement. Accordingly, His Majesty's Government are free to formulate their own policy, and after careful consideration, they have decided to adhere generally to the proposals which were finally submitted to, and discussed with, the Arab and Jewish Delegations.

The Mandate for Palestine [doc. 10], the terms of which were confirmed by the Council of the League of Nations in 1922, has governed the policy of successive British Governments for nearly twenty years. It embodies the Balfour Declaration [doc. 7] and imposes on the Mandatory four main obligations. . . . There is no dispute regarding the interpretation of one of these obligations, that touching the protection of and access to the Holy Places and religious buildings or sites. The other three main obligations are generally as follows:

a. To place the country under such political, administrative, and economic conditions as will secure the establishment in Palestine of a National Home for the Jewish people, to facilitate Jewish immigration under suitable conditions, and to encourage, in cooperation with the Jewish Agency, close settlement by Jews on the land.
b. To safeguard the civil and religious rights of all the inhabitants of Palestine irrespective of race and religion, and, whilst facilitating Jewish immigration and settlement, to ensure that the rights and positions of other sections of the population are not prejudiced.
c. To place the country under such political, administrative, and economic conditions as will secure the development of self-governing institutions.

The Royal Commission and previous Commissions of Enquiry have drawn attention to the ambiguity of certain expressions in the Mandate, such as the expression "a National Home for the Jewish people," and they have found in this ambiguity and the resulting uncertainty as to the objectives of policy a fundamental cause of unrest and hostility between Arabs and Jews. His Majesty's Government are convinced that in the interests of the peace and well-being of the whole people of Palestine a clear definition of policy and objectives is essential. The proposal of partition recommended by the Royal Commission would have afforded such clarity, but the establishment of self-supporting, independent Arab and Jewish States within Palestine had been found to be impracticable. It has, therefore, been necessary for His Majesty's Government to devise an alternate policy which will, consistently with their obligations to Arabs and Jews, meet the needs of the situation in Palestine.

His Majesty's Government are charged as the Mandatory authority "to secure the development of self-governing institutions" in Palestine. Apart from this specific obligation, they would regard it as contrary to the whole spirit of the Mandate system that the population of Palestine should remain forever under Mandatory tutelage. It is proper that the people of the country should, as early as possible, enjoy the rights of self-government which are exercised by the people of neighboring countries. His Majesty's Government are unable at present to foresee the exact constitutional forms which government in Palestine will eventually take, but their objective is self-government, and they desire to see established ultimately an independent Palestine State. It should be a State in which the two peoples in Palestine, Arabs and Jews, share authority in government in such a way that the essential interests of each are secured.

The establishment of an independent State and the complete relinquishment of Mandatory control in Palestine would require such relations between the Arabs and the Jews as would make good government possible. Moreover, the growth of self-governing institutions in Palestine, as in other countries, must be an evolutionary process. A transitional period will be required before independence is achieved, throughout which ultimate responsibility for the Government of the country will be retained by His Majesty's Government as the Mandatory authority, while the people of the country are taking an increasing share in the Government, and understanding and cooperation amongst them are growing. It will be the constant endeavor of His Majesty's Government to promote good relations between the Arabs and the Jews.

In the light of these considerations, His Majesty's Government make the following declaration of their intentions regarding the future government of Palestine:

The objective of His Majesty's Government is the establishment within ten years of an independent Palestine State in such treaty relations with the United Kingdom as will provide satisfactorily for the commercial and strategic requirements of both countries in the future. This proposal for the establishment of the independent State would involve consultation with the Council of the League of Nations with a view to the termination of the Mandate.

The independent State should be one in which Arabs and Jews share in government in such a way as to ensure that the essential interests of each community are safeguarded.

The establishment of the independent State will be preceded by a transitional period throughout which His Majesty's Government will retain responsibility for the government of the country. During the transitional period, the people of Palestine will be given an increasing part in the Government of their country. Both sections of the population will have an opportunity to participate in the machinery of Government, and the process will be carried on whether or not they both avail themselves of it.

His Majesty's Government make no proposals at this stage regarding the establishment of an elective legislature. Nevertheless, they would regard this as an appropriate constitutional development, and, should public opinion in Palestine hereafter show itself in favor of such a development, they will be prepared, provided that local conditions permit, to establish the necessary machinery.

At the end of five years from the restoration of peace and order, an appropriate body representative of the people of Palestine and of His Majesty's Government will be set up to review the working of the constitutional arrangements during the transitional period and to consider and make recommendations regarding the Constitution of the independent Palestine State.

His Majesty's Government will require to be satisfied that in the treaty contemplated by sub-paragraph (a.) or in the Constitution contemplated by sub-paragraph (d.) adequate provision has been made for:

1. The security of, and freedom of access to, the Holy Places, and the protection of the interests and property of the various religious bodies;
2. The protection of the different communities in Palestine in accordance with the obligations of His Majesty's Government to both Arabs and Jews and for the special position in Palestine of the Jewish National Home;
3. Such requirements to meet the strategic situation as may be regarded as necessary by His Majesty's Government in the light of the circumstances then existing.

   His Majesty's Government will also require to be satisfied that the interests of certain foreign countries in Palestine, for the preservation of which they are at present responsible, are adequately safeguarded.
4. His Majesty's Government will do everything in their power to create conditions which will enable the independent Palestine State to come into being within ten years. If, at the end of ten years, it appears to His Majesty's Government that, contrary to their hope, circumstances require the postponement of the establishment of the independent State, they will consult with the representatives of the people of Palestine, the Council of the League of Nations, and the neighboring Arab States before deciding on such a postponement. If His Majesty's Government come to the conclusion that postponement is unavoidable, they will invite the cooperation of these parties in framing plans for the future with a view to achieving the desired objective at the earliest possible date.

During the transitional period, steps will be taken to increase the powers and responsibilities of municipal corporations and local councils.

Under Article 6 of the Mandate, the Administration of Palestine, "while ensuring that the rights and position of other sections of the population are not prejudiced," is required to "facilitate Jewish immigration under suitable conditions." Beyond this, the extent to which Jewish immigration into Palestine is to be permitted is nowhere defined in the Mandate. But in the Command Paper of 1922 [doc. 9], it was laid down that for the fulfillment of the policy of establishing a Jewish National Home, "it is necessary that the Jewish community in Palestine should be able to increase its numbers by immigration. This immigration cannot be so great in volume as to exceed whatever may be the economic capacity of the country at the time to absorb new arrivals. It is essential to ensure that the immigrants should not be a burden upon the people of Palestine as a whole, and that they should not deprive any section of the present population of their employment."

In the view of the Royal Commission, the association of the policy of the Balfour Declaration with the Mandate system implied the belief that Arab hostility to the former would sooner or later be overcome. It has been the hope of British Governments ever since the Balfour Declaration was issued that, in time, the Arab population, recognizing the advantages to be derived from Jewish settlement and development in Palestine, would become reconciled to the further growth of the Jewish National Home. This hope has not been fulfilled. The alternatives before His Majesty's Government are either (1) to seek to expand the Jewish National Home indefinitely by immigration, against the strongly expressed will of the Arab people of the country; or (2) to permit further expansion of the Jewish National Home by immigration only if the Arabs are prepared to acquiesce in it. The former policy means rule by force. Apart from other considerations, such a policy seems to His Majesty's Government to be contrary to the whole spirit of Article 22 of the Covenant of the League of Nations, as well as to their specific obligations to the Arabs in the Palestine Mandate. Moreover, the relations between the Arabs and the Jews in Palestine must be based sooner or later on mutual tolerance and goodwill; the peace, security, and progress of the Jewish National Home itself requires this. Therefore, His Majesty's Government, after earnest consideration, and taking into account the extent to which the growth of the Jewish National Home has been facilitated over the last twenty years, have decided that the time has come to adopt in principle the second of the alternatives referred to above.

It has urged that all further Jewish immigration into Palestine should be stopped forthwith. His Majesty's Government cannot accept such a proposal. It would damage the whole of the financial and economic system of Palestine and thus affect adversely the interests of Arabs and Jews alike. Moreover, in the view of His Majesty's Government, abruptly to stop further immigration would be unjust to the Jewish National Home. But, above all, His Majesty's Government are conscious of the present unhappy plight of large numbers of Jews who seek a refuge from certain European countries, and they believe that Palestine can and should make a further contribution to the solution of this pressing world problem. In all these circumstances, they believe that they will be acting consistently with their Mandatory obligations to both Arabs and Jews, and in the manner best calculated to serve the interests of the whole people of Palestine by adopting the following proposals regarding immigration:

a. Jewish immigration during the next five years will be at a rate which, if economic absorptive capacity permits, will bring the Jewish population up to approximately one-third of the total population of the country. Taking into account the expected natural increase of the Arab and Jewish populations, and the number of illegal Jewish immigrants now in the country, this would allow of the admission, as from the beginning of April this year, of some 75,000 immigrants over the next five years. These immigrants would, subject to the criterion of economic absorptive capacity, be admitted as follows:
    1. For each of the next five years, a quota of 10,000 Jewish immigrants will be allowed, on the understanding that a shortage in any one year may be added to the quotas for subsequent years, within the five-year period, if economic absorptive capacity permits.
    2. In addition, as a contribution towards the solution of the Jewish refugee problem, 25,000 refugees will be admitted as soon as the High Commissioner is satisfied that adequate provision for their maintenance is ensured, special consideration being given to refugee children and dependents.
b. The existing machinery for ascertaining economic absorptive capacity will be retained, and the High Commissioner will have the ultimate responsibility for deciding the limits of economic capacity. Before each periodic decision is taken, Jewish and Arab representatives will be consulted.
c. After the period of five years, no further Jewish immigration will be permitted unless the Arabs of Palestine are prepared to acquiesce in it.

d. His Majesty's Government are determined to check illegal immigration, and further preventive measures are being adopted. The numbers of any Jewish illegal immigrants who, despite these measures, may succeed in coming into the country and cannot be deported will be deducted from the yearly quotas.

His Majesty's Government are satisfied that, when the immigration over five years which is now contemplated has taken place, they will not be justified in facilitating, nor will they be under any obligation to facilitate, the further development of the Jewish National Home by immigration regardless of the wishes of the Arab population.

The Administration of Palestine is required, under Article 6 of the Mandate, "while ensuring that the rights and position of other sections of the population are not prejudiced," to encourage "close settlement by Jews on the land," and no restriction has been imposed hitherto on the transfer of land from Arabs to Jews. The Reports of several expert Commissions have indicated that, owing to the natural growth of the Arab population and the steady sale in recent years of Arab land to Jews, there is now in certain areas, no room for further transfers of Arab land, whilst in some other areas, such transfers of land must be restricted if Arab cultivators are to maintain their existing standard of life and a considerable landless Arab population is not soon to be created. In these circumstances, the High Commissioner will be given general powers to prohibit and regulate transfers of land. These powers will date from the publication of this Statement of policy and the High Commissioner will retain them throughout the transitional period.

The policy of the Government will be directed towards the development of the land and the improvement, where possible, of methods of cultivation. In the light of such development, it will be open to the High Commissioner, should he be satisfied that the "rights and position" of the Arab population will be duly preserved, to review and modify any orders passed relating to the prohibition or restriction of the transfer of land.

In framing these proposals, His Majesty's Government have sincerely endeavored to act in strict accordance with their obligations under the Mandate to both the Arabs and the Jews. The vagueness of the phrases employed in some instances to describe these obligations has led to controversy and has made the task of interpretation difficult. His Majesty's Government cannot hope to satisfy the partisans of one party or the other in such controversy as the Mandate has aroused. Their purpose is to be just as between the two peoples in Palestine whose destinies in that country have been affected by the great events of recent years, and who, since they live side by side, must learn to practice mutual tolerance, good will, and cooperation. In looking to the future, His Majesty's Government are not blind to the fact that some events of the past make the task of creating these relations difficult; but they are encouraged by the knowledge that at many times and in many places in Palestine during recent years, the Arab and Jewish inhabitants have lived in friendship together.

Each community has much to contribute to the welfare of their common land, and each must earnestly desire peace in which to assist in increasing the well-being of the whole people of the country. The responsibility which falls on them, no less than upon His Majesty's Government, to cooperate together to ensure peace is all the more solemn because their country is revered by many millions of Muslims, Jews, and Christians throughout the world who pray for peace in Palestine and for the happiness of her people.

NOTES

1. Cmd. 5393.
2. Cmd. 5479.
3. Cmd. 5854.

15

Emergency Committee of Zionist Affairs

The Biltmore Program

May 11, 1942

With World War II preventing the Zionist Organization from holding a Zionist Congress, and with reports from Europe describing the dire situation of European Jewry, the American-based Emergency Committee of Zionist Affairs called for a special Zionist Conference. The Extraordinary Zionist Conference was convened May 6–11, 1942, in the Biltmore Hotel in New York City. Meeting in New York, rather than in Europe, not only was necessitated by the war but also reflected the movement of the center of Zionist activity from London, where it was based after the First World War, to New York and Washington. Some six hundred delegates from seventeen countries attended, including Zionist leaders such as Chaim Weizmann and David Ben-Gurion.

The Conference adopted the following eight-point declaration, known as the Biltmore Program. The program's most important parts included a demand for the establishment of Jewish sovereignty in Palestine as well as a rejection of the 1939 MacDonald White Paper (doc. 14) and a call for opening Palestine to Jewish immigration. The program was approved later by other Zionist organizations, including the Jewish Agency, and was renamed the Jerusalem Program. It became the basis for Zionist policy in the postwar years. By 1946 the Anglo-American Committee of Inquiry determined that "The Biltmore Program has the support of the overwhelming majority of Zionists.... The program has undoubtedly won the support of the Zionist movement as a whole, chiefly because it expresses the policy of Palestinian Jewry which now plays a leading role in the Jewish-Agency."

---

1. American Zionists assembled in this Extraordinary Conference reaffirm their unequivocal devotion to the cause of democratic freedom and international justice to which the people of the United States, allied with the other United Nations, have dedicated themselves, and give expression to their faith in the ultimate victory of humanity and justice over lawlessness and brute force.

2. This Conference offers a message of hope and encouragement to their fellow Jews in the Ghettos of concentration camps of Hitler-dominated Europe and prays that their hour of liberation may not be far distant.

3. The Conference sends its warmest greetings to the Jewish Agency Executive in Jerusalem, to the Vaad Leumi,[1] and to the whole Yishuv in Palestine, and expresses its profound admiration for their steadfastness and achievements in the face of peril and great difficulties. The Jewish men and women in field and factory, and the thousands of Jewish soldiers of Palestine in the Near East who have acquitted themselves with honor and distinction in

---

Source: Declaration adopted by the Extraordinary Zionist Conference, Biltmore Hotel, New York City, N.Y., May 11, 1942. Text taken from *The Israel-Arab Reader*, ed. Walter Laqueur (New York: Citadel Press, 1969), pp. 77–79. Reprinted in *The Jew in the Modern World*, ed. Paul R. Mendes-Flohr and Jehuda Reinharz (New York: Oxford University Press, 1980), pp. 470–71. Annotations adapted and used by permission.

Greece, Ethiopia, Syria, Libya, and on other battlefields, have shown themselves worthy of their people and ready to assume the rights and responsibilities of nationhood.

4. In our generation, and in particular in the course of the past twenty years, the Jewish people have awakened and transformed their ancient homeland; from 50,000 at the end of the last war their numbers have increased to more than 500,000. They have made the waste places to bear fruit and the desert to blossom. Their pioneering achievements in agriculture and in industry, embodying new patterns of cooperative endeavor, have written a notable page in the history of colonization.

5. In the new values thus created, their Arab neighbors in Palestine have shared. The Jewish people in its own work of national redemption welcomes the economic, agricultural, and national development of the Arab peoples and states. The Conference reaffirms the stand previously adopted at Congresses of the World Zionist Organization, expressing the readiness and the desire of the Jewish people for full cooperation with their Arab neighbors.

6. The Conference calls for the fulfillment of the original purpose of the Balfour Declaration [doc. 7] and the Mandate [doc. 10] which "recognizing the historical connection of the Jewish people with Palestine" was to afford them the opportunity, as stated by President [Woodrow] Wilson, to found there a Jewish Commonwealth.

The Conference affirms its unalterable rejection of the White Paper of May 1939 [doc. 14] and denies its moral or legal validity. The White Paper seeks to limit, and in fact to nullify Jewish rights to immigration and settlement in Palestine, and, as stated by Mr. Winston Churchill in the House of Commons in May 1939, constitutes "a breach and repudiation of the Balfour Declaration." The policy of the White Paper is cruel and indefensible in its denial of sanctuary to Jews fleeing from Nazi persecution; and at a time when Palestine has become a focal point in the war front of the United Nations, and Palestine Jewry must provide all available manpower for farm and factory and camp, it is in direct conflict with the interest of the allied war effort.

7. In the struggle against the forces of aggression and tyranny, of which Jews were the earliest victims, and which now menace the Jewish National Home, recognition must be given to the right of the Jews of Palestine to play their full part in the war effort and in the defense of their country, through a Jewish military force fighting under its own flag and under the high command of the United Nations.

8. The Conference declares that the new world order that will follow victory cannot be established on the foundations of peace, justice and equality, unless the problem of Jewish homelessness is finally solved.

The Conference urges that the gates of Palestine be opened; that the Jewish Agency be vested with control of immigration into Palestine and with the necessary authority for upbuilding the country, including the development of its unoccupied and uncultivated lands; and that Palestine be established as a Jewish Commonwealth integrated in the structure of the new democratic world.

Then and only then will the age-old wrong to the Jewish people be righted.

NOTE

1. The executive arm of the elected institution of the Jews in Palestine in the Yishuv era.

16

League of Arab States

Charter

March 22, 1945

The Arab League and its charter were the products of several compromises. After the collapse of the Ottoman Empire, Pan-Arab nationalism became the dominant ideological force in the Arab world. But the Arab world was divided into spheres of control and influence by the imperial powers that had been victorious in World War I. Some twenty years later, when the imperial powers had waned, the Arab states that had been formed or recognized by the peace settlement of 1918–22 had developed a vitality and a set of vested interests that stood in the way of unity. Nevertheless, in 1944, an association of Arab states formed at a conference in Alexandria, Egypt. This League of Arab States (Arab League) and its pact, signed in 1945, aimed to strengthen ties among Arab states and to coordinate policies on issues of mutual concern. The original members were Egypt, Transjordan (Jordan), Iraq, Lebanon, Saudi Arabia, Syria, and Yemen. The particular interests of these Arab states, the rival ambitions of the principal contenders for hegemony, and the lingering influence of Britain and France were reflected in the limited degree of unity achieved by the Arab League.

Article 1. The League of Arab State(s) shall be composed of the independent Arab States that have signed this Pact.

Every Independent Arab State shall have the right to adhere to the League. Should it desire to adhere, it shall present an application to this effect which shall be filed with the permanent General Secretariat and submitted to the Council at its first meeting following the presentation of the application.

Article 2. The purpose of the League is to draw closer the relations between member States and co-ordinate collaboration between them, to safeguard their independence and sovereignty, and to consider in a general way the affairs and interests of the Arab countries.

Article 3. The League shall have a Council composed of the representatives of the member States. Each State shall have one vote, regardless of the number of its representatives.

The Council shall be entrusted with the function of realizing the purpose of the League and of supervising the execution of the agreements concluded between the member States on matters referred to in the preceding article or on other matters.

It shall also have the function of determining the means whereby the League will collaborate with the international organizations which may be created in the future to guarantee peace and security and organize economic and social relations. . . .

Article 5. The recourse to force for the settlement of disputes between two or more member States shall not be allowed. Should there arise among them a dispute that does not involve the independence of a State, its sovereignty

---

Source: *A Documentary History of the Arab-Israeli* Conflict, ed. Charles L. Geddes (New York: Praeger Publishers, 1991), pp. 207–11. Copyright © 1991 by Praeger Publishers. Reproduced with permission of Greenwood Publishing Group, Inc., Westport, Conn.

or its territorial integrity, and should the two contending parties apply to the Council for the settlement of this dispute, the decision of the Council shall then be effective and obligatory.

In this case, the States among whom the dispute has arisen shall not participate in the deliberations and decisions of the Council.

The Council shall mediate in a dispute which may lead to war between two member States or between a member State and another State in order to conciliate them.

The decisions relating to arbitration and mediation shall be taken by a majority vote.

Article 6. In case of aggression or threat of aggression by a State against a member State, the attacked or threatened with attack may request an immediate meeting of the Council.

The Council shall determine the necessary measures to repel this aggression. Its decision shall be taken unanimously. If the aggression is committed by a member State the vote of that State will not be counted in determining unanimity.

If the aggression is committed in such a way as to render the Government of the State attacked unable to communicate with the Council, the representative of that State in the Council may request the Council to convene for the purpose set forth in the preceding paragraph. If the representative is unable to communicate with the Council, it shall be the right of any member State to request a meeting of the Council.

Article 7. The decisions of the Council taken by a unanimous vote shall be binding on all the member States of the League; those that are reached by a majority vote shall bind only those that accept them.

In both cases the decisions of the Council shall be executed in each State in accordance with the fundamental structure of that State.

Article 8. Every member State of the League shall respect the form of government obtaining in the other States of the League, and shall recognize the form of government obtaining as one of the rights of those States, and shall pledge itself not to take any action tending to change that form. . . .

Article 17. The member States of the League shall file with the General Secretariat copies of all treaties and agreements which they have concluded or will conclude with any other State, whether a member of the League or otherwise.

Annex on Palestine

At the end of the last Great War, Palestine, together with the other Arab States, was separated from the Ottoman Empire. She became independent, not belonging to any other State.

The Treaty of Lausanne[1] proclaimed that their fate should be decided by the parties concerned in Palestine.

Even though Palestine was not able to control her own destiny, it was on the basis of the recognition of her independence that the Covenant of the League of Nations determined a system of government for her.

Her existence and her independence among the nations can, therefore, no more be questioned (*de jure*) (than) the independence of any of the other Arab States.

Even though the outward signs of this independence have remained veiled as a result of (*force majeure*), it is not fitting that this should be an obstacle to the participation of Palestine in the work of the League.

Therefore, the State(s) signatory to the Pact of the Arab League consider that in view of Palestine's special circumstances, the Council of the League should designate an Arab delegate from Palestine to participate in its work until this country enjoys actual independence.

NOTE

1. The Treaty of Lausanne, signed July 24, 1923, was the formal peace agreement signed between Turkey and most of its foes in World War I—Britain, France, Italy, Japan, Greece, Rumania, and the Serb-Croat-Slovene state (later, Yugoslavia). The treaty replaced the Treaty of Sèvres (1920) that was imposed by the Allies on the Ottomans but was rejected by Turkey's nationalist government. The Annex refers to Article 16 of the treaty:

> Turkey hereby renounces all rights and title whatsoever over or respecting the territories situated outside the frontiers laid down in the present Treaty and the islands other than those over which her sovereignty is recognised by the said Treaty, the future of these territories and islands being settled or to be settled by the parties concerned. The provisions of the present Article do not prejudice any special arrangements arising from neighbourly relations which have been or may be concluded between Turkey and any limitrophe countries.

17

David Ben-Gurion, for the Jewish Agency Executive

Status-Quo Agreement

June 19, 1947

The Status-Quo Agreement provided a framework for determining the rules governing the relationship between church and state in Israel from 1948 onwards. The framework appeared in a letter sent June 19, 1947, by David Ben-Gurion, chairman of the Jewish Agency Executive, to the Ultra-Orthodox World Agudat Israel organization. The letter outlined the positions of the Jewish Agency (the "government in waiting" of the Jewish state that would be established on May 14, 1948) in respect to the "Jewish Nature" of Israel.

Four days earlier, on June 15, 1947, the United Nations Special Committee on Palestine (UNSCOP) began its fact-finding tour in Palestine, and Ben-Gurion sent the letter as part of his efforts to create a united Jewish front supporting the Zionist position. Though many aspects of the agreement have been transformed since 1947, the principle that underlines it remains a central pillar of regulating the relationship between church and state in Israel.

---

19 June 1947
To the World Agudat Israel Federation

Gentlemen:

The Jewish Agency Executive has heard from its Chairman your request to guarantee marital affairs, the Sabbath, education and kashrut [Jewish dietary laws] in the Jewish state to arise in our day.

As the Chairman of the Executive informed you, neither the Jewish Agency Executive nor any other body in the country is authorized to determine the constitution of the Jewish state-in-the-making in advance. The establishment of the state requires the approval of the United

Source: S. Ilan Troen and Noah Lucas, eds., *Israel: The First Decade of Independence* (Albany: SUNY, 1995), pp. 78–79. Reproduced by permission of the editors.

Nations, and this will not be possible unless the state guarantees freedom of conscience for all its citizens and makes it clear that we have no intention of establishing a theocratic state. The Jewish state will also have non-Jewish citizens—Christians and Muslims—and full equal rights for all citizens and the absence of coercion or discrimination in religious affairs or other matters clearly must be guaranteed in advance.

We were pleased to hear that you understand that no body is authorized to determine the state constitution retroactively, and that the state will be free in certain spheres to determine the constitution and regime according to the will of its citizens.

Along with this, the Executive appreciates your demands and realizes that they involve issues of concern not only to members of Agudat Israel but also to many defenders of the Jewish faith, both within the Zionist camps and outside party frameworks, who would understand fully your demand that the Jewish Agency Executive inform you of its position on the issues you raised and stipulate what it is prepared to accomplish regarding your demands on said issues, within the limits of its influence and decision-making powers.

The Jewish Agency Executive has appointed the undersigned to formulate its position on the questions you mentioned in the discussions. We hereby inform you of the Jewish Agency Executive's position:

THE STRUCTURAL FOUNDATION FOR RELIGIO-POLITICAL ACCOMMODATION

a. The Sabbath: It is clear that the legal day of rest in the Jewish state will be Saturday, obviously permitting Christians and members of other faiths to rest on their weekly holiday.
b. Kashrut: One should use all means required to ensure that every state kitchen intended for Jews will have kosher food.
c. Marital Affairs: All members of the Executive recognize the serious nature of the problem and the great difficulties involved. All bodies represented by the Jewish Agency Executive will do all that can be done to satisfy the needs of the religiously observant in this matter and to prevent a rift in the Jewish People.
d. Education: Full autonomy of every stream in education will be guaranteed (incidentally, this rule applies in the Zionist Association and "Knesset Israel"[1] at present); the Government will take no steps that adversely affect the religious awareness and religious conscience of any part of Israel. The state, of course, will determine the minimum obligatory studies—Hebrew language, history, science and the like—and will supervise the fulfillment of this minimum, but will accord full freedom to each stream to conduct education according to its conscience and will avoid any adverse effects on religious conscience.

Sincerely,

On behalf of the Jewish Agency Executive
D. Ben-Gurion
Rabbi Y. L. Fishman, Y. Greenbaum

NOTE

1. The members of the Jewish community in Palestine (1920–48) who participated in elections to the Asefat Hanivharim (Representative Assembly).

18

Ihud

Proposals to the United Nations Special Committee on Palestine

July 23, 1947

Alongside the Zionist mainstream, an alternative view of the Zionist relationship with the Palestinian Arabs was developed by a small but influential group of intellectuals that coalesced around Brith Shalom (Peace Pact). Prominent among them was Judah L. Magnes, president of the Hebrew University. In 1947, the Ihud (Union), an organization that continued Brith Shalom's task, presented a written statement to the United Nations Special Committee on Palestine that departed from the official Zionist line and advocated a bi-national solution to the Palestinian Problem.

From this material it will be seen that the Ihud Association advocates the following program:

POLITICAL

1. An undivided bi-national Palestine composed of two equal nationalities, Jews and Arabs.
2. The transfer of Palestine, for an agreed transitional period, to the Trusteeship System of the United Nations, under which a large measure of self-government under one Administrative authority is to be instituted from the very start and under which this self-government is to be developed increasingly.
3. After this agreed transitional period, the bi-national Palestine of two equal nationalities is to become an independent constitutional state.
4. Close cooperation between the independent bi-national Palestine and the neighboring countries of the Middle East within the framework of the UN. . . .

IMMIGRATION

5. The speediest possible immigration of 100,000 Jewish Displaced Persons.
6. During the period of trusteeship, Jewish immigration in accordance with the economic absorptive capacity of the country, the Jews being free to reach numerical parity with the Arabs.
7. Thereafter, immigration to be agreed upon between Jews and Arabs under the bi-national constitution.

LAND

8. Legislation for land reform, removing all discriminatory restrictions, and providing adequate protection for small land owners and tenant cultivators.

Source: Judah L. Magnes, M. Reiner, Lord Samuel E. Simon, and M. Smilonski, *Palestine—Divided or United? The Case for a Bi-National Palestine Before the U.N.* (Jerusalem: Achva Cooperative, 1947), p. 9.

DEVELOPMENT

9. A plan for the development of the economic potentialities of the country for the benefit of all its inhabitants.

COOPERATION

10. Cooperation between Jews and Arabs in Palestine and elsewhere in all walks of life—political, agricultural, industrial, social, scientific, cultural.

19
United Nations General Assembly
Resolution 181
November 29, 1947

In February 1947 the British government presented the Palestinian Question before the United Nations General Assembly and requested a reconsideration of the terms of the Mandate. The General Assembly appointed the United Nations Special Committee on Palestine (UNSCOP), composed of representatives of eleven countries, to study the conditions in Palestine and to present recommendations for the future of the land.

The majority report of UNSCOP, published at the end of August 1947, again recommended the partition of Palestine (see map 1). A minority of the members opted for a unified federal state. The UNSCOP report was considered by different bodies of the United Nations, and on November 29, 1947, the General Assembly adopted the partition resolution—Resolution 181 (II)—by a majority of thirty-three countries in favor, thirteen countries against, and ten countries abstaining. This result was made possible because both the United States and the Soviet Union came to support partition, although their reasons were different, even opposing.

The Jewish Agency, supported by additional sectors of the Jewish people, accepted the Partition Plan resolution of the United Nations, while the Palestinian Arabs and the Muslim countries of the Middle East rejected it and tried to overcome it by force of arms. A day after the resolution was passed in the United Nations, Palestinian paramilitaries launched guerrilla and terror warfare campaigns against the Jews. In early 1948, the paramilitaries in the north (Kaukji forces) and in the south (Egyptian Muslim Brotherhood) were joined by Arab volunteer forces.

The General Assembly,

Having met in special session at the request of the Mandatory Power to constitute and instruct a special committee to prepare for the consideration of the question of the future government of Palestine at the second regular session;

Source: *A Decade of American Foreign Policy: Basic Documents, 1941–49*, prepared at the request of the Senate Committee on Foreign Relations by the Staff of the Committee and the Department of State (Washington, D.C.: Government Printing Office, 1950), pp. 820–22.

MAP 1. U.N. PARTITION PLAN FOR PALESTINE, NOVEMBER 1947

Having constituted a Special Committee[1] and instructed it to investigate all questions and issues relevant to the problem of Palestine, and to prepare proposals for the solution of the problem, and

Having received and examined the report of the Special Committee (Document A/364)[2] including a number of unanimous recommendations and a plan of partition with economic union approved by the majority of the Special Committee,

Considers that the present situation in Palestine is one which is likely to impair the general welfare and friendly relations among nations;

Takes note of the declaration by the Mandatory Power that it plans to complete its evacuation of Palestine by 1 August 1948;

Recommends to the United Kingdom, as the mandatory Power for Palestine, and to all other Members of the United Nations the adoption and implementation, with regard to the future government of Palestine, of the Plan of Partition with Economic Union set out below:

Requests that

a. The Security Council take the necessary measures as provided for in the plan for its implementation;
b. The Security Council consider, if circumstances during the transitional period require such consideration, whether the situation in Palestine constitutes a threat to the peace. If it decides that such a threat exists, and in order to maintain international peace and security, the Security Council should supplement the authorization of the General Assembly by taking measures, under Articles 39 and 41 of the Charter, to empower the United Nations Commission, as provided in this Resolution, to exercise in Palestine the functions which are assigned to it by this Resolution;
c. The Security Council determine as a threat to the peace, breach of the peace or act of aggression, in accordance with Article 39 of the Charter, any attempt to alter by force the settlement envisaged by this Resolution;
d. The Trusteeship Council be informed of the responsibilities envisaged for it in this plan;

Calls upon the inhabitants of Palestine to take such steps as may be necessary on their part to put this plan into effect;

Appeals to all Governments and all peoples to refrain from taking any action which might hamper or delay the carrying out of these recommendations, and

Authorizes the Secretary-General to reimburse travel and subsistence expenses of the members of the Commission referred to in Part I, Section B, Paragraph 1 below, and to provide the Commission with the necessary staff to assist in carrying out the functions assigned to the Commission by the General Assembly.

Hundred and twenty-eighth plenary meeting, 29 November 1947.

NOTES

1. The U.N. Special Committee on Palestine was appointed by the U.N. General Assembly and carried out its task between June 15 and September 1, 1947. The committee spent six weeks in Palestine and also visited (in some cases, only in a subcommittee formation) Lebanon, Jordan, and Syria as well as camps for displaced Jewish Holocaust survivors in Austria and Germany. The committee held public hearings as well as private meetings.
2. The report was submitted to the U.N. General Assembly on September 1, 1947. It included a preface, eight chapters, an appendix, and a series of annexes. The first four chapters included factual information regarding the various phases of the committee's work and the background to the Palestine Question, as well as some of the solutions that were presented to the committee or were suggested before its creation. The following three chapters contained the recommendations and proposals. The final chapter provided a list of the reservations and observations by certain delegates on a number of specific points.

20

Zeev Sharef

Meeting of the National Administration and the Formation of a Provisional Government of Israel

May 12, 1948: Memoir

Zeev Sharef (1906–1984) began his public career and service in the Political Department of the Jewish Agency. Prior to independence he was close to the negotiations with King Abdullah of Jordan. As the first secretary of the cabinet, he was uniquely placed to observe the formation of the Israeli government. His career in public service was distinguished; he was later a member (Labor Party) of the Knesset, minister of housing, and minister of commerce and industry.

As the first part of this selection from Sharef's memoirs shows, Israel made early and persistent attempts to avoid a clash with the Arabs living in Mandatory Palestine. The history of such negotiations dates back to the meeting of Chaim Weizmann with King Faisal in 1919. Before the British withdrawal and the inevitable war with the neighboring Arab states, Israeli negotiators sought a political solution to what has since become known as the Palestinian Problem. Negotiations with Jordan (see also docs. 34, 71) are a recurring part of Israel's continuing efforts.

Source: Zeev Sharef, *Three Days* (London: W. H. Allen and Co., 1962), pp. 69–76, 154–57.

The term "Minister" for a member of Government had not yet been introduced and the title "Government" was being reserved for future use; but from the standpoint of responsibility for affairs and procedures, the actual existence of "Ministers" preceded the fact of the "Government," and the Government of Israel became a substantial fact on that day, the 12th of May. The meeting of Minhelet Haam, the National Administration, began at ten o'clock that morning and lasted—with intervals—until eleven o'clock that night, forty-nine hours before the expiration of the British Mandate. It may well be that upon dispersing to their homes after the meeting, the members of the National Administration felt that the body which would administer the State-to-be had been ushered in that day.

Neither the subject-matter nor the agenda of the meeting had been determined in advance—the agenda developed out of the proceedings; and the events within the territory of Palestine and along its circumambient frontiers, and the occurrences overseas, within the United Nations agencies, were the determinants of those proceedings. Half of the time was devoted by those present to hearing information about the threatened dangers from the neighboring countries, the position in the interior of the country and the fate of Jerusalem, and the attitudes of the Big Powers, both those sympathizing with and those hostile to the Jewish cause, as well as the implications arising therefrom.

At the meeting also were Mrs. Golda Meyerson (now Meir), director of the Jewish Agency's Political Department, and for part of the proceedings her two advisers on Arab affairs, Ezra Danin of Hadera and Eliyahu Sasson of Jerusalem.

The negotiations with King Abdullah of Jordan, on which Golda Meyerson reported, were in the nature of a last attempt to prevent an invasion by the Arab armies generally, or at least to forestall the entry of the Arab Legion into the arena of war. True, Arthur Creech-Jones, the British Colonial Secretary, had promised that the Arab Legion would leave Palestine before the 15th of May. Only four weeks previously, on the 16th of April 1948, the chief United Kingdom delegate at the United Nations, Sir Alexander Cadogan, had stated clearly and specifically in reply to a direct question by Moshe Shertok [Sharett]: "As regards the Arab Legion, we announced some time ago that Arab Legion units would be withdrawn from Palestine before the Mandate ended." It was now evident that not even this British assurance would be fulfilled. Only that morning Legion troops had stormed the positions of the isolated Ezion bloc[1] of settlements in the Hebron hills and it was patent to anyone that they would later be deployed against Jewish Jerusalem.

Moshe Shertok had only just returned from New York and a few days before his departure he had conferred with the U.S. Secretary of State, General George C. Marshall. His review at the meeting was intended to clarify the problem of whether the United States of America meant to interfere with the proclaiming of the State, and if so, the extent to which it would succeed in enlisting U.N. personnel for this purpose.

Part of the meeting was attended by Israel Galili (Hillel), Chief of the Haganah Command, and Yigael Sukenik (Yadin), its Chief of Operations Staff. Their reports were brief, penetrating and comprehensive, and left no room for illusion or misapprehension of the military position and of the possible upheavals within it one way or the other.

Eliezer Kaplan and Moshe Shapira, who had returned the previous day from Jerusalem, brought with them an impression of the feeling in the besieged city and the anxiety of its leaders. The meeting would have to decide on a reply to the British High Commissioner's proposal for a truce in Jerusalem, the supervision of which was to be in the hands of the Committee of Consuls (representing the United States of America, France and Belgium) set up by Security Council decision at the end of April, or of the Red Cross.

Zero hour had been fixed by the British Government when it announced that the Mandate would end at midnight of the 14th of May. But not all clocks were set to Greenwich time on the British plan. At Lake Success desperate efforts were being made to defer this zero hour by proclaiming a truce, the real significance of which would be to postpone the declaration of the Jewish State.

It was the accepted notion before that date that the regular Arab armies would launch their invasion only after the termination of the Mandate, but the attack launched by the Jordan Arab Legion against the Jewish settlements of the Ezion area was an anticipation of the British zero hour, and it was uncertain whether the other Arab armies might not behave similarly.

The duty which lay before the meeting was to assess all the complex information and to retain in Jewish hands the initiative in determining the course of events. Its chairman, David Ben-Gurion, defined its function in the following terms at the outset of the meeting: "Time is of the essence; it is pressing for two reasons: (1) Because of the danger of invasion which is liable to occur at any moment. It may already have started to a certain extent. The Legion's attack on the Ezion bloc may be called an invasion. The danger necessitates action, and not only by the security people. (2) Because of the date of 14th May. Ernest Bevin[2] anticipated the date and something is bound to happen on Friday night. Whatever happens, action is necessary."

The meeting continued, with a short interval, for thirteen hours. The lack of clarity at its outset had been dissipated by the time the meeting ended. The barque of Jewish history was no longer to be tossed about on the waves, driven by alien winds. Its sails had been unfurled, its course was set. "Jerusalem Time" had replaced "Greenwich Time."

Golda Meyerson told of her dramatic encounter with King Abdullah. It was her second meeting with him. The first had taken place in the middle of November 1947 in the Rutenberg house at the power-station on the River Jordan at Naharayim. That conversation had been friendly and had been conducted on the assumption that there would be no collusion between the Jews and himself. If the U.N. Assembly decided upon the partition of Palestine into two States, Jewish and Arab, he wanted, he said, to annex the Arab area to his kingdom. The reply given was that the Jews would not lend a hand to a breach of the U.N. Assembly's resolution. But it was no business of theirs as to what would happen in the Arab area. Obviously, if the Arabs attacked the Jews, then force would be met by force.

Abdullah rejoined that he understood this and promised that his friendship for the Jews remained. He spoke in derogatory terms of the strength of the neighboring states. The conversation concluded with an agreement that, after the U.N. decision, a second meeting would be arranged.

Two points during the colloquy aroused some doubts. Once he asked as to what the Jewish attitude would be to including their state (he called it "the Jewish republic") within his kingdom. When the response was a negative one, he did not pursue that line. Another time he remarked that he did not want Partition to be disappointing from the standpoint of the area which the Arabs would receive. He told the Palestinian Arab leaders that he would stand aside and give them no support whatever unless they submitted the Palestine case to his exclusive handling.

No further meeting had been held with him since then although contact was maintained through someone who had visited him twice. A little while earlier, Mrs. Meyerson said, this person had come from Abdullah with a query as to whether the Jews were ready to offer concessions in the area designated as the Jewish State in the Partition Plan, so that he could appear before the Arab world showing a territorial gain in comparison with what had been allotted by the United Nations. The answer via the emissary was that the Jews would make no concessions whatever in its area. Generally, he must know that the frontier proposed by the United Nations was a peace-time one and it would be honored so long as conditions of peace were observed. But if hostilities broke out, then each side would take what it could. No more news was received from him after that, as the disturbances which began at the end of November 1947 suspended all communications.

But contact was re-established a week ago and a meeting had been arranged, she said. This time Abdullah refused to come to the boundary of Jewish territory and they were compelled to go to him. While the previous meeting had been successfully kept secret, news about the second one filtered through to the public and even to the press before it took place, and consequently extraordinary precautions had to be taken for the journey. Owing to bad weather, Eliyahu Sasson's aircraft did not arrive from Jerusalem in time, and she was accompanied only by Ezra Danin. She drove in the car belonging to one of the King's faithful henchmen and was dressed as a Muslim woman. Ezra Danin wore Arab headgear.

The journey took several hours. They left from Naharayim, and after their identity was checked about ten times en route, they arrived in Amman and were taken straight to the meeting-place. The King received them in the presence of one of his confidants; he gave them a friendly welcome, but in general he seemed to be a different man—depressed, preoccupied, tense.

The go-between had conveyed Abdullah's proposals in advance: the country must remain undivided, and within it the Jews would have autonomy in the areas inhabited by them. This arrangement would be effective for one year, and at the end of that period the country would be amalgamated with Jordan. A joint parliament would be set up, with fifty percent Jewish membership; there might also be a government consisting of one-half Jews and one-half Arabs, but this was not clearly stated.

At the outset of the conversation the King asked whether his proposal had been transmitted, and Mrs. Meyerson answered affirmatively, adding that she had deemed it necessary to meet with him although his proposal was wholly unacceptable as a basis for negotiation. He repeated that he desired peace and did not want to see the destruction of agriculture and industry. But if his proposal were not accepted, then war became inevitable. Generally, he asked, why were the Jews in such a hurry to proclaim an independent and sovereign state?

Did he believe that expectation going back two thousand years could be called "haste"? Mrs. Meyerson countered. To our regret, we had lingered and delayed too long. There had been mutual understanding and friendship between the Jews and himself for years, she went on, and the friendship was also founded on the fact that they had common enemies. During the past five months, the Jews had hit hard at those enemies. The Mufti's[3] strength had diminished as a result of the Jewish military successes. The foreign mercenaries who had invaded the country had been beaten. As a result of our exertions the way had been cleared for him as well. If he returned to the previous plan and concentrated solely within the area set aside for the Arabs, then it was possible to establish an understanding. The Jewish strength today was nothing like that of four or five months ago, she asserted. If there had to be war, then we would fight with all our powers and would have no mercy upon any enemy.

The King said that he understood "you will have to repel any attack." While he desired to carry out the previous plan, several events had occurred in the meantime to prevent it. There was the massacre at Deir-Yassin (the Arab village west of Jerusalem attacked by men of the Irgun Zvai Leumi [Etzel]). He went on: "I was then alone but now I am one among five. I have no alternative and I cannot act otherwise."

Mrs. Meyerson declared that we were ready to honor the frontiers so long as there was peace. But if war came, we would fight wherever we could reach and so long as our strength lasted, and he must know, she repeated, that our strength was far greater than it was four or five months ago.

To this the monarch reiterated his warning, although in friendly tones, that he was sorry but had no alternative. He deplored the havoc and the blood of the young people which would have to be spilled as water. He offered to invite the Palestinian Arab leaders connected with him and several of his moderate followers, and suggested that the Jews should also send "moderate representatives" to such a meeting, at which the matter could be settled. He further said there would be no Jew-hating Arab extremists in government, but only Arab moderates.

When Mrs. Meyerson referred to the fact that he must remember that we were his only friends, among all those around him, who showed him friendly faces but were in reality seeking to do him evil, he replied the same as at previous meetings: I know it and I have no illusions on that score. I know them and their "good intentions." I firmly believe that Divine Providence has restored you, a Semite people who were banished to Europe and have benefited by its progress to the Semite East, which needs your knowledge and initiative. It is only through your help and guidance that the Semitic peoples will be able to regain their lost glory. The Christians will not do this because of their aloof and contemptuous attitude towards the Semites. If we do not help ourselves by our joint efforts, then we shall not be helped. All this I know and I have a profound belief in what I have said. But the situation is grave, and we must not err through hasty action. Consequently I beg of you again to be patient.

"We do not wish to delude you," she retorted, "but we cannot consider your proposal at all. It would not only be rejected by the responsible institutions, but there are not even ten responsible Jews who will be ready to support such a plan. The answer can be given at once: it is unacceptable. If you give up the agreement and want war, then we shall meet *after* the war."

King Abdullah stated he had heard that Shertok was in France, and perhaps one of his men could meet with him there. He added, "We don't need America and Europe. We, the people of the East, ought to show this miracle to the world. Let us sit down at one table and secure peace among us."

Finally, he turned to Ezra Danin and in a paternal tone asked why he, Ezra, a son of the East, had not helped him out in the conversation. Danin pointed out to him his fatal error. He had no friends in the Arab world and he relied on the armored cars of the Legion just as the French had relied on the Maginot Line. We shall smash these armored vehicles, Danin said. It was a pity that he stood to lose all that he had built up with such great effort. It was still not too late.

"I am very sorry," the King replied. "I deplore the coming bloodshed and destruction. Let us hope we shall meet again and will not sever our relations. If you find it necessary to meet me during the actual fighting, do not hesitate and come to see me. I shall always be glad to have such a meeting."

Before they parted Ezra Danin remarked that he, the King, would have to alter his gracious custom of allowing his flock to approach and greet him by kissing his hand or the hem of his robe. Townsmen were not the same as Bedouin tribesmen, and the guard upon him must be increased so as to avert the evil plotted by scoundrels, sons of Belial, against him.

"*Habibi*, my dear, I shall not change the customs of my fathers," King Abdullah rejoined. "I am a Bedouin and I shall not become the prisoner of my bodyguards. Let whatever happen, I shall not prevent my subjects from expressing their affection for me."

The impression gained from the conversation was that he did not contemplate the prospect of battle gladly or with self-confidence, and actually did not want it, as he feared defeat and was even afraid of his comrades-in-arms, the Arab States and the British together. But he had become entangled in complications, or the

British had entangled him, and he could no longer extricate himself.

On their way back to Naharayim, Mrs. Meyerson and her companion saw at a distance the invading Iraqi Army moving toward the front with its heavy equipment and extensive field artillery.

Such was the account of that historic meeting, the last diplomatic effort with an Arab leader on the eve of the invasion. . . .

The Ministries of Agriculture, Public Works and Labor existed only on paper. Their high officials were in Jerusalem. Aharon Zisling, who had taken the portfolio of Agriculture, and Mordecai Ben-Tov, who held Labor and Public Works, made every effort to organize nucleus staffs and enlisted people close to these fields of activity in various institutions quartered in Tel Aviv. Their prospective offices in Sharonah had not been handed over to them, and Zisling began work in the headquarters of Mapam, the United Workers Party (which then federated the Mapam of today and the Ahdut Haavodah–Poalei Zion Party). Mordecai Ben-Tov functioned in the editorial offices of the daily *Al Hamishmar*, where he was at home—he had been its editor-in-chief from the day it first appeared.

The other members of the National Administration occupied their former offices. Felix Rosenblueth [Pinhas Rosen] superintended the initial legislative work of the State at his law office. The personnel and records of other units scheduled to become part of the Ministry of Justice were in Jerusalem. Behor S. Shitrit, who had been a Magistrate until then, did his work in the Law Courts building; he was in charge of Arab affairs and Police. Arab affairs were then handled by local Emergency Committees, some of which were connected with Municipalities and others of which operated separately. Behor Shitrit, with the help of several advisers, tried to introduce some orderly procedure and unity into the administration of these matters. Most of the Arabs were displaced, far away from their homes and without means of livelihood, and it was necessary in some way to give them housing and support. His particular concern was with the Arab inhabitants who had remained in Haifa and those of Jaffa which was due to surrender in a few hours.

His other Ministerial responsibility was the Police. Its organization had been prepared by Yehezkel Saharoff (now Sahar) and Yosef Nahmias, who had been liaison officers of the Jewish Agency's Political Department in matters concerning the "legitimate" Jewish police formations, such as the Jewish Settlement Police and Auxiliary Constabulary. When the central Emergency Committee was set up and services began to be organized, they were invited to draft the scheme of police reorganization. Later on, Saharoff received his appointment from the Haganah's affiliates.

Registration for officers' courses was announced and several candidates were approved. But Saharoff failed to get the full quota of men he required to set up the force. The demand for combat troops was insatiable, and kept on growing. Both Saharoff and Nahmias had literally to struggle for the men they needed in each area.

Meanwhile they had to cope with a grave situation. The Irgun Zvai Leumi and Fighters for the Freedom of Israel [Lehi] took anything that came to hand, and there were even instances of Haganah units which did not exactly behave virtuously or with restraint. They needed, and commandeered, everything: autos, typewriters, tables, telephone instruments. Units were being formed, commanding officers set up offices, they required equipment and accessories. As there was no Quartermaster-General, they did their own foraging as they saw fit.

The IZL and FFI, former underground dissident groups, legitimized their position by the act of public appearance, and capitalized on this putative legitimacy by undertaking confiscations without any centralized control, even by their own commands. We therefore asked the commanders of the incipient police to post guards over the offices of the outgoing British government, of which we regarded ourselves as the successor authority. The combatant forces treated them as natural prey—the offices of a hostile government in disbandment; we saw them as our own future premises, upon which we had focused our past planning. But the fledgling police force had to decline the assignment as it was undermanned. The Jewish Agency also had its own worries over safety precautions. It used armed watchmen to guard valuable property and even called in the Military Police on special occasions. The latter were an entirely new phenomenon for the Jewish population: their smart uniformed appearance set them apart from other Haganah men, who generally wore an assortment of garments and were none too meticulous about the way they looked.

Very little was left of the vaunted Palestine Police. It had been methodically destroyed by the outgoing Government. Only a small number of officers and constables remained in the police stations under Jewish control. Vehicles in good condition were taken away, records were destroyed, laboratory paraphernalia and the Port Police motorlaunches were removed. The new Police H.Q. did its utmost to re-create the framework of organization with the aid of Jewish officers and men who had served in Mandate days. New men were taken on through the central military recruiting bureaux, but—as I remarked earlier—front-line drafts took precedence over the rear echelons. Yet in spite of the handicaps, the building-up of the force went ahead according to plan and along clear-cut purposeful lines.

The Health sector was organized by the late Dr. Avraham Katznelson (later Nissan), director of the Vaad Leumi Health Department. Moshe Shapira later took over this responsibility. Immigration was handled by the Agency's Immigration Department. Plans were readied for all other spheres of activity, but they were not put into effect owing to the truncation of Jerusalem.

Briefly, then, we were able to include on our table of organization a not inconsiderable number of active administrative components, part of which were housed in the seat of the future Government at Sharonah. Among them were the Controllers of Food and Stockpiles in the Ministry of Trade and Industry; the Public Works Department, which had already mustered the few Jewish workers in the districts but occupied itself mostly with getting the seat of Government ready for its tenants; Police Headquarters; the directorates of Posts and the Broadcasting Service; Immigration; and Transport.

But now the day and hour for the inauguration of governmental operations had been determined it was evident that demand outstripped supply in providing accommodation, and the pace of the last-minute preparations had to be stepped up. It was by no means a simple matter at the time. Normally a few groups of artisans and workmen would have been organized and set to work simultaneously on various parallel jobs. But men were being called up day after day by age-groups or categories. Only the day before, Emergency Order No. 17 published by the "Central Command for National Service" had summoned forthwith to the Colors all men aged twenty to thirty-five years, irrespective of family status, who had served in any foreign army in the Second World War. The Order further proclaimed that all soldiers in these classes who had previously received deferment or release for personal or economic reasons were now liable for immediate conscription, and all *previous decisions* were suspended for a period of sixty days.

The Order drew the attention of all institutions and industrial establishments to the following regulations: (1) The Central Command for National Service would not entertain any appeal against the Order except by the Palestine Electric Corporation, ports, hospitals, and waterworks. (2) Persons wishing to appeal against their conscription could do so only when they were on active service.

The watchword which had once been "We will do and be obedient" now became "Join Up and Appeal." The effect was that workmen and engineers, clerks and laborers, who had begun work on a certain day had to quit almost precipitately, leaving papers on their desks and tools at their jobs—and did not report for duty on the morrow. They vanished into thin air. During the evening or late at night they were called to arms and went; or the Military Police came to their homes and took the laggards. Pleas and excuses were unavailing: they had to go.

NOTES

1. The Ezion bloc (Gush Ezion) was a group of four Jewish settlements southeast of Jerusalem captured by the Arab Legion in May 1948. This area came under Israeli rule in 1967, and the settlements were reestablished.
2. Ernest Bevin (1881–1951), British foreign secretary, 1945–51, was a chief formulator of British Middle East policy, which during this period tried to court Arab favor.
3. Hajj Amin Al-Husayni (ca. 1895–1974), the most prominent leader of Palestinian Arab nationalism, was appointed *mufti* (Muslim religious leader) of Jerusalem by the British in 1921 and was dismissed by them in 1937. A religious fundamentalist who wanted Palestine to be an Arab state governed by Islamic laws, he militantly opposed both Zionism and Abdullah. His influence was felt in Palestine even from his exile in Cairo and Beirut.

CHAPTER 2

The New State of Israel, 1948–1956

1948

Independent State of Israel is proclaimed

League of Arab States attacks the new state

Israel Defense Forces is formed, incorporating various military forces under a single command

Mass immigration to Israel begins—more than 1 million Jews by 1951

United Nations establishes the Conciliation Commission for Palestine to assist in settlement of the Palestinian Question

1949

Armistice agreements are signed with Egypt, Jordan, Syria, and Lebanon

David Ben-Gurion heads Labor-led coalition government; Chaim Weizmann is elected first president

League of Arab States announces the establishment of a civil administration in Palestine

First Knesset meets in Jerusalem

1950

Law of Return gives every Jew the right to Israeli citizenship

1951

Palestine Conciliation Commission publishes its final report

1952

Luxembourg Agreement with West Germany arranges for reparations payments to Israel and individual victims of the Third Reich

1953

The Soviet Union breaks off diplomatic relations with Israel but resumes them in the thaw after Joseph Stalin's death

David Ben-Gurion resigns in December

1954

Moshe Sharett becomes prime minister

Israeli intelligence fiasco—the Mishap in Egypt—causes a scandal

1955

Israel Defense Forces attack an Egyptian base in Gaza in retaliation for acts of sabotage committed by *fedayeen*

Czech arms deal is concluded between Egypt and the Soviet Union

David Ben-Gurion becomes prime minister for a second time

1956

At Twenty-Fourth Zionist Congress, Nahum Goldmann assumes presidency of the Zionist Organization

Egypt nationalizes the Suez Canal

Sinai Campaign launched by Israel, France, and Britain against Egypt

Domestic Issues

21

Jewish Agency Executive

Proclamation of the State of Israel

May 14, 1948

On May 14, 1948, British rule over Palestine ended. At 8:00 A.M. the British lowered the Union Jack in Jerusalem. By midafternoon the neighboring Arab states had launched a full-scale attack. At 4:00 P.M., despite great pressure from the United States and the doubts of many of his colleagues, David Ben-Gurion, chairman of the Jewish Agency Executive, read the Proclamation of the State of Israel. The Jewish population of Palestine—except for Jerusalem, which was without electricity—heard the proclamation ceremonies as they were broadcast from the Tel Aviv Museum.

The Land of Israel was the birthplace of the Jewish people. Here their spiritual, religious and national identity was formed. Here they achieved independence and created a culture of national and universal significance. Here they wrote and gave the Bible to the world.

Exiled from Palestine, the Jewish people remained faithful to it in all the countries of their dispersion, never ceasing to pray and hope for their return and the restoration of their national freedom.

Impelled by this historic association, Jews strove throughout the centuries to go back to the land of their fathers and regain their Statehood. In recent decades they returned in their masses. They reclaimed the wilderness, revived their language, built cities and villages, and established a vigorous and ever-growing community, with its own economic and cultural life. They sought peace yet were prepared to defend themselves. They brought the blessings of progress to all inhabitants of the country.

In the year 1897 the First Zionist Congress, inspired by Theodor Herzl's vision of the Jewish State, proclaimed the right of the Jewish people to national revival in their own country [doc. 4].

This right was acknowledged by the Balfour Declaration of November 2, 1917 [doc. 7], and reaffirmed by the Mandate of the League of

Source: Palestine Post, May 16, 1948, pp. 1–2.

Nations [doc. 10], which gave explicit international recognition to the historic connection of the Jewish people with Palestine and their right to reconstitute their national home.

The Nazi Holocaust, which engulfed millions of Jews in Europe, proved anew the urgency of the reestablishment of the Jewish State, which would solve the problem of Jewish homelessness by opening the gates to all Jews and lifting the Jewish people to equality in the family of nations.

The survivors of the European catastrophe, as well as Jews from other lands, proclaiming their right to a life of dignity, freedom and labor, and undeterred by hazards, hardships and obstacles, have tried unceasingly to enter Palestine.

In the Second World War the Jewish people in Palestine made a full contribution in the struggle of the freedom-loving nations against the Nazi evil. The sacrifices of their soldiers and the efforts of their workers gained them title to rank with the peoples who founded the United Nations.

On November 29, 1947, the General Assembly of the United Nations adopted a Resolution [doc. 19] for the establishment of an independent Jewish State in Palestine, and called upon inhabitants of the country to take such steps as may be necessary on their part to put the plan into effect.

This recognition by the United Nations of the right of the Jewish people to establish their independent state may not be revoked. It is, moreover, the self-evident right of the Jewish people to be a nation, like all other nations, in its own sovereign state.

Accordingly, we, the members of the National Council, representing the Jewish people in Palestine and the Zionist movement of the world, met together in solemn assembly today, the day of the termination of the British Mandate for Palestine, and by the virtue of the natural and historic right of the Jewish people and of the resolution of the General Assembly of the United Nations, hereby proclaim the establishment of the Jewish State in Palestine, to be called Israel.

We hereby declare that as from the termination of the Mandate at midnight, this night of the fourteenth to the fifteenth of May, 1948, and until the setting up of the duly elected bodies of the State in accordance with a Constitution, to be drawn up by a Constituent Assembly not later than the first day of October 1948, the present National Council shall act as the Provisional State Council, and its executive organ, the National Administration, shall constitute the Provisional Government of the State of Israel.

The State of Israel will be open to the immigration of Jews from all countries of their dispersion; will promote the development of the country for the benefit of all its inhabitants; will be based on the precepts of liberty, justice and peace taught by the Hebrew Prophets; will uphold the full social and political equality of all its citizens, without distinction of race, creed or sex; will guarantee full freedom of conscience, worship, education and culture; will safeguard the sanctity and inviolability of the shrines and Holy Places of all religions; and will dedicate itself to the principles of the Charter of the United Nations.

The State of Israel will be ready to cooperate with the organs and representatives of the United Nations in the implementation of the Resolution of the Assembly of November 29, 1947, and will take steps to bring about the Economic Union over the whole of Palestine.

We appeal to the United Nations to assist the Jewish people in the building of its State and to admit Israel into the family of nations.

In the midst of wanton aggression, we yet call upon the Arab inhabitants of the State of Israel to return to the ways of peace and play their part in the development of the State, with full and equal citizenship and the representation in all its bodies and institutions provisional or permanent.

We offer peace and amity to all the neighboring states and their peoples, and invite them to cooperate with the independent Jewish nation for the common good of all. The State of Israel is ready to contribute its full share to the peaceful progress and development of the Middle East.

Our call goes out to the Jewish people all over the world to rally to our side in the task of immigration and development and to stand by us in the great struggle for the fulfillment of the dream of generations—the redemption of Israel.

With trust in the Rock of Israel, we set our hand to this Declaration, at this Session of the Provisional State Council, in the city of Tel Aviv, on this Sabbath eve, the fifth of Iyar, 5708, the fourteenth day of May, 1948.

22

David Ben-Gurion

The War of Independence

May 1948: Memoir

David Ben-Gurion was the single most important personality in Israel's early history. As leader of the largest political party, Mapai, he was elected in 1935 to chair the Jewish Agency Executive in Palestine and thus became head of the semiautonomous government of the Yishuv (the organized Jewish community in Palestine). When the State of Israel was proclaimed, he became prime minister, a position he held (with a brief interruption) until June 1963. By that time his personal political influence had begun to wane; he left Mapai and formed a splinter party, Rafi.

The following document is from Ben-Gurion's reflections during the War of Independence, which lasted from May 14, 1948, until January 7, 1949. Even before the British left Palestine, the Arab League undertook military preparations to negate the Partition Plan and began intermittent attacks on Jewish settlements and institutions. Simultaneously, the military forces attached to various Jewish parties—such as the Haganah and Palmach as the official forces of the Yishuv, and Etzel and Lehi as independent forces—were also preparing for the inevitable clash. Arab solidarity with the Palestinians, the intensity of the Palestinian Question, Pan-Arab unity, and interstate rivalries all played an important role in prompting the Arab League to initiate war. As soon as the British left, Israel was invaded by five Arab states—Egypt, Syria, Iraq, Transjordan (Jordan), and Lebanon. Saudi Arabia sent a military contingent that operated under Egyptian command. Yemen declared war on Israel but did not take any military actions.

The war began with an Egyptian air attack on Tel Aviv. When a temporary truce was declared (lasting from June 11 to July 7), Israel was cut off from the Negev (in the south) by the Egyptians, the Syrians had a foothold west of the Jordan River, Iraq controlled the headwaters of the Yarkon River (whose mouth is just north of Tel Aviv), and the Lebanese army and Fawzi al-Qawuqji's Arab Liberation Army consolidated themselves in much of the Galilee in the north. The Israelis had established a tenuous supply link to besieged Jerusalem.

Source: David Ben-Gurion, *Israel: A Personal History* (New York and Tel Aviv: Funk and Wagnalls, Inc., and Sabra Books, 1971), pp. 111–21. Copyright © 1971 by the American Israel Publishing Co. Ltd. Reprinted by permission of HarperCollins Publishers Inc.

Fighting flared up again immediately after the first truce. The turning point occurred during the ten days of July 9–18. Israel made major gains in the central region and in the Galilee. A second truce lasted from July 18 (July 17 in Jerusalem) until October 15. After fighting resumed, Israel made further gains. On January 7, 1949, the final cease-fire took effect (see map 2).

The war involved virtually the entire Jewish population of the new state, as Ben-Gurion's memoirs, excerpted here, show. The professional armies of the Arab states were fought by ill-equipped military forces originally operating under separate commands (see doc. 24) and by untrained civilians. Interstate rivalries undermined the Arab world's ability to mount an effective unified campaign against the young Israeli state. Nevertheless, the Jewish population of about 750,000 suffered heavy casualties.

May 16, 1948

At 11 A.M. Israel Galili and Shkolnik [Levi Eshkol] were called to Menahem Begin. He proposed that their (Etzel's) ship be purchased for a quarter of a million, and that the money be used to buy arms.

The Carmeli Brigade reached Rosh Hanikrah, where it blew up houses and bridges. Bridges on the northern road leading to Malkiya were blown up at Hanita as well. Acre is ready to surrender, but the situation in the eastern section of upper Galilee is quite bad. The battle for Malkiya was hard fought, with both sides suffering heavy losses. We have a hundred and fifty wounded in a battalion of five hundred men. An enemy unit holds the police station at Nebi Yusha. All the Arabs have left Safed. Two hundred men of the Carmeli Brigade have gone from the west to the east. Seventy men have reached there from Tel Aviv to replace the wounded. The first artillery pieces are now being unloaded. Among the immigrants was a French (Jewish) officer.

The Jordan Valley is under bombardment. They are asking for ammunition. The Syrians have descended from the hills. One of our planes is operating there with great effectiveness. The Alexandroni Brigade is facing an attack from Kalkilya, where some of Kaukji's [Fawzi al-Qawuqji] men are now located. The morale of the field units is very low, as a result of the losses they have suffered. Nahum [Sarig] in the Negev, demands that a high-ranking person

MAP 2. ISRAEL AFTER THE WAR OF INDEPENDENCE, 1949

be sent to discuss the situation in the area. Yigael Yadin is not certain about the situation there himself. Yesterday there were heavy attacks, led by tanks, on Nir Am, Nirim, and Kfar Darom. Our people don't think that they will be able to hold out. There are also reports of Egyptian columns along the coast, between Gaza and Mijdal.

A large force of Abdullah's men have entered Beersheba. Nahum has only two and a half companies that are not tied down. The south is wide open, Stone (Marcus) visited the Jerusalem road. Stone and Mundik (Moshe Ben Tikvah-Pasternak) have agreed on a plan of operations. Latrun was to have been attacked tonight, but I have not yet received a report about what happened. The Givati Brigade has established a Home Guard battalion of five or six hundred men. They are in Gedera digging trenches. We are holding all of our Jerusalem outposts, except in the Old City. We captured Allenby Barracks and Sheikh Jarrah. We are about to capture Su'afat. David Shaltiel says that if he is given piats,[1] artillery, and other equipment, he will be able to stand firm against the Arab Legion.[2]

Yizhak Sadeh feels that we should evacuate all settlements below Nir Am. In my opinion, there is no rush. Whatever time can be gained is important. Perhaps by Thursday units will be ready for offensive action in the Negev. An engineer has gone to the south to deal with fortifications and tank traps.

Yohanan Ratner is afraid that the Arabs are planning to seize the Akir airbase and says it is necessary to fortify it. We have one Sherman tank to operate against all enemy tanks. In the course of the week our brigades will suffer losses and we must establish new units. People should be taken from the settlements. We lose an average of one brigade per week, and need a brigade to hold in reserve. We should also send replacements to units suffering casualties.

Operating procedures for the Air Force have been worked out with Aharon Remez.

A delegation consisting of Yaakov Haft, Zekser, and Eli Bahir (Geller), has come from the Jordan Valley. Iraqi troops are attacking the Jordan Valley settlements. The attack on Ein Gev has ceased. Armored cars, and perhaps tanks as well, lead the way, followed by Iraqi infantry.

We must immediately dispatch machine guns, piats, and mortars to the Jordan Valley. Mordekhai Makleff should be sent there.

Tel Aviv was bombed again at 11:30.

Stone presented his plan for gaining control of the Tel Aviv–Jerusalem road. (1) Two battalions should entrench themselves along the ridges in order to prevent the enemy from reaching the road. (2) The enemy has four 75-mm field guns and we need similar weapons (65-mm) for operations in the Negev. Each company should be supplied with four mortars and four piats. The road must be kept in good condition. An engineering platoon and four armored cars should be ready to deal with problems arising out of air attacks, road blocks, or enemy ground action. (3) There should be a strong, motorized striking force at Shaar Hagai to defend convoys should they be attacked. The convoys should travel only at night. The General Staff accepted the Stone plan. The convoys will be organized tonight and tomorrow.

May 17, 1948

An attempt was made to bomb us again at 5 A.M., but our antiaircraft batteries drove off the "brave" pilots.

Tonight twenty-eight trucks are being loaded with supplies for the Harel and Ezioni Brigades.

Yigael Yadin reports: There is fighting within the Old City. Who started it? Yigael says the Arabs violated the cease-fire. The convoy carrying supplies to the Negev has been held up because the Arab Legion had entered the Iraq-Sudan police station. Stone flew to the Negev today. The Arab Legion has entered the Triangle with airplanes and armored vehicles. There is a report that Nebi Yusha has been conquered. Legion units at Sarafand attacked Rishon LeZion yesterday. The Etzel attack at Ramle is not going well. There is much Arab activity at the Lydda airfield. We are getting ready to bomb Lydda.

Beit Yosef in the Jordan Valley is under artillery bombardment. Radio Cairo announces that one Egyptian plane is missing. Radio Damascus announces that three Syrian planes have been shot down. An immigrant ship arrived this morning. An ammunition ship has been unloaded. Three cargo planes have arrived so far. Four piats, dynamite, and other matériel have been sent to the Jordan Valley.

Weapons are being collected from the settlements. Givati has already gathered 350 rifles, while Alexandroni expects to obtain 600. There are no reports yet from the Valley of Jezreel or from Galilee.

I asked Yigael whether we can fight on for another two weeks even without additional weapons from abroad. He is not certain. It will depend on the speed with which we can mobilize our own resources. Ratner reports: Kaukji's forces have been strengthened by the Arab Legion. If they are successful, local Arabs will join them. A commando operation must be carried out behind Arab lines. Moshe Dayan has been given responsibility for organizing a commando group in the central region. Ratner doubts whether we can hold out if we do not receive additional airplanes within two weeks. We are struggling against a coalition of states, which is a different matter from fighting a single nation. One side or the other will be knocked out.

Berl Repetur and Ben-Aharon came to see me; they quote Moshe Sneh and Israel Barzilai to the effect that airplanes can be obtained from Czechoslovakia and Poland if these countries are approached by the Provisional Government. When were Sneh and Barzilai there? Ten days ago—I asked Sneh to come and see me. Speaking on behalf of Berman (one of the heads of Left Poalei Zion), he told me that Poland would supply us with food (wheat from Danzig) for dollars or for goods that she needs. We will be able to receive full assistance from Yugoslavia and Czechoslovakia only if Russia approves. Sneh met with a Polish (Jewish) general, who told him: Poland's arms production is very small; everything was destroyed by the Germans and there is nothing much we can promise in the way of weapons. I asked: Were you there together with Barzilai? No, Barzilai was there before me. Did they promise Barzilai more? No, Sneh told Barzilai what he had been told and Barzilai had nothing to add. Sneh was also in Czechoslovakia, but he did not deal with these matters.

There was refreshing news in the evening: [V. M.] Molotov [Soviet foreign minister] answered Moshe Shertok's message by according us recognition (*de jure*). Austin, in the Security Council, demanded at a Council meeting that the Arabs cease their attacks on Israel for thirty-six hours. Air raids have begun again.

May 18, 1948

Twenty trucks with supplies for the army went to Jerusalem during the night. A twenty-five truck convoy to the Negev arrived safely. Armored cars accompanying Givati came back from the Negev without losses. The situation in the Old City is critical. But in the Jordan Valley it remains stable; the Arabs have retreated and are digging in. They are also digging in upper Galilee. Moshe Dayan has been appointed commander of the Jordan Valley front. The late-afternoon bombing of Tel Aviv wrecked the Central Bus Station: dozens of people were killed and more than a hundred were wounded.

Aryeh Bahir, a member of Afikim, called me from Haifa in the evening. He told me that the situation in the Jordan Valley is getting worse all the time. The settlements are under artillery fire. A great deal of assistance is necessary. A Palmach company from upper Galilee has arrived, but this is not sufficient.

Apparently David Namiri of Ashdot Yaakov has arrived from America. Good opportunities exist for purchases in Mexico, but only in lots of at least $1 million. Al Shwimmer, who is very capable, has gone into action. We must obtain two-engine bombers, single-engine fighters, cannon, and other equipment.

May 19, 1948

Ephraim Visnitski wired that we had taken all of western Galilee.

Bahir came from Haifa. He had been in contact during the night with all the Jordan Valley settlements. A bridge over the Jordan was built opposite Kinneret. A Palmach company arrived from the Galilee. Our counterattack began at midnight. It was made in an attempt to take the Zemah police station. The members of Massadah abandoned their settlement and went to Afikim. The members of Shaar Hagolan left theirs and went to Bet Zera. In both cases the settlers acted on their own initiative, without orders. They said that they had only eighteen rifles, which just was not enough.

May 20, 1948

There are 5000 members of the Arab Legion in action: 1500 between Jerusalem and Bet Gubrin, 300 near Latrun, 1500 to 2000 in the Triangle, 300 to 400 in the Jordan Valley and 400 to 500 in the Ramle-Lydda area.

We have a battalion of 500 ex-soldiers in Ein Shemer. They have 460 rifles, 460 Sten guns, 8 2-inch mortars (each one with 96 shells), 2 3-inch mortars, 20 machine guns, 560 Mills hand grenades, 140 mines, 3 piats, and 46 shells. There is also an armored battalion at Ein-Shemer composed of 9 half-tracks and 360 men, half of them trained. Their weapons are included in the previous list. [Haim] Laskov is at Ein Shemer.

At Tel Litvinsky, there are a unit of armored cars, 60 people, the battalion of Zvika Horowitz, 700 trainees, the heads of the Training Branch, 250 rifles, 15 machine guns, and 6 mortars.

The situation in Jerusalem: one column of the Arab Legion has reached Sheikh Jarrah. The Etzel unit there has fled. A second column has reached the Mount of Olives, and a third is at the Damascus Gate. Our forces are in control of Mount Zion. We have sufficient men and weapons there. Harel has 4 infantry companies and a heavy weapons company, altogether 700 men, but they are exhausted. On their return from Mount Zion they had an accident in which a truck overturned and 40 men were injured. They have 2 Davidkas,[3] 4 machine guns, 2-inch mortars, heavy machine guns, and 18 armored cars. All the outposts west of Latrun are in our hands, Kiryati has 240 men there, and Givati has a reserve unit.

I have discovered that the orders I gave Israel Galili about the appointment of commanders were not carried out.

May 21, 1948

The first Messerschmitt, a German plane built in Czechoslovakia, has arrived. Our planes tonight bombed Su'afat, as well as Gaza and Dir-Sunid in the Negev. All our pilots returned safely.

Four artillery pieces were sent to the Jordan Valley, where they raised the morale of the settlers. Gad (Mahnes), Jacobson, and Chizik (the Governor of Jaffa) complain about theft and anarchy in Jaffa.

May 22, 1948

A heavy attack was made yesterday on the Deganyah settlements. Six enemy tanks were put out of action. One of them is in our hands.

Eleven men have gone to Czechoslovakia to participate in a pilots' course. They are dressed in Czech Air Force uniforms: They have been given English-speaking instructors.

A ship is scheduled to arrive with weapons purchased by Ehud Avriel under the terms of Contract B: 10,000 rifles, 1421 machine guns, 16 million rounds of ammunition—altogether 800 tons of material costing $2,528,000.

In the evening a second Messerschmitt and a cargo plane arrived.

I was shown an urgent cable announcing that the Arab Legion had surrounded the Hadassah Hospital. Negotiations with the consuls and the Legion are under way. The Legion demands that the Haganah surrender, turn over its weapons, and allow its men to be sent as prisoners to Amman. I refuse to accept the Legion's conditions. I have cabled Yadin to mobilize a larger force and go on fighting.

May 23, 1948

A messenger arrived with a report from Stone (Marcus): The situation is critical, but there is no reason to panic. Yad Mordekhai, defended by 80 settlers and 25 other people, has suffered 50 casualties: 20 killed and 30 wounded. An Egyptian battalion is attacking. A motorized Egyptian brigade is operating in the Negev, where it has renewed its attacks on Bet Eshel and Nirim. Egyptians, not Arab Legionnaires, are in Beersheba. The Arab Legion has gone to Bet Gubrin. Heavy attacks were made on Kfar Darom (where we have 50 people). Our men went on the offensive and inflicted heavy losses on the Egyptians, who sustained about 100 casualties: several of their tanks were damaged. They retreated.

An emissary reports that the Iraq-Sudan police station has not been captured. It is held by the Egyptians and not by the Arab Legion.

The Arabs of the Negev are not active; a few of them are working for us.

Two hundred children were evacuated from the Negev tonight. Only in Dorot and Ruhama (with a total population of 350) have youngsters remained. Stone demands 300 rifles, 150 Sten guns, 30 to 40 heavy light machine guns, 15 heavy machine guns, 7 mortars, 50 piats, 100 flamethrowers, and smoke and tear-gas grenades. 250 Palmachniks have gone to the Negev; they have had a little training, and 70 percent of them are armed.

Yigael Yadin: After I left my office in the evening, a message was received from the Harel Brigade. Two companies have remained in outposts. We were asked to bomb Sheikh Jarrah at midnight. The message arrived late, but two planes nevertheless went out at midnight, by way of the university, and returned safely. Our forces were unable to break through into the Old City or to reach the university. The Arabs are in control of Mount Zion.

Benny Dunkelman (a Canadian) volunteered to deal with the production of 6-inch mortars. I gave him the necessary authorization to undertake the project.

Israel[4] reported from Ramat David that four Egyptian Spitfires had attacked the British airfield there, thinking we had taken it over. All four were shot down. Perhaps two can be salvaged.

I asked Nahum Kirschner to cable Cecil Margo in South Africa and request that he come to serve as an adviser on aviation to the Provisional Government.

8 P.M.: The situation at Yad Mordekhai is extremely grave. A column comprising dozens of Egyptian tanks and armored cars has arrived at Iraq-Sudan. Givati has sent another company to the Negev. Givoni cables that the Arab Legion has conquered Ramat Rahel and is entrenching itself in Sur Bahur. The Arab Legion has also moved into Ein Kerem, Bet Safata, and El Malha.

I have demanded that men under the command of Shlomo Shamir and Eliyahu Ben-Hur, who are trained and armed, be sent to Jerusalem. Those who are not trained should be dispatched to the Alexandroni Brigade and replaced with experienced men. These battalions should be provided with all available weapons: twenty-five guns, three hundred Molotov cocktails, ten piats, eighteen mortars, etc. The armored cars should be transferred immediately from Ein Shemer to Hulda. Latrun and all the villages in the vicinity should be taken and the road to Jerusalem opened up.

Our forces presently are distributed as follows: five thousand in service units, two thousand in the Central District, two thousand in Tel Aviv, twenty-five thousand in Givati, fifteen hundred in the Negev, three thousand in Jerusalem, twelve hundred in Harel, two thousand under the command of Shlomo, a thousand under the command of Eliyahu, three thousand in Golani, fifteen hundred in Carmeli, and two thousand in Galilee Palmach units.

May 23, 1948

Shaul Avigur cabled: Ehud Avriel has begun negotiations with the Czechs for the purchase of airplanes, tanks, and artillery on credit. But $1 million must be paid immediately and $5 million more in six months.

Another Messerschmitt arrived tonight; now we have three. Each plane has two cannons, two heavy machine guns, and bombs. Two of our planes attacked Napoleon Hill and Kfar Azariya tonight. The pilots returned safely.

The English are leaving Ramat David tomorrow. Our men will move in immediately. Engineers are already there. Vivian Herzog came from Jerusalem. He reports that the Arab Legion is in Sheikh Jarrah, the Police School, Mount Scopus, and has reached as far as the Damascus Gate. How many men do they have? We don't know. Both the Legion and the Iraqis are in the Old City. Rabbis Meisenberg and Hazan cabled the following message 3 o'clock yesterday afternoon to Rabbi Isaac Herzog and Yitzhak Ben-Zvi: "The community faces total annihilation. This is a desperate call for help. Synagogues—Or Haim, Sukat Shalom, Bet Hillel, Tiferet Israel, Nissan Beck, Porat Yosef, the Brisk Yeshivah, Ohel Moshe, etc.—have been destroyed and Torah scrolls burned. Misgav Ladah is under heavy fire. Bring our desperate plea to the attention of the entire world. Save us."

Two platoons of the Field Forces captured Ramat Rahel yesterday. We lost twelve men. Arab losses ran into the dozens. Six enemy armored cars were put out of action. We control all of Jerusalem except the Old City, Musrarah, the American Colony, Sheikh Jarrah, Wadi Joz, Bab El-Sahara, and Augusta Victoria. An attempt is now being made to penetrate the Old City by using flamethrowers. Mount Zion is in our hands. The enemy is bombarding Jerusalem day and night with shells falling everywhere. Morale is very low. People find it impossible to sleep and have practically nothing to eat. There is enough bread only for another two weeks, and no other food at all. Water is being distributed in the streets: a half tin per person every two days. There are plenty of seekers of peace, namely people willing to surrender. They are putting pressure on Rabbi Herzog.

We tapped a telephone conversation between Williams, the British Consul, and a BBC reporter. Williams said: "Amman doesn't make a move without first receiving orders from the Foreign Office." Dov Joseph is doing an excellent job. If there is any food at all, it is thanks to Dov Joseph. Our bombing raids have encouraged the population. All the members of Kfar Ezion were killed; settlers from other villages were taken prisoner. The Arab Legion has treated them very decently.

Almogi reports from Haifa: 250 immigrants arrived and disembarked on Friday. The (British) Army then ordered them to return to their ship. Abba Hushi [Mapai leader and mayor of Haifa] responded by calling a strike in the port. The stevedores surrounded the British Army units and told them to shoot. The British backed down and allowed the immigrants to leave the port. The next day another ship, the *Providence*, arrived with 960 immigrants of military age. The British Army did not interfere.

There was a meeting of the Provisional Government from 4 to 9 P.M.

I fell into bed dead tired, after forty-eight hours of constant strain.

May 24, 1948

Yesterday's experiment with 6-inch mortars was a success. Three have already been made, and two more are manufactured every day. They have a range of three and a half kilometers.

Yesterday an airplane arrived loaded with bombs.

Pressure on the Negev is very heavy. Dorot was shelled yesterday—its arsenal was hit. Yad Mordekhai is still holding out. An airplane of ours bombed Iraq-Sudan and Mijdal. Egyptian armoured cars advanced on Bet Mahsir but were repulsed.

The enemy bombardment of Jerusalem continues day and night. Our pressure on the Old City goes on. Ratner has returned from the central region and lower Galilee. We have taken Tantura, which has a good port. The Alexandroni Brigade has eleven hundred men from the Home Guards and eighteen hundred from the Field Forces.

There is no defense worthy of the name on the Jordan front. Kinneret miraculously holds out.

I met with a Mapam delegation on Israel Galili's role in defense matters. Ben-Aharon demanded that Israel have the right to issue orders to the General Staff. I replied that while I would not oppose Galili's being given the Defense portfolio, if I were to be responsible for defense, it was on condition that I alone give orders to the General Staff. Ben-Aharon argued that Israel would in fact be giving orders in accordance with my instructions. I rejected this approach, after which Israel announced that there was nothing more for him to do in the circumstances.

A freighter is being unloaded. Tomorrow we will have forty-five more artillery pieces and five thousand rifles—an important landmark.

Mikunis came to see me in the afternoon. He immigrated to this country in 1921, and became a communist in 1936. He has just returned from a visit to Rumania, Yugoslavia, Czechoslovakia, Poland, and Bulgaria. While there he discussed arms supplies. In Bulgaria he spoke to Dimitrov (they have no weapons themselves). In Yugoslavia he met Ramkovitch, in Rumania Luka, in Czechoslovakia Clementis, and in Poland Berman and Modolsky (both of them Jews). He asked whether we were unwilling to turn to the East for assistance, as *Al Hamishmar*[5] had reported. I told him the report was untrue. We had asked for and received assistance from the East even before the establishment of the State.

May 25, 1948

The commander of Yad Mordekhai came out of the settlement with eighteen wounded men in armored cars. Yad Mordekhai is surrounded by Arab villages. According to kibbutz members who also fought in Stalingrad, there is no comparison between that struggle and the present one.

May 26, 1948

Two Messerschmitts arrived last night. I asked the members of the General Staff whether a truce would be to our advantage. All of them (Yigael, Sadeh, Ratner, Zvi Ayalon, Lehrer) agreed that it would.

Yaakov Hazan came to me to speak about Galili. He said it was imperative that I should continue to handle defense matters, and have all the necessary authority to do so, but I could not handle everything myself. I should therefore have Galili coordinate matters under my direction. I would retain control of appointments. He believed that Mapai has been discriminated against in the High Command (almost all our commanders are Mapam members). I told him that I wasn't worried about discrimination and didn't care to which party the commanders belonged. It was my firm conviction, I added, that the Army should be absolutely nonpolitical. I told Hazan I would not agree to Israel's giving orders to the Army. I was unable to complete the discussion because of the pressure of other matters. We decided to meet again the next day. After four Cabinet meetings, the Israel Defense Forces Ordinance I drafted was approved [see doc. 24].

Large Arab forces are concentrating around Kiryat Anavim and Maale Hahamishah. It appears they want to conquer Jerusalem at all costs.

Simhah Blass, one of the heads of our arms industry, is producing seven piats and five to seven hundred shells per day. He fears that the 6-inch mortars may not be effective.

May 27, 1948

Ratner inspected fortifications in the south and found them satisfactory. However, they are not properly camouflaged, and can be detected easily.

Yehudah (Prihar-Friedberg) has come from Prague. Our representatives there are about to purchase another thirty Messerschmitts, thirty Spitfires, and nine Mosquitos. The Mosquitos are capable of flying directly to this country without refueling. The Czechs are also willing to sell us thirty sixteen-ton tanks now and thirty at the end of June, as well as twenty nine-ton tanks. Perhaps they will give us a $10 million credit for six months, if we pay 20 percent of what we owe them in cash.

Shmurak (a former British Army officer) came from Jerusalem this morning with a message from Dov Joseph. All the outposts that were in our hands, including Ramat Rahel, are still being held. Sheikh Jarrah and the Police School are under Arab control. Yesterday the Arabs delivered an ultimatum to the Jews in the Old City to surrender within twelve hours or the Hurva Synagogue would be bombarded. The Arabs are at Mar Elias. There is bread, sugar, and tea for another ten days and enough water for another three months. Our soldiers are waiting for ammunition; they think they will be able to hold out. The civilian population displays great courage. Rudi Klein (special operations officer in the General Staff) came to me from Sodom. All the members of Bet Haaravah and the North have been transferred to Sodom. They took all their weapons with them. The seven hundred people in Sodom have food for a month. There are sixty Arab Legionnaires in Safa, and a hundred or so in Mizra. There are four hundred rifles, eleven Lewis guns, three machine guns, one Spandau, three 331 mortars, six 221 mortars, four piats, and a great deal of ammunition.

Dov Joseph cabled from Jerusalem: each week the population requires a hundred and forty tons of bread, three tons of powdered eggs, ten tons of powdered milk, ten tons of dried fish, ten tons of lentils, ten tons of barley, five tons of yellow cheese, and five tons of jam.

May 28, 1948

Beit Susin has been captured. A large transport plane arrived last night with bombs and propellers. Only 20 percent of the goods on the ship have been unloaded; the process goes forward very slowly. There is no news from the Negev.

Stone came. We raided Gaza. We destroyed the Egyptian artillery. With fifteen hundred men we could have captured the town. Our army is excellent. The Egyptians have weapons, which we must seize. I sent Stone to Latrun to speed up the capture of the town and the liberation of Jerusalem. With Yigael's approval, I have appointed Stone as commander of the Jerusalem Front. He will be in charge of the Harel Brigade, plus the troops serving under David Shaltiel and Shlomo Shamir.

May 29, 1948

At 10:30 I attended a meeting of the Mapai Central committee for the first time since the establishment of the State. I gave a report on internal arrangements and on the security situation. I proposed that we halt negotiations with other parties about the appointment of government officials, as this was not a subject for interparty haggling.

Yitzhak Rabin came to see me. Seven hundred Old City Jews were freed by the Arabs and allowed to cross over to the New City. The Arab Legion occupied the Jewish Quarter on May 28, 1948, after its leaders decided there was no alternative to surrender. The conditions of surrender were: (1) weapons, ammunition, and military equipment to be turned in; (2) all men capable of bearing arms to be imprisoned; (3) all other residents, women, children, and wounded, to be transferred, under the supervision of a U.N. representative, from the Old City to the New City; (4) the officer signing the agreement on behalf of King Abdullah to be responsible, together with other Legion officers, for the safety of the civilians and wounded being evacuated from the Old City; (5) the Arab Legion to be given absolute control of the Quarter.

The Jewish Quarter was ablaze in the morning. The Legion treated the Haganah men and the prisoners very well. There is now tremendous pressure on Kiryat Anavim and Maale Hahamishah. Women, children, and cows have been evacuated from the settlements. The New

City is under heavy bombardment. One hundred and fifty trained men will join the Harel Brigade tonight. The bombing of Ramallah was successful; 75 percent of the men in one Harel Company and 50 percent in another have been put out of action. Three hundred soldiers remain, not counting those in outposts. According to Rabin, the Arab forces are concentrated at Bet Nuba, Imans, Yalu, and Latrun. Dir Ayub is almost empty.

I have drafted an oath of allegiance for the Israel Defense Forces.

Nahum Sarig arrived by plane from the Negev. I asked him whether it would be possible to conquer Beersheba. His answer: if we can leave the west undefended and concentrate all our forces on that objective, Beersheba can be taken. But he must have a decision by tomorrow if he is to carry out the operation.

May 31, 1948

Haim Laskov penetrated into Latrun with his armored force, killing some hundred and fifty Arab soldiers. But the two companies of Brigade Seven ordered to support him were frightened by the enemy bombardment and failed to move. Thus Haim was forced to abandon Latrun. Our losses were moderate: some twenty killed and thirty wounded.

Harel reports: The enemy is using poisoned mortar shells: two men who were scratched by shell fragments died of poisoning six hours later.

I was visited at 6 P.M. by Count Folke Bernadotte accompanied by Dr. Ralph Bunche. If an armistice is arranged, peace talks will be possible. During a cease-fire the Arab forces would be prohibited from moving from their positions. Food would be brought to Jerusalem by the Red Cross. Bernadotte realizes the problems involved in preventing the movement of arms across the borders, but hopes to overcome them after a period of time. Abdullah's entrance into Jerusalem after a cease-fire would be considered a violation of the cease-fire.

At 8 o'clock Haim Laskov and Shlomo Shamir came from Latrun. Yigal Allon came in from Galilee. If there is no cease-fire, we will prepare an operation to free Jerusalem. We have decided to bomb Amman and Cairo.

Laskov, who hadn't slept for eight days, reported on the Latrun operation. According to the battle plan, Prulov's battalion was to take Yalu, while Laskov's unit advanced toward the village of Latrun, the monastery, and the police station. In doing so, Haim lost about one hundred men killed, wounded, or missing. Four of his halftracks remained inside the police station; most of his drivers were killed or wounded. One of Zvika's companies went up with Prulov to the hills.

Two hundred men remain in the armored battalion, but they are in no condition to go into action immediately. Five hundred shells were pumped into Latrun in the course of the night. Had infantrymen from Brigade Seven advanced as they were ordered, the town would have been taken. Two companies occupy Beit Jis and Beit Susin, which permits us to open a new road to Jerusalem.

NOTES

1. Piat (acronym for projector infantry antitank) is a short-range antitank weapon.
2. The Arab Legion is the Jordanian army. It was created by Abdullah as the armed force of Transjordan and was developed into a modern army by John Bagot Glubb (Pasha) during World War II.
3. The Davidka was crude mortar developed and produced by the fledgling Israeli arms industry to meet the emergency situation of 1948. It was an effective noisemaker but, because of its inaccuracy and lack of firepower, an ineffective mortar.
4. Ben-Gurion is apparently referring to Israel Amir-Zovlotsky.
5. *Al Hamishmar* (On Guard) was the daily newspaper of Mapam. It was closed down in 1993.

23

Provisional Government of Israel

First Ordinance of the State of Israel

May 19, 1948

In Mandatory Palestine the Yishuv (the organized Jewish community) enjoyed a considerable degree of autonomy and developed a network of political and administrative institutions. It elected the Representative Assembly (Asefat Hanivharim), which in turn elected the National Council (Vaad Leumi or, as referred to by the British, the General Council). The National Council met between the infrequent sessions of the Representative Assembly and conducted most of the legislative business of the Yishuv.

In April 1948, in preparation for statehood, the government of the Yishuv was restructured. The National Administration (Minhelet Haam, People's Administration) was the new executive council; after May 14 it was called the Provisional Government. A legislative assembly, the Constituent Assembly, was elected by universal adult suffrage in January 1949. This assembly was transformed into the Knesset.

The authority and functions of the Jewish Agency prior to the establishment of the state were outlined in Article 4 of the British Mandate for Palestine (doc. 10), which provided that "an appropriate Jewish agency shall be recognized as a public body for the purpose of advising and cooperating with the Administration of Palestine" and that "the Zionist Organization . . . shall be recognized as such agency." Desiring to increase the scope of support of world Jewry for the Zionist program, the Zionist Organization created the Jewish Agency to act as an organ of all Jews (and not only of the Zionists) in furthering this goal. With the establishment of the State of Israel, the Jewish Agency automatically ceased to speak for the interests of the Jewish population in that country. It continues as an international nongovernmental body that coordinates all Jewish overseas efforts for Israel.

At the second meeting of the Provisional Council of State, on May 19, 1948, the following Law and Administration Ordinance (1–1948) was adopted after a brief debate. The texts of this and the following document demonstrate the fashion in which the new state coped with the formidable task of transforming the institutions of the Yishuv into governmental institutions of a sovereign state.

By virtue of the power conferred upon the Provisional Council of State by the Declaration of the Establishment of the State of Israel, of the 5th Iyar 5708 (May 14, 1948), and by the Proclamation of that date, the Provisional Council of State hereby enacts as follows:

Chapter 1. The Administration

THE PROVISIONAL COUNCIL OF STATE

1. (a) The Provisional Council of State consists of the Persons whose names are set out in the Schedule to this Ordinance. Representatives of

---

Source: David Ben-Gurion, *Israel: A Personal History* (New York and Tel Aviv: Funk and Wagnalls, Inc., and Sabra Books, 1971), p. 98. Copyright © 1971 by the American Israel Publishing Co. Ltd. Reprinted by permission of HarperCollins Publishers Inc.

the Arabs being residents of the State who recognize the State of Israel will be coopted on the Provisional Council of State, as may be decided by the Council; their non-participation in the Council shall not derogate from its power. (b) The Provisional Council of State itself prescribes the procedure for its meetings and business.

THE PROVISIONAL GOVERNMENT

2. (a) The Provisional Government consists of the persons whose names are set out in the Schedule to this Ordinance. Representatives of Arabs being residents of the State of Israel will be coopted on the Provisional Government, as may be decided by the Provisional Council of State; their non-participation in the Provisional Government shall not derogate from its power. (b) The Provisional Government shall act in accordance with the policy laid down by the Provisional Council of State, shall carry out its decisions, shall report to it on its activities, and shall be answerable to it for its activities. (c) The Provisional Government shall elect one of its members to be Prime Minister, and shall prescribe the functions of each of its members. A member of the Provisional Government shall be called "Minister." (d) The Provisional Government may confer any of its powers upon the Prime Minister and upon any of the Ministers, insofar as that is not repugnant to any of the Ordinances of the Provisional Council of State. (e) Decisions of the Provisional Government in respect of the division of Powers among the Ministers shall be published in the *Official Gazette*. (f) The Provisional Government itself prescribes the procedure for its meetings and business.

DISTRICT ADMINISTRATION

3. The Provisional Government may divide the area of the State into districts and subdistricts and shall demarcate their boundaries.

LOCAL AUTHORITIES

4. The municipal corporations, local councils, and other local authorities shall continue to act within the areas of their jurisdiction and scope of their authority.

24
Provisional Government of Israel
Ordinance on the Israel Defense Forces
May 26, 1948

Prior to statehood and independence, the underground or semi-underground military forces in the Yishuv sometimes clashed with each other. During the War of Independence the Haganah, as the military arm of the political establishment, had to transform itself into a regular army of the newly proclaimed state and to establish for itself and the new state a monopoly over military power.

Source: David Ben-Gurion, *Israel: A Personal History* (New York and Tel Aviv: Funk and Wagnalls, Inc., and Sabra Books, 1971), p. 109. Copyright © 1971 by the American Israel Publishing Co. Ltd. Reprinted by permission of HarperCollins Publishers Inc.

David Ben-Gurion designed this ordinance, adopted May 26, 1948, to regulate and centralize the various military forces under a single command, the Israel Defense Forces (a direct translation of the Hebrew, Zva Haganah LeIsrael, also frequently referred to by its acronym Zahal, or in English IDF). Etzel and Lehi agreed to discontinue independent activities except in Jerusalem. By September an IDF ultimatum forced them to place their forces under the central command as well. Nevertheless, the political nature of these forces and of their leadership meant that they were not fully integrated until after victory and independence were assured. Ben-Gurion also disbanded the Palmach as a separate unit of the IDF, thereby removing that arm of the former Haganah which was almost totally dominated by one political faction. His account of the adoption of the IDF ordinance by the Provisional State Council, and the ordinance itself, are reprinted here.

At a meeting of the Provisional Government on May 23, 1948, Prime Minister [David] Ben-Gurion presented the draft of an Ordinance on the Israel Defense Forces. [Haim Moshe] Shapira opposed the insertion of the word *haganah* (defense), but no one supported him. In accordance with the request of several members, a final decision on the Ordinance was postponed until May 26, 1948. On that date it was approved. The Ordinance reads:

> In accordance with Section 18 of the Law and Administration Ordinance No. 1–1948 [doc. 23], the following Ordinance is issued:
>
> 1. Herewith are established the Israel Defense Forces, consisting of ground, air, and naval units.
> 2. In times of emergency, conscription will be enacted for all formations and services of the IDF, with ages of those liable for conscription to be determined by the Provisional Government.
> 3. Every person serving in the ranks of the IDF will take an oath of allegiance to the State of Israel, its laws, and its lawful authorities.
> 4. The establishment or maintenance of any other armed force outside the IDF is hereby prohibited.
> 5. All orders, declarations, and regulations in regard to national service promulgated between November 29, 1947, and the date of this Ordinance by the Jewish Agency, the National Council for Palestinian Jews, the National Administration, the Provisional Government or one of its departments, will remain in effect until such time as they are changed, amended, or canceled.
> 6. All actions carried out in accordance with this Ordinance will be considered legal, even if they are in conflict with another section of an existing law.
> 7. The Ministry of Defense is responsible for carrying out this Ordinance.
> 8. This will be known as the Israel Defense Forces Ordinance–1948.

25

League of Arab States

Declaration of a Provisional Palestinian Civil Administration

July 10, 1948

While the Jews were quick to declare independence once the British left Palestine on May 14, 1948, the Palestinians lost control of their own fate as a result of weak and fractured leadership, a disorganized military force, and a determined Jordanian (and to a lesser extent, Egyptian) effort to gain control over parts of Palestine. The Arab League and especially the Jordanian king, Abdullah, became the dominant players on the Arab side during the Israeli War of Independence, thus leaving Palestinian interests largely underrepresented. On July 10, 1948, the Arab League took the first step toward promoting an independent Palestinian role and announced, in this document, the establishment of a civil administration in Palestine, headed by Palestinian dignitaries. However, the move was motivated more by a desire to block a U.N. plan to transfer parts of Palestine to Jordan (the Bernadotte Plan) than by an aspiration to allow a substantial Palestinian role: hence the minimalist declaration of a provisional civil administration rather than a sovereign Palestinian entity.

Not until September 1948 did the Arab League declare the establishment of a Palestinian government. King Abdullah fiercely objected to the new political entity and forbade its activities in the Jordanian-controlled parts of Palestine. Despite the official recognition conferred to the new government by some countries, it never assumed any significant role. The government relocated to Cairo in October 1948 and by September 1952 was practically disbanded by the Arab League, though officially it existed until the death of its eighty-year-old prime minister, Ahmad Hilmi, in June 1963.

The Political Committee of the League of Arab States has discussed the project of setting up a provisional civil administration in Palestine. Following consultations with the Palestinian organizations concerned, and having reached agreement therewith, it has approved the following:

1. A provisional civil administration shall be set up in Palestine, [whose functions shall be] to manage the public civil affairs and [to provide] the necessary services, on condition that it shall not have competence at present over the higher political affairs.

2. The administrative machinery shall be entrusted to a Council composed of a president and nine members, each of whom shall supervise and run one of the following civil departments:

a. The Presidency of the Council and the General Administrative Affairs. This Department shall perform the duties previously performed by the Secretary-General of the Palestine Government, and supervise the officers of areas, towns and districts.
b. The Judiciary. This Department shall super-

Source: Zvi Elpeleg, *The Grand Mufti* (London: Frank Cass, 1973), pp. 206–9.

vise the office of the Attorney-General, and the civil courts in towns and districts.

c. Health Services [Department]. This shall supervise hospitals, first-aid [centers], public health services, quarantines, etc.

d. Social Affairs [Department]. This shall supervise the affairs for the refugees, distressed persons, workers, education, etc.

e. Communications [Department]. This shall comprise public roads, communications, the Telegraph, Post, and Telephone Offices.

f. The Treasury. This [Department] shall comprise everything related to financial affairs, and the offices of income tax, municipal and rural taxes, customs, and the public Audit Office.

g. National Economy [Department]. This shall comprise everything related to matters of supply, import and export, and the two offices of trade and industry.

h. Agricultural Affairs [Department]. This shall comprise everything related to agricultural affairs, and the offices of forestry, veterinary (services), and fishing, etc.

i. Internal Public Security [Department]. This Department shall supervise everything related to the regular police, the maintenance of security, municipal and auxiliary police, prisons, and the national militia.

j. Publicity Affairs [Department]. This Department shall supervise the general [questions of] propaganda, publication, national guidance, newspapers, printed matter, and wireless broadcasting.

3. The jurisdiction of the Civil Administration Council shall extend to all areas at present occupied by the Arab armies or which may be occupied, until the whole of Arab Palestine is included.

4. The "Council of Directors" shall appoint all the officials it needs from among the Arab officials whose services have expired upon the termination of the British Mandate over Palestine.

5. All the above departments, together with social and other services, shall be conducted in accordance with the rules and laws in force at the time of the termination of the British Mandate, with the exception of those in conflict with Arab public interest.

6. The [said] Council shall, after the nomination and appointment of its members, meet on the summons of its President; during its meetings it shall determine the seat of the Civil Administration, the internal regulations of the Council, and the procedure [to be followed] in conducting its affairs.

7. All the services of the above civil departments shall be conducted in the interests of the whole population and in that of the occupying Arab armies.

8. The Council of the [Arab] League and the Governments of the Arab countries concerned shall define the competence of the Council [of Directors] and its members, together with the competence of the military governors, who may be appointed by the occupying Arab armies in the various areas.

9. The Civil Administration Council shall be guided by the decisions or directions that may be issued by the Council of the Arab League or by the Political Committee.

10. Should a member of this Council resign, die, or discontinue [his] work for any reason, the above Council shall nominate another member to fill the vacancy, with the approval of the Council of the [Arab] League or its Political Committee.

11. The Council of the [Arab] League shall issue a resolution [providing for] the setting up of this administrative machinery and the appointment of its members, and shall request all the inhabitants of Palestine to support it and facilitate its task.

12. This Council shall, at the first meeting held by it in Palestine, prepare its general budget, and [in doing so] shall aim at strict economy, as well as at the running of the necessary services with the least possible number of officials. The activities of [this Council] and its

various departments shall be expanded following the development of its financial resources.

13. As this administrative machinery cannot function unless assured of the necessary funds, particularly [those needed] for running the social, health, and other services, and until such time as the finance departments have been firmly established and have begun to collect the various taxes, the Council of the [Arab] League or its Political Committee shall decide to grant this administrative machinery a loan, an advance, or a gift, on condition that the amount [needed] shall be fixed when the Council begins its work and when the budget estimates for the first half of its financial year are submitted.

The Administrative Council shall be composed as follows:

1. Presidency of the Council and of the General Administrative Affairs: Ahmad Hilmi Pasha.
2. International Public Security: Jamal al-Husayni.
3. Social Affairs: 'Awni 'abd al-Hadi.
4. Health Services: Dr. Husayn Fakhri al-Khalidi.
5. Communications: Sulayman Tuqan.
6. The Judiciary: 'Ali Hasna.
7. National Economy: Raja 'ial-Husayni.
8. Publicity Affairs: Yusuf Sahyun.
9. Agricultural Affairs: Amin 'Aql.

In announcing this decision, the Political Committee hopes that it will herald the beginning of an era during which Palestinians will be able to conduct their own affairs, as well as lead to their exercising the attributes of their independence.

26

United Nations General Assembly

Resolution 194

December 11, 1948

By the summer of 1948, the refugee problem had emerged as the most serious international issue arising from the war, as hundreds of thousands of Palestinians fled the battle areas. A U.N. special envoy, Folke Bernadotte, had put forward a plan under which most refugees would be repatriated. On December 11, 1948, the United Nations General Assembly adopted Resolution 194 (III), which had no binding authority. The resolution called for two critical actions. It resolved that refugees "wishing to return to their homes and to live in peace with their neighbours" be permitted to do so and ordered the establishment of a Conciliation Commission composed of three states (France, Turkey, and the United States). Both met dead ends. Israel did not accept the recommendation for a right of return for refugees, and the commission was unable to lead the warring parties toward a peace agreement at the conference convened in Lausanne, Switzerland, April 15–September 15, 1949.

Source: A Decade of American Foreign Policy: Basic Documents, 1941–49, prepared at the request of the Senate Committee on Foreign Relations by the Staff of the Committee and the Department of State (Washington, D.C.: Government Printing Office, 1950), pp. 851–53.

The General Assembly,

Having considered further the situation in Palestine

1. *Expresses* its deep appreciation of the progress achieved through the good offices of the late United Nations Mediator [Folke Bernadotte] in promoting a peaceful adjustment of the future situation of Palestine, for which cause he sacrificed his life[1] and

Extends its thanks to the Acting Mediator [Ralph Bunche] and his staff for their continued efforts and devotion to duty in Palestine;

2. *Establishes* a Conciliation Commission consisting of three States members of the United Nations which shall have the following functions:

a. To assume, in so far as it considers necessary in existing circumstances, the functions given to the United Nations Mediator on Palestine by resolution 186 (S-2) of the General Assembly of 14 May 1948;

b. To carry out the specific functions and directives given to it by the present resolution and such additional functions and directives as may be given to it by the General Assembly or by the Security Council;

c. To undertake, upon the request of the Security Council, any of the functions now assigned to the United Nations Mediator on Palestine or to the United Nations Truce Commission by resolutions of the Security Council; upon such request to the Conciliation Commission by the Security Council with respect to all the remaining functions of the United Nations Mediator on Palestine under Security Council resolutions, the office of the Mediator shall be terminated;

3. *Decides* that a Committee of the Assembly, consisting of China, France, the Union of Soviet Socialist Republics, the United Kingdom and the United States of America, shall present, before the end of the first part of the present session of the General Assembly, for the approval of the Assembly, a proposal concerning the names of the three States which will constitute the Conciliation Commission;

4. *Requests* the Commission to begin its functions at once, with a view to the establishment of contact between the parties themselves and the Commission at the earliest possible date;

5. *Calls upon* the Governments and authorities concerned to extend the scope of the negotiations provided for in the Security Council's resolution of 16 November 1948[2] and to seek agreement by negotiations conducted either with the Conciliation Commission or directly, with a view to the final settlement of all questions outstanding between them;

6. *Instructs* the Conciliation Commission to take steps to assist the Governments and authorities concerned to achieve a final settlement of all questions outstanding between them;

7. *Resolves* that the Holy Places—including Nazareth—religious buildings and sites in Palestine should be protected and free access to them assured, in accordance with existing rights and historical practice; that arrangements to this end should be under effective United Nations supervision; that the United Nations Conciliation Commission, in presenting to the fourth regular session of the General Assembly its detailed proposals for a permanent international regime for the territory of Jerusalem, should include recommendations concerning the Holy Places in that territory; that with regard to the Holy Places in the rest of Palestine the Commission should call upon the political authorities of the areas concerned to give appropriate formal guarantees as to the protection of the Holy Places and access to them; and that these undertakings should be presented to the General Assembly for approval;

8. *Resolves* that, in view of its association with three world religions, the Jerusalem area, including the present municipality of Jerusalem plus the surrounding villages and towns, the most eastern of which shall be Abu Dis; the most southern, Bethlehem; the most western, Ein Kerem (including also the built-up area of Motsa); and the most northern, Shu'fat, should

be accorded special and separate treatment from the rest of Palestine and should be placed under effective United Nations control;

Requests the Security Council to take further steps to ensure the demilitarization of Jerusalem at the earliest possible date;

Instructs the Conciliation Commission to present to the fourth regular session of the General Assembly detailed proposals for a permanent international regime for the Jerusalem area which will provide for the maximum local autonomy for distinctive groups consistent with the special international status of the Jerusalem area;

The Conciliation Commission is authorized to appoint a United Nations representative, who shall co-operate with the local authorities with respect to the interim administration of the Jerusalem area;

9. *Resolves* that, pending agreement on more detailed arrangements among the Governments and authorities concerned, the freest possible access to Jerusalem by road, rail or air should be accorded to all inhabitants of Palestine;

Instructs the Conciliation Commission to report immediately to the Security Council, for appropriate action by that organ, any attempt by any party to impede such access;

10. *Instructs* the Conciliation Commission to seek arrangements among the Governments and authorities concerned which will facilitate the economic development of the area, including arrangements for access to ports and airfields and the use of transportation and communication facilities;

11. *Resolves* that the refugees wishing to return to their homes and live at peace with their neighbours should be permitted to do so at the earliest practicable date, and that compensation should be paid for the property of those choosing not to return and for loss of or damage to property which, under principles of international law or in equity, should be made good by the Governments or authorities responsible;

Instructs the Conciliation Commission to facilitate the repatriation, resettlement and economic and social rehabilitation of the refugees and the payment of compensation, and to maintain close relations with the Director of the United Nations Relief for Palestine Refugees and, through him, with the appropriate organs and agencies of the United Nations;

12. *Authorizes* the Conciliation Commission to appoint such subsidiary bodies and to employ such technical experts, acting under its authority, as it may find necessary for the effective discharge of its functions and responsibilities under the present resolution;

The Conciliation Commission will have its official headquarters at Jerusalem. The authorities responsible for maintaining order in Jerusalem will be responsible for taking all measures necessary to ensure the security of the Commission. The Secretary-General will provide a limited number of guards to the protection of the staff and premises of the Commission;

13. *Instructs* the Conciliation Commission to render progress reports periodically to the Secretary-General for transmission to the Security Council and to the Members of the United Nations;

14. *Calls upon* all Governments and authorities concerned to co-operate with the Conciliation Commission and to take all possible steps to assist in the implementation of the present resolution;

15. *Requests* the Secretary-General to provide the necessary staff and facilities and to make appropriate arrangements to provide the necessary funds required in carrying out the terms of the present resolution.

At the 186th plenary meeting on 11 December 1948, a committee of the Assembly consisting of the five States designated in paragraph 3 of the above resolution proposed that the following three States should constitute the Conciliation Commission: France, Turkey, United States of America. The proposal of the Committee having been adopted by the General Assembly at the same meeting, the Conciliation Commission is therefore composed of the above-mentioned three States.

NOTES

1. Folke Bernadotte was killed by Jewish extremists in September 1948 in Jerusalem.

2. U.N. Security Council Resolution 62 called for a truce in Palestine and the demarcation of armistice lines. See *Official Records of the Security Council,* Third Year, No. 126. ccp. rec.

27

Isaac Olshan

Jewish Religion and Israeli Democracy

1948–1953: Memoir and Analysis

Israel's history is marked by several deep political and ideological rifts that have their origins in the early Zionist movements of Europe and in the prestate Jewish community in Palestine. In a very rough way, three corners of a triangular "continuum" can be delineated, each characterizing a particular vision of the ideal Jewish state. Socialist Zionists envision a state organized along socialist, egalitarian, and democratic principles in which the economy is dominated by publicly owned and cooperative enterprises affording a high degree of workplace democracy and in which Jewish secular culture flourishes while religious institutions and culture are fully protected. The Revisionist Zionists envision an economically and militarily strong state that can provide a homeland and haven for Jews. They envision a state-directed or regulated capitalist economy able to compete favorably in international markets and ensure the state's economic prosperity and security. They also envision a state militarily strong enough to advance and defend the national interests of the state and of world Jewry. The Religious Zionists envision a theocratic state in the land given to the Jewish people by God where Jews can and do live completely religious lives, guided by religious leaders with the political power to ensure the theocratic integrity of the state and society.

One aspect of this theological and political competition was the struggle between the military units of various political movements for control of the emerging state (see docs. 22, 24). In the following document, the efforts of the religious parties to establish political influence within the state apparatus are discussed by Isaac Olshan (1895–1983), whose roots were in Socialist Zionist organizations. Olshan was one of the original five members of the Israel Supreme Court and its second president, 1954–65. His position, personality, and long tenure of office enabled him to enrich his memoirs of cases and events with insightful comments.

Immediately after the establishment of the state, the religious politicians began their efforts to secure strongholds with the intent of establishing life in the state on a firm halakhic[1]

Source: Isaac Olshan, *Din Udvarim* [Memoirs] (Jerusalem: Shocken Books, 1979), pp. 325–28. © World copyrights by Shocken Publishing House, Ltd., Tel Aviv, Israel. Reprinted by permission of Shocken Books.

basis, and in this way they tried to fortify positions in the various government offices by giving preference to members of religious parties in the bureaucratic apparatus. It must be admitted that politicians of other parties, too, as soon as they reached ministerial status, followed the same path. The only difference was that in the latter case these things were done out of a sense of obligation toward their own party members, whereas in the former case it grew out of an effort to create facts and customs, and by these means to achieve the penetration of halakhah in the management of the affairs of state and, in a roundabout way, in the life of the individual as well. To that end the leaders of the religious parties were most eager to widen the power and the authority of the rabbis. In the wake of a defective electoral system that actually corrupted the principles of democracy in the state and led to the fragmentation and multiplication of political parties, there arose the need to run the state by means of coalition governments. In those coalition governments, Mapai was the strongest party according to the number of representatives in the Knesset, but it never succeeded in achieving a majority in the elections.

Since it was the strongest party in the Knesset, Mapai always felt that it had the responsibility to form the governments in Israel during the entire period since the foundation of the state. Therefore it had to arrive, after each and every round of elections, at agreements with small factions. Here then was the possibility for the small parties to make conditions, which derived ostensibly from principles they professed but which were actually nothing but combinations of attempts to gain seats in the government. The negotiations about those conditions and the agreements concerning them were termed the "ground rules" of the coalition. Despite the fact that in the party newspapers as well as in public the politicians professed to be democratic in a general way, and despite the fact that in every interparty discussion the opponents pretended to base their viewpoints on principles of democracy—each according to a sophisticated reasoning all his own—when it came to determining those ground rules very little attention was paid to the needs of the community. The leaders cared little about whether they actually had received a mandate from the majority of the voting public to establish particular ground rules.

It would stand to reason that before the elections a number of parties would be forced to join together in order to form a coalition government on the basis of agreed-upon ground rules, and that each and every party entering into a coalition of this sort would present itself to the voter with its program, the principles of which were to be based on agreed-upon rules. But, instead of this procedure being followed before the elections, it was actually done after them, without giving the voters a chance to express their assent or opposition to the ground rules. What is called by the Israeli politicians in the area of legislation "the democratic system" was in actuality a party regimentation that allowed no choice but required compromise agreements and even conspiracies contrived by coalition members after the fact, i.e., after the elections. This situation was the cause of all kinds of mishaps in the public administration. The lion's share of the public service apparatus was party based, and even if this was not intended, at least the impression was created among the public at large that the affairs of such-and-such a department were in the area of such-and-such a party, and the affairs of another office lay in the power of a certain other party, and so forth.

Even in the government itself, it was impossible to create the efficient intermeshing between the different ministries because the relationships among them were most tenuous and every minister was careful not to intrude upon the territory of his colleague. As opposed to a government composed of the members of one single party, here every attempt by the head of the government, or the minister of one party, to respond to a subject under the jurisdiction of the leader of another party, was considered as impairing that leader's "sovereignty," and this could well lead to a government crisis because the injured party might throw down the gauntlet. It even happened that a particular minister or several of the ministers were opposed to the conduct of another minister, and although the majority of the ministers might be of the opinion that that opposition was justified, they hesitated to take measures in order to change the situation lest the stability of the government be undermined.

During the process of consolidation of the parties for the purpose of forming a coalition government, the parties "more fit" from the standpoint of the ruling party (Mapai) were the religious ones. It seemed that those parties represented only those aspirations that aimed at the penetration of religious laws into the life of the state, but that they knew very well that the promises, or most of them, would not be kept. Thus the formula of the status quo was created in the area of religious affairs. However when they were given such ministries as Religious Affairs, Interior, and Welfare, they were able to support, or defend, various institutions in keeping with their efforts to impose matters of religious interest on the nonreligious citizen as well. Parties such as Mapam and to a lesser extent Ahdut Haavodah appeared on the political stage with obsolete slogans of the kind used in the nineteenth century. These slogans were appropriate in that particular period, and at that time they really contributed to the growth and the progress of the socialist movement and to the protection of the working people from the exploiting classes. But now, in the second half of the twentieth century, during the period of the creation and the growth of the welfare state, when the government was forced to penetrate into all areas of individual life because of the responsibility placed on it for the livelihood and sustenance of every individual, these parties lost their vitality.

For example, in the nineteenth century the strike was an efficient and just instrument in the war of the workers against their unlimited exploitation by their employers. However, in the welfare state, as the government's responsibility to provide a livelihood for the masses has grown steadily, and with it the responsibility for the national economy, the unjustified use of the strike can increasingly be harmful, particularly when wildcat strikes at one enterprise threaten the economic viability of other enterprises. In such cases the strike weapon actually limits workers' power, especially if the national federation has lost influence over its local organizations. These observations apply particularly to a state that is forced to seek an opening into foreign markets and to compete there against the exports from other states with regimes not considered progressive in social policies. The prohibition against strikes in Soviet Russia is inevitable, and it can serve as proof as to the extent to which the doctrines of the previous century have become obsolete. The religious parties have been more reluctant than any others to profess socialist models for society or for anything connected with the economy of the state. For this reason, then, it was more convenient for the ruling party to ally itself through coalitions with the religious parties, in exchange for the preservation of existing affairs. In actuality, this alliance led to religious suppression, in many cases to halakhic decisions that had become totally obsolete, such as personal status laws (*ishut*) and others. In short, Mapai was able to make arrangements quite easily with the religious parties, as they did not demand doctrines that had a bearing on the economy of the state. On the other hand, the leftist parties that stood for anachronistic doctrines shut their eyes to the existing situation and did not recognize the danger lurking in the militant religious establishment.

For these reasons compromises, concessions, and intrigues occurred in the religious camp without consideration for the fact that the State of Israel had been established as a secular state on the basic principle of the rule of law.

As we said, the religious parties began as early as the first years after the establishment of the state to conquer strongholds in the direction of the religious coercion of the broad secular public. This occurred at a very slow pace, in order not to arouse instinctive reactions on the part of those wide circles that, although they were ready to grant all religious needs to those who required them, still were not ready to agree to a conversion of the state to one based on religious laws, many of which had been created under the force and conditions of life during the period in which they originated but were no longer suited for life and its conditions in our own era.

As already recounted, as early as the end of 1948 there arose, right after the declaration of the establishment of the state, the demand for a widening of the jurisdiction of the rabbinical courts. At that time, on the heels of the establishment of the Supreme Court, the religious parties demanded that among the five judges there should be named at least one religious judge, i.e., a rabbi. The matter was discussed by the Provisional Government, and in spite of the fact that there were members of Mapam within the government, who of course did not ask the opinion of their membership and did not get their approval to agree to this imposition by the religious parties, the demand was accepted without opposition. At that time, Rabbi Simhah Assaf was named, and his nomination was confirmed by the Provisional State Council (Moezet Hamedinah), which functioned on a temporary basis. That nomination was even against the law, according to which the conditions for the jurisdiction of the judges of the state were still anchored in the law of the Mandate, which had not yet been changed following the establishment of the state and was thus still in force.

The pill was sweetened by the fact that Rabbi Assaf—although he had no juridical training—was still an exalted personality, bright, progressive in his outlook, pleasant to deal with and not fanatical in his orthodoxy. He was easy to work with. All these qualities compensated in a large measure for the additional burden placed upon us—the four other judges—as we had to guide him along in connection with the application of various laws in cases brought before us. Cases that had a bearing upon questions of personal status, falling under the purview of religious rules, were decided in the religious courts; the instances in which we in the Supreme Court had anything to do with them were few. With respect to the majority of the cases, we had to explain to Rabbi Assaf the secular law.

In connection with the illegality of the nomination, a special law was afterward passed in the Knesset in order to make his nomination as judge legal. Wisecracks of that time termed it "Assaf's Law." In the years 1952–53 two of the judges of the Supreme Court resigned: Dr. [Menahem] Dunkleblum and Rabbi Assaf.

After the resignation of Rabbi Assaf there were those among the religious parties who demanded, on the basis of an established claim (*hazakah*), that another rabbi be named in place of Rabbi Assaf. Mr. Eliyahu Elyashar[2] even began to lobby for the appointment of a Sephardi judge to the Supreme Court. This time around, however, because it was well known beforehand that we as judges of the Supreme Court would take an unwavering stand that any nomination be made solely and entirely according to the qualifications of the candidates without religious considerations, the question was removed from the agenda of the various busybodies.

NOTES

1. Halakhah is Jewish religious law based upon the Pentateuch, Talmud, and other traditional rabbinic teachings.

2. Eliyahu (Elihu) Elyashar (ca. 1899–1981), president of the Sephardi community in Jerusalem, came from a long line of respected rabbinic leaders who had been in Palestine for centuries.

28

Israel First Knesset

The Debate on a Constitution

February 1 and June 13, 1950

Several of the chief problems confronting the State of Israel during the first years of independence are addressed in this and the following documents. The issue of a constitution reveals the depth of the ideological cleavage in the Israeli body politic at that time. Despite repeated attempts to draft such a document, fundamental differences could not be reconciled, and the idea of a constitution was eventually dropped. The minutes of the Knesset's debates in this matter present the full spectrum of opinion over the basic issues of life and politics in Israel: religious and antireligious parties, socialist and antisocialist parties, parties committed to the institutions that evolved from the Yishuv and parties opposed to the institutions of the Yishuv and the Zionist Organization. The inability to agree on the principles that should be embedded in a constitution reflects historical differences within the Zionist movement regarding the type of state and society that should be created. In the absence of a constitution, the Knesset has the formal power to legislate all laws.

At the end of the debate, Yizhar Harari (1908–1978), a lawyer and co-founder of the Progressive Party, proposed a compromise that was approved by a majority of 50 to 38. The proposal, which is part of the following document, established the basis for formulating what are known as Basic Laws that could become chapters of a future constitution. Eleven Basic Laws have been enacted: they deal with the Knesset (1958); Israeli lands (1960); the president (1964); the government (i.e., cabinet) (1968); the state economy (i.e., taxes and the budget) (1975); the army (1976); the Jerusalem Law (formally establishing Jerusalem as the capital) (1980); the judiciary (1984); the state controller (1988); human dignity and liberty (1992); and freedom of occupation (1994). Although the Law of Return (doc. 29) is not a Basic Law because it was not drafted according to the procedures outlined in Harari's proposal, it is generally agreed that in the (at present unlikely) event that a constitution is drafted, this law will be treated as if it were a Basic Law.

Debate on the Report of the Constitution, Legislative, and Judicial Committee regarding the Question of a State Constitution, February 1, 1950

NAHUM NIR (CHAIRMAN)

Until the conclusion of the Provisional State Council's term of office, there was no doubt that we were electing the Constituent Assembly—that was its title—and each of us included, within his party's platform, the content of the constitution as he saw it. However, as early as January 1949 the mood of the Provisional State Council had already shifted slightly, and when we met to adopt the Transition Ordinance, the majority of the Constitution Committee

---

Source: *Divrei Haknesset* [Knesset Minutes], February 1, June 13, 1950 (Jerusalem: Government Printer, 1950), 4:714–828; 5:1257–1722.

proposed the inclusion of a paragraph stating that the function of the Constituent Assembly is to draft a constitution, and that, until it does this, it serves as an ordinary House of Legislature. The debate began, then and immediately, and the first opinions opposing the need to prepare a constitution were voiced. But the arguments we heard in the Constitution Committee were not presented there. There only one point was made: Why should we obligate the Constituent Assembly? It is a sovereign body and will decide when it is elected; why then, should the Provisional State Council obligate it? We thought that if the Provisional State Council adopts an ordinance, it does not obligate the Constituent Assembly because the Constituent Assembly can nullify the ordinance, just as it can nullify any law. . . .

. . . It is said that there is no need to adopt a basic constitution but only basic laws. Dr. [Zerah] Warhaftig said, in the Constitution Committee, that the only difference between a basic constitution and basic laws is that a constitution is adopted ceremoniously, which is not the case with basic laws. This is not quite correct. There is another important difference. A constitution provides principles of the state's character, whereas basic laws are more like pieces of patchwork, such as we are accustomed to; and not only do the patches not always match, they sometimes clash dangerously.

I once gave this example in the Constitution Committee and I beg, in advance, the government's forgiveness. I don't think our government will do that. I speak only of the juridical circumstances. Our situation is such that, according to the basic constitution, the present government has the right to dissolve the Knesset. It need only refer to paragraph 9 of the Law and Administration Ordinance [doc. 23], which states that the government can pass emergency regulations which alter, or even nullify, an existing law, and are then brought before the Knesset for approval, for up to three months. I beg of you not to think that I suspect anyone, but this is the juridical situation, even though I am certain that the government would never take advantage of the possibility.

Yohanan Bader (Herut movement)

Don't trust it.

Nahum Nir

The juridical situation is such that it is possible to produce emergency regulations today that nullify last year's Elections Law, to dissolve the Knesset, to produce a new Elections Law, to hold new elections—all this within three months, and the new Knesset will approve the emergency regulations. And once again, I do not suspect anyone of such actions, but such a situation could occur in our circumstances, when we are without a constitution; for this reason, we must formulate a basic constitution—in order to set limits. . . .

Y. Bar-Rav-Hai (Mapai)

. . . There is one more point to which I would like to draw the House's attention. To the best of my knowledge, one does not create a constitution at the beginning of a revolution, but when it is completed. All constitutions are an attempt to "freeze" certain principles, to preserve them, inasmuch as it is possible to preserve any particular thing in the life of a nation. A state, of a people, which has arrived at a certain level and achieved certain principles, by revolutionary means or by casting off foreign rule, tries, by means of a constitution, to preserve and stabilize this development. Therefore all those constitutions that were created apropos the revolutionary process were nullified, exchanged, or altered as the revolution progressed. It is necessary to achieve a more or less stable situation that will enable the casting of a mold expressing the development level of a people or state at a particular stage. . . .

The constitution is created for that population which was in existence within the borders of the state. Ours is a different situation. Our population is fluid. We are not at the end of a revolutionary process but at its beginning. For our revolution is not the establishment of the state—that is only one of its stages. Our revolution is the ingathering of the exiles; it is the maximum concentration of Jewry within Eretz Israel. The question is, Can we, today, in these fluid circumstances, cast the decisive molds that will determine the permanent framework of the State of Israel?

... It is clear that this state needs laws, and we establish laws from time to time. Also, insofar as reality demands, insofar as it allows, we attempt to solve each problem without entering into meaningless, abstract debate about meaningless, abstract principles....

... Therefore, in conclusion, I should like to propose to this House that it charge the Constitution, Legislative, and Judicial Committee with the duty of preparing a list of laws necessary to ensure the efficient administration of the state and that will regulate the most pressing problems, on the basis of the principles established in the Proclamation of the State of Israel [doc. 21]. This committee will not only prepare the list of these necessary laws; it will also prepare—and I am confident that in this it will have the government's cooperation—the individual bills and will present them to this Supreme House. Then there will be a pointed debate on the proposals in this House—a debate about the fundamentals of our state, not about principles, not rhetoric, but rather about our real problems of living. This is the only way to guarantee us a basic constitution. I am not one of those who believe that states can usually exist indefinitely without a basic constitution. The unique spectacle of England does not repeat itself in history. I also reject the conventional notion that England has no written constitution. In the committee I attempted to quote the list of laws that, to all intents and purposes, determine the constitutional structure of England. I reject the view that a constitution is an immediate necessity; I merely state that it can be achieved stage by stage, and that only in this way will we draw closer to the objective....

Zerah Warhaftig (National Religious Front)

It is my opinion that the Proclamation of the State of Israel does not obligate us in any way to adopt a constitution—not on October 1, 1948, and not on any other date. The Proclamation of the State of Israel is a document connected with the political system and can only be explained in relation to that system's development.

As for the second question, Have we already a constitution? I think we do have one, according to that commitment that is contained in the Proclamation of the State of Israel. This commitment is not to the United Nations. We have undertaken such a commitment independently of the U.N. General Assembly decision, and we do not have to promise conditions that cannot be altered. We already have such a constitution, having adopted the Law and Administration Ordinance, the Transition Law, and the Knesset Elections Law, on the basis of which elections were held. A constitution is a system of laws that regulate the matters of government and law in the state. Such a system exists in our state, therefore we have a constitution.

To the extent that we know the difference between a written and an unwritten constitution, it may be said that we have no written constitution. But when one speaks of a constitution in the general sense, it includes both the written and the unwritten types. The study of constitutions distinguishes several types of constitutions, among them the written and the unwritten, although both are known as constitutions. If it says in the Proclamation of the State of Israel that we are committed to adopting a constitution, that means that we must make those arrangements which will enable the existence of a regulated government in the state. This we have done. Mind you, we did not do so on October 1, 1948, because the Knesset elections did not take place until January, but we have regulated the process of government in the country, though it can and must be improved. But it cannot be said that we have no constitution. . . .

. . . The Provisional State Council rejected by a majority vote the proposal of the committee majority to obligate the Constituent Assembly to adopt a constitution. It took the stand that the Constituent Assembly is under no obligation to adopt a constitution. I have no idea why Mr. Nir did not, at that time, use the Proclamation of the State of Israel as an argument, nor do I know why other members did not use that argument. But in any case, the Proclamation of the State of Israel already existed then, and the Provisional State Council, the same council that issued the proclamation, ruled that we are not obligated to adopt a constitution. . . .

. . . A Constitution consists of two sections: the executive section and the declarative. In our case, the executive section already exists—in the form of basic laws, which we have yet to complete. In concluding I will mention those basic laws we still lack and will have to adopt.

The declarative section of a constitution consists of an introduction and of vague principles that, lacking the executive section, without laws of implementation, have no practical value. Mr. Nir suggests deleting the introduction from the declarative section, for the reason that in the introduction, one may mention the "Rock of Israel," and of this he is afraid. . . .

. . . If the intention is to draw up a constitution based on some other constitutions, then it is unnecessary; not only that, it is actually harmful. Perhaps it is easy for MK [Member of the Knesset] Nir to draw up a constitution; to me it seems that the work demands inspiration, and that the Spirit of God must guide those who engage in such a project. Any who think that the granting of a constitution is nothing more than the drawing up of a number of superficial principles, a few platitudes, is mistaken. Take, for example, the collection of constitutions of the South and Central American countries, which was recently translated into English and published—I'm willing to wager any one of you that if you erase the names of the countries whose constitutions are included in this book, you won't be able to distinguish between that of Haiti and that of the Honduras, between that of Nicaragua and that of Costa Rica. If you want to adopt this sort of a constitution, it's possible, but it won't add anything to Israel's stature—not in our own opinion and not in that of other nations. Also such a constitution will not have any educational value, either in Israel or in the Diaspora.

Gentlemen, what is a constitution? A constitution must have educational value for the youth of Israel and for the Jewry of the Diaspora. The constitution is very important as an educational and cultural factor in the whole world. It must be a sort of calling card, an indicator of the character of this nation and of this state. The constitution that is being, or will be proposed, cannot serve these two functions. We are known in the world as the People of the Bible. We have no need of a second calling card. It will not add to our stature; on the contrary, it will detract from it.

Yisrael Bar-Yehudah (Mapam)

. . . The very opposing of the legislation of a basic constitution is a continuation of the system that I mentioned—a constant legislative irresponsibility, with all depending on the moment, the doer, or the circumstance. We must legislate permanent and stable basic elements that will obligate all. I want to remind all of you, my learned friends, who quote from all types of constitutions: You always mention three things that must be established in such basic laws—you mention that the constitution must determine the rights of the legislative authority, the executive authority, and the judicial authority. In my opinion, there is also a fourth very important point. Not only, What are the rights of those who are handed the job of governing the citizen-resident, but also, What are the rights of the citizen with regard to the government? What is the minimum beyond which the legislative, executive, and judicial powers must not go? We feel that in a state like ours this is one of the most important factors, and for this reason the drafting of a constitution is an urgent matter. There are some special circumstances that make the matter one of particular urgency in our case. I need only mention three such points. I could bring many examples, but in order to save time, I will concentrate on the main ones.

Don't forget that here we are the majority people, and that at our side there is a minority people—this after a bitter war—and coexistence will not be achieved so easily. Perhaps in this matter we should not depend only on the freedom to use emergency measures and various ordinances; rather, basic rules should be formulated, which will obligate everyone. I would like to continue and explain that principle which, in my opinion, should be first in importance and about which there is seemingly no debate or conflict of opinion among us. We live in this country, in the peculiar circumstances of the ingathering of the exiles, of different communities, coming from the four corners of the earth, with different habits, and—as Mr. Warhaftig mentioned—having all sorts of strange unwritten constitutions that sometimes contradict and oppose one another. Our goal is to create one nation out of this mixed multitude. To achieve this goal, we must act on all possible fronts: the educational, the organizational, in short, in all aspects of our lives, in order to live together and not as we do now—apart. This trend must find its expression in legislation as well—in the education toward a common legislation for all and in our taking account of each person and his needs when we legislate laws. This period of our history in our country is certainly not the end of our national revolution; it is the middle of it, perhaps only its beginnings. The expulsion of the British from this country did not conclude our national revolution; it simply initiated a new stage. After all, the ingathering of the exiles—the process of transferring masses of Jews to Eretz Israel, and that not only from the geographical aspect but also with the intention of turning them into citizens and workers in our country—this is one of the supreme commands of the continuation of our national revolution. Has this command already been fulfilled? . . .

Menahem Begin (Herut movement)

There is one thing you wish to prevent: the existence of a law of freedom, of justice, that will take precedence over all other laws and that you will not be able to nullify one fine morning by a mechanical majority. Look, gentlemen. When liberal thought flourished it was said of the state's authority that it ought to be limited to the role of "night watchman." That period is past, and every free man prays that we will not be forced to admit that it has gone forever. But in the meantime, generations have passed, and all of humanity is searching for the golden mean between the freedom of the individual and the aspiration for a world of justice. No nation has yet discovered that golden mean. Yet we, here, seem to have found the final answer to the question of the type of living regime we should establish in our state. Not only will we extend the authority of the government apparatus to all aspects of our life, but we will turn the state into a sort of "night thief." The citizen—surrounded by detectives, superintendents, policemen, clerks; the rule—suspicion; the exception to the rule—trust. The rule is that the citizen is a criminal; the exception to that rule is that he is law abiding. Therefore one must even enter private homes and search the refrigerator; one must pile supervision on supervision and carry out personal searches. . . .

. . . You have repudiated the mandate granted by the people in the elections. You have the right to make a change but on one condition—that you ask the people. The nation chose the Constituent Assembly; that is, it charged us all with the duty of legislating a constitution for the State of Israel. For whatever reason, impulsive or calculated, you do not wish to legislate a constitution. Go to the nation and tell it, We have no need of a constitution, we lack the inspiration, we hesitate to bind the coming generations, etc. Let the nation decide. (An interruption from the Mapai benches: The Constituent Assembly is the nation!) You are mistaken. The Constituent Assembly is merely the instrument of the nation, and in the event that it repudiates the will of the nation, the nation has the right to demand new elections. That is your philosophy—that your majority is superior to the nation, and that is why you oppose the constitution. If the Constituent Assembly legislates a constitution, then the government will not be free to do as it likes. At present, the government is superior to the law—the majority in the House does not control the government or guide it; on the contrary, the government imposes its will on the majority. Does the government want a particular law? Then, that law is adopted. Does it want to nullify a particular law? Then, that law is nullified. And so, you really are situated above the law. That's how it is in our state. We have a ruling sect, superior to the law, because there is no constitution to restrain it. You want to preserve this status quo; *that's* the real reason for your objection to a constitution, and *that* you do not reveal to the nation. Not only are you violating the law of the State, as I quoted from the Transition Law, 1949; you are ignoring the will of the people as it was expressed in the general elections. All of you ran for elections to the Constituent Assembly, each and every one of you; not one of you let the nation know that there would be no constitution. Therefore we demand of you one of the following: Either you fulfill the duty with which the nation has charged you and that is to legislate a constitution; or you hold a referendum, in which all the voters in the state will participate, and you will act according to their decision on the question of a constitution. Your first obligation is to enact a constitution. You do not have the authority to change your mandate.

The question is most grave. He who wants the public to respect the laws of the government is duty bound to make sure that the government respects the law of the state. If you violate the nation's will, if you repudiate the voters' mandate, there will be no law in Israel and no respect for the law. . . . I don't believe that the citizens of the State are obligated to expose their files for Dov Joseph. It is contrary to the natural right of the citizen and the man. But if you have decided to install such laws in Israel, then ask the nation if it releases you from your principal duty—to enact a basic constitution for the State of Israel. When the nation replies yes, then you can continue to legislate laws with a mechanical majority and from your position of supremacy vis-à-vis the law. As long as the nation does not speak thus, you have no right to decide for yourselves, no matter what your arguments.

Therefore, honored chairman, in order to conclude the debate on the constitution I wish to present two proposals, as follows: "The First Knesset, which is the Constituent Assembly, has decided to legislate a constitution for the State of Israel, in accordance with the duty with which the nation has charged the Constituent Assembly in the general elections." . . .

Knesset Decision regarding a State Constitution, June 13, 1950

The proposal of MK Y. Harari supported by Mapai, the Progressive Party, the Sephardim,[1] and WIZO [Women's International Zionist Organization]: "The First Knesset charges the Constitution, Legislative, and Judicial Committee with the duty of preparing a draft constitution for the state. The constitution will be constructed chapter by chapter in such a way that each chapter in itself will constitute a basic law. The chapters will be brought before the Knesset as the committee completes its work, and all the chapters together will form the state constitution."

NOTE

1. Sephardim are Jews who generally come from Mediterranean and Middle Eastern countries. Ashkenazi Jews, on the other hand, generally come from Europe or the United States; their different histories have led to somewhat different religious and cultural traditions. The traditional Sephardi community in Israel (as opposed to the Sephardim who entered the state during the years of mass immigration) organized a political party that was active in the early years.

29

Israel First Knesset

The Law of Return

July 5, 1950

On July 5, 1950, the Knesset unanimously passed the Hok Hashvut (Law of Return). This law reflects the messianic hope of the Jewish people for the "ingathering of the exiles" and the political goal of the Zionist movement to repatriate the "exiled" Jewish people into their ancestral homeland. But its significance is much more than symbolic. Following the experience of Jews attempting to flee Nazi persecution and massacres only to find the doors of all countries of refuge closed to them (including the gates to Palestine, which were closed by the British), this law assured all Jews throughout the world that there would always be at least one country whose gates would be perpetually open.

This open immigration policy had been impossible during the latter years of the Mandate period. Following the outbreak of the Arab Revolt in 1936, the British Mandatory government limited Jewish immigration and land ownership. In response, the Haganah and Etzel organized illegal immigration, which continued up to independence in 1948. Stories of this period have become "mythified" and are now part of the folklore glorifying the early haluzim *(pioneers).*

The Law of Return, based on the Zionist tenet of the centrality of Israel to Jewish life, continues to have political significance, particularly in terms of Israel's relations to the Diaspora (i.e., Jews living outside of Israel). From the late 1960s it has served as the legal basis for Israel's policy of encouraging immigration from Western nations and the Soviet Union, and later from Russia. Moreover, it has forced the state into legally defining "who is a Jew" (see doc. 48).

---

1. Every Jew has the right to immigrate to the country.
2. (a) Immigration shall be on the basis of an immigrant's visa. (b) An immigrant's visa shall be granted to every Jew who has expressed his desire to settle in Israel, unless the minister of immigration is convinced that the applicant (1) is acting against the Jewish People, (2) is likely to endanger public health or the security of the state.

Source: *Reshumot* [Official Record of the Laws of the State of Israel] (Jerusalem: Government Printer, 1951), 51:159.

3. (a) A Jew who comes to Israel and after his arrival expresses his desire to settle there is entitled, while he is still in Israel, to obtain an immigrant certificate. (b) The reservations detailed in section 2(b) will also be in force regarding the granting of an immigrant certificate, but a person will not be considered as endangering the public health as a result of an illness contracted after arrival in Israel.
4. Every Jew who immigrated to Israel before this law entered into effect, and every Jew born in the country, whether before or after this law entered into effect, shall be considered as having immigrated according to this law.
5. The minister of immigration is responsible for the enforcement of this law, and he is empowered to enact regulations in all matters concerning its implementation as well as the granting of immigrant visas and immigrant papers to minors under the age of eighteen.

30

Giora Josephtal

The Absorption of Immigrants

August 1951

Giora Josephtal (1912–1962) was born in Germany, where he was active in social work and the halutz *movement in the years prior to World War II. He immigrated to Palestine in 1938, where he helped establish Kibbutz Gal-Ed in 1945. After the war he began organizing the Jewish Agency's Absorption Department (later, Misrad Haklitah) and was successively its director and treasurer of the Jewish Agency Executive. In 1959 he became Israeli minister of labor, in which capacity he continued the work of absorption through the building of housing projects. His last post before his death was that of minister of housing and development.*

Josephtal's report in August 1951 to the Twenty-Third Zionist Congress, reproduced here, sheds light on a central aspect of Israeli life in the early 1950s—the absorption of hundreds of thousands of Jewish refugees and the regimen of austerity that this effort imposed upon the whole society. After the Arab-Israeli hostilities were brought to a close by the armistice agreements of 1949, most of the difficulties facing the new state revolved around the great number of immigrants. Josephtal's official duties brought him into direct contact with the emergencies that arose in every field connected with the absorption. Housing was the major problem. Immigrants were settled in abandoned Arab houses and former British army camps. Finally, beginning in January 1950 maabarot *(transit camps) were established to provide immediate temporary housing. The buildings were generally small prefabricated structures without central heating. By 1954 the* maabarot *were being steadily emptied as new methods of absorption were introduced, particularly the attempt to place newcomers directly in homes in new settlements or in development towns. Nevertheless, many* maabarot *eventually became permanent low-income residential areas.*

Source: Ben Halpern and Shalom Wurm, eds., *The Responsible Attitude: Life and Opinions of Giora Josephtal* (New York: Schocken Books, 1961), pp. 101–4. Reprinted by permission of Schocken Books, Inc.

The slogans "ingathering of the exiles" and "communal integration" have been so overworked by Israel and world Jewry that their precise meaning has begun to be vague.

During the three years since Israel's establishment, the bodies responsible for absorbing the immigrants have waged a constant battle with material, organizational, and spiritual problems in order to enable the mass immigration to continue. Even if the local Jewish community is showing certain signs of fatigue under the strain of taking in so many immigrants in such a short time, we are duty-bound to do everything possible before the gates of potential sources of immigration are closed, and not to wait for pogroms in countries where the Jewish community's political situation is today clearly unstable. This must constantly be borne in mind in doing our day-to-day work.

The most immediate task is to rescue the Jews living in the Arab lands. Two-thirds of them are already in Israel. We must save the remaining third as well. Only someone who regards the ingathering of exiles as an urgent rescue operation can possibly put up with some of the methods we are forced to use in settling the immigrants.

The Jewish people left us in a state of poverty at the decisive moment when Israel had to be saved. We are continuing to take in the waves of mass immigration and to conduct a desperate campaign against a shortage of raw materials and means of production, a shortage of funds, and a shortage of trained personnel.

What does every new arrival need the moment he reaches Israel? A roof over his head, a place of work, a bed, a mattress, blankets, cooking utensils, medical supplies, a doctor to look after him, a nurse, a place in a hospital, a kindergarten for his children, a school, a kindergarten teacher, a school teacher, an instructor, vocational training, and food (which the country is not yet producing). He also needs a warm and cordial atmosphere, because everyone who transplants himself from one country to another undergoes a spiritual crisis of some kind. We supply only some of these needs. We cannot supply all of them, because the Jewish people have given us only 20 percent of the means we need to integrate the immigrants fully.

Our greatest achievement has been the provision of employment for virtually all the new settlers, despite inadequate investments. We have arranged jobs for the immigrants and set them on the road to a productive future; we have freed them from a life of idleness and decay; but we have not yet fully exploited their productive potential, and we have not been able to instill in them the approach to work which they must adopt if this country is going to be built up. It will take years before we see the full fruit of the investments we have made in all branches of the economy. In agriculture this may take many years.

There are large areas of the country—such as Galilee and the Negev—where nature does not make intensive agriculture possible. Work villages, which prepare the ground for full-time farming, are a prerequisite for the expansion of the area under cultivation. And if we want to ensure a minimal supply of home-grown produce, we will have to prepare large tracts of land for cultivation for a long time to come.

We cannot live in the plains and valleys. If we want to safeguard Israel's security and provide food for its population, we will need a better appreciation of the importance of soil amelioration, we will have to understand its intrinsic value and not consider it a mere waste of manpower and money.

We have begun to adapt the form of the new agricultural settlements to the social structure of the immigrant families. Even if this means that the moshav (and not the kibbutz)[1] holds a leading place among the newly established settlements, can we forget that we are engaged in eliminating Diaspora patterns? Three generations come to Israel together: grandfather, son, and grandchild. All these have to be fitted into an appropriate framework for easy integration, and all these have to be helped to make a pioneering effort,[2] in accordance with the outlook on life accessible to each one. If 20 percent of the immigrants are working on the land, this can rightly be considered a tremendous revolution. Before the recent waves of mass immigration the number of Jewish wage earners working in agriculture was never as high as 20 percent.

After every unselective wave of immigration we find that some of the initial attempts at absorption do not succeed. Such trends as the flight from the villages to the town and the drift from manual labor to commerce are perfectly natural under the circumstances.

The most important factor in our efforts to ensure jobs for all the new arrivals was the immigrants themselves. If the immigrants had not shown initiative in finding work for themselves, in creating jobs for one another and for others, all our efforts would have been in vain. Anyone who visits the immigrant centers and sees what they have done to improve their situation by using their own resources, comes away with a deep feeling of confidence in the future of this nation and a conviction that its life force, powers of ingenuity, and common sense are no less important than all the efforts by all the organizations and the entire country. Of course, there are limits to the immigrants' ability to help themselves: and without the means of production and adequate capital no great and lasting enterprise can be established. We are still short of both. . . .

Second in the order of priority for immigrant services comes housing. However, it is obvious to us that the meager foreign currency at our disposal should first be placed in basic, productive investments, and only later invested in housing and services. We must spread the large sums of money needed for immigrant housing over many years. Rather than trying to build a small number of high-quality housing units, we should concentrate on giving every immigrant a roof over his head, even in the most primitive way. Here too we must avoid giving everything to a few people. A minimum must be provided for everyone. If we use wood, then every wooden unit takes the place of two canvas units; if we build with concrete, then every two concrete units takes the place of three wooden units. We will be able to erect better-quality housing if the immigration rate declines or if our foreign currency income increases. As long as neither of these two conditions has been fulfilled, we must continue following our present policy: as much as possible, as quickly as possible, as cheaply as possible.

Our greatest concern at present is the situation in the services, and social integration. A fundamental condition for successful communal integration is a change in the way of life of settlers from the more backward countries. One of the ways of achieving this is to support the weaker and underprivileged members of the family cell: the children and the women.

NOTES

1. A moshav is a cooperative agricultural settlement based on privately owned farms, as opposed to a kibbutz, which is a collective settlement with an agricultural base. In recent years kibbutzim have established many industrial enterprises as well. During the years of mass immigration immediately after the establishment of the state, many immigrants were settled in newly established moshavim, as the socialist ideology and collective way of life of the kibbutzim made them unsuitable for absorbing large numbers of these new immigrants.
2. The concept of *halutziut* (pioneering) was central to the Zionist ideology of the Labor movement. It had several important components, including self-fulfillment through labor (especially agricultural labor) and sacrificing for the common good and the realization of Zionist goals. Each member of the Zionist movement was expected to become a *halutz* in Eretz Israel.

31

Nahum Goldmann

The German Reparations

December 1951–March 1952: Memoir

Following the reconstruction of Germany after World War II, the West German government agreed, in principle, to pay reparations to those Jews who were victimized by the Nazi government. The Conference on Jewish Material Claims against Germany was established in October 1951 by world Jewish organizations to represent world Jewry in the negotiations, and an agreement was signed in Luxembourg on September 10, 1952. West Germany agreed to pay DM 3 billion ($750 million) in goods to Israel to offset the cost of absorbing the refugees, DM 450 million ($107 million) to Israel to be transferred to the Jewish Claims Conference for the rehabilitation of victims outside of Israel, and additional direct payments to the Jewish Claims Conference for compensation of individuals. These payments were to be made over a period of fourteen years. In addition, the West German Federal Indemnity Law of 1954, which provided for restitution to individuals oppressed by the Nazis, led to an influx of an additional DM 7 billion ($1.7 billion) into the Israeli economy over ten years.

It is now widely agreed that the decision to accept the reparations was correct and that the reparations money played an important role in consolidating Israel's economic foundation during a period in which the state was virtually bankrupt. At the time the agreement was negotiated, however, it was one of the most controversial issues of Israeli life. The experience of the Holocaust had affected much of Menahem Begin's political thinking, and Herut, under his leadership, opposed the negotiations, arguing that accepting reparations was tantamount to pardoning Germany for unpardonable crimes; the movement threatened to cause widespread violence during the massive demonstrations it organized.

Dr. Nahum Goldmann (1895–1982), a longtime Zionist leader and activist within the Zionist Organization, was instrumental in establishing contact with the West German chancellor, Konrad Adenauer, and in facilitating the negotiations that led to the Luxembourg Agreement. Goldmann, who headed the World Jewish Congress, 1953–77, had considered joining Israel's political system but made his home and political base in the Jewish Diaspora. In 1962 he left the United States (to which he had emigrated shortly after the outbreak of World War II) and became a citizen of Israel, spending part of his time there and part in Europe. In 1968 he became a Swiss citizen and made Geneva his home base. His insistence on emphasizing the distinction between Israel and the Jewish people as well as some of his policies embittered his relations with successive Israeli prime ministers (see, e.g., docs. 46, 63). In the following excerpt from his memoirs, Goldmann not only describes the delicate reparations negotiations but also presents the position taken by the majority of Israeli and Jewish institutions.

Source: Nahum Goldmann, *Memories: The Autobiography of Nahum Goldmann—The Story of a Lifelong Battle by World Jewry's Ambassador at Large*, trans. Helen Sebba (London: Weidenfeld and Nicholson, 1970), pp. 259–63. Reprinted by permission of Nahum Goldmann.

Next morning [December 6, 1951] at eleven o'clock, when I went with Dr. [Noah] Barou to see the chancellor at Claridge's Hotel, taking every precaution to avoid the press, I sensed that the coming conversation was going to be a momentous one. I asked [Konrad] Adenauer to allow me fifteen or twenty minutes to state my case and pointed out how significant it was that for the first time since [Adolf] Hitler, a representative of Jewry should be confronting a German chancellor. I told him of the heated, not to say passionate controversy in the Jewish world and of the violent attacks I myself had been subjected to for months, but said that my confidence in his statement to the Bundestag [West German legislature] had led me to arrange this conversation. I explained how important it was morally to atone for the crimes of the Nazi era, at least materially, by a great gesture of good will, and said that from the perspective of history, a contribution to the development of the Jewish state was an honor for Germany. The Jewish people would never forget what the Nazis had done to them, and no one should ever expect them to forget it, but a conspicuous symbol of atonement would show the Jews and the world that a new Germany had arisen. The form and extent of the restitution this Germany would make to the Jewish people would demonstrate, perhaps more clearly than anything else, the extent of Germany's breach with National Socialism.

At the same time I emphasized that whatever Germany did, could be no more than a gesture. Nothing could call the dead to life again; nothing could obliterate those crimes; but a symbolic gesture would have a deep meaning. The coming negotiations, I said, were unique in nature. They had no legal basis; they were backed by no political power; their meaning was purely an ethical one. If there was to be any haggling, it would be better not to begin the talks at all. If the negotiations were not to be conducted on the basis of an acknowledged moral claim, if they were not to be begun and ended in a spirit of magnanimity, then I, the sponsor of this claim, would advise the chancellor and Israel not to engage in them at all. Conducted under the wrong conditions, they would only poison relations between the Jews and the Germans still more.

I told the chancellor that I understood how difficult it must be for him to accept Israel's demands as they stood as the basis for negotiation and mentioned my talk with [Herbert] Blankenhorn[1] of the day before. On the other hand, I assured him that unless they were accepted, neither the Israeli parliament nor the Claims Conference would authorize the opening of negotiations and postponement would jeopardize the whole undertaking. Finally, I told him that I knew I was asking something unusual, something that by conventional standards might be considered incorrect. "But this is a unique case," I concluded. "Until now, Chancellor, I did not know you, but in the twenty-five minutes I have been sitting here opposite you, you have impressed me as a man of such stature that I can expect you to override conventional regulations. I ask you to take upon yourself the responsibility of approving the undertaking I have requested, not merely verbally, as I suggested to Blankenhorn, but in the form of a letter."

Chancellor Adenauer was visibly moved and replied: "Dr. Goldmann, those who know me know that I am a man of few words and that I detest high-flown talks. But I must tell you that while you were speaking I felt the wings of world history beating in this room. My desire for restitution is sincere. I regard it as a great moral problem and a debt of honour for the new Germany. You have sized me up correctly. I am prepared to approve the undertaking you request on my own responsibility. If you will give me the draft of such a letter after our talk, I will sign it in the course of the day." As a matter of fact, I dictated a text to his secretary in his apartment and, in the afternoon, on the occasion of an address the chancellor gave at Chatham House, Dr. Barou received the letter addressed to me. . . .

In Israel a majority of the coalition parties authorized the government to negotiate, after a stormy debate in parliament accompanied by tumultuous demonstrations from outside. The Claims Conference deliberately waited for Israel's decision, but after the resolution had been passed in the Knesset, I called a meeting in New York for January 20, 1952. That produced another very heated debate, although this time it ended in endorsement of the negotiations by a much larger majority. An executive committee, of which I was elected chairman, was appointed to direct the negotiations; its members included Jacob Blaustein of the American Jewish Committee, Frank Goldmann of the B'nai B'rith, Israel Goldstein of the American Jewish Congress, and Adolph Held of the Jewish Labor Committee, all of them from New York. Two European representatives were later co-opted: Barnett Janner of the British Board of Deputies and Jules Braunschvig of the Alliance Israélite Universelle.

We worked out a set of procedural directives. The main thing was to get the West German government to pass legislation applicable to all of the Federal Republic, so that claims for restitution and compensation could be handled uniformly. Up until then there had been great discrepancies in individual German states' handling of claims. Measures would also be required to make the Federal Republic responsible for enforcing this legislation, especially its financial provisions, since practice had shown how difficult it would be for several of the poorer states to meet legitimate claims. Finally, in addition to the individual claims, we demanded restitution of heirless Jewish property. A team of experts was asked to produce a detailed plan for implementing these directives and it did an excellent job.

In a joint session of the executive committee and the Israeli delegation, held in Paris on February 11, 1952, and attended by [Moshe] Sharett, the global claim of the Claims Conference was set at five hundred million German marks. This completed the necessary preliminaries on the Jewish side; the only thing that remained to be settled before negotiations could begin were some technical details of form and place, and I had already spoken to Adenauer in London on February 4 about these. During that talk, in which German Secretary of State for Foreign Affairs, Walter Hallstein, and Assistant Secretary Blankenhorn joined, we had agreed that the discussions should be held in Belgium or Holland in mid-March and that there should be two parallel negotiations, one between the Israeli delegation and the Germans and a second between representatives of the Claims Conference and Germany.

On March 16, 17, and 18 the executive committee of the Claims Conference held further meetings in London to appoint our team. We decided on Moses Leavitt of the American Jewish Joint Distribution Committee as leader of the delegation and Alex Easterman of the WJC [World Jewish Congress], Seymour Ruben of the American Jewish Committee, and Maurice Boukstein of the Jewish Agency for Palestine as its members. They were to be assisted by a number of experts, notably Dr. Nehemiah Robinson. . . .

On March 20, 1952, negotiations began in Wassenaar near The Hague. I deliberately took no part. I could not afford to spend months in Wassenaar and in any case I thought it better to remain in the background during the complicated and protracted discussions of detail, so that I could more effectively intervene in a crisis. It was only to be expected that difficulties would arise. In a great courageous gesture Chancellor Adenauer had accepted the Israeli claims of a billion dollars as the basis of discussions, but I knew that this gigantic sum was firmly opposed within his cabinet and by the party leaders, as well as by banking and industrial interests. I had been told by various sources that there was no hope of anything approaching that amount. I remained optimistic, trusting to the chancellor's word and his way of accomplishing what he desired, even in the face of opposition.

NOTE

1. Herbert Blankenhorn (1904–1991), political director of the West German Ministry of Foreign Affairs, 1950–55.

32

Moshe Dayan

The Transformation of the Israeli Army

1952–1955: Memoir

Moshe Dayan (1915–1981) was a dominant figure in the Israeli security establishment as chief of staff of the armed forces, 1956–58, and as minister of defense, 1967–74. As minister of foreign affairs, 1977–79, he played an important and constructive role in the Israeli-Egyptian peace negotiations. The following excerpt from his autobiography describes the reshaping of the Israeli army in the early 1950s as well as some of the major problems of Israeli defense policy.

On December 7, 1952, I was appointed head of the Operations Branch of the General Staff, and I held this post for one year until my appointment as chief of staff on December 6, 1953. During that year I applied myself to developing the operational capability of the army—the sole purpose of an army's existence—and sharpening the tools for doing that job—organizing the appropriate combat units and raising the standards of the individual fighting man.

My predecessor in Operations was Lt. Gen. Mordekhai Makleff who moved up to become chief of staff upon the resignation of Lt. Gen. Yigael Yadin. Our appointments came during a difficult financial period for the army. The War of Independence was behind us, and the country's priorities were the reception, absorption and settlement of the several hundred thousand new immigrants who had reached our shores in the few years since statehood. The treasury coffers had to be channelled to essential immigrant services and civilian development projects, and the budgets of other ministries, including defense, had to be drastically cut.

Makleff and I agreed in principle that the fighting units of the army had to be strengthened at the expense of the service units, and this principle was indeed reflected in the three-year program decided upon by the General Staff at sessions devoted to the reorganization of the army within the framework of our restricted budget. It was generally agreed that we had to change the character of the combat units. They were not what they had been in the War of Independence. Many officers had left. The best of the recruits doing their national service elected to join the Air Force or the Navy. Many of the new immigrants, without experience of the life and temper of beleaguered Israel, required longer training. Units were understrength and ill equipped.

We had seen the effects of lowered fighting standards in our infantry units reflected in the minor border actions that had taken place in the period since the War of Independence. At the beginning of 1953, the incidence of infiltration for sabotage and murder had increased, and several small-scale reprisal raids had been undertaken against terrorist bases in or near

Source: Moshe Dayan, *Story of My Life* (London: Weidenfeld and Nicholson, 1976), pp. 139–47. Reprinted by permission of the Orion Publishing Group.

Arab villages just across the border. The results were unsatisfactory. In some cases our detachments returned after one or two men were killed and a few wounded without having fulfilled their mission.

I considered it my job to change all this and to fashion fighting units that could always be relied upon to attain their objectives. This, I felt, should be the sole concern of the head of Operations. I was aware of the great importance of effecting the necessary organizational changes in the structure of the army. Abolishing military laundries, using civilian hospital services for army personnel, or reducing the number of field kitchens would make more funds available for armaments. But these changes could be made without anyone having to crawl on his belly through an enemy fence and risk getting a bullet in his back. It was the fighting man I was concerned with, for he was the cutting edge of the army's tool, and a soldier in the army of Israel, under constant threat from its neighbors, had always to be ready for battle. If we failed in minor border actions, as we had in the previous year, how would we stand up to the Arab armies on the battlefield? No amount of reorganization would alter the basic function of the Israel Defense Forces—to be fit for battle at all times.

It seemed to me that the recent failures were due to altered attitudes since the War of Independence in three spheres: the degree of the soldier's readiness to risk his life in fulfillment of his mission; the place and duties of the officer in battle; and the basic approach of the general Staff to casualty rates in a period of restricted hostilities.

It was not difficult to change the approach of the General Staff, and I accordingly met with the Operations officers of all the commands. I told them that in the future, if any unit commander reported that he failed to carry out his mission because he could not overcome the enemy force, his explanation would not be accepted unless he had suffered 50 percent casualties. The term "could not" was relative, and the question was how much effort was put into meeting enemy resistance in order to complete the mission. As long as the unit had not lost its combat power, it had to go on attacking. What I left unsaid when I spoke to the officers was transmitted by the expression on my face. They were left in no doubt that if they failed to carry out their assignment, they would have to face a detailed debriefing; and if their explanations did not satisfy me there would be little future for them in the army.

The factors that helped to bring about a practical change in combat standards during the year when Makleff was chief of staff and I was head of Operations were the channelling of the better-educated national service recruits to the fighting units and, above all, the establishment of a special unit known as Force 101. This was a volunteer unit which undertook special operations across the border. The commander was the daring and combat-wise Maj. Ariel Sharon, whom I had admired and known well since he had been my Intelligence officer at Northern Command. Arik, as everyone called him, gathered to his unit picked men, most of them reservists. I confess that when the proposal to establish this unit was brought before the General Staff in May 1953, I did not support it. I felt that our primary problem was not what to do to the Arab terrorists in reprisal, but how to improve the fighting capacity of our army. In fact, however, it was the practical influence of this unit which brought about the very aim I sought—raising combat standards. Force 101 operated with such brilliance that its achievements set an example to all the other formations in the army. It proved the feasibility of successfully carrying out the kind of mission at which other units had failed.

In January 1954, a few weeks after I became chief of staff, Force 101 was merged with the paratroops, and Arik became commander of the Paratroop Battalion. For some time thereafter, this unit alone undertook all the reprisal actions against Arab terrorists and raids across the border. Later, there was a growing recognition that such assignments should also be given to other units. The paratroops ceased to be solely an army formation and became a concept and a symbol—the symbol of courageous combat—that other formations in the army tried to live up to. Through the paratroops, the army recovered its self-confidence, and it was now rare indeed that a unit commander returned from action having to explain the failure of his mission.

My appointment as chief of staff placed me at the top of the army pyramid, and I knew that I had to safeguard the image of the Israel Defense Forces. But I also knew that I had to carry out those changes I thought essential and to mold the army into the shape I wanted. I recognized that I would now have to deal with matters which I had managed to steer clear of up to now. A chief of staff, particularly in times of comparative quiet, is occupied with administrative and technical problems—manpower, budget, armament, equipment, maintenance—and he is further away from the combat units in the field. As I rose in the military hierarchy, the gap between battle and me widened. Instead of fighting, I would tell others what to do. I would issue directives, give oral and written orders, but in the field, in battle, matters would be decided by the combatants. Sitting at General Staff headquarters, it would be difficult for me to determine, and at times even influence, the character of the fighting by our units in the distant Negev or on the Jordan border. I would have to live through them and their reports. It would be the commanders in the field who would tell me what could and could not be done.

I felt an understandable pride in becoming the number one soldier in the Israel Defense Forces. But even at the height of the ceremony, when [David] Ben-Gurion pinned on my badges of rank and I received the standard of the chief of staff, I had no sense of elation. I realized the weight of the responsibility, and I was ready to shoulder it faithfully and with devotion.

At the end of the ceremony, the secretary of the Cabinet came over to me and casually observed that I would now have to change my partisan character, be circumspect in my ways, become more respectable. I would have to "fashion a new Moshe Dayan," he said. I told him he was wide of the mark. It was not I who would change; the image of the chief of staff would change. It was not I who had made myself a new suit of clothes; it was the army that had acquired a new chief. I intended to change the style and content of the army, abolish the gap between the chief of staff and the private soldier, cut down on ceremonial, introduce more simplicity in the work habits of the army brass, and fill the higher echelon posts with talented and battle-hardened young officers who had fought in the War of Independence.

I started the change of style in my own office. I abolished the post of aide-de-camp to the chief of staff and I took over his room as my office. I brought in the field table covered by a khaki blanket and a glass top which I had used when I was head of Operations. I turned the large, well-furnished room which had been the office of the chief of staff, with its massive table and upholstered chairs, into a conference room. I wanted the field commanders who came to see me to feel that they had come to the headquarters of a higher command which was not very different and not cut off from their own. When I inspected units in the field, I wore fatigues, sat on the ground with the troops, got dirty and dusty together with them.

I paid a lot of surprise visits at night, mostly driving alone. I wanted to check whether units were in a constant state of readiness; ensure that there was always a responsible senior officer in every command headquarters; and talk to the soldiers returning from a night exercise or from guard duty at an outpost. Whenever there was an operational problem, I would see the head of the Operations Branch, the unit commander, and his junior platoon commanders. I wanted to hear what had happened, if it was after an action, or what special problems were envisaged, if it was before an operation. I wanted to hear things from them at first hand, without intermediaries, and I wanted the young officers to hear what I had to say directly from me, in my own words and in my own style. . . .

Since it was through the young officers that we could shape the kind of army we wanted, I would use the occasion of a graduation parade at an Officers' Course whenever I had something special to say. I remember one such occasion at the end of May 1955, and also what I said when I addressed the cadets on whom I had just pinned officer's insignia. A few days earlier, I had had the unpleasant duty of terminating the service of a young career officer who had ordered a soldier to proceed on a dangerous action while he himself sat in safety. A vehicle of ours was struck close to the border of the Gaza Strip and was under heavy fire from the Egyptians. The officer in charge sent a driver to retrieve it, while he himself lay behind cover and issued directions from there. I told the cadets: "I would not have dismissed this officer if he had decided that the danger was too great and it was better to abandon the vehicle rather than endanger lives. But if he decided to take daring action and save the vehicle, he should have advanced with his troops and laid his own life on the line together with theirs. Officers of the Israeli army do not send their men into battle. They lead them into battle."

Forging an army, however, requires more than talk, and officers require more than courage and moral leadership. They should also be well educated and of rounded intellect. Most of our officers at that time had fought in the War of Independence and stayed on, having had no opportunity before that war or since of attending the university. I thought that should be corrected, and we accordingly introduced a system of sending officers to the university at the army's expense. They could take a degree in any subject that interested them, from economics and Middle Eastern studies, to history and literature. One officer who later became commander of the Armored Corps studied philosophy. At the same time, we also started sending officers in the technical services, such as ordnance and engineering, to the Haifa Technion Institute of Technology to study subjects related to their work.

In mid-1955 we sent a detachment of volunteers on a daring reconnaissance mission through Sinai to find a land route to Sharm el-Sheikh, at the southern tip of the peninsula. Sharm el-Sheikh commanded the narrow Straits of Tiran at the entrance to the Gulf of Aqaba. The Egyptians had blockaded this waterway to Israeli shipping, thereby closing our sea lane to East Africa and the Far East and stifling Eilat port, as well as the development of its hinterland, the Negev. Egypt also closed the direct air route over the gulf for our civilian planes. The reconnaissance was part of our planning preparation for the capture of Sharm el-Sheikh if the Egyptians failed to lift the blockade. The results of the survey would make possible the extraordinary trek of one of our brigades in the Sinai Campaign a year and a half later.

On September 27, 1955, Gamal Abdul Nasser of Egypt opened a military exhibition in Cairo and announced that the week before, "we signed a commercial agreement with Czechoslovakia whereby that country will supply us with arms in exchange for cotton and rice." This was Nasser's innocent-sounding announcement of what was to mark a turning point in Middle Eastern affairs, for his "commercial agreement," which would soon be known as the Czech arms deal, revolutionized the scale and quality of arms supplies to the region, planted a Soviet foot firmly in an area which had been closed to her, opened a second front for the United States in the Cold War, and gravely threatened the existence of Israel.

Under this arms agreement, Egypt would be receiving from the Soviet bloc some 300 medium and heavy tanks of the latest Soviet type, 200 armored personnel carriers, 100 armored self-propelled guns, several hundred field howitzers, medium guns, and anti-tank guns, 134 anti-aircraft guns, and 200 MIG-15 jet fighters and 50 Ilyushin bombers, in addition to transport planes, radar systems, 2 destroyers, 4 minesweepers, 12 torpedo boats, ammunition, spare parts, ground equipment for aircraft, and hundreds of battle vehicles of various types. All small arms and light weapons were to be replaced by huge quantities of the Russian semiautomatic rifle.

These arms, types and quantities may not seem startling by today's standards. But at that time, they represented a stunning acceleration of the pace of rearmament in the Middle East. In quantity alone, they tipped the arms balance drastically against Israel; in quality, the tilt was even more drastic. We had never imagined that we could match the size of the arsenals possessed by the Arab states. But we believed we could bridge the gap by the superior fighting capacity of our troops, as long as we could match the quality of their weaponry. In modern warfare, however, the elements of range, speed and fire power in technologically advanced aircraft, naval vessels, and armor can be so superior that inferior weapons are simply unable to stand up to them. For every rise in standards of an enemy's arms, there must be a minimum means of reply. Without it, no amount of courage can get the better of objective technical superiority. A brilliant pilot in a propeller aircraft has no chance against mediocrity in a jet. A daring tank gunner in an obsolete Sherman, which is the tank we had, would find his shells bouncing off the armor of a Stalin-3 tank, which was what the Egyptians were about to receive. The Czech arms deal placed in doubt the capability of the Israeli army to give expression to its qualitative human advantages.

It was clear to us in Israel that the primary purpose of this massive Egyptian rearmament was to prepare Egypt for a decisive confrontation with Israel in the near future. The Egyptian blockade, Egyptian planning and direction of mounting Palestinian guerrilla activity against Israel, Nasser's own declarations, and now the Czech arms deal left no doubt in our minds that Egypt's purpose was to wipe us out, or at least win a decisive military victory which would leave us in helpless subjugation.

The Soviet arms began flowing into Egypt at the beginning of November 1955, and at meetings of the General Staff we considered that it would take the Egyptian army from 6 to 8 months to absorb and digest most of its new weapons and equipment. We therefore had to expect an Egyptian attack at any time from late spring to late summer. In that time, we had to acquire at least some planes and tanks which could match their Russian counterparts. The problem for us was that our sources were limited. The United States and Britain produced quality planes and tanks, but at that time they were refusing to sell us arms. There was talk that America might change her policy and consider letting us have defensive weapons, but even that was dubious. The only possible source for new tanks was France, but she produced only the light AMX tank. We would try to get that and make do with it, and also to recondition some obsolete American tanks which we had acquired from World War Two surplus stores in Europe. On planes, the only European manufacturers, apart from Britain, were Sweden and France. We would try to get them quickly from France.

33

Benyamin Givli

Memorandum on the Mishap in Egypt

October 1954

In July 1954 eleven Egyptian Jews organized by Unit 131, a special operations unit of the Israel Defense Forces Intelligence Branch, exploded bombs at an Alexandria post office and the American information center in Cairo. A third action was supposedly planned, and other targets were considered. The bombings, which caused minor property damage and an injury to the fingers of one postal clerk, were apparently meant to strain the United States' relations with the Arab world at a time when the United States was increasing its arms sales to Arab countries.

*Following this ill-conceived act of Israeli intelligence warfare, the Egyptian government arrested and tried eight Egyptian Jews. Two were sentenced to death and executed; the others received prison terms. Three of the participants in the bombings escaped arrest. This so-called Mishap (*esek bish*) subsequently developed into a political scandal that shook the Israeli political system in the early 1960s (see docs. 47, 49). Serious questions were raised about the Mishap: Who gave the order to carry out the operation? Who was responsible for the operation? Was it the defense minister, Pinhas Lavon, or the chief of the IDF's Intelligence Branch, Benyamin Givli?*

Pinhas Lavon (Lubianiker) (1904–1976), Israeli defense minister from 1953 to 1955, was at the center of this controversy. Despite his position as Ben-Gurion's heir apparent, he was forced to resign his cabinet position. Givli was also dismissed.

The document reproduced here—a top secret memorandum of October 1954 from Givli to the General Staff—is one of the original documents around which the controversy has raged. It was printed in an account of the Mishap and its consequences by Haggai Eshed, an Israeli journalist commissioned by Ben-Gurion to research and document the event. Eshed's version is obviously only one among several.

Pursuant to your request, I am listing herewith the details in connection with the operations [of Unit] 131 in Egypt and the mishap that occurred there:

1. For prior reference, see: (a) report on operation in Egypt, July 1954, dated 8/8 of this year, (b) arrest of IDF officer in Egypt of 9/24 of this year, (c) report on events in Egypt July–September dated 10/5 of this year.
2. On 7/16/54 a discussion took place in the home of the defense minister on the topic "Significance of British evacuation of Suez"; the participants were the defense minister, Brigadier (Aluf) Avidar, Lieutenant

Source: Haggai Eshed, *Mi natan et hahoraah?* [Who Issued the Order?] (Jerusalem: Edanim Books, 1979), pp. 258–59. Reprinted by permission of Haggai Eshed.

Colonel Yuval Neeman, Mr. Ephraim Evron, and myself.

During the discussion I was asked about the possibility of putting Unit 131 into action against British targets and my reply was affirmative from the operational point of view.

After the conclusion of the meeting, I was requested by the defense minister to stay on. In the conversation between us the subject of the operations [of Unit] 131 against British targets was again raised.

The targets that seemed acceptable to me were British missions and vehicles as well as other British institutions and personnel. British soldiers were not designated as such because of the assumption that they would not move beyond the area of the canal zone, in view of the prevailing tension there.

Thereafter the defense minister told me that I should issue instructions to 131 to operate against British elements. In that conversation, we talked about two additional matters that have no connection with the present subject. After the meeeting, I invited to my home the commander of Unit 131 and another commander.

The commander of 131 informed me that he hoped the men would be in a position to act, since during the last meeting the need for a state of readiness was emphasized in view of the unsatisfactory situation in the ranks, and I instructed him to transmit operational directions by way of proper communication channels.

The other officer was unable to make any concrete suggestions and informed me that he would examine the matter and let me know. Several days later the press published stories of arrests and operations in Cairo and Alexandria, taken from broadcasts by Radio Damascus and Radio Cairo.

The officer on location received the instructions transmitted by Kol Israel in a garbled and unclear form, and operated according to his best judgment.

From reports that reached us afterward it became clear that operations in the post office and in the American information offices were carried out by the men on location, according to their best judgment and based upon the instructions that had been issued for planning purposes only.

Foreign Policy Issues

34

Abdullah al-Tal

The Jordanian-Israeli Negotiations

March 22–23, 1949: Memoir

The Jordanian-Israeli negotiations in 1949 differed from the other armistice negotiations that ended the War of Independence in two important respects. There were prior contacts and "feelers" between Jordan and Israel. Perhaps more important, the armistice lines between Israel and Jordan affected numerous civilians, both Jewish and Arab, and village boundaries.

The following discussion of the negotiations that led to the armistice agreement between Jordan and Israel on April 3, 1949, is from the memoirs of Abdullah al-Tal. Al-Tal was a Jordanian officer who, as lieutenant colonel, became commander of Jordanian Jerusalem. As an anti-British and anti-Hashemite Arab nationalist, he tried to obstruct all attempts at Jordanian-Israeli understanding. Nevertheless, his memoirs of the Jordanian-Israeli negotiations reflect the special relationship between King Abdullah and the Israeli government as well as the centrality of negotiations with Jordan to Israeli peacemaking efforts (see doc. 20).

In the evening of March 22–23, 1949, at precisely eight o'clock, the Jewish delegation arrived at El-Shuneh. They were received at the palace by the protocol officials, who escorted them into the parlor, and there they awaited the king's arrival. After a short while, His Royal Highness entered and shook hands with the members of the delegation, which included [Walter] Eytan, [Yigael] Yadin, [Moshe] Dayan, and [Yehoshafat] Harkabi, i.e., those men who participated in the meeting with the Jordanian governmental mission in Jerusalem. On behalf of the government were present at this time Said Al-Mufti, the acting prime minister, Fallah al Madadkha, Muhammad al-Shunkeiti, and Hussein Saraj, and for the army Major Cooker,

Source: Abdullah al-Tal, *Zikhronot Abdullah al-Tal* [Memoirs of Abdullah al-Tal] (Tel Aviv: Maarakhot Publishing House, 1960), pp. 366–77. Reprinted by permission.

head of the Operations Branch of the Arab Legion, and Lieutenant Abdal Rakham Rassas representing the cartographic division. The stay in the reception hall was not long, since the king invited all present to follow him into the dining room. There he placed each of the guests into the seat prepared for him.

At the table the discussions were mostly carried on between the king and Eytan. The king entertained the guests by speaking about the universities in Britain and about living languages. After that, His Royal Highness proceeded to talk about Ben-Gurion and asked Eytan about the fields of knowledge in which Ben-Gurion had shown a special interest.

Eytan replied that [David] Ben-Gurion was interested in philosophy and that he was also a great scholar in the field of history. Following that, the king turned to Dayan and asked him why his knowledge of Arabic was so weak, despite the fact that he was born in Palestine. Dayan replied that the reason was a lack of contact with the Arabs.

At the conclusion of the meal, His Royal Highness rose and proceeded to the meeting room, with the guests and government representatives following him in his steps. . . .

In addition to those mentioned above, Doctor Shaukat al-Sati[1] and Hashem al-Dabas, one of the king's entourage, also participated in this meeting. The king opened the session by directing his remarks to Dr. Eytan and expanding upon the problem of Palestine and how it had developed. His Royal Highness spoke to the Jews as if he were addressing members of his own government, without paying attention to the results of his frankness, which revealed to the Jews his entire way of thinking. He did not hesitate to reveal and explain to the Jews that the Arab Legion was not fighting against the Jews and that it had no such aim. Among other things the king said:

> The Jews are a progressive and cohesive nation, and the Arabs a weak and backward nation. The West is against us and I swear to God that we did not receive even one single bullet from abroad in this war. The foreigners support you and give you every possible assistance. The Arabs had hoped for victory, but exactly the opposite happened. Our intention was not to fight; but we were forced to enter this war against our will, since they refused to accept our advice. I personally am not afraid, and I am ready to accept all the responsibility to bring this problem to a conclusion and to come to an understanding with you. That is my goal, and you know that I am a frank person.

Following this, His Royal Highness reviewed his trip for a meeting with the regent of Iraq at "H3"[2] and the results of that meeting. . . .

The king spoke for about an hour and concluded with the warm request that the Jews should make his task easier by not exaggerating their demands, since that would have a negative influence upon his own standing in the Arab world—something, according to his estimate, even the Jews would not want. Then the king stated that he would name the same commission, with the addition of Major Cooker, in place of Abdullah al-Tal, who did not want to participate in this commission since he was now out of the army.

The king concluded his remarks with these words: "And now I would like you to tell me a thing or two, so that I might find out to what extent my words have influenced you."

Major Harkabi translated the king's remarks to Eytan in Hebrew, and after that Hussein Saraj translated Eytan's words which had been spoken in English, into Arabic.

Eytan began by conveying to His Royal Highness the greetings of Ben-Gurion and his appreciation for the honor with which he received the Jews who had come to meet with him. Then Eytan proceeded to the main topic and said that he was in full agreement with regard to most of the points the king had raised during his remarks and that he was interested that a final peace between Israel and His Royal

Highness be reached as soon as possible. Eytan continued by stating that in the past the Arabs had neither understood nor believed that the Jews wanted to live, both in Palestine and in the rest of the Arab states, in peace and harmony with the Arabs. But now this is what we are hoping for. The emergence of Israel and its becoming a reality will not be merely a historic event but an event of importance to the entire Middle East. Eytan said further that friendship and understanding would have to be founded on a firm basis and that therefore the Jews were asking for certain territorial changes in the Triangle sector[3] as a fundamental factor in the mutual understanding with His Royal Highness.

In explaining the factors that prompted Israel to demand certain changes in the Triangle as a condition for its agreement to the occupation of that area by the Arab Legion, Eytan stated that Israel was suffering great difficulties because of the shape of the state in that particular sector and that every day men and women were slain as the result of constant clashes originating in that abnormal situation in the sector that threatens Israel's peace and its very existence. Following that, Eytan said frankly that if King Abdullah's government were to refuse to accede to Israel's demands, he would suggest that Transjordan should cease to interfere between the two sides—i.e., between the Jews and the Iraqis—but that it should be left to those two sides to arrange matters among themselves in a way suitable to Israel. Eytan continued by promising that the demands of his government would be realized if the matter would be left to direct negotiations with Jordan or with Iraq, since these demands were, in his eyes, justified and would secure for Israel peace and quiet and would strengthen the link between North and South.

When Eytan finished his talk the king replied by stating that he agreed the demands of the Jews were indeed vital to them but that he would ask them to give up several villages, such as Umm El Fahm, Baqa al-Gharbiyya, and El-Taybeh, in order that the refugee problem not become even more complicated. When the hour of eleven at night approached, the king said, "Let us leave the study of the problem to the two delegations, and I promise you that I shall not retire to bed and shall not sleep until I am informed of the success of the meeting."

NOTES

1. Shaukat al-Sati was the king's physician.
2. H3 is a cluster of three airfields in western Iraq, 270 miles west of Baghdad.
3. The Triangle is three triangular areas of Palestine inhabited almost exclusively by Arabs. The Arab or Large Triangle is the northern section of the West Bank, roughly bounded by the towns of Tulkharm, Jenin, and Nablus (Shekhem). The Israeli Triangle borders the Large Triangle in the western Sharon district and includes the villages of Baqa al-Gharbiyya, Kfar Kasem, and Taybeh. It has been under continuous Israeli control since 1949. The Little Triangle is near Haifa in the Carmel Mountain range and extends to the seacoast. It was conquered by Israel in Operation Hashoter (Policeman). The area discussed in this document includes the Little Triangle and the Israeli Triangle, which are contiguous.

35

Armistice Agreement between Syria and Israel

July 20, 1949

The War of Independence ended with a series of armistice agreements, secured through the mediation of the United Nations (see doc. 36), that were to have been replaced by peace treaties. Since they were not, they had to regulate a complex and hostile set of relationships for eighteen years, despite the fact that negotiations continued through various channels to seek a broader Arab-Israeli peace.

The Armistice Agreement between Syria and Israel was signed on July 20, 1949. Israel had already signed armistice agreements with Egypt on February 24, Lebanon on March 23, and Jordan on April 3, 1949. Iraq did not become a party to these agreements. Map 2 shows the 1949 armistice lines, which were the same as the cease-fire lines.

The following excerpt from the Syrian-Israeli Armistice Agreement exemplifies both the complexities and the provisional nature of these agreements.

Preamble

The Parties to the present Agreement:

Responding to the Security Council resolution of 16 November 1948,[1] calling upon them, as a further provisional measure under Article 40 of the Charter of the United Nations[2] and in order to facilitate the transition from the present truce to permanent peace in Palestine, to negotiate an armistice;

Having decided to enter into negotiations under United Nations Chairmanship concerning the implementation of the Security Council resolution of 16 November 1948; and having appointed representatives empowered to negotiate and conclude an Armistice Agreement:

The undersigned representatives, having exchanged their full powers found to be in good and proper form, have agreed upon the following provisions:

Article 1. With a view to promoting the return of permanent peace in Palestine and in recognition of the importance in this regard of mutual assurances concerning the future military operations of the Parties, the following principles, which shall be fully observed by both Parties during the armistice, are hereby affirmed:

1. The injunction of the Security Council against resort to military force in the settlement of the Palestine question shall henceforth be scrupulously respected by both Parties. The establishment of an armistice between their armed forces is accepted as an indispensable step toward the liquidation of armed conflict and the restoration of peace in Palestine.

2. No aggressive action by the armed forces—land, sea or air—of either Party shall be undertaken, planned or threatened against the people or the armed forces of the other; it

---

Source: Meron Medzini, ed., *Israel's Foreign Relations: Selected Documents, 1947–1974* (Jerusalem: Ministry of Foreign Affairs, 1976), 1:192–97, 202–3, 205–7. Reprinted by permission of the Director General, Ministry of Foreign Affairs, Jerusalem.

being understood that the use of the term "planned" in this context has no bearing on normal staff planning as generally practised in military organizations.

3. The right of each Party to its security and freedom from fear of attack by the armed forces of the other shall be fully respected.

Article 2. With a specific view to the implementation of the resolution of the Security Council of 16 November 1948, the following principles and purposes are affirmed:

1. The principle that no military or political advantage should be gained under the truce ordered by the Security Council is recognized.

2. It is also recognized that no provision of this Agreement shall in any way prejudice the rights, claims and positions of either Party hereto in the ultimate peaceful settlement of the Palestine question, the provision of this Agreement being dictated exclusively by military, and not by political, considerations.

Article 3.

1. In pursuance of the foregoing principles and of the resolution of the Security Council of 16 November 1948, a general armistice between the armed forces of the two Parties—land, sea and air—is hereby established.

2. No element of the land, sea or air, military or para-military, forces of either Party, including non-regular forces, shall commit any warlike or hostile act against the military or para-military forces of the other Party, or against civilians in territory under the control of that Party; or shall advance beyond or pass over for any purpose whatsoever the Armistice Demarcation Line set forth in Article 5 of this Agreement; or enter into or pass through the air space of the other Party or through the waters within three miles of the coastline of the other Party.

3. No warlike act or act of hostility shall be conducted from territory controlled by one of the Parties to this Agreement against the other Party or against civilians in territory under control of that Party.

Article 4.

1. The line described in Article 5 of this Agreement shall be designated as the Armistice Demarcation Line and is delineated in pursuance of the purpose and intent of the resolution of the Security Council of 16 November 1948.

2. The basic purpose of the Armistice Demarcation Line is to delineate the line beyond which the armed forces of the respective Parties shall not move.

3. Rules and regulations of the armed forces of the Parties, which prohibit civilians from crossing the fighting lines or entering the area between the lines, shall remain in effect after the signing of this Agreement, with application to the Armistice Demarcation Line defined in Article 5, subject to other provisions of paragraph 5 of that Article.

Article 5.

1. It is emphasized that the following arrangements for the Armistice Demarcation Line between the Israeli and Syrian armed forces and for the Demilitarized Zone are not to be interpreted as having any relation whatsoever to ultimate territorial arrangements affecting the two Parties to this Agreement.

2. In pursuance of the spirit of the Security Council resolution of 16 November 1948, the Armistice Demarcation Line and the Demilitarized Zone have been defined with a view toward separating the armed forces of the two Parties in such manner as to minimize the possibility of friction and incident, while providing for the gradual restoration of normal civilian life in the area of the Demilitarized Zone, without prejudice to the ultimate settlement.

3. The Armistice Demarcation Line shall be as delineated on the map attached to this Agreement as Annex 1. The Armistice Demarcation Line shall follow a line midway between the existing truce lines, as certified by the United Nations Truce Supervision Organization for the Israeli and Syrian forces. Where the existing truce lines run along the international boundary

between Syria and Palestine, the Armistice Demarcation Line shall follow the boundary line.

4. The armed forces of the two Parties shall nowhere advance beyond the Armistice Demarcation Line.

5. (a) Where the Armistice Demarcation Line does not correspond to the international boundary between Syria and Palestine, the area between the Armistice Demarcation Line and the boundary, pending final territorial settlement between the Parties, shall be established as a Demilitarized Zone from which the armed forces of both Parties shall be totally excluded, and in which no activities by military or para-military forces shall be permitted. This provision applies to the Ein Gev and Dardara sectors which shall form part of the Demilitarized Zone. (b) Any advance by the armed forces, military or para-military, of either Party into any part of the Demilitarized Zone, when confirmed by the United Nations representative referred to in the following sub-paragraph, shall constitute a flagrant violation of this Agreement. (c) The Chairman of the Mixed Armistice Commission established in Article VII of this Agreement and United Nations Observers attached to the Commission shall be responsible for ensuring the full implementation of this Article. (d) The withdrawal of such armed forces as are now found in the Demilitarized Zone shall be in accordance with the schedule of withdrawal annexed to this Agreement (Annex 2). (e) The Chairman of the Mixed Armistice Commission shall be empowered to authorize the return of civilians to villages and settlements in the Demilitarized Zone and for internal security purposes, and shall be guided in this regard by the schedule of withdrawal referred to in subparagraph (d) of this Article.

6. On each side of the Demilitarized Zone there shall be areas, as defined in Annex 3 to this Agreement, in which defensive forces only shall be maintained, in accordance with the definition of defensive forces set forth in Annex 4 to this Agreement.

Article 6. All prisoners of war detained by either Party to this Agreement and belonging to the armed forces, regular or irregular, of the other Party, shall be exchanged as follows:

1. The exchange of prisoners of war shall be under United Nations supervision and control throughout. The exchange shall take place at the site of the Armistice Conference within twenty-four hours of the signing of this Agreement.

2. Prisoners of War against whom a penal prosecution may be pending, as well as those sentenced for crime or other offence, shall be included in this exchange of prisoners.

3. All articles of personal use, valuables, letters, documents, identification marks, and other personal effects of whatever nature, belonging to prisoners of war who are being exchanged, shall be returned to them, or, if they have escaped or died, to the Party to whose armed forces they belonged.

All matters not specifically regulated in this Agreement shall be decided in accordance with the principles laid down in the International Convention Relating to the Treatment of Prisoners of War, signed at Geneva on 17 July 1929.

5. The Mixed Armistice Commission established in Article 7 of this Agreement shall assume responsibility for locating missing persons, whether military or civilian, within the areas controlled by each Party, to facilitate their expeditious exchange. Each Party undertakes to extend to the Commission full co-operation and assistance in the discharge of this function.

NOTES

1. Resolution 62 adopted by the Security Council on November 16, 1948, states:

The Security Council, ...

Decides that in order to eliminate the threat to the peace in Palestine and to facilitate the transition from the present truce to permanent peace ... an armistice shall be established in all sectors of Palestine;

Calls upon the parties directly involved in the conflict in Palestine, as a further provisional measure under Article 40 of the Charter, to seek agreement forthwith, by negotiations conducted either directly or through the Acting Mediator on Palestine, with a view to the immediate establishment of the armistice including: (a) the delineation of permanent armistice demarcation lines ... ; (b) such withdrawal and reduction of their armed forces as will ensure the maintenance of the armistice during the transition to permanent peace in Palestine.

2. Article 40 of the U.N. Charter states: "In order to prevent an aggravation of the situation, the Security Council may . . . call upon the parties concerned to comply with such provisional measures as it deems necessary or desirable."

36

United Nations Conciliation Commission for Palestine

Report Conclusions

November 20, 1951

The Conciliation Commission for Palestine was formed by the United Nations in December 1948 to assist in a final settlement of the Palestinian Question (see doc. 26). It included representatives of France, Turkey, and the United States. The commission's report, published in 1951, marked not only the termination of its work but also the realization by the international community of the complexity of the Arab-Israeli conflict. The report also revealed the gap between the Arab and Israeli positions on the fundamental issues of the conflict, as the conclusions printed here demonstrate. Although the commission suspended its activities after three years, it has never been officially dissolved.

In its work during the past year—and indeed during the three years of its existence—the Conciliation Commission has been unable to make substantial progress on the task given to it by the General Assembly of assisting the parties to the Palestine dispute towards a final settlement of all questions outstanding between them.

In the course of its efforts to accomplish that task, the Commission has successively employed all the procedures which were at its disposal under the relevant General Assembly resolutions. At Lausanne, in the spring of 1949, it tried to render that assistance in the role of an intermediary between the parties; at Geneva, in 1950, the Commission attempted to bring about direct negotiations between the parties through

Source: Meron Medzini, ed., *Israel's Foreign Relations: Selected Documents, 1947–1974* (Jerusalem: Ministry of Foreign Affairs, 1976), 2:279–80. Reprinted by permission of the Director General, Ministry of Foreign Affairs, Jerusalem.

the medium of Mixed Committees; and, finally, at its recent conference in Paris, the Commission assumed the function of a mediator and, in that role, submitted to the parties for their consideration a comprehensive pattern of concrete proposals towards a solution of the Palestine question.

This pattern of proposals comprised practical arrangements for a solution of the refugee question, and a method of revising or amending the Armistice Agreements concluded between Israel and her neighbours with a view to promoting the return to peace in Palestine.

In linking those two issues together in a comprehensive pattern of proposals the Commission took account of two factors: (a) that the Armistice Agreements, although of a military character, were designed as a means of transition from war to peace and provided for procedures by which that aim could be attained; and (b) that positive progress in the transition from war to peace in Palestine is impossible if the refugee problem remains unsolved.

This final effort at the Paris conference was no more successful than the prior attempts by the Commission during the past three years. Despite that lack of progress, the Commission recognizes that both sides have expressed their desire to co-operate with the United Nations towards the achievement of stability in Palestine; but the Commission believes that neither side is now ready to seek that aim through full implementation of the General Assembly resolutions under which the Commission is operating.

In particular, the Government of Israel is not prepared to implement the part of paragraph 11 of the General Assembly resolution of 11 December 1948 which resolves that the refugees wishing to return to their homes and live at peace with their neighbours should be permitted to do so at the earliest practicable date.

The Arab Governments, on the other hand, are not prepared fully to implement paragraph 5 of the said resolution, which calls for the final settlement of all questions outstanding between them and Israel. The Arab Governments in their contacts with the Commission have evinced no readiness to arrive at such a peace settlement with the Government of Israel.

The Commission considers that further efforts towards settling the Palestine question could yet be usefully based on the principles underlying the comprehensive pattern of proposals which the Commission submitted to the parties at the Paris Conference. The Commission continues to believe that if and when the parties are ready to accept these principles, general agreement or partial agreement could be sought through direct negotiations with United Nations assistance or mediation.

The Commission is of the opinion, however, that the present unwillingness of the parties fully to implement the General Assembly resolutions under which the Commission is operating, as well as the changes which have occurred in Palestine during the past three years, have made it impossible for the Commission to carry out its mandate, and this fact should be taken into consideration in any further approach to the Palestine problem.

Finally, in view of its firm conviction that the aspects of the Palestine problem are interrelated, the Commission is of the opinion that in any further approach to the problem it is desirable that consideration be given to the need for coordinating all United Nations efforts aimed at promotion of stability, security and peace in Palestine.

37

Ehud Yaari

The Challenge of the *Fedayeen*

February–August 1955: Analysis

In the years following the establishment of the State of Israel, the political dimensions of the Arab-Israeli conflict were superseded by escalating violence. Arab infiltration (both spontaneous and organized) from across the borders and Israeli retaliation led to a deepening cycle of conflict. This cycle was reinforced by numerous border and armistice problems and by violent fallout from the frequent political contests between Israel and its Arab neighbors, such as Arab resistance to Israel's diversion of Jordan River waters. Internationally, Israel was feeling threatened and isolated. The United States was increasing arms sales to Arab countries, and some of its State Department officials were publicly critical of Israel. Soviet-Egyptian relations were growing closer, and more weapons were being supplied to Egypt from the Soviet bloc. In 1955 what became known as the Czech arms deal was negotiated between Egypt and the Soviet Union, and Egypt began receiving the latest Soviet military equipment from Czechoslovakia (see doc. 32). Within Israel there was considerable debate on Israel's policies: Was it wise to retaliate for Arab acts of aggression, or should remedies be sought through diplomatic channels? In a somewhat simplistic fashion the two sides of this debate in the 1950s and early 1960s have been identified with David Ben-Gurion and Moshe Sharett respectively (see doc. 39).

In this essay, Ehud Yaari, an Israeli journalist specializing in Arab affairs, uses Egyptian military and intelligence documents captured in Gaza to shed interesting light both on the conduct of the anti-Israeli irregular warfare in the 1950s and on Israel's policy of retaliation. He recounts the turning point in Egyptian policy toward Palestinian commando raids from Gaza and Jordan into Israel. These terrorists came to be known as fedayeen *(from the Islamic term meaning "martyrs"). On February 28, 1955, an Israeli paratroop unit attacked an Egyptian base near Gaza in retaliation for acts of sabotage and murder committed by* fedayeen *from bases there. Thirty-eight Egyptian soldiers and two civilians were killed, and many were wounded.*

The raid of the Israel Defense Forces [IDF] into Gaza on February 28, 1955, was, in the opinion of everyone, an important milestone in Egyptian-Israeli relations. [Gamal Abdul] Nasser and a number of Western diplomats and researchers have for many years suggested that it represents the turning point in Cairo's policy. Nasser himself declared on numerous occasions that this was the hour of truth and that only then did he realize the futility of continuing his previous policy and grasp the extent of the Israeli problem, and on this basis turned to accept Soviet arms. This is not the place to discuss the complications or the principles involved in that action and its results, although it is clear that Nasser's explanation is much too simplistic

Source: Ehud Yaari, *Mizraim vehaFedayun, 1953–1956* [Egypt and the *Fedayeen*, 1953–1956] (Givat Havivah: Center for Arab and Afro-Asian Studies, 1975), pp. 18–23. Reprinted by permission.

and one-sided even if we supposed that there is a grain of truth in it. But it is difficult to connect the Israeli raid with the activity of infiltration, because the Israeli action came precisely during a period of relative calm in that area and in the wake of major efforts on the part of the Egyptian regime to stop infiltrations in the Gaza Strip. Hence it is necessary to look in another direction for an explanation for [David] Ben-Gurion's decision to call for the raid a few days after his return from Sdeh Boker to the Ministry of Foreign Affairs.

Immediately after the raid into Gaza, which raised a great commotion in the entire world, several large demonstrations occurred throughout the Gaza Strip that raised questions about the achievements of the Egyptians in stabilizing their rule there. In the town of Gaza itself the Egyptian army opened fire and killed four demonstrators when the ruling governor Abdullah Rif'at was wounded by a stone thrown at him. Two U.N. vehicles went up in flames. In Dir Al-Balakh demonstrators smashed windows in the police building, and Egyptian soldiers were beaten in the streets. In Khan Yunis a food warehouse was burned. And there were many other incidents. Demonstrators demanded that weapons be distributed to civilians and that the border be fortified against Israeli incursions. There were also slogans condemning Egypt and its army in particular. Order was restored only after widespread arrests among the demonstrators and those responsible for inciting the people and after extended patrols by vehicles with loudspeakers declaring that the army would disperse further demonstrations with an iron hand.

The list of those arrested reveals the opposition to Egyptian policy among important and influential portions of the local Palestinian establishment at that period. Among the names: Munir Al-Rayyes, shortly to become head of the Gaza municipality; his grandson Zvheir Al-Rayyes, a lawyer and publisher of the local paper *Akhbar Falastin*; Gamal Al-Surani, son of the well-known Sheikh Moussa Al-Surani, for some time member of the executive committee of the Palestine Liberation Organization; Faisal Al-Husayni, a pillar of an old family in Gaza; Muhammad Yusuf Al-Najjar, an official of the UNRWA [U.N. Relief and Works Agency] who was among the founders of the PLO; and others.

The very fact that these men openly stood up against the Egyptian regime is significant and shows the difficulties Cairo had in imposing a strict rule and harnessing the old local leadership in its direction. The Egyptian regime was able to overcome the opposition on the fringes: the cells of the Communist party were by and large destroyed around the time of the court case of Hassan Makki and his men at the end of 1952, and the circles of the Muslim Brotherhood were already no longer a security threat, as we learn from the plentiful reports of the secret police. Egypt's problem was how to handle the old members of the Mufti movement and the local leadership.[1]

Nasser announced on March 1 that his country was "not going to take a quick revenge," but late in May there occurred a sharp turnabout within the regime regarding the problem of infiltration, and the change is evident from the official correspondence. The term *fedayeen,* with a positive connotation, now comes in place of the term *infiltrators.* Reinforcements of the Egyptian army are brought into the Gaza Strip, and instead of expressions of condemnation and worry about the penetrations into Israel, the secret documents now speak in terms of glorification and encouragement. On May 8 the intelligence office of the army command in Sinai even issued a circular describing the crisis in Israeli border kibbutzim as the result of the infiltrations.

According to Moshe Dayan, the Egyptians began to form the *fedayeen* units in April 1955 in order to carry out terrorist operations against Israel. But actually, when the Egyptians activated the *fedayeen* for the first time according to their plan—at the end of August—the job was given to the men of the national guard. In other words, the arm that had been established to stop the infiltration movement and to preserve order and control in the refugee camps was now mobilized for fedayeen operations. This arrangement indicates a change of policy from relying on professional infiltrators to relying on new groups, subject to the discipline of the Egyptian command. The old infiltrators were apparently considered of doubtful loyalty, and some of them were identified with anti-Egyptian political factors.

The succession of *fedayeen* operations at the end of August came in the wake of the occupation by the IDF of widespread areas and the gun battle at Kilometer 90 in the course of which one Egyptian officer and two volunteers were killed. A classified official circular, distributed in all army units, states clearly that the activization of the *fedayeen* was in retaliation for those clashes: it had been decided "to carry out revenge operations against the Jews by the forces of the Egyptian national guard and the national Palestinian guard."

The national guard of Egypt carried out four encounters on the border of the Gaza Strip on the night of August 25–26, but the main assignments were given to four groups of the Palestinian national guard, one of which was able to penetrate up to eighteen kilometers from Tel Aviv. On August 31 the IDF responded to the *fedayeen* incursions with the large-scale attack on the Khan Yunis police station.

The Egyptian press published at length—and for the first time—a number of glowing reports about the feats of the *fedayeen*, complete with maps and exaggerated descriptions about their success. (By the way, two of the *fedayeen* who had participated in these activities were taken captive.)

Beginning with these events toward the end of August, the *fedayeen* entered upon the Arab-Israeli scene. Their first operation characterizes in large measure their future activities: the Egyptians established firm control over the activities of the Palestine national guard, and those men became *fedayeen* only at the orders of Egypt. Orders were issued at the discretion of the higher echelons, first and foremost—as we shall see further—as military instruments within the framework of military encounters with Israel in order to increase the element of surprise and the Egyptian army's ability to inflict damage.

The Egyptians succeeded, thus, in doing away with the infiltrators, and in their place came the *fedayeen* who had demonstrated back in August that they were an efficient and sharp weapon in the struggle against Israel. From the series of the first *fedayeen* operations, the Egyptians learned to look on them as an extreme and drastic instrument that could not be utilized for uninterrupted action. Therefore the Egyptians attempted to widen the scope of the national guard as a reservoir for the *fedayeen* in times of need and also to set a limit to their operations, and even to divert part of them to actions from the direction of the Jordanian border.

In any event, there is not the slightest doubt that the appearance of the *fedayeen* under Egyptian guidance belongs to the period subsequent to the incursion of the IDF into Gaza. This was one of the clearest indications of a developing change in the Middle East, whether it came as a direct result or was evident only in its wake.

NOTE

1. After deposing King Farouk in 1952, the Egyptian officers almost immediately neutralized all possible opposition to their political hegemony except for the Muslim Brotherhood. During 1953–54 there was a struggle between the new regime and the brotherhood, which wanted a full partnership in the government. General Muhammed Naguib, who led the junta in its first years, was more sympathetic to the brotherhood than was Nasser, and the differing approach was one of the internal conflicts connected with Nasser's seizure of power from Naguib.

38

Moshe Sharett

Israel's Foreign and Middle Eastern Policy

May 28, 1955

In 1955, Prime Minister Moshe Sharett prepared this review of Israel's foreign affairs and policies and presented it to a senior forum in the Ministry of Foreign Affairs. Of particular interest are his statements on Israel's "retaliations policy" in response to the irregular warfare conducted against Israel from across the Jordanian and Egyptian borders (see doc. 37).

In the evening [May 28, 1955], the final meeting for consultations with the ambassadors. The invitation was extended not only to the limited circle but also to all heads of department at the Ministry of Foreign Affairs. Teddy [Kollek] and Isser [Harel], who in any case participated in all the meetings, were also there. There were close to twenty people. I spoke for over an hour. I explained to those who were displeased with the timing of the briefing that if we had not convened now our meeting would have had to have been deferred until after the meeting of the General Assembly, that is until the beginning of 1956 owing to U Nu[1] and [Eric] Johnston's continued schedule of visits in May and June, the U.N. Convention in San Francisco at the end of June, the election campaign in July, the trials and tribulations of forming a new government in August, which would bring us to the opening of the General Assembly in New York in September continuing until December. I refrained from adding that had we not held our briefing now, it is doubtful whether I would have participated in it.

Following an analysis of the situation and policy of the United States, on the one hand, and England on the other, I stated that our aim of achieving a defense treaty with the United States was a central tenet of our policy. It was not improbable that we would succeed in signing a treaty with the United States only, because of an agreement between her and England concerning the Baghdad Pact, to which England had become a party while the United States had not. It is not clear what the prospects are of achieving this goal, but it is worth investing every effort. Its advantages: it would guarantee our security through a mutual pact; it would strengthen us in relation to the Arab states; it would assist peace; it would increase our worth in the eyes of the world; it would provide an incentive for capital investment; it would constitute a message to Jewry. The treaty should be explained to the Soviet bloc and the Asian states as arising exclusively out of our concern for security in the face of Arab hostility and as a conclusion drawn from the Bandung Conference.[2] We did not see that Yugoslavia's ties with the Balkan Alliance[3] were damaging to her relations with the Soviet Union. On the contrary. On the other hand, Yugoslavia cannot be a model for us in its independent maneuvering owing to the

Source: Moshe Sharett, *Yoman ishi* [Personal Diary], ed. Yaakov Sharett (Tel Aviv: Maariv, 1978), pp. 1924–25. Reprinted by permission of Yaakov Sharett.

Arab peril, the Jewish link, and the necessity of economic assistance, all of which differentiate us from her. In the final analysis, she also has more armed divisions than we do. We do not request a defense treaty merely because we are exposed to danger from the Arab countries on account of their ongoing hostility toward us. Our request derives from the formation of alignments that the policy of the Western powers has generated in the structure of the Middle East. In other words, we are not sounding the alarm, nor are we pleading to be saved; we are merely stating the responsibility of the powers and leaving them to draw their conclusions, to respond or not. We are not asking them for favors, but we are asking them to accept the responsibility for the change in the situation against us, which was brought about through their initiative. I warned that in the discussion the supporters of the treaty had not indicated any concern for the intrigues of U.S. policy toward us. Since the absence of peace in the Middle East obstructs its inclusion in the defense setup, there is likely to be an attempt to achieve peace by putting pressure on us to give in on the issues of territory and refugees. I also warned against any thought of returning tens of thousands of people even as a price for peace, and on this question I adopted a firmly negative position. I also warned against talking lightly of adjusting the borders as an intermediate stage. It would be a distortion of the facts to assume that the strange state of the Jordanian border is the cause of infiltration. When the [Arab] Legion does what it is supposed to, there is no infiltration even when the border divides villagers from their lands. On the other hand, if the Jordanian authorities become careless or neglect their job, there will be large-scale armed infiltration even if the border is as it should be. In any event, no straightening of the borders is possible unless they are fixed once and for all, and that is not possible except within the framework of a peace treaty. A different kind of border adjustment is possible only as an amendment in cease-fire treaties. Are the Arabs ready for this? How long will negotiations take, and who knows how they will end? For all these reasons, it would be better to put our efforts, not into clarifying possibilities of altering the borders as a precondition for a defense treaty, but rather into striking this problem completely off the agenda of our negotiations over the treaty—particularly in view of the fact that the slogan of adjusting the borders camouflages a trend to extract much more from us than they would be willing to give to us. The direction for advancing in a practical manner toward achieving an intermission in the tension between us and our neighbors (as an interim step toward signing a defense treaty) lies in compensation for refugees in exchange for lifting the hostile embargo and boycott, an agreement with Johnston concerning water affairs, and stabilizing the peace on the border. All three matters depend on the attitude of the opponent.

At the end of my talk I devoted some time to the issue of retaliations. I opposed the facile charge brought by ambassadors and other members against the policy adopted by the government. I claimed that this was not merely a question of pure political reason, and the problem should not be viewed only as a reflection of foreign affairs of state. The representatives should state their opinion about the internal affairs of the country. At the core of the question lie deep-rooted ideas that could not be eradicated by persuasion alone. The soul of the nation, the youth, and the army are subject to waves of depression and disequilibrium that create serious crises; not releasing this tension at the appropriate time would be perilous. I described the growth of Revisionism[4] in the 1920s and 1930s and told them that [Chaim] Weizmann and his system could not be absolved from responsibility for this pestilence. He [Weizmann] also had political reason on his side, but his fault lay in not understanding the soul of the movement. The disease of dissent might be revived in the state if we attempt to pull the string too taut. The machinations of Kibbutz Beitar on the one hand and the vengeance wreaked by the young men of Ein Harod and Deganyah Bet on the other give an indication of what awaits us. Practically speaking, the account cannot be set straight so simply either. The assumption that incidents can be prevented from occurring simply by being on guard is absolutely superficial. On the other hand, it is a fact that the Kibiyah and Nahlin [operations] brought the Legion to the front line of border protection and thus obstructed murderous infiltration.[5] Kibiyah was a political and moral disaster because of the slaughter of women and children, but a distinction must be drawn between the vigorous retaliatory action in itself and the cruel, ugly character it had in this case, which was by no means mandatory. Verdicts of Jordanian courts and articles in the Jordanian press indicate an understanding there of the fact that murderous attacks by gangs ultimately result in disasters befalling peaceful villages, and for this reason they should be viewed as a national crime that ought to be eradicated. All in all, a bitter, determined struggle is being waged, sometimes even a desperate one, against the desire for reprisal, and for every action that is given approval, several much more drastic ones are forbidden or prevented. I expressed my grievance at the fact that the criticisms and complaints leveled against me had not taken into account the fact that I had stated, that with much effort we had been saved from the greatest calamities to the state. In conclusion, I pointed out in a positive light Teddy's criticism of the low level of the Ministry of Foreign Affairs' activity in the field of internal propaganda among our people both concerning the problems confronting foreign policy and relating to its achievement.

NOTES

1. U Nu (1907–1995) was prime minister of Myanmar (Burma) from its independence until he was deposed by a coup (with two minor interruptions), 1948–62.
2. The Bandung Conference, first conference of African and Asian states, held in Bandung, Indonesia, April 18–24, 1955, provided the setting for the organization of a Third World bloc in international relations and for the spread of nonalignment as a conscious collective strategy of these states. Israel did not attend. Gamal Abdul Nasser of Egypt emerged from the conference as a major leader and spokesman for this bloc.
3. The Balkan Alliance among nonaligned communist Yugoslavia and Turkey and Greece (both members of NATO, the North Atlantic Treaty Organization), was signed in 1953 at the height of Joseph Stalin's hostility to Yugoslavia's independent policies. This pact had a silent birth and death.
4. World Union of Zionist Revisionists.
5. During this period *fedayeen* attacks on Israeli settlements were common, and Israel responded with reprisal raids. One was led by Meir Har-Zion and his friends, young men of Ein Harod and Deganyah Bet, who undertook a private revenge against a Bedouin whose men murdered Har-Zion's sister and her friend while they were on a trip to Petra. In 1953 and 1954, Unit 101 retaliated against two Jordanian villages, Kibiyah and Nahlin, whose inhabitants had committed acts of murder. Many civilians were killed in the raids. All these incidents aroused Israeli public opinion.

39

Moshe Sharett

The Clash with David Ben-Gurion over Defense Policies

July 31, 1955

The Egyptian Officers' Revolt deposed King Farouk in 1952, and by 1954 Gamal Abdul Nasser had emerged as the dominant figure in Egyptian politics. These events were crucial in the development of the Arab-Israeli conflict. Nasser espoused a militant philosophy of Arab unity that included the call for a military, as opposed to political, solution to the conflict with Israel. As a result, his popularity and influence rose within the Arab world, while Egyptian-Israeli relations deteriorated, culminating in the Sinai Campaign. The following selection records the process from an Israeli perspective.

Moshe Sharett kept a personal diary from 1953 to 1957, meticulously recording the events in which he participated and his reflections on them. The diary illuminates numerous issues as well as the workings of the innermost circles of Israel's political system. The following excerpts dated July 31, 1955, when Sharett was prime minister, describe two Israeli attempts to negotiate with Arab leaders in search of accommodation and then the difference of opinion between himself and David Ben-Gurion over the very foundations of Israel's foreign and defense policies.

The meeting ended early so that I was able to spend some two hours in the Foreign Ministry.

I listened to the first chapter of the report by Gideon Raphael, who had returned about a week before me from a trip to Europe. He informed me about two interesting meetings—one with the ex-prime minister of Syria, Hosni Barazi, and with one of the idols of Egyptian capitalism, Aboud Pasha.

Husni's aim was to return to power, and to this end he was willing to accept the assistance of whoever was at hand—Turkey, in exchange for a promise to join the Ankara-Baghdad axis;[1] the United States, in order to identify himself with the West; Israel, with whom he was willing to make a peace treaty. It was clear that just a hint from Turkey against the liaison with us, lest it interfere with her pact with Iraq, would be sufficient to make him betray us. In the meantime he wanted things from us: money for newspapers, money to buy people, money to buy political parties. Gideon tried to infuse him with ideals—here he was himself a large landowner, and he should get together a group of estate owners and should initiate a large program of resettling refugees, including draining swamps and utilizing water from the Orontes for irrigation, for this would gain him merit in the opinion of the United States, he would be the recipient of extensive funding and genuine political support. Husni lent a willing ear, said that these were the words of the living God but that these matters would receive his attention after he had returned to power; but until such time, he needed an advance on the account.

Source: Moshe Sharett, *Yoman ishi* [Personal Diary], ed. Yaakov Sharett (Tel Aviv: Maariv, 1978), pp. 1100–1102. Reprinted by permission of Yaakov Sharett.

Aboud turned out to be [Gamal Abdul] Nasser's confidant. He was evidently able not only to maintain his position and entrench himself under the new regime of hostility toward big capital but to make himself a pillar of support for this regime, which he cleverly used for his own purposes. A serious person, who carefully considered his words. Nasser once told him that he saw two dangerous elements in Israel that prevented him from making peace with her: the danger of economic competition and the danger of expansionism. Aboud responded that the danger of competition was nonsense, but as far as the expansion was concerned, he was not qualified to pass an opinion. He asked Gideon for proof to contradict this claim, and the explanations he received satisfied him. He expressed his willingness to act to achieve a mitigation of the Suez embargo—free passage for all cargoes including fuel in non-Israeli ships. He reminded us that immediately after the cease-fire he had proposed that we renew permission for the Khedive ships [belonging to the Egyptian State Company] to anchor in the ports of Haifa and Jaffa. We replied that we would agree to this only on a reciprocal basis. To this day he was still amazed at our shortsightedness. If we had accepted his proposition, we would have thereby knocked the blocks out from under the Arab embargo.

According to Aboud's description, Nasser's position among his own supporters was shaky. He was subject to perpetual nervousness and was at a loss with whom to begin reconciliation. The top echelons of his faction were in discord, and the officers, each of whom derived his support from one of the forces—infantry, navy, and air force—were at odds with one another. The setup was completely out of equilibrium, and there was no telling what would happen. In short, there was no peace in the Land of the Nile. . . .

. . . At three o'clock in the afternoon a meeting of our "friends" was held at [David] Ben-Gurion's request. The nine ministers were present as well as Teddy [Kollek] and Zeev Sharef. I was of the opinion, and had also heard this from someone, that it was Ben-Gurion's intention to clarify the moves toward forming a coalition, but he had not been candid about his position. He arrived tense and taut as a violin string, in quite a state. He announced that I had demanded a policy clarification in the pertinent party institution. He had called this meeting in order to state his position and was not willing to participate in any discussion held under any other auspices, for experience had shown that anything said in a larger circle was leaked to the press. At the behest of Golda [Meir] and [Mordekhai] Namir, who had appealed to him at Sdeh Boker, he had returned to accept the defense portfolio upon [Pinhas] Lavon's resignation and he explained why he had complied at the time—solely out of a concern for the Israel Defense Forces. When I had approached him later, he informed me that in his opinion cease-fire matters should return to the Defense Ministry, simply "because these are matters of defense." I had disagreed, and we had not settled our differences. Later he had written me that only on this condition would he return to the government, but he had found out—I don't know when or from whom—that I had not managed to read his letter before I put the changes before the Knesset. And so cease-fire matters had remained under the control of the Foreign Ministry, and he had accepted the verdict and had fallen in with my decision as prime minister. Here I thought he was going to say what he had said to the government—that since these affairs had been transferred to the Foreign Ministry, great steps forward had been made—but he did not say it this time and left the impression that he held the same opinion: Nevertheless he did add that, ultimately, the question of which ministry was in charge of cease-fire affairs was an administrative matter and not a matter of principle. As far as the principle was concerned, he wished to clarify his position beyond all shadow of doubt. Here he began to read from a detailed written declaration the main contents of which were: he was in favor of peace, and opposed to initiating any war, and considered it obligatory to keep the cease-fire agreements faithfully, but if the opponent broke them and the United Nations was unable to prevent this, the response should be force, regardless of the consequences. He would only be a member of a government that acted in this way. He would not participate in a government that acted in any other way either as prime minister or as minister of defense or in any other capacity, and he would not only not be a minister in such a government but would also not support that government from outside it (this was a softening of the version he had expressed to Nahum Goldmann, in which he stated that he would fight against such a government to the bitter end).

The extreme tension prevailing was not dispersed by my words. I said that it was no secret to the opposition members that things had come to a head in the last few months between myself and Ben-Gurion regarding national security. Had it not been for the imminent elections and anxiety for the fate of the party—and by implication the fate of the country—I would not have hesitated to tender my resignation since I remained in the minority in my party faction in the government concerning several momentous decisions. In the future I was not prepared to give in or to swing the balance against Ben-Gurion and the majority of party members by means of the minority together with members of other factions [in the government]. For that reason I had come to the conclusion that it was better for me to resign now while at the same time preserving the good name of the government, rather than to resign over a specific matter that was liable to weaken the status of the government. In the meantime, however, the results of the election were publicized. The party had been dealt a death blow [Mapai lost five seats—dropping from forty-five to forty seats], and I was reluctant to heap yet another calamity upon it. But my position remained unchanged—I was certainly, and with no personal difficulty, to become once more the foreign minister in a government headed by Ben-Gurion as prime minister, but as foreign minister I would not undertake to implement a foreign policy to which I was totally opposed and that all my confidants, from within and without, know I negate completely. I would not betray my soul—and no one would ask it of me—and so, if such a conflict were to arise, I would leave and Ben-Gurion would have to find himself a new foreign minister. But I felt that first of all, policy should be thrashed out in the competent institutions of the party so that a clear stand could be decided upon. I added that I did not rule out a preliminary discussion in the present circle, although I knew the opinions of all the members. But I was not willing to make do with this. And in any case, I was not prepared for such a discussion at present—Ben-Gurion had arrived ready for it but I had had no idea that he was going to present this problem for discussion and I was also in a hurry to go to Tel Aviv to [Shmuel] Elyashiv's memorial service.

Ben-Gurion reiterated that there would be leaks from any larger forum. [Levi] Eshkol and Golda supported me—for some time no discussion had been held in the party on this penetrating question and a framework should be found that would be able to maintain the secrecy.

I did not state before that Ben-Gurion also spoke about coalition problems in general and proposed convening the Histadrut Committee for a public debate with the left-wing factions on the subject of the status of the laborer in Israel; his spirit compelled him to settle his account with Tabenkin, to reply to those who were decrying the leadership of Ahdut Haavodah, and to vent his wrath on Mapam. The discussion moved to this subject, and before it had come to an end I left the meeting.

NOTE

1. Ankara-Baghdad axis is the unofficial name for the alliance based on the defense treaty of February 24, 1955, between Iraq and Turkey, sometimes called the Baghdad Pact. This treaty was to be the cornerstone of

U.S. plans to "contain" Soviet expansionism in the area through a comprehensive Middle East defense treaty to include the United States, Britain, and the Northern Tier of friendly Middle Eastern states. Britain, Pakistan, and Iran joined the pact in 1955. Egypt and other states denounced it as "imperialist" and turned to the Soviet Union. With the fall of the Iraqi monarchy in 1958, the Baghdad Pact collapsed, although there were later attempts to resuscitate it as the Central Nations Treaty Organization (CENTO).

40

Shimon Peres

The Quest for Arms

1948–1967: Memoir

The early 1950s were difficult years for Israel's foreign policy. Shortly after the establishment of the state, Israel drew away from the Soviet Union but was not willingly accepted by the Western powers, which were bent on preserving or obtaining the goodwill of the major Arab states. Shimon Peres, one of David Ben-Gurion's closest aides, was director general of the Ministry of Defense from 1953 to 1959. In that capacity he played a major role in developing the French-Israeli alliance in the mid-1950s and in procuring French and other weapons for the Israeli army, which was still being transformed into a military organization that could meet the young state's security needs (see doc. 32). In the following excerpt from his memoirs, Peres discusses some of the ways in which Israel dealt with two of its most persistent and crucial foreign policy problems: overcoming international isolation and procuring arms for its defense needs.

What water is to agriculture, armaments are to security. Israel suffers from a shortage of both. Revolutionary efforts to utilize every drop of water have led to revolutionary achievements in an arid land. Similar efforts in the field of local arms manufacture have also produced significant gains. But there were basic weapons like warplanes, tanks and heavy guns, vital in modern warfare, for which Israel had to rely—and to a great extent has still to rely—on outside sources. It is difficult to exaggerate the importance of such armaments for the establishment and maintenance of an effective defence and deterrent force for Israel. Without them, Israel would have been in a calamitous situation.

Getting arms has thus been one of the central tasks of Israel's leadership. At times it has given rise to their sharpest anxiety; for while Israelis feel the urgency, it has been excessively difficult to get outsiders to feel the same. At times, such as the arrival of a clandestine arms shipment at a critical moment in battle, it has excited their deepest sense of relief.

If there was a genocide in Biafra—irrespective of the political issues involved—it was because the Biafrans failed to secure the arms they needed, while the Nigerians received planes and guns from Russia and Egypt. Israel was saved from this fate because she managed to acquire some of the armaments she needed. Israelis

Source: Shimon Peres, *David's Sling* (London: Weidenfeld and Nicholson, 1970), pp. 31–64. Reprinted by permission of Shimon Peres.

were naturally sensitive to this problem, with the memory still fresh of the six million unarmed Jews who were crushed and murdered by the Nazis in Europe.

The need to secure arms for a regular army was born with Israel's birth, since she came under attack by the regular armies of six neighbouring Arab States within hours of her proclamation of independence. The majority of the members of the United Nations had voted for the establishment of the Jewish State; but they refused to supply even the elementary types of arms she required for her defence. They followed a curiously paradoxical policy of political amiability coupled with an arms embargo, though it was evident that a formal signature on a piece of paper was not sufficient to create a State. A country under attack cannot defend itself with a verbal decision alone, even if the words come from members of the United Nations.

The open declaration of war by seven Arab States—and no-one disputes who was the aggressor in Israel's war of independence—did not alter the policy on arms supply of those countries who supported the establishment of Israel. Israel had to face the invaders alone, and with her hands tied by an arms embargo. The invaders already enjoyed a preponderance of arms, and could get virtually unlimited additional supplies. The world certainly knew what had happened to the Jews of Europe, and knew, too, that many of Israel's inhabitants were among the few survivors of the Holocaust. Despite it, beleaguered Israel had the utmost difficulty in securing even simple rifles, to say nothing of tanks and planes.

The United States refused arms. Britain refused. So did Russia. (Russia, incidentally, had also voted for the U.N. resolution calling for a Jewish State.)

The arms which nevertheless reached the Israel Army during the War of Independence came through "illegal" channels, in small quantities, and always at the last moment.

Some came from Czechoslovakia, which at that time was still governed by a coalition of communists and non-communists. . . .

The rifles from Czechoslovakia arrived just in time to be distributed to the units who were about to go into action to break the siege of Jerusalem. They were issued to some of the troops who were actually en route to the front.

Czechoslovakia also sold us some old Messerschmitts, the German fighter planes of World War Two. (Even though the price for these second-hand craft was sky high at that time—$200,000 apiece—some of them were found to suffer from a serious technical defect. The plane was equipped with machine-guns which fired through the propeller space, but the synchronization device did not always work, so that at times the burst hit the propeller and shattered it.) They sold us some heavy machine-guns which were very useful in both ground and anti-aircraft defence. The Czechs also helped us in training, and they put an airfield at our disposal.

Until then, Israel's General Staff had had the most trying time deciding on how, when and where to allocate the four guns they possessed, the total artillery force in Israel's arsenal. These were four old 65 mm weapons which had somehow survived, and still managed to work, from World War ONE!

One of the historic decisions of the General Staff was to send one of these guns to the northern front, to save Deganyah, Israel's first kibbutz, which was under pressure from a formidable force of Syrian tanks. The gun arrived without sights and the gunners had to test its range and workability by firing across the Sea of Galilee. To its credit—and to that of its operators—it must be said that age had not weakened its powers, and it fulfilled its task with efficiency and honour.

Small quantities of arms, including planes, were brought to Israel under ingenious circumstances which today evoke the image of a James Bond tale rather than that of a young country fighting for its life. For instance, some of our arms procurement people set up a film company in England and the first sequence of the script of the first film, which was of course a war film, called for shooting an air battle. They went out on location, the cameras were in place, and the planes took off. The cameras went on whirring and the planes went on flying—all the way to Israel, where the actions in which they were subsequently engaged were rather more realistic than those envisaged in the script.

Other arms were acquired in France and Italy, and three American Flying Fortresses made the long flight, filled with incident, via the Caribbean to Israel. Most of these planes were flown by non-Israeli Jewish pilots who had volunteered to fight in Israel's War of Independence.

Despite delays, defects and meagre quantities, these overseas weapons enabled the Israel Army to hold out for a year, to beat off their enemies and ultimately to chase them from Israel soil.

The end of the War of Independence did not bring an end to the arms embargo. For the next seven years, this ban remained in operation, whether official or unofficial, complete or partial. Israel followed with an anxious heart the steady accumulation by the Arab States of heavy and sophisticated weapons of war.

In 1951, America, France and Britain publicly announced their tripartite agreement on an arms policy for the Middle East.[1] After some obscure references to the need to maintain the status quo in the area, the three signatories undertook to co-ordinate their individual supplies of weapons to the Middle Eastern States. This meant the continued denial to Israel of supplies from any of the three powers. The Arab States suffered no such restrictions with the signatories; and other sources were also open to them. The British, for example, under the Anglo-Jordanian Treaty, supplied weapons to Jordan's Army and officers to train and command it. Saudi Arabia continued to receive arms under its treaty with the United States. Egypt acquired arms from France and Italy—additions to the not inconsiderable supplies which had been left behind after World War Two.

This policy was due largely to inertia. The British continued to be sensitive about routes to India—even after they lost India. The French clung to their "Levant Policy" even when they had lost their position in the Levant. The United States faithfully supported these two countries who could not seem to make up their minds whether to maintain the posture of great powers or resign themselves to the status of middle-ranking States. They conducted their affairs with indolence, hesitancy, and the pusillanimity of closed minds.

The vacuum in the Middle East created by the gradual departure of Britain and France began to be filled by powers who had had no major historic associations with the region and whose diplomatic representatives scorned both the table manners of the British and the subtlety of the French.

Soviet Russia appeared on the scene in the spring of 1955 in the form of a handsome, outgoing, middle-aged man, quite unlike his reserved predecessors. Indeed, he seemed to live in the eye of the camera, and pictures of him feeding the pigeons in Cairo squares soon appeared on the pages of the world press. Mr. [Dimitri] Shepilov, soon to become the Soviet Foreign Minister, was welcomed with open arms—and he did not disappoint his hosts. He seemed uninhibited by the cautiousness that characterized the experienced Middle East representatives of the former world powers. He did not argue with the Egyptians over their requests, did not bargain with them over each detail in the long shopping list of armaments which, in quality and quantity, were quite new to the region. The demands were wholesale; so was the response.

What followed Shepilov's visit was the "Czech Arms Deal." Within a short time, jet planes, tanks, guns, destroyers and submarines began to reach Egypt from Czechoslovakia. All were of the latest type, and they arrived in quantities which seemed fanciful. Up to then, the normal arsenals of the Middle Eastern States had been made up of obsolescent weapons (by western standards), and even those in comparatively small quantities.

The Czech arms deal thus violently upset the arms balance, and with it the security of Israel. To Egypt's great new military strength, Israel had no answer. The menace grew more grave as Egypt grew more confident—her threats now had a bite. Nasser charged that King Farouk had armed the army with "rotten weapons" and that was why Egypt had lost the 1948 war with Israel; but now Egypt had acquired great supplies of spanking new armaments and equipment, and would know what to do with them.

Israel again had to cast about for even minimal quantities of arms to safeguard her existence. The entire nation well understood that its fate depended on the results of that quest.

Arms procurement thus became the principal aim of Israel's foreign policy (and it has remained one of the central purposes to this day).

Constant technical advances in the development of weaponry have turned the supply of arms into a complicated issue. Highly sophisticated armaments can no longer be manufactured and sold within the commercial framework. The enormous investment required in research and development, and the need for coordination between numerous plants (often, plants in different countries), have led more and more to the transfer of arms production from private to governmental control. . . .

When jets started to become the bread and butter of the air force, the sources of supply were extremely limited. Whereas the prop plane had long been manufactured by numerous countries and stocks were available all over the world, from Japan to Canada, the basic production of jets was confined to five countries alone: the United States, the Soviet Union, Britain, France and Sweden. The governments themselves were involved in their development and manufacture, and kept scrupulous supervision and control over their disposal. No country could acquire them from any one of the five in a simple commercial transaction. The considerations were almost wholly political. Indeed, the sale of jets was a marked expression of political friendship.

From 1955 onwards, Egypt, Syria and Iraq were able to buy these planes from Soviet Russia, and since the political rather than the economic factor was the prime ingredient the terms were unusually favourable. The Russian price tag for a MIG was $400,000 (as against more than a million dollars for the comparable French jet, the Mirage); and long term credits were granted at the remarkably low interest rate of 1½ percent.

The reasons prompting Russian generosity in its arms dealings with the Arab States were also the reasons for the deterioration in Russia's relations with Israel—frigid in times of relative quiet, downright hostile in periods of tension. It is largely with the coin of Israel that Russia has tried to buy the Arabs, wean them away from the western world, and pursue her historic ambition of penetrating into the Middle East. Her cold-shouldering of Israel undoubtedly increased the spread of her influence in the region.

It was quite clear, therefore, that Israel could expect no supply of jets from Russia. She was thus left with four possible sources of supply, at least theoretically. Sweden had to be excluded from the start. Sweden follows a policy of scrupulous neutrality, and she does not sell arms to "areas of tension." . . .

America would appear to have been the most likely country from which to get them. But United States' policy during the 1950s was expressed by President [Dwight D.] Eisenhower: "We are not prepared to become the major supplier of arms to the Middle East." The reasons for this ran the range of the spectrum. The cold war was at its height. The world was divided into blocs, and the countries of each were bound by military treaties. NATO[2] and SEATO[3] had just been launched, and they were treated by their creators with a reverence that was almost holy. The United States supplied the armaments of their members, and this was America's great contribution to strengthening these two treaty organizations. But Israel was a member of neither. She was bound by no treaty, either bilateral or multilateral, with the United States. Moreover, this was a period in which Congress was reluctant to approve the supply of arms unless the American Government could exercise supervision. Such supervision, however, again involved agreements with conditions which excluded Israel. For Israel's enemy was not communist, and only countries "favoured" with an enemy recognized as belonging to the communist camp were able to receive American military help. . . .

As for Great Britain, she was still very much a power in the Arab Middle East right up to 1955, and was heavily involved in Egypt, Jordan, Iraq and the Emirates and principalities of the Arabian peninsula. She had an army in Suez. Her officers commanded the Arab Legion. Nuri Sa'id, Prime Minister of Iraq, was the pampered favourite of the Foreign Office, who regarded him as the wisest statesman in the Middle East and the most faithful ally of the British Crown. British administration of the Arabian principalities was backed by the Royal Navy. The wealthy sheikhs of Kuwait and Bahrein kept their vast deposits in British banks. Marked friendship for Israel would have endangered this British presence in the Arabian world. So Britain could be eliminated as a supplier of jets to Israel.

There remained France. France at that time was not yet out of the military mess in Indo-China; she was conducting independence negotiations with the exiled leaders of Tunisia and Morocco; and she was almost wholly concerned with the grave situation in Algeria and the more than a million French *colons,* the "pieds noirs,"[4] whose fate rested on the outcome of the growing Algerian rebellion. The France of the Fourth Republic, split as it was, was forced to determine anew her international status in the postwar world, to re-establish her shattered and obsolete economy. She was faced by the powerful challenge of an advancing technology which could lead to a regrading in the status of countries, great and small, old and young.

In Israel's search for weapons to match those of her enemies, the cardinal question was whether or not there was a chance of getting jets from France. . . .

Many of the new leaders of the Fourth Republic had spent terms in Nazi concentration camps. There they had seen what was done to the Jews; they had seen the gas chambers, and seen the ovens, smelt the smoke. For many, therefore, the Jewish tragedy was felt as a personal experience. . . .

The emergence of Nasser on the Egyptian scene was also viewed differently by these new French leaders. To them, he was no romantic new Pharaoh who had suddenly been unwrapped from a 4,000 year old mummy, but a pale shadow of the dictators whose lives had ended in Germany and Italy only ten years earlier. Guy Mollet,[5] leader of the Labour Party, termed him "an apprentice dictator" who aroused instinctive revulsion.

They did not regard Nasser's intervention in the Algerian rebellion—his supply of arms and instructors to the FLN[6]—as revolutionary altruism, but as an ingredient in a new "Pan" movement—Pan-Arabism—which was as distasteful to them as Pan-Germanism or Pan-Slavism.

Israel, on the other hand, stirred their imagination. It was a democratic country, a haven for the survivors, the persecuted and the dispossessed, a challenge to young Jewish pioneers from the lands of comfort, a country of social equality, whose people sought to bring life to the desert and to create a new society and who were determined to fight to defend their independence and their future.

This did not mean that these new men of France favoured an attitude of friendship towards Israel without any of the reservations of traditional French diplomacy which the Quai d'Orsay [French Foreign Ministry] expressed so skilfully. Because the territory had been administered by a British Mandate, Israel was widely regarded as belonging to the English-speaking world, and it was the French feeling that her problems should be tackled by the "Anglo-Saxons," whose centre had shifted from London to Washington. "Where is the logic," I was once asked by Couve de Murville when I was on an arms shopping expedition, "in the proposal that France should turn itself into the 'lone knight of the Middle East' when Britain, who once governed you, and the United States, who is so friendly to you, refuse your requests with such stubbornness?"

Another reservation stemmed from the traditional competition for influence in the Middle East between France and Britain. The competition was still there, but it had already been overtaken by history. The new competitors were the United States and Soviet Russia, whose eyes were on its warm-water ports. Nevertheless, France tried its utmost to hold on to its positions in Syria and Lebanon whose political leaders, military commanders and professional classes spoke French, who had cultural and economic ties with France, and whose currencies were based on the French franc. A closer French relationship with Israel was likely to endanger French influence in these two Arab States, an influence which France believed was being seriously undermined by British agents.

There were divided opinions as to the effect of French policy in the Middle East on the Algerian revolt. Some leaders, notably those responsible for defence matters, held that clipping Nasser's wings would limit his ambitions and impact on the Algerian front. Others, particularly those in charge of French diplomacy, believed that closer friendship with the Arab world would induce it to stay out of what was an exclusively French issue, even though the site of the conflict was Arab.

France's foreign policy had thus to take into account contradictory considerations: a natural feeling of warmth towards Israel, and the need to strengthen France's weakened status in the Arab States; a conflict over interests with Britain, and the need to join in partnership with Britain and America to provide the basic core of NATO; anger over Nasser's intervention in Algeria, and the prospect of nullifying it by drawing closer to Egypt.

Each view had its partisans in the governments of the Fourth Republic, coalition regimes made up of statesmen of different schools, several of whom exercised considerable individual influence on decisions when they were in power. But they were not always in power. Change of government was frequent—there were twenty-two in twenty years. Any one of those twenty-two might have favoured a policy of friendship with Israel only to find the position reversed by any one of its successors. Conversely, a hostile attitude by one of these governments was also not necessarily immutable. . . .

At the end of 1954, I went to Paris with a personal letter in my pocket from Ben-Gurion to General Pierre Koenig, France's Defence Minister. I arrived on a Friday evening after all offices were closed, and so it was only next morning that I could telephone for a meeting. It was promptly arranged for an unlikely day and hour—4 P.M. next day, Sunday. I teamed up together with our Defence Ministry representative in France, Yosef Nahmias. General Koenig, hero of Bir Hakim, with a reputation both as a great fighting commander and as a man of few words, knew quite a lot about Israel and the fate of the Jews, and he had met our units during the war in the Libyan desert. He listened to our arms requests, asked some pertinent questions, and then gave his decision on the spot with characteristic brevity: "I agree. Give me your list."

I promised to let him have our requirements by about 10 o'clock next morning. Never will I forget the telephone call I received at precisely that hour. Koenig was on the line, and his tone was impatient: "It's already ten. Where's your list?" That was the start of a long and deep friendship between the General and Israel, a friendship which saw us through many critical situations and called for considerable personal courage on his part.

It was, indeed, as a result of this meeting that the first practical moves were made to supply us with tanks and guns. The tanks were the AMX-13, a fast and light tank which was to prove its worth in the Sinai Campaign. The gun was the 155 mm, and we got this first. . . .

Throughout 1955, and particularly in the final months, the situation in Israel became steadily worse. The first shipments of Soviet-bloc arms began to reach Egyptian ports, and the scale of these supplies shocked the Israel public and its leaders. The Arab States, notably Egypt, sent in more and more infiltrators to carry out acts of terror and sabotage. The mounting actions of these Arab fedayeen called forth counter-operations from Israel along three borders—her borders with Syria, Jordan and the Gaza Strip (which drew down upon her American pressure to exercise restraint).

The Czech arms deal with Egypt produced a "backs to the wall" feeling in Israel. She possessed no weapons sufficient in quality and numbers to meet the new situation. In the absence of a better immediate alternative, the Israel Government announced an interim "Israel deal"—to strengthen the fortifications of the land. Israel became a nation of volunteers as young and old, workers and professional men, shopkeepers and housewives, the Prime Minister and secondary school pupils, took up picks and spades and went out to build fieldworks.

As France's election day approached, in the final month of 1955, we could sum up the results of our year's activities with a certain measure of satisfaction but also with one clear disappointment. We had established direct contact with many of France's leaders; we had broken through the arms-supply barrier; and we had already received some guns and tanks. But as far as jet planes were concerned, apart from a few Ouregans which we had been allowed to buy, the obstacles were still there. We now had to prepare for the future, for the new year and for the new Government that would come into power. . . .

The results of the French elections became known at the beginning of 1956. With the left and right wing blocs fairly evenly matched, the balance was held by the Socialist Party, and contrary to all political expectations, Guy Mollet became Prime Minister. Maurice Bourgès-Maunoury got the Ministry of Defence. Shortly after his assumption of office, Guy Mollet invited us to Paris. When we arrived at his official residence at the Hotel Matignon for dinner on our first evening, he put forth his hand and, before I had a chance to congratulate him, he smiled and said: "Now you will see that I will not be a Bevin." We found the new chief of government a man of his word, the word he had given us on election eve when he was still only chief of a party.

It was the start of a new era in Franco-Israel relations, an era that was to last without interruption for twelve years, enabling Israel to overcome most of her security problems during this period, and having the vital international impact of changing the balance of forces in the Middle East. This was a friendship almost unexampled in the history of international relationships. Being utterly informal—there was no official treaty, no formal alliance—it blossomed on a degree of mutual trust and mutual understanding rare among governments. . . .

With the landing of the planes, something else happened. Our close relationship with France had started, after all, through the somewhat circumscribed fields of arms procurement, and that had been carried through almost as an underground operation. But the news spread very quickly, and was greeted with extraordinary enthusiasm by the people of both countries. There was, indeed, a spontaneous fusion of friendship between the two nations, and this mood suddenly took on a life of its own, going far beyond the bounds of anything envisaged in the preliminary cooperation between the two administrations. Frenchmen and Israelis found themselves personally involved, each moved by this common bond which had just been created. Its expression was everywhere apparent in the two countries. Israelis arriving in France found it in the warmth of their reception from the moment they stepped off the plane, and it was echoed in parliament and the press. Frenchmen found the same on visits to Israel. This deep and wide-spread feeling of mutual affection was a rare phenomenon in international relationships—the spontaneous coming together of two nations.

The basis of this relationship was mutual interest. But it would be utterly false to the very nature of this bond to conceive of it in terms of interest alone. It had about it a romantic quality—a strange manifestation in a cynical world—the kind of quality that at times lifts man from the prosaic greyness of a calculating pragmatism and gives him the inspiration to gaze anew at human values.

Official France and official Israel were also seized by this intangible new dimension of friendship. At no time did France seek to dictate conditions, request supervision over the arms we acquired, or demand that she be consulted over their use—or non-use. France's specific and prescribed aim was to help, not to control. Her purpose was to strengthen our army without encroaching on our independence. Her behaviour was that of an equal, not of a patron to one in need. This attitude was hailed by most Frenchmen, proud that their Government was helping "courageous little Israel" to defend herself. Israelis on their part were profoundly grateful to "the centre of civilization" for coming to their aid at a critical moment. The new Franco-Israel relationship showed that traditional policies of "what's in it for me," based on self-interest, could give way to policies informed by generosity, understanding and comradeship.

The association between the two countries was to stand the test of the Sinai Campaign a year later, and also to yield fruit eleven years later. In 1959 we started negotiating for Mirage jets, and in the summer of 1960, Isser Penn, our representative in Paris, and I signed the first agreement on their supply. In the Six-Day War, June 1967, Israel pilots flying these Mirages played a key part in overcoming the air forces of the enemy and thus stifling the new danger that threatened to engulf the nation.

NOTES

1. The Tripartite Declaration was a statement of policy for the Middle East issued by the United States, Britain, and France in 1951. It stated in part: "The three Governments take this opportunity of declaring their deep interest in and their desire to promote the establishment and maintenance of peace and stability in the area and their unalterable opposition to the use of force or threat of force between any of the states in that area. The three Governments, should they find that any of these states was preparing to violate frontiers or armistice lines, would, consistent with their obligations as members of the United Nations, immediately take action, both within and outside the United Nations, to prevent such violation" (*U.S. Department of State Bulletin* 22, no. 570, June 5, 1950, p. 886).

2. The North Atlantic Treaty Organization (NATO) was originally a mutual defense pact of the United States, Canada, and most of Western Europe. Established in 1949, NATO was the cornerstone of the Western bloc's defense policies and strategies during the Cold War.

3. The Southeast Asia Treaty Organization (SEATO) was a mutual defense pact among the United States, Great Britain, France, Australia, New Zealand, Pakistan, Thailand, and the Philippines, established in Manila in September 1954. It was part of the U.S. policy of containment and formally extended the U.S. sphere of influence in Asia.

4. *Colons* were the French who went from the metropole to the colonies. The *pieds noirs* were the *colons* who returned to mainland France.

5. Guy Alcide Mollet (1905–1975) was secretary general of the French Socialist Party and prime minister of France, January 1956–May 1957. His was the longest lasting government of the Fourth Republic.

6. The Front de Liberation Nationale (FLN) was a national liberation movement in Algeria fighting for independence from France, which was achieved in 1962.

41

Yaacov Herzog

The Anderson Mission

January–March 1956: Memoir

The exacerbation of tensions between Israel and the Arab states, especially Egypt, and the growing estrangement of Egypt, prompted President Dwight D. Eisenhower to send Robert Anderson, U.S. secretary of the treasury, on a mission to Egypt and Israel. Anderson visited both countries twice in January 1956 and once at the beginning of March. At his first meeting in Jerusalem he met with Prime Minister David Ben-Gurion, Foreign Minister Moshe Sharett, and their two aides, Teddy Kollek, director general of the Prime Minister's Office, and Yaacov Herzog, director of the United States Division of the Foreign Ministry.

From a perspective of more than a decade later, Herzog recalled this mission and its relationship to U.S. and Soviet diplomacy in the Middle East. His reflections in the following memoir provide his analysis of how the events of this period became a critical turning point for Israel in Middle East and global arenas.

My impression at the time—and it is not contradicted by anything I have learned since—was that the mission was doomed to failure from the beginning. It came a year and a quarter after the beginning of the deterioration in the relations between the Egyptian revolutionary regime and Israel. At that time, Nasser was starting his efforts to undermine Arab regimes that, in his view, were anti-revolutionary and pro-Western, and he appeared to be advancing towards the realization of his dream of Egyptian hegemony throughout the Middle East. At the same period, [Gamal Abdul] Nasser also embarked on his policy of "neutrality" leaning to the Soviet Union, and after the Czech-Egyptian arms deal of September 1955, extensive Soviet arms supplies began to flow into Egypt.

His first aim was absolutely fundamental to the Egyptian revolutionary outlook on the place of the Land of the Nile in the Arab world. Nasser's attitude towards the Cold War—the chilly winds of which had started to blow in our region before the Egyptian revolution—was either the result of his world outlook, a reaction to the inclusion of Baghdad in a Western defence treaty (in January 1955), or an expression of his quest for status, prestige and the international and regional advantages involved in manoeuvring between the two blocs. Possibly a combination of all these considerations made up Nasser's motives.

From 1953 (when the American Secretary of State, John Foster Dulles, visited the area) until the beginning of 1955, the United States hoped to base a Western defence treaty on Egypt, and it was this consideration that led it to press Britain to respond to the Egyptian revolutionary regime's demand for the withdrawal of the British forces from the Suez Canal zone. When America despaired of this possibility, she started to work for the "Northern Tier" treaty, in which she included Baghdad in response to the demands of the British. The Soviet Union

Source: Yaacov Herzog, *A People That Dwells Alone: Speeches and Writings of Yaacov Herzog,* ed. Misha Louvish (New York: Sanhedrin Press, 1975), pp. 237–42. Reprinted by permission of Pnina Herzog.

wanted to outflank the Baghdad Treaty by jumping over the Northern Tier into our region. It met with a response from Nasser, who had already started to draw inspiration from the neutralist policies of [Jawaharlal] Nehru and [Joseph Broz] Tito and saw himself as a potential partner in the leadership of the "non-identified" world bloc. The feelers between the Soviet Union and Egypt over the arms deal started, apparently, in the spring of 1955 at the Bandung Conference, with Chou En-lai—strangely enough—as the go-between. In September 1955 the Czech-Egyptian deal was born, opening a new chapter in the history of the Middle East. Into this new situation President Eisenhower's emissary made his entry at the beginning of 1956.

The struggle between pan-Arabism, or Arab unity under Nasser's leadership, and the independence of the Arab states, became intertwined with the Cold War, each struggle influencing the other, with the focal points of the combined struggle at Baghdad on the one side and Cairo on the other. An outstanding example of the combination of the two tensions was the violent outbreak in Jordan in November 1955, when the visit of the British Chief of the General Imperial Staff, who came to discuss the inclusion of Jordan in the Baghdad Pact, ended in failure. Five months later, early in 1956, Glubb Pasha, the British Commander of the Jordanian Arab Legion, was dismissed.

While he was still struggling for supremacy in the Arab world as the chief spokesman and leading representative of the region on the international scene, it is difficult to see how Nasser could have let go of the Israel-Arab problem, even had he so wished, especially as the problem was connected with the two other struggles in the Arab world. Nor are there any grounds for the assumption that at the time of the mission, at the beginning of 1956, he really had any such intention. Had he wished, even without taking the risk of direct contact with Israel, he could have discussed proposals for a settlement in the region as put forward by (John) Foster Dulles [U.S. secretary of state] in the summer of 1955 and Anthony Eden, the British Prime Minister, in his Guildhall speech towards the end of that year. Both involved an Israeli withdrawal from part of the Negev to enable a direct link to be established between Egypt and Jordan. It seems, therefore, that even the political isolation of Israel was not so important in Nasser's eyes as his dream of subduing her by force. It is clear, at any rate, that the emissary himself, at the end of his mission, did not have the impression that there was any sense in continuing to attempt to arrive at a settlement, and his opinion was shared by his superiors in Washington. In any case, we have never heard any accusation that Israel was to blame for the failure of the mission.

Although the emissary concentrated on Egyptian-Israeli and Arab-Israeli relations during his discussion with us, it may be stated with confidence that with Nasser he also tried to clarify all the aspects of U.S.-Egyptian relations after the Czech-Egyptian deal. It was my impression that the emissary made no greater progress in this matter than he had in connection with an Israeli-Arab settlement. In any case, a few months after the end of the mission, the United States announced the withdrawal of her financial support for the building of the Aswan Dam and informed Egypt accordingly in quite an offensive fashion. Even on the limited question of border pacification, with which the emissary dealt, together with his quest for a fundamental settlement, he did not receive satisfactory replies from Nasser.

The Secretary-General of the United Nations [Dag Hammarskjold] visited the Middle East during the same period and came again in April 1956 for the purpose of finding some arrangement, even a temporary one, to stop the killing on the borders. His attempt also ended in failure. The argument that Nasser repeated to various visitors, including the emissary, that it was very difficult for him to impose his authority on the *fedayeen* in the Gaza Strip, was proven baseless after the Sinai Campaign: between 1957 and 1967 he was perfectly capable of preventing the murderous infiltration.

To sum up, during that period Nasser was trying at one and the same time to undermine the pro-Western regimes in the region, to gain advantages from the Cold War in the Middle East and to appear as the standard-bearer of "the liberation of Palestine," first through the fedayeen and later by all-out war. When we come to analyse Nasser's attitude during his talks with the emissary, it should be remembered that at the time of the mission—from January to March 1956—Nasser still hoped to get American finance for the Aswan Dam project. He was apprehensive of the increasing influence of Nuri Sa'id, the Iraqi Prime Minister, through Western support. He also wanted to convince the United States that the Czech-Egyptian deal, which had been born four months previously, did not mean that he was sliding into the Soviet sphere of influence. Nasser's policy was based on the desire to balance—if only in appearance—his relationships with the Great Powers.

His great success in this regard was the support he received from both the United States and the Soviet Union after the Sinai Campaign. The break came in the summer of 1958, when the U.S. Government landed marines in Lebanon, and Britain sent troops to Jordan to prevent Nasser from gaining control over both countries. From 1958 to 1960, Nasser was out of favour with Washington. But when [John] Kennedy became President, Nasser renewed his hopes to balance his relations with the Powers and indeed gained American recognition for the revolutionary government in Yemen. The failure to achieve a solution in Yemen over a period of five years again disturbed his relations with Washington, though not completely. Even in our own period, the quest for balanced relations, if only outwardly, continues to be an element in Egyptian policy.

This is not the place for an extensive analysis of Nasser's place in the Israel-Arab dispute, but anyone who follows the course of events cannot escape the impression that he added to the conflict a new historic dimension in that it was his contention that so long as Israel existed there could be no complete success for Arab nationalism. During the entire period of Nasser's rule, some argued that he was the only man who was capable of making peace with Israel. This view has evaporated, I believe, since his death.

It was not only to the emissary, but to Western visitors in general, that Nasser alleged that the Gaza raid was the turning-point in the prospects of a settlement with Israel and even hinted that this was what compelled him to appeal for arms to the Soviet Union in order to wipe out the stain on the honour of the Egyptian Army. This story gained currency in the Western literature of the period. Without belittling the shock that the operation caused to the Egyptian Army, and without analysing the political situation at the time, it is difficult to regard this argument of Nasser's as sincere. Nasser was a master of calculated moves. He was perfectly capable of restraining his emotions and refraining from changes in basic policy under the impact of emotional impulse (until May 1967). His numerous failures were due rather to mistaken evaluation of the effectiveness of his military strength than to lack of planning and cold calculation. It is hardly conceivable that because of the Gaza raid—which the Egyptian people did not even hear about—he decided overnight to change Egyptian policy if, indeed, he sincerely wanted a settlement with Israel (especially as the Israeli-Egyptian border had already been in a ferment for many months). Moreover, in considering his allegation that it was the Gaza raid that drove him to contact the Soviet Union, it is impossible to ignore the fact that the same month in which the raid took place also saw the signature of the Baghdad Pact which Nasser regarded as a fundamental Western challenge to the prospects of his leadership in the Middle East. The rivalry between Egypt and the Northern Tier countries over the fate of the Middle East goes back to the beginning of its history.

The Arab world at the time was convinced of two fundamental axioms, that time was on their side and that Israel's doom would be sealed in a much shorter period than that of the Crusaders. Moreover, many of the world's capitals had grave doubts about the long-term survival of Israel. In my opinion, the Arab world lived on this plane of thought until after the shock it received in the Six-Day War. True, the axiom has not been abandoned, but it is burdened with doubts, which have even been uttered in public by Arab spokesmen. In 1956 no Arab leader dared use the name of Israel expressly in public. It was as if Israel were a leper among nations, or some kind of nightmare that would soon vanish. To talk of peace with Israel was certainly impossible, if only for emotional reasons, and, with the exception of a remark by President [Habib] Bourguiba of Tunisia, this situation continued until 1967.

In 1956 Israel was faced by a multi-dimensional siege: the attacks of the *fedayeen*; the Egyptian blockage of the Straits of Tiran and the Suez Canal; Egypt's military preparations for war; the West's wholehearted support for part of the Arab world and the Soviet Union's for the other part, with no one favouring Israel; the danger of Nasserism gaining control over the Middle East; the American and British plans for a settlement, which would have weakened Israel's prospects of independent survival and, above all, the lack of response to Israel's desperate requests for defensive arms. In 1955 and 1956, Israel felt more isolated than at any other period since the establishment of her independence. Without underestimating the dangers of today, it is hard to see how anyone can argue that time has worked to Israel's disadvantage. Despite the more extensive Russian support, the Arabs themselves are not sure that time has been and still is on their side. Our great challenge today is to protect our security while seeking every crack in Arab consciousness that may lead to peace.

At the beginning of 1956, Washington believed—or wanted to believe—that there was still some possibility of an Israeli-Egyptian settlement. Not only had Jerusalem stopped believing in such a possibility at that stage, but it was afraid that the pursuit of a settlement would have only one result: namely, a prolonged delay in meeting Israel's urgent demand for defensive arms. On the one hand the emissary was busy for a few months shuttling between Cairo and Jerusalem. On the other, the hands of the clock moved on: the Czech arms were being absorbed into the Egyptian Army, and the threat of an unannounced air attack on Israel's cities cast a lengthening shadow. The late Moshe Sharett, then Foreign Minister, believed that but for the Kinneret Operation, which was carried out in December when he himself was in Washington for talks on the supply of arms, our request would have met with a positive response at the time. I believe there was no solid basis for this view, though the operation undoubtedly served as an excuse for delay. For fear of injuring her position in the Middle East, the United States did not want to become a supplier of arms to Israel, but after the failure of the 1956 mission she tried, for lack of any alternative, to help us get arms from Canada and France. Her efforts in this direction were not totally effective; in a few months we concluded an extensive arms agreement directly with France.

If the United States had responded in time to our demands, the history of the Middle East might have been different. In the course of time, it appears that the lesson that Israel must not be left defenceless—both for fear that she might be driven to take desperate action and because her deterrent power is a central factor in the prevention of war—began to make an impression on the American consciousness. The process was gradual and passed through several stages. The principle won full recognition in President [Lyndon] Johnson's public statement in 1968 about America's responsibility for the preservation of the balance of forces in the region, and the measures that President [Richard] Nixon took with this end in view.

The mission of the U.S. President's emissary to Jerusalem and Cairo between January and March 1956 was indeed one of the most unsuccessful attempts to break the fifty-year deadlock in Arab-Israeli relations, but I believe the historian will have to designate it as one of the central events and turning-points in the development of the Middle East in our time.

42

Yaacov Herzog

The Background to the Sinai Campaign

November 1956: Memoir

Yaacov David Herzog (1921–1972) was active at the highest levels of Zionist politics prior to the founding of the State of Israel and until his death. Under the British Mandatory government he was a member of the clandestine Jewish intelligence network in Palestine. After Israel was established he quickly became one of the most influential members of Israel's foreign policy-making elite and served as ambassador to Canada, assistant director general of the Ministry of Foreign Affairs in charge of economic affairs, and director general of the Office of the Prime Minister under Levi Eshkol and Golda Meir. He was the son of Rabbi Yizhak Halevi Herzog and the brother of Chaim Herzog. In the following interview published November 11, 1966, on the tenth anniversary of the second major war of the Arab-Israeli conflict, he discusses the background to the Sinai Campaign.

Following the Czech arms deal, Egypt instituted a blockade against Israeli shipping, confiscating Israeli ships in international waters and imprisoning Israeli sailors. Then, on July 27, 1956, Egyptian president Gamal Abdul Nasser nationalized the Suez Canal, canceling the Anglo-Egyptian agreement under which it was to be operated by Egypt. Britain and France vehemently opposed this step and undertook a joint military venture to regain control of the canal.

Yaacov Herzog explains how and why Israel became involved in this operation. Most immediately, Israel was concerned about fedayeen *attacks (see doc. 37), but the rise of Nasserism (see doc. 38) and Egypt's recent acquisition of large quantities of Soviet weapons convinced David Ben-Gurion and Moshe Dayan, chief of staff, that a preemptive strike against Egypt was a necessity. Britain and France attacked Egyptian airfields and began moving their fleets in the Mediterranean toward Egypt. For Israel the Sinai Campaign (code name Operation Kadesh) lasted from October 29 to November 11, 1956. Israeli forces swept through the Sinai Peninsula and reached the Suez Canal. From Israel's standpoint, its three major goals—the eradication of the* fedayeen *bases in Gaza and Sinai border areas, the prevention of an Egyptian attack by the destruction of Sinai airfields, and the opening of the Gulf of Eilat to Israeli shipping—were all achieved. Pressure from the international community brought the joint operations to a halt in two weeks.*

Source: Yaacov Herzog, *A People That Dwells Alone: Speeches and Writings of Yaacov Herzog,* ed. Misha Louvish (New York: Sanhedrin Press, 1975), pp. 229–36. Reprinted by permission of Pnina Herzog.

An important element in the background to the Sinai Campaign was the personal rivalry between [Gamal Abdul] Nasser and Prime Minister Nuri Sa'id, which reflected the national rivalry between Egypt and Iraq. The efforts to integrate Egypt into the Western defence system had failed. After the conclusion of the Baghdad Pact in 1955, Nasser went to Bandung. According to one account, it was Chou En-lai who advised Nasser at Bandung to approach the Soviet bloc for arms. In the summer of 1955, Dimitri Shepilov, then editor of *Pravda,* visited Cairo; he was followed by the Soviet Foreign Minister. And in December 1955, the Czech-Egyptian arms deal was signed.

Anyone who follows international developments can perceive that Nasser was already moving away from the West in the autumn of 1954, after the signature of the agreement for the evacuation of the Canal zone by the British forces. Nasser wanted American arms without an accompanying American military delegation, but, in keeping with their policy, the Americans insisted on a delegation going with their armaments, as they did with other countries in the Middle East. The Soviets, on the other hand, supplied Nasser with arms "unconditionally." With his approach to the Soviet bloc, Nasser began his political game. Although he had failed in every one of his external efforts in the Middle East (with Syria, Lebanon, Jordan, Iraq, Yemen, etc.), he succeeded in strengthening his international position by playing East and West against each other. At one and the same time, he convinced the West that if his regime fell it would be replaced by a Communist one, and the East that an extreme rightist regime would emerge from the ruins of his own.

In view of these developments, little importance should be attached to the Israeli raid on Gaza at the beginning of 1955, . . . despite the views of those, including some Israelis, who regard it as the main reason for Nasser's appeal for arms to the Soviet bloc [see doc. 37]. The Gaza raid may have somewhat stimulated the process, but it may be assumed that, even without it, Nasser would have made the same change in his policy.

If Nasser had only asked for defensive arms against Israel, the Americans would probably have been prepared to supply them. In fact, the United States was very eager to establish the Western defence system with a base in Egypt, or at least with her participation, and this aroused serious anxiety in Israel. Against the background of Nasser's inter-Arab activity and the international position he adopted for reasons that have no particular connection with Israel, Israel was the touchstone in the inter-Arab struggle. Each side wanted to prove that its international policy would serve Arab interests against Israel. The more Nasser denounced Nuri Sa'id as an agent of Western imperialism, the greater was Nuri's pressure on his partners in the Baghdad Pact—especially Britain and the United States—to reduce their support for Israel.

The Western attempt to establish a defence system in both the north and the south of the Middle East aroused the Soviet Union to look for a way to penetrate into the region. The Czech-Egyptian deal was signed as a counterbalance to the Baghdad Pact and a "prize" for Nasser's non-adhesion to the Western defence system, and not in order to give him arms superiority over Israel—although this was the inevitable result.

It is possible that Nasser aspired from the beginning to neutralism as he understood it, a fact that was not perceived in 1953–54 by the Americans, who had great hopes for him. This trend facilitated the growth of Indian influence, especially in view of the establishment of the Baghdad Pact. [Jawaharlal] Nehru's influence was considerable at the time and the Indian Ambassador in Cairo influenced Nasser to adopt the neutralist position in the inter-bloc struggle.

On the Israeli side, a main feature of the background to the Sinai Campaign was concern at any strengthening of Egypt, whether by plans that did not come to fruition—such as MEDO

(Middle East Defense Organization) and [U.S. Secretary of State John Foster] Dulles's plan to base the Western defence system on Egypt—or through the Czech arms deal. Foreign Minister Moshe Sharett's journey to Geneva (where the first Summit Conference was taking place) at the end of 1955 was meant to bring home to the Powers the gravity of Israel's position as a result of the upsetting of the balance of forces. Later, Sharett and Eban [then Israeli Ambassador to the United States] had talks in Washington with Dulles about the supply of arms—especially planes—to Israel. If the Secretary of State had responded to Israel's request in December 1955, it is highly possible that the Sinai Campaign would not have taken place. Ultimately, he agreed to arrange to have Israel supplied with planes by other countries.

Why was U.S. action in this regard delayed for several months more? Sharett believed that the Kinneret Operation at the end of 1956 was the reason. (On 11 December 1956 Israeli forces attacked Syrian army posts east of Lake Kinneret, from which Israeli farmers and fishermen had been harassed.) True, the operation did not make Washington's efforts any easier, but there can be no certainty on this subject. In the U.S. State Department there was a conflict between various evaluations. Some took the Czech arms deal as proof that Nasser had fallen victim to Soviet influence, while others—headed by Henry Byroade, the American Ambassador in Cairo—argued that the deal was a one-time event and that Nasser had made it in despair. Byroade claimed that Nasser could still be saved from Soviet influence.

In November 1955, shortly before the Geneva Summit Conference, Dulles summoned Byroade and the late Edward Lawson, then U.S. Ambassador in Israel, to Paris. He agreed to wait six months to test Byroade's view that Nasser could still be won over for the West. As part of the effort to repair relations with Egypt, negotiations continued during the following months for American aid for the building of the Aswan Dam. Dulles did not believe that Israel was in any immediate danger. He apparently thought that from Israel's point of view action on aircraft supply could be put off, thus avoiding a step that might have interfered with the process of testing relations with Nasser. At the same time, Washington did not give up the hope, which it had cherished since 1954, that somehow or other it would be possible to prevent a deterioration on the Egyptian-Israeli borders and perhaps to improve relations between Cairo and Jerusalem. In fact, during the first few months of 1956 there was some American activity to this end. President Eisenhower sent a special envoy to the area, who met several times with Ben-Gurion and Sharett in Jerusalem and Nasser in Cairo [see doc. 41].

During the critical period of early 1956, the United States was thus operating on three levels at one and the same time: examining the possibilities of improving her diplomatic relations with Egypt, including continued talks on an American grant for the building of the Aswan Dam; attempting to persuade Israel that she was in no immediate danger, while promising to work for the satisfaction of her immediate requirements in aircraft through France and Canada, but without taking energetic steps to speed up these supplies; and a last and supreme effort to find out whether it was possible, despite the growing tension, to arrive at a reconciliation between Egypt and Israel. If I am not mistaken, the question of the agreements for the supply of planes from France and Canada—twenty-four Mysteres (for which American approval was necessary) from the former and twenty-four F84s from the latter—was on the way to settlement between March and May 1956. During the same period it became clear that there was no hope of an improvement in Cairo's attitude to Israel.

In July 1956, two successive crises broke out: the first over the Aswan Dam and the second over the Suez Canal. Various accounts have been published of the reasons for America's ultimate withdrawal from the Aswan project. According to one version, it was doubtful whether

Congress was prepared to budget the enormous sum required; according to another, the United States found out that the Egyptian Government was conducting parallel negotiations with the Soviet Union to finance the dam. In any case, it may be assumed that by this time Washington had come to the conclusion that Ambassador Byroade had been mistaken in his evaluation of the situation. During that summer, tension in Israel grew. In the face of the threat to our security, France agreed (after negotiations in which Shimon Peres, then Director-General of the Ministry of Defence, played a major role) to supply Israel with arms [see doc. 40]. The nationalization of the Suez Canal and the failure of the efforts to reach a political settlement that would satisfy France and Britain intensified the crisis in relations between these two countries and Egypt.

Israel felt that she was engaged in a race with time. The operations of the *fedayeen* (terrorists based in Egypt, Gaza and Jordan who raided Israeli territory) intensified and there was growing concern at the unknown dimensions of Egyptian power and the pace at which new Soviet arms were being absorbed by the Egyptian Army. In addition, the situation deteriorated in Jordan: on the one hand, pro-Nasserist forces were attempting to overthrow Hussein's regime and, on the other hand, the Iraqi Army stood ready to enter the country. In October, pro-Nasserist elements gained a majority in the Jordanian parliament, and the unification of the Egyptian, Jordanian and Syrian armies under Egyptian command was proclaimed. Jordanian-Israeli relations were extremely tense, and Britain warned Israel against any military action in case of the entry of Iraqi forces into Jordan. It was clear in Jerusalem, however, that the real focus was in Cairo.

The Sinai Campaign, which began on 29 October, and the accompanying events were no mere episode. They were of historic significance for Israel, the Middle East and the world as a whole. From Israel's point of view, the campaign led to a fundamental change in her regional and world position, as well as in political and military thinking both in Israel and in the Arab States. For the Middle East as a whole, the campaign strengthened the trend towards greater independence of the countries of the region as against the doctrine of Nasserist hegemony under the mask of Arab unity. For the Great Powers, the campaign emphasized the consequences of a local outbreak in the Middle East for the relations between them. From the international point of view, the events of 1956 were followed by a transformation in the system of external influences over the area.

In the United Nations, 1956 marked the beginning of the appearance of the Afro-Asian bloc, which was then relatively small, as a force of great international importance. In the maelstrom of the 1956 crisis, the United Nations international police force [United Nations Emergency Force], which has since played its part in foci of international tension in Africa and elsewhere, was born.

The direct results of the Sinai Campaign—the crushing of the threatening Egyptian force, the stoppage of *fedayeen* activities and the opening of the Straits of Tiran to free navigation—were perceptible immediately, but in the course of the years it transpired that the campaign also had demonstrated that Israel is a permanent factor in the Middle East. This recognition has since struck roots in the international consciousness and has also begun to penetrate the Arab consciousness. At the end of the War of Independence, it was believed that the armistice agreements would be a preface to peace in a few years, but it became clear that Arab hostility had not only not declined, but was steadily growing, and peace was still far away. Israel suffered from isolation and discrimination. In the various proposals for international military arrangements in the region, there was no place for her. She found it difficult to get defensive arms in the face of the growing threats from the Arab countries. From the international point of view, the solution to the Israel-Arab problem appeared to involve concessions by Israel, including border revisions to which Israel could on no account agree. In the eyes of the Powers, Israel was regarded, in a way, as a nuisance.

The Sinai Campaign was a turning-point in the relations between Israel and the Powers. When, a few months later, the Eisenhower Doctrine[1] for the Middle East was enunciated, Israel was recognized equally with the Arab countries. Until a few months before the Sinai Campaign, the tripartite declaration by the Powers, issued in 1950, calling for the maintenance of the balance of forces in the Middle East, was still on record, but it was never carried out in practice. Before the campaign, the arms embargo was broken in regard to France. During the succeeding years, diplomatic struggles were needed to ensure the opening of significant sources of arms in other Western countries. Today it is generally agreed that a careful balance of forces is the most effective guarantee against war in the region. Without such a balance, Israel is liable, whenever the Arabs received large quantities of arms, to find it necessary to take action in self-defence. Since the Sinai Campaign, the voices that called for Israeli territorial concessions have died down. True, the Israeli Army returned to the armistice lines, but since its return it has made them permanent, and none of the Western Powers has expressed any reservations regarding them.

It is also true that the Sinai Campaign exacerbated the relations between Israel and the Soviet Union, but against the background of Soviet activity in the region, which was then in its earliest stages, it is doubtful whether the relations would have improved very much even had the campaign never taken place. Today, ten years later, it appears that it is not the memory of the campaign that is the major reason for the lack of progress in improving relations between Israel and the Great Powers.

It is a fact that since 1956 Israel's relations with the non-Arab countries in and around the Middle East have improved. It seems that the campaign has been followed by a growing recognition in these countries that Israel is strong and her position in the area is firm. Against the background of the serious clash in the United Nations between Israel and the Afro-Asian bloc, many were anxious lest the campaign and the charges that were flung against Israel might in the future raise a barrier between ourselves and the peoples of Africa and Asia, many of which were then on the threshold of independence. In reality, the African and Asian peoples were not influenced for long by Arab propaganda about Israel's motives in the Sinai Campaign. Friendship and real understanding between them and Israel continued to develop and were strengthened on the practical plane by the opening of the sea routes from Israel to these two continents.

Most critical of Israel's moral position in connection with the campaign was the Government of India, and for many years Prime Minister Nehru continued to rebuke Israel for her reaction. He saw the campaign against the background of his fundamental prejudice, regarding Israel as a foreign body in the region, and even without the campaign it is doubtful whether his attitude would have been any different.

According to Zionist political thinking during the decades preceding the establishment of Israel's independence, Arab hostility to the Zionist enterprise was not fundamental, but was the consequence of Arab social structure, local interests, a temporary failure to understand the Zionist contribution to the progress of the entire area and continual mischief-making by external factors. A historian who studies the history of the Zionist effort may reach the conclusion that a more accurate and comprehensive perception by the Jews and world public opinion might have made greater difficulties for the realization of the Zionist idea.

In any case, it is very doubtful whether many people could have foreseen in 1947 that, after almost twenty years, Israel-Arab relations would be as they are today. With the signature of the armistice agreements it was believed that peace was around the corner, though this faith was gradually undermined as the years went by. However, the alternative, the continuation of a prolonged state of war, was in such glaring contradiction to the original assumptions that it seems there were psychological barriers to its acceptance in Israeli consciousness.

From 1954 to 1965 there were, therefore, two schools of thought about the prospect of settlement with the Arabs. After the Sinai Campaign, out of a feeling of strength, it was easier to absorb the idea that we should have to stand firm for many years to come with our deterrent force in the hope that historical processes would have their effect on Arab consciousness. It transpired that even the shattering of a threatening Arab military force does not necessarily mean peace. The hope, which was born after the military victory in the first week of the campaign, that we might get direct negotiations for peace in return for the evacuation of Sinai, was not realized. Nor were the Great Powers ready to sacrifice world interests on the altar of Israeli-Arab relations. Israel, therefore, adapted herself to the thought that peace would be the result of a slow and gradual process, which must be carefully watched and stimulated whenever possible. In the meantime, Israel must protect her security and prevent war by strengthening her deterrent force.

Arab hostility to Israel is founded on a failure to understand the true nature of Israel and the spiritual and historical roots that bind the Jewish people for all eternity to its homeland. Just as the Jews did not understand the Muslims, so they did not understand us. This lack of understanding still dominates Arab consciousness, but Arab thinking today is not the same as it was ten years ago. The change was emphasized after the Summit Conference [see doc. 57], which was convened in 1964 under the same banner of hostility that was brandished in 1948 and in the framework of the same crude thinking that called for the immediate crushing of Israel by force. If this were so at the beginning of the Summit Conference, however, three main trends were apparent in Arab thinking during the course of it. The first trend, for which Syria was the spokesman, called for the launching of war against Israel without delay and with no concern to the relations between the forces. This trend recalled the Arab thinking that was dominant to the eve of Israel's independence and that was revived during the years 1954–56. The second trend, which was expressed by Nasser, might be called "Arab Zionism." It called upon the Arabs to continue to cherish the ardent conviction that Israel is a foreign growth in the area. In order to uproot her, the Arab world must first achieve unity, strengthen its military forces, improve the international position of the Arab countries and consolidate the Arab economies. In the course of time, all these endeavours would endow the Arab countries with superiority over Israel and at the same time tighten the siege against her. Time and logic would inevitably have their effect. This trend, then, calls for patience and the long view. The third trend is publicly represented by President [Habib] Bourguiba of Tunisia. It argues that the Arabs have lost the opportunity to solve the problem of Israel by war. Hence they must try to realize their claims, or part of them, by negotiations and international pressure. (The Tunisian President's ultimate goal is still wrapped in obscurity.)

We cannot exclude the possibility that the changes and differences in the Arab approach during the past few years are ultimately due to the shock caused by the Sinai Campaign. The campaign proved that there was no basis for oversimplified Arab thinking about the prospect of overwhelming Israel by force, which reigned previously. The fruitless efforts to achieve Arab unity and Nasser's attempt to dominate the Arab world continued, in stages, also after the Sinai Campaign. The fact that the other countries did not rush to give Egypt military aid during the campaign did not remain without effect on the Arab consciousness. Though this cannot be stated with certainty, it may be assumed that the shattering of the legend of Egyptian power dwarfed Nasser's image to some extent in the eyes of the masses, at least outside Egypt, and released the other Arab rulers from the complex of Nasser's exclusive supremacy in the region. It is possible, therefore, that the Sinai Campaign made an important contribution to the inculcation of the principle that the Middle East is a pluralistic region, in which there is room for various peoples, each with its own political character and its sovereign independence.

The events of 1956 also shook international public opinion. Rightly or wrongly, the conviction grew that the grave tension among the Middle East countries involved the danger of an international conflagration. There is the impression that the Powers are interested in preventing a major outbreak in the region: but if there is some contradiction between the desire to prevent war and the Powers' acts of commission or omission that lead to an increase in tension, it is due to the fact that the Powers are more influenced by global considerations than by the interests of the peoples in the region.

In 1956, the United States took vigorous action to stop the fighting. In the political struggle that followed, it pressed relentlessly for the evacuation of the Israeli forces from Sinai, thus perhaps saving Nasser's regime. This intervention not only aroused among Americans the feeling that perhaps the United States had not given fair consideration to Israel's situation before the campaign, but also led to the conclusion that just as America had not allowed Nasser's regime to be overthrown by force, so it should not allow Nasser to overthrow other regimes by force. Only a year and a half after the events of 1956, American marines landed in Lebanon to protect Camille Chamoun's regime against pro-Nasserist forces, and British troops, with American encouragement, were sent to Jordan to save Hussein's regime from Nasserist subversion. Anyone who was intimately familiar with the situation in the Middle East during the period before the Sinai Campaign will find it difficult to imagine any such American action at that time. This development was not only a paradoxical result of 1956; it also symbolized the appearance of the United States as the major Western factor in the Middle East.

NOTE

1. Eisenhower Doctrine, U.S. policy statement on the Middle East issued by President Dwight Eisenhower on January 5, 1957. It granted military and economic assistance to Middle Eastern states requesting aid and promised the use of U.S. military forces to protect the territorial integrity of any state threatened by communist aggression (see doc. 52).

43

Walter Eytan

Israel and the Jewish Diaspora

1948–1959: Analysis

The establishment of a Jewish state inhabited by a small portion of the Jewish people created a complex relationship between Israel and the Jewish Diaspora. What did the creation of Jewish sovereignty mean for the public position of the major Jewish communities in the world? What were the repercussions on Jewish life and political Zionism in the Diaspora? How dependent was Israel on Jewish help from abroad? Was Israel to become the political and spiritual center of Jewish life? How were Israel's relations with the Diaspora to be regulated? These were just some of the questions that had to be answered. Even the use of the term Diaspora (galut) *seemed to imply support of the central Zionist tenets of the "abnormality" of a Jewish people without a sovereign state and of the centrality of Israel to the Jewish people.*

An Israeli outlook on these issues is presented in this article by Walter Eytan. Like many other leading Israeli diplomats, Eytan began his public career in the Political Department of the Jewish Agency. He was Israel's first director general of the Ministry of Foreign Affairs, a position he held until 1959.

It is a commonplace of our Foreign Service that every Envoy Extraordinary and Minister Plenipotentiary of Israel has a dual function. He is Minister Plenipotentiary to the country to which he is accredited—and Envoy Extraordinary to its Jews. This has come to be accepted generally—by other governments in the "free" world, by the Jews of the diaspora, and by everyone in Israel. It is, in fact, a natural enough situation. King George VI once startled the Chief Rabbi of the Commonwealth by mentioning to him, at a Buckingham Palace reception, that he had the day before received "your ambassador," meaning the ambassador of Israel in London.

In each country the foreign residents constitute what in their circles and in the diplomatic corps is known as a "colony." There is a French colony in Italy, a Swedish colony in Japan, a British colony in Peru. The Jewish community in many countries is seen by gentiles as the Israeli colony. In September 1955, at a climax of the Cyprus crisis, when Jewish property in Istanbul was plundered by anti-Greek rioters, the Turkish Government thought it perfectly natural to instruct its representative at Tel Aviv to express its regrets to the Government of Israel and to assure it that there existed in Turkey "no intention or inclination to prejudice in any way the security or the rights of the Jews of Turkey." The Swiss minister to Brazil once envied his Israeli colleague on the size of his colony; he himself had only 12,000 fellow countrymen—and there were ten times as many Jews.

These colonies can be extremely helpful to their country of origin, and it is one of the duties of every ambassador, minister and consul to keep in close touch with them. The Jews are exceptional, however, and nowhere form a colony in the accepted sense. Members of a Danish

---

Source: Walter Eytan, *The First Ten Years: A Diplomatic History of Israel* (London: Weidenfeld and Nicholson, 1958), pp. 192–200. Reprinted by permission of Walter Eytan.

colony, for example, are Danish citizens or they may at most, if their own and the local laws allow it, have dual nationality—their Danish nationality of origin and the nationality of the country in which they reside and perhaps were born. Jews in general do not have Israeli nationality; the only Israelis are those who are or have been domiciled in Israel—and the overwhelming majority of Jews in the world have never been to Israel even on a visit. Yet the ties which bind Jews everywhere to Israel are very strong, and Jewish communities abroad are often "colonies" in at least as real a sense as the Germans or Danes or Swiss. Israel does not claim their political allegiance. The Jews are citizens of their own countries, and the question of double loyalty does not arise. But they are bound to Israel by sentiment, and to some extent by self-interest. Exposed as they often are to discrimination, and in many countries fearful for their future, they have felt more secure since Israel came into existence. Just as Americans of Swedish, Irish, English or Italian origin have a "home country" in which they take a pride and an interest even after many generations, Jews all over the world can take a pride and an interest in Israel; and just as Irish Americans and Greek Americans support their "home country," its institutions and villages and their own families, so Jews support Israel, materially and morally.

When Herzl first gave the dream of Jewish independence political shape, he did so in a pamphlet entitled *Der Judenstaat*, "The State of the Jews." He did not call it *Der Jüdische Staat*, "The Jewish State." The difference may seem subtle, but it is real enough. Israel is not merely a state predominantly Jewish in the race, religion or way of life of its people. It is a state for all Jews. The principle was laid down in its Declaration of Independence [doc. 21]: "The State of Israel will be open to the immigration of Jews from all countries of their dispersion." Legislative effect was given to this in the Law of Return [doc. 29], passed unanimously by the Knesset on July 5, 1950. Israel is the only country in the world which confers citizenship on an immigrant automatically at the moment he steps off the boat or plane. Every Jew knows that he can migrate to Israel whenever he feels like it. The gates are always open. At the same time, Israel places no Jew under compulsion to exercise this birthright of his. He is perfectly free, as far as Israel is concerned, to stay where he is. But inevitably a special relationship has sprung up between Israel and Jews everywhere who share the age-old attachment to the Land of Israel. Even if they are unwilling or unable to link their personal lives with it by coming as immigrants, they are animated by a powerful sentiment of solidarity and love. Mr. [David] Ben-Gurion, in an Independence Day message in 1957, defined succinctly the links which join Israel and the Jews all over the world: "The unity of the Jewish people, its sense of common responsibility for its fate, its attachment to its spiritual heritage, and its love for the nation's ancient homeland, have become more and more intense as a result of the rise of the Third Commonwealth. The ingathering of Israel's exiled and scattered sons is the common task of all sections of the Jewish people wherever they may live. Everything that has been created in this country is the common possession of the Jews of all lands."

Few would quarrel with this definition; it reflects indisputable fact. But it has not been easy to adjust the relationship between Israel and the Jewish communities abroad, particularly in the United States. Before Israel attained political independence, a Jew could either be a Zionist or not. If he was, he believed in Jewish statehood as a political ideal and goal and did his best to help achieve it. If he was not, he would be either indifferent or hostile to the idea, believing it not worth striving for or incapable of realization or, in extreme cases, positively harmful. With the rise of Israel, there had to be a reorientation of attitudes and action. The Zionist's goal was achieved—what was there left for him to do? The non-Zionist and anti-Zionist found themselves faced with a fait accompli—Israel existed, whether they were interested or pleased or not, and they were forced to think again.

The adjustment of Jews outside Israel to the reality of Israel has not yet been completed. It is now less a problem of action than of ideas. It was not simply for the sake of talking that as late as August 1957 an "ideological conference" was called at Jerusalem and attended by Jewish leaders and thinkers from all over the world. There is genuine confusion, even distress. The classical concept of Jewish "exile" presents itself in a new form. In traditional Jewish thought, reflected in Mr. Ben-Gurion's Independence Day message, the Jewish people had been in exile since the destruction of the Second Commonwealth in the year 70. The concept of "exile" applied in some measure even to those who lived in Palestine, for they were living there under foreign rule. With the establishment of the Third Commonwealth, Israel, the exile came to an end—in the sense, at least, that there was again a Jewish state and that any Jew who wished to return to it was free to do so. It became natural to distinguish, if not always explicitly, between those Jews who were "at home" or "in their own country"—that is, in Israel as Israeli citizens—and those who continued to live "in exile," anywhere outside Israel. Instinctively, the majority of Jews accepted this distinction, though no undue stress was laid on it either in Israel or abroad; the essential unity of the Jewish people, in terms of race, tradition and faith, was too strong to brook differentiation along hard and fast lines of any kind.

An ideological crisis arose in the United States, however, where Jews resented any suggestion that they were living in "exile." America was their home, Americanism their creed, the American way of life their heritage. This denial of an American "exile" implied a break with almost two thousand years of Jewish thought and teaching. Israeli leaders, steeped in Jewish tradition, found it difficult to adjust themselves to the idea that America was excluded from the "exile," and they continued to think, and sometimes speak, in terms of two Jewish worlds—Israel and the rest. Each time such a thought found expression in speech there would be a protest from American Jewish leaders, deeply sympathetic though they were by nature to Israel and her aspirations. In the end, a modus vivendi was achieved. The problem was aired exhaustively in June 1957, when a delegation of the American Jewish Committee, an influential "non-Zionist" group, visited Israel. After much discussion, Mr. Ben-Gurion, as Prime Minister of Israel, defined his position in terms which proved acceptable to the Committee's leaders:

> While Israel is open for all Jews who desire or need to come and live in it . . . the State of Israel represents and speaks only on behalf of its own citizens and in no way represents or speaks on behalf of Jews of any other country. The attachment of Jews throughout the world to Israel is based on a joint spiritual and cultural heritage, and on a historical sentiment toward the land which was the birthplace of the Jewish people and of the Book, and which today as the Third Commonwealth of Israel enshrines the regeneration of a people in its ancient homeland and revival of its civilization. Jews throughout the world give expression to this attachment and dedication in various ways. But these, in whatever form they may be expressed, carry no political connotation whatsoever.

This was taken to mean that in Israel's official view American Jews were American citizens, no more and no less, and that they were not necessarily looked upon as children of Israel in exile. Anything they did to express their "attachment and dedication" to Israel, they did as Americans, and not as the detached limb of a foreign state.

Events have robbed the term "Zionism" of much of its original meaning and the old

"Zionist movement" of much of its strength. Mr. Ben-Gurion, in his personal capacity, has in recent years made a point of declaring that he is not a Zionist—he is a Jew first, an Israeli second, and that is all. Jews who live outside Israel cannot, in his conception, be partners in Israel's cause, but only "helpers." His attitude has caused some resentment on the part of veteran Zionists who, having devoted their lives to this cause, find they can no longer claim a monopoly of support for Israel. All they can do, differently from others, is to take pride in having been right all along. Support for Israel is now universal among Jews everywhere, apart from a handful of eccentrics. (Here and there one may find a Jew who gives comfort to Abdul Nasser, propagandizing for him actively against Israel, impelled by a form of self-hate which borders on the abnormal.) The fact that so many "Zionists" continue to live in the diaspora has served to blur the distinction between them and other Jews; logic would dictate that Zionists come to Israel to live, but not everyone acts logically. For Israel it is important, indeed vital, that support for her be not confined to any single group. The Jews who in their thousands close their shops and line the streets of Buenos Aires cheering when the ambassador of Israel drives to the Casa Rosada [Brazilian president's house] to present his letters of credence may not all have been "Zionists" ten years ago, and the term "Zionist" hardly applies to them now. It is sufficient that today every single one of them takes a pride in Israel, glories in her achievements, worries when things go wrong for her and feels a personal obligation to do whatever he can, financially or otherwise, to help.

Israel has received massive financial support from the Jews of the diaspora. It came to be agreed that the Israeli taxpayer would bear all the normal burden of government expenditure, including defense, thus making Israel responsible for her own budget, like any other state. On the other hand, the costs of immigration would be borne primarily by the diaspora, which had a long tradition of succoring Jews and had for generations financed Jewish rescue and relief work and Jewish migration to every part of the world. In practice, the division of responsibility has worked out rather differently. Israel herself has had to carry an increasing share of the cost of immigration, and particularly of settlement and integration. At the same time, the diaspora has invested large sums in Israel, either directly in industrial enterprises and the like, or through successive bond issues launched in the United States and in countries of Latin America and Western Europe. These loans have gone a long way toward financing Israel's development budgets; the larger the income from them has been, the more Israel herself has been able to divert from development to defense and other urgent domestic needs.

The two-way relationship between Israel and the Jews of the world has a profound significance, politically, materially and morally. It takes up much of the time of all Israel's diplomatic representatives abroad, and most of the time of some. They do their best not to get involved in the internal controversies of local Jewish communities, but they cannot avoid being asked for advice or, when necessary, giving it. At all costs they must refrain from taking sides. In particular, they are careful not to interfere in matters at issue between the Jewish community and the government of the country in which they serve. A Jewish community will sometimes look to them for help of this kind, but it would clearly create an impossible position if the representative of Israel appeared as the protagonist of local Jews in dealings with their governments. Generally speaking, the limitations of an Israeli ambassador in this field are understood and respected, but the latitude he can allow himself in practice will vary. It has happened more than once that a government, on its own initiative, has discussed with the representative of Israel some problem concerning the local Jewish community. He will normally report to his own Government on important

Jewish affairs, particularly when they may affect Israel's interests. He and his staff will be in demand as speakers at Jewish functions and will concern themselves with cultural and educational work. Jews planning investments in Israel will look to the embassy or legation for advice; others will have problems connected with Israeli relatives. All this, with the normal duties of diplomacy, leaves Israel's representatives little time for idling.

CHAPTER 3

From the Sinai Campaign to the Six-Day War, 1956–1967

1957
U.S. President Dwight D. Eisenhower issues the Eisenhower Doctrine, a policy statement meant to bolster pro-Western Arab regimes

Israel withdraws from the Gaza Strip and Sinai Peninsula

1960
Nazi leader Adolf Eichmann is captured in Argentina; he will be tried in Jerusalem and found guilty of "crimes against the Jewish people and humanity"

1963
Levi Eshkol succeeds David Ben-Gurion as prime minister

1964
First Arab Summit Conference

Palestine Liberation Organization is proclaimed at the Arab Palestinian Congress

1965
David Ben-Gurion and his supporters form a new party, Rafi

1967
Egypt closes the Straits of Tiran to Israeli shipping

Egypt and Jordan sign a defense pact

Israel launches the preemptive Six-Day War

Domestic Issues

44

Emmanuel Marx

The Development Town

1956–1966: Analysis

Development towns were built to accommodate the masses of new immigrants who arrived in Israel in the 1950s. In the following document Emmanuel Marx, a professor of anthropology at Tel Aviv University, discusses both the policies of settling new immigrants in these towns and some of the social consequences. "Galilah" is the code name he chose for the development town in which he conducted his research.

The little town of Galilah is situated in the mountains of Galilee. It was founded in 1956, and almost all of its 3,000 inhabitants are immigrants from various parts of Morocco. The town lies off a main road leading to the nearest town, Nahariyah, a resort on the Mediterranean seashore. Buses ply the Galilah-Nahariyah route at half-hourly intervals, and there is also a regular taxi shuttle service. A small number of Galilah people are employed in Nahariyah; many others make a weekly trip to Nahariyah for their shopping (or window-shopping) and entertainment.

The town's appearance is that of a neat and moderately prosperous residential suburb. There are various types of new-looking houses, ranging from tiny whitewashed bungalows often surrounded by well-tended gardens, to five-storied grey blocks of flats, with litter-strewn courtyards. All dwellings are connected to the central water and electricity networks. The house roofs are studded with solar water heaters and the occasional television aerial. The paved streets are maintained in good repair. On all but the main road there is little traffic. The townspeople themselves own only five or six trucks and commercial vehicles, and the only private cars are the mayor's and the anthropologist's so most of the traffic consists of buses, taxis, and the cars of visitors. The smaller children use the streets at most times for play and expect drivers to watch out for them. In the late afternoon they are joined by the older children back from school, and on summer evenings their elders also come out into the street, men

---

Source: Emmanuel Marx, *The Social Context of Violent Behaviour: A Social Anthropological Study in an Israeli Immigrant Town* (London: Routledge Kegan Paul, 1976), pp. 19–26. Reprinted by permission.

and women gossiping in their separate small clusters.

Most of the public institutions are centered on the pleasant little town square, which is planted with trees and shrubs. The most prominent buildings are the local Council and the Trade Union offices, standing next to each other. On the square one also finds the bank, the post office and the "café," a small snack bar frequented by men only. Then there is the First Aid and ambulance station, the main bus stop and the "kiosk," a soda-fountain. Just off the square are the Sick Fund's[1] clinic, the Jewish Agency, the Labour Exchange, the Housing Corporation and the Welfare Offices, as well as the largest of the town's eleven synagogues and the ritual bath. On top of a hill in the town centre a large modern sports hall has been built. It has not yet been equipped, and is therefore mainly used as an improvised cinema; performances are given once a week. Not far from it is a well-stocked public library. The three schools are housed in modern airy buildings. For a town of this size, Galilah is well provided with public services.

In contrast, there are only fifteen shops, which fall into the following categories: five grocers; four greengrocers (one of whom also sells fish); one butcher; one poulterer; seven shopkeepers selling durable goods (household goods, furniture and electric equipment, tools and building materials, and clothing). The shops selling provisions are usually packed with customers, and their turnover of staple foods is considerable. The grocers and the other shopkeepers selling provisions often extend short-term credits to their regular customers. The other shops keep small stocks and their few customers usually require long-term credits. Therefore their prices are rather higher than in neighbouring towns. Cash-paying customers prefer to shop outside Galilah, where prices are lower and the choice of goods is wider. It appears that the townspeople do not control enough money to provide livelihoods for a larger number of shops selling durable goods. But there could be more grocers' and greengrocers' shops, if there were suitable premises. The town's planners did not take these requirements into account and, in the interest of orderly planning, the Local Council sees to it that traders and artisans set up only in suitable premises. Even if suitable commercial promises were to be constructed, the potential entrepreneurs would not possess the necessary capital to buy them (according to the rules, such premises are only to be sold, not to be let); therefore whoever wishes to set up in business has to do so illegally. One man hawks his wares on the pavement, another sets up a wooden shack next to his house, and all become involved in litigation with the local authority. Only a few have the perseverance to fight it out with the authorities, and these are the men who ultimately obtain permission to stay in business.

Industry too has not developed in Galilah. The authorities laid the groundwork for an industrial estate on the town's outskirts; they built approach roads and a few halls, and then waited for suitable applicants. In spite of official inducements in the form of government loans and tax concessions, few firms moved into the industrial estate. Most of them lacked capital and, after a short and troubled life span, closed down. Only a workshop maintained at a loss by the Trade Unions [Histadrut], and a small private firm producing building materials, some of which were used locally, held out for several years.

The town was planned within the framework of a national settlement policy. Immediately following the establishment of the State of Israel in 1948, large numbers of Jewish immigrants entered the country, increasing the Jewish population from 700,000 in 1948 to 1,400,000 in 1951. The authorities did their best to absorb the immigrants, while taking into account both the available accommodation and national strategic requirements. Many were settled in deserted Arab quarters of the cities and in smaller towns. Others were temporarily housed in tent-towns, and later in tin-shack towns, set up and run by the Jewish Agency. At the same time plans were drawn up to establish a large number of co-operative villages all over the country, and to turn immigrants into small farmers. This scheme sought in particular to settle the strategically sensitive regions along the Egyptian and Jordanian borders. Galilee was more sparsely endowed with new Jewish villages, and these were mostly located in a semi-circle around the western, southern and eastern fringes of Galilee, where plains provided good farmland. In mountainous central Galilee most of the indigenous Arabs and Druzes had stayed on after the Israeli forces occupied the area. Although there was a contiguous Arab population in central Galilee and in southern Lebanon, the Israeli defence authorities felt no urgent need to establish many Jewish settlements in Galilee, as the Lebanese border stayed peaceful. Therefore the local Arab population was left undisturbed, and only a few selected areas were reserved for Jewish settlement. One of these was located near the site on which Galilah was later established. There, within a radius of 7 km (about 4 ½ miles) from Galilah, eight new settlements were established, in addition to the existing eight villages inhabited by Druzes, Christians and Muslims. Two of the new settlements were communal (kibbutzim), and the other six were co-operative villages (moshavim).

By the mid-fifties agricultural settlement had reached saturation point, and the authorities began to build more new towns. These towns were intended to offset the tendency of an ever-increasing proportion of the population to converge on the three large cities, Jerusalem, Tel Aviv and Haifa. The new towns were to supply services to the surrounding villages, to process farm produce, and to develop other light industries. It was left to the future inhabitants of the towns to attract investments with the help of generous financial concessions offered by the government. At that time the Egyptian government, which had until then been concerned with internal reform, returned to full participation in Middle Eastern politics. One of its chief aims became the military encirclement of Israel. This caused the Israeli authorities to renew their interest in settling central Galilee. Galilah was established in 1956, and the following year a Jewish town was founded on the outskirts of Arab Nazareth. A third town, Karmiel, was set up in 1964, astride the main east-west road of central Galilee.

The town of Galilah was settled by some of the new immigrants who were still arriving in great numbers. The rate of population growth was determined by the numbers of houses available for occupation. In 1957 there were already 1,000 inhabitants, in 1961 nearly 1,700, and in 1964 about 3,100. Towards the end of 1964 immigration came to a standstill, and Galilah's population has remained stationary since. It attracted none of the immigrants who again began to arrive from 1967 onwards. Most of the immigrants who were settled in the town had undergone a twofold selective process. During Galilah's first years, most of the immigrants to Israel came from Morocco. Many of the professional and skilled Moroccan emigrants settled in France, and a relatively small number of them made their way to Israel.[2] Numerous people in Galilah had close kinsmen in France; among them were doctors and lawyers, technicians and skilled artisans. A second selection took place when the immigrants arrived in Israel. Every immigrant was entitled to subsidized housing and other material privileges, but had to accept a house anywhere if it was vacant. Families with able-bodied members who were willing to become farmers could still in those years join a co-operative farm. They established in their countries of origin contacts with an Israeli emissary, who would then arrange for them to join a settlement affiliated to his political party. People with suitable professional qualifications or with capital insisted on going to places where work could be found or where they could set up profitable businesses. They often dispensed with the Jewish Agency's services, or used force and influence to obtain accommodation where they wanted it. The immigrants who agreed to move to the outlying towns like Galilah were those whose freedom of choice was restricted, and who depended on the accommodation and assistance offered by the authorities. Many of the new arrivals in Galilah were destitute, lacked skills and educational qualifications, and had large families. A considerable proportion of them were elderly and infirm.

The decision where to send the new immigrants was made at the Jewish Agency head office. There the Absorption Department collated weekly lists of the available accommodation submitted by Amidar Housing Corporation[3] with reports from the Jewish Agency's Immigration Department on the number of immigrants due to arrive. The reports included details on their social characteristics and local preferences. But the Department's main concern was to settle immigrants in the available accommodation and it considered other factors only when suitable pressure was applied. The Department was responsible for the immigrant only during his initial three months in the country, and from then on he was formally on his own, and had to deal as best he could with various bureaucratic organizations, although the Department often continued to assist him. As the Jewish Agency officials were not concerned with his long-term problems, they dealt only with those that faced him immediately upon arrival. That meant first and foremost the provision of a roof over his head. The Absorption Department also contributed to the immigrant's maintenance during his first three months and, where required, provided welfare assistance. It issued him with some household equipment, beds, chairs and blankets. The Jewish Agency attended mainly to his immediate needs: the provision of suitable employment was a long term problem, involving re-training, language study and other preparations. The Jewish Agency sent the immigrant to intensive Hebrew language courses, to vocational training centres, but by the time the training was completed it was no longer responsible for him. It helped him to find work, but was not unduly concerned when he could find only a temporary job or was employed on relief work, as it had solved his short-term problem of employment. A senior official of the Absorption Department made it clear where his Department's primary concern lay when he proudly asserted that "never yet has an immigrant left without a roof over his head." He thus expressed satisfaction that the Department's main task had been properly accomplished.

Galilah is a town only in the administrative sense. While its inhabitants lack the capital and skills to make it economically viable, it is also too small to be able to develop the complex division of labour associated with town life. There is not only very little industry in the town, but few businesses and almost no places of entertainment. Neither is it a village, however, for its inhabitants do not own or cultivate land. There are only limited employment opportunities locally available. Official statistics in 1966 put the number of unemployed, and employed on relief work, at about half of the working population, a figure which understated the reality.

Galilah is located in a region of relative underemployment. The townspeople are worse off than some others living in the region, as they are restricted in their search for work to the area under the jurisdiction of their local Labour Exchange. This is a branch office of the Labour Exchange in the neighbouring town, Nahariyah, a seaside resort of nearly 20,000 inhabitants, which also has some industry. The people of that town are served first by their Labour Exchange, so that hardly any jobs are left for Galilah men, although an exception is made at one industrial plant, where a number of places are reserved for them. The Arab and Druze villagers of the area supplement their incomes from farming by working in towns, and compete successfully for jobs with the men of Galilah. They engage in trade, crafts and clerical work, and have come to occupy an important place in farm work and construction, two branches of the economy which rely largely on seasonal labour.

The skilled and semi-skilled work on building sites in the areas is often done by Arabs. Most of the fifty to sixty Galilah men regularly employed in construction, and even those working in the town itself, are semi-skilled or unskilled workers.

The kibbutzim and moshavim in the area directly employ only two or three persons from Galilah, and altogether contribute very little to the town's economy. Both types of settlement are affiliated to national political and economic organizations based in the main cities. They market their produce and obtain their supplies through central co-operatives, and do not provide much custom to the small towns. Their political regional and national organizations seek to protect sectoral rather than local interests. While they do not adhere strictly to the ideological injunction against employing hired labour, the settlements in the Galilah region are not sufficiently developed to require workers from the town. The links between the town and its hinterland are thus very tenuous.

The Labour Exchange's policy always to prefer local people for local jobs was initially designed to curb the tendency of the population to converge on the main cities. One result was to keep people from depressed areas out of work, unless they moved their domicile to the region in which work was available. Most of the inhabitants of Galilah are not in a position to take such a momentous decision. Few could collect the amount of money needed to acquire a flat or to rent accommodation or to maintain themselves during a transitional period. This applies particularly to large families which, therefore, are seldom able to move away from Galilah and improve their condition.

The economic opportunities in the town are too limited to attract individual settlers from other parts of the country. Only a handful of old-established Israelis have found employment and only some of them actually live there. For instance, of the sixty teachers employed in Galilah's schools, ten live locally. The others either commute daily or were sent to the town to serve an obligatory period as teachers, either as soldiers or as civilians, and leave at weekends and during vacations.

Against this background, Galilah's present condition can be understood. The town is inhabited mainly by people who have no better economic chances elsewhere, or are unable to leave the town for lack of resources and who do not possess the capital and skills to develop the local economy unaided. They depend largely on material resources provided by governmental and other public organizations. The two most important sources of income available to the inhabitants are relief work and welfare assistance.

Relief work is supplied by the Ministry of Labour, or by the Jewish National Fund (KKL)[4] acting as its agent. The work is allocated mostly to men responsible for households, and only when there are no able-bodied males in the house will a woman be employed. In 1966 there were 342 persons employed on relief work, of whom 287 were men and 55 women. Relief work is often productive and useful, in spite of its welfare connotation. Most of the men are employed in road construction, land reclamation and afforestation, and women usually in afforestation. Physically handicapped men are employed as part-time relief workers, on light menial tasks such as road-sweeping. Land reclamation is physically very demanding work, and some of it semi-skilled. Basic pay equals that of unskilled farm hands, but some of the harder jobs, such as work on a pneumatic drill or blasting, are paid at a slightly higher rate. Gross pay ranges from IL 11.40 to IL 14.80 (£1.35 to £1.75 approximately) per day. While wages of relief workers are relatively low, they are then comparable with those for ordinary unskilled work. Relief work has some important attractions: it is paid regularly, by a monthly or fortnightly cheque; it is available throughout the year, unlike seasonal farm work; and a person can remain on the job as long as no better one is available. Many of the Galilah men have been on relief work since their arrival in the country seven or eight years ago, and they are confident that the government will provide this type of work as long as required. They feel quite secure in their employment and, in a sense, consider themselves to be employed by the state. Relief work cannot, however, be fully equated with ordinary work because of the manner of its distribution. It is allocated to families according to their requirements. Single men and women were in the past employed between ten to fifteen days monthly, and only family heads were given the full twenty-two days or more. During my field-work period, some of the lighter kinds of relief work were still rationed in this manner. The local Labour Exchange treated relief work as suited only to persons otherwise unemployable; it was considered to be undignified. Only elderly, unskilled heads of large households were thought to be fit for such work, and young men were only reluctantly engaged in it. They came under moral pressure from officials not to degrade themselves by accepting this kind of job. Thus I heard a foreman in charge of relief work remonstrate with a young unmarried worker: "This is no place for someone like you who served in the army. You must help yourself, no one else will. If you cannot find work here, there is nothing left for you but to seek it elsewhere." He felt that the young man had no need to be "supported" by the state. Yet pay in relief work was often as good as, or better than that in local industry. A young carpenter who had been dismissed from his job in a local workshop took to relief work only unwillingly, after several attempts to regain his job had failed. But he admitted that he was now better paid than in the workshop.

Relief work, however exacting and useful, does not give the workers a sense of achievement and satisfaction, for it is categorized as a social welfare benefit handed out by the state. Men thus employed understand that they obtain this work in order to maintain their families on a standard appropriate to their needs. They subscribe to the state's socialist principles, manifested in relief work, welfare assistance and in many other ways. They feel that being new immigrants without resources of their own they have a right to be supported, and do not usually realize that they are providing valuable labour in return.

The income of many relief workers is supplemented by regular welfare assistance. Out of the town's 620 households, 340 are on the lists of the Ministry of Social Welfare, and 240 of these receive regular monthly welfare grants. Some households obtain several types of welfare assistance, and their income from this source may exceed that derived from relief work. There are also some who depend almost entirely on welfare aid. When there is a married adult male in the household, the welfare office considers him to be the provider, and the assistance is given to him. A wife may plead with the welfare officer for aid just as her husband does, but as a rule the monthly welfare cheque is made out in his name. The combined income from these two main source of income, and the additional services supplied gratis, are just enough to give people a decent standard of living, to allow them to meet demands made upon them and to provide in addition a modicum of security. While most of the industries hitherto established in the town have closed down after a short time, relief work and welfare assistance payments have continued regularly over the years. People realize that, in the balance, dependence on the state may be as good as a job in industry and they express this insight in a frequently-quoted equation: Welfare and relief work = Isas-best. Individual economic enterprise is at a disadvantage in these conditions, particularly as it is linked with less social security and loss of welfare benefits.

The inhabitants of Galilah depend on a number of officials in a variety of ways. I have already referred to some of these: the officials who allocate relief work and welfare aid, the main sources of income; the housing official, who is the sole landlord of all the real estate; the Jewish Agency representative, who assists immigrants in their first steps in the new country or helps them to move to another locality if they so desire. These are the officials on whom almost everyone depends. There are some others whose resources are valuable only occasionally or for certain sections of the population: one of them is the local doctor who functions like an official, as all the inhabitants are members of his organization, the Trade Unions' Sick Fund, and entitled to free treatment. People who are absent from work because of illness or convenience require medical certificates if they do not wish to lose their pay. Then there is the bank clerk, who decides whether a man is good for a personal loan. A number of Local Council officials can help, or cause obstructions, in such matters as admitting children to schools and nurseries, hygienic inspections in shops, Local Council contracts, or admission to interviews with the mayor. All these officials are supervised by the mayor, appointed by the Minister of the Interior. While funds for relief work, welfare, housing and education are, in this new and economically non-viable town, allocated by the appropriate government office, the mayor bears the overall responsibility for their use. He is very influential—not because the officials are formally subordinated to him, but rather because he has access to their superiors and can cause them inconvenience. Therefore officials do not lightly reject the mayor's demands even when they have doubts about their justification.

NOTES

1. Kupat Holim (Sick Fund, or Fund for the Ill) is a system of health care that is provided without charge to all members of the Histadrut (i.e., to about 70 percent of the population of Israel). The Kupat Holim operates clinics and hospitals throughout the country. In 1999 Kupat Holim was separated from the Histadrut but has remained the largest healthcare provider in Israel.
2. Citizens of the French colonies in North Africa were French citizens and thereby entitled to emigrate to France.
3. The Amidar Housing Corporation is the Israeli national immigrant housing company owned by the state (75 percent of all shares) and the Jewish Agency (25 percent). In recent years Amidar's construction activities have been transferred to other companies. It is the proprietor and administrator of public housing.
4. Keren Kayemet LeIsrael (KKL, Jewish National Fund) was established in 1901 by the World Zionist Organization to purchase land in Palestine for Jewish settlement. Today its activities have shifted to land reclamation and afforestation.

45

David Ben-Gurion

Social and Ethnic Tensions in Wadi Salib

1959: Memoir

Wadi Salib, a poor neighborhood in the "lower town" of Haifa, was deserted by its Arab inhabitants in 1948–49 and subsequently settled by impoverished immigrants from North Africa. In July 1959 an outburst of violence

Source: David Ben-Gurion, *Israel: A Personal History* (New York and Tel Aviv: Funk and Wagnalls, Inc., and Sabra Books, 1971), pp. 561–63. Copyright © 1971 by the American Israel Publishing Co. Ltd. Reprinted by permission of HarperCollins Publishers Inc.

in Wadi Salib shocked the Israeli public and alerted it to the explosive potential created by the overlapping of poverty and feelings of communal and ethnic discrimination. The following account is from David Ben-Gurion's memoirs.

About a month after the last recess of the Third Knesset, a sad occurrence in Haifa agitated the entire country. On Friday, July 12, 1959 the Minister of Police Behor Shitrit, told the story in the Knesset:

> On the night of Wednesday, July 8, and on Thursday, July 9, regrettable events took place in Haifa. At 6 p.m. on Wednesday a police sergeant in a patrol car encountered a drunken man obstructing traffic on Shivat Zion Street in Haifa (a quarter with largely Oriental residents). The policeman persuaded him to leave the street and left him in the hands of local residents who promised to take him home.
>
> A short time later a patrol car came to one of the cafés on that street. The owner of the café stated he had had trouble with a drunk who had caused damage, seized a panful of hot coals, injured one of the customers, and run away. The policeman later found the drunk imbibing alcoholic beverages in one of the nearby cafés. Two policemen asked him to accompany them to the sergeant in the car. He did so but when requested to get into the car refused, ran back into the café, and began throwing bottles at the policemen. At this point policemen fired four or five shots from two revolvers, under circumstances that are now being investigated.
>
> The subject of the complaint, a resident of the Wadi Salib Quarter, was injured by one of the shots and was immediately taken to the hospital by the police. The disturbance and the shooting led to a gathering of local inhabitants. When a car of the Criminal Investigation Department arrived, it and the men in it were attacked by the crowd. A policeman who happened on the scene and saw the policemen in trouble fired one pistol shot in an attempt to rescue them. A local resident who lived on the top floor also fired a pistol, for which he had a permit. Additional police reinforcements arrived, including a Subdivision Commander who expressed his regret at the occurrence, announced that an investigation would be held, and asked the inhabitants to calm down, and they complied.
>
> The next morning there was a procession of some two hundred people carrying black flags and the national flag smeared with blood. The procession reached the area in front of police headquarters and a delegation on its behalf was received by the Subdivision Commander. The Commander expressed his regret at the incident and denied all rumors to the effect that the injured man had died. He provided information regarding his condition and the delegation appeared to calm down. The crowd finally dispersed.
>
> After this demonstration, a number of incidents of hit-and-run vandalism were perpetrated by small groups of inhabitants of the Quarter. In these disturbances a number of shops and cafés in the lower city and in the Quarter itself were damaged and a number of private automobiles were overturned and set on fire. The Mapai club and the Labor Council club in the Quarter were destroyed. In several of these disturbances the participants included young people, children, and even women. The police, quickly arriving on the scene, were stoned. They did their best to soothe tempers and

were successful in many cases, while in others they were compelled to use force to disperse the crowd and had to make arrests.

Around 6 o'clock a serious outbreak occurred when a small group of youngsters from Wadi Salib ran up the steps of the Quarter and through the main streets of Hadar Hakarmel[1] breaking shop and kiosk windows indiscriminately, injuring anyone in their way and overturning automobiles. This outbreak lasted only a very short time and its perpetrators vanished into the narrow streets out of which they had come. At 8 p.m. demonstrators armed with stones again made their way up to Hadar Hakarmel and began throwing them. The police dispersed them by force before they caused any damage.

A total of thirty-two persons, including two women, were arrested. On Friday, July 10, when things had quieted down, all the arrested persons were released. In the course of the disturbances thirteen policemen were injured; two of them required treatment though their condition is not serious. Two civilians were injured and hospitalized.

At its meeting on July 12 the Cabinet heard a report by the Minister of Police and decided to appoint a committee of inquiry headed by a judge. The other members were the Rabbi of Ramlah, Yizhak Abuhazeira and Knesset member Yishar Harari. The assignment of the committee was (1) to determine how and under what circumstances the police acted on Wednesday and Thursday, July 8 and 9; (2) what factors and circumstances led bystanders to take part in the incidents; (3) whether any organization was involved in the riots.

In the debate that followed, the first speaker was Aryeh Ben Eliezer: "This is one of the most serious events since the renewal of our political life, and one of the gravest since the arrival of the exiles in the Homeland in which they hoped to become one nation. We must call for an assuagement of tempers, the imposition of order, and the insurance of justice." He proposed that a parliamentary committee be set up instead of the committee the Government had appointed. Israel Rokah suggested that the existing committee be enlarged by the addition of two Knesset members.

Israel Yeshayahu Sharabi said that for many years we had been worried by the possibility of just such a flareup of communal passions as had occurred in Haifa: "The ingathering of the exiles from all corners of the world had revealed a distressing situation, for though we are one nation in our historic awareness and our Jewish religion, we find ourselves after two thousand years of exile a people that not only has been dispersed among the nations but fragmented by sharp differences of language, food, dress, customs, concepts, ways of thinking, and other things. Nor is this the result of any conscious desire but a curse, perhaps the harshest one that has been imposed upon us by exile."

"The way of life developed in Israel before and especially after the rise of the State," he continued, "has generally been directed not only to upbuilding of the country's desolate areas but to the rehabilitation of its people. In actual fact our achievements in this area have exceeded expectations. From my personal experience of thirty years in this country I know that there is no comparison between the relations among the various communities thirty years ago and today. However, in three areas—economic, social, and educational—progress has not been completely satisfactory. I would request that in speaking and writing about this unfortunate incident, we do not implicate an entire community."

After the debate the Herut proposal for a parliamentary committee was rejected and the Knesset adopted the proposal by Hanan Rubin and Akiva Govrin which said: "After hearing the Government's statement, the Knesset refers the matter to the Knesset Interior committee."[2]

NOTES

1. Hadar Hakarmel is a major commercial center in Haifa with shops that cater to middle-income groups.

2. After these events the government officially recognized the problem of the "social gap" and instituted a few programs aimed at alleviating it. In particular, efforts were made to increase the number of Israelis of North African and Asian descent in the higher grades of the educational system. For the next decade and a half, however, there was virtually no social mobility among this group. Protest movements such as the Black Panthers (see doc. 64) were one consequence of this failure of social policy.

46

David Ben-Gurion

The Capture of Adolf Eichmann

May 24 and August 8, 1960

In May 1960, Adolf Eichmann (1906–1962), head of the Gestapo section that dealt with Jewish affairs in Nazi Germany and the deportation of Jews to death camps, was abducted by Israeli security agents from Argentina, where he had been hiding since 1950. The abduction created diplomatic tensions between Israel and Argentina, which claimed that its sovereignty and Eichmann's rights had been violated. The Israel Supreme Court ruled that Eichmann could be tried in Israel. He was charged with "crimes against the Jewish people and humanity," a charge punishable under Israeli law. The trial took place before the Jerusalem District court, April–December 1961. Eichmann was found guilty, and in May 1962 he was hanged in an Israeli prison.

During the trial the grim facts of the Nazi Holocaust were presented throughout the world by the news media, and the historical and moral issues they engendered were raised. Within Israel a generation that had experienced the Holocaust used the trial and the events surrounding it to educate their children and their non-European co-citizens about the centrality of this experience, and European antisemitism in general, to their collective historical memory. Because of the importance of the Holocaust to Jewish national identity, the Eichmann trial evoked strong emotions among most of Israel's Jewish population as it simultaneously reinforced one aspect of this national identity.

This reading includes, first, David Ben-Gurion's announcement in the Knesset of Eichmann's capture. With these few words Ben-Gurion set in motion a trial that would remain at the center of Israeli public life and debate for two years. Illustrating the kind of controversy the trial aroused is the second section of this reading, Ben-Gurion's reply to an article by Nahum Goldmann (1895–1982), head of the World Jewish Congress, arguing that Eichmann ought to be tried by an international tribunal instead of an Israeli court.

Source: "Eichmann Found by Security Services; To Be Tried Here for Crimes against Jews," *Jerusalem Post,* May 24, 1960, p. 1. Reprinted by permission. David Ben-Gurion, *Israel: A Personal History* (New York and Tel Aviv: Funk and Wagnalls, Inc., and Sabra Books, 1971), p. 575. Copyright © 1971 by the American Israel Publishing Co. Ltd. Reprinted by permission of HarperCollins Publishers Inc.

Announcement in the Knesset

I have to inform the Knesset that a short time ago one of the greatest of the Nazi war criminals, Adolf Eichmann, who was responsible, together with the Nazi leaders, for what they called "the final solution of the Jewish question," that is, the extermination of six million of the Jews of Europe, was found by the Israel Security Services.

Adolf Eichmann is already under arrest in Israel, and will shortly be placed on trial in Israel under the terms of the Law for the Punishment of Nazis and Nazi Collaborators, 5710–1950.

Reply to Nahum Goldmann

American journalists, who have not suffered from the Nazi atrocities, may be "objective" and deny Israel's right to try one of the greatest Nazi murderers. But the calamity inflicted on the Jewish people is not merely one part of the atrocities the Nazis committed against the world. It is a specific and unparalleled act, an act designed for the complete extermination of the Jewish people, which Hitler and his collaborators did not dare commit against any other people. It is therefore the duty of the State of Israel, the only sovereign authority in Jewry, to see that the whole of this story, in all its horror, is fully exposed—without in any way ignoring the Nazi regime's other crimes against humanity, but as a unique crime without precedent or parallel in the annals of mankind.

It is perhaps the first such episode of historic justice in history when a small nation, beset by many foes, is able on its sovereign territory to try one of its chief enemies for atrocities against hundreds of thousands of its sons and daughters. It is not the penalty to be inflicted on the criminal that is the main thing—no penalty can match the magnitude of the offense—but the full exposure of the Nazi regime's infamous crimes against our people. Eichmann's acts alone are not the main point in this trial. Historic justice and the honor of the Jewish people demand this trial. Historic justice and the honor of the Jewish people demand that this should be done only by an Israeli court in the sovereign Jewish State.

47

J. L. Talmon

The Lavon Affair

1961: Analysis

*In the early 1960s the Lavon Affair (*Haparashah, *Affair) became a central issue in Israeli politics. The affair involved David Ben-Gurion's drive to depose Pinhas Lavon, secretary general of the Histadrut, for his alleged role in the 1954 Mishap in Egypt (see doc. 33). Immediately after the Mishap, Prime Minister Moshe Sharett appointed Isaac Olshan, president of the Supreme Court, and Yaakov Dori (Dostrovsky) (1899–1973), president of the Technion, to investigate what happened and who was responsible. Besides holding responsible and respected positions at the time, both had backgrounds in the military and in Mapai. Olshan's military career*

Source: J. L. Talmon, "The Lavon Affair: Israeli Democracy at the Crossroads," *New Outlook* 4, no. 5 (1961): 23–30.

began during World War I when he was a member of the Jewish Legion attached to the British army. He was active in the Whitechapel branch of Poalei Zion while in England as a student and served as liaison officer between Labor leaders in Palestine and the British Labour Party. He was also a former commander of the Tel Aviv district of the Haganah. Dori was commander of the Haifa District of the Haganah, 1931–39, and then the Haganah's first chief of staff, 1939–45, 1947–48. He was chief of staff of the Israel Defense Forces through the War of Independence.

The Olshan-Dori Committee report, submitted December 12, 1955, did not present clear-cut answers. The government approved the report, with Ben-Gurion's partisans (i.e., Ben-Gurion, Abba Eban, Giora Josephtal, and Behor Shitrit) abstaining. The issue remained dormant, but not dead, until suddenly in a 1959 trial in camera *of an army officer convicted of disclosing secret information to enemy agents (unrelated to the Mishap), the court stated, in passing, that the accused had been persuaded by the officer in charge of Unit 131 to perjure himself before the Olshan-Dori Committee. This statement renewed the debate. Lavon demanded that his name be cleared once and for all. When Ben-Gurion refused to do so, the debate was continued within the party and in Knesset committees. Eventually the Committee of Seven, chaired by Pinhas Rosen, minister of justice, was formed to look into the matter once again. This committee reported that Lavon did not give the order that resulted in the Mishap. Although this report was endorsed by the government and the Knesset, Ben-Gurion rejected it and attacked the committee members. The controversy moved once again to the inner circles of Mapai. Finally, on February 4, 1961, Minister of Finance Levi Eshkol, apparently acting under pressure from Ben-Gurion, introduced a motion in the Mapai Central Committee that Lavon be removed from leadership of the Histadrut. The motion was approved by a vote of 159 to 76. But Ben-Gurion continued to demand another inquiry into the Mishap, thus widening the rift that the affair had caused in Mapai. In 1964, supporters of Lavon formed the Min Hayesod (Back to Basics) faction in Mapai, and in 1965 Ben-Gurion and many of his supporters, including Moshe Dayan and Shimon Peres, left Mapai to form a new party, Rafi.*

Jacob Leib Talmon (1916–80), one of Israel's foremost historians, joined other intellectuals in challenging the moral basis of Ben-Gurion's conduct. He published the following article in New Outlook, *an English-language journal reflecting Socialist Zionist viewpoints that used to be edited by some of Israel's most prominent left-oriented intellectuals.*

Is the tempest over the Lavon Affair—the greatest public scandal since the founding of the State—only the result of the Lavon Affair itself, or is it rather an explosion of pent-up forces, an accumulation of festering frustrations?

Mr. Lavon had every right to try to clear his name, nor can there be any complaint because he was not more moderate or deliberate in his attempts. He was certainly straining things when he attacked what he called the arrangements in the Defence Ministry and in the defence forces as responsible for his dismissal from the post of Minister of Defence. Anyone is justified in objecting to bad management. But by mingling personal with public factors, Lavon became guilty, in the opinion of many, of rationalizing a private grievance. He lost some of the support naturally his as a man wronged, and also raised doubt as to the justice of his fundamental arguments altogether.

Furthermore, if army officers and officials of his own ministry really did conspire against him, one is tempted to conclude that a minister whose subordinates act thus lacks the authority necessary to inspire respect and discipline, like an incompetent schoolmaster whose students misbehave during class. There was considerable naivete in his complaint that the Director of his Ministry—when he was summoned to do so by the committee appointed by the Prime Minister of that time—testified "behind his back." It is naive to expect that in the Ministries or in human relations in general, people will behave like robots without impulses of their own, or to be shocked at acts of intrigue, maneuver or competition.

Certainly it is a sacred principle that the army should always be subservient to the civil authority. In England the situation from this point of view is almost ideal, but nevertheless, in 1940, British generals delivered an ultimatum to Neville Chamberlain, then Prime Minister, that he either fire Hore-Belisha, the Minister of War, or accept their own resignations. Theoretically, the Prime Minister should have chased them out of his office, but he did not. Instead, to the surprise of the whole world, he dismissed Leslie Hore-Belisha, and this put an end to the ministerial career of the brilliant man whom many considered a new Disraeli.

Lavon's position as Minister of Defence was difficult and uncomfortable. His predecessor had been the idol of the army, acclaimed as the architect of the forces and victor in the War of Independence. Lavon's past, on the other hand, was not only civilian but also pacifist. Nor was he blessed with the quality of supreme leadership which inspires loyalty, enthusiasm, and the willingness to obey which is the portion of Mr. Ben-Gurion. It is no wonder that in those difficult circumstances Lavon failed to develop the needed self-confidence: his work showed nervousness and instability.

In the course of his efforts to clear his name, Lavon often fell short of good taste, and he was tactless toward both foe and friend. However, when Mr. Ben-Gurion started his counterattack, he went immeasurably further than Lavon. Lavon represented nothing but himself—not even the Histadrut. Whereas the Prime Minister stood for the State, its policies and self-respect.

Pinhas Lavon can hardly be classed among the saints, but the minute he was brought up before the forum of Mapai, to account for his behavior in the "Affair" (while Mr. Ben-Gurion was not required to give any accounting) he became a symbol of the struggle for justice, decency and liberal ideals. It is the way of History, with her fondness for Mephistophelian irony, to choose as symbols of higher values men who are not exactly charming. [Alfred] Dreyfus[1] was hardly an enchanting personality, not even likeable. In eighteenth-century England, John Wilkes,[2] according to all opinion an evil man, became for many years the symbol of justice. His affair was the touchstone of the struggle against strong government, and the democratic uprising against the dictates of those in power and the selfishness of the oligarchy ruling Parliament.

What happened to Mr. Ben-Gurion, who at first declared that he was not a party to the affair, since he had neither charged Lavon nor was the one to acquit him? He suddenly attacked and did not desist until he had achieved Lavon's immediate dismissal from his job as Secretary of the Histadrut under pressure of the ultimatum "either he or I," and not because of anything that Lavon had done or not done in this post.

It is said that Ben-Gurion as Minister of Defence had refused in 1955 or 1956 to promote the "High Ranking Officer" [Benyamin Givli], who had meanwhile been transferred to another post, on the ground that a trace of suspicion clung to him. But in 1960, Ben-Gurion identified this officer completely with the status and honor of the Israel Defence Forces, and thus began a series of events and circumstances without solution. The worst thing of all is the deterioration or degeneration of the best. The Prime Minister deserves admiration for his deep feeling of responsibility for the good name of the Army. However, it is very dangerous when someone in these circumstances develops a the-army-and-I-are-the-same, or I-am-Defence complex such as King Louis XIV's "L'Etat, c'est moi." A thin line divides a deep sense of responsibility from self-glorification, a feeling of mission from the arrogance of the tyrant. Who can say where deep loyalty ends and idol worship begins? Where is the boundary between fiery devotion and the Machiavellian theory that the end justifies the means? These are things which cannot be measured, nor can subjective "feeling" help much. Personal sincerity is no guide either, but rather, and here we are talking about statesmen, the way things look in the eyes of the people.

In Mr. Ben-Gurion's letter of resignation, as in the arguments of his partisans, there is heard only one objection on matters of principle: the matter of the judiciary committee, which—so we have been told with much emphasis—is a matter of conscience for Ben-Gurion. Justice must be done to the High Ranking Officer through the courts, for the Committee of Ministers confounded authorities (executive and judicial) and produced a verdict without resort to judicial procedure. Lavon's deposition from his post as secretary of the Histadrut, on the other hand, is attributed to "new circumstances." Thus at this stage the problem came up for political decision according to the rules of power politics and not as a moral question, or a matter of principle or ideology.

One of the most astonishing things in the whole affair is the behavior of the High Ranking Officer, in opposition to all the rules of chivalry. What kept this officer from dropping his cloak of anonymity and publishing a letter to Mr. Pinhas Lavon in something like this fashion: My name is thus-and-so. You have libeled me and made me one of the central figures in a national and even international crisis. This you have done as a member of the Knesset before a body (the Committee for Security and Foreign Affairs) which guarantees you immunity. I hereby challenge you to repeat those same accusations in circumstances which will permit me to take legal action against you.—If a man is quite sure of the justice of his case, and if the matter is not simply a private affair but one that has set fire to the whole country, then he has no reason to take shelter, like any common criminal, in procedural technicalities. Why does he hide behind a statute of limitations which would be exceedingly difficult to change ex post facto without doing violence to the due process of law?

There was no possibility of holding the government together after the words that passed between the Prime Minister and the Committee of Seven, or rather, the members of the Cabinet who by a large majority endorsed the findings of that Committee. The question here is not whether the Committee was right in its findings or its methods of work, for who can say whether we shall ever know the whole truth? It seems that there will always be things unrevealed about how Lavon tried to come to an agreement with the High Ranking Officer on a joint version of the "sorry business." How could the Prime Minister invite Lavon to head a public committee for national security on the eve of the Sinai Campaign when he already knew about the "capriciousness" of his former Minister of Defence during his time in office?

NOTES

1. Alfred Dreyfus (1853–1935), a Jewish captain in the French army, was convicted and jailed for an act of treason he did not commit. When it was revealed to the French public that he was convicted solely because, as a Jew, blame could be easily placed upon him, one of France's major political scandals erupted; it is still referred to in France as "the Affair." While covering Dreyfus's trial, Theodor Herzl became aware of the nature and severity of European antisemitism.

2. John Wilkes (1727–1797) was a popular hero in England who continued to publish criticisms of the king and government even after he was jailed for this offense. The cry of "Wilkes and Liberty" was a popular slogan among eighteenth-century English advocates of freedom of the press and representative government.

48

Israel Supreme Court

Jewish Religion and Israeli Nationality: The Brother Daniel Case

March 14, November 19, December 6, 1962

Persistent religious controversies within Israel have given rise to legal and political problems for the state (see docs. 27–29). In what became known as the Brother Daniel Case, a convert to Christianity applied for Israeli citizenship under the provisions of the Law of Return (doc. 29), and the courts were forced to deal with the problem of defining "who is a Jew." The Supreme Court ruling, excerpted here, was a landmark decision that still stands. It has not, however, ended the controversy. Factions of the religious parties have frequently demanded a Knesset law giving the religious courts sole jurisdiction over defining "who is a Jew" as a condition for their participation in a government coalition. To date these factions have been unsuccessful. Moreover, non-Orthodox religious movements have attempted to pass resolutions in Zionist Congresses and elsewhere, calling on the Israeli government to recognize marriages and conversions performed by their rabbis, thus, in effect, giving them some authority over defining "who is a Jew."

The applicant was born in Poland, in 1922, to Jewish parents and received a Jewish upbringing. In his youth he was active in a Zionist youth movement, spending two years, approximately, in a pioneer training farm in preparation for his immigration to Palestine. With the outbreak of war between Germany and Russia, in June 1941, he was imprisoned by the Gestapo, but fled. After managing to acquire a certificate stating that he was a German Christian, he became secretary and translator for the German police station in Mir, the district capital. While in Mir, he used to notify the Jews of German plans for anti-Jewish actions. When he discovered the German intention of destroying the Mir ghetto, he informed the Jews of the city and the surrounding area and provided them with weapons. On the basis of his information, many fled from the ghetto and joined the partisans; most of the survivors now live in Israel. He was denounced, interrogated by the police and jailed, but once again he fled. For a long time he hid in a convent and, at the first opportunity, joined the ranks of the Russian partisans. The Russians suspected him of being a German spy and sentenced him to death, but he was saved thanks to evidence given in his favor by a Jewish survivor of Mir; in the end he received a Russian medal of honor for his partisan activity. In 1942, during his stay in the convent, he converted to Christianity; in 1945 he became a priest, entering the Carmelite order because it would give him the opportunity to join the Carmelite monastery in Israel. During our War of Independence, and many times after, he requested permission from his superiors to immigrate to Israel; his request was granted only in 1958. In all his appeals to the Polish authorities

---

Source: Supreme Court Decision 72/62, *Osvald Rufeisen v. Minister of the Interior* (1962) 15 P.D. 2428.

he emphasized that, despite his conversion to Christianity, he had never stopped thinking of himself as a nationalist Jew, tied heart and soul to the Jewish people. The travel certificate issued to him by the authorities was of the kind issued only to Jews immigrating to Israel and leaving Poland forever; as far as his native country was concerned, he came to Israel as a Jew. His request for an immigrant's certificate and to be registered as a Jew on his identity card was refused by the minister of the interior on the basis of a government decision from July 20, 1958, which determines that only a person who declares in good faith that he is a Jew, and has no other religion, will be registered as a Jew.

The applicant's claims were (1) that the concept "nationality" is not identical with the concept "religion" and that a Jew by nationality need not be a Jew by religion; (2) that according to Jewish religious law [halakhah] he is a Jew because he is the son of Jewish parents; (3) that the decision of the government from July 20, 1958, which served as the basis for the minister of the interior's refusal, has no legal basis and is therefore not binding; (4) that the minister of the interior's refusal to grant him rights is arbitrary, that it is based on considerations outside the legal framework, that it is an affront to the law and to the rights of the applicant, and that it constitutes an act of discrimination against him. On the basis of the above claims, the minister of the interior was served with an *order nisi* to come and explain his reasons for not granting the applicant an immigrant's certificate in accordance with paragraph 3(a) of the Law of Return (1950), and an identity card in accordance with paragraph 7 of the Registration of Inhabitants Ordinance (1949), in which it would be registered in the column "Nationality" that the applicant is Jewish.

The question facing the court in simple legal terms is, What is the meaning of the term "Jew" in the Law of Return (1950), and does it also include Jews who have left Judaism and been baptized as Christians, but consider and feel themselves to be Jews in spite of their conversion?

The Supreme Court, nullifying the *order nisi* by a majority decision, ruled:

1. The dominant opinion in Jewish law is that an apostate is a Jew in all regards, with (perhaps) the exception of some peripheral laws that have no essential importance with regard to the question of principle; the laws of Judaism are not merely the laws of Judaism but they are laws that obligate Jews, and if the halakhah applies them to the apostate, then he also is a Jew.

2. (a) The opinion is unacceptable that even according to the religious ruling the apostate is not a total Jew but only a "partial Jew," a half, a third; the evidence for this opinion: he is not considered a Jew in matters of inheritance, interest (usury), and participation in a quorum [minyan] of ten males required for a communal prayer. (b) First, the opinion is unacceptable on principle. Judaism is a status, and status is indivisible; we have found such an arithmetical division only in the case of a slave who has two masters; the Jewish religion, like every other religion, is total in its essence, comprehensive, exclusive. The Israelite character of the apostate, which finds clear legal expression in laws of marriage, divorce, and levirate marriage, is a status that does not allow for any split or relativity. (c) Second, the opinion is also unacceptable by its very nature. It is absurd to think that an apostate, who believes in another deity, could participate in a religious quorum in which the rest of the members are praying to the God of Israel. (d) Then again, there is a real doubt as to whether one may lend money with interest to an apostate. The question of inheritance is also a matter of dispute among the authorities; in opposition to Rabbi Hai Gaon's opinion, there are other authorities who think that according to the Biblical law [the Torah] an apostate inherits his father, but the court or the elders have the authority to fine him so that he does not inherit. Even if we follow those who ruled that an apostate may be lent money with interest and that he does not inherit his father,

these rules in themselves do not turn him into a "non-Jew" in matters of interest and inheritance; if that were the case, his "Gentileness" would work both ways: the very split—i.e., borrower as opposed to lender, inheritor as opposed to testator—is a clear indication that the question is not one of detraction from the Jewishness of the apostate but of whether to deal strictly or leniently, for various reasons that are based not on the status *Rem* but on the possession of that status *in Personam*.

3. (a) Clearly the term "Jew" as used in the Law of Return (1950) does not have the same meaning it does in the Rabbinical Courts Jurisdiction (Marriage and Divorce) Law (1953). The latter is religious in meaning, as prescribed by the laws of Judaism; the former is secular in meaning, in accordance with its ordinary meaning when used in popular language and by Jews. (b) The logic of the matter is that the Rabbinical Courts Jurisdiction Law is meant to increase the authority of the rabbis, and it is common knowledge that this authority was requested and granted in order to broaden the application of Jewish religious law to Jews. (c) It follows that the question of "who is a Jew" must also be solved on the basis of Jewish law, for if any other criterion—external, secular, non-halakhic—becomes the determining factor, then Jewish laws will not be applicable.

4. (a) This is not so in the Law of Return. It is a secular law, the terms of which, having no definition in either law or verdict, we must interpret according to their popular meaning, taking into consideration, so as to avoid stereotyping, the legislative aim that led to the legislator's directive. (b) The Law of Return being an original Israeli law, and not an adapted law, it would seem that the term "Jew" should be interpreted as we, the Jews, understand the content and the essence of the term "Jew." (c) In the light of the popular, Jewish meaning of the term "Jew," a Jew who has converted to Christianity is not called a Jew. (d) For this reason the applicant, despite his many positive qualities and the sincere love of the Jews that he has proved, does not have the right to call himself by the name "Jew."

5. (a) Israel is not a theocratic state, because it is not religion that orders the lives of its citizens but the law. And this present case is evidence of that fact; had we applied the religious categories of Jewish law to the applicant, then he would actually be considered a "Jew." (b) The basic attitude, that "Jew" and "Christian" are two mutually exclusive titles, is shared by all, whether it be the mass of the people or the scholars; none of these can consider an apostate as a member of the Jewish nation.

6. (a) The applicant, Brother Daniel, is not a member of the Jewish nation, nor is he a member of the Polish nation, since he relinquished that right before leaving Poland. He is a nationless person and will be so registered in his identity card. (b) The space above which is written the item "Nationality," according to paragraph 4 (a) of the Registration of Inhabitants Ordinance, will remain blank and unfilled. And there is no anomaly in this, because not every applicant for an identity card can fill in all of the items in it, for instance, an atheist.

49

Teddy Kollek

The Transition from David Ben-Gurion to Levi Eshkol

June 1963: Memoir

The Israeli political system and its constituent parties underwent considerable changes during the late 1950s and the first half of the 1960s. One major development was David Ben-Gurion's political decline. Aspects of this process—the antagonism between Ben-Gurion and his chosen successor Levi Eshkol, the conflict between "veterans" and "youngsters" within Mapai, Ben-Gurion's insistence on a thorough investigation of the 1954 Mishap (see docs. 33, 47)—are described in Teddy Kollek's autobiography and in the excerpts that follow.

Teddy Kollek was the mayor of Jerusalem, 1965–93. As director general of the Office of the Prime Minister, he was particularly well placed to observe the transition from Ben-Gurion to Eshkol.

On June 15, 1963, the Saturday night before Ben-Gurion resigned, I brought Golda [Meir] to Ben-Gurion's home. The conversation was about the German scientists in Egypt and other aspects of our relationship with Germany. I didn't think that Ben-Gurion would make the decision to resign that night, but I saw his despair at not being able to convince Golda about that matter. The conflict over the subject was probably so sharp because there was already a rift anyway, not because this particular problem was insurmountable. Their conversation didn't end with an explosion. It was more like an estrangement, an abyss in their thinking. Ben-Gurion did not accept the appraisal he was given on the matter. He didn't think the situation was dangerous, and he didn't believe the scientists—if, indeed, there were any—were working with the backing and approval of the German government. Ben-Gurion had met with Carlo Schmidt, the chairman of the German parliament and a key figure in the Social Democratic Party, who had always been a friend. When he came to Jerusalem bearing a message from [Konrad] Adenauer and swore there was no truth in the accusations, Ben-Gurion knew he could believe him. But a whole campaign had been organized by Ben-Gurion's adversaries through the Press Office. It included sending reporters all over the world to speak out against Germany and the scientists, and that made Ben-Gurion furious.

The morning following that meeting with Golda, Uri Lubrani (who had temporarily replaced Yizhak Navon) came into my office very alarmed and said Ben-Gurion was about to gather the party leadership and announce his resignation. I was dumbfounded. Of course, I know Ben-Gurion was unhappy, but I hadn't thought he was actually planning to leave. During the day I tried to persuade him to reconsider—as did many others—but to no avail. He would not be moved from his decision.

Source: Theodore Kollek, *For Jerusalem: A Life*, with Amos Kollek (London: Weidenfeld and Nicolson, 1978), pp. 152–61, copyright © 1978 by Teddy Kollek. Used by permission of Random House, Inc.

Perhaps a great many people in Israel and all over the world, common citizens and statesmen alike, were relieved that the stubborn old man was leaving and now there would be an easier regime. They may have hoped that some badly needed young blood would be injected into Israeli politics. But being well acquainted with Eshkol and the group surrounding him, I knew this would not happen. Israel was losing a great leader, and there was no one to take his place. The next generation of leadership—Eshkol, Pinhas Sapir, Zalman Aranne—none of them "young blood," had no real understanding of what statehood was about. They still acted as though they were living in an enlarged shtetl[1] and dwelled on the old concepts they had brought with them from Eastern Europe. Perhaps if Ben-Gurion had stayed on for a few more years, the third generation—Dayan, Peres, and their contemporaries—politically more sophisticated men—would have taken over. But by the time that generation finally did take over, things had already become much worse.

I don't know to what extent the people in Israel realize even today that the battle Ben-Gurion fought over the Lavon Affair was for a principle no democracy can exist without. With all the attention focused on corruption now, I doubt that if a similar incident occurred it would be treated any differently. I am afraid that most of the people in the country have not yet grasped the importance of Ben-Gurion's stand. Basically, it is the same principle that I invoked in my long battle against what I call "Sapirism."...

Sapir had been director-general of the treasury, then minister of trade and industry, and later minister of finance and the Labor Party secretary, the two jobs which made him a tremendously powerful political figure. His last appointment was as chairman of the Jewish Agency. He was a big, tall, bald-headed man who looked a lot like Kojak.[2] I, on the whole, rather liked him. Furthermore, it is quite rightly said that there was practically no development town, no development scheme, no industry, and no institution of learning that Sapir had not been involved in and had not helped. No man got up earlier and worked harder or with more consistency and more devotion. He was indefatigable, and economic progress in Israel was his main concern. He was a great fundraiser, and people had confidence in him.

It is very difficult to be critical now, so soon after he died in harness. But without analyzing the influence he had on the country, it will be impossible to understand many things that have happened here and even more difficult to repair them. For a long time even before his death, Sapir had been a controversial figure, and during the last few months of his life much of the disastrous economic situation and low morale was blamed on him. There were accusations against the "Sapir system" and the "Sapir Fund" and many other facets of the economy. My own relationship with Sapir was an ambivalent one. I had the greatest admiration for his work capacity and for his ability to cut through red tape, make quick decisions, and make them stick, so that his officials could not revoke them. But I did not feel this qualified him to set the direction for the workings of Israel's economy. And while Sapir's practical achievements were noteworthy, the legal, orderly, and moral basis of his transactions was regrettably lacking.

I criticized Sapir openly on various occasions, frequently in his presence. (I must say that this did not affect the personal relationship between us, and even when he was most occupied, I had free access to him.) My argument with Sapir was not personal; it was over the "Sapir system." He judged many matters not on their merits but by who had brought the problem before him and how it had been presented. Thus an important matter might be pushed aside because the "wrong" person advocated it; a poor policy may have found favor because it was advocated by someone who was close to Sapir and willing to call on him in his modest home and implant the idea over a glass of tea on a holiday afternoon. It was also a method by which Sapir personally made decisions on an ad hoc basis, and the Ministry of Commerce and Industry and the Ministry of Finance lacked clear guidelines and standards for dealing with big business. Thus industrialists had far more to gain by currying the favor of ministry officials, or of Sapir himself, than by trying to improve their production or cutting down on their labor costs. It was easier to make a profit this way than to work hard and achieve increased sales or lower costs.

This same attitude also led to some give and take in connection with the "Sapir Fund," which must inevitably have led to some abuses—though I was sure that as far as Sapir personally was concerned, it was absolutely aboveboard.

Sapir was linked with some unsavory incidents, although he himself was of the highest personal integrity. There is not a soul, not even among his most violent critics—most of whom have halted their criticism since his death—who believed that he stood to gain personally in these dealings. But that is not the point. The issue was not the man, but the system. And the system is not restricted to the minister himself.

Basically I always believed in approaching people to donate money for a specific educational or civic project. That would allow the donors to see the results of their generosity. Under Sapir, however, government officials dealt with people who were investing and building in Israel, so that the very same people were offering gifts and applying for certain concessions. When you combined donations and the Sapir method of conducting business, disaster was inevitable. It was impossible to establish priorities when the methods befitted the small-town leader who knew everybody's problem and could conduct business out of his waistcoat pocket. A minister of finance, even in a small country like Israel, must be a statesman.

As to Jerusalem, Sapir supported many of its institutions but not the city itself. Whenever I claimed that Jerusalem was not getting its share, he showed me long lists of industrial and educational institutions that had been showered with funds. He had no understanding of the fact that when you invest hundreds of millions of pounds in a university, for example, you also have to invest an appropriate amount at least in building the roads leading to it. The same surely is true about the new suburbs going up around the city and a parallel strengthening of the central city. We have not yet entirely overcome this negative tradition. It was very difficult to fight Sapir, and it is astonishing that we did make progress in getting some governmental support, in spite of his attitude.

Perhaps the gravest danger of all, however, was not to recognize immediately after the Yom Kippur War that the time had come to bring home to the people the need to lower sharply our standard of living. Sapir saw the solution in going out and collecting more donations from the Jews all over the world, rather than in changing policy at home. I am perfectly convinced that in a few years' time nobody will be able to understand how we survived for years and years under Sapir's shortsighted economic dictatorship.

It was principles of this kind that played a major role in the Lavon Affair, the battle Ben-Gurion undertook and lost. When he resigned in June 1963, Levi Eshkol was Ben-Gurion's choice to succeed him, and naturally Ben-Gurion's friends wanted him to be successful. I had known Eshkol a long time and had worked closely with him while he was minister of finance. I usually called on him on Saturday mornings to discuss the affairs of the week and bring about some coordination between Ben-Gurion and his chief lieutenant in the Cabinet. We had many talks during the Lavon Affair. He felt that Ben-Gurion was exaggerating its importance but supported him because of a sense of loyalty that came naturally. He knew it would be tough for anyone to follow Ben-Gurion, and those of us inside the Prime Minister's Office tried hard to adjust to Eshkol and help him. Yizhak Navon, Ben-Gurion's personal secretary, had gone to Latin America on a mission when Ben-Gurion resigned. Uri Lubrani, who had been working on Arab affairs in the Prime Minister's Office, had temporarily replaced Navon and continued to act as Eshkol's private secretary during his first few weeks in office. But soon it become clear that Eshkol had to have people of his own choice.

Eshkol brought in some people recommended by Yaakov Arnon, the director-general of the Finance Ministry, and I remained with my vague and many-sided role as director-general of the Prime Minister's Office. But the whole style of things was completely different. As the months went by, Eshkol began to take a much greater interest in the details pouring into the Prime Minister's Office than Ben-Gurion ever had. His interest went beyond deciding on policy or principle; he intervened in the smallest decisions. Moreover, you might arrive at a decision with him and the next morning, having talked to someone else, he had changed his mind. Sometimes he even forgot to tell you so. Still, it was impossible to dislike Eshkol, and we remained on good personal terms for the rest of his life.

After he became prime minister, Eshkol remarried (he had been a widower). There were quite a few candidates, but Miriam [Zelikovitz] was the lucky one. It was a sudden marriage ceremony squeezed into an overburdened schedule, as Eshkol had become a very busy man. A rabbi was provided for the wedding on a few hours' notice. I remember that at the last moment Eshkol said jokingly, "Maybe we should postpone it?" He always hated making crucial decisions. "You'll have to decide one day," we said almost in unison. Finally, at eleven o'clock, it was decided to hold the wedding at noon. I rushed home, Tamar grabbed half a cake and a bottle of champagne, and we rushed off to what was a very small and pleasant wedding party at Eshkol's home. It became a happy marriage indeed.

Miriam had a strong influence on Eshkol, and I think she directed him on to the wrong course in his rift with Ben-Gurion. She apparently felt that Eshkol should assert himself and be a strong prime minister and that this was the only way he could demonstrate leadership to the country. It may have been a legitimate attitude on her part, but left to his own devices, Eshkol might have found ways to compromise with Ben-Gurion. Such accommodation might have lessened the tensions that eventually led to the split in Mapai, which had a long-term negative influence on Israel's affairs. Even though the party was reunited a few years later, the wound was not entirely healed. Sometimes a little stone on the tracks can derail a large train.

My final break with the Prime Minister's Office resulted mainly from the continuing argument about secret, absolutely personal reports from the head of Intelligence to the prime minister. Eshkol appointed Meir Amit, a former general and deputy chief of staff and an extremely intelligent and capable person, to head the Mossad. I tried to persuade the prime minister to implement the Yadin-Sharef committee's[3] recommendations by appointing a permanent liaison in the Prime Minister's Office. I even wanted him to make this a condition of Amit's appointment. But Amit opposed the idea as not being in the tradition of the service, and Eshkol gave in.

I believed that this situation might one day cause disastrous results, as it had in the past. Although I had no direct connection or responsibility in this sphere, I did not want to remain in the Prime Minister's Office if the loose arrangements of the past were perpetuated. I finally decided to leave. Eshkol made several attempts to persuade me to stay (in general he didn't like upheavals), but I felt that my usefulness had come to an end.

Some time after the changeover from Ben-Gurion to Eshkol, I had a long conversation with Isaiah Berlin on the difference between the two regimes. Isaiah tried to explain to me that it was time to bring the "heroic period" to a close. We could not go on demanding heroism from the people all the time, as Ben-Gurion did. The country should be able to relax a little, and whatever our personal feelings were, we should be happy that a shift toward relaxation had taken place. I tried to convince him that our roots were in many ways still very shallow, and another four years with Ben-Gurion as prime minister would have been tremendously advantageous. Now, many years later, I still believe that.

NOTES

1. A *shtetl* (Yiddish, small town) was a small, predominantly Jewish town; the majority of Eastern European Jews lived in these towns.
2. Kojak was a shaved-headed hero of an American television program popular in Israel in the 1970s.
3. Yadin-Sharef Committee, consisting of Yigael Yadin and Zeev Sharef, was appointed by Ben-Gurion to investigate lines of command and responsibility in Israel's intelligence services—the Israel Defense Force's Intelligence Branch and the Mossad. The committee's report, recommending that a special adviser to the prime minister be appointed for intelligence affairs, was submitted in mid-1963, after Ben-Gurion had left office, and his successor, Levi Eshkol, did not take action.

50

Yohanan Bader

The Formation of a Center–Right-Wing Bloc

February–May 1965: Memoir

While the conflicts within Mapai contributed to the eventual weakening of the Labor parties, their historic rivals—the center and right-wing parties—were laying the groundwork for the formation of a center–right-wing bloc.

Yohanan Bader (1905–1995) was a leader in the Herut movement and an active member of the Knesset for more than two decades. His memoirs are an indispensable source for the history of the Herut movement as well as Israeli parliamentary and political history in general. In this excerpt, Bader, a close associate of Menahem Begin, describes in detail the negotiations that led to the establishment of Gahal (the Herut-Liberal bloc) in 1965.

What was the matter with the Liberals, that they reacted negatively to [Menahem] Begin's attempt to establish a joint bloc in the Knesset in August 1961, and then in the beginning of 1965 they themselves suggested the establishment of Gahal? One difference must have influenced the change: in the beginning of the Fifth Knesset they wanted to be accepted in the coalition, and in 1965 they awaited the outcome of the elections. But they also had additional reasons. At the time the Liberal Party was established in 1961, the Progressives convinced the General Zionists that it would be necessary to invite some new forces into the partnership, and so they introduced into the list of candidates and into the Knesset list Baruch Uziel as a "new

Source: Yohanan Bader, *Haknesset veani* [The Knesset and I] (Jerusalem: Efdanim, 1979), pp. 170–73.

force," as well as Professor [Yizhak] Hans Klinghoffer and Mrs. Rachel Kagan who, according to their own outlook, were much closer to the Progressives than to the General Zionists. At the head of the list they placed Pinhas Rosen (and not [Perez, or Fritz] Bernstein), and he was elected head of the party after Dr. Nahum Goldmann examined the situation and found that his participation [in the election] would not secure for him the foreign portfolio in the government. Another Progressive was elected as head of the faction: Yizhar Harari. Thus the General Zionists became the secondary partner in the framework of the united party, quite in contrast to their relative strength among the supporters of the partnership.

The Progressives were not so happy either. It was to be expected that some Mapai followers would be in the coalition and candidates for any office that Mapai, for reasons of its own, preferred not to yield to its own members (e.g., Dr. Yeshayahu Foerder as director general of the Bank Leumi LeIsrael).[1] And thus, because of the partnership with the General Zionists, they became a large, oversized faction. In this role they had to demand a high price for the coalition, but for Mapai the partnership of Ahdut Haavodah (eight Knesset members) was enough to assure them a majority in the Knesset. Both of the coalition partners complained about their bitter lot as the second largest opposition faction. They sense in this a constant frustration and debasement. And it is true that in the parliamentary system there really is no position less comfortable than to be a second opposition and to have to rehash in most of the debates the words of the spokesman of the first and large opposition.

And so, after Begin had once again called for the establishment of the Gush [bloc] in the convention of the Herut movement, the Liberals discussed it all over. Harari gave us a speech that was full of contempt. In his opinion the Herut movement was nearing bankruptcy. The public did not like it, on the other hand the chances of the Liberals were excellent. Only Bernstein and [Yosef] Serlin, who had opposed the Ihud [unification] in 1957, expressed their support for the establishment of the Gush.

Begin's proposal came for a vote and was turned down 42 to 8. Avraham Krinitzi, head of the Ramat Gan municipality, and his deputy Shalom Zisman, announced that they would continue to work for a partnership with us. I held lengthy and friendly sessions with Krinitzi, but without results.

After Mapai had decided to establish a common front (Maarakh) with Ahdut Haavoda (in November 1964), Begin turned to the Liberals again, and this time the reaction of the erstwhile General Zionists was positive. Only Simhah Ehrlich was bitterly opposed to a partnership with Begin and with Herut. The leadership of the Liberals decided (20 to 15) on their readiness in principle to ally themselves with us in the forthcoming elections. In this decision I found a confirmation of my suspicions that they were planning to enjoy the partnership with us in the elections but that they would, once the elections were over, prefer a coalition with Mapai. I warned Begin, but he was more optimistic than I. Moshe Kol, Dr. Foerder and even Nahum Goldmann also participated in the internal arguments among the Liberals. All of them opposed the creation of a close tie; the General Zionists, on the other hand, met in the home of an American Zionist to establish the bloc. Actively participating in this meeting were Yosef Sapir, Dr. Elimelech Rimalt, Shalom Zisman, and Aryeh Dulzhin, all of them General Zionists, and also a number of former Progressives. In the meeting they decided to establish a bloc with us, and a joint faction in the coming Knesset. A number of important personalities in the Liberal party, such as the industrialists Dr. Mossberg, Kalir, and also Gershom Schocken (*Haaretz*),[2] tried to salvage the unity of the party, but they did not succeed in convincing Pinhas Rosen to agree on the establishment of a bloc with the Herut movement.

At the end of January 1965, Krinitzi invited the leaders of the Liberals and us to his home.

Of the liberals, there appeared Yosef Sapir, Elimelech Rimalt, Aryeh Dulzhin, and Yosef Tamir; from our side Begin, [Aryeh] Ben-Eliezer, [Yosef] Shufman, [Nahum] Levin, and myself, as well as the secretary of the faction, Yehiel Kadishai. We did not talk about problems of principle or the actual proposal; we knew that we had plenty of material on hand from the old negotiations in 1957–58 and that we would somehow be able to "arrange things." The Liberals proceeded at once to practical questions: they demanded that the list of candidates for the Knesset and the entire relationship between us be on a basis of parity, or fifty-fifty, because in this Knesset the number of seats was equal for each of the two parties. Begin and Ben-Eliezer replied to them: All of you here are only General Zionists, without so much as one Progressive, and we know very well that you find yourselves on the threshold of a split in your party, and according to our information, only a small majority of the members of our faction will go with you, and how can we then agree to parity? They replied with absolute self-confidence—for which they deserve credit—that the General Zionists are the only serious force in their party, and that if the Progressives would split off, they would at most capture two seats in the Knesset. They did not convince us. We had no trouble remembering that at the time they were unified, the General Zionists had eight seats in the Knesset and the Progressives six, and on that basis they created their unified group (Ihud). The Liberals (one or two among those present) responded that the most important thing is to establish the bloc, but at the same time they demanded parity. I saw that we had arrived at a dead end, and I drafted for myself and read the text of a final proposition according to the system used by Mapai, namely point-counterpoint: they demand parity and we could not agree to that for good reasons. We all resolved to start negotiations about the establishment of a joint bloc. This summary was accepted (the slip of paper is still with Kadishai).

The negotiations were conducted at a speedy tempo. Only practical matters were discussed. In the beginning they met in my house: from our side Levin, Shufman, and myself; from their side Rimalt and Zvi Zimmerman. They spoke of parity and hinted at a small change in our favor. We want to know: How many will they be after the split? My associates and they even exchanged assessments about our mutual strength and about the chances in the elections. I notified Begin: There is no real progress.

We actually broke off contact. After a number of days, Aryeh Dulzhin appeared in the Knesset building to talk with me and then to Begin. They agreed among themselves that the negotiations should start again. Begin invited me to a discussion and brought up his own proposal. He agreed to distribute the first ten seats on the list according to parity, one for one—the first seat for us. He thought that six of the seats (21–26) [slot numbers on the party list] belonged entirely to us and that the rest of them should be distributed again on the basis of parity. Likewise we had to demand that if the bloc obtained thirty seats in the coming Knesset, we should get at least one seat on top of the seventeen that would be ours. It was not likely that the group of Liberals going with us, representing hardly more than nine Knesset members, would obtain twelve seats and that we would have only sixteen or seventeen.

I thought he went out of his way to accommodate the Liberals. But he was interested in the establishment of the bloc and optimistic as to its success (although at the same time careful).

We met again in the King David Hotel. From our side: Nahum Levin and myself, from their side Rimalt and Zimmerman. He spoke at length and profusely. We made a little bit of progress. We set up another meeting. Again I consulted with Begin; he was ready for giving up more . . . we met again with Rimalt and Zimmerman—we made progress—but there was still a gap between our positions, one seat this way or that. I reported to Begin by telephone, and he came to the King David Hotel. I explained the situation to him. He agreed to give up more. We finished our work (I with a heavy heart), and we signed the agreement (2/28/65).

After the agreement concerning the composition of the Knesset list was reached, we proceeded to negotiate officially and openly. A meeting between the two delegations was arranged—each consisting of twelve members—and speeches were made. There was great optimism. Two committees were set up. Begin was at the head of our delegation to the Political Committee, which was to prepare the Gahal agreement and the statement of principles. I was at the head of our delegation to the Municipal Committee, whose task was to determine the order of candidates on the list of the Gahal candidates for the municipal elections that would take place on the day of the Knesset elections. The basis was the prevailing situation (in the 1959 elections the Liberal party did not exist). Our members in the municipalities argued, and rightly so, that in a general way our strength as a party had grown and their strength had also risen in different locations (since 1955), but that the strength of the General Zionists had dropped. However there was no possibility of determining a different basis. We also agreed to make some special arrangements. In place of a seat in Jerusalem (where heretofore not one single General Zionist had been elected), we were to get "compensation" in Ramat Gan. On the basis of the "status quo," the Liberals will get the first seat in Tel Aviv. I tried to obtain a change at least with respect to Tel Aviv, but without success.

The negotiations in the municipal committee were difficult and drawn out. Simhah Ehrlich, the head of the Liberal delegation, was quite headstrong, and I had a few members who were quick to suggest compromises. But I saw to it that we would not yield to the Liberals more than necessary.

The agreement for the establishment of Gahal was signed on April 25. On May 25 the Knesset committee confirmed the establishment of the Gahal faction, comprising twenty-seven members, seventeen from the Herut faction, eight General Zionists, and two from the "new force," Uziel and Professor Klinghoffer.

The Progressives set in motion their "protection" channels to Mapai in order that their new faction may carry the designation the "Liberal party." I talked about that with Baruch Azaniah of Mapai, chairman of the Knesset Committee. He finally agreed that on the basis of the rules and regulations this title belongs to the larger splinter group, i.e., to our own Liberals. Contrary to this, I agreed (with the consent of my friends) that the smaller splinter group be called the "Independent Liberals." We also agreed that the letter "L" belongs to our Liberals and that the Independent Liberals would use the letters "LI."[3] This arrangement was part of the arrangement of the change in election laws, and I shall talk about it later.

In the negotiations surrounding the establishment of Gahal I had a task to fulfill as representative of the faction, but I had my doubts as to the conditions about its formation, and in particular about the part of the Liberals on the combined list. Krinitzi and Shalom Zisman, the initiators of the talks, emphasized over and over again that the formation of the Gush was only a first step toward the full unity of both parties. The rest of their members, too, used to speak of their readiness to unite both parties after the elections to the Sixth Knesset. If it had not been for those hopes I would certainly have been opposed to the "key" (the order of the list) according to which we surrendered to the Liberals quite a few Herut seats. In the course of the negotiations, my doubts concerning the chances for a unification increased, and in the Central Committee of the movement I voted against the establishment of a Gahal executive in addition to the executive of the Knesset faction that was already in existence. These doubts of mine appeared to have been justified during the subsequent years. The chances for a unification of both parties evaporated, and more than once I proposed to break up Gahal.

There are those who think that the formation of Gahal, and afterward also the formation of the Likud, paved the way toward the Likud government in 1977. As far as I am concerned, the process leading to the decline in strength of the Left in Israel and to the downfall of the Maarakh in the elections was inevitable, and the Herut movement would have achieved what it did even without the formation of Gahal, and by its own strength, in cooperation with the other parties, on the basis of a coalition. But the fact is that Menahem Begin came to power not as the head of the Herut movement but as the candidate of the Likud. The internal difficulties of this government also stem from this situation.

NOTES

1. Bank Leumi LeIsrael, B.M. (National Bank of Israel, Ltd.) is Israel's largest commercial bank. Established in 1902 as the Anglo-Palestine Bank, Ltd., it was reincorporated in 1951 as Bank Leumi. From 1948 until the creation of the Bank of Israel in December 1954, Bank Leumi was the government banker and bank of issue.

2. *Haaretz* is one of Israel's leading independent daily newspapers, published by the Schocken Publishing Company.

3. Political parties in Israel are represented at the polls by a letter or series of letters.

51

Itamar Rabinovich

From "Israeli Arabs" to "Israel's Palestinian Citizens"

1948–1996: Analysis

Israeli-Palestinians are the biggest minority group in Israel. In 2006 they numbered more than 1.3 million out of 7 million Israelis. In the following text, Itamar Rabinovich (a co-editor of this collection) discusses the complex relationship between the state and the Arab-Palestinian minority over the years.

In the original terminology of the Arab-Israeli dispute the conflict in and over British Mandatory Palestine was conducted between an Arab side and a Jewish side. It was only after the establishment of the State of Israel and the conclusion of the 1948 War that a stark distinction was drawn between Israelis and Palestinians as the successors of the Jewish and Arab communities in Palestine. In Israeli usage, the term "Arab" came to refer to the larger Arab world, while the term "Palestinian" referred to the Palestinians residing outside Israel. Israel's Arab or Palestinian citizens were strictly referred to as "Israeli Arabs," members of Israel's "Arab minority" or "sector." This was a curious choice of terms which reflected Israeli uneasiness about

Source: Itamar Rabinovich, *Waging Peace: Israel and the Arabs at the End of the Century* (New York: Farrar, Straus and Giroux, 1999), pp. 156–63, with revisions.

the Palestinian issue. It was, in a way, easier to cope with a national minority pertaining to an amorphous Arab world than with part of the Palestinian people who laid a specific claim to Israel's own land.[1]

For twenty years or so, Israel's Arab citizens accepted this terminology and used it, but by the 1970s they began to refer to themselves as Palestinians or as Palestinians who are Israeli citizens. This was but one of many profound changes in the complex relationship between the Israeli state and its Arab citizens as it has unfolded through three principal phases: 1948–1967, 1967–1993, and 1993 to the present.

When the 1948–49 War of Independence ended, some 130,000 Palestinian Arabs remained in the territory of the independent Jewish state and became its citizens. The fledgling State of Israel had a population of just over a million and its Arab citizens constituted a national minority of about 11 percent.

In the aftermath of a brutal war, the victorious Jewish side saw the Arab minority as a potential fifth column, liable to be used by a hostile Arab world in an inevitable, imminent "second round." This underlying attitude was translated into a policy of control embodied first and foremost by the imposition of a system of "military government" on the Arab population. It was only in 1966 that Israel's third Prime Minister, Levi Eshkol, abolished this mechanism of control.

This policy of control was carried out in a context of ambivalence. Israel as a Jewish state was hard put to decide whether it wanted to separate the Arab minority from the mainstream of Israeli public life or whether as a democratic state, dominated by a social-democratic political establishment, it chose to integrate it. Ironically, integration was first accomplished, after a fashion, in the political realm. As full fledged citizens of the State of Israel (though not equal members of Israel's body politic and society), most Israeli Arabs voted for Zionist parties through satellite lists and in fact played a role in perpetuating Labor's hegemony.

During Israel's early years, the Arab minority, predominantly rural and Muslim, can be best described as powerless, traumatized, and confused. Its members had to adjust to defeat, to minority status, to isolation from the other parts of the fragmented Palestinian community, and from the larger Arab world. There was an acute problem of leadership—the pre-1948 Palestinian Arab elites were on the other side of Israel's borders and those who stayed tended to be poorer and less educated.

Arab political opinion and activity in Israel spanned the spectrum—from pragmatic acceptance of the reality of the Jewish State to nationalist opposition and rejection. Pragmatism was manifested by the majority's affiliation with the major Zionist parties while opposition was manifested primarily through the Communist Party. All attempts to form a local Arab nationalist party (most notably a grouping called *al-Ard*—"The Land") collapsed against an insurmountable obstacle—in order to qualify as such the party would adopt a platform negating Israel's very existence and legitimacy as a Jewish state and would be cited by the government and the courts as seditious.

A subtler, politically easier way for members of the intellectual Arab elite in Israel to express their rejection of the Israeli state was in literary prose and verse.

As in so many other respects, 1967 was a watershed in the evolution of Israel's Arab minority. The reemergence of an authentic and effective Palestinian nationalist movement and the removal of the physical barrier that had previously separated them from the larger Palestinian and Arab worlds induced a process of Palestinization. The balance that had been achieved in practice between the Israeli and Arab nationalist components of the community's makeup was upset. It was a measure of this change that the terminology of "Israeli Arabs" was discarded by Israel's Arab citizens who came to refer to themselves as Palestinians.

The nationalist awakening of the late 1960s coupled with socioeconomic changes (higher standard of living, higher level of education, partial breakdown of extended family system, and the transformation of several villages into towns) led to a new phase of political activism. On March 30, 1976, a massive protest was organized under the title "The Day of the Land" against the expropriation of Arab-owned land in the Galilee. In clashes with security forces six persons were killed. March 30 was set as an annual day of protest in which Palestinians in Israel and in the West Bank and Gaza express the gamut of their grievances.

Yasir Arafat and the PLO turned "The Day of the Land" into an all-Palestinian event, but as a rule the PLO did not view Israel's Arab minority as part of its constituency. Long before the PLO formally accepted the notion of a two-state solution, its leadership had predicated its conduct on that assumption. The Arabs in Israel, in turn, while galvanized by Palestinian nationalism, continued to see their future within the State of Israel. Individual Israeli Arabs crossed a physical and mental line and joined the PLO and its orbit, but the vast majority continued to pursue its life within the Israeli state and system. This was manifested most significantly by the failure of Israel's Arab minority to join either the violent conflict between the PLO and Israel between 1967 and 1987 or the *intifada* of the late 1980s.

But the patterns of organization and activity in the Israeli Arab political arena during the same years underwent profound changes. The Zionist parties' satellite lists disappeared and nationalist Arab parties were formed that found a way of operating within the boundaries of Israeli law (most notably Abdul Wahhab Darawsha's Arab Democratic Party, founded in 1988). Semi-political civic groups like the Committee of Heads of Local Arab Councils emerged. In the late 1970s, a powerful fundamentalist movement appeared, partly as a reflection of regional trends and partly in response to particular local conditions. Muslim fundamentalists in Israel operate primarily as a religious and social movement, but their potential political power is enormous.[2]

The Oslo and Washington Accords of August–September 1993 were another watershed; its impact had been mixed.

On the one hand, the agreement and mutual recognition between the State of Israel and the Palestinian national movement released Israel's Arab citizens, as it did other Arabs, from their all-embracing commitment to the Palestinian cause and have enabled them to pursue their particular cause and interests. Most Arabs living in Israel see themselves as Palestinians and support the ideas of Palestinian self-determination and statehood, but they are not interested in becoming part of that state. They rather view themselves as a Palestinian component of that state and are primarily interested in their status and position within the Israeli system.

To an Israel encumbered with difficult problems of segmentation and coping with contending definitions of its political community, the Arab minority's new focus on its relationship with the state is a compounding development.

Nor is the challenge alleviated by the diversity of Arab opinion. Most Arab citizens of Israel are interested in the more mundane issues of integration and equality—educational opportunities, a larger slice of the national economic pie, and the like. The intellectual and political elites address and challenge the very foundations of the Israeli state and system as they are presently constituted. Their platforms vary. Some demand that Israel "dezionize" itself and become "a state for all its citizens," or, in other words, cease to define and conduct itself as the national state of the Jewish people and become a state in which Arabs can be full members of the political community rather than members of a national minority with less than full civil and political rights. Others speak of autonomy or a return to the old notion of a "bi-national state."

Such ideas are given greater volume by a converging "post-Zionist" ideology that has been adopted by parts of the Israeli Left. Whether they argue that Zionism was or is inherently wrong or whether they feel that Zionism had accomplished its original mission, they, too, advocate a reformulation of the underlying ethos of the Israeli polity and a commensurate constitutional and political change.[3]

But of far greater potential is the import given to these ideas by the growing significance of the Arab vote in Israeli politics. At the end of 1996, there were 1,122,000 non-Jews in Israel who constituted 19.5 percent of the total population. This figure includes 180,000 Palestinian residents of East Jerusalem (who were annexed to Israel but choose not to vote in Israeli elections) and 50,000 non-Arab Christians. If these two figures are deducted, there remain 900,000 Arab citizens of pre-1967 Israel, who constitute 15.5% of the general population.

The present Knesset has 12 Arab members out of 120. Four of them were elected in Zionist lists (three in the Labor Party's list and one through the left-wing Meretz) and eight through Arab, non- or anti-Zionist lists (formally speaking the New Communist List is a non-sectarian Arab-Jewish Party which has Jewish members and activists and sent one Jewish member to the Knesset, but essentially it is an Arab party). It is also important to look at the breakdown of Arab vote to the Knesset in 1992 and 1996.

	1992 (PERCENT)	1996 (PERCENT)
Unified Arab List	23.2	37.0
(Arab Democratic Party and the Islamists)	15.2	25.4
Total Vote for Jewish Parties	61.6	37.6
Labor	20.3	16.6
Meretz	9.7	10.5
Likud and Religious (Jewish) Parties	19.3	5.2
Others	12.3	5.3

The change from 1992 to 1996 is striking. In 1992, a clear majority of Israel's Arabs voted for mainstream Zionist parties and under 40 percent voted for non- or anti-Zionist Arab lists. In 1996, the figures were reversed.

In weighing the significance of this change it is important to consider the effect of the new electoral system introduced in the 1996 elections. Like other groups in the Israeli electorate that could now split their vote, Arab voters tended to cast their "responsible" ballot for the prime minister's post and "to go ethnic" with their party-list ballot. Arab voters gave overwhelming support to Shimon Peres against Benjamin Netanyahu but drifted away from Zionist party lists to Arab nationalist ones. The change in the electoral system clearly accelerated trends that had been set in motion much earlier.

The full impact of these trends had thus far been blunted by the fragmentation of the Arab vote. But the role of the Arab vote and consequently of Arab politicians and groups in Israeli politics is bound to increase dramatically in the coming years. Such a development is likely to be followed by more vociferous complaints by the nationalist right wing which view the Arab vote as less than fully legitimate. The argument was raised in the early 1990s that the Rabin and Peres governments relying as they did on the votes of Arab members of the Knesset did not have a "Jewish majority." In the 1996 elections Benjamin Netanyahu defeated Shimon Peres by the slim edge of some 16,000 votes. But Netanyahu had a clear majority of 55% among Jewish voters. Had the numbers been reversed the right wing would have probably complained that Peres had been elected by "the Arab vote" and had no mandate to make concessions not acceptable to "the Jewish majority." . . .

AUTHOR'S NOTES

1. For two basic and very different books on the subject, see Jacob Landau, *The Arabs in Israel: A Political Study* (London, 1969); and Ian Lustick, *Arabs in the Jewish State: Israel's Control of a National Minority* (Austin, 1980).

2. See Majid Al Haj and Henry Rosenfeld, *Arab Local Government in Israel* (Tel Aviv, 1988); Jacob Landau, *The Arab Minority in Israel, 1967–1991: Political Aspects* (London, 1994); C. Klein, *Israel as a Nation State and the Problem of the Arab Minority in Search of a Status* (Tel Aviv, 1987); David Kretzmer, *The Legal Status of the Arabs in Israel* (Tel Aviv, 1987); Sammy Smooha, *Arabs and Jews in Israel,* vols. 1–2 (Boulder, 1989–92); Elie Rekhess, "Resurgent Islam in Israel," *Asian and African Studies* 27, nos. 1–2 (March–July 1993); Elie Rekhess, ed., "Arab Politics in Israel at a Crossroad," *Occasional Papers* 119 (Tel Aviv: Dayan Center, 1991); Nadim Ruhana, "The Political Transformation of the Palestinians in Israel from Acquiescence to Challenge," *Journal of Palestine Studies* 18, no. 3 (1989): 38–59.

3. A particular radical formula of this position was offered by Dr. Azmi Bishara, then a member of the Knesset, in a lengthy interview he gave to *Haaretz* weekly magazine, May 29, 1998.

Foreign Policy Issues

52

Dwight David Eisenhower

The Formulation of the Eisenhower Doctrine

January–March 1957

The Eisenhower Doctrine was a policy statement on the Middle East issued by the U.S. president, Dwight David Eisenhower, on January 5, 1957; its provisions were authorized by Congress in March. The doctrine was meant to bolster the pro-Western Arab regimes (e.g., Lebanon, Jordan, and Iraq) by granting military and economic assistance to Middle Eastern states requesting aid and promising the use of U.S. military forces to protect the territorial integrity of any state threatened by communist aggression. This doctrine did not prevent the Lebanese Civil War or the fall of the Iraqi monarchy in May and July 1958 respectively. Following the military coup in Iraq and fearing destabilization of the region, both Jordan and Lebanon invoked this clause for direct military intervention. In the summer of 1958 the United States sent troops to Lebanon and Britain sent troops to Jordan.

Israel's response was ambiguous. On the one hand, it wanted to see stabilization and increased Western influence in the area. On the other hand, particularly in light of U.S. opposition to the Sinai Campaign, Israel feared that the doctrine might lead to the strengthening of its enemies. Nevertheless, David Ben-Gurion articulated support for the Eisenhower Doctrine despite this slight uneasiness and in the face of opposition from Ahdut Haavodah and Mapam, whose socialist orientations led them to oppose Israeli involvement in the cold war, and from Herut and the General Zionists, who believed that the doctrine did not go far enough in protecting Israel and the region.

The formulation of the Eisenhower Doctrine and the American response to Soviet advances in the Middle East and to the challenge of regional anti-Western forces are described here from the president's personal vantage point.

Source: Dwight D. Eisenhower, *The White House Years: Waging Peace, 1956–1961* (New York: Doubleday, 1965), pp. 180–83. Copyright © 1965 by Dwight D. Eisenhower. Reprinted by permission of John S. D. Eisenhower.

At 7:50 on the morning of Saturday, January 5 [1957], I arrived at my White House office. It was still dark outside. I dictated an insert for the Special Message to the Congress on the Middle East. At noon, I went up to Capitol Hill to deliver it in person before the legislators assembled in a Joint Session.

Weaknesses in the present situation and the increased danger from International Communism, convince me that basic United States policy should now find expression in joint action by the Congress and the Executive. Furthermore, our joint resolve should be so couched as to make it apparent that if need be our words will be backed by action. . . .

The action which I propose would, . . . first of all, authorize the United States to cooperate with and assist any nation or group of nations in the general area of the Middle East in the development of economic strength dedicated to the maintenance of national independence.

A further purpose was to authorize the President to undertake programs of military assistance and cooperation with any nation desiring them, such programs to include United States military aid when requested, against armed aggression from any nation controlled by international Communism.

The message recommended financial support in reasonable amounts and pledged, "These measures would have to be consonant with the treaty obligations of the United States, including the Charter of the United Nations."

That same day the administration bill, House Joint Resolution 117, was introduced into the Congress.

The members of the Congress did not move as one man to endorse the administration's proposal. Far from it. Some thought it would confer on the President constitutional authority belonging to the Legislative branch. Others, friends of Israel, did not like helping any Arab nation. Still others feared it would weaken our ties with either Western Europe or the United Nations or both. One suggested the far-fetched possibility that if the Soviet Union did some minor meddling in the Middle East, the Resolution would authorize "an all-out attack" on the Soviet Union.

Speaker [Sam] Rayburn circulated among his colleagues on Capitol Hill a substitute—a thirty-four-word declaration, "The United States regards as vital to her interest the preservation of the independence and integrity of the states of the Middle East and, if necessary, will use her armed force to that end."

When asked, "Would the administration accept this substitute?" Secretary [of State John Foster] Dulles, with my approval, gave a flat "No." A resolution in these words, he said, would look like an effort to establish an American protectorate over the countries of the Middle East; it would call for a guarantee, by the United States alone, of existing Middle East boundaries; it would violate the U.N. Charter by calling for military action to overthrow any regime which comes under communist control by peaceful means; and it would ignore the importance of economic aid.

From around the world reports came in of varying responses to the suggested new policy.

Britain and France generally favored the plan. Communist China and the Soviet Union condemned it as a "substitution for British and French imperialism." The Moslem countries divided: Syria was hostile, Iraq and Saudi Arabia were cautiously critical, while Turkey, Pakistan, Lebanon, and Iran saw the doctrine as the best possible guarantee of peace.

Prime Minister [Jawaharlal] Nehru wrote to me of his dislike of a "military approach to these problems"—an approach which, he thought, might excite ". . . passions and create divisions among the Arab countries and thus add to the tension. . . ."

"I do not think that, in existing circumstances," Nehru continued, "there is any danger of aggression in the Middle East from the Soviet Union. The Soviet Union is too much tied up with its difficulties in the Eastern European countries. Even otherwise, nationalism is a far stronger force in the Middle East than any other."

The next day I dictated a reply, assuring him that the United States' purpose was to help stabilize the area and promote the rise of living standards.

> We have no thought that any country in the group would want, or indeed could afford, great armaments. When we speak of assisting in a military way, we mean only to help each nation achieve that degree of strength that can give it reasonable assurance of protection against any internal rebellion or subversion and make certain that any external aggression would meet resistance. . . .
>
> . . . It is my belief that this announcement will tend to diminish, if not eliminate, any chance of this kind of aggression. . . .
>
> But we are far more interested in bringing about conditions that will tend to lessen tensions and provide a climate that will bring about the possibility for conciliation even among the Israelis and the Arabs. We stand ready to make considerable sacrifices to bring this about, and in return we want nothing whatsoever except the confidence that these nations are gradually developing their economic strength and living standards and are achieving the ability to live more happily and peacefully among themselves and with the world.

At the first news conference of my second term on the morning of January 23, I was asked whether I had any comment on the Democratic criticism that in asking for advance approval to use the armed forces, I was creating a tradition which might restrict and embarrass future Presidents.

"What we want now," I said, "is an expression of the convictions of the vast portion of the American people without regard to party. . . ."

". . . I would like the nations to know that America is largely one in our readiness to assume burdens and, where necessary, to assume risks to preserve the peace, because this peace is not going to be obtained in any cheap way and it is not going to be maintained in any cheap way."

On January 30 the House passed the Middle East Resolution 355 to 61.

After extensive consideration of the Joint Resolution the Senate, on March 2, voted down 58 to 28 a proposal by Senator Richard Russell to eliminate any funds for economic and military assistance. This rejection came after Senator Knowland read on the floor of the Senate a letter from me opposing this cut and deploring any suggestion that "our country wants only to wage peace in terms of war." For the Russell amendment, which would have cut the heart out of the Resolution, only five Republicans lined up with twenty-three Democrats.

Three days later, the Senate passed the Joint Resolution by a vote of 72 to 19 and on March 9 [1957] the Resolution was signed into law. As in similar cases in the past, the doctrine acquired the name of the president who proposed it and came to be known as the "Eisenhower Doctrine."

With the help of statesmen of both parties, against the grumbling of some opposing congressmen and senators, and against the well-intentioned counter-suggestions of some leading Democratic foreign policy thinkers, we had effectively obtained the consent of the Congress in proclaiming the administration's resolve to block the Soviet Union's march.

The next day Senator J. William Fulbright of Arkansas demanded that Secretary Dulles submit a white paper justifying in detail the conduct of American foreign policy in the Middle East since 1952.

Secretary Dulles made the obvious response: nothing he could think of would do more damage to our relations with England and France than such a rehearsal of events now past, dredging up the painful memories of recent division, and "reopening all the wounds" in the Atlantic Alliance. After modifying his original proposal to take the policy review back to 1946, Fulbright finally abandoned it.

In the course of the Senate's deliberations, I wrote a letter of thanks to former President Truman in appreciation for a syndicated newspaper column urging prompt passage of the Resolution. "I feel that your attitude," I said, "is in the high tradition of non-partisanship on foreign policy matters of grave national concern," to the Mediterranean, to the Suez Canal and the pipelines, and to the underground lakes of oil which fuel the homes and factories of Western Europe.

53

Michael Bar-Zohar

David Ben-Gurion and the Policy of the Periphery

1958: Analysis

The years following the Sinai Campaign saw a marked improvement in Israel's international position. The United States, which had opposed that campaign, came to regard Egyptian president Gamal Abdul Nasser as a Soviet proxy. Hence by the late 1950s Israel was partially emerging from the regional and international isolation that had characterized its position earlier in the decade. It now had the opportunity to find its place within the regional and global policies of the Western powers that were trying to establish a network of regional treaty organizations and security alliances committed to resisting Soviet influences. David Ben-Gurion's biographer offers an account of Israel's successful attempt in the late 1950s to develop a semialliance with Iran, Turkey, and Ethiopia.

While Israel was getting more than its fill of bitter pills and frustration from the United States, it was establishing, under cover of darkness, a clandestine pact in the Middle East. Around it, in dead secrecy, rose a ghost organization, which grew and spread until it ringed the entire Arab Middle East. We must be forgiven our picturesque language: in this case, expressions like "under cover of darkness," "in dead secrecy," "ghost organization" are not at all extravagant. Even they pale in the presence of the actual circumstances which formed the backdrop for these events, and which would fire the wildest imagination. For some years, in hidden underground conditions, Israel engaged in very intensive activity throughout the Middle East. Using various disguises, fictitious names, forged passports, night flights, circuitous paths, [David] Ben-Gurion's many messengers took off for and returned from the capitals of the new allies. Special envoys, high officials, ministers and experts were all involved in the complex operation. The secret action encompassed different spheres, most of which have not been

Source: Michael Bar-Zohar, *Ben-Gurion: A Political Biography* (Tel Aviv: Am Oved, 1977), pt. 3, pp. 1321–26. Reprinted by permission.

revealed to this day. Many of those involved, including some of its initiators and thinkers, will remain anonymous for a long time to come. Only a tiny fraction of these activities have leaked into public knowledge as the years passed, and it is known as the "peripheral pact."

The affair began even before the Sinai Campaign. Secretly, special relations were forming between Israel and two states on the edge of the Middle East: Iran in the north, and Ethiopia in the south. [Gamal Abdul] Nasser's subversion and his expansionist aspirations wakened growing concern in Iran and Ethiopia. And not only in those two countries. Other states also shuddered at the thought of the Egyptian lust for power. Moshe Sharett mentioned one in his diary. "Concrete possibilities of joint action with the Ummah Party[1] in Sudan have been clarified," he wrote just a few days prior to his resignation, "and one of its leaders is planning a visit to Israel for more serious talks." He later added: "I asked myself, over and over again, what will happen to all these if and when I leave."

Sharett had no cause for worry. The Prime Minister, the new Foreign Minister, and their aides were no less aware of the matter's importance.

The blow dealt to Nasser by Israel in the Sinai Campaign reverberated throughout the Middle East and its periphery with an intensity beyond all expectations. States fearful of Nasser's ambitions suddenly found an element capable of overcoming him. Leaders concerned about Communist infiltration via Egypt realized that there was someone capable of halting the Soviets. Ethiopia, an isolated Christian enclave in Africa, was particularly worried, and observed Nasser's pan-Islamic and pan-African expansionist tendencies with growing anxiety. Shortly after the Sinai Campaign, a high-level Israeli official, who was in charge of an important political sector in the Israeli government, arrived in Ethiopia. He met with Emperor Haile Selassie. The two discussed joint political action against Nasser's subversion, as well as economic and development cooperation. The envoy met with some of the Emperor's senior officials, and procedures and ways of action for a plan of broad scope were established. The plan included the assignment of Israeli experts to Ethiopia, and the sending of Ethiopian trainees to Israel, the establishment of joint projects, and courses of study. But something additional came of the meeting in Ethiopia. In the course of time, a secret trip was planned for Ben-Gurion so that he could meet with the Emperor Haile Selassie. Ben-Gurion also expressed his willingness for such a trip, but at the last minute he was prevented from implementing it. Israel coordinated its actions with France, which had vital interests in black Africa. Some of the missions to Ethiopia were carried out by Yosef Nahmias, who had returned from his work as head of the Defense Ministry delegation in Paris. But the pact with Ethiopia expanded and grew, and was expected to be long-lasting.

Meanwhile, Israel was looking eastward as well. Widespread activity was begun in Persia, parallel with the Ethiopian connection. Ben-Gurion's envoys came to Teheran, and met with the Shah of Iran [Muhammad Reza Pahlavi],[2] with his Prime Minister and with senior officials of his retinue. Iran also hoped to halt the Nasserist and Communist influence in the Middle East, especially considering its border with the Soviet Union and its feeling of being in real danger. Iran was aflutter with powerful anti-Arab feelings, which eased the making of contact with Israel. The state was grappling with serious problems in the spheres of agriculture, development, and the exploitation of science. Israel was prepared to offer assistance in all those spheres: many Israeli envoys arrived in Iran, and the ties were gradually strengthened. On top of all that, came cooperation, the exchange of information and coordination of outlooks and actions in the face of developments in the Middle East. In 1958 a letter was delivered to the Shah from Ben-Gurion, in which the Old Man mentioned the works of Cyrus, King of Persia,[3] for the sake of the Jews. The Shah asked that Ben-Gurion be told, in his reply, that "the memory of Cyrus' policy regarding your people is precious to him, and he strives to continue in the path set by this ancient tradition."

The unwritten pact with Iran became the basis for the establishment of a "triangle." In April 1958, a meeting was held between Ambassador Eliyahu Sasson and [Fatin Rustu] Zorlu, the Turkish Foreign Minister. The Turkish Minister expressed his country's concern about the new reality which was consolidating in the Middle East. Only months earlier, a revolutionary change had occurred on Turkey's southern border: some of the traditional Syrian leaders, fearful of the rapidity with which Soviet influence was infiltrating their country, suddenly flew to Egypt and placed the fate of their country in Nasser's hands. Egypt's ruler was surprised and discomfited, but saw only one way out of the imbroglio: the establishment of a "United Arab Republic," by uniting Egypt and Syria into one state, consisting of two "districts." This event raised a scare in the pro-Western countries of the Middle East. Jordan and Iraq, which hoped to block the Nasserist influence, hurried to establish the "Arab Unity." A sort of weak blending of the two states.

The Turkish leaders worriedly followed events in Syria. During 1957, they sensed a clear threat to their country's existence when a treaty was drawn up between their northern neighbour, the Soviet Union, and their southern neighbour, Syria. Nasser's appearance in Syria quickened their sense of danger, since he was known for his subversive activities. With the struggle between Israel and between Syria and Egypt as the background, they lit on a revolutionary idea for joint action. Zorlu and Sasson met once more, and agreed on a timetable and on topics, with the intention of arranging further meetings on the senior levels. One of those most active in forming the ties with the Ankara government was Reuven Shiloah. Israel decided to establish a tie with its two new friends in the north—Iran and Turkey. It was aware of the fact that those two countries were the principal strongholds of American influence in the Middle East, and its most forward positions against Russia.

Now, on the backdrop of the promising connections with states in both north and south, Israeli political thought turned to the idea of a comprehensive plan for a "peripheral pact": the establishment of a bloc of states situated on the periphery of the Middle East, and connected to Israel in a "triangle," with Turkey and Iran in the north, and Ethiopia in the south. The common denominator of these states was expressed mainly in their political position: sharp opposition to Nasserist expansionism and subversiveness, and the aspiration to halt Soviet influence. The unwritten pact had a clear implication for the West. The United States was most concerned in view of the Soviet penetration of the Middle East: the Eisenhower Doctrine [doc. 52] did not succeed in arresting the deterioration of the situation. For the first time, Israel sensed that it had something to offer the Americans: no longer would it be a small, isolated ally, hated and ostracized by all the Arab countries, but the leader and the connecting link of a bloc of states, one of which was a member of NATO, two—of the "Baghdad Pact," and one—an important African state. Here was a bloc whose population exceeded the number of Arabs in the Middle East, and which was prepared for far-reaching cooperation with the Americans in opposing Soviet ambitions in the area. Israel realized that it was terribly important to win America's political and financial support for the clandestine organization.

The first to propose arousing the United States' interest in the peripheral pact was Moshe Dayan. He came to Ben-Gurion with a suggestion: to "sell" the "pact" idea to Field Marshall [Bernard] Montgomery, who would pass it on to his friend [Dwight] Eisenhower, with whom he had fought side by side in the Second World War. A few months earlier, Dayan, on a visit to Europe, had been invited for a long talk with Montgomery. The experienced warrior had unfolded a plan for the solution of the problems of the Middle East. The programme was naive, and it is doubtful whether it could have been implemented. Montgomery was interested in Ben-Gurion's opinion of the plan, and intended to present it to President Eisenhower. Ben-Gurion and Dayan had not been enthusiastic about the plan; now, however, with the peripheral pact beginning to take shape, Dayan thought that it might be possible to make use of Montgomery's good services in order to inform Eisenhower of what was happening, in an unconventional way. Ben-Gurion gave his approval, and Dayan flew to Europe and met with the Field Marshall. He described, for Montgomery, the pro-Western pact in the Middle East, the oil pipeline as an alternative to the Suez Canal, and the strength and ties of the north and south countries of the triangle. After the meeting, Montgomery set out for Washington and a visit with Eisenhower. Ben-Gurion, for his part, reported this development to [Abba] Eban, who was Israel's ambassador in the United States capital. "The proposed plan contains one weak link—Turkey," admitted Ben-Gurion.

> because it is a member of NATO, not only of the Baghdad Pact, and is not dependent for its security on the Baghdad Pact. Turkey also receives much° more American aid than does Iran. And its hatred of the Arabs is not as great as that of Iran. Turkey's present principal leaders are hypocrites. Nevertheless, the plan has some basis . . . there is an objective reality in the Middle East which provides a slight hope for my plan. Jordan is hanging on a shoestring. Iraq's situation is also shaky.
>
> Should America take over this idea—the connection between Iran, Turkey, Israel—and, we must add, Ethiopia as well—there is a chance that something important might come of it. And we should stand guard during Montgomery's visit.

It seems that Montgomery did not even raise the subject with Eisenhower. And at the same time, Eban expressed doubts as to the pact's chances of success. But Ben-Gurion was very enthusiastic about the subject, and as usual, he kept moving forward; nothing could stop him any more. "Our ties with Iran and Ethiopia are on the highest level," he wrote to Eban. "In Iran—with the Shah, in Ethiopia—with the Emperor."

> There is no need to establish a pact immediately. But the development of ties of friendship and cooperation—even if they are secret in the meantime—in the fields of science and in economic affairs as well, particularly if we construct a wider oil pipeline—have much value. . . . The ties with these countries (Ethiopia and Iran) are becoming closer and closer: and if the meeting with the Turks really does take place, and the expected connection is established—it will be a triple thread with many possibilities . . . together with the budding signs in Ghana, Liberia, Nigeria, Burma, these relations are of great significance and may provide many opportunities. The good will of the United States (even without its knowing yet of all our cooperative ventures with Iran and Ethiopia) will move things forward.

The "weak link," as Ben-Gurion pointed out, remained Turkey. After the Sasson-Zorlu meeting, a high-level delegation arrived in Turkey from Israel. The background of the meeting was exotic: the representatives of Israel and Turkey met on board a grand ship, floating on the waters of the enchanting Marmara Sea. Here, at least, they could be sure that no one would see them and that their secret would not be discovered. But this was not the meeting referred to by Ben-Gurion, when he spoke of "the meeting with the Turks." To ensure himself that it was possible to establish the pact, he wanted to hold a high-level discussion with the Turkish government.

It is doubtful whether the meeting would ever have taken place had it not been for the storm which broke out in the Middle East in the summer of 1958, and swept a number of states into a powerful whirlpool. In May, civil war erupted in Lebanon between the Christian groups, gathered around the retiring Lebanese Prime Minister, Camille Chamoun, and the Moslems, working to integrate Lebanon within the Arab Nasserist bloc. The armed uprising, which began as an internal conflict, was fanned by the propaganda of Nasser's agents, and fed by the support of Egypt and Syria in the form of money, weapons and soldiers. The situation in Lebanon deteriorated dramatically; pro-Western elements in the Middle East tried to provide weapons for the anti-Nasserist elements in Lebanon, but their help was limited. In July, the crisis struck Iraq and Jordan as well. When the situation in Jordan worsened, and the throne was endangered, the Iraqi government sent help in the form of a motorized division under General [Abd al-Karim] Qasim. But half-way, Qasim ordered his troops to turn back, and attacked Baghdad. He, together with his friends in the "Free Generals" action, carried out a speedy military coup and took power. Faisal, King of Iraq, was put to death in his palace, while kneeling, still in his nightclothes and begging for his life. The heir to the throne, Abdul Illa, was murdered in his palace. The Prime Minister, Nuri Sa'id, the "strong man" of Iraq for many years, fled for his life, disguised as a woman. But the next day, as he walked through the streets, he was recognized by the crowds; they tore him to bits. Qasim, in his first broadcasts to the people, announced that Iraq was to be a "People's Republic."

When Iraq collapsed, it seemed that all the strongholds of the West in the Middle East were crumbling one after the other. Nuri Sa'id was the confidante of the British; Iraq was the heart of the Baghdad Pact, and the central link in the "Northern Tier," which the West had set up against the Soviet Union. Now it seemed that Iraq would become a Soviet satellite. Iran and Turkey, both of which shared borders with Iraq, sensed, with terror, that the Soviet noose was gradually tightening around them. . . .

. . . The Soviet Union didn't just stand by, either. Nikita Khrushchev advised Nasser, who came to Moscow for a visit, to fly to the Middle East immediately. Nasser flew to Damascus, where he declared his full support for the Iraqi revolution. The Soviet Union, for its part, announced maneuvers involving 24 divisions to be carried out in the Caucasus, along the border with Turkey. The latter, together with Iran, put heavy pressure on the United States to intervene also in Iraq. Ben-Gurion too, urged the American government to "put down the rebels (in Iraq)." The Iraqi coup spurred the Turkish leaders to overcome their remaining hesitations, and to tighten their ties with Israel as quickly as possible. "'A,' our envoy, was invited to Zorlu in Istanbul," wrote Ben-Gurion excitedly in his diary, five days after the Iraqi coup, "and (Zorlu) told him that they are acting parallel to our actions, and that he will be pleased to see full cooperation between our political activities and theirs. We are in historic times, and the opportunity for this action will not come again. He also notified me of the agreement, in principle, for a meeting between the two Heads of State . . . (but) should this become known, the whole matter will explode and then the Americans will also interfere."

Ben-Gurion did not agree with Zorlu about the possibility of American interference; on the contrary, now that he had Turkey's agreement to strengthen the ties—and to solidify the last layer of the peripheral pact—the Old Man decided to move on to the next stage: to arouse American interest in this pact. The next day, he convened a consultation in Golda's [Meir] house, in order to discuss the "tightening of ties with Iran, Turkey and Ethiopia, with America's help, in other words, by applying pressure to America which would in turn apply pressure and offer aid to those countries." Ben-Gurion believed that if he could interest the United States in the peripheral pact, then the United States would encourage the countries of the periphery to consolidate their ties with Israel; this would in turn help to consolidate the pact. The Middle East conflagration provided a once-in-a-lifetime opportunity for such an appeal. Ben-Gurion immediately formulated an urgent memo to President Eisenhower, in which, for the first time, he revealed the matter of the peripheral pact.

First Ben-Gurion described the gravity of the present situation and the dangers which threatened Jordan, Lebanon and Saudi Arabia. "Nasser's take-over of the Arab Middle East, with the assistance of the tremendous might of the Soviet Union, would have serious implications for the West." Among those implications, he listed: the failure of France's efforts to solve the Algerian problem and to retain its friendly relations with Tunisia and Morocco; the breakdown of Libya's independence and of American and British influence there; the danger of a communist revolt in Iran; Egyptian and Soviet domination of Sudan; the endangering of Ethiopia's independence; a sweeping assault by Nasser of "Black Africa" with the intention of gaining control over that area.

"There is no need for me to emphasize the significance of such a process, for Israel and Turkey," wrote the Old Man, placing the emphasis on Turkey in particular, since he was aware of the special American interest in that country's security.

> We have begun to strengthen our ties with neighbouring countries on the outer circle of the Middle East: Iran, Ethiopia and Turkey, with the purpose of creating a powerful dam against the Nasserist-Soviet torrent. We have established friendly relations and an attitude of mutual trust with the government of Iran and the Emperor of Ethiopia. Recently, our ties with the Turkish government have become more intimate, above and beyond our normal diplomatic relations.
>
> Our purpose is the creation of a group of states, not necessarily an official and public pact which . . . will be capable of standing firm against the Soviet expansionism with Nasser as its middleman, and which may be able to save the independence of Lebanon; perhaps, with time, that of Syria as well. This group will include two non-Arab Moslem countries (Iran and Turkey), one Christian country (Ethiopia), and the State of Israel.

Ben-Gurion described Israel's possible role to Eisenhower: "I don't want to exaggerate my estimation of our ability. I am aware of our limitations in material resources and man-power . . . nevertheless I can say that it is within our power to help . . . in those countries." Ben-Gurion made much of the peripheral states' fears of foreign "domination," stating that this fear did not exist regarding Israel. "We are capable of carrying out our mission, which is a vital need for us and also a source of tangible might for the West in this part of the world." He detailed the help which Israel could extend: technical assistance, scientific and research assistance, help in the fields of agriculture and education; he described the importance of laying an oil pipeline between Eilat and the Mediterranean Sea, "to diminish Nasser's extortion power and the chance of Soviet domination in this region."

With the above as background, Ben-Gurion presented Israel's demands: It is vital and urgent to grant Israel full security with regard to the integrity of its borders, its sovereignty and its capability for self-defense.

"I am not speaking of a distant vision. The first stages of this plan are already in the process of implementation. But two things are necessary: political, financial and moral American support, and the instilling, in Iran, Turkey and Ethiopia, of the feeling that our efforts in this direction have the support of the United States."

In concluding, Ben-Gurion emphasized the fact that the group of states in whose name he spoke could save freedom in the central part of the Middle East and even in some of the North African countries. "When the flanks of the region are guaranteed, it will be easier to develop a resistance to Soviet and Nasserist penetration in the other parts of the Middle East."

A similar memo, worded slightly differently, was sent by Ben-Gurion to the French Prime Minister.

Now came the dread and tension of awaiting the American reaction; and when Eban delayed one day in delivering the memo, he burst out angrily: "We've lost a very precious day in such a critical time . . . instead of rushing off to Washington, Eban stayed an extra day in New York and had a talk with [Dag] Hammarskjold. . . ."

Late in the evening of July 24th, Eban met with [John Foster] Dulles and handed him Ben-Gurion's memo. Dulles read the message on the spot, and immediately handed it to one of his aides. "Get this to the President at once," he said, and repeated: "at once!" He turned to Eban, and added: "This is a very important letter. It must be handed to the president immediately."

Eban suggested that the Secretary of State encourage the governments of Turkey and Iran to cooperate with Israel. Dulles replied: "I see no reason why I shouldn't notify Turkey and Iran of our satisfaction with the development of ties between you and these countries."

The next day, the first reaction from Eisenhower reached Ben-Gurion. "I was deeply impressed by your comprehensive perception of the grave problems faced by the free world, both within the Middle East and beyond it . . . since the Middle East includes Israel, you can be assured of the United States' interest in the wholeness and independence of Israel. I discussed your letter with the Secretary of State, who will write to you in more detail, in the near future."

Ben-Gurion was somewhat disappointed by this reply. In his letter to the President, he had hinted of his willingness "to have an urgent discussion with the United States on these questions"; he had hoped to be invited to Washington for official talks. Some of this disappointment was expressed in a conversation with a high-level visitor from the United States. "Why doesn't the President invite me," he complained, "when he invites heads of government from large and small countries?"

Dulles and Eisenhower were still cautious; but finally, when Dulles replied to Ben-Gurion, he expressed a positive opinion and encouraged Ben-Gurion to establish the peripheral pact.

Ben-Gurion gave the green light for intensified action. But not all of his friends favoured the idea—in consultations with "our friends," [Levi] Eshkol expressed doubts about the operation. There were also some ministers who were critical of the idea, but Ben-Gurion was convinced that the operation would succeed. Contacts with Turkey entered an advanced stage. Golda Meir met with the Turkish Foreign Minister, Zorlu, for two detailed talks in which it was definitely agreed that the two Prime Ministers should meet. During the last days of August, Ben-Gurion convened his close aides for decisive consultations.

NOTES

1. Ummah (Nation) is the Sudanese political party that took a pro-Western line while Egypt was moving more and more into the Soviet camp. Immediately after Sudanese independence in early 1956, Egypt—Britain's former partner in the Sudanese condominium—began pressing for new borders with Sudan. In part because of this crisis, the Ummah Party became the dominant party in a new coalition formed in July 1956.
2. Muhammad Reza Pahlavi (1919–1980) was shah of Iran from 1941 until he was overthrown and exiled in the Iranian revolution of January 1979. By the mid-1960s he had established a virtual police state.
3. Cyrus, king of the Persian empire in the sixth century B.C.E., promoted the reestablishment of a Jewish community in Judaea, thus ending the first Babylonian Exile, which had begun in the years 597–586 B.C.E.

54

Michael Bar-Zohar

David Ben-Gurion and Israel's Regional and International Position

1958: Analysis

Although under David Ben-Gurion's leadership Israel successfully placed itself as an ally of the Western powers and of the anti-Nasserist, anti-Soviet states in the area (Iran, Turkey, and Ethiopia), it still faced the enmity of many nations and the threat of international isolation from the growing "neutralist" Third World bloc. The following pages from Michael Bar-Zohar's biography of David Ben-Gurion, known affectionately, by this time, as the Old Man, are based largely on Ben-Gurion's own diary. Ben-Gurion's outlook at the time was clearly influenced by the successes of the Nasserist movement in the Arab world, and particularly by the formation of the United Arab Republic (UAR), which formally united Egypt and Syria from February 1958 until September 1961. Of particular interest, in light of the Six-Day War, is Ben-Gurion's assessment of the importance of a modern air force to meet Israel's security needs.

On 4 March 1958, at the beginning of an event-filled year, [David] Ben-Gurion attended a political session of Mapai's Foreign Affairs Committee. In his pocket was the carefully worded agenda he had prepared. But suddenly,

> Something happened to me that had happened several times before, but not for a long time: all of a sudden I saw before me a picture of the world, and I sensed our position in it very clearly; and when it came to my turn to speak, I didn't use one word of what I had prepared but instead described what I had suddenly seen, and I knew that this picture was right even if it was "cruel." And it seemed that those who heard also felt that this was an accurate picture of how we were seen by the Arab world, Russia, China, India, the small nations of Asia and Africa—and the countries of America and Europe—and the political line that we must take.

At this same moment of elation, which he himself saw as prophetic, Ben-Gurion turned his attention to each of the political problems facing Israel. The spontaneity with which the words flowed belied his methodic thought as he constructed layer after layer of sober analysis and logical conclusions, each becoming the foundation for the subsequent layer. At the very basis of this structure he placed the Israel-Arab relationship, and described the Land of Israel, "as the Arabs see it."

"To Arab eyes," he claimed,

> it seems as if ten years ago or more, people came from Poland, Rumania, Russia, and took over this country, this Arab land. And

Source: Michael Bar-Zohar, *Ben-Gurion: A Political Biography* (Tel Aviv: Am Oved, 1977), pt. 3, pp. 1359–62. Reprinted by permission.

> for them a country inhabited by Arabs for 1500 years is Arab . . . why should they give this country up. It stands as a wedge between the Arab countries. Abba Eban, with his skillful turn of phrase, has called it not a wedge but a bridge. That's from Eban's standpoint. But when I put myself in an Arab's place, I see it as a wedge, . . . but if we put ourselves in the Arab's place, the conclusion we arrive at is bitter. But a bitter conclusion that is true is preferable to an illusion, however sweet. . . .

Ben-Gurion stated categorically: "I have come to a bitter conclusion, that at the present time there is no prospect of an Arab-Jewish peace.

"Two questions arise: if there is no prospect now, is there no prospect forever? But there is a still graver question. If there is no prospect now, is our existence secure?"

He asked and responded: "The two questions are linked together. . . . There is no possibility, I am deeply convinced, to bring about peace before the Arabs are convinced that it is impossible to destroy us. It's the only road to peace."

At this point he began to review the global factors shaping this reality. He admitted that [the attainment of] this [goal] has become more difficult in recent years because of Russia. He emphasized that the Soviet Union was hostile to Israel for two reasons: "its interests in the Arab world and the problem of Soviet Jewry. . . ."

Ben-Gurion's conclusion was that Israel will receive no help from Russia, Communist China or [Jawaharlal] Nehru's India; these states will not make it clear to the Arabs that it is impossible to destroy the state of the Jews.

Nor did he find the U.S. very helpful. "Now, America is in a state of ebb. The America of [Dwight] Eisenhower and [John Foster] Dulles is so perceived by the Americans as well as by the whole of Europe. . . ."

"So, who is left?" he asked. There are small nations in Asia and Africa. There is America, North America, the U.S. and Canada and the countries of Latin America. And there is Western Europe. We have hope and prospects in all these countries and only in them. . . ."

He then moved to analyze the actual current problem. He reported the information that the UAR might form a Palestinian government in exile in the Gaza Strip, to add it to the UAR and launch a campaign designed to push Israel back to the time of partition. The Old Man recommended that Israel refrain from any reaction at that point. But in view of the growing danger to Israel's existence a rapid build-up was crucial. The major source of weapons, France, was facing serious difficulties due to the Algerian problem. "It cost them money and blood. They need friends and the most important friend for them is Germany." Hence his conclusion that Israel should develop her ties with Germany in order to obtain the aid that France was hard put to provide. "But the aim is not just Germany, though she holds the central position but Germany, France, the Netherlands, Belgium." He also alluded to the alliance that was then taking shape in the Middle East without mentioning the names of the members of the alliance of the periphery [see doc. 53]. "I won't talk about them, we are merely beginning and it should remain unpublicized. . . ." Thus he reached the summing up of his political outlook:

> The Arab unions could pose a big danger if Russia is behind them. In view of this we should strive to achieve guarantees for the status quo in the Middle East. It will be a great achievement if Russia could be made part of this guarantee. . . .
>
> . . . And if we can bolster our security with an air-force that cannot be defeated in a surprise attack, then we can face the power of the Arabs themselves even if they are equipped with Soviet weapons. And we

should strive for guarantees by global forces that Russia will not and does not want to challenge seriously. . . . [And if] the Arabs realize that Israel cannot be destroyed, then there may be people among the Arabs who would begin to think that this "quarrel" should be stopped and peace should, perhaps, be made with Israel.

55
Ehud Avriel
Israel's Beginnings in Africa
1956–1973: Memoir

In the early 1950s Israel tried to break out of its partial international isolation by establishing relations with the emerging Asian and African nations. Burma was the first of the developing countries to establish diplomatic relations with Israel and enter into economic cooperation and aid programs. Ghana, in 1957, was the first African state to do so. In the following years, through trade agreements, training programs, and economic cooperation programs run by both the state and the Histadrut, Israel successfully established diplomatic ties with all black African states except Somalia and Mauritania, which did not recognize Israel. The relationships were mutually beneficial until the aftermath of the Yom Kippur War, when most African states suspended formal diplomatic relations with Israel. Guinea had severed relations following the Six-Day War; Uganda did so in 1972.

Ehud Avriel, an early member of the Israeli Foreign Ministry and an aide to David Ben-Gurion, was one of the architects of Israel's African policy. His memoirs describe the "golden" era of the African-Israeli relationship. Most of Israel's relations with sub-Saharan African states were restored in the aftermath of the 1979 peace treaty between Israel and Egypt (doc. 104).

With joy one remembers how we in Israel threw ourselves, with verve and boundless enthusiasm, into cooperation with the fledgling movement of emerging African nationalism. The latter half of the fifties was not a period of idealistic optimism regarding the future of our planet and society. The cold war was sobering to hopes entertained during the brief euphoria immediately following the victory over Hitler's Axis. Commercialism had replaced the magnanimous expectations engendered by the new beginning after the darkest interlude in human history; the war-time Alliance had disintegrated; European powers were on the verge of

Source: Michael Curtis and Susan Aurelia Gitelson, eds., *Israel in the Third World* (New Brunswick, N.J.: Transaction Books, 1976), pp. 69–74. Copyright © 1976 by Transaction Publishers. Reprinted by permission of Transaction Publishers.

decline; the adjustment to life in the shade of the two giant superpowers was beginning to take its awkward shape.

The sound of cheerful drumming from remote Africa, announcing the stirrings of [Kwame] Nkrumah's[1] national liberation movement and its scattered echoes from other parts of the black continent were the one encouraging message in an otherwise most unimaginative world. Israel was among the first to derive courage from these signs on the firmament; we were looking for kindred souls, people in hope for justice, equality, purposeful social development, unorthodox politics, daring foresight, readiness for sacrifice. We had just received an inkling of these from a different source. David Hacohen, Israel's first ambassador to Burma, had evolved unprecedented schemes for practical cooperation. Rather than content himself with the analysis of political trends in the country in which he represented us, he attempted to dig more deeply. His enthusiasm infected the leadership of the Burmese People's party. Soon Israeli technicians, advisers and experts arrived in faraway Burma to help avoid the repetition of mistakes we had made, just recently, when we began to develop our own country with the new elan that came with independence.

Our first encounter with the new Africa occurred thanks to one of Israel's most stable friends, President [William V. S.] Tubman of Liberia. Ambassador Daniel Lewin went in 1956 to the president's third inauguration to represent Israel. On the late president's pilgrimage to the American Congress in 1935 (for the resumption of relations) he was shunned by most and scorned by many. Congressman Emanuel Celler[2] was the one person who comforted and encouraged President Tubman in his despair. Ever since Tubman remained a true friend of the Jewish people whom he regarded as equal only to Africans (and blacks in America) in terms of suffering and disdain on the part of the "superior races." At that inauguration Lewin met two representatives of the Gold Coast. The Israeli and the Africans spent hours on end telling each other about their respective countries, comparing the underlying philosophies of the Zionist movement and of the Convention People's party, and found that they had much common ground.

In search for new sea routes—in view of the barring of the Suez Canal to Israeli shipping—a representative of the National Shipping Line (Zim) explored the West Coast of Africa at that time for suitable harbors. He found what he had looked for—and more—in Accra. Shalom Klinghofer returned from his search for new outlets for Zim's initiatives with glowing reports about the Convention People's party and their leaders: high-minded, dedicated young men who thought along much the same lines as the Haganah (volunteer defense forces before Israel became a state) and the pioneering movement in Israel.

Ambassador Lewin, then in charge of African and Asian affairs in the Foreign Office, added a file inscribed "Gold Coast" to his lean archives and started to look around for an emissary to the newly discovered territory. As independence was still some way off, the first representative of Israel was to be a consul rather than an ambassador. Luckily, Lewin was able to obtain the most suitable candidate for the mission into the unknown. Hanan Yavor, a kibbutznik without the protocol air but with devotion to the heritage of the pioneering movement that built Israel and love for exciting adventure. He went to Accra and planted the Israeli flag in the center of what was to be for a number of years the Jerusalem of African nationalism; Kwame Nkrumah's capital city, Accra.

During the winter of 1956–57 the Foreign Relations Department of the Histadrut received a telegram from four African trade unionists, who had attended an Asian trade union conference in Bandung. There they had heard so much invective against Israel that their curiosity was aroused: where there was so much smoke there must be some fire. If, they had argued, Arab countries with no free trade union movement whatsoever, inveighed so aggressively against the one country in their area that had a model trade union movement—they would like to have a look for themselves at the object of Arab tirades. Could they spend a few days as guests of the Histadrut on their way home? Reuven Barkatt was delighted and cabled immediate acceptance. They came, led by John Tettegah of the Ghana Trade Union Congress (TUC) and at that time a close aide of Kwame Nkrumah's, and stayed not for a few days but for a few weeks. They were overcome with admiration for the achievements of Israel during the short time that had elapsed since the end of "colonial rule" and overwhelmed by the warmth of their comradely reception. Also they were impressed by the fact that they were not exposed to anti-Arab polemics. Instead of hostile instigation against their nonaligned Arab friends, they were led from one serious discussion about the real problems concerning the social and technological development of their territories to another. As they returned to their respective countries (Ghana, Nigeria, Northern Rhodesia [later Zambia] and Upper Volta), human contacts had been established stronger than any vitriolic Arab incitement against the "Zionist imperialists." (Incidentally, one of the issues that remained unexplained during this crucial encounter, and was to remain a moot point throughout most of the ensuing relationship, was the speed of Israeli development; when we insisted that we had begun to lay the foundations for independent statehood right under the nose of the Mandate we were often judged overmodest or exaggerating unavoidable insignificant initiatives. How, the Africans asked, could you begin to build the infrastructure of your educational system, your agriculture, your industry, and moreover your armed services while foreign power is still all-pervasive. The fact that this attitude was the source of their weakness—as ours was the secret of our relative strength—remained clouded to the end.)

The proclamation of Ghana's independence was welcomed by high tides of warm love from all over the world. Delegations of all sovereign countries and of most underground movements still struggling for their freedom congregated in Accra. The emergence of the first black African state from colonial rule was regarded as a momentous event. The fact that this emergence had become possible by mutual consent and compromise between the British and the Ghanaians augured well for future relations. It was generally assumed though, that for quite a while Ghana would be alone. No other British colony and certainly no French dependency would soon follow the path of Ghana to independence.

At the end of the Ghanaian festivities, the Israeli delegation had a private audience with Kwame Nkrumah. He presented them (David Hacohen with his Burmese experience was a member) with exactly the same list of urgent requirements he expected from the older states: a shipping line to transport the countries' exports, mainly cocoa, to overseas markets, advice on modernization of agriculture, technical assistance in the production of import replacements, schools, frameworks for the mobilization of youth in the service of the new state's development.

Under Golda Meir's energetic leadership, the Israeli Foreign Office vastly expanded its technical assistance program that had just been installed. Ambassador Aharon Remez was given the task of coordinating Israeli government agencies, public and private entrepreneurs, universities, the Histadrut, the kibbutz movement and the Israeli Army in an effort to meet Ghana's demands.

Less than one year after Ghana's proclamation of independence, Israel had already installed an embassy in Accra. Before the first year was out, every single requirement on Nkrumah's list had become a subject for intensive cooperation between Ghana and Israel. We provided the top men. We received first-rate Ghanaians to understudy and serve as second-in-command to prepare to take over as soon as possible from our specialists. Ghana, still in possession of vast foreign exchange reserves, provided most of the capital necessary. Over two hundred Israelis were busy on the many schemes. As a matter of policy we very seldom seconded personnel to existing departments in Ghana, and later, as cooperation expanded, in other African countries. We preferred to assist in the creation of new enterprises or new departments of public administration, better suited to the requirements of an independent state than the carry-overs of colonial structures.

India and Israel were at that early stage the countries closest to Nkrumah's mind. He venerated [Jawaharlal] Nehru's continuous neutralism, antiimperialism and nationalistic pride that offered no favors to the technologically more advanced white nations. He admired Israel's tenacity in the face of widespread hostility, its military prowess in the face of more numerous and more heavily equipped, long established armies, its success in "making the desert bloom" through hard work and the application of unorthodox technical and social devices. Nkrumah shrewdly calculated that his acceptance of our enthusiastically and massively offered aid would have to constitute sufficient reward for a people accustomed to dwell in solitude and unpampered by the support of like-minded power blocs.

It was in this spirit that major strides forward were made in our cooperation with Ghana during the initial period of our friendship. The Black Star Line—the first African shipping line ever—was founded on only a fraction of the investment deemed necessary by older (and more self-centered) seafarers than has Israel; a nautical college was installed to provide officers and engineers for the merchant navy when we discovered, to our consternation, that black Africans had been kept down to the level of unskilled deckhands. Chicken farming was most successfully introduced with negligible capital investment to overcome the trauma left along the West African coast by a grandiose but wholly inexpert scheme the British had tried out and which had left behind the myth that eggs cannot be produced in the tropics and that the few eggs necessary—only whites would need them anyway—would be forever imported from Northern Europe. Alumni of the Israeli pioneering movement, the kibbutz and the paramilitary defense-cum-settlement movement Nahal arrived in Ghana to instill patriotic dedication into the members of the Youth Brigade, established to take unemployed youngsters from idleness to productivity.

These and many other programs deepened the relationship between Israel and Africa's first decolonized model country. A major breakthrough into wider expanses was to occur on this background during the All-African-People's Conference, held in Accra in December 1958. This meeting of the movements of national liberation from all over Africa could have easily been overshadowed by extremist Arab incitement against recognition and cooperation with Israel. The competition between [Gamal Abdul] Nasser and Nkrumah for leadership of the oppressed was fierce. While Nasser had the necessary funds and ambition, Nkrumah knew well how to use his kingship and the uniqueness of his constitutional achievement in making Ghana the African symbol of decolonization.

Golda Meir was on a state visit to Ghana just as the conference convened and Accra abounded with resistance fighters from all corners of the continent. George Padmore, venerated father of Pan-Africanism, suggested that Nkrumah's guest, the foreign minister of Israel, meet in special session with the participants of his revolutionary gathering. With the president's blessing Golda Meir entered a conference hall containing mostly people who had little—or utterly negative—information about Israel. George Padmore acted as host and moderator. Mrs. Meir, in her outspoken simplicity, repelled the attack of Algeria, orchestrated by the immensely popular Algerian delegates. As they remonstrated against Israel's involvement with France (still our "friend and ally"), Mrs. Meir patiently and convincingly explained Israel's true philosophy to an increasingly interested and warmly affected audience. Padmore's affirmation of the Israeli position elevated her statements to a level beyond any possible doubt. Within that afternoon Israel had sown the seeds of future attachments with otherwise completely unattainable personalities. The pessimistic timetables of the leaders of decolonization were soon to be overturned by [Charles] de Gaulle's ruse and by Britain's sudden awareness of "the winds of change." Within less than one year the subversive ringleaders who had congregated at Accra to prepare for a long-drawn struggle found themselves in positions of acknowledged legitimacy as heads of states. Many of those present who had listened to Mrs. Meir's talk, gladly grasped the hand of Israel proffered to initiate cooperation on the Ghana model.

When the lights went out in one Israeli embassy in Africa after another many an Israeli was deeply saddened. Not only those who had actively participated in our cooperative effort; not only the diplomats and commentators whose business is the analysis of political events. The severance of diplomatic relations was—when it came right during the Yom Kippur War—a heavy blow: we felt abandoned by countries we had helped in their own hour of need and rejected by people for whom we felt great warmth.

The African decision to break relations with Israel is partly the result of the self-imposed law of unanimity that prevails at the Organization for African Unity: the Arabs of Northern Africa, shedding all pretense, forced the Middle Eastern conflict upon a forum designed mainly for the purpose of dealing with problems more directly pertinent to Africa's own survival in a troubled world.

Israel has no regrets concerning its role in the emergence of African independence. If we were privileged to add even the tiniest particle to the liberation of the oppressed Africans and to the amelioration of their cruel living conditions, we shall always regard ourselves vastly rewarded for whatever efforts we may have invested in a great human enterprise.

NOTES

1. Kwame Nkrumah (1909–1972) was head of state of Ghana from its independence in 1951 until he was deposed by a coup in 1966. Nkrumah had been a leader of the Pan-African movement since the 1940s and was a major figure in African and Third World politics.

2. Emanuel Celler (1888–1980) was a Jewish member of the U.S. House of Representatives from Brooklyn, New York, 1923–73.

56

Shimon Peres

American Arms for Israel

1960–1964: Memoir

In the early 1960s President John F. Kennedy tried to reopen a dialogue with Gamal Abdul Nasser's Egypt, and that meant attempting to resolve the Arab-Israeli conflict. David Ben-Gurion, however, was skeptical of any fundamental change in the Arab states' stance (see doc. 54). Israel's anxiety that its security might be affected

Source: Shimon Peres, *David's Sling* (London: Weidenfeld and Nicolson, 1970), pp. 87–108. Reprinted by permission of Shimon Peres.

was relieved by major American-Israeli arms deals. In the first of these, announced in September 1962, the United States agreed to sell the short-range defensive Hawk missiles to Israel. This sale was not only the first time that a nation outside of the Western bloc received ballistic weapons and supporting equipment; it was also a reversal of U.S. policy not to be a major source of weapons for any nation in the Middle East. This policy reversal grew out of the U.S. Defense Department's concern that the amount of Soviet military equipment recently furnished to Egypt, Iraq, and Syria would tip the military balance of forces in the Arabs' favor and that such an imbalance might lead either to an Arab attack on Israel or to a "preventive" attack by Israel upon one of the Arab states with offensive military power.

Following the Hawk missiles deal, arms negotiations between Washington and Israel accelerated. Growing Soviet involvement in the Middle East and the failure of the attempt at a U.S.-Egyptian rapprochement led to a reevaluation of Israel's role in U.S. strategic planning. As a result, the United States overcame some of its earlier objections to a close military relationship with Israel. During Lyndon Johnson's presidency U.S.-Egyptian relations deteriorated even further as tension and conflict within the region increased. The following reading presents these processes from the perspective of Shimon Peres, who had been near the center of Israel's defense planning since the early 1950s.

The story of America's refusal, until fairly recently, to help Israel achieve an arms balance seems almost as unreal today as the account of France's generous response to Israel's arms pleas up to the Six-Day War. The unreserved friendship of Paris and the restraining hesitations of Washington now read like forgotten chapters of a distant past. Yet as with many events of the past, they have a relevance for the future: what has happened before *may* happen again. The interests of Israel demand—as they always have and always will—that she not be dependent on a single source of arms supply, for she may find herself the victim of a change in attitude by the supplying country. Such change may occur without any special action on Israel's part. It may be—and most often is—motivated by extraneous factors, notably by changes in relationships with other countries and not necessarily with other countries in the Middle East. The birth of new international relationships, unlike that of humans, cannot always be anticipated; nor is the gestation always apparent. Their death, similarly, is not always, if ever, a function of age or accident. A small State, much affected by international political changes, must therefore always preserve its power of initiative, seek alternative forms of insurance, follow a pluralistic policy in its international associations.

The United States did respond in some measure to Israel's arms requests even before the middle 1960s; but her modest compliance was far outweighed by her reservations. These were due primarily to what in those earlier years was considered to be the relative insignificance of a major political factor powerfully in evidence today—the Soviet presence in the Middle East. Soviet penetration was then thought to be slight, and John Foster Dulles, Secretary of State in President [Dwight] Eisenhower's Government, believed it could be contained. He had high hopes of "rescuing" [Gamal Abdul] Nasser from the overtures of Russia, and had no wish to jeopardize his efforts by delivering major arms to Israel. Dulles was further inhibited from so doing by his attachment to the aim of winning the hearts of the "unaligned" States, led by India, Yugoslavia and Egypt. (It proved equally fruitless.) It must also be added that he and his President did not always approve of Israel's policies.

However, neither was completely indifferent to Israel's arms needs, and after a time they enabled her to acquire certain types of defensive weapons—recoilless anti-tank guns, anti-aircraft guns and radar systems. But Dulles specifically demanded a softening of Israel's reactions to the terror and sabotage raids by the Arab States. . . .

Shifts in America's arms policy towards Israel followed major changes not only in the situation in the Middle East but also in the world. By the time Presidents [John] Kennedy and [Lyndon] Johnson reached office, the special enterprise of winning over the "unaligned" States was no longer relevant; the India-Yugoslavia-Egypt bloc had crumbled (particularly after the death of [Jawaharlal] Nehru). Also no longer relevant was the design, demonstratively pursued by Dulles, to gain favour with the Arab States by dissociating America from the colonialism of her allies, Britain and France. The departure of France from North Africa, and Britain from her remaining territories in the Middle East, left the United States with no "imperialism" to decry. The principal major change, however, was the increasing penetration of the Soviet Union in the Middle East, which developed deeper and deeper in the years that followed until it ultimately evolved into a full-scale presence. The Russians had operated shrewdly: they were careful not to take unnecessary risks, but they were energetic and alert enough to seize every opportunity to extend the range of their influence.

An important factor, too, was the growing awareness in the United States of the independence-minded qualities of Israel. She had shown that she was able to stand up for herself, and even to withstand Soviet pressures. These qualities, of course, sprang from sources that were wholly Israeli. But Israel's determination not to become a victim of Soviet penetration—nor indeed to become anyone's puppet—was nonetheless congruent with wider American interests.

These international developments and their constant review and reappraisal by America's leaders eventually brought about a revolutionary change in the American response to Israel's requests for arms—from a virtual embargo in the early fifties to the supply of tanks and planes in the middle sixties. . . .

The Hawk missiles, which [David] Ben-Gurion had requested in his first talk with Kennedy as President, were the first major weapons to breach the wall of America's arms embargo. They were to play a valuable part in strengthening the deterrent and defence system of Israel. . . .

My second memorable visit to Washington took place a year later. On the last day of May 1964, I accompanied the late Levi Eshkol, who had followed Ben-Gurion as Prime Minister of Israel, on his first official visit to the American capital. President Johnson, in a special gesture to Mr. Eshkol, had given it the status of a State visit, and Mr. Eshkol was a guest of the President. . . .

Before leaving for Washington, we had reviewed our prospects. We were reasonably certain of getting some of the things we would ask for, hopeful about others. We also thought there might be subtle political pressures on some points. In the event, we found we had exaggerated the danger of pressures, and had been slightly optimistic about securing all we wanted. We had not yet learned that in a visit of a few days, one can do no more than open doors. Practical results take longer.

We felt that the visit would have several useful effects. It would demonstrate to the world the warmth of Israel-American relations. It would enable us to gauge at first hand the Administration's attitude towards Egypt. It would give the Israeli Prime Minister the opportunity to seek directly an American declaration to support Israel if she were attacked. It would also give us the opportunity of trying to break the partial arms embargo which the United States still maintained against us. We were particularly interested in tanks—we were still getting aircraft from France—for disturbing reports had reached us of a new arms deal between Russia and Egypt, as well as information on the development of two types of ground-to-ground missiles which the Egyptians were carrying out with the aid of German scientists.

There were two other items on which we sought American help. One concerned an idea we had been working on to establish a nuclear desalination plant, and we thought the United States might aid us in a joint project—for lack of water was becoming a problem for some regions of America as well. Finally, we were very worried about the fate of the Jews in Russia, and we hoped the United States might use her good offices to secure an easing of their lot.

As against our requests, we thought we might find ourselves under pressure from the United States Government on two subjects. One was the possible American demand that we take back Arab refugees before any Arab-Israel agreement and without any permanent political arrangement for peace in the region. The other was that we accept an inverted arms balance, namely, a reduction in the quantities of arms in the Middle East, which would leave us woefully short.

On the morning of 1 June 1964, the President's helicopter landed us on the White House lawn, and through the windows of the craft we could see the honour guard already drawn up in the form of three sides of a square, composed of Navy, Marines, Air Force and Infantry detachments. Near them stood two military bands and the official welcoming party. As soon as the door of the helicopter was opened, the President stepped towards us, accompanied by Lady Bird [Johnson's wife], and greeted us warmly. After a short and graceful speech by the President and Mr. Eshkol's response, Mr. Johnson led us into his working office. It seemed much the same as in Kennedy's day, except that the model of the PT-boat was no longer there, and against one wall was a small bust of the assassinated President.

After polite exchanges, Mr. Johnson hinted that he would like to conduct part of the talk with the Prime Minister alone, and we all left them. When we were asked to come in again, Eshkol was beaming. As I took my seat beside him, and while the rest of the party were going to their places, he had time to tell me that the President could not have been more friendly, saying that "the United States stands four-square behind Israel"; that America would "not be idle if Israel is attacked"; and that this undertaking, given by both his predecessor and himself, was a "solemn and serious commitment."

The talks now entered the formal stage, and the President opened by making clear America's position on five points: on water, he said that the United States would support the implementation of the "Johnston Plan"—the plan drawn up by President Eisenhower's special envoy, the late Eric Johnston, on the division of the waters of the Jordan and Yarmuk rivers between Israel and Jordan; on tanks: America would help Israel get them; on the defence of Israel: America stood behind her; on missiles: the United States was against proliferation of nuclear weapons in the world, and she was certainly against their proliferation in the Middle East; on desalination: the United States would extend her help.

The President enlarged on all these points, and he concluded by saying that he regarded Mr. Eshkol's visit as an expression of the friendship that existed between the two peoples. Turning to the Prime Minister, he added, with a smile: "Some say that we're alike. Well, that's not all bad."

It was now Eshkol's turn to speak. This was certainly one of the most dramatic moments of his life, and one heavy with responsibility. He had come a long way from his father's flour mill in the Ukraine, and from the swamps in the Jordan Valley which he had helped to clear as a young labouring pioneer in Palestine. He was now a guest in the White House, the official representative of his people. He spoke with his usual simplicity, his mind firmly focused on essentials. After outlining the dangers which still encompassed Israel, he said that he certainly appreciated the "American commitment," but he could not go back and tell his people that they could rely on that alone. A nation had to rely on itself, its soldiers and its weapons for its defense. It might be true, as the President had said, that the Egyptian missiles were "primitive" and not very accurate; but they could cause much damage in our populated areas. The balance of forces was in Nasser's favour—or Nasser might think so—and it was impossible to depend only upon "the nice words said about Israel's Defence Forces." Israel wanted tanks. He hoped the President would understand that the defence of Israel had to be a "do it yourself" undertaking. It would be worth helping Nasser only when he agreed to transfer the resources of Egypt from the military to the economic field. He ended by urging the President to speed up the joint desalination project.

The opening statements by the two principals were followed by a discussion in which the rest of us took part. This first meeting established the framework of our negotiations, though it did not exhaust the subjects we would be taking up....

The negotiations ended with America's agreement to supply Israel with Patton tanks (which the Jordanians were already getting) and Skyhawk planes. (Jordan preferred the F-104.) This brought to an end the policy of the United States "not to be the major supplier of arms to the Middle East." This, to my mind, became inevitable the moment the Russians took that function upon themselves—but becoming the chief supplier to one side only. This was the side of the Anti-Western Arab States, whose enmity of Israel had brought them to the abandonment of their vaunted "non-alignment" stand in the global conflict and bound them tightly to the policy of Moscow. This policy, for all Moscow's pretensions to be the pioneers of Marxist revolutionary ideology, was but a continuance of the imperialist ambitions of Czarist Russia.

57

Gamal Abdul Nasser

The Arab Summit Conferences

May 31, 1965

The Sinai Campaign was followed by a lull in the Arab-Israeli conflict. Israel acquired the means for a policy of deterrence, and Egypt was determined not to be dragged into another war without proper preparation. The debate over the issue of the Jordan River waters serves to illustrate both the Egyptian outlook at that time and the interlacing of the Arab-Israeli conflict and inter-Arab rivalries.

Shared usage of the Jordan River waters has been a persistent issue in the Arab-Israeli conflict. Eric Johnston's mission in the early 1950s led to a de facto agreement between Israel and Jordan regarding the distribution and utilization of the waters that allowed Israel to build its National Water Carrier System in stages. In 1964, during the final stages of its completion, Jordan and Syria attempted to divert the Jordan River, the sources of which are primarily in Syria, and thereby deprive Israel of most of these waters.

The First Arab Summit Conference, held in Cairo in January 1964, was called by Gamal Abdul Nasser to

Source: Israeli Foreign Broadcast Information Service, *Daily Report,* no. 55 (June 3, 1965), pp. B5–B7.

counter Israel's plans to pump Jordan River waters to the Negev. At the meeting the Arab League decided that its members should proceed with plans to divert the river waters. The Arab kings and heads of state also addressed broader issues. They affirmed that "they will regulate their political and economic relations with other countries according to the stands of these countries towards the Arabs' legitimate struggle against Zionist designs in the Arab world." They accused Israel of "continuous acts of aggression," "practicing racial discrimination against the Arab minority," having "evicted the Arab Palestine people from their home," and subjecting Afro-Asian states to "Zionist, imperialist dangers and designs—particularly in Africa." To put teeth into these accusations, they placed their armies under a Unified Arab Command. The conference also began the discussions that led to the establishment and support of the Palestine Liberation Organization, which was proclaimed in March 1964 at the Arab Palestinian Congress in (Jordanian) Jerusalem.

With the diversion of the Jordan River waters thus approved by the Arab League, Israel responded by artillery and tank fire to obstruct the project and finally, in November 1964, attacked construction sites by air. Israel had long maintained that any attempt to deprive it of its rightful share of the Jordan River waters would be considered a casus belli. *The Second Arab Summit Conference, held in Alexandria in September 1964, dealt with essentially the same set of issues, as did a meeting of Arab heads of state held in Cairo in May 1965.*

The following excerpts are taken from a speech delivered by President Nasser to the Palestine National Council on May 31, 1965, shortly after the meeting of Arab heads of state in Cairo. It addresses the controversies among the Arab states, particularly Egypt and Syria, over implementation of the resolutions of the conferences. The issues at stake—the diversion of the tributaries of the Jordan River waters, the Palestinian entity, the Unified Arab Command—ultimately produced the crisis of May 1967.

On 23 December [1963] I stood and called for a conference of the Arab kings and presidents to discuss the question of Palestine and for a unified Arab action in regard to Palestine. The question was that Israel had diverted the Jordan River, that resolutions had been made in the Arab League since 1960 providing for the diversion of the Jordan River tributaries, and that some other resolutions had been made at the Arab League since 1960 providing for the setting up of a Unified Arab Command but that these resolutions have not been implemented.

For this reason, at the time I felt the great danger to our action and felt that work within the framework of the Arab League in the normal way would not bring us a step forward toward collective Arab action and that it was our duty to make another attempt. Thus I called for the conference of Arab kings and presidents. This was another or second course of unified Arab action.

The Arab kings and presidents met. All of us were aware of the conditions of the Arab states at the time and of the disputes and clashes and how imperialism and Zionism relied on these disputes and clashes and fanned them. The conference represented a course of Arab action. In my personal opinion, it worked for the accomplishment of one marginal or secondary task (*muhimah janibiyah aw fariyah*). It tackled one of the complications of the danger which faced us at the time, namely, the waste of the unified Arab effort in the face of the Israeli action.

Again in order to be well informed about things, we ask ourselves: is this conference, the first conference of Arab presidents and kings and the second conference of Arab presidents and kings, and the conference of heads of states or the one Arab action which resulted from the summit conference—are they the road to the liberation of Palestine? We ask ourselves this question in order to reply to it and find out what the state of affairs is among Arab nations. There are contradictions among the Arab states. There are problems among the Arab states. There is a lack of confidence among the Arab states. There is war among the Arab states. In Yemen, there is a conflict between Yemen and the UAR [United Arab Republic] on the one side and Saudi Arabia on the other, and the British as well.

There are these contradictions. Shall we forget them and shall we close our eyes and say that all the matters have been settled, all the problems have been solved, and that the way is now paved? Shall we say that we have held a conference for the kings and presidents, that some speeches were made at this conference, and that some resolutions were adopted and, therefore, the Palestine problem is solved?

I say that we must view things realistically. . . . Differences could be gradually settled through meetings and conflicts could also be overcome gradually. We can adopt a unanimous attitude on certain things but we will not be able to be unanimous about everything. Everyone has his own interests. Everyone has his apprehensions about the other. This shows that there are suspicions and conflicts. This is evident in not allowing the Arab armies to move from one Arab country to another. This is a reality which we must admit.

There are problems between Syria and Iraq; there are problems between Syria and Egypt; and there are problems between Saudi Arabia and Egypt. There are, of course, suspicions in Lebanon—they do not accept any Arab force. We are experiencing these situations and, therefore, we must accept them and not overlook them. But how could the unified Arab action be of help to us? Unified Arab action which was the result of the conference of kings and presidents had pushed us a step forward from the point where we were before in the Arab League. Therefore, unified Arab action is only one way of Arab action.

Palestine cannot be liberated by holding conferences. When the Arab countries meet, as they met last week, some try to outbid the others; some launch attacks; some write articles and make broadcasts. We read of some Arab countries—that we must open all the Arab fronts against Israel and that a joint Arab action should be taken when Syria is attacked. We also read that the Arab unified command did not take any action when Syria and Jordan were attacked. And every Arab country tries to put the blame on another Arab country claiming that it is carrying out its duties fully while the Unified Arab Command failed to fulfill its task. Such countries hold that the Unified Arab Command should have done this or that. We can do nothing unless air and land protection is provided for us and we cannot divert the Jordan tributaries without land and air protection, and so everyone puts the blame on the other.

58

Syrian Ba'ath Party

The Conflict with Israel

March 1966

The Ba'ath (Renaissance) Party, founded in Syria in the 1940s, is Pan-Arab and calls itself socialist. It won seats for the first time in the Syrian elections of 1954 and began to spill over into Jordan, Lebanon, and Iraq. After 1958 pressure from Egyptian president Gamal Abdul Nasser forced it underground, but it seized power in Syria in 1963 and in Iraq in 1968.

On February 23, 1966, one faction of the Ba'ath Party in Syria staged a military coup and ousted its rivals from power. The coup resulted in the emergence of a radical regime that preached and implemented a more militant policy in a number of spheres, including the Arab-Israeli conflict. The new line was clearly articulated in this statement of purpose adopted at the regional (Syrian) congress of the Ba'ath held in March 1966.

The traditional presentation of the campaign for the liberation of Palestine and the resolutions of the summit conferences which were cast into this would in the end lead only to the piling up of arms in the various Arab countries. Military preparations are indeed necessary, but they must be made within the framework of a program which has a time limit. It has become absolutely clear that time in no way favours the Arabs, and that each passing day increases Israel's military and economic strength. The time factor will progressively work in her favour now that she has decided to exploit the atom both for peace and for war. It is therefore necessary to consider decisive revolutionary action, which will deny Israel the benefit of the time factor and frustrate the plans she has based on it. It is essential to begin the campaign; obviously, this presentation of the problem demands a definition of the nature of the struggle, its methods and its instruments. The experiences of the peoples struggling against Imperialism have proved that the only way to make war against superior forces is by means of a people's war of liberation. This war has to take on a certain form, suited to the given Arab reality. This demands an analysis of the problem in revolutionary terms which lays bare the actual possibilities and describes their development and growth in the future: the world powers, both east and west, regard the Middle East in a special way. The traditional policy strives to maintain this region free from war and its accompanying phenomena, since any escalation towards war would endanger the maritime passages and the oil lines, a result affecting the whole world. Until now this concern has been directed towards the preservation of Israel's existence, as a consequence of the Arabs' weakness and their surrender to pressure and their reluctance to act. The time has come for us to exploit this concern in our favour, and we will not be able to do this unless we prove that we are stronger than this pressure and that our firm decision to open the campaign will be accompanied by a real readiness to make enormous

---

Source: Abraham Ben-Tzur, ed., *The Syrian Ba'ath Party and Israel: Documents from the Internal Party Publications* (Givat Havivah: Center for Arab and Afro-Asian Studies, 1968), pp. 19–21. Reprinted by permission.

sacrifices. We must be psychologically prepared to bear the consequences (of beginning the war), however dire they may be, even if the price demanded is the total destruction of all that we have built up within the sphere of civilization, or of all the development projects which we thought of building; because all of these things can be created again after the elimination of Israel, and then we will direct our enormous resources towards economic development and prosperity.

59
Yitzhak Rabin
The Last Stages of the Crisis
May 1967: Memoir

Tensions between Israel and the neighboring Arab states increased in the spring of 1967. Egypt, Syria, and Jordan were mobilizing their troops and preparing for a possible military confrontation. When Egyptian president Gamal Abdul Nasser declared on May 22 that the Straits of Tiran (see map 3) were closed to Israeli shipping, he committed a belligerent act that Israel had long maintained would be a casus belli.

Yitzhak Rabin (1922–1995), Israel's prime minister in the years 1974–77, 1992–95, was chief of staff of the Israel Defense Forces when war broke out in June. In the preceding years, when Levi Eshkol was prime minister and minister of defense, Rabin had played a crucial role in shaping Israel's defense policies. The following is a brief account by Rabin of the development of the May Crisis that led to the Six-Day War.

The Syrian government passed the information on to Egypt[1] and requested an urgent consultation with the Egyptian chief of staff. Eager to prove that he was capable of deterring Israel from carrying out her "aggressive designs," [Gamal Abdul] Nasser began to undertake a series of steps. On 14 May I received the first report—vague and laconic—that something was afoot in Egypt. The chariots of war were beginning to roll.

The following day, as I stood in the reviewing stand in Jerusalem watching the IDF's [Israel Defense Forces] Independence Day parade, firm reports of Egyptian troop movements were whispered into my ear. The Egyptian army was moving through the streets of Cairo on its way eastward toward the Suez Canal. I immediately instructed Southern Command to step up its reconnaissance activities and Northern Command to refrain from superfluous troop movements (so as not to foster the impression that we were planning to attack). The next day our government also took a political step by notifying the American and French ambassadors that the reports of Israeli troop concentrations on the northern border were unfounded. What, then, was going on?

Source: Yitzhak Rabin, *The Rabin Memoirs* (Jerusalem and London: Weidenfeld and Nicolson, 1979), pp. 133–39. Reprinted by permission of Leah Rabin.

GHQ's Intelligence Branch submitted its assessment that we were facing a repetition of Operation Rotem[2] and that the Egyptians would withdraw their forces to the west of the Suez Canal after a time. Nevertheless over the next few days we continued to take precautions: heightening the alert of our forces, deploying regular armoured units in the south, placing reserved armoured brigades on mobilization alert, and laying minefields at vulnerable spots along the Egyptian border. At the same time, standing orders were to refrain from overt movements to avoid an escalation of tension. It was a very delicate situation. We had to react to the military moves in Egypt, both to protect our security and keep up our deterrent posture. Had we failed to react—giving the Egyptians the impression that we were either unaware of their moves or complacent about them—we might be inviting attack on grounds of vulnerability. On the other hand, an overreaction on our part might nourish the Arabs' fears that we had aggressive intentions and thus provoke a totally unwanted war.

As we constantly monitored Egypt's moves, events moved slowly but steadily toward a more alarming situation. As early as the evening of 16 May, I spoke to the prime minister about the option of beginning to mobilize reserves. The Egyptian 4th (Armoured) Division—whose movements were considered highly indicative of Egypt's intentions—had not yet left its camps near Cairo. But if it were to move into Sinai, I felt there was no way of postponing partial mobilization. [Levi] Eshkol was understanding of my position and approved the call-up of a reserve armoured brigade.

The next day, 17 May, we learned that the Egyptians had stepped matters up another notch by demanding that the U.N. forces stationed along the Sinai border be removed from their positions and transferred to Gaza and Sharm el-Sheikh. This move was a radical departure from the pattern of Operation Rotem and sufficient reason for alarm. Still, it was a calculated step and did not necessarily call for an immediate, belligerent response. First of all, as many people throughout the world expected, rather than respond to Nasser's dictates the U.N. might categorically refuse to remove the UNEF [United Nations Emergency Force] force. At the very least it would take time for the General Assembly or Security Council to meet and debate the matter, which would slow down the momentum of developments. On the other hand, by focusing world attention on his martial posturing, Nasser might only be using the U.N. as a tool to impress his point on Syria and other Arab states: he was not hiding behind the UNEF force. On the contrary, he was trying to remove it and, by doing so, was sufficiently intimidating Israel to defer any warlike actions on her part. Seen in this light, Nasser might even have been banking on the assumption that the U.N. would turn down his request.

But even if the U.N. let him have his way, Nasser assumed that as long as he did not order the UNEF to leave the Gaza Strip and Sharm el-Sheikh (guarding the sea lane through the Straits of Tiran), he would not be confronting Israel with a *casus belli*. Instead, he would be manoeuvring us into the uncomfortable position of having to deal with a potentially explosive situation that none the less fell short of being a clear-cut pretext for war, while he would remain free to dictate all the moves. Or so he thought.

The one possibility that Nasser overlooked was that the U.N. would not necessarily play the game by his rules. Commentators and historians have spent much ink on speculations about what would have happened if Secretary-General U Thant had agreed to Nasser's demand for a limited withdrawal of U.N. forces. But on 17 May we learned that U Thant had presented Nasser with only two options: either the U.N. troops remained in all their positions or they withdrew from the Middle East entirely. Given that choice, Nasser was left with the problem of saving face. His reply was quick in coming: the U.N. force was to withdraw from all its positions. In the chain of events that drew

Nasser into war—perhaps contrary to his original intention—U Thant's action proved to be a vital link.

Our response was no less unequivocal. A GHQ order placed all land, sea and air units on top alert. On the evening of 17 May, Aharon Yariv, the head of Intelligence Branch, reported that the Egyptian forces in Sinai were equipped with ammunition containing poison gas. At that time we were unprepared for chemical warfare and our anxiety deepened. Moreover, for the first time in the current train of events, Yariv altered his basic assessment: if Nasser were to order all the U.N. units to withdraw, we should regard the move as a clear indication of Egypt's aggressive intentions.

Early on the afternoon of 18 May our final uncertainties about the U.N. forces were dispelled. The Egyptian foreign minister officially demanded the total withdrawal of all U.N. units from Egyptian territory. I asked the prime minister to approve the mobilization of additional reserves primarily for the defence of our border with the Gaza Strip, where a Palestine division with forty-four tanks was stationed. I also notified Eshkol that the entire Syrian army was now on emergency footing, and he consented to the mobilization of one battalion in Upper Galilee. Yet we still felt bound to act cautiously since any mobilization exceeding our vital needs was liable to lead to further escalation, which we were anxious to prevent.

I held a further conference with the prime minister at eleven o'clock that night and submitted my assessment that the Egyptians were liable to close the Straits of Tiran within two or three days, placing Israel in a situation that would oblige her to go to war. I added, however, that even if the Egyptians refrained from blockading the straits, our situation would be no less difficult. We simply could not keep our reserves mobilized for long, as demanded by the presence of large Egyptian forces in Sinai. Whether or not the Egyptians were bent on leading the situation to war at present, we were inevitably moving in that direction.

By that evening, 19 May, the U.N. forces had been withdrawn and we faced the imposing order of Egypt's forces in Sinai. Yariv's new assessment was that the Egyptians would continue their build-up and choose one of four options: (1) undertaking no further action but reaping the fruits of victory by declaring that Egypt had deterred Israel from carrying out her "aggressive designs"; (2) instigating a provocation in order to bait us into striking back; (3) initiating an attack without prior provocation, to make the most of surprise; or (4) opting for a long period of tension—thereby forcing us to keep our reserves mobilized—and then choosing a comfortable opportunity to attack.

It was clear to me that whichever option Egypt adopted, Israel would stand alone in its forthcoming struggle. I ordered all commanding officers to make it clear to their men that we were heading for war. Without doubt we now faced the gravest situation Israel had known since the War of Independence. Yet any immediate action on our part was bound by a severe political drawback: the Egyptians had still not presented us with a concrete *casus belli* to justify launching a full-scale war. I agreed with our political leadership that we must not attack as long as the Egyptians had not undertaken some blatantly warlike act—such as blockading the Straits of Tiran or attacking targets in Israel. But deep inside I was convinced that this was only a matter of time; and I naturally assumed that, given a *casus belli*, the IDF would be ordered to attack. In the meanwhile, however, Nasser was still dictating the moves, and the delicate balance had to be maintained.

NOTES

1. The Soviet Union fed the Syrian government false information that the Israel Defense Forces had mobilized between eleven and thirteen brigades on the northern border and was about to launch a full-scale attack.
2. Operation Rotem was Israel's code name for its deployment of troops in early 1960 after Egypt began to deploy troops in the Sinai. No shots were fired, and a "minicrisis" (Rabin's term) was avoided. Rabin was chief of operations at the time.

60

Zayd al-Rifa'i

The Nasser-Hussein Reconciliation

May 1967: Memoir

Zayd al-Rifa'i (b. 1936) is from one of the few Palestinian families who became fully integrated into the Jordanian political elite. He was a member of the king's entourage and served as prime minister, 1973–76, 1985–89. His account of Jordan's drift into an alliance with Egypt just before the Six-Day War illuminates the relationship between inter-Arab relations and the Arab-Israeli conflict.

When [Gamal] Abdul Nasser closed the Straits of Tiran, the king [Hussein] became convinced that war was inevitable. Just as with the withdrawal of the U.N. Emergency Force, Jordan was not consulted and not given warning. We gathered these two important pieces of information by listening to radio broadcasts from Cairo, just like the rest of the Arab world and Egypt's Soviet allies—a fact about which Moscow complained bitterly.

This is the sequence of events:

On the morning of Monday, May 22 [1967], I was sitting, as usual, at my desk in the palace when I received a telephone call from Radio Amman. I was informed that Cairo Radio had just announced the closing of the Gulf of Aqaba [Gulf of Eilat to the Israelis].

At one o'clock the king arrived at his office and called me in. He had already heard the news and was most disturbed.

"This is very serious," he said. "I feel that war is now inevitable." But we contented ourselves with noting the event and nothing more.

The truth is that for the past year, Jordan had been isolated in the Arab world and had to accept abuse and vilification from Egypt. We therefore refused to get in touch with Egypt in order to hear her explanation. We were tired of always being the ones to make the first move. Since the withdrawal of the U.N. forces from Gaza, the king—who certainly derived no satisfaction from the events—had made several moves toward Cairo. We wanted to revive the machinery of Arab unity, which was more important than ever when we were confronted with this peril. All these moves had been of no avail, for Cairo kept silent.

For a few days nothing happened. After the initial moment of shock had subsided life returned to normal. The tension abated. We followed the diplomatic feelers that were put out after the "Gulf affair."

Meanwhile, forty-eight hours after the closing of the gulf we requested reinforcements from Saudi Arabia and Iraq through diplomatic channels. This was a cautious step in view of the deteriorating circumstances, a step that was entirely in accord with the principle of the collective defense pact that the Arab states had signed in Cairo in 1964 [see doc. 57]. The reinforcements took their time to arrive. To be more specific, the Saudi forces arrived after

---

Source: Zayd al-Rifa'i, *Hussein holekh lamilhamah* [Hussein Goes to War], ed. A. Kam (Tel Aviv: Maarakhot, 1974), pp. 46–48. Reprinted by permission.

everything was over and done with. The Iraqis responded with a downright refusal.

On May 28 another stage was reached in the process of escalation: President Abdul Nasser stated in Cairo at a press conference for three hundred reporters: "If Israel wants war then I say 'welcome.'" In other words, "Gentlemen, you will fire the first shot!"

With my ear attuned to the radio on my desk, I followed Abdul Nasser's press conference from beginning to end. Then I realized that His Majesty's fears were well founded. After all this, there could be no doubt that war would ensue.

The king also heard the Egyptian president's speech and immediately decided to send the chief of staff of the Jordanian army, Major General Amar Hamash, to Cairo. General Hamash's task was to contact the Unified Arab Command, whose headquarters had been in Egypt ever since the first summit meeting. He was to find out from the heads of the command their plans for withstanding a possible Israeli attack.

Upon his return from Cairo, Hamash informed the king that the end was looming over the Unified Arab Command as a result of disagreements between Egypt and the other Arab countries. These disputes caused a complete breakdown in all the command's activities.

Hamash also discovered that the command had played no role whatsoever in the present events. Egypt was acting according to a bilateral accord with Syria in these matters.

On the same day the Egyptian parliament invested Abdul Nasser with full authority and declared a state of emergency in all Egyptian airfields.

Faced with a clear deterioration in the situation, the king decided to make one last attempt to achieve a reconciliation with Egypt. He invited the Egyptian ambassador in Amman, Othman Nuri, to a meeting and informed him of his desire to meet with Nasser as soon as possible. The king stressed the importance of the meeting for coordinating our defense systems against the Israeli threat.

This desire to meet with Abdul Nasser may appear strange in the light of the insults broadcast on Cairo Radio over the preceding year, but there was no rhyme or reason at all for evading an issue in which clearly the whole Arab world was to become involved.

Cairo's response was received late at night on May 29. It was Sa'ad Juma'a, the Jordanian prime minister, who let the king know immediately by phone: Abdul Nasser welcomes the king's initiative.

On the morning of Tuesday, May 30, at sunrise, the king ordered a Caravel airplane from the Jordanian airlines Alia (named after the king's eldest daughter). At seven in the morning the plane took off from Amman airport. It carried a full crew, but, as usual, the king took the cockpit. King Hussein is too active a man to allow others to take the wheel, whether he is in a car or plane. He himself said, "Flying a plane soothes me and gives me great pleasure." One interesting detail: the king wore a khaki combat uniform and a beret bearing the emblem of the crown and his rank of supreme commander. He was armed with an American Magnum 357 revolver in a cloth holster attached to his belt above his left hip. Since the dispute broke out, the king had been in uniform like all of us.

Not a single bodyguard or member of the secret service or even a policeman accompanied him: this was one of the king's characteristic acts of bravery.

Before takeoff His Majesty said, "I shall probably be back for lunch," which in Jordan is at about 1:30 P.M.

The discussion with Abdul Nasser took longer than the king thought. He did not return at the time he had stated but ate with Nasser at the Kubbeh Palace, which had once been the residence of King Farouk.

The king's trip to Egypt had been kept secret, and so here at the palace in Amman the whole staff listened to the radio. This was a habit we had developed over the past fifteen days. Since Cairo had adopted her independent path, this had become the only means at our disposal for keeping up-to-date with the latest developments.

In my office, adjacent to the king's, I was also glued to my transistor.

At 3:30 P.M. Radio Cairo interrupted its broadcast with a news flash: "King Hussein and President Abdul Nasser are about to sign a mutual defense pact. The ceremony will be broadcast over the radio."

We all heaved a sigh of relief.

CHAPTER 4

Years of Euphoria, 1967–1973

71967
Israel occupies former Egyptian, Syrian, and Jordanian areas, including the Sinai Peninsula, Golan Heights, Gaza Strip, East Jerusalem, and West Bank

The Soviet Union breaks off diplomatic relations with Israel

Fourth Arab Summit Conference issues the Khartoum Resolutions

U.N. Security Council Resolution 242 provides a framework for settling the Arab-Israeli dispute

1968
Palestine Liberation Organization adopts a new charter

Israeli-Egyptian War of Attrition begins

1969
Levi Eshkol dies in office, and Golda Meir becomes prime minister

In the War of Attrition, Egyptian bombardments along the Suez Canal escalate into hostilities that end with a renewed cease-fire in 1970

1970
Actions by Palestinian fighters in Jordan plunge the country into civil war, known as Black September

Israeli-Egyptian War of Attrition ends

1971
The number of Soviet Jews immigrating to Israel begins to increase

1972
Arab terrorists kill eleven Israeli athletes at the Munich Olympics

1973
On the Day of Atonement, Egypt and Syria, aided by other, mostly Arab countries, launch a surprise attack on Israel, starting what is known as the Yom Kippur War

Domestic Issues

61

Shabtai Teveth

Administering the West Bank

June 1967: Analysis

At the end of the Six-Day War, the Israelis found themselves in control of territories containing about 1 million Arabs and other non-Jews (see map 3). At the end of 1967 the estimated population of the West Bank was 585,700; the estimated population of Gaza and northern Sinai was 380,700. The population of the Golan Heights—comprised almost totally of Druze, a sect that broke away from Islam centuries earlier and does not consider itself Arab—was unknown. One of the first steps to facilitate the transition from wartime control to peacetime governance of these territories was to declare them "nonenemy" areas and to place them under a combination of military and civilian administration. (Eastern Jerusalem was incorporated into the municipal administration of Jerusalem, and the city soon became administered as a unified city.) In the following account, Shabtai Teveth, one of Israel's leading journalists and political analysts, examines this transitional process as it occurred in the West Bank.

Moshe Dayan did not place himself personally in the governing apparatus handling the occupied territories. First Colonel Yehuda Nizan and afterwards Colonel Dan Hiram functioned with his deputy, Zvi Zur, as coordinators of the committee of Director-Generals, which was responsible to the Ministerial Committee headed by Finance Minister Pinhas Sapir. In August he established a coordinating committee and put Brigadier-General (then Colonel) Shlomo Gazit in charge. But this committee too was not given official status. Shlomo Gazit himself was subordinate to the Army General Staff. Thus, Dayan functioned through bodies responsible to other Ministers or directly subordinate to the General Staff.

Lack of a special apparatus in his own office created a situation whereby Zahal [Israel Defense Forces] alone was responsible for the Military Government. Perhaps the real reason was

Source: Shabtai Teveth, *The Cursed Blessing: The Story of Israel's Occupation of the West Bank* (London: Weidenfeld and Nicolson, 1970), pp. 96–105. Reprinted by permission of Shabtai Teveth.

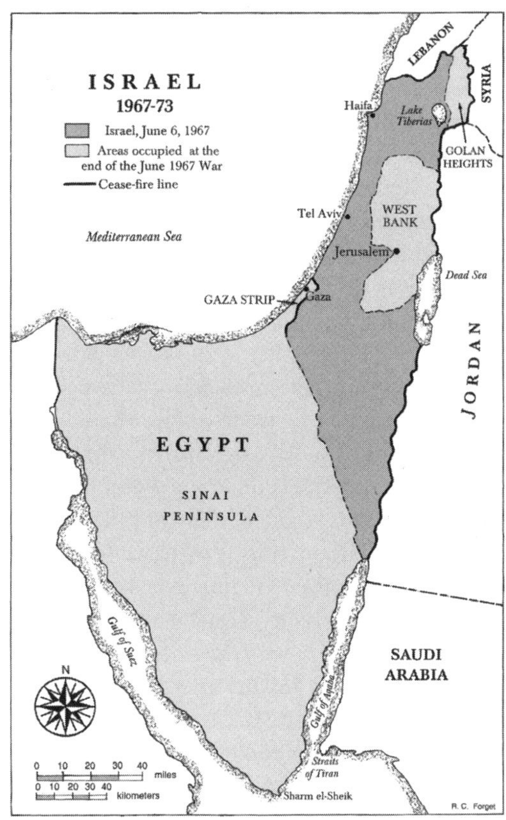

MAP 3. ISRAEL AFTER THE SIX-DAY WAR, 1967

that Dayan did not wish to create a new structure and fragment responsibility for the handling of the occupied territories. Absence of such machinery in his office brought about direct contact between Dayan and the military commanders in the various districts. This method of action not only put Dayan in the driver's seat of the government machine in the territories, but also made him the engine behind it. There were obvious inherent disadvantages in this method, as well as the advantages of daring and speedy action and maximal use of Dayan's talents and personality.

Initially, [Chaim] Herzog's command functioned in Jerusalem and the West Bank and Dayan maintained direct contact. While Herzog's HQ was in process of organization Dayan was still engaged in directing the war. On Friday 9 June the battle for Ramat Hagolan commenced and was ended the following day, Saturday 10 June, with the cease-fire order of the Security Council. During the battle in Ramat Hagolan Dayan visited the front, arriving there by air from Tel Aviv. In the week commencing Sunday 11 June and ending the following Friday he was still occupied with war problems and Army and Government meetings which laid down the principles of administration in the occupied territories. It was only on Saturday 17 June that he managed to pay a visit to the West Bank, Jerusalem, Nablus and Jenin.

It was a busy week even for someone who delegated authority in every aspect of his work. For Dayan, who wanted to personally get the feel of every problem and to set the administrative machine in motion by both steering and propelling the wheels, it was a particularly crowded week. During this week he was able to lay down only the most general of principles for Herzog's Command, which were to concentrate on Jerusalem and to return services to normal as speedily as possible.

However, for the first week of its existence absolute confusion reigned in Herzog's Command. His staff officers were personally the finest of their kind—and each, by virtue of his personality and his high position in the managerial and economic life of Israel, was entitled, at least in his own opinion, to participate in the supreme forum of the Command. Since no prior format for orderly staff work had been devised, General Herzog was forced to preside over large meetings where everyone was given the right to air his views as if it were some home circle for the clarification of questions of universal moment. The Command did not function through channels of bureaucracy, handing down of reports, executive functions and supervision. In addition the Command lacked an administrative base. In the first few days there was no one to prepare food for the scores of Command personnel crowded in the Ambassador Hotel.

A regular soldier like Brigadier-General—then Colonel—[Raphael] Vardi was concerned not with the shortcomings of the Command in dealing with civil matters, but with the fact that this was a command of Zahal forces supposed to be in charge of all units in the area, and, as a military command its main deficiency was that it lacked the means of communication with its own units.

Herzog, who was aware of these defects, agreed that the only way out of the confusions was to return matters to their previous state, namely, that the Central Command serve as both Army command and civil administration. The Central Command had an efficient headquarters, and means of communications with all units which had proved efficient during the war. One week after his appointment as Commander of Zahal Forces in the West Bank General Herzog returned the authority vested in him to General Narkis. From 15 June General [Uzi] Narkis was both General of the Central Command and the commander of Zahal Forces on the West Bank and, in everyday language, Military Governor. The military section of Herzog's HQ was annulled, there being no need for it, while the civil section was reorganized and added to the Central Command as a fourth branch. General Narkis had two chiefs of staff, his regular military chief of staff and a chief of staff for civil affairs, Colonel Raphael Vardi.

The timing of the annulment of General Herzog's command coincided with the Cabinet meeting at which it was decided to set up the Committee of Director-Generals. Government offices began sending their representatives to the West Bank Command and they replaced the various reserve officers and volunteers. The civil administration under Narkis and Vardi was divided into three departments—economic, services, and special affairs.

During his week as OC Zahal Forces in the West Bank, Herzog put a stop to the looting of shops and houses, order was established in the eastern section of Jerusalem and the services got moving. On Friday 9 June water and electricity supplies were resumed. Herzog even took upon himself responsibility for clearing the square in front of the Western Wall.

On Thursday 8 June at 4 P.M. Herzog called a meeting of the heads of religions in the Ambassador Hotel. About thirty priests were present, among them heads of the Christian Churches, the Greeks, Armenian, Syrian, Latin Lutheran, Anglican, Coptic, the Apostolic Representative of the Vatican and others. As General Herzog entered the hall the heads of the clergy rose to their feet. After thanking them for the honour showed him, he informed them that he had come to assure them in the name of the Israeli Government that there would be freedom of religious worship in the holy city. Despite the fact that for the nineteen years of Jordanian rule Jews from Israel had been forbidden access to holy places or to worship in the eastern city, Israel would act not in accordance with the precept of an eye for an eye but according to the rules of liberty and fraternity.

General Herzog spoke in a very personal vein. He knew many of the leaders of the clergy from the house of his father, the late Chief Rabbi of Palestine, Rabbi Yizhak Halevi Herzog. On opening his talk he mentioned this fact. "I know many of you from my father's house and I regard it as a great privilege that it has fallen to me to represent the Government of Israel before you and to be the person authorized to pledge full freedom of religion and rites to all denominations and sects." On the day of the meeting Legionnaires who had discarded their uniforms but retained their arms were still hiding in Christian religious institutions, many of whose religious officials were Arabs. General Herzog promised that no harm would befall these soldiers if they were handed over to Zahal. But while guaranteeing freedom of religion and worship, he announced that he would take strong measures against violators of law and order.

The Greek Patriarch, His Highness Gregorianus, replied in the name of those assembled there. Speaking in Greek, which was translated into English by one of the bishops accompanying him, he thanked the Government of Israel in the name of his colleagues for the polite and humane attitude displayed by the conquering Zahal soldiers. He then said that representatives of Christianity were not politicians and that their desire for freedom of religion and worship was very strong. Accordingly, he welcomed General Herzog's announcement assuring full freedom of religious worship. He concluded on a personal note. He personally regarded it as a sign from heaven that it should be the son of Rabbi Herzog who was given the task of passing on the tidings of freedom of religion in Jerusalem in the name of the Government of Israel, because he knew that the son of Rabbi Herzog understood the full significance of this promise.

The speakers following the Patriarch also warmly recalled the late Rabbi Herzog. After the head of the Lutheran Church had spoken in Arabic, Bishop McReas spoke in the name of the Anglican Church. He particularly stressed the significance of the fact that Rabbi Herzog's son was the harbinger of the communication from the Government of Israel and he regarded the fact that the Rabbi's son was the Governor as God's will. The Anglican commended Zahal for the fact that even at the cost of the lives of its soldiers it had made every effort not to damage the holy places in the heat of war. History would credit Zahal with this fact.

The representative of the Lutheran Church asked, "Why are our friends, the shepherds of the Moslem Community, absent from this gathering?" This was said as if he wished to assure their welfare. Herzog replied that he had intended to invite the Moslem priests but had been unable to locate them. He solemnly vowed that he would meet with the heads of the Moslem religion and decree their freedom of religion just as he had done with the leaders of the Christian sects. At the conclusion of the meeting champagne goblets were filled and everyone toasted the President of Israel.

General Herzog did not manage to meet the Moslem leaders and a meeting was held in special circumstances by Dayan. But on Friday afternoon 9 June Herzog called the Jordanian Commissioner of the Jerusalem District, Mr. Anwar El Khatib, to meet him. The Jordanian Commissioner was in a state of shock, a fact noted by Herzog himself. "Only on Tuesday afternoon, I was speaking to King Hussein and he told us: 'Hold out—we are coming to your aid,' and then on Wednesday morning I had to meet Colonel Mordechai Gur and inform him that all resistance had ceased." El Khatib told Herzog that he had appealed to the Legion not to fight from the Temple Mount, but they had paid him no heed and had stationed snipers in the Al-Aqsa Mosque.[1] He was touched by the humane attitude of the Zahal soldiers and admitted: "I never dreamed it would be this way." He too, like many Arabs, imagined that an Israeli victory would mean slaughter. Anuar El Khatib explained the set-up of the Jordanian administration in Jerusalem and offered his services getting the regional services functioning again and in returning life to normal. Herzog, however, had no reply for him since no policy on activation of Jordanian Government departments in the West Bank had as yet been decided upon.

At the end of the meeting Anuar El Khatib made a request which quite unintentionally was to be of political significance. He asked that the families of consuls from Arab states in Jerusalem, who had been stranded with no source of livelihood, be permitted to cross to the East Bank. He requested this specially for those among them who were his personal friends, for humane reasons. General Herzog promised him his full cooperation and even decided on an arrangement whereby on an appointed day, buses would be waiting at Nablus Gate to provide transport for whoever wished to get to the Jordan crossings. From there they could go to Jordan and the East Bank. El Khatib found it difficult to believe him.

"Whoever wants to go?" he asked.

"Whoever wants to go. We won't ask questions. We only want those who leave to sign that they are doing so of their own free will and not under duress."

Anuar El Khatib agreed and in this way he and General Herzog started an exit service to the East Bank. Herzog's Command issued an order stating that commencing on Thursday 15 June special arrangements would be made for the transport of Jordanian citizens wishing to cross from East Jerusalem to Jordan. They would be taken from the Nablus Gate to Jericho in special buses and from there would cross the Jordan on foot to the East Bank. Following this arrangement similar ones were made in other West Bank cities. In this way organized emigrant traffic from the West Bank to the East was being carried on in addition to that which had taken place before and during the war. Many others reached the river independently, by vehicle or on foot, and from there crossed to the East Bank. In all about 200,000 Arabs emigrated from the West Bank during and after the Six-Day War.

In spite of its deficiencies General Herzog's command instituted a series of measures which were later to be of great help to the Military Government. It was his command that decided to make a census of the population and before this was executed, gathered statistical data from Jordanian Government records. An inspiring example of quick Israeli action under impromptu circumstances was the survey on employment in the West Bank, including East Jerusalem, carried out by Hanoch Smith. This report was presented to the West Bank Command on Friday 9 June. The data was based on reports received from governors of various regions and on observations. Smith's report was interesting in that it estimated the population on the entire West Bank up to Thursday 7 June at under 800,000 persons. In the census run by the Central Bureau of Statistics on 11 July 1967, just under 600,000 inhabitants were counted on the West Bank (excluding East Jerusalem, which was then included in Israeli territory). A registration of inhabitants carried out by the Ministry of the Interior on 26 June 1967 put the population of East Jerusalem at just under 60,000 inhabitants. Taking into account the emigration, which was at its height in June, and which was estimated at 150,000 persons for that month, the final number comes to exactly Hanoch Smith's estimate.

In the reorganization of the West Bank Command, there was a portent of the general character of the future administration. General Narkis did not appoint Colonel Yehoshua Werbin as chief of his HQ Staff, but Colonel Raphael Vardi. Werbin had been a Military Government man in Israel and afterwards headed the GHQ department which had inherited the responsibilities of the Military Government in the Arab-populated areas of Israel, which had been annulled by [Levi] Eshkol before the Six-Day War. Narkis dubbed him a *moshlan,* that is to say a professional governor, and many copied the term. Since Dayan's method was to function through regular Army units in all matters pertaining to administration, General Narkis also thought that what he needed was a Regular Army man like Vardi as chief of staff, and not a specialist in government. Dayan had objected to the ways of the former Military Government in Israel and had no desire to repeat them on the West Bank. Also, Narkis felt more at home with field soldiers. This step subsequently led to the appointment of field officers as governors in various areas.

The first decision by Narkis and Herzog on the West Bank was routinely military in nature. Permits and check-points were strictly controlled both within and on the outside. The first thing the Zahal spokesman announced on 8 June was that a strip of land fifty metres wide along the length of the borders of the occupied territories was closed by the military authorities and any trespasser endangered his life. Since there had been no time for the West Bank administration to make advance preparations and Herzog's Command lacked communication with the units in the area, even this regime of permits and barriers lacked uniformity. Each commander issued his own permits and decided on his own checkpoints. The West Bank Command did not manage either to control the situation or to issue a uniform license form. Entry permits were issued by GHQ, by Herzog's Command, by brigade commanders, battalion commanders and company commanders.

NOTE

1. Al-Aqsa Mosque, part of the Haram al-Sharif (in Arabic, Noble Sanctuary), a complex of religious buildings on the Temple Mount in Jerusalem considered the most sacred place to Muslims after Mecca and Medina. The Al-Aqsa Mosque and the Qubat al-Sakhra (Dome of the Rock) are the two most important buildings in the complex.

62

Shabtai Teveth

The Conflict between Moshe Dayan and Pinhas Sapir

1968: Analysis

Since June 1967, the single most important debate within the Israeli political system has been the debate on the future of the West Bank and the Gaza Strip. The debate has divided the Israeli political spectrum along numerous lines. The profound difference between two key members of Levi Eshkol's government, Moshe Dayan and Pinhas Sapir, illustrates the complexity of the issues and the way in which several separate issues were superimposed on the dividing line in the debate over the Palestinian issue.

In 1967 [Moshe] Dayan opposed Israeli-Arab partnerships and demanded that the Arabs manage their own affairs and provide the public services they were accustomed to, even if these were on a much lower level than those provided in Israel; in 1968 he maintained that Israel was obliged to develop the public services in the Administered Territories and raise the standard of living as much as possible. He demanded that the government double the sums spent on services in the Territories. It was against the background of this demand that the first public confrontation occurred between Dayan and Pinhas Sapir, the Minister of Finance.

Sapir put all the weight of his considerable influence against the duplication of the Services Budget and objected to opening the entire Israeli economy to the Arabs of the Administered Territories. In the end, he managed to thwart Dayan's plan. The Cabinet, led by Eshkol, was mostly in Sapir's favor and limited the development of public services and investment in the Administered Territories. Permission to employ labor from the Territories was restricted and temporary, designed only to ease immediate problems of unemployment in the West Bank and the Gaza Strip. At first the government set a limit: no more than 5,000 workers from across the "Green Line."

Source: Shabtai Teveth, *Moshe Dayan* (Jerusalem, 1972), pp. 349–51. Reprinted by permission of Shabtai Teveth.

Sapir was candid about the reasons for his objections. He had no need of the confederacy Dayan was striving for and was quite content with a Jewish State with borders very similar to the "Green Line." He feared that employing Arabs from the Administered Territories in industry and manual labor within Israel would change the country's image, and the Israelis would cease to be a "nation of workers." Sapir was also concerned that a million and a half Arabs would threaten the demographic status of the country's Jewish majority. In a meeting of functionaries of the Labor Party (created out of the union of Mapai, Ahdut Haavodah and Rafi) held on November 11, 1968, he stated: "I am against adding a million Palestinian Arabs to the 400,000 Israeli Arabs in the country, who would then constitute a minority of 40% in Israel's population. And if their rate of natural increase continues to be three or more times greater than that of the Jewish population, it is not too difficult to calculate when there will be an Arab majority in the country."

The differences between Dayan and Sapir were clearly a function of their different outlooks on Israel. In Dayan's view, the two nations in the area formerly called Palestine could function within a single economy, even though they belonged to different cultures and sovereign states. The basic principle in his approach was neighborliness, or, in his phrase, "a joint way of life." Sapir's concept of a Jewish State was modeled on the first twenty years of Israel's existence, and even if peace came in the future, the marked differences that existed between Israel and its Arab neighbors would serve as a guarantee for the survival of the Jewish identity. Sapir would apparently have been content to dig a giant trench along Israel's borders and cut the country off from the Middle East. Dayan envisioned a land of many dimensions; Sapir relied on the conventional concepts that a Jewish State meant congruent geographical, demographic, political, and cultural borders.

Dayan saw the country as an integral part of a region and only its geographic and economic borders were identical. They contained two distinct demographic and cultural entities whose political demarcation did not follow strictly demographic lines. Thus an Arab from Jerusalem and an Arab from Nablus, though belonging to the same demographic and cultural group, could belong to different political entities. Both would work in the same economy but would vote for representatives in different countries and enjoy different civil rights. Dayan's overall aim was to blur the identification between the geographic and the demographic lines of demarcation. He therefore proposed that the government establish four Jewish cities along the mountain ridge extending from Hebron and Nablus, thereby breaking up the Arab demographic continuity. When he presented part of his plan to the public for the first time, he suggested that the Hebron-Beersheba area be turned into a single economic-administrative region. Another integrated area, in the north, could include Afula and Jenin.

The Jewish State Dayan envisaged was not defined by a geographical border but by demographic and cultural criteria. The same applied to the Palestinian entity, although he had not yet decided whether it should be a state in its own right or a part of the Hashemite Kingdom of Jordan whose inhabitants live in Israel. He did not care whether the Palestinian inhabitants of the West Bank temporarily remained Jordanian citizens or whether his "country-as-part-of-a-region" concept was complicated by the fact that Arabs living in a sovereign Israeli framework would be the citizens of and vote in another sovereign framework.

63
Amnon Rubinstein
The Israeli Left
1970: Analysis

Israel's military victory in June 1967 did not bring about the hoped-for political solution to the Arab-Israeli conflict. As it became clear that peace would not automatically follow the war, public debate centered increasingly around the political and diplomatic policies that Israel should be willing to pursue. A relatively small but vocal and well-organized network of left-wing groups emerged in opposition to the policies of the Labor-dominated National Unity government. In general these organizations believed that in any peace settlement Israel should be willing to return all territories captured during the war and recognize the legitimate national rights of the Palestinians; therefore Israel should not establish permanent civilian settlements in the captured territories.

Amnon Rubinstein (b. 1931), a legal scholar and a longtime member of Knesset, 1977–2003, and minister, 1984–87, 1992–96, discusses the emergence of this left-wing dissent in an article, excerpted here, published in the New York Times Magazine.

A wave of public disagreement with Government policy was brought about by the Goldmann affair. Dr. Nahum Goldmann, the 75-year-old president of the World Jewish Congress, has voiced growing dissatisfaction with what he regards as the Israeli Government's rigid policy, but until recently few Israelis paid any attention to him. The old-time Zionist leader has never been a popular figure in Israel. His Swiss passport, his departure from Israel before the June war, and his private diplomacy have not endeared him to the public. When, on April 2, *Haaretz*, Tel Aviv's independent daily, began publishing a series of articles in which Goldmann expounded his credo, his seemed an ancient voice in a new reality. Three days later, in an ironic twist of public mood, Goldmann, who had long felt rejected and forgotten, became the newly acclaimed hero of an angry opposition, a campus idol overnight. This change was brought about by a short communiqué on April 5, in which the Israeli Government announced that it had declined to sanction a Goldmann mission to Cairo to meet President [Gamal Abdul] Nasser.

The communiqué reflected the Israeli Government's notorious talent for ruinous public relations. The pompous language used was characteristic of Israeli bureaucracy. The Government failed to give reasons for its rejection and also omitted to add that it had no objection to Goldmann visiting Cairo on his own and not as a representative of Israel.

Many Israelis were astounded by the Government's announcement. Most Israelis believe that every possible crack in the wall of Arab enmity ought to be explored, and many felt that the alleged invitation to Goldmann constituted such a crack. At Tel Aviv University, a student assembly voted—by a clear majority—for the

---

Source: Amnon Rubinstein, "And Now in Israel a Fluttering of Doves," *New York Times Magazine*, July 26, 1970, pp. 8–9, 44–45, 47–48. Reprinted by permission of Amnon Rubinstein.

Goldmann visit, and against the Government. Newspaper columnists denounced the Government in unprecedented terms. *Haaretz* threw its weight into an all-out campaign against the Cabinet's policies in general and its handling of the Goldmann affair in particular; a random poll by that paper showed 63 percent against the Government on this issue. Even *Davar,*[1] Labor's own newspaper, demanded a more satisfactory explanation of the Cabinet's refusal to sanction the visit.

Fifty-six Jerusalem high-school pupils, including the son of a Cabinet minister, signed a letter addressed to Mrs. [Golda] Meir in which they bluntly questioned whether their forthcoming military service was justified in the light of the Government's decision. In Jerusalem, about 100 demonstrators tried to break into Mrs. Meir's house[2] and were repulsed by the police. Demonstrators sat down at three major road junctions and stopped traffic for an hour until they were forcibly removed by the police. For Israeli radicals, the Goldmann affair had at least one virtue: it removed the "stigma" of national consensus. They can now wear a "we, too" badge and look their Western colleagues straight in the eye.

The new voices of dissent emerged not out of any organized opposition to the Government, but spontaneously from amorphous groups. In Israel's centrist politics, this is a welcome innovation all the more surprising since it comes while the country is fighting a brutal war under siege conditions. Part of the explanation for this expression of nonconformist moods actually may be found in the united front and wide-coalition Government itself.

The Government commands a majority of 102 out of the 120 seats in the Knesset. Friction inside the Cabinet is not uncommon and the rule of collective government responsibility is honored more in its breach than in its observance. Yet, the very existence of this wall-to-wall coalition and the virtual disappearance of a real opposition have produced an atmosphere of political tranquility. A minority of Israelis find this consensus stifling and almost instinctively rebel against it. "Someone," said a high school student on a recent radio program, "has to say 'no,' otherwise we may forget what democracy is all about."

The nay-sayers comprise a number of small, divergent groups. The original nucleus came from the Hebrew University of Jerusalem, where, after the Six-Day War, a group of professors founded the Movement for Peace and Security. Among the members and supporters of this movement are some of the university's leading names: Yehoshua Bar Hillel (philosophy), Yaakov Talmon and Yehoshua Arieli (history), and Avigdor Levontin (law). The movement, which has a substantial following among younger faculty members and the student body, was formed as an antidote to the Greater Israel Movement. It has pleaded, at meetings and through newspaper advertisements, against annexation of Israeli-occupied areas and the creation of *faits accomplis* in the new territories, and for a moderate policy which would leave open every option for a peaceful settlement.

Out of the Jerusalem campus sprang the Peace List which, in November, 1969, ran in the Knesset elections. It was headed by two young professors: Gadi Yatziv, a sociologist, and Saul Fogel, a mathematician, and failed to win even one seat. The beating at the polls weakened the movement and dulled its edge. Yet the nucleus of dissenting professors is still there and their peace offensive has gathered momentum as a result of the Goldmann storm.

The Jerusalem group has recently initiated a public campaign against the Government's plan to build 250 houses for Jewish settlers in Hebron. The campaign began with an advertisement which said the project would "antagonize the Palestinian Arabs and hinder peace efforts"; the public was invited to pay for and sign further advertisements. The results were impressive: seven long ads and hundreds of signatures. Among the signatories were artists, authors, journalists, scientists and prominent Israelis from all walks of life. Surprisingly, the list included names of persons highly placed in the establishment, such as the Inspector of Banks and the former Director of the Treasury.

The Hebron ads are part of an almost daily press war fought between doves and hawks. They include petitions for and against annexation, direct talks, and Government rigidity; eccentric, far-fetched peace solutions spelled out by a Jerusalem doctor; cartoons against administrative arrests of suspected *fedayeen*; farmers lashing out in Agnewish[3] terms against the loud minority of professors and journalists; peace poems lamenting the dead, denouncing annexationists, glorifying peace. All these quite expensive ads are paid for by individuals—often from their meager funds—and testify to the Israelis' inherent need to speak out, not despite the war, but because of it.

Siah, a new radical-left group, does not participate in this ad war. It has been involved in noisy demonstrations and occasional clashes with the police. The members of this group have taken much of their terminology and some of their tactics from the New Left in Europe or America. Protesting against the planned settlement in Hebron, a number of Siah members carried a coffin which bore the slogan: "Here lies the last chance of peace," and buried it next to Government offices. Because of its noisy carryings-on, Siah has been accused of anti-Israeli sympathies and has even been equated with the Mazpen, the extreme pro-Fatah, and anti-Zionist group. Yet Siah's philosophy is Zionist and its only quarrel is with the Government's policy.

Siah has no ordinary membership. About 500 people participate in its activities and another 500 are regarded as supporters. They come from three sectors: members of left-wing (Mapam) kibbutzim, who are disillusioned with their party's participation in the coalition Government; ex-Communists who frown upon their leadership's return to the fold; intellectuals and artists who associate themselves with the New Left. Prominent members are two students at Tel Aviv University: Ran Cohen, 31 (economics), member of Kibbutz Gan Shmuel and a reserve officer in the paratroop corps, and Yossi Amitai, 33 (Middle Eastern Studies), member of Kibbutz Gvulot.

Says Ran Cohen:

> We regard ourselves as Zionists and radicals. Our philosophy is based on self-determination within Palestine, for Arabs and Jews. We regard the Six-Day War as a justified defensive war, but because [it was this], we are against any annexation and any Jewish settlement in the occupied territories. We believe in the possibility of a peaceful settlement which will give the Palestinians their inherent right to self-determination and will, at the same time, insure Israel's security. We are also committed to the radical left—not in its Soviet perversion—but in its true meaning. Yet we are different from the New Left in the West. First, we, unlike them, have to insure our national existence. Secondly, our whole background and society are different from theirs. But we have things in common: a belief in direct action, a rejection of the old dogmatic left, a burning need to change the present reality.

Though tiny, Siah has played an important role in the new dissent. It has, in some ways, saved the radical tradition in Israel. With the traditional left in Government, and the Israeli (Jewish) Communist party domesticated and respectable, Siah remains the bearer of Israeli radicalism. By its acceptance of basic Zionist tenets, Siah has demonstrated that the ideas of the New Left do not necessarily lead to a rejection of Israel as a Jewish state. The facts that almost all of Siah's members are recruited from the younger generation and that its leaders play their part in the defense of the country, have made its role significant. Unlike Mazpen, Siah has managed to be virulently anti-Government without associating itself with the Arab cause.

On the contrary, Siah criticizes the Arab left for denying the Jewish people the inherent right to self-determination.

Haolam Hazeh is another advocate of nonconformist ideas. This small party has two members of Knesset, and its leader, Uri Avnery, was the first political figure to wave the flag of a Palestinian entity and to draw public attention to the growing role the Palestinians play in the Arab world.

All these groups make up a small part of the Israeli public. The reason the new dissent has the impact that it does is that it occasionally appeals to a broader section of public opinion. This broad section encompasses people from most political parties: they are united not by any definitive ideology but by an almost instinctive rejection of nationalist myths and annexationist creeds. They believe that some compromise solution must be found to bring an end to the tragic conflict between Arabs and Jews.

This mood is tested daily by the brutal *fedayeen* attacks on civilians and the venomous anti-Jewish propaganda emanating from Arab radio stations and press. Yet the mood persists; its motto is: "If the Arabs are ready for real peace, we would be ready to give up a lot." In other words, these dissenters believe, the national consensus is being kept in existence by the continuous Arab "no."

The Goldmann affair and its aftermath indicate how deeply divided public opinion in Israel would have been had there been any positive Arab response. For a moment, when it seemed that there was a faint rumor of an Arab voice whispering "yes," the whole country seemed to have been rent asunder.

It is this phenomenon and not the noise emanating from small radical groups which is indicative of the strength of the peace lobby in Israel. The great majority of Israelis would give up territory, dispense with diplomatic paraphernalia and go out of their way to put an end to the war. At the same time, they are ready to fight with the courage and valor which have made them famous, provided they know that there is *ein breirah,* that there is "no alternative," and that war and death are forced upon them.

Mrs. Meir and her Government are impressed by the new sounds of protest, not because of their volume but because, for a time, they seemed to have shaken the solid rock of *ein breirah* on which national consensus has been built. Mrs. Meir has sensed that in this case the qualms of the young and the question marks of the journalists have to be tackled and answered immediately.

It is no secret that Mrs. Meir and some of her colleagues were alarmed specifically by the outcry against the Government's rigidity. As a senior Cabinet minister admitted off the record, Mrs. Meir's recent statement in the Knesset in which she accepted the Security Council's settlement-terms resolution of Nov. 22, 1967, should be ascribed not only to external factors—mainly American prodding—but also to internal pressure: the Government wanted to appease the determined minority which was unhappy about Israeli *nyets.* It was this anxiety which, at least partly, was responsible for the Government's relatively moderate reaction to the recent American initiative [the Rogers Plan, described below].

This sensitivity to under-current moods of public opinion is not characteristic of Israeli politics. On the contrary, because of the completely proportional electoral system, under which members of the Knesset are picked by party nomination committees, there is a tendency to disregard minority groups. Only a few months before the Goldmann fiasco, the Government had disregarded strong secular feelings on the "Who-is-a-Jew" issue and high-handedly pushed the quasi-orthodox definition through the Knesset. This new response to public mood does not usher in a new atmosphere; it merely attests to the magnitude of the issue involved. On this issue of *ein breirah,* of no alternative, even a small minority of nay-sayers succeeds in shaking the political establishment.

How strong are the moderates? In a public-opinion poll conducted last May [1969], 22 percent of Israelis defined themselves as doves and 31 percent stated that they had not yet decided, and 15 percent gave a "don't know" answer. This poll explains the dilemma of the liberal, moderate Israeli. Most Israelis would trade almost all of the new territories in return for peaceful relations with neighboring countries. But nobody offers Israel such a peace. Not even friendly intermediaries talk of the type of peace which would allow Israel to reduce its armaments and live in security. Nobody offers Israelis the kind of peace they aspire to, that which Abba Eban calls a "Benelux peace": diplomatic relations and trade agreements with neighbors and, above all, open borders. In the utopian image of a peaceful Middle East harbored by Israelis there are Israeli tourists in Cairo and Beirut. This image, still clung to in the popular songs, is nowadays further from reality than ever before.

All the American peace plans mapped out since the Six-Day War exclude diplomatic relations and do not insure open borders between Israel and her neighbors. The "contractual peace" provided for by [U.S.] Secretary of State [William Pierce] Rogers's formula seeks to squeeze out of the Arabs hardly anything more than a legal recognition of Israel and its borders. Israeli withdrawal from the west bank of the Jordan River, under present circumstances, would restore the pre-1967 closed borders and would bring the *fedayeen* from the Jordan Valley to the outskirts of Tel Aviv.

It is this reality which explains why so many Israelis cannot define themselves as either doves or hawks. Not that they cannot make up their minds, but rather that they lack the facts which would enable them to decide. It is generally assumed that this silent majority—silent, not out of apathy but because of the bewildering reality—is mostly made up of "tentative doves" who would give up almost everything in return for that which, at present, seems unattainable. The strength of the radical peace groups stems from their blaring appeals to the wishful thought of the great majority of Israelis.

The Arab governments could easily exploit the prevailing Israeli mood to sow dissention and disruption inside the country. They could, without giving up any real point of advantage, encourage opposition to the Meir Government by speaking softly in Israeli ears. The fact that they have not done so, and that they continue their incessant barrage of anti-Semitic propaganda, indicate the depth of their unfathomable hatred of Israel. Every time a powder keg of dissent builds up inside Israel, the Arabs douse it with a cold shower of curses and abuse. Radio Cairo was not content with denying the alleged Egyptian invitation to Goldmann, but declared emphatically that the Arabs would never deal with any Jew who had Zionist aspirations.

And after Goldmann met King Hassan of Morocco, a new campaign followed. Aksan Abdul Kadus, one of the leading Egyptian columnists, writing in *Akhbar El-Yom,* the Cairo daily, compared the earnest president of the World Jewish Congress with Rudolf Hess: "He attempts to fulfill the same task as that performed by Hitler's envoy, who flew to Britain in World War II in order to negotiate an end to war." And he goes on to accuse Goldmann of supporting a "racist" (i.e., Jewish) state in Palestine.

Jordanian press and radio outdo Cairo. Yacob-al-Salti wrote in the reputable Amman daily, *A Difa,* last April: "It is a serious mistake to link Nazism with Zionism and its activities. The Zionists and their followers claim that Nazism used modern methods to liquidate the Jews, burning them alive and killing them in masses. If Nazism had only completed this humanitarian task and had it carried out this social service, in other words, had it done what it is accused of doing by the Zionists, the universe would have been purged of the Zionist existence and the nightmare of plotting and evil would have been removed from the face of the earth." Such statements do not exactly encourage Israelis to believe that moderation will be met with moderation from the other side. . . .

But the deepest and most significant expression of dissent is to be found not in the mass media, but in contemporary Israeli literature. There one can find the most stirring, controversial and soul-searching words written on the Arab-Jewish conflict. The young generation of authors has, almost without exception, expressed an empathy for the Arab side which comes as a shock to the uninitiated. In their novels, poems and short stories the Arab appears not as an enemy, never as a villain but as the innocent victim of a tragic conflict. *Khirbet Hizeh* and *The Prisoner of War* by S. Yizhar, *The Swimming Match* by Benjamin Tammuz and *The Acrophile* by Yoram Kanyuk are four pieces representative of the period after the 1948 war. When these authors write of the Israeli war of independence they do not neglect to portray the Arab *fellahin* [village peasants] uprooted, displaced and killed in the war. . . .

A younger group of authors, bewildered by the apparent endlessness of the war, continued this tradition in a more dramatic fashion. Amos Oz in *My Michael,* perhaps his most mature novel, writes of a deranged Jewish woman in Jerusalem who cherishes the memory of Arab twins who grew up with her in Mandate Jerusalem: the woman imagines the twins across the border . . . the playful children of yesteryear have turned into menacing figures, desperate marauders, and the book ends with an apocalyptic scene in which the twins sneak across the border and blow up a Jewish settlement. A. B. Yehoshua, 34-year-old novelist and playwright, has another symbolical ending in *Facing the Forests:* the hero, a student employed as a forest guard, watches an Arab set fire to a forest planted by the Jewish National Fund on a site which had once been an Arab village.

The feeling of guilt toward the Arab is the theme which dominates the latest Israeli literature. Yehoshua says that the "feeling of guilt is there and it would be dangerous to repress it." . . .

This inherent empathy for the Arab, this amazing understanding for a brutal enemy, has perhaps no immediate practical relevance. Yet poets and writers often echo a palpable sense of reality, which looms above and beyond the world of current events and newspaper headlines. . . .

And, above all, they provide spiritual and philosophical justification for the Israeli dove: a compromise between Arab and Jew is needed not only because war is hateful, but also because a compromise is a just and moral solution to a tragic conflict between two types of "justice"—the Jewish justice and the Arab justice. Yet, as Amos Oz has pointed out, the conflict is asymmetrical: while the Israelis are ready for compromise and coexistence, the Arabs seek to annihilate Israel. As long as this asymmetry persists, this inherent understanding for the Arabs will not be translated into action. But no one will deny that this understanding represents a powerful force in Israel society and culture.

What are the specific issues on which dissent is centered? Practically all Israelis agree that there should be no withdrawal without a peace agreement with neighboring Arab states. Almost all Israelis agree that Jerusalem must remain united and under some measure of Israeli control. From this point onward consensus gives way to divergence.

Attacks against Government's rigidity—and again it should be emphasized that we are dealing with a minority, sometimes a very small minority—have been aimed at different issues. Since Golda Meir's latest speeches in the Knesset, the voices of critics have been lowered. But they still aim their arrows at the Government's failure to do anything about the Palestinians; its intention to build the Jewish settlement near Hebron; its rejection of the limited cease-fire proposed by Rogers; its insistence on contractual peace and the Rhodes formula; its failure to formulate a positive peace plan which could be presented to the Arabs and to world public opinion.

The dissenters' case is often encumbered by the very fault which they ascribe to the Government. The dissenters criticize the Government but rarely point to a constructive way which would lead to peace or even to a state of non-war. Their strongest point is their emphasis on the need for a direct rapprochement with the Palestinians, but even here they are hampered by the lack of any real response from the Palestinians. Their arguments seem to be somewhat academic and are often founded upon wishful thinking—of an expected *volte face* in the Arab world, a naive belief that moderation will be countered by moderation, a rational analysis of an irrational hatred.

Their greatest frustration is the total absence of any corresponding voice of dissent from the other side. The only voice for Arab moderation is that of Cecil Hourani, a Westernized Arab, who opposes Arab war tactics against Israel. But even this courageous and lonely voice in the wilderness rejects the idea of a Jewish state in Palestine and sees Arab moderation as a means toward diluting and then eliminating Israel. Yet the existence of Israel as an independent Jewish nation, the right of Jews to self-determination, is a condition *sine qua non* to all dissenting groups, excepting Mazpen.

Often the peace dissenters themselves admit that, in the present circumstances, nothing Israel can do unilaterally will help. Occasionally, they concede that their alternative policy is aimed not at a foreseeable solution but at a slow, gradual process which may eventually produce a corresponding mood in the Arab countries. Some go even further and regard their activities as of essentially psychological importance. Listen to this *cri de coeur* by Gadi Yatziv, who headed the Peace List and who figures prominently in the camp of no-sayers:

"A reality in which the best political alternative left in the hands of the Government is to send its sons to death is not a reality to which a mentally healthy people can acquiesce. Anyone who does not understand this truth shows that he is unable to fathom the monstrous dimension of our life. This refusal to accept the present reality does not necessarily have political implications and is not always reflected in political solutions. This nonacceptance is not a sign of defeatism: it is one of the healthy instincts of a life-loving social organism. This type of protest is an important element in our capacity to hold our own. This protest against the present reality is the real 'realism.'" Protest is needed not as a means to immediate political action but as an almost symbolic rejection of deadlock.

Moreover, the Soviet menace has overshadowed the internal argument. The intervention of the Soviet empire with its tradition of ruthlessness and anti-Semitism has given a new dimension to the conflict. The Russian bear, casting an ominous shadow across the canal, dwarfs the Arab masses shouting for revenge. The Soviet intervention has diminished the debate inside Israel. The issue now is not what to do about the west bank or the Palestinians but how to insure the survival of the Jewish state. The Soviet danger looms, like some monstrous evil, over the whole Middle East.

Some observers tend to regard the emergence of dissenting groups in Israel as a sign of weakness and the result of the war of attrition. There is some indication that both the Arabs and the Soviets see the recent outbursts as symptoms of disintegration, the beginnings of a disruptive process inside Israel. It is perhaps understandable that governments which rule by repression, censorship and police-state methods should misinterpret the sounds of clogs and brakes in a democratic machine. It was a similar kind of miscalculation which led the Soviets to misjudge Israel's strength on the eve of the Six-Day War, when the country was plagued by an economic recession and public morale under the nonleadership of a nongovernment seemed to have reached its lowest ebb. Actually, the rise of dissent in Israel is proof that the war of attrition waged upon Israel by the Arabs and the Soviet Union has failed at least in one respect. Against all odds, Israel at war retains all the features of a peaceful democracy.

The visual image of Israeli democracy is the frank, often even wild, debate heard through the sounds of war. It is the image of Ran Cohen, who returns from army duty on the canal to join in a demonstration against the Government's policy, or of the author, Yizhak Orpaz, a reserve lieutenant colonel, who in his recent novel, *Daniel's Dream,* describes the plight of the questioning Israeli and the tragedy of his enemy. It is the image of Prof. Dan Patinkin, who volunteered to serve as a private in an infantry reserve unit and who opposes the Government's policy in the press and on television. It is the image of *Keshet,* a literary magazine, which devoted its last issue to an academic and objective examination of postwar Arab literature and poetry. It is the image of Capt. Israel Guttman, killed on the Suez front on May 19, three days after he had written a letter to a class of Beersheba pupils, in which he assured them that "the Egyptians on the other side of the canal are human beings who want to live like us—and to return safely home to their wives and children," and urged them not to hate the Arabs. It is the image of a tiny, odd, occasionally exasperating, always intriguing people attempting, in peace and war, to do the seemingly impossible.

NOTES

1. *Davar* was the daily newspaper of the Histadrut. It was established by Berl Katznelson, who was its first editor, in 1925. As Mapai gained control over the Jewish Agency Executive, it also became the unofficial newspaper of the Jewish semiautonomous government. The paper was shut down in 1996.
2. Actually, the demonstrators broke into the courtyard.
3. The term refers to Spiro T. Agnew (1918–1996), vice-president of the United States, 1969–73, who was known for his invective attacks on the press, liberals, and intellectuals. He was forced to resign because of a graft scandal.

64

Lea Ben-Dor

The Black Panthers

1971: Analysis

The years following the Six-Day War saw an exacerbation of sociopolitical tensions in Israel that derived from the government's preoccupation with foreign and defense affairs, the acceleration of economic activity, and the reaction of underprivileged social groups to the privileges extended to new immigrants from the West and the Soviet Union. The absorption of the latter group has not been free of problems, but it was an irritant that induced young, non-Western Jews, mostly of North African descent, to articulate their grievances through the formation of a protest movement, the Black Panthers, in 1971. (This protest movement of young Sephardim from poor urban neighborhoods in Tel Aviv and Jerusalem had no connection, other than choice of name, with the American Black Panthers of the 1960s.) The Black Panthers tried to focus attention on what they regarded as

Source: Lea Ben-Dor, "A Dream of Panthers," *Jerusalem Post Week-End Magazine,* May 21, 1971, p. 7. Reprinted by permission.

systematic discrimination against non-Western Jews by the European establishment in areas such as housing, employment, and education. Lea Ben-Dor, a senior journalist and commentator for Israel's English-language newspaper, the Jerusalem Post, *analyzes this phenomenon.*

"So you see the panthers are real; they aren't just an invention of the press," said a sympathiser in a radio discussion of the panther riot on Wednesday evening.

They are real. But they are not black, and "Panther" is no more than wishful thinking. The ones I have met, or seen, are mostly undersized, even rather underfed looking. They are no match for husky policemen, with or without batons. The grievance of many, after all, started with the fact that they were rejected by the army. Their school attendance was sketchy in most cases. Some were ill, others were caught out in petty crimes and drifted into delinquency; for others, hashish provided solace against the hardships of poverty.

Their battle-cry, not very loud but increasingly persistent, has been "discrimination." Who runs the country, who has the good jobs? The Ashkenazim. Who lives in overcrowded housing, who does the poorly paid work? The children of the Oriental families. The answer seems close to hand and has long lurked around the corner.

Except that it is just not true and those of the Panthers who think about their situation—and not a few of them do—know that is so. The Black Panthers of Detroit or Chicago had no difficulty in pinning down the exact points at which there is discrimination. Their namesakes in Jerusalem have now been able to claim a specific grievance, which is that immigrants of today get incomparably better housing than their parents did in the early years of the state.[1] But other young Israelis, or old Israelis for that matter, do not get cheap housing any more than do the Panthers.

What has really emerged is a terribly deep sense of frustration that here they are, an Israel-born generation, and little better equipped for a competitive society than their fathers were in the confusing years after their arrival here; less well off possibly than their grandfathers, who suffered varying degrees of discrimination in Arab countries but had learned how to live in that world. It is worse than discrimination: it is failure.

Little is heard today of A. D. Gordon and the healing dignity of manual labour, except in kibbutzim that still constitute isolated communities, and it was always a concept that could appeal only to those who had a choice in the matter. There is unskilled work to be had, but its acceptance has become more difficult in a place like Jerusalem where the shortage of manual labour has been solved by Arabs from East Jerusalem and beyond. The Panther's relationship to an Arab fellow-worker is likely to be both closer and far more problematical than that of a European Jew, rather as European Jews who lived through the Holocaust find contacts with today's Germans more difficult than does a Yemenite or a South American.

The Panthers are kids who not only know that they have not got a proper job now, a job with what they call "status," but that they are never going to have one, because they have neither the training nor the habit of work; that not only do they still have to share a bed with another brother in a cramped flat full of squabbling people, but that they are never going to be able to get a proper home of their own, or not the way things are at the moment.

Casual jobs provide enough money for a few jazzy clothes and the cinema. But for marriage and a home? Nor is the situation made any easier by the fact that plenty of boys of their own communities have made good, learned a trade, carried on with it in the army, became foremen in a factory; sweated their way through high school, to head a department in the post office; or struggled into university and escaped altogether into a different world.

The Panthers blame others for their troubles, and they are right. The basic, original trouble was not discrimination, but the lack of it. All over the Western world, but specifically in Eastern Europe, the Jews have been mobile. They have escaped persecution and, scarcely arrived in their new country, fought for security. Fathers in factories pushed their children through school and into university, to arm them with knowledge, to make them secure. Nobody really gave much thought to whether the large and disorganized families from Arab countries who arrived here after 1948 were equally ready to pull themselves up by their own bootstraps.

The remnants from the camps in Europe made this effort. In the Orient, fathers take precedence over sons, they do not slave and scrape to send them to college. In any case a small family is no credit to anyone, there was never enough room for the large families in the small flats we provided, and the children drifted out into the street and fell behind at school. In the early years of the state, with a small population and mass immigration, there was a simplistic assumption that merely being in Israel, where a school was provided, would create equal learning conditions for the ten children of an illiterate and the two of a professor. Belatedly, an attempt was made to even things up with long school days in some of the schools, with extra tuition, special classes in summer and easier admission to high school. But only lucky ones, or the capable ones, escaped the trap of overcrowding, which prevented children from making use of the education they were offered. . . .

If there is one single thing we could do to reduce the gap between those who can make a living and those who see nothing but odd jobs in their future it is to provide public housing for rent, quickly, on an emergency basis, like we build armies or roads or industries. The fact that a man cannot get a place to live without a down payment that is astronomical for the unskilled labourer is destructive of his sense of independence and self-confidence. If flats are rented, a man can move to a new job, an unproductive factory can be closed down, older couples can move to a smaller flat when the children have grown up. Flats that must be bought become straitjackets.

Today the Panthers are not a political movement but a group that has banded together, more or less, in the hope of getting unspecified satisfaction for the fact they are not equipped to get anywhere, even into the army. They are already split on whether they should press the issue of "discrimination" or poverty.

They are equally split on whether to accept political and financial help from the left-wing groups, Mazpen and Siah. Some money is handy for any organization, but these donors are the privileged, students, professors even, very few of them of Oriental background. The Panthers may seek to be a revolutionary group, but most have no left-wing ideology, nor socialist or Maoist, that is for intellectuals. Their would-be friends put out stenciled broadsheets signed "Solidarity Committee for the Black Panthers," because the Panthers do not want to be identified with any of the existing political groups. Perhaps the Panthers have a healthy suspicion that their wealthier friends are only enjoying the pleasures of slumming. The friendship is one-sided.

As a group looking for help the Panthers have made many mistakes. The name itself, borrowed from a bitterly anti-Semitic organization, is an affront. Their first target seemed to be immigrants from Russia who have themselves barely escaped from danger and genuine discrimination—but they hurried to the Wall now to tell the demonstrators there that this is not what they meant. Their next target in Tuesday's demonstration, was the police, the great majority of which consists of the sons of other Oriental immigrants whose living conditions are removed a bare half step, if that much, from that of the Panthers themselves. Fighting the police is the fashion in America, it seeps in like pop music and nudity.

Because of their real grievances, the Panthers in fact received a great deal of public interest and attention. One result is that they have developed a hunger for continuous publicity and excitement. Talking to the press and ringing up the police has the missing "status." Can you feel equally important talking about job training?

They are going to have to struggle hard for their identity, or else they will be swallowed up by busy leftists looking for a cause, or anyone ill-disposed towards Israel. Even flats are easier to conjure up out of nothing than the dream of status that hides in the name "Panthers."

NOTE

1. The provision of public housing in Sephardi neighborhoods still frequently reflected the conditions of the early 1950s (see doc. 30).

Foreign Policy Issues

65

Government of Israel

The Land-for-Peace Principle

June 19, 1967

In the days following the end of the Six-Day War, the Israeli government moved quickly to formulate a policy regarding the future of the areas gained from Egypt, Syria, and Jordan in the course of the war. On June 14 and 15, the government's subcommittee for security debated the matter, and on June 16–19, the discussion was expanded to include the rest of the ministers.

The final decision authorizing withdrawal from areas occupied in the Six-Day War reflected Israeli willingness to give up almost all its territorial gains in return for peace, coupled with an inability to decide over the future of the West Bank. The proposal, printed below, was presented to the Egyptian and Syrian governments through the services of the United States. The flat Arab rejection of the offer led to an erosion in Israel's position, and by late October 1967, the government, in effect, rescinded the June 19 offer. However, the underlying principle of the decision, "land-for-peace," appeared in all of Israel's future peace agreements.

Egypt

Israel proposes forging a peace treaty with Egypt on the basis of the international boundaries [from the British Mandate period] and Israel's security needs. According to the international boundary, the Gaza Strip is located within the State of Israel territory.

Commitments of the Peace Treaty to include:

1. Guarantee of freedom of navigation through the Straits of Tiran and the Gulf of Solomon
2. Guarantee of freedom of navigation through the Suez Canal
3. Guarantee of overflight rights over the Straits of Tiran and the Gulf of Solomon
4. Demilitarization of the Sinai Peninsula

Until a peace treaty with Egypt is forged, Israel will continue to hold territories it holds today.

Source: Reuven Pedazur, *Nizahon hamevukhah: Mediniyut Israel bashtahim le'ahar milhemet sheshet hayamim* [The Triumph of Embarrassment: Israel and the Territories, 1967–1969] (Tel Aviv: Bitan, 1999). Reprinted by permission.

Syria

Israel proposes to forge a peace treaty on the basis of the international boundary (as above) and the security needs of Israel.

Commitments of the peace treaty to include:

1. Demilitarization of the Golan Heights, today held by IDF [Israel Defense Forces] forces.
2. Absolute guarantee of non-obstruction of flow of waters from sources of the Jordan into Israel.

Until the forging of a peace treaty with Syria Israel will continue to hold territories it holds today.

Refugees

The establishment of peace in the Middle East and the associated regional cooperation will create opportunities for international and regional settlements for the resolution of the refugee problem.

66

Alexei Kosygin

The Soviet Union and the Six-Day War

June 19, 1967

The diplomatic barrage against Israel, led by the Soviet Union and the Arab states, began almost simultaneously with the Six-Day War itself. Alexei Kosygin, premier of the Soviet Union from 1964 until his death in 1980, presented the Soviet line in a speech, excerpted here, before the United Nations General Assembly on June 19, 1967.

Representatives of almost all States of the world have gathered for this special emergency session of the United Nations General Assembly to consider the grave and dangerous situation which has developed in recent days in the Near East, a situation which arouses deep concern everywhere.

True, no hostilities are under way there at this moment. The fact that a cease-fire has been brought about is a definite success for the peace-loving forces. This is in no small way due to the Security Council, although it failed to discharge fully its obligation under the United Nations Charter. The aggression is continuing. The armed forces of Israel are occupying territories in the United Arab Republic, Syria and Jordan.

As long as Israeli troops continue to occupy the territories seized by them, and urgent measures are not taken to eliminate the consequences of aggression, a military conflict can flare up with renewed force at any minute.

Source: Yaacov Roi, ed., *From Encroachment to Involvement: A Documentary Study of Soviet Policy in the Middle East, 1945–1973* (Tel Aviv: Shiloah Center, 1974), pp. 450–55. Reprinted by permission of the Dayan Center.

That is exactly why the Soviet Union took the initiative in convening an emergency session of the General Assembly. We are pleased to note that many States supported our proposal. They have displayed their awareness of the dangers with which the situation is fraught and manifested their concern for the consolidation of peace.

The General Assembly is confronted with the primary task of adopting decisions that would clear the way for a restoration of peace in the Middle East. This task concerns all States irrespective of differences in social or political systems and philosophical outlook, irrespective of geography and alignment with this or that grouping. It can be solved only if the multiple and complex nature of today's world does not relegate to the background the common bond that joins the States and peoples together, and above all the need to prevent a military disaster. . . .

Not a single people wants war. Nowadays no one doubts that a new world war, if it started, would inevitably be a nuclear war. Its consequences would be disastrous for many countries and peoples of the world. . . .

The nuclear age has created a new reality in questions of war and peace. It has laid upon States an immeasurably greater responsibility in all that pertains to these problems. . . .

However, the practice of international relations abounds in facts which show that certain States take quite a different approach. Continuous attempts are made to interfere in the internal affairs of independent countries and peoples, to impose upon them from outside political concepts and alien views on social order. Everything is done to breathe new life into military blocs. A network of military bases, the strong point of aggression, flung far and wide all over the world, is being refurbished and perfected. Naval fleets are plying the seas thousands of miles from their own shores and threaten the security of States over entire regions.

Even in those cases when the aggravation of tension or the emergence of hotbeds of war danger is connected with conflicts involving relatively small States, not infrequently big Powers are behind them. This applies not only to the Middle East, where aggression has been committed by Israel, backed by bigger imperialist Powers, but also to other areas of the world. . . .

If we analyze the events in the Middle East, we are bound to conclude that the war between Israel and the Arab States did not result from some kind of disagreement or inadequate understanding of one side by the other. Nor is this just a local conflict. The events that recently took place in the Middle East in connection with the armed conflict between Israel and the Arab States should be considered squarely in the context of the over-all international situation in the world. . . .

We should note that the main features in the relations between Israel and the Arab States during the past year were the ever-increasing tension and mounting scale of attacks by Israel troops on one or another of Israel's neighbor States. . . .

On 7 April last, Israel troops staged an attack against the territory of the Syrian Arab Republic. . . .

. . . Israel was warned by a number of States about its responsibility for the consequences of the policy it was pursuing. But even after that the Israeli Government did not reconsider its course. Its political leaders openly threatened "wider military actions against Arab countries." . . . On 9 May 1967 the Israeli Parliament authorized the Government of Israel to carry out military operations against Syria. The Israeli troops began concentrating at the Syrian borders, and mobilization was carried out.

At that time the Soviet Government, and I believe others too, began receiving information to the effect that the Israeli Government had chosen the end of May as the time for a swift strike at Syria in order to crush it and then planned to carry the fighting over into the territory of the United Arab Republic [see doc. 58].

When the preparations for war had entered the final stage, the Government of Israel suddenly began to spread, both confidentially and publicly, profuse assurances of its peaceful intentions. It declared that it was not going to start hostilities and was not seeking conflicts with its neighbors. Literally a few hours before the attack on the Arab States, the Defence Minister of Israel swore his Government was seeking peaceful solutions. "Let diplomacy be put to work," the Minister was saying at the very moment when Israel pilots had already received orders to bomb the cities of the United Arab Republic, Syria and Jordan. This is indeed unprecedented perfidy.

On 5 June, Israel started war against the United Arab Republic, Syria and Jordan. . . .

What followed is well known.

Here, within the United Nations, I shall only recall the arrogance with which the unbridled aggressor ignored the demands of the Security Council for an immediate cease-fire.

On 6 June the Security Council proposed (Resolution 233 [1967]) an end to all hostilities as a first step towards the restoration of peace. Israel expanded operations on all fronts.

On 7 June the Security Council (Resolution 234 [1967]) fixed a time limit for the cessation of hostilities. Israel troops continued their offensive, and Israel aircraft bombed peaceful Arab towns and villages.

On 9 June the Security Council (Resolution 235 [1967]) issued a new categorical demand providing for a cease-fire. Israel ignored that too. The Israel army mounted an attack against the defensive lines of Syria with the purpose of breaking through to the capital of that State, Damascus.

The Security Council had to adopt yet another, fourth, decision (Resolution 236 [1967]); a number of States had to sever diplomatic relations with Israel, and a firm warning was given that sanctions might be applied, before Israel troops halted their military activities. A large part of the territory of Arab countries now actually occupied by Israel was seized after the Security Council had taken the decision on the immediate cessation of hostilities.

67

Fourth Arab Summit Conference

The Khartoum Resolutions

September 1, 1967

The Khartoum Conference, convened in September 1967, was the first Arab summit to be held after the Six-Day War. It formulated the Arab consensus that underlay the policies of most Arab states participating in the conflict until the early 1970s. The following is an excerpt from a summary of the summit prepared for the U.S. Senate Committee on Foreign Relations.

Source: U.S. Senate Committee on Foreign Relations, *A Select Chronology and Background Documents relating to the Middle East,* 2nd rev. ed. (Washington, D.C.: Government Printing Office, February 1975), p. 249.

The Arab heads of state have agreed to unite their political efforts on the international and diplomatic level to eliminate the effects of the aggression and to ensure the withdrawal of the aggressive Israeli forces from the Arab lands which have been occupied since the 5 June aggression. This will be done within the framework of the main principles to which the Arab states adhere, namely: no peace with Israel, no recognition of Israel, no negotiations with it and adherence to the rights of the Palestinian people in their country.

68

United Nations Security Council

Resolution 242

November 22, 1967

With hindsight, it is easy to see the cycle that led from the Six-Day War to the Yom Kippur War. By the end of 1967 the euphoric hopes of the Israelis for a quickly negotiated peace settlement were dashed, and it was clear that a stalemate between Israel and the Arab states would prevail (see doc. 65). The U.N. Security Council Resolution 242, November 22, 1967, terminated efforts to legislate a solution to the Arab-Israeli conflict in the United Nations in the aftermath of the Six-Day War. The general nature of the resolution and the ambiguity of language that made the resolution acceptable also made it largely inoperative. In the decades following 1967, Resolution 242 served as an agreed-upon basis between Israel and its Arab partners in peace. Resolution 242 is mentioned in the peace agreements with Egypt (1979), the Palestine Liberation Organization (1993), and Jordan (1994), as well as a basis for the 1991 Madrid Middle East Peace Conference (doc. 118).

The Security Council,

Expressing its continuing concern with the grave situation in the Middle East,

Emphasizing the inadmissibility of the acquisition of territory by war and the need to work for a just and lasting peace in which every State in the area can live in security,

Emphasizing further that all Member States in their acceptance of the Charter of the United Nations have undertaken a commitment to act in accordance with Article 2 of the Charter,

1. *Affirms* that the fulfillment of Charter principles requires the establishment of a just and lasting peace in the Middle East which should include the application of both the following principles: (a) withdrawal of Israeli armed forces from territories occupied in the recent conflict; (b) termination of all claims or states of belligerency and respect for and acknowledgement of the sovereignty, territorial integrity and political independence of every State in the area and their right to live in peace within secure and recognized boundaries free from threats or acts of force;

Source: U.S. Senate Committee on Foreign Relations, *A Select Chronology and Background Documents relating to the Middle East,* 2d rev. ed. (Washington, D.C.: Government Printing Office, February 1975), pp. 249–50.

2. *Affirms further* the necessity (a) for guaranteeing freedom of navigation through international waterways in the area; (b) for achieving a just settlement of the refugee problem; (c) for guaranteeing the territorial inviolability and political independence of every state in the area, through measures including the establishment of demilitarized zones;

3. *Requests* the Secretary-General to designate a Special Representative [Gunnar Jarring] to proceed to the Middle East to establish and maintain contacts with the States concerned in order to promote agreement and assist efforts to achieve a peaceful and accepted settlement in accordance with the provisions and principles of this resolution;

4. *Requests* the Secretary-General to report to the Security Council on the progress of the efforts of the Special Representative as soon as possible.

69

Palestine Liberation Organization

The Palestine National Charter

July 17, 1968

In addition to launching the War of Attrition (see doc. 70), the Arab states put their collective weight behind the Palestine Liberation Organization in order to break the deadlock in Arab-Israeli relations. Frequently these states sought to further their own competing policies and approaches by manipulating factions of the PLO—or even by organizing new factions.

After drafting the original Palestine National Charter in 1964, the PLO underwent several important changes. Ahmad Shuqeiri, the first chairman, was replaced in 1967 by Yahya Hamudeh, who was in turn replaced in 1969 by Yasir Arafat, head of al-Fatah. During the transitional period that followed the Six-Day War, the PLO became increasingly independent of the Arab states and served as an umbrella organization of semiautonomous Palestinian groups. Fatah, the largest of these, has continued to dominate it. Following the May 1983 Lebanese-Israeli agreement, Arafat's leadership of Fatah was seriously challenged for the first time.

The Popular Front for the Liberation of Palestine (PFLP), headed by George Habash, was organized in December 1967. In 1968 Nayef Hawatmeh and his followers seceded from the PFLP to form the Popular Democratic Front for the Liberation of Palestine. The Palestine Liberation Front was reorganized by Ahmad Jibril into the Palestine Front for the Liberation of Palestine—General Command. In 1968 the Syrian Ba'ath Party established Al-Saiqa (Vanguard of the People's War of Liberation), and in 1969 the Iraqi Ba'aths established the Arab Liberation Front, which later also gained the support of Libya.

To accommodate the changes occurring in the PLO, new institutions were established and a new char-

Source: Yehoshafat Harkabi, *The Palestinian Covenant and Its Meaning* (London: Vallentine, Mitchell and Co., 1979), pp. 119–24.

ter was formulated. The charter adopted by the Fourth Palestine National Council, meeting in Cairo, on July 17, 1968, is reproduced here. An amendment to the charter made by the Palestine National Council in 1996 is reproduced as document 138.

This Charter shall be known as "the Palestine National Charter."

Articles of the Charter:

1. Palestine, the homeland of the Palestinian Arab people, is an inseparable part of the greater Arab homeland, and the Palestinian people are a part of the Arab Nation.

2. Palestine, within the frontiers that existed under the British Mandate, is an indivisible territorial unit.

3. The Palestinian Arab people alone have legitimate rights to their homeland, and shall exercise the right of self-determination after the liberation of their homeland, in keeping with their wishes and entirely of their own accord.

4. The Palestinian identity is an authentic, intrinsic and indissoluble quality that is transmitted from father to son. Neither the Zionist occupation nor the dispersal of the Palestinian Arab people as a result of the afflictions they have suffered can efface this Palestinian identity.

5. Palestinians are Arab citizens who were normally resident in Palestine until 1947. This includes both those who were forced to leave or who stayed in Palestine. Anyone born to a Palestinian father after that date, whether inside or outside Palestine, is a Palestinian.

6. Jews who were normally resident in Palestine up to the beginning of the Zionist invasion are Palestinians.

7. Palestinian identity, and material, spiritual and historical links with Palestine are immutable realities. It is a national obligation to provide every Palestinian with a revolutionary Arab upbringing, and to instill in him a profound spiritual and material familiarity with his homeland and a readiness for armed struggle and for the sacrifice of his material possessions and his life, for the recovery of his homeland. All available educational means and means of guidance must be enlisted to that end, until liberation is achieved.

8. The Palestinian people is at the stage of national struggle for the liberation of its homeland. For that reason, differences between Palestinian national forces must give way to the fundamental difference that exists between Zionism and imperialism on the one hand and the Palestinian Arab people on the other. On that basis, the Palestinian masses, both as organizations and as individuals, whether in the homeland or in such places as they now live as refugees, constitute a single national front working for the recovery and liberation of Palestine through armed struggle.

9. Armed struggle is the only way of liberating Palestine, and is thus strategic, not tactical. The Palestinian Arab people hereby affirm their unwavering determination to carry on the armed struggle and to press on towards popular revolution for the liberation of and return to their homeland. They also affirm their right to a normal life in their homeland, to the exercise of their right of self-determination therein and to sovereignty over it.

10. Commando action constitutes the nucleus of the Palestinian popular war of liberation. This requires that commando action should be escalated, expanded and protected, and that all the resources of the Palestinian masses and all scientific potentials available to them should be mobilised and organised to play their part in the armed Palestinian revolution. It also requires solidarity in national struggle among the different groups within the Palestinian people and between that people and the Arab masses, to ensure the continuity of the escalation and victory of the revolution.

11. Palestinians shall have three slogans: national unity, national mobilisation and liberation.

12. The Palestinian Arab people believe in Arab unity. To fulfill their role in the achievement of that objective, they must, at the present stage in their national struggle, retain their Palestinian identity and all that it involves, work for increased awareness of it and oppose all measures liable to weaken or dissolve it.

13. Arab unity and the liberation of Palestine are complimentary objectives; each leads to the achievement of the other. Arab unity will lead to the liberation of Palestine, and the liberation of Palestine will lead to Arab unity. To work for one is to work for both.

14. The destiny of the Arab nation, indeed the continued existence of the Arabs, depends on the fate of the Palestinian cause. This interrelationship is the point of departure of the Arab endeavour to liberate Palestine. The Palestinian people are the vanguard of the movement to achieve this sacred national objective.

15. The liberation of Palestine is a national obligation to the Arabs. It is their duty to repel the Zionist and imperialist invasion of the greater Arab homeland and to liquidate the Zionist presence in Palestine. The full responsibility for this belongs to the peoples and governments of the Arab nation and to the Palestinian people first and foremost. For this reason, the task of the Arab nation is to enlist all the military, human, moral and material resources at its command to play an effective part, along with the Palestinian people, in the liberation of Palestine. Moreover, it is the task of the Arab nation, particularly at the present stage of the Palestinian armed revolution, to offer the Palestinian people all possible aid, material and manpower support and to place at their disposal all the means and opportunities that will enable them to continue to perform their role as the vanguard of their armed revolution until the liberation of their homeland is achieved.

16. On a spiritual plane, the liberation of Palestine will establish in the Holy Land an atmosphere of peace and tranquility in which all religious institutions will be safeguarded and freedom of worship and the right of visit guaranteed to all without discrimination or distinction of race, colour, language or creed. For this reason the people of Palestine look to all spiritual forces in the world for support.

17. On the human plane, the liberation of Palestine will restore to the Palestinians their dignity, integrity and freedom. For this reason, the Palestinian Arab people look to all those who believe in the dignity and freedom of man for support.

18. On the international plane, the liberation of Palestine is a defensive measure dictated by the requirements of self-defence. This is why the Palestinian people, who seek to win the friendship of all peoples, look for the support of all freedom, justice and peace-loving countries in restoring the legitimate state of affairs in Palestine, establishing security and peace in it and enabling its people to exercise national sovereignty and freedom.

19. The partition of Palestine, which took place in 1947, and the establishment of Israel, are fundamentally invalid, however long they last, for they contravene the will of the people of Palestine and their natural right to their homeland and contradict the principles of the United Nations Charter, foremost among which is the right of self-determination.

20. The Balfour Declaration [doc. 7], the Mandate Instrument [doc. 10], and all their consequences, are hereby declared null and void. The claim of historical or spiritual links between the Jews and Palestine is neither in conformity with historical fact nor does it satisfy the requirements for statehood. Judaism is a revealed religion; it is not a separate nationality, nor are the Jews a single people with a separate identity; they are citizens of their respective countries.

21. The Palestinian Arab people, expressing themselves through the Palestinian armed revolution, reject all alternatives to the total liberation of Palestine. They also reject all proposals

for the liquidation of internationalisation of the Palestine problem.

22. Zionism is a political movement that is organically linked with world imperialism and is opposed to all liberation movements or movements for progress in the world. The Zionist movement is essentially fanatical and racialist; its objectives involve aggression, expansion and the establishment of colonial settlements, and its methods are those of the Fascists and the Nazis. Israel acts as cat's paw for the Zionist movement, a geographic and manpower base for world imperialism and a springboard for its thrust into the Arab homeland to frustrate the aspirations of the Arab nation to liberation, unity and progress. Israel is a constant threat to peace in the Middle East and the whole world. Inasmuch as the liberation of Palestine will eliminate the Zionist and imperialist presence in that country and bring peace to the Middle East, the Palestinian people look for support to all liberals and to all forces of good, peace and progress in the world, and call on them, whatever their political convictions, for all possible aid and support in their just and legitimate struggle to liberate their homeland.

23. The demands of peace and security and the exigencies of right and justice require that all nations should regard Zionism as an illegal movement and outlaw it and its activities, out of consideration for the ties of friendship between peoples and for the loyalty of citizens of their homelands.

24. The Palestinian Arab people believe in justice, freedom, sovereignty, self-determination, human dignity and the right of peoples to enjoy them.

25. In pursuance of the objectives set out in this charter, the Palestine Liberation Organisation shall perform its proper role in the liberation of Palestine to the full.

26. The Palestine Liberation Organisation, as the representative of the forces of the Palestinian revolution, is responsible for the struggle of the Palestinian Arab people to regain, liberate and return to their homeland and to exercise the right of self-determination in that homeland, in the military, political and financial fields, and for all else that the Palestinian cause may demand, both at Arab and international levels.

27. The Palestine Liberation Organisation shall cooperate with all Arab countries, each according to its means, maintaining a neutral attitude vis-à-vis these countries in accordance with the requirements of the battle of liberation, and on the basis of that factor. The Organisation shall not interfere in the internal affairs of any Arab country.

28. The Palestinian Arab people hereby affirm the authenticity and independence of their national revolution and reject all forms of interference, tutelage or dependency.

29. The Palestinian Arab people have the legitimate and prior right to liberate and recover their homeland, and shall define their attitude to all countries and forces in accordance with the attitude adopted by such countries and forces to the cause of the Palestinian people and with the extent of their support for that people in their revolution to achieve their objectives.

30. Those who fight or bear arms in the battle of liberation form the nucleus of the popular army which will shield the achievements of the Palestinian Arab people.

31. The Organisation shall have a flag, an oath of allegiance and an anthem, to be decided in accordance with appropriate regulations.

32. Regulations, to be known as Basic Regulations for the Palestine Liberation Organisation, shall be appended to this Charter. These regulations shall define the structure of the Organisation, its bodies and institutions, and the powers, duties and obligations of each of them, in accordance with this Charter.

33. This Charter may only be amended with a majority of two thirds of the total number of members of the National Council of the Palestine Liberation Organisation at a special meeting called for that purpose.

70

Ezer Weizman

The War of Attrition

1968–1970: Memoir

In the fall of 1968 Egypt began bombarding Israeli positions on the Suez Canal. This action led to an escalation of hostilities known as the War of Attrition and to an arms race as Egypt introduced new Soviet ground-to-air missiles and Soviet personnel.

During this period Ezer Weizman (1924–2005) was chief of operations of the Israeli General Staff. He had served in the British Royal Air Force in World War II and then helped establish the Israel Air Force, in which he held numerous commands. He also rose to become one of the leaders of the Herut faction of Gahal, and in 1969 he entered the National Unity cabinet. His political influence grew when the Likud came to power in 1977, and he was named defense minister, but his personal and political conflict with Menahem Begin forced him to resign his position and leave the Likud. He later served as Israel's president, 1993–2000.

These excerpts from Weizman's autobiography echo the debate that took place in Israel over the strategy employed by the government during the War of Attrition with Egypt.

In August and September 1968, while we were battling with the guerrillas and building up our army, the new Skyhawks [missiles from the United States] arrived, and our hearts felt a little lighter. We re-organized the armoured units and the paratroopers. Although there was no telephone call from down there, the Egyptian border was quiet. And then, in October, the blow landed. Fourteen soldiers were killed in an Egyptian bombardment at Kantara on the Suez Canal. We sensed that a new era had begun. It didn't have a name yet; later it was called the War of Attrition. Fortunately, we did not fall into the snare of thinking that the Egyptians had struck once and would not do so again. After the bombardment in October, there was an interval of a few months before the static battle was renewed, but, all the same, we took matters in hand. The first thing was to erect fortifications. A number of officers, headed by Elhanan Klein, the chief engineering officer, brought up an idea: "It's a long affair to pour concrete into fortifications so that they can stand up to bombardments. Let's strip down the Egyptian railway line in Sinai and use its rails as steel shields."

Haim Bar-Lev hesitated. We didn't know if it would stand up to bombardment. We built a wall like the one they proposed and conducted experiments on it. We fired 120-mm and 160-mm mortar shells straight at it, as well as 105-mm, 130-mm and 155-mm cannon shells, and the Russian 122-mm, and the wall didn't collapse. The detonating layer held out. We stripped down the railway line, ordered used rails from abroad and built the first fortresses. Between March 1969 and 1 August 1970, we lost 250 dead and about 1,000 wounded on the

---

Source: Ezer Weizman, *On Eagles' Wings: A Personal Story of the Leading Commander of the Israeli Air Force* (London: Weidenfeld and Nicolson, 1976), pp. 269–75, 280–82. Reprinted by permission of Ezer Weizman.

Canal. Only a few were killed inside the fortresses; all the rest were hit when they were outside them or on their way to or from the line.

March 1969 is usually regarded as the beginning of the War of Attrition. I was in my second year as head of General Staff Division. There were two things troubling me. First, never having conducted a static war, our ground forces were unaccustomed to it and could not bring their full potential to bear, as they weren't storming forward to put a stop to Egyptian provocations. Second, our magnificent air force was sitting back; other than photographic missions and intercepting enemy planes, it wasn't doing a thing. It was forfeiting its image as the arm whose absolute superiority could decide every war.

During the months of March–June 1969, 20,000 Soviet advisers poured into Egypt, penetrating into the lowest command echelons of Egyptian armour, artillery and infantry battalions. Soviet planes, with Russian pilots, were stationed in Egypt. Our soldiers were being killed daily. The Egyptians were growing more and more arrogant. We were faced by an army with 1,000 tanks and as many artillery pieces, and, yet, Israeli forces weren't doing what they should and could do. Even when they did act, it was often too little, too late. They made the grievous error of reverting to outdated methods, which may have been good enough for attacks on Jordan or Gaza during the fedayeen raids preceding the Sinai Campaign but were hardly suitable now. "Deep penetration" was the slogan. The army carried out demolition attacks: destroying a transformer station deep inside Egypt; blowing up a bridge; a deep penetration raid with armour. These showed a great deal of courage, daring and resourcefulness, but all this was no more than tickling the Egyptian army. Such actions earned the Israeli army world-wide renown and threw tasty morsels to Israeli public opinion, but they didn't decide the war; they didn't bring it to an end, nor even dampen it.

Whether I was listened to or not, I repeated, over and over again, "A war like this can't be won by commando raids! It won't work! The Israeli army has to be employed in full and overwhelming force, not only to put an end to the War of Attrition—important enough unto itself—but also to check the Egyptian army before it launches more dangerous offensives!" But mine was a lonely voice. A state with a strong standing army that has just defeated its enemies in a brilliant lightning campaign and yet chooses to conduct commando raids instead of making full use of its strength does so either because it doesn't believe in its ability to employ that strength to the utmost or because of the illusion that some commando raid can solve the problem. The facts proved that the problem wasn't solved until the air force went into action on a large scale.

My efforts to convince my General Staff colleagues to give up these commando pricks and prods and to deploy the army in earnest, so as to put an end to the War of Attrition, were not successful. Another prod and another prick, and the next day, there'd be 1,000 Egyptian shells, 2,000, 5,000, 10,000. Soldiers were getting killed, and the mood in the streets was swaying between grim and grotesque.

If I didn't succeed in conveying to my colleagues how essential it was to employ the army's full strength and to desist from commando raids—and events proved that I did not—I tried to persuade them at least to use the air force effectively, to strike such painful blows at the Egyptians that they would cease to regard the War of Attrition as profitable. Here, too, I encountered opposition. For the first time in the history of Israel, the air force commanders said that, because of the Egyptian SAM anti-aircraft system, they could not conduct operations unless the United States supplied us with some missile or other. I regarded this view as extremely dangerous. Never before had such a contention been put forward. When there had been nothing better, the Pipers of the War of Independence were good enough for the aerial missions required at the time, and no one ever contended that we could not cope because the

Egyptian air force had better planes. The Israeli soldier—with his daring, his skills, his devotion, his patriotism, his inner motivation, his readiness to sacrifice his life—was the guarantee of our ability to survive. To trade this mighty treasure for the contention that we lacked some contraption or missile and that as long as we didn't acquire them from our friends or manufacture them ourselves we were powerless to defend Israel's security was, without any exaggeration, acquiescing to a death sentence on the Jewish state. . . .

Finally, on 20 July, we carried out the operation; we sent the air force in for a powerful surprise strike along the whole Egyptian line. We also had sixteen helicopters on stand-by, with 150 paratroopers awaiting permission to cross over to the other side and demolish a considerable portion of the Egyptian line. The plan was ready, and we were fully convinced of its prospects of success, but permission was not received. From one of the air force bases, the deputy commander called me up on the telephone: "Sir, it's just like the Six Day War. They're fleeing their dugouts like mice, we can take the whole line!" Indeed we could have. I was sure of that.

Despite the great success of the air operation, when we discussed it that night there were still some officers who opposed continuation of the bombings. I pressed for further attacks, contending that we should exploit our success and continue to strike at the Egyptians. Permission was given for bombing to be resumed the next day. But I didn't get much satisfaction from my success. Systematic recourse to the air force involved great difficulties and the loss of planes and pilots. After the air force succeeded in knocking out the ten missile batteries along the Canal, Russian involvement increased, and so did the number of batteries. Instead of regarding the air force as one of the components of the war against the Egyptians, instead of committing ground forces and armour on a large scale to pulverize the Egyptian line, with its artillery and missiles, the whole task devolved upon the air force, which came to be considered the sole solution, while the ground forces continued digging in. The Egyptians got used to living under bombing and did not give up their campaign of attrition. They were also reassured by the success of their attempts to lay ambushes in between our fortified positions. It was here they learnt the lesson they were to apply so successfully in the Yom Kippur War: leave the fortified positions alone and establish footholds in between.

Throughout the War of Attrition, there were apprehensions about the Russians, which was why the ground forces were not used for any decisive purpose, and also why the air force attacked here and there, causing the Egyptians—and itself—casualties and damage, but without employing its full strength.

As the war dragged on, without any army finding a way to put a stop to it, I, unlike others, became gradually convinced that this was the first time we were not winning. I said so countless times: we failed in this war. We did not comprehend it correctly. When the Egyptians agreed to a cease-fire, in August 1970, we interpreted it as an admission on their part that they couldn't stand our bombing any more. Without detracting from the great suffering inflicted on them by our air force, I don't have a shadow of a doubt that the Egyptians wanted a cease-fire in order to move their missile system forward to the Canal, so that it could neutralize our air force when their units crossed the waterway. All this backs up both of my contentions. First, the War of Attrition, in which our best soldiers shed their blood, resulted in the Egyptians gaining a free hand, over a period of three years, to prepare for the great war of October 1973; if so, it is no more than foolishness to claim that we won the War of Attrition. On the contrary, for all their casualties, it was the Egyptians who got the best of it. Second, by our errors between March 1969 and August 1970, and, subsequently, by our tragic acquiescence when the Egyptians violated the cease-fire and moved their missiles ahead, we, with our own hands, smoothed Egypt's path to the Yom Kippur War.

When our blindness caused us to misread Egyptian intentions and prevented us from applying an accurate interpretation—or taking action to forestall the enemy—it was then that the Yom Kippur War began, with all its ensuing results....

In 1948 and 1967, and during all the difficult times up to 1970, we never budged from the concept, without which Israel's existence would have been inconceivable, that our safety would be ensured not by parity of armament, but by the quality of the Israeli soldier; that it wasn't technological superiority which made us stronger than our enemies, but our great spiritual pre-eminence; that it wasn't arsenals crammed with the weapons and missiles which maintained us in the Middle East, but resourcefulness and cunning and brains, following the precept, "By ruses shall you make war." All through the War of Attrition, there wasn't a day when we didn't talk of our moral preponderance, but we contented ourselves with talk; without being convinced of these truths, all this was mere lip-service. Of the great conviction that we could overcome the Arabs, even if we didn't have some weapon or missile—ground, air or naval—nothing was left but words whose meaning had vanished. Either we got the Shrike [missile]—or what? Indecision. Lack of initiative. Acquiescence. Thus, the War of Attrition was the first one in which we gave in to technological limitations.

To use the terms of ground warfare, our Phantoms hacked through the barbed-wire fences of missiles and broke through the aerial fortifications, despite the losses they suffered; but they weren't backed up by the force that should have swept the objectives, demolishing the Egyptian positions and hurling them back from their footholds on the west bank of the Canal. The Egyptian surface-to-air missile system, which was the cause of our air losses and glumness, could have been eliminated in 1970. It would have required sending in infantry and armour, in addition to the air force. Whoever came to the conclusion that we lacked the strength to do so decreed that for the first time in her history, Israel would back down before the superior weapons possessed by the Arabs, thereby condemning the state to face the Yom Kippur War and concede its political positions, until it stood in real peril. And those who did so committed a further sin: in the course of the years 1970–3, they cultivated the delusion that we had won the War of Attrition, thus lulling our senses. Instead of saying: "We have failed to destroy the missiles system. Let's prepare for the eventuality that this system will fulfil a decisive role in the next war, and let's find ways of eliminating it!" we said: "Once again, we've won, once again, the Egyptians have had to rely on American favours to get them out of trouble" (and they were, indeed, in trouble). Thus, we created a myth, instead of dealing with the facts. We may have improved public morale, but we did so at a high price.

The results were not long in coming. Two or three weeks after the cease-fire ending the War of Attrition went into effect, in August 1970, the Egyptians took a meaningful and highly important step towards the Yom Kippur War: they moved their missile bases right up to the edge of the Canal, under cover of the agreement and in express defiance of it. The Israeli leadership did not have the courage to order a full-scale attack to annihilate the missile system, because they didn't believe it could be done. Then, by appealing to the Americans, they sowed the seed of total dependence on U.S. wishes.

71

Yitzhak Rabin

The Jordanian Crisis

September 1970: Memoir

Israel was hard put to devise a solution to the Palestinian Problem, both in strategic terms and to the challenge of terror. But the problem has plagued several of the Arab states as well. As the Palestine Liberation Organization grew in strength—diplomatically and militarily—it tried to establish a territorial base for itself, first unsuccessfully in Jordan and then with limited success in Lebanon. During the late 1960s and the Lebanese civil wars of the 1970s the PLO achieved virtual sovereignty over large areas of Lebanon.

In September 1970 the Palestinian organizations attempted first to assassinate King Hussein, then to overthrow him by waging war against him. During the first week of September there were sporadic attacks and hijackings; by mid-September Jordan was torn by a full-scale civil war. On September 18, Syrian forces tried to intervene on the side of the Palestinian organizations. This development alarmed Israel, which threatened to intervene in Jordan against the Syrian forces. Moreover, the United States acted quickly to deter the involvement of the Soviet Union on behalf of its client-state Syria. In the end Syria's attempt to intervene proved abortive, and Hussein's army dealt a crushing blow to Palestinian organizations in Jordan, who called this clash with Jordan their Black September.

The Jordanian crisis of September 1970 was an important turning point. The diplomatic maneuvering is described here by Yitzhak Rabin (1922–1995), who was Israeli ambassador in Washington and, together with the U.S. secretary of state, Henry Kissinger, played a major role in coordinating American and Israeli policies during the crisis.

Ever since the guns fell silent along the Suez Canal, a grave crisis had been brewing in Jordan. The Palestinian terrorist organizations based there were at the peak of their strength and conducted themselves like a state within a state. As control progressively slipped out of his hands, King Hussein realized that the hour of decision was drawing near, and in September he launched a life-or-death battle against the terrorists. It was a cruel conflict, with the army using tanks and artillery against Palestinian refugee camps. Official casualty figures have never been published, but they are estimated to run into the thousands. With the terrorists on the defensive during what they called their "Black September," Syria saw an opportunity to send armoured units across the borders—ostensibly to aid the terrorists, but actually to gain effective control of Jordan. The Jordanian army deployed for defence, but it was pathetically inferior to the Syrians in armour and air power.

By that time Golda Meir had completed her visit to Washington and on her last evening in the United States was scheduled to address a large United Jewish Appeal dinner at the New York Hilton. It was there, at eight in the evening,

Source: Yitzhak Rabin, *The Rabin Memoirs* (Jerusalem and London: Weidenfeld and Nicolson, 1979), pp. 146–48. Reprinted by permission of Leah Rabin.

that I was asked to call Henry Kissinger immediately at his Washington office. When the call was put through, he spoke with a ring of urgency in his voice: "King Hussein has approached us, describing the situation of his forces, and asked us to transmit his request that your air force attack the Syrians in northern Jordan. I need an immediate reply."

"I'm surprised to hear the United States passing on messages of this kind like some sort of mailman," I told Kissinger. "I will not even submit the request to Mrs. Meir before I know what your government thinks. Are you recommending that we respond to the Jordanian request?"

"You place me in a difficult position," Kissinger begged off. "I can't answer you on the spot. Perhaps in another half-hour."

After we rang off, I stole Golda away from the cocktail party in progress, moved off into another room, and told her of my conversation with Kissinger. We decided to notify Acting Prime Minister Yigal Allon of this latest development and ask for his opinion. In the meantime, minutes were ticking by and Kissinger had not called back. Golda spoke with both Allon and [Moshe] Dayan and found that opinions back home were split down the middle: the former inclined toward fulfilling the request, while the latter was far more reserved. I suggested that reconnaissance flights be made over the combat zone to northern Jordan and asked our people to explore the feasibility of establishing direct contact between the IDF [Israel Defense Forces] and the Jordanian command. Battles unfold swiftly, and it would be absurd to have to communicate via Washington.

Over an hour later Kissinger finally called back: "The request is approved and supported by the United States government," he said.

"Do *you* advise Israel to do it?" I pressed.

"Yes," he said, "subject to your own considerations."

That the Americans were eager to ensure our intervention in the Syrian-Jordanian conflict was underscored by the fact that Kissinger arranged for a special White House plane to fly me back to Washington that same night. I accompanied Mrs. Meir to Kennedy Airport for her own flight back to Israel, and at 2 A.M. a plane was waiting at La Guardia to take me to Andrews Air Force Base near Washington, where I was picked up by a White House limousine and taken home. I called Kissinger again, even though it was already three-thirty in the morning, and while talking to him I had the impression that someone was listening in on our conversation. I later learned that it was the president [Richard Nixon].

When I met Kissinger at nine the next morning, the American reports on the military situation were still sketchy. But the reports from Israel were encouraging, and I now became the major source of intelligence on the conflict. Although the Syrians had penetrated northern Jordan, Hussein's armoured units were holding on to the two routes leading south and had inflicted losses on the invasion force. In response, the Syrians were massing further armoured units near the border, but they had refrained from using their air power.

Although Golda had not yet arrived in Israel, the government had worked out its general lines of approach to the United States. I was notified that Israel was prepared to take action, but (one of the few times that I could address this word to the Americans) should our intervention in Jordan lead to a renewal of fighting along the Suez Canal, we wanted the United States to back our response. I also told Kissinger and [Joseph] Sisco that we wanted a written undertaking to provide us with an American "umbrella" vis-à-vis the Russians if the Soviet Union threatened Israel directly and that we wanted additional arms. Their response was affirmative on the arms, but when it came to the "umbrella" they were in a predicament.

As we were bargaining, events in the Jordanian-Syrian conflict continued to unfold, as with the IDF reinforcing its forces in the Golan Heights, the Jordanians succeeded in halting the 300 Syrian tanks and the American moves bore fruit. Israeli-U.S. co-operation in planning the IDF intervention, together with the Israeli troop concentrations near the Syrian border convinced the Russians and the Syrians that they should halt the advance into Jordan. In weighing up their options, the Russians could not have been oblivious to the fact that the Sixth Fleet's[1] aircraft carriers were moving eastward in the Mediterranean and that a group of American officers took off from one of the carriers and came to Israel to discuss operational coordination. "Hints" of that nature may or may not have been subtle, but they were certainly effective, for soon afterward the Syrians withdrew from Jordan and the risk of a broader war was averted. At the same time, these events had a far-reaching impact on U.S.-Israeli relations. Israel's willingness to co-operate closely with the United States in protecting American interests in the region altered her image in the eyes of many officials in Washington. We were considered as a partner—not equal to the United States, but nevertheless a valuable ally in a vital region during times of crisis.

On 25 September Kissinger phoned me and asked me, on behalf of the president, to convey a message to our prime minister: "The president will never forget Israel's role in preventing the deterioration in Jordan and in blocking the attempt to overturn the regime there. He said that the United States is fortunate in having an ally like Israel in the Middle East. These events will be taken into account in all future developments." This was probably the most far-reaching statement ever made by a president of the United States on the mutuality of the alliance between the two countries. I had never heard anything like it and still look back on that pronouncement with nostalgia. Now we waited to see how the sentiment would be translated into concrete policy.

NOTE

1. The Sixth Fleet is the U.S. naval force stationed in the Mediterranean.

72

Palestine Liberation Organization

Political Program

January 12, 1973

This political program of the Palestine Liberation Organization, written in late 1972–early 1973, is interesting in several respects. It reflects the political outlook of the PLO leadership after the clash with Jordan in September 1970 (Black September) at a period of an apparent Israeli success before the changes that the Yom Kippur War introduced. Yet there were already signs that the collective power of the Arab world was rising and that the PLO was to be a major beneficiary of that trend.

Source: Yehoshafat Harkabi, *The Palestinian Covenant and Its Meaning* (London: Vallentine, Mitchell and Co., 1979), pp. 132–39, 141–44, 145–46.

Prologue

Throughout its glorious struggle for liberation, democracy and unity, our Arab people has been persistently subject to conspiracies from the colonialist and imperialist forces and their lackey local reactionaries. These colonialist and imperialist forces see in our Arab homeland ample opportunity for imperialist plunder of its unlimited natural resources. They regard it, also, as an important strategic take-off point, owing to its unique central position amidst the three continents of Asia, Africa and Europe, and to its control over vital air and sea routes, especially the Mediterranean Sea, the Suez Canal, the Red Sea, the Arabian Gulf and the Indian Ocean. They also view it as a center of gravity for whoever dominates it in international politics.

In their invasion of our Arab homeland, the colonialist and imperialist powers feared that the rising patriotic and national struggle would stand in the way of their schemes. Neither were they confident of the ability of their local reactionary mainstays to hold out against the rising national tide. Hence, using the world Zionist movement, they plotted the usurpation of Palestine, intending to create therein a colonialist racist entity which would constitute both an outpost for the protection of colonialist and Zionist domination over our Arab homeland and a heavy club to be raised by world imperialism in the face of the ever-growing Arab struggle for liberation.

In collusion with the reactionary forces which ruled the whole area—except Syria where a nationalist regime existed—the colonialist and imperialist forces succeeded in planting the colonialist Zionist entity in Palestine arbitrarily and forcibly. They also succeeded in uprooting the Palestinians from their land. The Palestinian Arab people, however, did not submit. On the basis of its right to defend its homeland and its existence, and in view of the responsibility it bears as a forward defense line against the imperialist-Zionist assault on the Arab nation, the Palestinian Arab people, for thirty years, put up a heroic and relentless struggle. In each of its revolutionary uprisings, which culminated in the 1936 and 1947 revolts, the reactionary and lackey forces played a role in undermining the Palestinian struggle and bolstering the position of its enemies and the enemies of the Arab nation.

This was the situation on January 1, 1965, when the vanguard of our Palestinian people initiated the contemporary armed national revolution against the Zionist entity, which exists on Palestinian soil through aggression and the force of arms, and which has never desisted from using violence to expel our people and to finalize the realization of its schemes for the usurpation of the whole of our land. In this revolution, which erupted on that glorious first day of 1965, the vanguard of our people embodied the noble revolutionary traditions of our people and of our Arab nation. They also raised anew the flag of the struggle for liberation against imperialism and Zionism, the flag in whose defense tens of thousands of martyrs have fallen everywhere in the Arab homeland.

This vanguard (with it the Palestinian people, the Arab masses and the free of the world) believed that armed struggle is the correct, the inevitable and the main method of liberating Palestine. For such an antagonistic contradiction with the Zionist enemy cannot be resolved except through revolutionary violence.

When the Palestinian revolutionary vanguard resorted to armed struggle, it aroused the Palestinian and Arab masses, filling them with the will to fight. This led to a violent transformation of Arab realities in the direction of insistence upon rejecting the defeat and determination to take the offensive against the Zionist enemy and to defeat the American imperialist plots. Consequently, Jordan became a base for armed struggle and a take-off point for both the escalation of armed struggle and its protection on Palestinian soil. In addition, extended battle fronts were opened against the enemy which included the Suez Canal and the whole of the Palestinian frontier with Transjordan, Lebanon and Syria. Armed popular resistance was escalated in the West Bank and in the Palestinian territory occupied prior to June 1967. The Gaza Strip witnessed heroic deeds of armed struggle to the point where semi-liberated neighbourhoods in Gaza itself were created.

The Palestinian revolution moved from one victory to another and grew quickly, in spite of all the imperialist and Zionist plots and notwithstanding all difficulties. It was able to emerge victorious from all the battles in which it confronted imperialist conspiracies and counter-revolutionary forces in Jordan and Lebanon from November 1968 up to June 1970. The Zionist enemy, too, failed in the extermination campaigns which it conducted against the bases of the revolution. The revolution was able to turn these campaigns of the enemy into victories, as witnessed at Al-Karameh and Al-Arqub.[1]

However, the revolution began to face an extremely difficult situation due to the American initiatives and the plans they spawned (such as the Rogers Plan [see doc. 63]). These initiatives were accompanied by large scale encirclement of the revolution and the spread of the spirit of defeatism. This situation provided the counter-revolutionary forces in Jordan with a valuable opportunity to exploit some of the negative features that characterized the course of the revolution in order to implement the American-Zionist-Hashemite schemes. These schemes aimed at administering a harsh blow to the Palestinian revolution as a preliminary step towards its elimination and towards the liquidation of the Palestine problem. The Palestinian revolution and the Palestinian-Jordanian masses fought gloriously in Jordan in September 1970, in defense of the principle of armed struggle and for the Palestinian and Arab cause. Their battle shall forever remain an epic of incredible heroism and historic resistance under the harshest of conditions. But in July 1971, the lackey Jordanian regime eliminated the public presence of the Palestinian revolution in Jordan and began to follow policies which carried the threat of (a) an official capitulation to the enemy concerning the West Bank and Jerusalem, (b) the liquidation of the unity of the Palestinian presence, (c) the encouragement of dissension among the ranks of the Palestinian people and of divisions between Palestinian and Jordanian, between soldier and *fedayi,* (d) the conversion of the East Bank into a buffer favoring the Zionist entity and into a military, political and economic sphere of influence for Israel, which means transforming it into an American, West German and British backyard where imperialist influence dominates, (e) the repression, pillage and impoverishment of the Jordanian masses, the suppression of their democratic freedoms, in addition to the wrecking of their national economy. It is no secret that the American schemes aim at rebuilding the Jordanian army so it can be directed against Syria and Iraq also. These circumstances presented the Zionist enemy with the golden opportunity for making its occupation more secure by concentrating its efforts on trying to wipe out the armed resistance in the Gaza Strip and pacify the situation in the occupied territories. Thus the Gaza Strip was subjected to the harshest forms of repression and population expulsions; while in the West Bank local municipal elections were imposed to create favorable conditions for the occupation, divide the Palestinian people and attempt at promoting phony political leaders to substitute for the Palestinian revolutionary leadership. This went simultaneously with King Hussein's plan for the establishment of a so-called United Arab Kingdom with goals identical to those of the Zionist plot.

On the other hand, American imperialism intensified its assault according to a broad plan to securely contain and liquidate both the Palestinian revolution and the Arab liberation movement. For this purpose, American imperialism resorted to numerous manoeuvres and plots under such signboards as the so-called American initiative, peace proposals, interim settlements and United Nations Security Council resolutions. In this they were abetted by active defeatist forces, bound by strong economic and political ties to the imperialists.

The blow that was administered to the Palestinian revolution in Amman in mid-1971, the intensification of the American and Zionist imperialist assault against the Palestinian revolution and the Palestinian masses in the occupied territories and outside, and finally the growing deterioration in the official Arab situation in favor of capitulation, have all continued to generate a crisis for the Palestinian revolution and the Palestinian and Arab masses. This general crisis has, on the one hand, captivated the whole Arab nation throughout the greater Arab homeland and, on the other, produced a series of conspiratorial schemes aiming at the liquidation of the Palestinian revolution, of the Palestinian people's unified national existence and of its patriotic cause. These conspiracies have taken such forms as the Allon Plan,[2] the proposed Palestinian state on the West Bank and the Gaza Strip, annexation, judaization, as well as the absorption and assimilation of the Palestinians in the societies where they lived in the diaspora.

In this atmosphere of crisis, we find our Palestinian Arab people moving with firmness and determination to defend its armed revolution, its unified national existence and its right to liberate its entire homeland. Our people will allow neither the liquidation of this just cause, nor of its revolution, both of which constitute a central point from which military and revolution radiate onto an area over which the imperialists and the Zionists want to extend their full domination. . . .

In these new and dangerous circumstances and in the face of the responsibilities which the Palestinian revolution bears, the Palestine Liberation Organization, with all its groups and forces, has agreed to an interim political program based on four principal strategic axioms:

1. The continuation of the mobilization and organization of all our people's potentials, both within and without the homeland, for a protracted people's war in pursuit of total liberation, and the creation of a democratic state in accordance with the aspirations of the Arab nation for comprehensive unity and national liberation.
2. The tight linking of our people's struggle with that of our brothers the Jordanian people in a Jordanian-Palestinian liberation front to be entrusted (in addition to its tasks in Palestine) with the conduct of the struggle for the liberation of Jordan from the lackey reactionary royalist regime, which acts both to mask actual Zionist domination over the East Bank and to guard fiercely the said Zionist occupation of Palestine.
3. The linking of the Palestinian struggle with the overall Arab struggle via a front of all the national and progressive forces hostile to imperialism, Zionism and neo-colonialism.
4. Solidarity with the world struggle against imperialism, Zionism and reaction, and for national liberation.

The Palestine Liberation Organization defines its tasks as follows:

First: On the Palestine Scene

1. To continue the struggle, particularly armed struggle, for the liberation of the entire Palestine national territory and for the establishment of a Palestinian democratic society which guarantees the right to work and to a decent life for all citizens so they can live in equality, justice and fraternity, a democratic society opposed to all forms of prejudice due to race, color or creed. This society will guarantee the freedoms of thought, expression and assembly, freedom to demonstrate, strike and form national political and labor organizations, freedom of worship for all creeds; such that this democratic Palestinian society will constitute a part of the entire united Arab democratic society.
2. To militate against the compromising mentality and the plans it spawns which are either contrary to our people's cause of national

liberation, or aim to liquidate this cause through "proposed Palestinian entities" or through *a Palestinian state on part of the Palestinian national soil.* Also to oppose these plans through armed struggle and political struggle of the masses connected to it.

3. To reinforce the bonds of national unity and joint struggle between our compatriots in the territory occupied in 1948 and those in the West Bank, the Gaza Strip and beyond the occupied homeland. . . .

Second: On the Jordanian-Palestinian Scene

The Jordanian-Palestinian national front is called upon to direct the struggle of the two peoples towards the following strategic aims:

1. The establishment of a national democratic regime in Jordan which shall: create the appropriate atmosphere for the continuation of the struggle for the liberation of the whole of Palestine; guarantee the national sovereignty of both Jordanian and Palestinian peoples; guarantee the renewal of the union of the two banks on the correct basis of the complete national equality between the two peoples, so that the full historical national rights of the Palestinian people and the present national rights of the two peoples are safeguarded; ensure common national development economically, socially and culturally; strengthen the ties of brotherhood and equality between the two peoples by means of equal legal constitutional, cultural and economic rights and by means of placing the human and economic resources of each people in the service of their common development.
2. The consolidation of the struggles of both the Palestinian and Jordanian peoples with that of the Arab nation so as to: complete national liberation; oppose imperialist plans aiming at imposing solutions and conditions in the Arab homeland that mean surrender to the enemy; eradicate all forms of Zionist and imperialist presence (economic, military and cultural), as well as all the forces connected with them which act as mediators for neo-colonialism and its policies.

NOTES

1. Al-Karameh is the Palestinian base located in Jordan that was attacked by Israel on March 21, 1968, in the largest such Israeli attack at that time. A joint Palestinian-Jordanian defense inflicted relatively heavy losses on the Israeli forces, heavier than the damage the Israelis inflicted.

Al-Arqub is an area in southeast Lebanon, near the Syrian and Israeli borders, that was taken over by the Palestinians in the late 1960s and controlled by them until 1982. Israelis commonly referred to the area as Fatahland.

2. The Allon Plan was developed in 1968 by Yigal Allon in the wake of the Yom Kippur War to retain Israeli military control over the West Bank through strategically placed military and paramilitary bases while returning most of the populated territory to Jordan (see map 4).

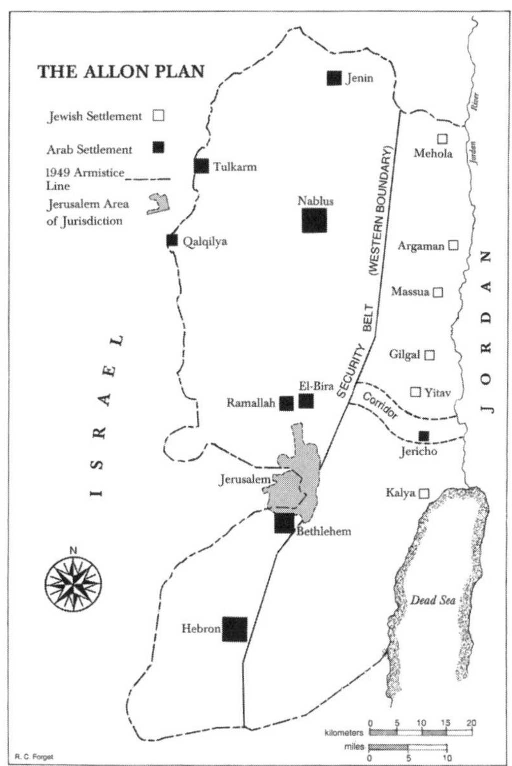

MAP 4. THE ALLON PLAN, 1968

73
Hanoch Bartov
The Eve of the Yom Kippur War
Spring–Summer 1973: Memoir

Israel's intelligence failure—the assessment that, numerous reports notwithstanding, Egypt was not going to launch war—was a crucial fact underlying the developments of October 1973. Hanoch Bartov, an Israeli writer and journalist, illuminates this failure through his biography of General David (Dado) Elazar (1925–1975), the Israel Defense Forces' chief of staff from January 1973 until April 1974. Elazar was forced to resign on April 2, 1974, because of the findings of the Agranat Commission of Inquiry established to investigate the intelligence failure (see doc. 76). Elazar came out of the Labor movement and began his military career in the Palmach. He was Northern Area commander during the Six-Day War. After the Yom Kippur War he represented Israel in signing the Egyptian-Israeli separation-of-forces agreement on January 18, 1974, at Kilometer 101 (see doc. 91).

This excerpt deals with the outlook of the Israeli political and military elite in the spring and summer before the war.

A week after [Anwar] Sadat put together his new government and took over as its head, Arnaud de Borchgrave published an interview with him in *Newsweek* (on April 2) whose purpose was to reinforce the impression that Egypt was indeed preparing for an all-out confrontation with Israel. Sadat warned the United States that the evolving situation in the Middle East would prove worse for America than the "national trauma" of Vietnam, from which she had recently emerged. The picture of stalemate in the region would change radically when Egypt renewed the fighting, Sadat told the *Newsweek* correspondent. Official sources deliberately leaked word of Egypt's intentions; a military exercise was publicized; and civil defense exercises were held. By April 8 the *Sunday Times* correspondent in Cairo was moved to write that there were signs that Sadat really intended to land a limited military blow against Israel. He was not aiming for the defeat of Israel—which Egyptian generals did not believe they could achieve—but a move to break the deadlock in the Middle East, which could be accomplished with Syrian and Libyan aid. The scenario called for capturing part of the Sinai Peninsula and fielding as much weaponry as possibly in order to inflict considerable damage on the Israelis. Presumably this action would open up new political options for Egypt, which undoubtedly meant the intervention of the superpowers to impose a solution on Israel.

The background to this burst of activity in Egypt was Leonid Brezhnev's forthcoming visit to the United States, which was heralded by a flurry of diplomatic activity on the part of the

---

Source: Hanoch Bartov, *Dado: 48 shanah veod 20 yom* [Dado: 48 Years and 20 More Days] (Tel Aviv: Maariv Book Guild, 1981), pp. 188–96. Reprinted by permission.

superpowers. The third round of talks in Helsinki, laying the groundwork for the Foreign Ministers' Conference on European Security, was coming to a close at about that time, and the conference itself was scheduled to open in June. Thus the Israeli chief of staff viewed the *Newsweek* interview and Sadat's speech upon unveiling his new government as part of an Egyptian political offensive. Sadat's remarks were addressed to two audiences. Domestically, they were meant to draw attention away from the country's economic and social problems, which were growing worse every day. Outside Egypt, they hinted at developments that would be undesirable to the United States and other countries, so that the recipients of the message would pressure Israel to give in to the Arab position.

Yet conflicting reports on a state of alert also began to come in from Egypt at that time. On the one hand, there was talk of Russian military advisers returning to Egypt and considerable amounts of military equipment arriving from Libya by airlift. In contrast, Jim Holland of the *Washington Post,* for one, reported an "expert's" opinion that the Egyptian air-defense network had been destroyed and the little that had been redeemed in the meanwhile was merely "first aid." He likewise reported that the maintenance of the army's equipment was worse than ever, civil defense was in a bad state, and that the consistent weakness of the Egyptian military machine made it obvious that renewing the war would be the equivalent of "suicide."

Dado [David Elazar] believed that there was a good deal of exaggeration in the reports of the total inefficacy of Egypt's anti-aircraft and missile networks and warned that "we shouldn't regard it as an inoperative system." Moreover, despite the fact that there were no concrete signs of a war-footing in Egypt, the chief of staff cautioned against ignoring the risk that matters would deteriorate, so that "our readiness remains high." Yet his assessment of the situation did not fill Dado with any sense of apprehension, and he was confident of the IDF's [Israel Defense Forces] ability to overcome the missile system, regardless of its degree of efficacy on any given day.

We have already described the general mood in Israel during this period, placing special emphasis on the political and military outlook of the minister of defense. We have also noted that [Moshe] Dayan's influence over the military establishment was considerable, by virtue of both his formal status and the senior command's admiration for him. That influence extended to the interface of political and military evaluations—meaning such questions as the probability vs. intent—as well as such purely military subjects as the acquisition of certain types of hardware and operational decisions. At the beginning of April, Dayan aired his assessment of the situation publicly, and it proved to run contrary to Dado's view that in the absence of political progress Israel could expect hostilities to be renewed. "Until recently I wasn't sure," Dayan stated at a convention of paratroopers in Jerusalem, "but now I believe that we are on the threshold of the crowning era of the Return to Zion." This feeling had been roused not only by the Six-Day War itself but by the cease-fire on the Bar-Lev Line,[1] the collapse of the eastern front and the terrorist organizations, and the expulsion of the Russians from Egypt, "which has ensured stability without war." In a speech delivered atop Massada[2] before members of the Israel Exploration Society, he characterized the times as being blessed by a constellation of circumstances "the likes of which our people has probably never witnessed in the past, and certainly not since the modern Return to Zion." The first of these factors was the power of Israel's army, "the superiority of our forces over our enemies, which holds promise of peace for us and our neighbors." The second feature was "the jurisdiction of the Israeli government from the Jordan to Suez."

Speaking more explicitly in closed sessions with the senior command of the army at the beginning of April, Dayan was more specific:

Israel was now at the end of war. The Russians had gone home, and he didn't have the impression that the region was on the brink of an explosion. The cuts in expenditures for equipment—meaning the latest reductions in the five-year plan "Ofek A"—were not the last, for the nation had more pressing priorities. Everything had to be planned with an eye to the needs of the next war, which was not expected before 1976—if at all. Israel would not start a war, for it was not in her interest to do so, and the Arabs knew that they hadn't a chance of defeating Israel. Therefore, Dayan concluded, Israel would continue to man the present lines for at least another three years—or slightly different lines if an interim agreement was concluded in the meantime.

This assessment was also reflected in the decision about purchasing fording equipment. Dayan believed that it was preferable to postpone ordering such equipment for a year, in view of his assessment of the situation, budgetary considerations, and the fact that it was an election year. But the chief of staff opposed him on the question of amphibious craft, arguing that what you put off today won't be available tomorrow. And Dado would not give in on that point, even if it had to be brought before the prime minister, though he wanted to settle the matter then and there.

Moreover, as if to belie Dayan's unqualified confidence and optimism, Dado's attention was taken up with the insistent reports that Egypt was preparing to renew hostilities in the near future. Sadat had paid a visit to Libya and proclaimed the inauguration of "the stage of total confrontation." Libya's [Muamar] Qaddafi had visited [Houari] Boumedienne in Algeria. A squadron of sixteen Iraqi Hunter fighter planes and their pilots had reached Egypt on April 7. And following the Libyan airlift, on April 10 sixteen Mirage fighter planes that France had sold to Libya were transferred on to Egypt. Undercover sources suddenly began to supply very specific information that was not made public, even though it was remarkably similar to the reports published in the *Sunday Times* on April 8. The gist of the information was that Sadat had decided to go to war on May 15. His plan was to have five infantry divisions cross the Canal while helicopters landed commandos deep inside Sinai and attacked Sharm el-Sheikh. Once the infantry divisions had made it across the Canal, armored formations would follow into Sinai. This is essentially the plan that was carried out on Yom Kippur afternoon. But it was back on April 8, when everything was still tinged by the effect of the Beirut raid,[3] that the "countdown" began. From mid-April into the summer of 1973, the possibility that Egypt would opt for a surprise attack preoccupied the IDF and the Israeli government. And for weeks there would be ups and downs, endless discussions and operational planning sessions, the institution of measures to bolster the IDF's fighting ability, until slowly but surely the idea would take hold that it was all a false alarm. In mid-August, seven weeks before the outbreak of the Yom Kippur War, this alert footing in anticipation of an Egyptian attack—code named Blue-White—was finally and formally cancelled.

Was Sadat really capable of pulling off a war in 1973, or were the circumstances that led to Blue-White merely posturing with an empty gun? This was the problem that faced the General Staff and the government in the spring of 1973. Despite the detailed intelligence reports—including the basic outline of the Egyptian war plan, the forces that were to cross the canal, their targets and the timetable of the two-stage assault—the probability of an Egyptian-initiated war remained an open question. And though that question would be kicked around by many people during the long wait from the middle of April onward, the three main characters in this drama-before-the-drama were the chief of intelligence, the chief of staff, and the minister of defense.

Before we follow the development of Blue-White, however, a word or two about procedure. If we were to construct a flow-chart for the Intelligence Branch, it would show the raw intelligence data moving toward the chief of intelligence and his aides, each of whom was an expert in his field. These are the men responsible for the final sifting of the data and for transforming it into concentrated summaries that include both the relevant information and an assessment of its reliability, significance, and implications. At the time, the Intelligence Branch was Israel's only broad-based, experienced, and efficient apparatus for constructing a comprehensive political-military intelligence picture. What's more, even though the purpose of the branch was primarily to aid the army's various command levels in making the best possible "command decision" by providing them with data and assessments, its influence did not stop at the chief of staff's office.

This state of affairs had come in for sharp criticism from the Yadin-Sharef Committee, which had submitted its conclusions in mid-1963. But in essence nothing had changed over the next ten years. The Research Department of the Foreign Ministry had not been upgraded, and it was totally incapable of providing the prime minister with independent political appraisals. The Mossad [at this time under the direction of the Prime Minister's Office] had not been elevated to a status that would enable it not only to gather information but submit its own political-military assessments to the government. Although the head of the Mossad had a standing invitation to General Staff meetings, and in the period under discussion Maj. Gen. Zvi Zamir also had easy access to both the prime minister and the chief of staff, everyone's attention naturally gravitated toward the body that had the tools to effect a solid job of evaluation. After all, in making its assessments the Intelligence Branch availed itself of the data collected by the entire "intelligence community."

Finally, the need for selectivity in drawing up an intelligence report is inevitable, since it is impossible to imagine a situation in which all the "raw data" is regularly passed on to the chief of staff, the minister of defense, and the prime minister as the summary accompanying the assessments is. The reliability of intelligence evaluations depends to no small degree upon the good judgment of the men and women responsible for sifting and evaluating the data all along its treacherous path to the top and the degree of confidence they enjoy from the recipients of the final product.

It is at the end of this mine-strewn path that the chief of intelligence comes together with the chief of staff and the minister of defense. The meeting that took place between them on April 13, 1973, three days before Passover, was not between three "incumbents" but three very singular men. Maj. Gen. Eli Zeira drew his authority from both his formal standing at the apex of the intelligence pyramid and his reputation for a sharp mind, articulate tongue, and forceful views. Everyone has remarked upon his direct and close relationship with the minister of defense, and the two men were known to share a long acquaintanceship and remarkably similar political outlooks. Dado also placed great faith in Zeira, even though throughout that summer they continued to differ in their appraisals of the probability of war—and all that followed therefrom. Suffice it to say here that all evidence leads to the impression that there was direct contact between each of the three vertices of the Dayan-Elazar-Zeira triangle, and a triangle—rather than a linear hierarchy—is precisely how this relationship should be understood.

As in November 1972, Zeira again concluded that nothing in the new intelligence data merited a change in his fundamental assessment—namely, that the Egyptians could not possibly be as foolish as their war plans made them appear. Hafez Ismail[4] was to meet with Henry Kissinger on May 19. Brezhnev was scheduled to visit the United States in June. An all-out war at this point would mean a resounding military defeat for Egypt, and there was no reason to believe that Sadat had revised his own assessment that he was incapable of waging a war on such a scale. Thus the inescapable conclusion was that Sadat merely wanted to create a menacing atmosphere in order to boost the Arab bargaining position before the talks scheduled for May and June.

The situation also called for certain conclusions to be drawn vis-à-vis the United States. Despite reports of Egypt's martial intentions, Israel must beware of pressing the panic button and leading the Americans to believe that she is alarmed by the threats of war emanating from "the great Sadat." Any sign of squeamishness would probably invite negative political consequences, for in order to head off a military crisis the Americans would undoubtedly be quick to advance their own proposals for a political settlement; and if precedent were any guide, their proposals would most likely be unacceptable to the Israeli government.

Dayan's assessment of the situation that spring was much more circumspect than Zeira's. He too believed that Sadat was merely putting on a show of muscle-flexing before the series of political meetings, but could anyone be absolutely sure that the latest threats were merely bluster? The Egyptians might open fire precisely in order to spur some progress on the political front, and the detailed intelligence data did appear to be reliable. There was no doubt that the odds of a war breaking out were higher than they had been at the end of 1972. But the question remained whether by "war" Sadat meant a full-scale attack or a more modest and manageable undertaking. One way or the other, Dayan agreed with Zeira that "crying wolf" to the Americans would only invite pressure to return to the path of negotiations. So although the intelligence must be passed on to the United States, Israel should refrain from appending any definitive assessment of its significance.

Dado, for his part, basically accepted Zeira's analysis, but he could not get away from the political factor: the very passage of time and perpetuation of the stalemate in themselves constituted a motive for Egypt to go to war. He confessed that he had not yet seen the data upon which Zeira had based his evaluation, so that he could not judge whether "it is certain that they will open fire." But he believed that "there's a very good chance it can happen" because he could see the beginning of an erosion in the situation and preparations for war. "Instinctively I feel that this time it's more serious than the previous warnings," he remarked. But since there was at least a month before fighting would break out, the IDF would have time to prepare for war, and that included the adoption of deterrent or pre-emptive measures.

Dayan advised that any plans should take into account the Arab brand of logic, which is likely to dictate that if they've lost planes anyway, they might as well have a full-blown war. Sadat, for example, maintains an army of half a million soldiers on salary; why shouldn't they do something productive to earn their keep?

Three days later, on the eve of Passover (April 16), when Dado convened a General Staff meeting, Eli Zeira reiterated his assessment that Egypt's strength had not changed in any significant way since the end of 1972, and the additional Libyan Mirages and Iraqi Hunters did not create a new balance of power in the air. The probability of war was low, Zeira concluded—perhaps even very low—but it did exist. And if Egypt wished to create the impression that she might resort to an act of desperation on the eve of the Nixon-Brezhnev summit, Israel must not let it be thought that she was susceptible to the threats, had put her forces on alert, or was asking the world to deflect the Egyptians from their resolve to make war. An overreaction on Israel's part would only contribute to the making of a war scare, which would be exploited by whomever wants to exert pressure.

Many of the participants in the discussion shared Zeira's feelings. The commander of the Southern Area, Ariel Sharon, believed that the southern front was prepared for the contingency of war and was generally in good shape insofar as control systems, communications, command posts, and access roads were concerned. A special road was in the process of being paved for the roller bridge, but even if it were not completed, the troops could get along without it.

What's more, all combat plans had recently been reviewed and updated. Sharon also aired his standard view on reducing the number of strongholds: only the absolutely necessary minimum should be maintained along the waterline in areas where it was in Israel's interest to maintain a presence for the purpose of effecting a quick crossing. Incidentally, Sharon viewed the crossing itself as a very attractive operation but believed its importance to be marginal and felt that it could definitely be waived. He was not concerned with the appraised strength of the Arabs' armor; another 1,000 Egyptian tanks and 500 Syrian tanks would not endanger the existence of the State of Israel or challenge its defensive capability as long as the IDF occupied its present lines, he felt.

Contrary to Sharon, the chief of Training Division, Maj. Gen. Shmuel Gonen, felt that the IDF must not treat the information it had recently received as though nothing had changed. Quite the opposite, serious preparations should be made for war. Essentially he too believed that nothing would come of it all; but in case something did happen, he reasoned, we would never be able to explain to ourselves or anyone else that we simply didn't believe a war would break out. Obviously the army should not adopt tactics that would create a war scare—e.g., mobilizing reserves or making changes in troop deployments and scheduled maneuvers. But plans should be reviewed, the level of alert upgraded to anticipate the opening artillery barrage, and the units slated to cross the canal should be given special training. Gonen was concerned by the rise in the number of tanks at the disposal of the confrontation states. He therefore concluded that changes should be made in the long-range armament programs to increase the tank force at the expense of equipment for the other ground forces. But not only was Gonen's voice a lonely one in that room, it sounded oddly out of tune.

Before bringing the meeting to a close, the chief of staff went into a lengthy analysis of the components that made up the present situation. Although he again granted the logic of the intelligence assessment that an Egyptian decision to go to war immediately was unlikely, he also explored the antithetical logic, citing Egypt's frustration over the continuing deadlock and the passage of time, which added up to "a feature, politically speaking, that worries the Egyptians." Hafez Ismail's more recent visit to Washington had been fruitless, whereas Golda's [Meir] visit had brought Israel assurances of continued weapons supplies. Egyptian hopes of renewed Soviet support were also disappointed. Added together, all this clearly aggravated the dilemma facing President Sadat and explained his preoccupation with planning for war.

In all likelihood, Dado stressed, the latest flurry of Egyptian activity was merely meant to raise Sadat's political capital in the eyes of the superpowers and Israel. But it was impossible to predict whether or not he would cross the Rubicon that separates threats from acts. Perhaps he had another aim in mind. Perhaps Sadat hoped "that there will be a brief round of fighting, and even if it ends in a draw—without any tragedy befalling Egypt—within a few days, the Egyptians will again be a fighting nation, and the war will have launched the entire problem back into the headlines and onto the negotiating table." Illogical as that may sound, it was possible to imagine the Egyptians harboring such illusions, "for that is essentially the only thing that would really solve Egypt's problem for a few years," Dado summed up. "And the subjective temptation, desire, and ambition are so strong that despite the great risk, Sadat might try it. It's illogical. The risks are much greater than the prospects, and I presume that in the end he will be dissuaded. But I can't be fully confident of that."

The more Dado went into his analysis, the greater the political element took precedence over the military and heightened his feeling that his latest warning should be treated more seriously: "A war can be tempting to Egypt today, as we come to the end of the sixth year since the Six-Day War and the years of stalemate create a more established situation." Yes, a war might indeed break out.

Did Israel have any reason to allow such a war to break out? "My answer is unequivocal," Dado pronounced. "We are not interested in a war. And if it's possible to go on for another five, six, seven years without a war, that would be the best for the people of Israel . . . from both a strategic viewpoint and the standpoint of Israeli domestic affairs. Israel fought very well in the Six-Day War because it felt that it had been forced into a war that it did not want and did not instigate."

So it was clear that the Egyptian and Israeli interests were diametrically opposed on this point. But the question remained whether Egypt really would initiate a war. And if so, how could Israel make the best of it?

Dado did not believe that any kind of war would bring about peace, but a serious Egyptian defeat could change the situation in the region for a few years and postpone for five years or so the pressures to arrive at a settlement that might well be unpalatable to Israel. If that kind of war broke out, Israel's aim must be not to solve the conflict but to win a military decision as quickly as possible while causing maximum damage to the enemy and securing long-range military and political benefits. That being the case, the warning that Israel received should be taken very seriously, and the coming month should be devoted to feverish preparations. First priority immediately after the Passover holiday should go to speeding up the construction of bridging equipment, updating operative plans, upgrading the level of alert, and the like. "And if war breaks out in another month or month and a half, we'll have the maximal means to carry on a war with optimal effect."

Many things that were said and done in anticipation of that war appear in retrospect—after the Yom Kippur War—to assume a tragic dimension on both personal and national planes. During Passover 1973 and the weeks following, Israel's political and military leadership "knew no sleep," and despite the different assessments on the question of probability, the chief of staff directed the General Staff to act as if war were a certainty.

A number of questions that arose during that Passover eve meeting were destined to crop up again during the containment phase of the Yom Kippur War. Should the strongholds on the waterline be held, for example, or would the troops retreat into the interior of Sinai and wage the decisive battle with the Egyptian armor there? Dado reasserted his decision of the previous year—expressed during the discussion on the defensive system in Sinai—that the strongholds must be manned and held. However,

> if I know that they are going to attack in the morning, we could say—as an intellectual exercise—that under certain circumstances 30 kilometers in Sinai could be completely evacuated. We let them move five divisions into Sinai, and then we slam the door on them. Such a battle implies a number of political risks, but it's a beauty, and I'm sure it will make it into the military history books. . . . We must be completely free to choose a modus operandi and decide on a last-minute plan, and I'm open to any plan. I am not committed to anything. I have no biases. We may hold down a fortification here and evacuate another one there. . . . We have no interest in war, but if one breaks out in 1973 it's a historic opportunity to deal a crushing military and political blow that will last for a very long time to come.

NOTES

1. The Bar-Lev Line is an Israeli fortification—a series of hardened concrete and steel-reinforced bunkers—built along the east bank of the Suez Canal between October 1968 and March 1969.

2. Massada is the fortress in the Judaean desert built by King Herod about two thousand years ago, where a small sect of Zealots—the last of the Jewish rebels—made their futile stand against the Romans after the destruction of the Second Temple in 70 C.E. In the spring of 73 C.E. it became clear that the Roman army would breach the walls of the mountain fortress; rather than be killed by the enemy, the Zealots killed each other. Massada thus came to be a symbol of Jewish resistance and bravery. Since the completion of the archaeological excavations directed by Yigael Yadin, the site has become a popular spot for IDF ceremonies.

3. The Beirut raid, an Israeli intervention in Lebanon on April 10, 1973, again inflamed the Lebanese-Palestinian conflict. An Israeli commando unit, landing by night on a Beirut beach, rendezvoused with seven Israeli secret agents who had arrived earlier with European passports. These agents, passing themselves off as tourists, rented cars to transport the Israeli hit-team to their objectives in four Beirut neighborhoods. They killed three Fatah leaders—Kamal Nasser, Abu Yussouf, and Kamal Radwan—in their apartments. Several innocent bystanders and two military police were killed or wounded. In addition, an office building of the Popular Democratic Front for the Liberation of Palestine was blown up. The Israelis encountered no interference from the Lebanese army, and the Lebanese premier then resigned over a dispute with the president about the army's reluctance to defend the country. This episode resulted in increased tensions between the presidency and the Muslim communities that were critical of the appointment of weak premiers and thus solidified the centralization of power in the hands of the Maronite rightist president.

4. Muhammed Hafez Ismail (1918–1997) was Sadat's special adviser for national security, 1971–74.

74

David Elazar

The Turning Point in the Yom Kippur War

October 16, 1973

Despite advance intelligence information, Israel was caught unprepared when it was attacked by Egypt and Syria on October 6, 1973. That day was Yom Kippur (Day of Atonement), the holiest day of the year in the Jewish religious calendar and a national holiday in Israel. In several of his writings and speeches on the Yom Kippur War, Chaim Herzog has suggested that the Arabs made a mistake in choosing this day, when virtually all Israelis were at home or in synagogues and could therefore be immediately contacted and mobilized.

Nevertheless, during the first days of the war Israel suffered heavy casualties as its positions in Sinai and the Golan Heights were overrun by the Arab armies. The turning point occurred on October 16. On October 22 a cease-fire with Syria took effect, and two days later, on October 24, fighting with Egypt ended (although the cease-fire agreement was not signed until November 11). Hanoch Bartov's biography of David Elazar, known as Dado, based on the Israeli chief of staff's war diaries, provides a detailed description of the developments of October 16 when an Israeli expeditionary force crossed the Suez Canal and established itself on its western bank.

Source: Hanoch Bartov, *Dado: 48 shanah veod 20 yom* [Dado: 48 Years and 20 More Days] (Tel Aviv: Maariv Book Guild, 1981), pp. 482–89. Reprinted by permission.

01:32

Back at midnight, when he discovered that the pontoons were not making it through the traffic jams, Arik [Ariel] Sharon ordered his men to hurry the Gilois rafts[1] up to the crossing site. At about the same time, the paratroops began to move out from Tasa in the direction of the [Suez] Canal.

Right now the paratroops are beginning to cross the canal silently in rubber dinghies and are clambering onto the waterway's western bank completely unnoticed. The following report immediately reaches the senior command waiting in Southern Command's war room: the paratroops are past the waterline to the west of the canal.

03:00

Sharon's forward headquarters reaches the Compound.[2] All together he has ten tanks with him there.

The chief of staff contacts Col. Dani Matt, the commander of the paratroop brigade, who is now with the advance forces across the canal, and congratulates him.

04:00

The Gilois rafts reach the Compound along with ten more tanks. So do two bulldozers, which immediately begin to create a breach in the section of the embankment specially preconstructed so that such a breakthrough would be quick and easy.

At the High Command—for all intents and purposes, now ensconced in Southern Command headquarters—a decision is taking shape to have Bren's [Avraham Adan] division cross the canal first.

06:00

Only now does the overall picture come into focus for the senior command: the paratroops have made it across the canal; the Gilois rafts are assembled alongside the embankment ready to cross; a passage is being dug through the embankment; and finally a battle continued to rage against an Egyptian antitank position at the Tirtur-Lexicon[3] crossroad. Evidently the IDF [Israel Defense Forces] is in for a hard time and heavy casualties. Moreover, Arik Sharon is asking for help in opening up Tirtur, and he wants one brigade from Bren's division.

Despite the snags, however, the High Command decides against retrieving the paratroops from the west bank and in favor of pursuing the plan. If they manage to get the brigades up before the day is out, fine; if not, tomorrow is another day. This is not an easy decision to make, for up to now nothing has gone according to the original schedule, and no essay has been consummated.

06:15

[Moshe] Dayan talks with the prime minister [Golda Meir], assuring her he is not concerned about the paratroops being cut off on the west bank. "I am convinced that what we need more than anything else is a victory over the Egyptian army. And the way to achieve that victory is to cross the canal," he tells her.

06:52

The first Israeli tank reaches the west bank of the canal. Following it on Gilois rafts come additional tanks, but the real problem is still the antitank position at the Nahala-Tirtur crossroads and the fact that the bridges are being held up. Only now does the High Command realize that there's been another hitch with the roller bridge: one of its hinges has broken and will take some time to repair.

It also becomes evident now that Bren's division must join the battle for the bridgehead to stave off the Egyptian assaults that are both blocking Tirtur and preventing the flow of traffic along Akavish.[4] From now on Bren's division will also assume responsibility for transporting the pontoons to the Compound so that the first bridge can be assembled.

09:00

The chief of staff decides to return to the Pit.[5] His colleagues will be let in on his grim mood during the meeting that takes place upon his return.

10:00

A whole day—brimming with expectations, enormous tension, anxiety, and anger—has passed since the chief of staff was last in the Pit. But even though the review he now conveys to his colleagues is as clear and orderly as ever, he is exhausted and unable to suppress his anger over a number of slipups that occurred during the night: the lack of a realistic time estimate, the manner in which the battle was being conducted, and more than anything else, the sloppy reports coming in from the crossing site, "in a vein I never heard before, in all my years of warfare, coming over the communications network all night long!" Dado would subsequently recall his impressions of that night as follows:

> Our plan was a very good one, except for one flaw. I noticed at the very beginning of the night the whole thing was built around having Arik capture a bridgehead and cross the canal. Early on in the night I said to Haim and Shmulik:[6] "Listen, things will go much faster around here if Arik's forces stick to extending the bridgehead." The operation was going all right and you couldn't have expected more than that. The Egyptians didn't understand what was happening. They didn't read the attack correctly; they thought it was some kind of a raid, so they didn't call for reinforcements to dam up the breach. And when we finally got Dani Matt's paratroops across, there were no Egyptians there. The shore was absolutely deserted, and that's the way it went on for hours. At first light we began to send tank after tank across, and they still did not hinder us. There was no deployment of any kind facing us.
>
> In the midst of all that tumult, however, an obstacle emerged. At first it was referred to as an "ambush," then an "antitank position," "something we've gotten messed up in." To this moment I don't know how extensive it was, because the boys got stuck in the mess at night, and when they began to unravel it in the morning it turned out to be more formidable than we thought: antitank weapons, missiles, and tanks all in one. So first it was necessary to sort out the imbroglio before they could penetrate and attack.

By then, Dado went on to explain, it had become clear to him that Sharon's division alone would not be able to mop up and secure the crossing zone and cross the canal in strength. When Sharon was asked whether he would be able to accomplish both, he asked for a brigade from Bren's division to help in the battle for the bridgehead. But when he was ordered to clear a corridor to the canal, so that Bren's division could begin to cross in the meantime—since at that stage it was hardly involved in the fighting—Sharon replied that he had sufficient forces to cross as well. "Fortunately," Dado now explains to his colleagues in the Pit, "it took the enemy until nine in the morning to catch onto what was happening—and perhaps he still doesn't realize it and hasn't closed off the sector. When I left, we already had a bridgehead on the west bank—paratroops plus twelve tanks."

In the meantime, someone remarks, the number of tanks on the west bank has grown to twenty-eight and some half-tracks and APCs [armored personnel carriers] have also been sent across.

But the chief of staff is far more worried about the east bank and that "little snag" that still hasn't been overcome and is blocking Tirtur, so that all traffic must flow on a single axis along the shore of the Great Bitter Lake. "There are two bridges here that can be there by the afternoon." Dado points to the map. "And the advance force is screaming that the Egyptians still haven't grasped what's going on. Here it's still empty; here it's still wide open. We're already in, at the sweet-water canal and we're waiting! In short, that was the situation. And it hurts like hell, because that whole business is wide open. If the bridge had been up by ten, Bren could have gone in and wreaked havoc!"

"He'll do it yet," Talik [Israel Tal] consoles him.

"Hold on. I haven't lost the war yet. It's just that it makes your heart ache. If ever there was a golden opportunity, this is it."

In a little while it will be eleven o'clock, and the element of complete surprise—which could have been exploited to the hilt if a large force had penetrated the deserted area of the "seam" between the two Egyptian armies that night—is rapidly being lost. Had a tank force from Bren's brigade sped further west toward the screen of anti-aircraft missiles immediately after crossing and attacked it with tanks and artillery, then "everything would have been wide open for the air force, all our hopes would have been fulfilled."...

The men in the Pit are monitoring Southern Command's communication networks, and there, too, the command is waiting expectantly for the armor to deal with that "little snag" and hoping that by afternoon two bridges will be spanning the canal. It is highly doubtful whether Southern Command or the General Staff has any idea of the scope of the losses or the fierceness of the fighting in the bridgehead. And they certainly don't even begin to envision the kind of battle awaiting the IDF in the next twenty-four hours for the roads leading to the crossing site. By that hour, it would later come out, 200 men had already fallen and fifty tanks had been lost in this battle. And certainly no one imagined that the fortified localities menacing the bridgehead from the north—Missouri and Televiziah—would not be overcome before the cease-fire, though much blood would be shed over them.

All in all, the men in the Pit are expecting a dramatic turn in events—and within a few hours, at that. But the roller bridge is still stuck on the road linking Akavish and Tirtur, and the latest estimate is that its repair will take another twenty-four hours. What's more, while flying back from Sinai this morning, Dado was stung by anxiety at the sight of columns of vehicles jammed along the few arteries—an easy target for enemy planes—so he ordered his helicopter to land, summoned the commanders in charge, and ordered them to spread out as much as possible to forestall a catastrophe. And stuck somewhere in the midst of this "mess" that extends for miles are the pontoons, still not making any headway.

As Dado is relating all this in the Pit, [Shmuel] Gonen had reached Bren's forward headquarters and continued by jeep (together with the division's second in command, Col. Dovik Tamari) to see for himself how matters stood with the roller bridge. On the one hand, he was relieved to hear that the repair would be completed in another half hour. But he also discovered that the entire area was under tank fire. As Gonen and Tamari strode westward, they found that countless Egyptians were dug in all around the Chinese Farm[7] (Amir) and that the Akavish axis was also blocked by fire now. While they were still standing there peering westward, a solitary tank headed toward them. Its turret had been knocked off by a direct hit, two of its crew were dead, and a third was wounded. The driver told them that he had just been hit by an antitank missile on Akavish.

All of this brought Gonen to the conclusion that Bren's division should be sent in to reopen Akavish and assume responsibility for transporting the pontoons to the "yard" without further delay. Upon his return to Southern Command headquarters, Gonen relayed his impressions to Bar-Lev, and as a result Sharon was ordered not to float any more tanks across the canal on rafts until further notice. The divisional commander was also informed that from now on Bren's division would take over the fight to open the two blocked axes and see to it that the pontoons were brought forward to the waterline.

Sharon greeted this order—which he received at 11:00 [A.M.]—with a shower of bitter criticism, for he viewed it as a cardinal military error—and had no intention of keeping his opinion to himself. That same evening, for example, when he returned to the Pit from the south, Ezer Weizman told the chief of staff that junior officers in Sharon's division had complained that hundreds of tanks could have crossed the canal on the rafts but were being held back. The outspoken rivalry and friction that Israelis refer to as "the wars of the Jews" are not even tempered in time of war and will grow even sharper during the coming days.

NOTES

1. Ariel Sharon, frustrated by high command decisions to delay the crossing of the Suez Canal since October 9 and convinced that once under way the operation should proceed rapidly, decided to cross the canal on rafts before bridges could be built to provide logistical and tactical support.

2. Preparations for crossing the Suez Canal began after the Six-Day War while Sharon was commander of the Southern Area. Plans included the construction of a leveled area (approx. 150 × 400 yds.) surrounded by a high earthen rampart that could be easily breached by Israeli equipment. Located at the juncture of the canal and the north end of the Great Bitter Lake, the Compound was the staging area for crossing the canal.

3. Tirtur is an east-west dirt road about 6 m wide that links the Compound with more easterly positions. Lexicon is a road that runs parallel to the east bank of the canal.

4. Akavish is the main road south of and parallel to Tirtur. Troops and supplies for the crossing operation were to be delivered via the Tirtur and Akavish roads.

5. The Pit is the war room of Israeli General Headquarters in Tel Aviv.

6. Elazar is referring to Haim Bar-Lev, who, on October 10, was asked to be Elazar's "special representative" at the Southern Command, and to Shmuel Gonen, commander of the Southern Area, who three months earlier had been Sharon's subordinate and was now—with the arrival of Bar-Lev—again de facto second in command.

7. The Chinese Farm is the former Japanese-operated agricultural station near the Tirtur-Lexicon crossroad.

75

Mordechai Gazit

The Yom Kippur War

October 1973: Analysis

The 1974 Agranat Commission report (doc. 76) determined that a limited number of officers, including the chief of staff and the director of military intelligence, were responsible for the lack of readiness for the Egyptian-Syrian surprise attack on October 6, 1973, that began what is known as the Yom Kippur War. However, the Israeli public perceived the political leadership as equally responsible. Prime Minister Golda Meir and Minister

Source: Based on a lecture delivered by Mordechai Gazit at a Hebrew University conference on the Yom Kippur War in October 1998. Published by permission of Mordechai Gazit.

of Defense Moshe Dayan resigned under public pressure, and less than three years after the war, the Labor Party, which had ruled Israel since 1948, was voted out of power.

In the three decades that followed the war, Mordechai Gazit, director general under Prime Minister Meir, had become the leading defender of Israel's pre-1973 leadership arguing that there was, in fact, very little Israel's political leadership could have done to prevent the Yom Kippur War. The following text presents his core argument.

The Yom Kippur War has had a traumatic effect on Israelis. Twenty-five years later Israelis still look back on the war in anger and frustration. They consider it a low point in Israel's history. Most Israelis remain convinced that something very serious must have gone wrong in the period preceding October 1973 and firmly believe that the political and military leadership of the country was accountable for what happened. That Prime Minister Golda Meir, Defense Minister Moshe Dayan, Chief of Staff David Elazar (Dado), and others resigned or were forced to resign has not assuaged Israeli public opinion and, in particular, the Israeli media.

Three main accusations are leveled against the then Israeli leadership. In what follows, the first two will be dealt with less extensively than the third. The third accusation, that the war could have been averted altogether had Golda Meir reacted "positively" and "creatively" to President Sadat's presumed peace signaling in February 1971, is subjected to a closer scrutiny.

The first accusation postulates that the Israeli leaders failed to take the right decision in the immediate period preceding the Arab attack on October 6, 1973. Their negligence, some would call it inexcusable negligence, resulted from their having fallen prey to a certain concept (in Hebrew, *kontzeptziah*) which had a soporific effect on them. The so-called *kontzeptziah* induced them to believe that Sadat would not go to war unless he first obtained from the Soviets more quality aircraft and some ground-to-ground missiles. The conviction that such was Sadat's policy was based on reports Israel received from a good intelligence source. However, and this is the crucial question, is it a proven fact that it was indeed the *kontzeptziah* that caused Golda, Dayan, and the Chief of Staff David (Dado) Elazar not to take the obviously necessary military precautionary measures, namely, to call up some, if not all, the army reserves in the week preceding the outbreak of the fighting? Intelligence data was detailed and specific—both armies, the Egyptian and Syrian, were fully arrayed and in jump-off positions, there was no doubt about that.

Yet, no reserves were called up. This was so even though the Israeli leaders were by temperament and experience too chary of the Arab leaders to let their guard down. True, military intelligence opined that the probability of war was low. That estimate was probably influenced by the *kontzeptziah*. But Israeli national and military leadership did not call up the reserves because it was confident that the regular army (in Hebrew, Hasadir), that is the Israeli forces along the cease-fire lines as built up since 1967, and the Israeli air force would suffice to contain and, hopefully, even repulse the attackers. The military thinking at the top was that the Hasadir was able to do this even in case of a surprise attack launched from all fronts.

This was the conventional wisdom of all Israeli military luminaries. Yitzhak Rabin affirmed in an article, "There is no need to mobilize even when threats are heard and [the enemy] deploys. . . . Today such a call-up is not required as long as Israel's defense line is on the Suez Canal."[1] The chief of military planning, General Avraham Tamir, wrote, "All war scenarios forming the basis for planning and organization, order of battle of the Israeli army . . . assumed a situation of war which began with an all-Arab surprise attack which would be contained by the Israeli standing army."[2] A most revealing testimony is that of General Yitzhak Hofi, commander of the Northern Sector during the Yom Kippur War. While blaming himself for not "banging the table and demanding additional forces," before October 6, he adds significantly, "I don't know if it would have helped because they [Hofy's superiors] did not want to mobilize the reserves."[3]

It makes a world of difference if the contention is that the Israeli leadership did not call up the reserves until October 6 because of a weird belief in a *kontzepziah* originating in reports from an intelligence source or if it refrained from mobilizing because of an apparently reliable military defense plan that put its trust in the regular army and in the air force. Not in vain does General Tamir point out that Israel invested huge sums of money to create an army capable of repulsing all kinds of attacks. He affirms that it was just not true "that the Israeli army was not ready for a surprise attack."[4]

Too many things went wrong and were badly done on October 6 to justify blaming what happened early in the fighting solely on Israel Defense Army's decision to entrust the defense of the cease-fire lines to the regular army. The belief that Hasadir alone could do the job satisfactorily long enough for the reserves to be called up and be sent to the fronts would have been vindicated if everything had worked smoothly. This is not, however, what happened and the hope that it might was obviously overly optimistic. Dayan and Dado should have thought it prudent to call up some reserves early in October. But it was their complete trust in the Hasadir, and not their addiction to the *kontzepziah*, as is commonly argued, that prevented them from ordering mobilization.

That much for the first accusation. The second charge avers that King Hussein of Jordan met with Golda Meir on September 25, 1973, ten days before the joint Egyptian-Syrian attack, and warned her that a coordinated attack by the two armies was imminent.

There is no truth in this; the facts are quite different. Hussein had been meeting with Israeli leaders since 1963. In a meeting in late September 1973, he discussed with Golda the Syrian army's deployment on the Golan and correctly pointed out that the Syrians were poised to launch an attack and could do so without further preparation. Israel, however, was well aware of these facts.[5] Thus Hussein did not add much to what Israel already knew. Hussein did not refer at all to the Egyptian army concentrations along the Suez Canal. Egypt came up in the conversation only when Golda Meir asked him whether he thought that Syria would venture to attack Israel on its own, without Egypt participating. Hussein agreed with Golda that such an eventuality was unlikely since Syria must clearly be aware of Israel's absolute military superiority that had been brought home to it by a recent (September 13) air combat during which the Israeli air force destroyed nine Syrian fighter planes with no loss to Israel.[6]

Throughout the years, Hussein had referred several times to the rumors that he had passed on a warning to Israel prior to the war. In a long and nearly complete account of the history of his secret meetings with Israeli leaders, which he gave in 1996, he said: "In 1973, I wasn't part of it. . . . I had embarked on a course of trying to achieve peace and I could not be double-faced about it even if they [Sadat and Assad] had told me about the plan to go to war. Thank God, I wasn't told anyway."[7] Hussein's statement is trustworthy, and there is abundant evidence to support it.

Evidence that Hussein did not know of the decision to go to war is contained in the memoirs of the PLO [Palestine Liberation Organization] leader Abu Iyad (Salah Halaf).[8] Abu Iyad notes that Yasir Arafat, Faruk Qaddumi, and he himself were received by [Anwar] Sadat on September 9, just before Sadat met with Hussein. Sadat assured them that "he had no intention of breathing a word to Hussein about the war plans."

It is apposite to show that Hussein was ignorant of the Sadat-Assad plan to go to war because it refutes unjust allegations made by some Israeli intelligence officers. According to them, the information their organization (Aman, military intelligence) had passed on to Golda, Dayan, and Chief of Staff Elazar, coupled with Hussein's warning given directly to Golda, was more than enough to alert them to the impending danger ahead. True, the intelligence officers acknowledge that they had consistently added a reservation to the detailed and precise data they had passed on to Golda, Dayan, and Dado. Their repeated caveat was that in their estimate the danger of war was low. Yet they affirm that their caveat should have been ignored by Golda, et al., since she had been the direct recipient of Hussein's message. Golda and her associates allege the officers took an offhand attitude toward Hussein's warning. This allegation is totally unfounded. What King Hussein told Golda was thoroughly discussed in two military consultations on the morrow of the Golda-Hussein encounter. One was chaired by the Chief of Staff and the other by Moshe Dayan.[9] A complete report of what had transpired at the encounter was given to the participants at the two military consultations. They could not fail to notice that the King had *not* said that the Egyptian army was about to launch an offensive or that Syria and Egypt were coordinating a military move. This explains why Dayan declared himself insouciant concerning Egypt's intentions on two occasions a few days prior to the war. He said that he was firmly convinced that Egypt was not about to start a war.[10] There is no gainsaying that Dayan would not have remained calm if Hussein's "warning" had included Egypt.

Dayan's conviction that Egypt was not about to launch a war against Israel was based on his strictly military analysis of the terrain. He pointed out that the Suez Canal (200 meters wide) was too formidable an obstacle for enemy armor to cross. The Egyptians would not be so foolish as to launch a major military assault on the Israeli lines. Should Syria attempt an offensive on its own, the Israeli standing army, supported by the Israeli air force, would easily stop them.

If more proof is needed to convince that Hussein was not privy to Sadat and [Hafez al-] Assad's plans, it can be found in his address to the Rabat Summit Conference in October 1974. Israeli intelligence apparently failed to notice a remarkable passage in it. Hussein mentioned that some Arab leaders had criticized him for not joining Egypt and Syria in the war immediately and "automatically." He explained the reason: "We were not in the picture as regards the operation, the preparations, and dispositions made for it or its timing, so that we were not in a position to take advantage of the surprise element."[11] Clearly Hussein would not have dared to make this statement in the presence of Sadat and Assad who were both in the hall had it not been the truth. Hussein knew that his statement could not be refuted by either Sadat or Assad. In a sense, he challenged them to dare refute it.

The third accusation that the Israeli government missed an opportunity in 1971 when President Sadat supposedly signaled Egypt's readiness to favor some kind of agreement with Israel, such as an interim one, is also unfounded. A close look at what Sadat in effect proposed in a speech on February 4, 1971, shows that he was talking about a comprehensive settlement, meaning an agreement between all the Arab states and Israel, on condition that Israel first committed itself to withdraw from *all* the Arab territories it controlled since 1967. Sadat was then in the first year of his presidency, far from being the established leader he became after the 1973 War. In 1971 or 1972, he was neither ready nor strong enough to deviate from the consensual Arab position insisted on since 1967. To maintain the contrary is to turn a blind eye to what Sadat himself repeatedly and emphatically declared.

However, before looking at the evidence furnished by Sadat and other Egyptians, one must also briefly review the then Israeli position. Israel's position in 1971, when Golda Meir was prime minister, was not any different from what it had been under her predecessor, Levi Eshkol and his National Unity Government. In any peace talks with the Arab leaders, Israel would insist on border rectifications in its favor. Accordingly, the eastern part of Jerusalem, including the Old City, would be in perpetuity part of sovereign Israel. Concerning Sinai, Israel would not go back to the old pre-1967 line (Eshkol's Cabinet resolution of October 31, 1968). Golda Meir stated her government's policy in similar terms (see, e.g., Meir's Knesset statement of March 16, 1971). Even one of Israel's most dovish parties, the United Workers Party (Mapam), adhered to this line and confirmed it in a party resolution in the years 1967 to 1973 (e.g., in the Sixth Mapam Convention in December 1972). Clearly, then, the gap between the Arab position, including Sadat's insisting on a prior Israeli commitment to withdraw to the 1967 lines on all fronts, and Israel's position that there would be border changes in its favor and no going back to the 1967 lines, was unbridgeable.

Can one, however, be altogether certain that Sadat, a leader who pioneered the peace moves after 1973, was not already beginning to contemplate a first, albeit prudent, step toward peace? The answer to this question is unambiguous: one must strongly resist the temptation to imagine the Sadat that one came to know in 1977 and thereafter as identical with the Sadat of 1971.

Why, then, is there a time-resistant impression that there was a peace opening in 1971? Probably because American diplomats, in a buoyant mood, accepted Sadat's invitation of March 5, 1971, to President [Richard] Nixon to "launch a diplomatic effort to bring about an interim agreement along the lines of his [Sadat's] February [4th] peace."[12] U.S. Secretary of State William Rogers promptly responded by visiting Cairo (May 4, 1971), the capital of a country with which the U.S. had cut off diplomatic relations in 1967. As would not have been unusual for a mediator or facilitator, Rogers must have assumed that there existed some "give" in Cairo, otherwise Sadat would not have sent him his message. Rogers was undeterred by Sadat's specific reference to his February 4 speech to the Egyptian National Assembly. He probably assumed that Sadat's insistence in that speech that he was merely thinking about a "first step in a timetable to be laid down with a view to implementing all the other provisions of the Security Council Resolution,"[13] was no more than an opening gambit. But this was a mistaken assumption. On May 1, three days before Rogers arrived in Cairo, Sadat, anxious not to be misunderstood, clarified in a speech that he had not meant to offer a separate agreement with Israel. He viewed the limited first-step Israeli withdrawal as a "procedural move organically linked" with the total solution to *all* provisions of the Security Council, notably "Israel's withdrawal from *all Arab territories.*"[14]

Still not sure that Rogers had gotten the point, Sadat again defined his position two weeks after Rogers' visit. In an address to the Egyptian National Assembly, he stressed that what he was proposing was not a partial or separate solution, "it is a *stage* in the *complete* Israeli withdrawal in accordance with a timetable." To dispel any lingering doubts as to what he meant, Sadat spelled it out: "Our [i.e., Arab] territory is what it was before the 5th of June [1967] and this applies to *all* the Arab territories."[15] It is altogether unthinkable that Sadat misled the Egyptian Parliament in making this statement, especially since he stressed that he was quoting from a message he was about to send to Rogers.

There was a very good reason why Sadat was so concerned that the U.S. might misunderstand him. As far back as late 1968, two years before Sadat became president, the U.S. attempted to prod Egypt into a separate agreement with Israel. Egypt rejected the U.S. initiative out of hand. Mahmoud Riad, Egypt's Foreign Minister, told Secretary of State Dean Rusk that Egypt's Arab commitments did not allow it to conclude a separate agreement with Israel, leaving out Jordan and Syria. "It would be unethical on our

[Egypt's] part . . . leaving out the rest of the occupied Arab territories . . . there [also was] a legal commitment in the joint defense agreement between Egypt and the other Arab states."[16] That Riad's response to Rusk in 1968 was still relevant in 1971 and later is unquestionable. Sadat severely criticized the U.S. role throughout 1971. He argued that "a big process of deceit and misrepresentation is going on. The U.S. said that Egypt had agreed to a partial solution. . . . We shall not agree to a settlement in stages if not part of a comprehensive peace."[17] That this position was still strongly linked to the Riad-Rusk episode of 1968 was made quite clear by Sadat as late as February 13, 1972, when he referred pointedly to that meeting, noting that the U.S. had not given up its efforts "to turn Security Council Resolution [242] into a resolution for a separate and independent agreement with each Arab country separately. . . . [But] I presented my [February 4, 1971] initiative as a prelude to a comprehensive Arab settlement of the question of peace in the Middle East."[18] Clearly, he mentioned the old Rusk attempt in order to give vent to Egypt's displeasure with America's unvarying efforts since 1968 to drive a wedge between Egypt and the other Arab countries.

Significantly, this particular Sadat speech was made shortly after Israel had informed the U.S. that it accepted all the demands deemed necessary by the U.S. to enable a negotiation for an interim agreement for the opening of the Suez Canal. However, this was precisely the kind of proposition that Sadat dreaded. He gave frequent expression to his apprehension. Ridiculing the U.S. proposal of 1971 to coax Egypt into what he called a "partial agreement," and sardonically, "a partial agreement of a partial agreement," he said that such an agreement "means that I was supposed to be happy and delighted when they told me that they would open the Suez Canal and that would be all [and not] a step towards a comprehensive settlement for *all* the Arab territories, *not just Egypt*. . . . What I want is to get my land back and to get all Arab lands back."[19]

In July 1972, on the 20th anniversary of the July Revolution, Sadat again mocked Israel's "plans" to create a *fait accompli* by means of partial or interim agreements. "Israel will want to stay where it is now for another 10–15 years and after that long period everything would be over. All the territories where Israel is would be lost: Sinai, the West Bank, and Gaza."[20] Sadat's foreign minister, Mahmoud Riad, told *Le Monde*, "Could anyone imagine that Egypt would allow Israel to keep their conquest in exchange for an open canal?"[21] As Sadat saw it, the Americans had reduced his original initiative of February 4, 1971, and "twisted" it to a mere "opening of the Canal agreement." This, he insisted, would gravely damage not only Egypt's interests but the interest of all the Arabs (Syria, Jordan, and the Palestinians).

In the face of all this evidence, and there is plenty more, it is incomprehensible why many Israelis and some Americans continue to believe that Sadat could have come around to accepting a limited or interim agreement. They blame Israel (i.e., Golda Meir) for shortsightedness and for aborting the effort. In fact, however, Israel would have gladly accepted an interim agreement because it would have given it years of peace with Egypt in return for a small withdrawal from the east bank of the Canal. The Americans should have realized that what they had in mind was not realizable and was definitely not on Sadat's agenda. The Americans, however, are still reluctant to admit that they were treading water back in 1971–1972, the reason being that they had then committed some of their diplomatic prestige. But it is an interesting fact that U.S. Secretary Rogers, the man directly responsible for these unsuccessful American efforts, did admit to Moshe Dayan, Israel's defense minister, in November 1972, that the "Egyptians do not deviate from their position that Israel must first of all declare its readiness to total withdrawal."[22] The way Rogers put it to Dayan shows that he knew that the Egyptians had been adamant from the start in demanding linkage between the Canal agreement and total Israeli withdrawal.

There remains one more argument often made. The diplomatic efforts could have succeeded if only Golda Meir had listened to Moshe Dayan. While Dayan was ready to consider a 15 to 20 mile Israeli withdrawal from the Canal, Golda insisted on a more limited one. This argument does not make sense. Sadat's refusal to start negotiation had nothing to do with the question whether Israel should withdraw 10 or 30 miles from the Canal. It is significant that Dayan himself acknowledges this. In his autobiography, Dayan says that he was ready to consider the greater distance withdrawal from the Canal only if Sadat undertook to put the war behind him and to no longer resort to arms in order to settle the border question.[23] In a Cabinet meeting Dayan explained, "For this [the greater distance withdrawal] to come about, we must be convinced that this is not the beginning of a withdrawal in stages [to the old 1967 lines]."[24] Dayan's conditions equaled a demand that Egypt and Israel enter into a radically changed relationship from one of hostilities to one of non-belligerence for an unspecified period of time—the very "ten to fifteen years" that Sadat dreaded. Dayan's military secretary, General Y. Raviv, in a long and well argued analytical article published in the spring of 1975, at a time when heart searching in Israel had already been going on for some time, concluded on the basis of all available evidence, that Sadat had been throughout 1971 and 1972 unwilling to accept a partial agreement.[25] The precise distance of Israeli withdrawal from the Canal, whether it be Golda's 12 or Dayan's 30 miles, is nowhere mentioned by Raviv as having influenced Sadat's decision.

What Sadat was supposed to have proposed in February 1971 was altogether different from what America's well meaning diplomats assumed. One must also bear in mind that Egypt had been made aware by Israel since 1967 that it would not oppose an Egyptian decision to reopen the Canal. It was Egypt that had decided to block it in 1967—as it had done also in 1956—and it was up to Egypt to unilaterally open it. What deterred Egypt from doing it was the realization that this would have implied a *de facto* acquiescence in Israel's presence in Sinai for who knows how long. Egypt would have been viewed by all other Arab countries as acting against the general Arab interest, which was the recovery of all Arab occupied territories. What Sadat was ready to do at Camp David in 1978, he was not yet ready to do in 1971.

The Judicial Commission's report (The Agranat Report [doc. 77]) cleared Dayan but held Elazar (Dado) accountable. The report blamed Dado for not having reached a judgment about the imminence of the war independent of that of his subordinate chief of military intelligence. The chief of staff should not have gone along with the "low probability" estimate of military intelligence. He should have insisted on calling up the reserves. It was right, the Commission ruled, to expect this from a top military commander. Inexplicably, it escaped the Commission's notice that Dayan's military background at least equaled Dado's. Dayan was an internationally acclaimed military figure. The Commission's assertion that a minister of defense was a civilian of whom one ought not to expect to reach an independent intelligence estimate, while true in general, did not apply to Dayan's case.

The Israeli public refused to go along with the Commission's verdict. The public sensed intuitively that Dayan was as guilty as Dado. Dayan shared Dado's absolute reliance on the Hasadir to stop an enemy attack for at least 12 to 24 hours. Consequently, the call-up of the reserves could wait. Had the Commission inculpated Dayan, its message would have been clear and simple—that the *Mehdal* (blunder or fault) was entirely the army's. The unfounded claims about Hussein's warning ten days before the war and about Golda Meir neglecting a peace opportunity in 1971 would not have arisen and, had it arisen, would certainly not have been given credence.

AUTHOR'S NOTES

1. Yitzhak Rabin, in *Ma'ariv,* July 13, 1973.
2. Avraham Tamir, *Hayad shocher shalom* (Idanim, 1988), pp. 104–5 (Hebrew).
3. Yitzhak Hofy, lecture at Hebrew University conference, October 27, 1998, in *Milhemet yom hakippurim* (Davis Institute and Ministry of Education, 1999), p. 98.
4. Tamir, *Hayad shocher shalom,* p. 104.
5. Hofy, lecture, p. 91; Hanoch Bartov, *Dado* (Maariv Publishers, 1978), p. 280.
6. Bartov, *Dado,* p. 283.
7. Hussein, interview with Professor Avi Shlaim, *New York Review of Books,* July 15, 1999.
8. Abu Iyad, with Eric Rouleau, *My Home, My Land* (Times Books, 1978).
9. Arieh Braun, *Moshe Dayan in the Yom Kippur War* (Idanim, 1992), pp. 39, 40 (Hebrew).
10. Braun, *Moshe Dayan,* pp. 55, 61.
11. Hussein, address to Rabat Summit Conference, October 1974, *International Documents on Palestine (IDP),* 1974, p. 521.
12. William B. Quandt, *Peace Process: American Diplomacy and the Arab-Israeli Conflict since 1967* (Berkeley, Calif., 1993), p. 124.
13. BBC Monitoring Service, February 6, 1971; War Ministry of Information, State Information Service, *Speeches by President Sadat,* Cairo, March 1971, pp. 23–41.
14. Anwar Sadat, speech, May 1, 1971, *IDP,* 1971, p. 458; see also Mordechai Gazit, "Egypt and Israel: Was There a Peace Opportunity Missed in 1971?" *Journal of Contemporary History* (London) (1997), pp. 97–115.
15. Sadat, speech, *IDP,* 1971, p. 469.
16. Mahmoud Riad, *The Struggle for Peace in the Middle East* (London: Quartet Books, 1981).
17. Sadat, speech, September 16, 1971, *IDP,* 1971, pp. 533–35.
18. Sadat, speech, *IDP,* 1972, pp. 274–76.
19. Sadat, speech, January 13, 1972, *IDP (1972),* pp. 274–76.
20. Sadat, speech, *IDP,* 1972, pp. 333–34.
21. Riad, in *Le Monde,* 18 June 1971.
22. Yitzhak Rabin, *Pinkas sherut* (1979), p. 379 (Hebrew).
23. Gad Ya'acobi, *Kechut hasearah* (Idanim, 1989), pp. 150–51 (Hebrew).
24. Moshe Dayan, *Avnei Derech* (Idanim, 1982), p. 527 (Hebrew).
25. Y. Raviv, "Early Efforts for an Interim Agreement between Israel and Egypt (in the Years 1971–1972)," *Maarakhot,* nos. 243–44 (April–May 1975), p. 13 (Hebrew).

CHAPTER 5

War, Peace, and War Again, 1973–1982

1973

The Organization of Petroleum-Exporting Countries (OPEC) raises oil prices to penalize Western countries that supported Israel in the Yom Kippur War, causing international shortages and inflation

Israel and Egypt agree to a cease-fire

Sixth Arab Summit Conference in Algiers formulates a new consensus on terms for settlement of the Arab-Israeli conflict

1974

Talks at Kilometer 101 produce an interim separation-of-forces agreement with Egypt; four months later a similar agreement is reached with Syria

Antigovernment protests force the resignations of Golda Meir and Moshe Dayan; Yitzhak Rabin becomes prime minister

Seventh Arab Summit Conference in Rabat recognizes the Palestine Liberation Organization as the sole legitimate representative of the Palestinian people

1975

A second disengagement agreement with Egypt further resolves issues outstanding since the Yom Kippur War

U.N. General Assembly passes the Anti-Zionist Resolution

1976

A threatened general strike in the Arab sector ends in violence; thereafter Land Day has been observed as an annual protest by Arab Israelis

1977

Shimon Peres becomes prime minister

Menahem Begin leads a Likud victory over Labor and becomes prime minister

Egyptian president Anwar Sadat declares he is willing to travel to Jerusalem to find a solution to the Arab-Israeli conflict, and Begin invites him to address a special session of the Knesset

1978

Israel takes action (Operation Litani) against terrorist camps in southern Lebanon

U.N. Security Council Resolutions call for Israeli withdrawal and establishment of a U.N. force in southern Lebanon

Camp David Accords establish a basis for peace between Israel and Egypt

1979

Peace treaty with Egypt ends three decades of hostility

1982

Israel completes withdrawal from the Sinai Peninsula

Israel invades Lebanon, following an assassination attempt on the Israeli ambassador in London; Israeli forces remain in the southern part of Lebanon until 2000

U.S. President Ronald Reagan offers a peace plan, which is rejected by Israel and also by Arab parties that were not consulted

Domestic Issues

76

Agranat Commission

Interim Report

April 1, 1974

On the eve of the Yom Kippur War, Israel's intelligence services provided the Israel Defense Forces and the Israeli government with information about Egypt's and Syria's intention to launch a war (see doc. 73). The military and civilian leadership accepted the evaluation of the IDF's Intelligence Branch that the threat of war was not serious. This evaluation was changed at the last moment, and Israel entered the war unprepared, its reserve army only partially mobilized. This intelligence failure largely accounted for the military reverses sustained during the initial phases of the war (see doc. 74). At the end of the war a commission headed by Shimon Agranat, president of the Supreme Court, was appointed to investigate the chain of events that preceded the war and the army's performance. Members of the commission also included Moshe Landau, Yitzhak Nebenzahl, Yigael Yadin, and Haim Laskov. They decided to restrict the investigation to the military level and not to deal with the cabinet's performance. The following document is a summary of the commission's interim report, together with Chief of Staff David Elazar's reply, prepared for the Foreign Broadcast Information Service. The full text of the final report remains classified.

Summary of Report

The committee investigating the Yom Kippur events this evening published an interim report containing conclusions and recommendations on institutional and individual affairs.

The committee is recommending that the chief of staff, Lt. Gen. David Elazar, end his service; that Maj. Gen. Shmuel Gonen not fulfill an active role in the IDF [Israel Defense Forces] until the committee completes its investigation of matters connected with the continuation of the fighting; that Maj. Gen. Eliahu Zeira not continue to serve as chief of intelligence in the

Source: Israeli Foreign Broadcast Information Service, *Daily Report: Middle East and North Africa* 5, no. 65 (April 3, 1974): N1–N7.

General Staff; and that the services of Brig. Gen. Aryeh Shalev, Lt. Col. Yonah Bandman, and Lt. Col. David Gedalyah in intelligence duties end.

The committee, headed by the president of the Supreme Court, Judge Shimon Agranat, rules that the defense minister, Moshe Dayan, was not obliged to order additional precautionary measures or precautionary measures different from those ordered by the IDF General Staff according to joint evaluation and consultations between the chief of intelligence and the chief of staff.

The committee also notes that on May 21 the defense minister issued a directive to the General Staff in which he predicted that the war would break out in the second half of last summer. The defense minister, the committee rules, was not responsible for the operational details of the deployment of forces and that this was under the jurisdiction of the chief of staff. Also, no request or proposal was submitted to the defense minister to mobilize the reserves before Yom Kippur.

The committee says that in view of Mr. Dayan's special abilities in army affairs it was possible to reach a conclusion different from that which was proposed to him unanimously by his technical experts, but a matter of this kind does not come under the jurisdiction of the committee. . . .

The committee says that it questioned the defense minister and the prime minister as to whether their decision on the mobilization of the reserve forces was influenced by the fact that the elections for the Knesset were scheduled to take place at the end of October. The two emphatically denied this, and the committee believes that Mrs. [Golda] Meir and Mr. Dayan did not think of letting party considerations take preference over their obligations to the state on this matter.

It was right for the prime minister to give information about the situation on the borders during the cabinet meeting convened two days before the war broke out, the committee says. The prime minister was also not expected to know of the [absence?] of ministers who were not in Tel Aviv on the eve of Yom Kippur.

At the same time, the committee is convinced that the activities of the prime minister in the decisive days which preceded the war indicate an approach appropriate to the heavy responsibility which the prime minister shouldered.

The committee points out that the prime minister had the great right [of decision making] and that she made correct use of the right of decision making on the morning of Yom Kippur. Mrs. Meir adopted a decision with wisdom, good sense, and speed in favor of mobilizing the reserves despite weighty political considerations, and thus carried out a very important act for the defense of the state.

The committee rules that with the passage of time, confusion has taken place in regard to the duty the government has to fulfill in discussions and adoption of decisions on defense matters at the highest level. This confusion is connected with the absence of the ministerial committee for security affairs in its original framework and the fact that the cabinet has turned into a ministerial committee for security affairs. The leaks from cabinet discussions made it difficult to bring information to cabinet sessions, and the investigating committee recommends the setting up of a ministerial committee with a limited number of members and adherence to the implementation of the law and government regulations which ensure secret discussions on security matters. The investigating committee says in this way there will be no excuse for transferring the center of gravity of the discussion of security matters to an ad hoc body outside the cabinet.

Regarding the personal responsibility of Lt. Gen. David Elazar, the investigating committee says the following: "We reached a unanimous decision that the chief of staff bears personal responsibility for what happened on the eve of the war, both with regard to the evaluation of the situation and to the preparedness of the IDF." The committee says this with particular regret because the person in question is a soldier who has served the state for many years with dedication and distinction and has accomplished glorious achievements.

The committee also regrets the fact that the interim report does not deal with the subject of fighting after the firing broke out, because it is known that despite the grave crisis in the first stages of the fighting, the chief of staff led the IDF in the fighting to check the enemy at our gates. However, even if it is found that in later stages the chief of staff carried out great deeds, this does not obliterate the impressions of the initial mistakes.

The committee says the chief of staff should have recommended a partial mobilization of the reserves on October 1 and by October 5 at the latest. The committee rules that it did not accept Lt. Gen. David Elazar's explanation that he did more than necessary when he ordered an alert in the regular army. The chief of staff also erred in his excessive confidence that there would always be sufficient warning to mobilize the reserves and that the IDF would always and under all circumstances be able to repulse a general offensive by the enemy on both fronts through the use of regular forces alone.

The committee rules that the chief of staff did not use the means at his disposal to evaluate the situation correctly on the eve of the war. He did not tour the front lines to receive impressions from the warning signs which were discovered through observation or to consult commanders in the field. The chief of staff was content with information that lacked operational clarity—information that he received from the Southern Area commander—and thus in the difficult circumstances which occurred our forces were denied the measure of preparedness and deployment that they could have achieved. The result was that when the war broke out the armored force in the south was caught in improper deployment and the enemy gained an initial advantage. However, in the emergency situation that prevailed on the morning of Yom Kippur the chief of staff should have seen to it that his intentions were translated into clear operational orders.

The committee ends this chapter with the following: "In view of the above facts, we view it as our obligation to recommend the ending of the services of Lt. Gen. Elazar as chief of staff."

Maj. Gen. Shmuel Gonen, who was the Southern Area commander during the war, the committee says, did not carry out his duties properly when the war broke out and in the days that preceded it. Maj. Gen. Shmuel Gonen is also partially responsible for the dangerous situation in which our forces were caught on Yom Kippur. What has been found out about his activities and failures regarding the evaluation of the situation and the preparedness of his command in the days which preceded the war and on the day it broke out is sufficient for adopting the serious conclusion that the committee has reached regarding him.

The committee points out Maj. Gen. Gonen's command received enough information to arouse grave concern in the heart of a commander. But two days before the war, Maj. Gen. Gonen was outside his area of command on a private visit. During the entire week that preceded the war he accepted the chief of intelligence's evaluation that what was taking place in Egypt was only an exercise. But his main failure was on Yom Kippur itself. While he should have deployed the Armored Corps with two-thirds of that corps near the canal and the other third in the rear, Maj. Gen. Gonen kept the corps on a contrary arrangement. He told the committee that he ordered the implementation of the correct deployment two hours before the hour of the expected attack. But the operational documents of that day do not contain such an order, and when the enemy opened fire, no force from the rear began to move forward to the front line. Not only that, but according to the command orders, the forward force did not deploy near the canal at the right time, and when the armor began to move forward it was confronted with an Egyptian ambush east of the canal. Artillery and tank fire was opened on these armored forces, and its functioning was thus disrupted and it was seriously hit.

The committee rules that the order not to deploy the Armored Corps in time was an unfortunate order. Maj. Gen. Gonen gave as a reason for that action that he did not want to cause nervousness among the enemy, but the committee says it is not clear what source Gonen [word indistinct] this limitation and his fears [about arousing the enemy] did not justify the failure.

The committee rules that Maj. Gen. Gonen did not act in accordance with his ability to use the force he had at his disposal to break the surprise thrust of the enemy forces.

The committee says that at this stage it is not making a final recommendation regarding the ability of Gonen to carry out duties in the IDF, but it recommends that he not continue on active duty until the investigation regarding the stage of the war to check the enemy is completed.

Regarding the chief of intelligence, Maj. Gen. Eliahu Zeira, the committee says that he is respected at higher political levels, but that he adopted a concept with such inflexibility that it prevented him from maintaining the flexibility necessary to tackle the information which flows into the Intelligence Branch, and Maj. Gen. Zeira even strengthened this concept. Zeira tended to view himself as the decisive factor in the state on intelligence matters. The committee rules that in view of his serious failure, Maj. Gen. Zeira cannot continue his duties as chief of intelligence in the General Staff.

The committee also criticizes and places personal responsibility on three other officers whom it recommends should end their services in the Intelligence Branch.

The committee rules that there were three reasons for the failure to evaluate the situation before the war. These are the clinging of certain elements to the idea that Egypt would not go to war until it had assured aerial capability to attack deep inside Israel and paralyze the Israel Air Force. A second reason was Maj. Gen. Zeira's assurance to the IDF that intelligence would give advance warning regarding enemy intentions to launch an all-out war and the fact that this assurance was the mainstay of the IDF's defensive operations. The committee rules that there was no basis for giving such an assurance. A third reason for the failure was the readiness . . . to justify the enemy's preparations on the front line on the assumption that the matter did not go beyond defense preparations in Syria and exercises in Egypt. This was the result of the theory detailed above.

The chief of intelligence failed to adopt other measures that could have been adopted and which could have revealed important complementary information. Thus, the enemy was able to mislead and surprise the IDF.

The committee points out that two weeks before the war broke out the Northern Area Commander expressed concern over the limitations of receiving sufficient warning in view of the dangerous situation that developed in the Golan Heights following the reinforcement of the Syrian deployment. The defense minister was impressed by the concern of Maj. Gen. [Yitzhak] Hofi. He visited the area and voiced a warning to the Syrians. It was decided then to strengthen the armor and artillery on the Golan Heights.

When the prime minister returned from her trip to Europe she convened, on the initiative of the defense minister, a military and political meeting in which Ministers [Yigal] Allon, [Israel] Galili, and [Moshe] Dayan participated three days before the war. The chief of staff and Brig. Gen. [Aryeh] Shalev also took part. In that meeting, Brig. Gen. Shalev presented the Intelligence Branch's evaluation that war was not a likely possibility and none of the participants questioned his evaluation. It was then decided to hold a cabinet meeting on Sunday, October 7. On Friday, the defense minister and the chief of staff met, and then there were consultations at the prime minister's office with the defense minister, the chief of staff, and the chief of intelligence. The chief of staff announced that on Yom Kippur there would be a very high alert in the army. The prime minister decided to call a meeting of the ministers present in Tel Aviv that day. The chief of staff and the chief of intelligence said in that meeting that war was not a likely possibility although there was no proof that the enemy did not intend to attack. The chief of staff said that for the time being there was no need for a call-up. The participating ministers authorized the prime minister and the defense minister to decide on the mobilization of the reserves if the need arose.

On Saturday morning news was received of the enemy's plan to go to war. The chief of staff recommended to the defense minister that all reserve units be mobilized in preparation for a counterattack. The defense minister was of the opinion that the largest number of forces that the chief of staff thought would be necessary for defensive duties should be mobilized, but there was a delay of about two hours in calling up these forces because the chief of staff was waiting for the prime minister's decision regarding the mobilization.

At 0905 the prime minister approved the call-up. The defense minister was convinced that it was convenient to limit the mobilization to defense needs so that no friendly state could accuse Israel of causing an escalation of the war. The defense minister's reasoning was connected with arms purchases. The committee says that this was a political stand that can be disregarded as a justification that was rejected. The prime minister did not agree to this contention. In the discussion at the prime minister's office, the chief of staff suggested launching a deterrent attack but it was decided not to launch an attack for political reasons.

The committee concludes its interim report by saying that in the Yom Kippur War, the IDF was faced with a task that was one of the most difficult that any army could face. The IDF came out of this war with the upper hand despite the dangerous circumstances under which the war began and despite the mistakes committed in that stage. Moreover, the IDF was able to mobilize large and complex reserve units with unprecedented speed. While mobilizing its forces, it also halted a massive invasion carried out by the enemy's armies after preparing and training on this invasion plan for years.

The victory of the IDF was achieved through many dear sacrifices and thanks to the supreme heroism of its troops of all ranks, and thanks to the presence of mind of its commanders and the stability of its structure.

These facts strengthen the committee's opinion that the IDF cannot only stand up against criticism and draw the painful conclusions, but also that it will be able to increase its strength. . . .

Lt. Gen. David Elazar's Reply, Read to the Cabinet

Madame Prime Minister: I have just read for the first time the report of the [investigating] committee. I am convinced that I do not agree with a number of the committee's rulings which are not in my favor. I shall here give examples of some of them. The committee ruled that according to information which the chief of staff had in his possession he should have recommended a partial call-up of the reserve units of the land forces at the beginning of the week preceding the war in order to establish the right balance between the enemy forces, who were in a full state of alert and who were prepared against us, and our forces. I state that during my service as a chief of staff, and before that, the IDF has never had the right balance between the prepared enemy forces and our forces for a number of basic reasons which are known to all responsible elements. Among these reasons was our reliance on intelligence warning. This time, there was no such warning, and the committee rules that I was not to blame for that.

I reject the committee's ruling that no proper defense plan was prepared for the eventuality that the regular army would have to halt by itself a general enemy attack on both the Egyptian and Syrian fronts at one and the same time. The truth is that there was such a plan in the Northern and Southern commands. The plan was known and trained for, even in the lower ranks.

I reject the ruling that on that morning no clear directions were given to the Southern Area commander. The truth is that in addition to the operational plan that was prepared in advance, I gave directions to the area commanders on the morning of October 6 and I even invited them to a meeting at noon to make sure of their readiness for the fighting. The committee itself does not say anything about the directions which were given to the two area commanders in the same way.

It is not the duty of the Chief of Staff and it is not within his ability to go into minor tactical details. I testify that during my service as Northern Area commander in 1967 I submitted general plans to the then chief of staff, but I did not receive detailed directions either for defense or for attack.

I reject the committee's ruling that the difference between me and the defense minister on the morning of October 6, 1973, was in connection with the forces needed for defense as though I requested additional forces only for a counterattack. My demand for the mobilization of the entire reserve force emanated from a general concept regarding the need for forces for war when counterattacks are an organic part of a useful defense plan.

My request proves that I did not have excessive confidence in the IDF's ability to stand up against a general enemy attack on two fronts with the regular forces alone. This is an unfounded claim. I never said or thought so. I said the opposite. I do not know what the committee bases this assumption on. My request to mobilize reserves on a larger scale was approved by the Prime Minister, proved to be justified and decisive in the course of war. Had it not been adopted, undoubtedly there would have been a disaster at least in the Northern Area Command.

There is no truth in the claim that the chief of staff awaited the prime minister's decision regarding the mobilization of all the reserves. The defense minister did not approve my mobilization of reserves that morning. The approval for the mobilization was given afterwards during a discussion with the prime minister and on the basis of my proposal.

I reject the basic approach that the committee adopted regarding the authority of the defense minister and the chief of staff. This incorrect approach has misled the committee.

According to the standing authority, the defense minister is the operative authority above the chief of staff, and all operational plans and questions were brought to him for approval before the war. Only during the war itself did the defense minister cease in practice to constitute an operational authority.

I do not accept the committee's ruling that the chief of staff did not make a genuine effort to evaluate [word indistinct] on his own. According to information that I had in my possession I could not reach an evaluation different from that of the Intelligence Branch. Only through the investigating committee did I learn of intelligence information of warning value that I did not know about. Had I known of that, perhaps I would have made a different evaluation, as happened in April and May 1973.

I reject the committee's ruling that I engaged in planning counterattacks instead of concentrating on [word indistinct] the warning. I acted in the two spheres and it was my duty to lead the IDF a number of stages forward. I did so throughout the war.

Why does the committee believe that I should have reached the conclusion that reserves should be mobilized on October 5, 1973, when the defense minister was unable to reach the same conclusion, although both of us had the same information, and when no one in the General Staff thought of or suggested mobilizing the reserves? This can only be explained by saying that the committee did not treat both of us equally.[1]

NOTE

1. Elazar ended his letter by saying that he did not see any possibility of continuing his duties and that until further notice they should be carried out by the head of the General Staff, Maj. Gen. Yitzhak Hofi. Mordekhai Gur was appointed to succeed Elazar as chief of staff.

77

Motti Ashkenazi

The Protest Movements in the Aftermath of the Yom Kippur War

June 7, 1974

The recommendations of the Agranat Commission did not satisfy the Israeli public, who felt that the failure on the eve of the Yom Kippur (1973) War could not be ascribed to only one group of officers. Several protest movements arose spontaneously and demanded far-reaching change in Israeli society and the political system. The pressure of these movements was an important part of Golda Meir's decision to resign as prime minister in early April 1974 despite her electoral victory a few months earlier. Motti Ashkenazi, a reserve officer, was a leader in the protest movements and wrote the following article for Haaretz.

If one wants to understand what have been commonly known as the "protest movements" (in actuality they are nonconformist movements), one would err by seeking their roots in the Yom Kippur War. That war—which was and is a catalyst for a new type of social unrest in Israeli society, lying quite deep beneath the surface—can be seen as an outstanding characteristic of Israeli society in its entirety, as well as a mirror of its state of affairs.

On the one hand, this society has magnificent potentials, qualities, and abilities of a personal and social nature that enabled us, in times of crisis, to wrestle successfully, even under the most gruesome conditions, with a situation that made other societies totter, even if only temporarily. On the other hand, this society unwisely and wastefully uses those resources. This exacts from us a bloody price, in more than one sense, far beyond what is necessary given the reality in which we live. This situation has led to a frustrated society that is able to utilize only a part of its latent potential and that drowns in a destructive process of debilitating apathy.

The Yom Kippur War shocked many of those for whom social indifference served as a refuge from this frustration, and it also served as a catalyst arousing those who had even before

Source: Motti Ashkenazi, "Tafkidei tnuot i-hahashlamah " [The Tasks of the Nonconformist Movements], *Haaretz,* June 7, 1974, p. 17. Reprinted by permission.

found it difficult to make peace with the direction and deterioration of the society in which we live. Those who were among the first to give expression to the speed of this social nonconformism were precisely the people who formed themselves into groups and called themselves, in the communications media, "protest movements." The role of those groups was to act as a catalyst in the process of deep social change, on whose threshold we find ourselves.

The public's lack of understanding of the ongoing change makes it likewise difficult for those groups to fulfill the roles for which they were destined, because they now feel themselves urged more and more by public expectation to carry out a task they are not at all fit for at this moment—namely the establishment of alternative leadership that could utilize the national potential and could find the best possible solutions to the national challenges we are facing.

The task I see for the nonconformist movements is based on my belief and judgement that after decades of mistaken groping and lack of understanding of the era in which we live and the geostrategic arena in which we function—an era during which Israeli society placed at its head men whose outlook and understanding were anchored in a world and an environment that had long since disappeared—we find ourselves in the process of building a leadership that is the product of the environment and the era in which we live today, and in which we shall be living in the immediate future.

There is a reciprocal relationship between a leadership and the society it leads. A healthy society knows how to place at its head a leadership able to utilize a given situation for future achievement and to utilize all the potential of society in order to arrive at those achievements.

Israeli society is not a healthy society, at least in this sense, but in my view it finds itself at the beginning of a recuperative process. In each and every society such a process is prolonged and erratic even with regard to the social framework in which it takes place. A revolutionary change occurs because a different human being has to be created, who has different personal and social needs that the new society, different from its predecessor, has to learn to adopt. That is a slow process which takes its time. It is difficult to accomplish it in one leap.

In a society laboring under enormous internal and external pressures such as Israeli society, care should be taken so that this process is accomplished as quickly as possible without leading in the wrong direction. Here, in my view, lies the role of the nonconformist movements; they must be a strong and forward-pushing stimulant that does not mistakenly create processes of self-destruction and needless waste of social energies, processes that very often render social changes ineffective. If we are able to understand and recognize this role we shall ourselves, as individuals as well as a society, be in a position to prevent exaggerated expectations that can only lead to frustration.

We see our task in the following areas:

- Building public awareness of the destructive processes and shortcomings in the structure and the function of society, and a public struggle to prevent them from occurring. In that light we have to see the political fight we are now waging to establish such basic social values as the sharing of public responsibility, the accountability of publicly elected officials to their constituencies, the placing of national interests over narrow group interests, and the setting of a personal example of leadership, the closing of "social gaps," and so forth.
- The search for, discovery of, and presentation of better and more up-to-date solutions to social problems, with the aim of enhancing the quality of life. Toward this end we must increase the involvement of those individuals who are part of these networks but for some reason—conservativism, bureaucracy, or whatever—are unable to utilize their abilities. In this light we

must applaud the attempts to forge a group of activists from among social workers, community workers, and the underprivileged strata who will dare challenge rote bureaucratic methods, suggest unconventional ideas, put experimental models into practice, and through public debate teach the Establishment how to implement the lessons.

- Educating the individual toward personal involvement in society and a firm understanding of the meaning of "quality of life," as well as fostering the social standards that will lead to these goals. In this light we have to see and understand the demonstrations and the discussions of social and political problems among young people and adults in civil service, schools, and meetings.
- Formation of a political "pressure group" that will activate its members toward a struggle for content and for values within the framework that now exists among parties and other sociopolitical configurations. And all this—in order to hasten the social change so necessary for our survival. In this light we have to see the building of contacts and the creation of common ground among all the different groups included in the nonconformist movement. It may be assumed that this process will find a political and parliamentary expression if and when it becomes clear to these groups that the current establishment actually prevents, and not merely hampers, that process of change.

In this case it seems to me necessary to get a wide agreement on the following three basic principles: (1) a revision of the operating procedures of the existing system in the direction of an open and much closer relationship between the voters and those elected; (2) heightened efforts to narrow the social gap, even if this should lead to a freezing of the present standard of living of large classes of people and to its decline among the elite; (3) an active wrestling with the Palestinian problem, and that means acknowledging that this problem is at the center of the Arab-Israeli conflict and that there is room for a sovereign Palestinian state on the soil of historical Eretz Israel.

If we learn to appreciate this task correctly, and to work toward its realization along democratic lines, we shall succeed in building a mature society that knows how to solve its national problems in such a fashion that the citizen who lives in it will utilize his own potential within its framework and will be proud to belong to it. Such a society will be a social and economic focal point in the Middle East and will, at the same time, realize the values of Zionism.

It is worthwhile to remember that one should not judge the achievements of the nonconformist movement from moment to moment but rather in terms of its contribution to the process described above. The contribution during these first four months of its existence has been far beyond expectations, but it is still not enough compared to what must be achieved in the near and distant future.

78

Hanna Herzog

Israel's Road to Feminism

1973–2000: Analysis

Israel's initial public image was of an egalitarian society with regard to women. Equal status for women was a result both of the dominance of socialism in the Zionist movement and of the military's need for women in combat units in the War of Independence. However, as Hanna Herzog, a leading Israeli sociologist, demonstrates in the following reading, women's role in Israeli society is far more complex.

First Wave

The first wave of feminism in Israel washed over the country as early as the prestatehood Yishuv period. It was manifested in the voices that clamored for inclusion in the public sphere. Phrased in terms rooted in socialist discourse, women from the Left sought a way to enter the male world as equals, chiefly in the *hachsharot* (pioneer training camps), in the "labor battalions," the kibbutzim, and in political activity within the workers' parties and the Histadrut.[1] Women's voices in civil circles at the same time sought to preserve their distinctiveness as women and to gain civil equality in recognition of their contribution as women and mothers.[2]

At that period, the peak of the feminist struggle was in 1919–26, with the fight to obtain the right to vote for Yishuv institutions. As was the case across the world, women in Palestine also believed that achieving suffrage would bring equality. And like women around the world, their counterparts in Palestine would also need a few more decades to free themselves from the illusion that equality would necessarily result from the formal right of participation.

Second Wave

The second wave of feminism in Israel started evolving, though very slowly, around the time of the 1973 Yom Kippur War, though more emphatically after it. Only a calamity of that war's magnitude could manage to impel the issue of women's inequality into the awareness of a group of women, who started a still unfinished effort to place that issue on Israel's social and national agenda.

In the United States and Europe, the wave of feminism during the 1960s was one aspect of the waves of civil protest that flooded through the West. The liberal wave that washed over the West left Israel untouched, though not totally. Voices of social protest against ethnic discrimination were first heard in the early seventies, with the emergence of the "Black Panther" phenomenon [see doc. 64], a movement that demanded the reallocation of economic and political resources, and of social prestige. In 1970, upon her return from the United States, Shulamit Alloni—founder of the Citizens' Rights Movement—was the first to ask, "Does Israel need a women's rights movement?" In 1972, the first radical women's movement was set up.[3]

Source: Hanna Herzog, "Women in Israeli Society," in *Jews in Israel: Contemporary Social and Cultural Patterns*, ed. Uzi Rebhun and Chaim I. Waxman (Hanover and London: University Press of New England, for Brandeis University Press, 2004), pp. 206–17. Notes have been adapted.

It is noteworthy that this period marks the onset of the second feminist wave in Israel, signified by the establishment of Nilahem (a Hebrew acronym standing for "Women for a Renewed Society" but also meaning "we will fight"). It is not surprising that, in a society where the dominant discourse is military, the women who challenged that dominance chose to call their movement by a name taken from the military lexicon, with the intention of transposing its meaning.

The initiative for the foundation of this movement came from two professors at the University of Haifa: Marcia Freedman, a philosopher, and Marilyn Safir, a psychologist, both originally from the United States. Their seminar engendered a radical movement that was critical of the degree to which women were suppressed in a male-dominated society. Ostensibly these changes can be viewed within the framework of the liberal social movements that flooded the West during the 1960s. In practice the Israeli story is more complicated. In the West, and especially in the United States, that decade was marked by the students' revolt, and the struggles against the Vietnam War and against discrimination suffered by blacks and women. In Israel, by contrast, a very different frame of mind prevailed. Caught up in the euphoria that followed victory in the 1967 Six-Day War, the country experienced a surge of national pride and deep admiration for the armed forces. This was attended by a belief, both explicit and implicit, that brute force constituted the way to resolve international problems.

Post-1967 Israel was preoccupied with the question of borders and territories. In a society where the army, and more particularly a fighting army, is the centerpiece of social identification, civil society and civil demands are marginalized. Moreover, with the army as the fulcrum of the social ethos, the emphasis was naturally on men and on masculinity as the almost ultimate model of the "civilian" who participates in and contributes to the life of the community. The collective identification with the Six-Day War encompassed men and women alike.

The appointment of Golda Meir as prime minister in 1969, together with the economic boom that followed the 1967 war, which enabled large numbers of women to enter the labor market, helped entrench the dominant myth of equality in Israeli society. Women were not aware that in practice they were channeled into "feminine" occupations and were secondary players in the work force. They did not internalize the fact that the majority of their social functions revolved around family- and home-based activity. In post-1967 Israel, women constituted less than 7 percent of the members of the Knesset, and only 4 percent of local government representatives. They were almost completely absent from the decision-making level in the economic, political, and social spheres.

In many areas of Israeli society, the Yom Kippur War of 1973 was a watershed. For women, the war served as a kind of magnifying mirror that reflected with painful clarity Israel's social structure and their place within it. The three weeks of hostilities until the cease-fire, together with the subsequent months of stepped-up mobilization of reservists, revealed the full intensity of the gendered role division that existed between men and women, and the marginality of women in the public sphere. The massive and swift mobilization of the country's males when the war erupted almost brought civilian life to a complete standstill. Factories, businesses, offices, and schools shut down. Without men the national economy virtually ground to a halt. Public transportation was sparse: there were no women bus drivers. For the first time it was disclosed that the two bus cooperatives that monopolize public transportation in Israel (Egged and Dan) neither allowed women to become members nor employed women as drivers on a contract basis.

In 1973, then, women were excluded from the three major role systems of the war effort: the military leadership, civilian administration, and war production. Many women reported a feeling of helplessness during the war. However, the feelings of anger and frustration were soon channeled into areas of activity that are considered legitimate for women: concern for the soldiers and helping to treat the wounded, the widows, and the orphans. Women baked and knitted for the men at the front, inundated the hospitals that cared for the wounded, and of course looked after family members who had remained at home. The longer the hostilities persisted, the greater became the number of caring and integration roles that were added to female tasks.

As hostilities died down, the mobilized reservists began returning home. First to be released were those who held key positions in various sectors, so that the civilian economy could be revitalized. The war had been relatively short in terms of social change. Unlike World War II, which lasted for several years and in the aftermath of which many women entered the work force, in Israel the war of 1973 only intensified the traditional role division between men and women. However, the war did have the effect of creating an awareness of what that role division meant in relation to women and their place in the society, and also in relation to the society overall. The waste of human capital that occurs in a gender-stratified society was fully manifested in the first three weeks of full hostilities, before the cease-fire took effect.

The first body to react to the situation was the Israel Defense Forces (IDF). The process of self-criticism carried out by the military high command after the war, combined with the need to bolster combat units with males and the growing recourse to advanced technologies, led the army to reassess its policy toward women. The adoption of the new technologies, whose operation required trained and high-quality personnel, opened many new military fields to women and afforded them new opportunities. Women's functions in the army became more diverse, a trend that has continued ever since.

While the IDF always makes new missions available to female soldiers on the basis of need—generally in order to offset manpower shortages—it does not pursue this policy in order to promote gender equality. A legal battle was required before the Air Force would allow women into the pilots' training courses, at least formally. The military advocate general did not oppose on grounds of principle against women pilots the attempt by the plaintiff, Ms. Alice Miller, to enter the course—that would have been too blatantly a sexist stance. Instead, he cited "defense expenditures." The military's logic was that, given Israel's security situation, the investment involved in setting up a special course for women would be incommensurate with the high costs of maintaining Air Force preparedness and combat capability. Gender equality is perceived as a luxury. That was the IDF's position after the Yom Kippur War, and it remains unchanged a quarter of a century later.

Many women were actively involved in the large number of protest movements that sprang up in the wake of the Yom Kippur War. Nevertheless, the increasing attention paid to feminist concerns after the war should not be considered a foregone conclusion. We should bear in mind that two contradictory voices made themselves heard after the Yom Kippur War. One was trenchantly critical of the government and of the social order that had consolidated itself in Israel. But another—which became increasingly dominant—demanded national mobilization and the closing of ranks. The strength of this latter call made it difficult for the protest movements, and doubly so for women, to cut their way through to the political center. Besides, feminism as a social movement was received in Israel with deep reservations. It was perceived as an American import, alien to the Israeli spirit. Worse, the demands of feminism were seen as a threat to the collective solidarity and to women's readiness to accept the dominant national agenda, which—certainly in the aftermath of the 1973 war—revolved around the security discourse and the centrality of the Arab-Israeli conflict.

It was precisely because the gendered role division had reached an unprecedented level during the war that the seeds of the feminist approach, which had been sown before the war, could thereafter flourish. The offspring, although initially small, proved sturdy. Politically, this was first seen in the success of Ratz, the Citizens' Rights Movement (CRM), in the elections to the eighth Knesset held on December 31, 1973, soon after the formal conclusion of the Yom Kippur War (the elections had originally been scheduled to take place on October 30 of that year). Ratz was the first party in Israel to be formed by a woman, Shulamit Aloni, and to espouse human rights, civil rights, and women's rights as policy guidelines. Marcia Freedman, a declared feminist, held the third place on the Ratz list.

The public protest against the blunders associated with the war, together—undoubtedly—with the frustration generated among women by the status to which they were relegated during the hostilities were translated into votes. In the event, Ratz won four seats. Ratz was the first Israeli political party to indicate the connection between the dominance of the security discourse and the inequality of women. Ratz placed the issue of women's rights and women's status in the family and in society—and not just in legislation affecting marriage and divorce—on the national agenda. In the eighth Knesset the conspiracy of silence about violence against women in the family was broken. For the first time the subject of battered women was discussed. (It was during this period that Ruth Resnick, a member of Ratz and of the feminist movement, established the first shelter for battered women.) The question of abortions was also dealt with extensively, and the feminist argument relating to a woman's right to her body was voiced. Admittedly, the Knesset did not enact legislation to legalize abortions. But the mandates of the official committees that it formed were sufficiently broad to include, for instance, the "social clause"—which defined the social conditions in which women lived as legitimate considerations in decisions about whether to permit abortions.

A perusal of the press and of the official Knesset Record from that period shows that neither the legislature nor the public was sympathetic or enthusiastic about these new themes that had been placed on the political agenda. Nevertheless, they could no longer be ignored. This was amply demonstrated in 1975, which was designated International Year of the Woman, when the then-prime minister, Yitzhak Rabin, appointed a commission to examine the status of women in Israel. It took the panel some time to get organized and to prepare its report, which in fact was not submitted until 1978—to the new prime minister, Menahem Begin. The report examined the place of women under the law and in education, the army, the labor market, the family, and in decision-making centers, and investigated the plight of women in distress. The findings revealed the scale of the inequality between the genders and constituted an eye-opener for many women (and men). Appended to the report was a pamphlet containing 241 recommendations for action that were required in order to promote the status of women and bring about equality between the genders in Israel. The marital status of women was the only issue on which the commission could not reach unanimity: this was due to the lack of separation between state and religion, and because of the dominance of Jewish tradition.

The importance of the report drawn up by the Commission on Women's Status was not only in its recommendations, but also in the opportunity it provided for women from different spheres to work together. Some one hundred women participated in the commission's efforts, and it was the first encounter between women politicians and women academics. Participating in the conferences and the sessions of the subcommittees became a means for raising consciousness. It was clear that the work invested by all those involved in preparing the commission's report was a formative experience for a new generation of leadership. One of the few resulting political achievements was the creation of the position of Advisor to the Prime Minister on the Status of Women. Only a few items in the commission's report drew attention and were dealt with. Still, the report of the Commission on Women's Status should be seen as a breakthrough. Even though some years would elapse before its implementation began—and women's organizations continue to battle for its full implementation—the report serves as a symbolic document of Israeli society's commitment to make changes in women's status.

From the late seventies onward, feminist organizing in Israel intensifies. Its features are varied, and it comprises different forms of social-feminist endeavors: feminist writing, translations of leading international feminist articles, texts written locally, and a feminist journal, *Noga.* Shelters for battered women and rape crisis centers are established. Various mutual support groups are set up by women. A women's party is founded in 1977, and although it does not attain the minimum percentage required, it is clearly another milestone in the feminist fight.

The chief characteristics of this organizing are conscious defiance, grassroots initiatives, and the absence of direct dependence on parties or institutionalized political parties. Many organizations highlight a single issue—violence against women, rape, *agunot* (women who are refused, or unable to obtain, a divorce), injurious advertising, and so on.[4] Although most of them are small and marginal, one can still claim that, to a great extent, the merging of the different voices changed the public climate on the issue of women's status.

Alongside the radical feminist organizations, the Women's Network is established, defining its main mission as advocacy work with Knesset members, decision makers, and policy setters. The Women's Network was yet another innovation in the community of women's organizations in Israel. Most of its founders came from the academy. Their entry to feminist activities constituted more than crossing over the line separating the academy from politics, for it was those women who eventually opened gender and women's studies tracks in Israel's universities and colleges, thereby helping to expose the gendered-political aspects of the academic discourse.

Under the influence of the feminist organizations, the concept of feminism was interpreted as less and less threatening in the institutionalized organizations too. Increasingly, Na'amat, WIZO [Women's International Zionist Organization], and even Emunah, embarked on consciously feminist activities, linked with consciousness-raising through training, journalism, and political efforts. Greater willingness to collaborate with other organizations on specific issues was also displayed. In 1992, during the thirteenth Knesset, the Commission on Women's Status was established. This Knesset, in comparison with its predecessors, was more "women-friendly." The majority of the women MKs were members of the Women's Network, that is, they defined themselves explicitly as feminists: "When the Commission was set up, we didn't 'reinvent the wheel,' but a new engine was added to the wheel, a feminist, militant engine that crossed the lines of party, origin, age, and religion."[5] It is an attempt by women to go beyond party squabbles, and to cooperate with each other on shared issues that have an impact on the status of women.

The commission chalked up more than a few achievements. Some are linked to setting up frameworks dedicated to dealing with women's status (such as the state authority to promote women's status), and to creating supervisory mechanisms for state institutions—for example, the commission's authority to request reports from state institutions on issues concerning women. Others relate to legislative initiatives, introducing to the agenda of the Knesset and of the public topics such as educating for gender equality, fighting injurious advertising, single families, lesbian and homosexual rights, women in sport, preventing sexual harassment, police attitudes to victims of rape and violence, the status of Arab women, and the Basic Law—Rights of Women. The agenda of issues that were discussed by the commission attests to an attempt to address different groups of women, as well as to widen public debate concerning people suffering as a result of their gender. On these issues, too, the Commission made a significant contribution in institutionalizing a feminist agenda.

It should be noted, though, that the most noticeable phenomenon in the community of feminist organizations in Israel is that radical grassroots organizations raise new issues that are gradually adopted by the large organizations. In consequence, the former, and their leaders, remain permanently at the margins as a kind of eternal avant-garde, constantly initiating new ideas that a priori are considered radical and impossible. Over time, the issues they raise are adopted by establishment women's organizations and, to some extent, they are eventually institutionalized and enter the public agenda and the Knesset. Notable examples are the issues of domestic violence, sexual harassment, and rape. Thus, the boundaries between the extra-establishment feminist discourse and the political discourse are no longer impermeable.

Since the late 1970s, but more emphatically in the past decade, there has been an outburst of voices: secular and religious women, Mizrahi women, Palestinian women living in Israel, lesbians, single mothers, mothers of soldiers, women in black, women in green, women with political views from the Right and Left, liberal, Marxist, and radical feminists, as well as women who consider gender an essentialist social category, and those who see it as constituted by social process and thus reinterpretable. All these voices are involved in the public political discourse, some loudly raised, some whispered, and others in deafening silence.

The logic of feminist thinking rules out delegitimizing any of that chorus of voices. If gender is a result of power-oriented social construction, then any idea of a single, all-inclusive gendered identity must have a coercive element. Attempts to describe this identity and to act in its name are power-driven, normalizing, and exclusionary endeavors. Feminism's attempts to speak in the name of "The Group" has been negated in light of the demand to keep feminist discourse open and constantly changing. Implementing such an idea in the political arena is highly problematic. A political movement must have a group identity in order to mobilize political power: in the absence of consensus over a common identity, it is almost impossible to mobilize politically. Hence, feminist politics in Israel, as in many other places, is divided and there are more than a few disagreements between the feminist organizations. One solution is to conduct politics of identities, attempting to bridge or, more correctly, to neutralize disagreements that extend beyond the issues that can be agreed on. For example, the modus operandi of the Women's Network, or that of Women in Black—which agreed on a single slogan, refusing to debate on other feminist issues apart from that of "End the Occupation"[6]—or other attempts to set up an ad hoc coalition (like Ikar's struggle to deal with the issue of *agunot* and recalcitrant husbands who refuse to grant their wives a divorce).

The feminist voice is growing ever more diverse, preventing the formation of a uniform feminist identity that can unite women around it and crystallize them into a single political force. The multivocal, nonunified participation of feminist organizations in the formal, institutionalized political arena leaves the feminist women's organizations outside the power foci of decision makers, but they have clearly become an influential social force that must be reckoned with. Obviously, this is the achievement of a "movement," though not a movement that wins seats in the Knesset. It is a movement that aims to change the public agenda and, in this sense, in addition to being a political force, it is extending the borders of politics.

Women, Motherhood, and Politics

The dilemmas over what constitutes feminist discourse are embodied in the most dramatic way in the growing phenomenon of women who mobilize their female or maternal status to enter the political discourse. As an issue, this is not new, and it has existed ever since the feminist movement came into being. The first suffragettes were divided on the question of whether to demand electoral rights because of their unique contribution as mothers, or because of their universal civil right—a right that is blind to gender and role.

Repeated attempts by women to enter the heart of Israel's political discourse were doomed to repeated failure, as the analysis has shown so far. Israeli politics—which presents itself as gender-blind—replicated gender-based distinctions by perceiving women as being first and foremost mothers and wives. From the 1980s on, we see attempts by women to challenge this pattern, using those gendered definitions; that is, women mobilize the substantial legitimization that Israeli society grants to motherhood and femaleness, as a means of joining in the political discourse from which they are excluded.

Influenced by the dominance of the security discourse, women started to recruit mothers on the basis of their worries about their children, in order to make their political voice heard.[7] Women protested the protracted War in Lebanon under the banners of "Parents against Silence," "Bring the Boys Home," and the "Four Mothers" organization. Calls to evacuate the Occupied Territories were accompanied by parents organizing under the slogan "Parents against Silence" and "Mothers for Peace." The "other" voice that was uttered was the female voice, which was perceived to be at variance with the dominant male voice. Though their concern was accepted with understanding, it was also disparaged—"because it's natural for women to worry"—or, as Knesset member Geula Cohen said as she observed a demonstration of Women against Silence, "The mothers have forgotten they have a brain, and are thinking via their wombs." Often, mothers' protests were excoriated by military staff, who claimed that they should encourage the spirits of their warrior sons. Still, their voices did not die down. The Four Mothers organization played a leading role in the calls for the Israeli army to get out of Lebanon, and those calls were indeed answered. The female voice of concern was not only recruited by the Left to promote peace, but also by women from the Right, to intensify demands to settle in Judea and Samaria. Accordingly, women from Rachelim justified a settlement outpost as a means of safeguarding their children's physical security.[8] Like their sisters from the Left, they called to shift the maternal practices of concern and caregiving from the private sphere into the public, thus aiming to politicize the maternal voice. Terrorist attacks and the army's incursion into the territory of the Palestinian Authority in the "Defensive Shield" operation both generated other women's movements: "The Fifth Mother" and "The Seventh Day," which call for evacuating the territories and returning to the Green Line borders; as well as a new Right-wing movement, "Many Mothers" and "White and Blue Mothers," opposing the movements of women from the Left.

In contrast, with the use of mothers to claim a right of participation, and also as a means for defying the boundaries between private and public, the Women in Black, who protested against the occupation, and Women in Green and Blue and White Women, who supported continued settlements in the occupied territories, all intended to take part in the political discourse as women, and not necessarily as mothers. This attitude is particularly prominent in Women in Black, an organization that sought to relinquish women's taken-for-granted identity, in which every female is a mother or a potential mother. Through the response to Women in Black, we can see that it was easier for society to "accept" a maternal-female message than a female-feminist message. In the message of Women in Black there was a dual challenge—to the dominant security-oriented discourse and also to the gendered order, including worldviews that limit the world of women to motherhood. They sought to join the political discourse simply by virtue of being women, not by virtue of the social roles that channel them into the world of home and family. They emphasized what is common to women everywhere, and to both Palestinian and Jewish.[9]

Even if the women's movements that were based on being women and mothers did not attract many women, they placed fresh questions on the political-public agenda and challenged the gendered borders of Israel's political discourse. Without doubt, the most outstanding feminist achievement of those women is that they dismantled the obstacles to entering the security discourse.

Concluding Remarks

Women's politics, or alternatively, feminist politics, implies the demand to recognize women as a social category suffering discrimination and deprivation. It is a demand to recognize the gendered social world, a demand made on society to observe itself and to examine the presupposed assumptions that form the social orders, and especially the sexual roles prevailing within it. Has this voice been heard in Israel? At what intensity?

To a considerable degree, the pincers of the simultaneously inclusionary and gendered culture have determined women's political prospects. As a generalization, it can be asserted that women who were elected were women in politics, but women who did not necessarily implement women's politics. True, the majority of women Knesset members and the women involved in local authorities sat on committees engaged in "female" issues, and they were without doubt among the supporters and promoters of legislation and policy influencing the world of women. However, the majority did so on an isolated basis, by virtue of their position, and to a substantial extent did so subject to the dominant agenda that is principally set by men. Without detracting from the value of their endeavors, their lack of awareness of the gendered social order made the few women who were active in political endeavors partners in reproducing the existing order.

Political culture in Israel, as outlined here, had reservations about feminist activity and marginalized it. However, since the end of the seventies, feminist organizing has grown and flourished in Israel, but women have remained mainly in the ex-parliamentary arena. The prime characteristics of this organizing are challenging awareness, grassroots growth, and the lack of direct dependence on parties or the establishment's political organizations. Many organizations focus on a single issue: combating violence against women, rape, *agunot,* offensive advertising, Mizrahi women, Palestinian women, peace, and so on. Although most such organizations are still small and marginal, it can be claimed that the conjunction of this spectrum of voices is slowly penetrating the feminist organizations and deserves a separate discussion; it exceeds the goal of this study, which focuses on formal politics and women's representations within it.

As the winds of feminism blew stronger, the formal sphere did not remain unaffected. Women brought about legislative changes that were aimed at enhancing equality. Among the laws that were passed were those that assured women's representation in directorships of government and public firms, stipulated equal wages for women in return for equal work, and prohibited sexual harassment. Growing awareness of the issue led to increased activity around the enforcement of laws, and greater reliance on the Law of Human Rights, in order to establish the right to equality. Some symbolic expressions of the burgeoning attempts to blur the gendered dichotomy were effected in the army by gradually admitting women to combat positions, dismantling the Women's Corps—a mechanism that had institutionalized the separation between women and men in the army—and creating frameworks for military tasks shared by men and women. This last endeavor is an interesting example of the ongoing negotiations over the social boundaries of the gendered world in Israel. Together with the attempt to blur the boundaries and to include women in the world of men, another stubborn struggle continues—that of religious groups resisting such inclusion, and the allied struggle by religious men to avoid conscription and to remain in the world of the *yeshivot,* a world that remains closed to women in Israel.

Finally, the political culture of exclusion and inclusion of women in Israeli politics as analyzed here is not unique to the political sphere. It can equally be found in the army,[10] in the labor market,[11] in the literary world,[12] and in the sphere of art and culture.[13] In all these areas, the past decade has witnessed attempts to blur the gendered dichotomy, and to bring about the more egalitarian inclusion of women in various public domains.[14] However, realizing the challenge of blurring the gendered dichotomy is also strongly linked to the degree of weakening of the other mechanisms that previously reinforced the gendered boundaries. Although the myth of equality finally disintegrated a short while ago, which certainly prepared society to show greater openness to the issue of women's status, the sustainability of other mechanisms is not clear-cut. A study is required of the trajectories of development in traditional Jewish and Palestinian cultures, the intensity of the separation processes between religion and state, and the path that the Arab-Israeli conflict is taking. Even a superficial examination supports the claim that the processes occurring in each sphere are not necessarily moving along the same trajectory. Thus, for example, some changes are taking place in Palestinian and Jewish cultures that may lead to greater equality between the genders; changes in the world of religion and in the status of women in religious communities constitute only one such aspect.[15] In contrast, at the start of the century, the Israeli-Palestinian conflict, which had seemed close to resolution, was exacerbated. Not only did the Al-Aksa *intifada* cut off the dialogue between Palestinians and Israelis beyond the Green Line, it also filtered into the delicate fabric of relations between Israel's Jewish and Palestinian citizens. As a result, cooperation between Palestinian and Jewish women within Israel was markedly reduced, and the feminist voices that called for change were hushed.

The simultaneous existence of inclusionary and exclusionary processes explains, to a great extent, the weakness of the feminist movement in Israel, in view of the unequal economic, cultural, and political opportunities, as well as inequalities in terms of income, power, and social prestige. At the same time, I would like to claim that, while exclusion creates subordinated social feminine enclaves, it also has the potential for social change. An ongoing segregation that exists alongside growing awareness of the need for women's inclusion in the collective has the potential for creating a new agenda, and even for crystallizing a feminine claim challenging the existing social norms and sociopolitical institutional arrangements.

AUTHOR'S NOTES

1. Deborah Bernstein, *The Struggle for Equality: Urban Women Workers in Prestate Israeli Society* (New York: Praeger, 1987); Sylvie Fogiel-Bijaoui, "The Struggle for Women's Suffrage in Israel, 1917–1926," in *Pioneers and Homemakers: Jewish Women in Prestate Society,* ed. Deborah S. Bernstein (Albany: State University of New York Press, 1992), pp. 275–302; Dafna N. Izraeli, "The Zionist Women's Movement in Palestine, 1911–1927: A Sociological Analysis," *Signs* 7 (1981): 87–114.
2. Hanna Herzog, "The Fringes of the Margin: Women's Organizations in the Civic Sector of the Yishuv," in *Pioneers and Homemakers,* ed. Bernstein, 283–304.
3. Marcia Freedman, *Exile in the Promised Land: A Memoir* (Ithaca, N.Y.: Firebrand Books, 1990); Uri Ram,

"Emerging Modalities of Feminist Sociology in Israel," *Israel Social Science Research* 8 (1993): 51–76.
4. Sylvie Fogiel-Bijaoui, "Feminine Organizations in Israel: Current Situation," *International Problems: Society and Politics* 31 (1992); 65–76 (Hebrew).
5. Committee for the Advancement of Women's Status, *Report to the Knesset* (Jerusalem, 1998), p. 4.
6. Sara Helman, and Tamar Rapoport, "Women in Black: Challenging Israel's Gender and Socio-Political Orders," *British Journal of Sociology* 48 (1997): 682–700.
7. Yael Azmon, "War, Mothers, and Girls with Braids: Involvement of Mothers' Peace Movements in the National Discourse in Israel," *Israel Social Science Review* 12 (1997): 109–28; Nurit Gilath, "Women against War: 'Parents against Silence,'" in *Calling the Equality Bluff: Women in Israel*, ed. B. Swirski and M. Safir (New York: Pergamon Press, 1991): 142–46; Chaya Zuckerman-Bareli and Tova Benski, "Parents against Silence," *Megamot* 32 (1989): 27–42 (Hebrew).
8. Tamar El-Or and Gideon Aran, "Giving Birth to Settlement Maternal Thinking and Political Action of Jewish Women on the West Bank," *Gender and Society* 9 (1995): 60–78.
9. Helman and Rapoport, "Women in Black."
10. Dafna N. Izraeli, "Gendering Military Service in Israeli Defense Forces," *Israel Social Science Research* 12 (1997): 129–66.
11. Dafna N. Izraeli, "Gendering the Labor World," in *Sex, Gender, Politics: Women in Israel*, ed. D. N. Izraeli, Ariella Freedman, Henriette Dahan Kalev, Sylvia Fogiel-Bijaoui, Hanna Herzog, Manar Hasan, and Hanna Naveh (Tel Aviv: Hakibbutz Hameuchad, 1999) (Hebrew).
12. Hannah Naveh, "*Leket, Pe-ah, Veshikha:* Live outside the Canon," in ibid., 49–106.
13. Yael Amzon, ed., *Will You Listen to My Voice: Representation of Women in Israeli Culture* (Tel Aviv: Van Leer Jerusalem Institute and Hakibbutz Hameuchad Publishing House, 2001) (Hebrew).
14. See data of the Israeli Women's Network, *Women in Israel: Concentration of Data and Information, 1999–2000* (Tel Aviv: Israel Women's Network, Center for Information and Research of Policy, 2001) (Hebrew).
15. Tamar El-Or, *Next Pesah: Literacy and Identity of Young Religious Zionist Women* (Tel Aviv: Am Oved Publishers, 1998) (Hebrew).

79

Menahem Begin

Prospects for the New Government

May 19–20, 1977

The shock caused by the initial Israeli reverses during the Yom Kippur War was a catalyst for profound changes in Israeli politics. The Agranat Commission report (doc. 76) blamed professional army officers for the intelligence and military failures during the first days of the war. But public reaction (see doc. 77) forced Golda Meir to resign despite her recent electoral victory. Her replacement by Yitzhak Rabin was insufficient to preserve the Labor Party's rule. In the May 1977 elections the Likud, under Menahem Begin, gained a plurality and formed a new government.

The Likud's victory was significant in several ways. It resulted in the first transfer of power from one wing of the Israeli political system to the other. The new government sought to implement a different social and economic philosophy affecting both domestic and foreign policies. This interview with Menahem Begin on May 19–20, 1977—immediately after his electoral victory and before he assumed office—reveals his ideas and frame of mind before his actual encounter with the realities of power.

Source: Israeli Foreign Broadcast Information Service, *Daily Report: Middle East and North America* 5, no. 99 (May 23, 1977): N2–N6.

May 19

Two hours with Menahem Begin, the next prime minister. The time: yesterday morning. A new reality. Bodyguards and policeman stationed at the entrance to the small apartment in Tel Aviv, symbolically making real the change which has occurred in Israel's political world. No longer the opposition leader, but the one who will shortly form the cabinet and lead it.

"Reb[1] Simhah (on the telephone to his friend in the Likud leadership, Simhah Ehrlich, of the Liberal Party), listen Reb Simhah, if you agree, I want to send (here comes the name of a man which I was asked not to publish at this stage) [Shmuel Katz] to the United States at once. Yes, yes, at once, even today or tomorrow . . . he will meet with senators, congressmen, famous journalists and will appear on coast-to-coast television programs. Yes . . . it is important and urgent . . . we must explain . . . we must speak to the American people. . . . Fine, I'll let him know at once that he should be set off. . . . Thank you Reb Simhah."

MK Zevulon Hammer is proposing that the National Unity cabinet be established without any basic policy lines and that it should debate each question separately. Is this possible?

No. Definitely not. My dear friend Hammer was wrong. It is a legal commitment binding the whole cabinet to bring agreed basic policy lines to the Knesset for authorization—as well as to present itself to the Knesset and request the confidence of the house. This is demanded by Clause 15 of the Basic Law for the cabinet, as follows: "As soon as the cabinet has been formed it will present itself before the Knesset, announce the basic lines of its policy, its composition and the division of tasks among the ministers and ask for an expression of confidence."

What are you prepared to offer the [Labor] alignment?

What is demanded by the law . . . exactly: Negotiations over the basic policy lines of the cabinet and over the division of tasks among the ministers.

What will you offer them on the personal level?

We can reach understanding on the personal level too. . . . It is possible, . . . it is still too soon to determine things. It was only last night that I managed to get some normal sleep. I slept wonderfully. First I had a nice doze in the armchair and then went quietly to bed. It was wonderful. If the alignment agrees—we will begin negotiations seriously, both on the basic policy lines and on the manning of government ministries with ministers.

And the negotiations with the Mafdal, the Democratic Movement for Change, Agudat Israel, and Poalei Agudat Israel?

Everything in its proper time. We will certainly discuss things with everyone and we will look for ways to reach understanding and agreement for the sake of a cabinet which enjoys the confidence of the nation, a cabinet which initiates, thinks, does things. Of course . . .

What improvements will you make in the government ministries?

There will be ministries which we will eliminate completely. For example, the Ministry of Police will cease to exist. It will become a branch of the Ministry of the Interior. We will establish a ministry of social betterment, which will include the ministries of welfare and labor. A new ministry will be established—a ministry of publicity abroad. The emphasis, please, on the word abroad. Not internal publicity. It was a mistake to establish such a ministry. This is an institution only befitting a totalitarian country. In a democratic country such as ours there is no need for a ministry of internal publicity. The citizens explain to themselves what they see with their own eyes, how they must behave and how they should judge the acts of their government. But a ministry for publicity abroad—this is definitely needed from the political point of view. We must speak not only with governments, but to the people as well. I have the most talented candidate for this task, but I will not say his name until I consult both with my colleagues and with him. . . .

Is that the man you are sending to the United States now?

Exactly! That's the man! A wonderful man!

Is the rumor correct that says that you intend to appoint as ministers experts in their professions, who have not been members of any of the Likud factions, but that you are meeting with opposition on the part of powerful men from among the Likud parties?

I deny this completely! Public honesty demands that the important tasks be given to people who must be talented and capable, but who have toiled and labored diligently, even suffered, for many years, and when the time comes . . . they must prove themselves in senior tasks. As against this I am sure that all the members of the Likud leadership and of the factions will agree that a talented man who is not in one of the Likud factions can certainly serve as a cabinet member. I will give you an example, just to illustrate, since there has not yet been any consultation and we have not yet received the agreement of the man himself—but to me Prof. Yuval Neeman[2] is certainly suitable to be a cabinet member.

And Ariel Sharon?

Certainly! Ariel Sharon and his friends will support the Likud cabinet and he certainly could and should be one of its members.

Do you intend to man the senior posts in the cabinet with your people? To change the senior ambassadors in the different capitals and appoint people beneath them who are loyal to you?

We have a great rule and that is of "civil service." Civil servants can rest easy. There will be no dismissals in the civil service. Those with political and economic views different from those of the Likud from among the civil servants can be sure that this will under no circumstances be an obstacle to the continuation of their work. I call on them to continue doing their jobs.

There will undoubtedly be a number of central jobs where there will be changes. But the reference is to a very few jobs. We came to serve and not to set traps. And this applies to ambassadors. Only in a few embassies will there be changes.

And in senior IDF [Israel Defense Forces] appointments?

Even more so: All the commanders will continue to serve in their jobs and it is not to be imagined that because of any views whatsoever there will be a change in the status of a commander in the IDF, neither in relation to his promotion or in relation to holding up his promotion. There will be no such thing!

President [Jimmy] Carter's announcement that the change of rule in Israel will not influence relations between the two countries and will not detract from the U.S. commitments to Israel's security . . .

The announcements by President Carter and the new American ambassador to Israel, Mr. [Samuel] Lewis, made us rejoice. I will tell you a secret: Before I felt ill I was about to write an article for a paper in which you and I are partners, under the heading: "An Open Letter to President Carter." However, because of the illness I did not finish it. In one sentence I expressed my view that if there is a change of power in Israel as a result of the elections, that fact would increase the honor of Israel in the eyes of the U.S. president—since he himself is used to this and knows from experience what is the real sign of a democratic regime: changes in power. I was happy to hear the president's words and I am sure that Israel's honor will indeed increase in his eyes.

I was also happy to hear that he will send me an invitation to visit him after the formation of the cabinet. It will be an honor to exchange views, information and evaluations with him—as two free men.

When do you assume your meeting will be held?

Not before the beginning of July. And I will have enough time to prepare myself, to prepare myself most exactly.

You will no doubt also talk about the Bible . . .

Oh, certainly. There is reason to assume that we will discuss the Bible very much indeed, since both of us know it. And allow me also to welcome the new American ambassador. His first announcement in the country and his warm words about democracy were wonderful, really. I will call him today and bless him for his words.

Will the Likud cabinet really try to fight inflation by creating controlled unemployment?

There will be no unemployment under the Likud cabinet: there will not! The alignment people again slandered my friend Simhah Ehrlich and accused him of causing unemployment. Unemployment is inconceivable. I remember, and none of us have forgotten, the slump and the unemployment under the alignment regime. That was a national tragedy, which principally harmed the development towns. We will not go back to those dark days.

How, then, will you fight inflation?

We can certainly curb inflation by up to 15 percent a year. We will do this through a tripartite agreement between the cabinet, the Histadrut and the employers. For a period of two years there will be no increase in taxes, prices will not go up and the workers will refrain from any demand to increase their wages. Thus we will succeed in curbing inflation, we will bring back stability to the currency, we will increase output and production. After the first two years we will check on what can be done to add to the real wages of the worker. We will seek with all our strength to enable the worker to support himself on his wages with confidence and honor.

Will the Likud cabinet remove the controls on foreign currency or at least appreciably increase the allocation to travelers abroad, so that citizens will not be currency smugglers and criminals against their wishes?

Yes. Definitely! We will very seriously and urgently consider completely eliminating controls over foreign currency. It is well known that where there is control, the black market flourishes. We learned this in the days of Dov Joseph, when control over food brought out a flourishing black market in food commodities. Control over foreign currency is also one of the obstacles to foreign investments and from this aspect as well it is harmful. . . .

May 20

Mr. Begin, in the political sphere, we hear of concern in Washington in view of the establishment of a Likud government headed by you. Do you think that Israel now faces the choice between confrontation with the United States and a territorial compromise that is unacceptable to you?

No, I do not think we are going toward a confrontation with the United States. Of course, I do not determine Washington's policy. Yet, I am convinced that we, Israel and the United States, have a mutual interest and that we can explain it in the United States. I am certainly doing so now. I have heard various announcements. This morning, for example, we heard that the *New York Times* published an article by Mr. Reston[3]—he is well known to you, he is one of the most important commentators in America—to the effect that it may ultimately be desirable to have such a government. Well, then, if this is desirable, this is certainly good. At any rate, I want to correct the term territorial compromise, as Mr. [Shimon] Peres and Mr. [Yigal] Allon say for example, what is actually said? We say that we are giving part of Judaea and Samaria[4] and keeping part to ourselves. I want everyone to remember that the Arabs answered with an absolute no to this. Allon's plan was presented to King Hussein three times. He said: Totally unacceptable. I think that it is exactly those using this deceptive term who have blocked the path toward the agreement with the Arabs.

I am not claiming that the Arabs will accept our plan. They do not agree to any Israeli plan. The difference is that those who say that they will give up Judaea and Samaria, while they do not and really cannot reach an agreement with the Arabs, only invite pressure—from America as well. That is to say, we are told: You are not prepared to withdraw enough, withdraw a little more. The proof is President Carter's announcement before the elections. He made the announcement concerning the withdrawal to the 1967 borders with slight modifications, which is in fact the famous Rogers Plan, a few weeks before May 17. This term is totally deceptive. It has a certain sound. How did the late [Levi] Eshkol put it: "Everyone is fond of his own compromises." However, we are not discussing love here but a policy. Therefore, I wish not to use this deceptive and misleading term. I think that we will act to explain this mutual interest between Israel and the United States. There does not have to be a confrontation, there does not have to be American pressure.

But your policy is unacceptable in Washington, Mr. Begin. From my experience I know that there is no single senator, no administration official in the United States who is prepared to put up with a policy that will impose Israeli law on Judaea and Samaria.

The problem of imposing the law is a problem involving a discussion, a special decision of the Knesset. I would like to ask you: Has any Israeli representative ever told a senator that Judaea and Samaria should, by law, justice, and right, be an integral part of Israeli politics? What can you or any other Israeli expect from these senators when you tell me that they are not prepared to accept the policy according to which Judaea and Samaria should be an integral part of Israel? Should they be more Israeli than the Israelis themselves? They received lessons from Mr. Allon, Mr. Peres, Mr. [Yitzhak] Rabin and Mrs. Golda Meir to the effect that we are prepared to give up Judaea and Samaria. Thus they have come to believe that this is in fact a just policy since the Israelis themselves preach it.

Now, I hope, we will start to explain it properly for the first time in ten years, we will begin to explain that this is not so, that the retention by Israel of Judaea and Samaria is the thing that guarantees the chance for peace. If we give up Judaea and Samaria, there will not be any chance for peace. We have not started yet; that is, we have just started. I have not yet visited President Carter. I have not yet spoken before the Congress. Let us have the possibility of carrying out this task. For ten years all Israeli representatives said that we are withdrawing, that we will leave Judaea and Samaria. Mr. Allon presented his own plan before the American representatives. They do not accept it. The American representatives have never said that they favor Allon's plan. On the contrary, I know that in Washington King Hussein's words were said again—totally unacceptable. What is the difference then? I think that the Israeli policy and information campaign were totally wrong. We should now turn over a new leaf.

NOTES

1. Reb is a traditional Yiddish term of respect.
2. In 1979 Yuval Neeman (1925–2006) and Geula Cohen (b. 1925) led a faction out of the Likud and formed the Hatehiyah (Revival) Party, which opposed the withdrawal of Israeli forces from the Sinai. Many members of the Gush Emunim (who opposed any territorial compromise on the West Bank) also joined Hatehiyah. It won three seats in the 1981 elections. After the return of the Sinai had become a *fait accompli,* Hatehiyah joined the Likud coalition as a separate party, and Neeman was given a portfolio in August 1982. The party disintegrated in 1992.
3. James Reston, "Israel: Second Thoughts," *New York Times,* May 20, 1977, p. A25.
4. Judaea is the biblical name of the area around Jerusalem and Bethlehem; Samaria, biblical name of the

Central Hills region north of Judaea. In modern Hebrew these names are used to designate these historically significant geographic regions. One of the early symbolic acts of Menahem Begin's government, revealing his attitude toward the land conquered from Jordanian rule in 1967, was to instruct all government personnel (including ambassadors abroad) to use these terms to designate the political entity previously called the West Bank.

80

Yehuda Ben-Meir

The Ideology of the National Religious Party

1977: Analysis

The victory of the Likud alignment in 1977 had an impact on the role of the religious parties in the government. For the first time Agudat Israel was included in the coalition along with the National Religious Party (NRP). Moreover, the 1977 coalition agreement accorded the religious parties a larger role than they had been given by the Labor governments.

Dr. Yehuda Ben-Meir, MK, was one of the leaders of the NRP and served as deputy minister of foreign affairs. This ideological profile of the party addresses both domestic and foreign policy issues.

The National Religious Party (NRP) is a direct offspring of the Religious Zionist movement established over seventy-five years ago. As such, and in common with other parties whose ideological and organizational roots lie in the Zionist movement of prestate days, the NRP's ideology is an expression of its unique concept and particular brand of Zionism. Indeed, the original name of the Religious Zionists was Mizrahi, which stood for Merkaz Ruhani (Spiritual Center), thus expressing the religious-spiritual approach to Zionism and to the Zionist ideal.

The NRP, as its Mizrahi forerunner, has always been part and parcel of the Zionist movement and participated actively in all its activities and endeavors, perceiving it as the movement of and for Jewish National Liberation. At the same time, the NRP championed, most vehemently, the idea that in order for Zionism to be a truly *Jewish* movement for National Liberation, and for it to succeed, it must be rooted in Jewish tradition, which is synonymous with Jewish religion. Thus the NRP advocated, consistently and strongly, that Zionism must and should reflect, in its outward expression, Jewish religious values, norms, practices, and institutions. The NRP saw as its goal and purpose the guaranteeing of the traditional Jewish character of Zionism, of the State-in-Being, and eventually of the Jewish state itself.

Central to NRP ideology throughout the years was the close relationship between nationalism and religion. The *duality,* combining nationalistic fervor with religious belief, can be traced throughout Jewish history, emerging at key periods of that history as a factor of paramount importance, exercising a key influence on the Jews of that day. The nationalist-religious

Source: Written by Yehuda Ben-Meir specifically for the 1st edition of *Israel in the Middle East.*

relationship—even symbiosis—is rooted in the unique self-definition of the Jew and of the Jewish people, as being at one and the same time a nation and a religion. No less a secularist than David Ben-Gurion always stressed that for a Jew, being a member of the Jewish nation and of the Jewish religion was one and the same, totally indivisible and inseparable. And it was the Israeli secular Supreme Court that ruled that the state could not recognize someone as being a Christian Jew, because such a definition is self-contradictory and goes against the universally accepted definition of a Jew [see doc. 48]. For the NRP the concept of the *unity* of nationhood and religion, and the total indivisibility of the two, is the very cornerstone of its ideology and system of belief.

A prime example of the close relationship between Jewish nationalism and religion can be found in the person of Rabbi Akiva. Rabbi Akiva, who lived in Israel a generation after the destruction of the Second Temple (70 C.E.), is considered one of the greatest Torah scholars and sages of all times. He is the symbol of religious learning and scholarship and was compared by the rabbis to Moses himself. And it was the same Rabbi Akiva who was the spiritual and political leader of the great Bar-Kokhba rebellion against Roman rule over Israel.[1] It was Rabbi Akiva, the great religious luminary, who was also the fierce freedom fighter, willing to risk all in order to liberate the Jewish people and the Land of Israel from foreign domination, from the yoke of Roman rule and subjugation. Interestingly enough, the NRP's youth movement—considered by many to be the most successful one in Israel and indeed throughout the Jewish world—is called Bnei Akiva (Sons of Akiva) after the same Rabbi Akiva. Indeed, no better a symbol of the NRP's ideology could be found than Rabbi Akiva.

The twin pillars of nationalism and religion, which form the basis and heart of Religious Zionism, are clearly and explicitly expressed in the very name given to the political arm of the movement in Israel, namely the National Religious party. The same idea was clearly enunciated, close to eighty years ago by Rabbi [Yizhak Yaakov] Reines, the founder of the Religious Zionist movement, when he coined the famous phrase, "The Land of Israel for the People of Israel by the Torah of Israel" and determined that this objective is the goal and purpose, the raison d'être of the Mizrahi movement. During the past eighty years the emphasis has moved, back and forth, from the national to the religious, from the Land and People of Israel to the Torah, but the essential synthesis has remained the core belief of the Religious Zionist movement as a whole, and of the NRP in particular, and has been the guiding factor in forming its policies and approaches to the various issues facing Israel.

The overall ideology and the specific policies of the NRP are the result not only of the joint effect of these two forces or values but also of the interacting effects of one on the other—both the reinforcing effects as well as the tempering effects. It should be clear that Jewish nationalism and Jewish religion can and do reinforce one another, but no less significant is the tempering effect of these two forces each on the other. Indeed, it is only through an awareness and realization of these far-reaching tempering effects that one can understand how and why the NRP evolved as a center party and as a centrist force of the political spectrum. It was the deep sense of Jewish nationalism, of the unity of the Jewish people, of the need for national liberation that tempered the religious fervor of the Religious Zionist, countering the trend to isolationism and preventing the creation of a closed caste and the erection of a wall between the religious and the nonreligious Jew. Herein lies the basic difference between Religious Zionism, between the Mizrahi, and the Agudah movement [Agudat Israel]. The ultra-orthodox Agudah saw secularism as the prime danger to the Jewish people, a danger that must be met and fought at all costs and with which there could be no cooperation and no truce. Thus the Agudah was vehemently anti-Zionist. The Mizrahi was no less religiously committed than the Agudah, and no less opposed to secularism than the Agudah, but its strong sense of nationalism led it to be willing to cooperate—within the framework of the Zionist movement, within a framework dedicated to the national liberation of the Jewish people—with the nonreligious and even with the antireligious. The NRP fought Agudah isolationism, claiming that for the sake and in the cause of the Land of Israel and Jewish liberation all Jews, regardless of their religious convictions or behavior, must stand together and work together.

To the same degree it was the pragmatism, the worldliness, the practicality of Jewish religion that tempered the nationalistic fervor of the religious Zionist, preventing nationalism from turning into chauvinism, guaranteeing moderation and countering extremism. Thus, although sympathizing with the Revisionists and supporting many of their positions, the Religious Zionist movement refused to follow Zeev Jabotinsky out of the Zionist movement, rejecting separatism, and chose to remain an integral and active part of the World Zionist movement. The NRP sympathized deeply with many of the political positions of the Revisionists, including, to a large degree, rejection of the Partition Plan; yet it chose to ally itself with the Practical Zionism[2] of the Labor movement. Ben-Gurion's Practical Zionism, which stressed practical activity and the upbuilding of the Land of Israel through a "step-by-step" (or, as it was called in Hebrew, "dunam after dunam") process, appealed to the religious side of the Religious Zionist because it struck a responding chord and a common vein with the pragmatism, worldliness, and down-to-earthness so characteristic of the precepts, values, and norms of the Jewish religion.

Having laid the basic ideological foundation, we can try to follow the development and formation of NRP policy during the past thirteen years—from the Six-Day War to the signing of the Egyptian-Israeli Peace Treaty. In so doing, we must never forget that these policies are deeply rooted in an overall ideological framework—an ideology that is part of a total way of life and world approach, an ideology at whose heart lies a synthesis between religion and nationalism and an attempt to reach a synthesis between a deep commitment to basic values and a recognition and acceptance of political realities of our world.

Thus the NRP has consistently *differentiated* between its approach to Judaea, Samaria, and Gaza on the one hand, and toward the Sinai and Golan Heights on the other. The NRP has maintained, steadfastly, since 1967 that Israel's position regarding Sinai and the Golan Heights should be determined *solely* by security considerations although such security considerations can, of course, lead to radically different results regarding the two different areas. But the main point always was and remains that the *sole* criterion in determining the final boundaries for the area should be Israel's security—in the broadest sense of the word. To the same degree the NRP has maintained, with the same tenacity and consistency, that Israel's position on Judaea, Samaria, and Gaza must be based on *national-religious* considerations and sentiments side by side with the security criterion. The inalienable right of the Jewish people to their ancient homeland—the Land of Israel—the heart of which, by both geography and history, is Judaea and Samaria, is a basic and undeniable tenet of faith of both Jewish nationalism and Jewish religion.

The NRP supported the position that the Sinai Peninsula was not essential for Israel's security and that in the context of a genuine and permanent peace with Egypt the Israeli military presence could be replaced and substituted by a demilitarization of Sinai and that specific and guaranteed arrangements on the ground, such as demilitarized zones and buffer zones, could effectively maintain Israel's security. For this reason the NRP supported the resolution of the National Unity government taken in June 1967 and transmitted to the American government—namely, that Israel would be willing to conclude a peace agreement with Egypt on the basis of the international boundary in Sinai. Based on the same logic, the NRP in March 1979 supported the peace treaty between Israel and Egypt on the basis of the Camp David Accords [doc. 103]. The NRP's opposition to the removal of the settlements in the Rafiah Salient[3] was based on security considerations and on the national-religious significance attached to Jewish settlement once already established and inhabited. One should remember that the settlements were established for security reasons and on the basis of a strategic-security concept and not as a result of religious significance attached to the area itself. In this respect, the NRP always rejected the Greater Israel movement's claim that an active Israeli military presence in Sinai is vital for Israeli security.

The NRP's approach to the Golan Heights is also based on security criterion. One need not be a military strategist to realize the vital significance of the Golan Heights for the defense of Israel. One need only to stand on the top of the heights, and to see the entire Galilee in the palm of his hand, to realize that a strong military and civilian presence on the Golan Heights is absolutely essential for the defense of the entire North and for the very security of Israel. Thus the NRP is part of the national consensus which holds that Israel will never go down from the Golan Heights. Yet, since the basis for Israel's adamant stand on the Golan Heights is security, the NRP supports the government's position that while Israel remains on the Golan she is willing to negotiate with Syria—in the context of a permanent peace treaty—on the final borders of the Golan, which need not be identical to the present lines.

Judaea, Samaria, and Gaza present an entirely different picture. The NRP's attachment to these areas is founded *both* on security grounds and on their national-religious significance as an integral part of Eretz Israel, the Land of Israel. The NRP has always refrained from determining the *relative* importance of each of these two factors, stressing the vital importance and centrality of each one in its own right and the fact that each complements and reinforces the other—both jointly leading to the same conclusion and both forming the joint basis for the NRP's position. Thus, the NRP firmly rejects a territorial compromise in Judaea and Samaria, claiming that such a compromise does not meet either the requirements of Israel's security or of the maintenance of her national right.

The NRP's position is that while the Allon Plan [see map 4] *might* be an answer to the external threat to Israel's security, it leaves the question of internal security and terrorism wide open. The presence of Israeli forces on the Jordan River, as envisaged by the Allon Plan, *might* deter Arab aggression from the East, although the need for such a force to be maintained and reinforced through narrow corridors in hostile territory could seriously impair its effectiveness and its deterrent capability. But the creation of a sovereign Arab entity—be it Jordanian or Palestinian—inhabited by close to a million Arabs, raised and educated on hatred and on a dream of revenge, adjacent to Israel's population centers, would mean a hotbed of irredentism and terrorism that would be uncontrollable and make life in Israel unbearable and unlivable. The only answer to such a possible nightmare in the future is a strong Israeli presence in these areas, with Israel enjoying the prime responsibility for internal security for the entire area west of the Jordan River.

Similarly the NRP believes that once Israel returned to parts of its historic homeland—as a result of an aggressive war waged against it by Jordan—it cannot permit itself to sever these areas from any relationship or contact with the Jewish people. The NRP's position is that there must be some relationship and some contact between the Jewish people and Israel and between these areas.

Nevertheless, the NRP supports a compromise solution for Judaea, Samaria, and Gaza, a compromise that falls far short of meeting the just national aspirations of the Jewish people. For this reason, the NRP has *not* demanded the annexation of Judaea and Samaria. On the contrary, it has opposed legislation calling for the annexation of Judaea, Samaria, and Gaza or parts of these areas, as for instance, has been proposed by Gush Emunim [see doc. 81]. The NRP supports the Autonomy Plan of the present government and is actively involved in the autonomy negotiations. In fact, the NRP is not demanding Israeli sovereignty in Judaea and Samaria but is willing to support a *functional compromise,* by which authority, government, and effective sovereignty would be shared by the Palestinian Arabs and Israel. This is the essence of the Autonomy Plan, and the NRP sees in this plan, or in a similar approach, the only viable compromise with which both sides can live.

NOTES

1. Bar Kokhba (d. 135 C.E.) was the leader of the Jewish revolt against the Romans, 132–35 C.E. The great rabbinic leader of the period, Akiva, considered Bar-Kokhba to be the Messiah. The revolt was put down, and both leaders were killed.
2. The First Zionist Congress endorsed Political Zionism as espoused by Theodor Herzl. According to Herzl, the Jewish Question could be solved only by large-scale migration and settlement of Palestine, which could be attained only through the political assistance and consent of the community of nations. On the other hand, many Eastern European Zionists advocated practical Zionism—i.e., the building of the Jewish state through acquisition of land, settlement, and the creation of an economic infrastructure. Chaim Weizmann's program of Synthetic Zionism maintained that both kinds of activities should go on simultaneously to complement each other.
3. The Rafiah Salient is the area in the northern part of the Sinai immediately south of the Gaza Strip.

81
Gush Emunim
Opinion Paper
January 1978

The cardinal issue in Israel's domestic politics following the Yom Kippur War has been the debate over the fate of the territories captured in 1967, particularly the West Bank and Gaza. In the late 1970s the signing of a peace treaty with Egypt (doc. 104) and the return of the Sinai served to exacerbate the debate on the Palestinian issue inside Israel.

One side of this issue was argued by Gush Emunim (Bloc of the Faithful), a group of ultra-right-wing religious nationalists who believe that Jews have a holy obligation to retain sovereignty over western Palestine. The group was led in its early phases by Rabbi Moshe Levinger and Hanan Porat. Before the formation of a sympathetic government in 1977, Gush Emunim established settlements on the West Bank illegally, forcing the Labor governments either to compromise and allow the settlement to remain or to use military force to remove the illegal settlers. The Labor governments usually compromised. The Likud governments have been more openly supportive of such settlements. The following opinion paper was published in Gush Emunim's newsletter.

Source: Ohadei Gush Emunim [Friends of Gush Emunim], January 1978, pp. 2–5.

The hope for peace has captured the people of Israel of all ages. The people of Israel—its blessing is peace, the end of its prayers is for peace, and even upon leaving for battle it calls out to its enemies for peace.

But just because of our strong desire for peace, we need great strengths of wisdom and courage not to mistake a deceitful peace for a real peace, a weak peace for a peace of honor and strength, a peace of crisis and retreat for a peace of renewal and creation.

We must painfully conclude that the peace plan proposed by the government of Israel has no truth, no honor and strength, no redemptive power. The basis of this plan is a deceitful peace; its spirit, one of breakdown and weakness; and its results, crisis and retreat.

This "peace plan" is based on three main points of distortion:

1. Readiness for complete withdrawal down to the last centimeter, to the borders before the Six-Day War. This withdrawal would signify acknowledgment of the Arab claim that the "obliteration of the traces of Israeli aggression" is a condition for peace. This claim is false and deceitful, and willingness to accept it as a basis for a peace plan, and to retreat indiscriminately now from all of Sinai and the Golan Heights, is an unethical step lacking the propriety in which the prime minister prides himself.
2. Readiness to remove all the Jewish settlements from the Rafiah Salient and Sharm el-Sheikh from Israeli sovereignty and to transfer them to Egyptian sovereignty. This readiness reflects an approach lacking in national responsibility and represents not only a mortal blow to the ability of these settlements to exist but also a basic undermining of the ideological foundation of Zionist fulfillment, which determined from its beginnings that settlement of the land is the basis for sovereignty. A blow to the practical and ideological roots of settlement undermines the motivation to settle, and therefore whoever thinks that it is possible to call upon the people of Israel to become pioneers and go out to settle the land in great numbers on the basis of this plan is mistaken and deceiving.
3. The idea of administrative autonomy for the Arabs of Judaea and Samaria and the Gaza District.[1] The autonomy as it is proposed is not limited to the regional municipal framework but represents a basis for Arab national institutions to be elected in general democratic elections. One would be completely blind not to realize that this autonomy will lead directly to the establishment of a Palestinian state that will enjoy—despite Israel's opposition—recognition by the overwhelming majority of the countries of the world. There is not one Arab leader, not even the "most moderate of the moderates," who will not see autonomy as the basis for a Palestinian state and who will not do everything to bring this about. This proposal does not bring a solution to the Palestinian question any closer. On the contrary, it exacerbates the question and will force the question that much sooner. Therefore, it not only does not contribute to peace and tranquility but actually brings closer the time at which the War of Palestinian Liberation is likely to set off a war in the entire Middle East.

In conclusion, we reject this plan from the start and call for a public struggle for its abolition. This is not a personal struggle against the prime minister. It is a deep moral struggle against the spirit of deceit, the weakness inherent in the very basis of the plan; it is a struggle for the spirit of the great renaissance.

Our sages have said, "A bit of light pushes much of the darkness aside," and we will proceed likewise. We will raise the light of revival, we will arouse the power of Israel through great public outcries of honor and strength; we will rejoice in the land with settlements and waves of immigration; we will, through education and information, open our eyes to see what is this peace we are yearning for, and what the difference is between true peace and a deceitful peace. Rav [Abraham Isaac] Kook, of Blessed Memory, said, "The truth is not shy or cowardly." We shall follow in his footsteps and not be deterred from stating loudly the truth of renaissance, even if it is not the kind of peace that can be attained from one day to the next, one that is all lies and illusion.

We believe that the people will yet awaken from the illusion of this imaginary peace and will strengthen itself in its onward struggle.

We pray that this awakening will not be accompanied by the sufferings of despair and as a result the hope for true peace, of strength, brotherhood, honor, and light will not be lost.

We pray that this awakening will not be accompanied by the sufferings of despair and as a result the hope for true peace, of strength, brotherhood, honor, and light will not be lost.

God will grant His people strength
God will bless His people with peace!

Come, let us go up and settle the land!

Shiloh

Shiloh, at which the members of Gush Emunim intend to lay the cornerstone for a new city today, has been the target for settlers since the middle of 1974.[2]

Shiloh has great significance and holds a special place in the history of the Jewish people. According to tradition, Shiloh is one of the holy places for the people in which the Divine Presence abided. Here the land was divided up among the tribes, and the Tabernacle and Ark of the Covenant arrived here. It is said that the graves of Eli the Kohen and his two sons are here.[3]

The site, at which archeological excavations have long been held, is near the Arab village of Turmus-Aya in Samaria, about two miles east of the Ramallah-Nablus road, about fourteen miles north of Ramallah. At the mound itself, remnants have been found of buildings, walls, burial caves, and more—remnants of an Israelite city that existed before Jebusite Jerusalem was conquered and reached the height of its development in the tenth century. When the renowned Jewish traveller Ishtorai Hafarhi visited it in 1322, he saw ruins, among them a mosque. Its remains can be found in the area today.

Next to the mound is the Valley of Shiloh, which is intended to serve the city the settlers plan to establish. In Arabic the valley is called Marg-el-eid (lit., Valley of the Holy Day), in which, it seems, large public gatherings were held in the days of its glory. Among the vineyards of the valley, the tribe of Benjamin laid in ambush for the daughters of Shiloh, in order to kidnap them and take them for wives, as told in the Bible.

NOTES

1. The Autonomy Plan is a proposal for "administrative autonomy" for the West Bank and Gaza first developed by the Begin government in late 1977 and presented as a twenty-six-point plan to Egyptian president Anwar Sadat in December of that year (doc. 100). The plan agreed to at Camp David used the term "full autonomy," and autonomy talks began in May 1979 but made no real progress.

2. Shiloh is a Gush Emunim settlement established in January 1978 and officially classified as an archaeological site despite Gush Emunim's public statement that it intended a permanent settlement. By March 1979 Shiloh was officially included in the list of settlements under the jurisdiction of the Settlement Section of the Jewish Agency.

Elon Moreh is another Gush Emunim settlement that created controversy. Members of Gush Emunim originally tried to establish a settlement near Nablus in 1972, but the government forcibly removed them. In June 1979 Elon Moreh was established with the government's support. In October 1979, however, the Supreme Court ruled that civilian settlement on land privately owned by Arab residents was illegal, rejecting the government's argument that the land was appropriated for security reasons and stating that no such justification existed in this instance. The court ordered that the settlement be evacuated by November 18, 1979. Both the settlers and the government ignored this deadline at first, but the settlement was finally evacuated in 1980.

3. Eli the Kohen (priest) was priest at Shiloh in central Samaria, one of the major religious centers of the Israelites before the Temple was built. Eli trained Samuel. See 1 Sam. 1–3.

82

Simon Markish

A Soviet Jewish Intellectual Abroad

December 1978

The 1970s witnessed a large emigration of Jews from the Soviet Union, and in the early part of that decade many went to Israel. By the mid-1970s it was clear that Soviet Jewish immigrants were encountering serious problems in Israel, and many chose other destinations. The nature of these problems, especially for the class of intellectuals, is explained by a Soviet Jewish emigrant who chose not to settle in Israel.

Simon Markish (1921–2003), son of the Yiddish writer Peretz Markish, was trained in classical philology. He left the Soviet Union in 1970 and moved to Geneva. The article excerpted here appeared in Commentary, *the intellectual journal published by the American Jewish Committee.*

Once an intellectual is abroad, and has passed through the period of shock which every emigrant from the USSR must inevitably experience—it is largely a mixture of alarm and rapture—he begins to adapt psychologically. His mind, and especially his emotions, formulate a set of responses to his new situation. Whether the response will be predominantly gloomy or bright depends as much on physical circumstances as on mental baggage, though possibly the latter is more important. With all the difficulties of life in Israel, material conditions there are, with rare exceptions, greatly more favorable than in the USSR. But neither Israel nor the West is like the preconception of them which the future émigré has before his departure, and that is because his preconceptions are made up of Soviet components. It might be said that this is not more true of the present-day émigré than it was of the Jewish émigrés from Russia at the turn of the century, and that the real America was sharply different from the Realm of Gold dreamed of in the shtetl. But the mental baggage of Jews was different then, the disparity between ideal and real was experienced differently.

The very departure from the USSR is felt by the émigré to be something of a feat, and in many cases it is just that: months and even years of "refusal" status, letters of protest, arrest, prison, and so on. But even if everything has gone smoothly, the émigré has had to overcome his terror of the all-powerful state and authorities, a feeling which is incomprehensible to anyone in a free society. Every émigré, moreover, has to tolerate all manner of humiliation and loss to the very last, at the various customs checkpoints—and not only in the USSR; if he goes by train, he is openly robbed by the Poles and the Czechs—and his sufferings acquire the nature of virtues in his mind. He is a hero and a martyr, and therefore has a legitimate claim to retribution.

Judging as he does by Soviet standards, he is not capable of understanding that his retribution begins from the moment he steps off the train or the plane in Vienna. Everything that comes his way he accepts as his just dessert. This

Source: Simon Markish, "Passers-by: The Soviet Jew as Intellectual," *Commentary* 66, no. 6 (December 1978): 34–38. Reprinted from *Commentary* by permission; all rights reserved. © 1978 by the American Jewish Committee.

is not only because he is a hero and a martyr, but because everything has already been paid for by the American Jews. And Israel has nothing to do with it, he owes nothing to Israel. Hence the fierce aggressiveness of some émigrés in their very first moments on Israeli soil, in the immigration hall at the airport. Hence the frank discussions in Vienna. The immigration official from the Jewish Agency asks one of those who have announced their intention to go straight to the U.S., Canada, or Australia, "But what if you could only have gone to Israel; would you have emigrated?" And without any hesitation the "straighter" answers, "No."[1]

Judging as he does by Soviet standards, he is not capable of understanding that the country he has come to has its own laws and customs, its own difficulties, and that it is trying to overcome them in its own way. He does not understand that the only way to get used to the place and to feel at home is to accept the rules of the game, and not to stand on the doorstep and demand that they be abolished or fundamentally altered. This is not to say that the rules are ideal; many of them are no good at all. But if you want to tidy up the house, you might at least wait until you are inside. The "noisy minority," however, do not go beyond the doorstep; their sense of superiority does not allow it. We have suffered more than anybody else, they seem to say, we know better than anybody else, we will explain everything and teach everything.

The passion for preaching overcomes new émigrés from Russia, regardless of their origin, Jew and non-Jew alike. In essence there is no difference between the repatriate, hardly able to express himself in kitchen Hebrew but already discoursing on the poverty of spiritual life in Israel, and the professional émigrés traveling around different countries and answering all questions without hesitation, settling any problem without the least difficulty. Though there is one important distinction. The émigré knows his place after all, he knows he is a stranger whom nobody has asked or especially invited, and so he knows how far he may go in his attacks and exposures. It is one thing to hear the view expressed at dinner in a private home that Harvard University is worse than Elets Teachers' Training Institute; this is hardly a view to put into a newspaper or to pronounce from the lecture platform. The repatriate, however, knows no such limitations or inhibitions.

Coming to the concrete reasons for dissatisfaction and disillusionment, we should exclude the obvious and well-known ones like the hard climate in Israel or the rude civil servants. All new arrivals suffer from these, whatever country they come from. The former Soviet Jewish intellectual, especially if he belonged to, or numbered himself among, the so-called creative intelligentsia, is shaken, apart from everything else (and sometimes above all else), by the change in his accepted scale of values. He is no longer in an elite, or at any rate not in the only elite, and not the most important of elites. To be a writer is no more honorable than to be an engineer or a doctor. Poverty and lack of success are no longer evidence of a proud and independent talent, but more likely the result of hopes that have been dashed. The accepted scale of values is overturned, and there remains only the choice between adopting a new one and living in a fantasy world of old and hurriedly renovated values—or repudiating any scale of values altogether.

The first course represents, strictly speaking, a completely different subject of discussion: namely, the successful adaptation and integration of immigrants. It is worth pointing out that the quickest to adapt are those who have inner resources, people with convictions and ideas. For example, and above all, believers or new believers. Or old-school Zionists, although even they are not immune from disillusionment, irritation, and straightforward rebellion. We need not dwell on the loud protests made by Georgian Jews about religious life in Israel, since their psychology is a mystery to many besides myself; complaints about inadequate piety of the state of Israel and of its scandalous godlessness are clearly not the monopoly of the old

Hasidic inhabitants of Meah Shearim.[2] The point is, however, that the first course, the course of adaptation, is most accessible to those who bring with them or quickly acquire some positive spiritual equipment: to put it simply, a love of God, of freedom, of the Jews, of Israel, but only the real Israel, and not the one dreamed up in the Soviet vacuum, bathed in tears of humiliation or drunkenness. These people grow quickly in their new soil, put down roots, forget the discrimination of their Soviet existence, forget even their existence itself, the land of the Soviets, Russia, and their past hatred for it, once so fierce as to serve virtually as the chief content of their lives.

The second course is the most interesting to the outside observer and, most likely, the most bitter to those who follow it. It is a course taken by many a Soviet intellectual in Israel. He who felt himself to be a Jew in Russia, and for that very reason "returned to the historic homeland," finds himself once there to be a Russian, not because of Israeli phraseology, not because it is generally accepted that immigrants from Russia are called Russians, but because he suddenly feels for certain that he is a Russian. In Russia, being a Jew was the most important mark of self-identification, whether personal or social; it was the main motive and factor in any interpretation of one's destiny; it marked the conscious or subconscious frontier between one's own and what was not one's own, between "ours" and "not ours." This is perhaps natural in any diaspora, and almost inevitable in the process of reidentification in the new environment, Israel.

If the mind recoils from the new circumstances, once so desired when they were a dream and a goal, and if the mind does not want to harbor this new feeling of hostility but cannot overcome it, and also cannot or does not want to change the circumstances, then in order to avoid self-destruction it will return to the past, reshape it, shifting the emphasis, reassessing evaluations. All the old forms, standards, and patterns are preserved. We are not like the others, we are better, we know more; but they do not value us, they envy us, they don't want to help. Everything around us is alien; we are not interested in "their" petty concerns and primitive pleasures; we are aristocrats of the mind, we live our own internal lives, we are intellectuals, we are members of the Russian intelligentsia, we are the third wave of the Russian emigration. We are in Israel by chance, just as we could be in Canada or in France, by chance.

Passers-by were they there, passers-by are they now here.

NOTES

1. A conflict with world Jewry regarding the settlement of Soviet Jewish émigrés arose in the 1970s and 1980s. The Israeli government argued that Jewish philanthropic funds should be given only to those Soviet Jews emigrating to Israel, with the exception of those uniting with their families elsewhere.
2. Meah Shearim (One Hundred Gates) is an Orthodox neighborhood in Jerusalem with a large concentration of militantly Orthodox organizations.

83

National Committee for the Defense of Arab Lands

Manifesto

March 25, 1979

The Six-Day War and the Yom Kippur War generated processes that radicalized Israel's Arab citizens and fostered the development of political groups to the left of the Communist Party, such as the National Committee for the Defense of Arab Lands.

One government policy contributing to this radicalization was the expropriation of Arab-owned land. On March 30, 1976, a general strike was planned in the Arab sector to protest such expropriations. In the attempt by the authorities to suppress the general strike and in the accompanying antigovernment riots, six Arabs were killed and many more were wounded. Since then Land Day has been commemorated with rallies and demonstrations by Israeli Arab nationalists and the Jewish Left. The following manifesto was published by the National Committee for the Defense of Arab Lands on the third anniversary of Land Day.

Few days separate us from the 30th of March, the third anniversary of Land Day, the day the Arab minority in Israel commemorates as a symbol of its struggle to defend Arab-owned land and as an act of protest against the policy of land expropriation and the demolition of Arab houses. The decisions adopted in the conference held in Nazareth by the National Committee for the Defense of Arab Lands on February 17, 1979, form the basis for this anniversary. These decisions are as follows:

1. The Arab masses in Israel, joined by democratic forces in Israel, will commemorate the Land Day by holding four mass rallies on March 30 in the following places: Dir-Hanna village, Kfar Kanna village (Galilee), Taibeh village (Triangle), and Tel El-Sabi' (Negev). At these rallies representatives of the committee, local councils, and public figures—both Jews and Arabs—will speak.
2. This anniversary takes place while the impetuous policy and actions of land expropriations and the expulsion of Arabs from the land continue, especially in the Negev where Bedouins are forced out of the houses and lands on which they have lived for hundreds of years. The criminal acts perpetuated by the Green Patrol[1] against the Bedouin livestock should move people of conscience, Jews and Arabs alike, to demand an end to these brutal measures that are in violation of law and justice and are fundamentally opposed to basic human rights. These actions are threatening the mere existence and fate of those unprotected citizens in their own homeland.
3. The Arabs in Israel express their resolve to continue their just struggle relentlessly against all acts of land confiscation and the demolition of Arab houses and for safeguarding their rights for full equality as citizens and as human beings.

Source: Press release distributed by the National Committee for the Defense of Arab Lands, March 25, 1979.

4. It is naturally expected that any peace policy should begin at home by guaranteeing equality for the Arab citizens and by recognizing their right to ownership of their lands. Peace policy should mean the banning of all manifestations of national oppression and discrimination that are being carried out against the Arabs, including the policy of dispossessing them of their lands and homes. The National Committee for the Defense of Arab Lands calls for the withdrawal of all court cases against Arabs who were charged since 1976 with disturbing law and order on the eve of the Land Day.
5. The committee will intensify its propaganda campaign to mobilize public opinion in Israel and elsewhere toward solidarity with the just demands of the Arabs in Israel. In addition the committee has appealed in a letter to the president of the state that its efforts toward a genuine solution to the suffering of the Arab masses be given a hearing.
6. The committee wishes to make it known that if all appeals fall on deaf ears, it will find itself bound to step up its struggle by using all legitimate means including strikes and demonstrations in order to win justice, equality, and democratic rights.
7. The Arab masses in Israel consider their struggle for full equality, for the abolition of national oppression and discrimination expressed first and foremost by dispossession, as part and parcel of the general democratic struggle for a just peace and for ensuring democratic rights and coexistence among the peoples of the region. This peace is what all of us desire and seek.

NOTE

1. The Green Patrol is the police force established in the Ministry of Agriculture during Ariel Sharon's tenure in order to guard state lands, especially in areas contested by Bedouins.

84

Peace Now

Platform

1980

Peace Now is an unstructured political movement that emerged as a dovish pressure group during the Egyptian-Israeli negotiations resulting in the Camp David Accords (doc. 103). It aspired to counterbalance the activities of the Gush Emunim and other right-wing and religious movements that advocate militaristic or hawkish policies and the further expansion of Israeli settlements on the West Bank. Its leadership included reserve officers. The 1980 platform of Peace Now is excerpted here.

1. The Peace Now movement was founded and exists out of a deep concern for the peace and security of the State of Israel.

The movement acts with the cognizance that *peace* is the basis for attaining the goals of the State of Israel.

Source: Leaflet distributed by Peace Now, 1980.

The movement is opposed to government policy since it believes that it will lead neither to peace nor to security.

The movement has a broad, comprehensive perception of the concept "security" that is not confined to territorial superiority alone but has additional components: the strength of the Israel Defense Forces and its soldiers' conviction that they are following the right path; the quantity of arms that Israel receives; assistance from and liaison with the United States and other countries of the world; security arrangements that are determined by negotiation; preparedness of the other party for peace; demilitarization of evacuated territories; the time factor in the peace settlements; mutual confidence between the two parties willing to find a peaceful solution; the success of the peace processes; the moral, social, and economic vigor of the State of Israel. All these, not just a single factor, are the components of security. Without these and without their perpetual reassessment, no peace will be established, nor will there be security.

The Peace Now movement will use democratic means to oppose any government in Israel that does not take into account these broad aspects of security and peace and is not open to options which might lead to a solution by negotiation. The movement does not deny the existence of historical and religious ties in themselves but believes that Israel's peace and security take precedence.

The movement demands from any government in Israel that it view the subject of security in its broadest sense, taking all its components into account, and that it be prepared for any negotiations which are not damaging to broader considerations of security. The movement opposes any extreme positions that might further postpone negotiations.

The movement demands from any government in Israel that it maintain the traditional aims of Zionism that work toward a Jewish state, and not one that negates the rights of some of its inhabitants; that does not rule over another nation, just as it would not allow another nation to rule over it; and exists by virtue of its own labor. It encourages *genuine settlement* but not expansion at the expense of others. . . .

3. The Autonomy Plan [doc. 101] is merely an interim plan that should be implemented only with the cognizance that Israel has no rightful claim of sovereignty over the West Bank and the Gaza Strip.

Israel will express willingness to withdraw to secure boundaries that will be agreed upon in comprehensive negotiations and according to security considerations alone. The lack of real progress in the negotiations about the future of the autonomy is liable to affect the stability of the peace with Egypt.

4. Israel must halt its settlement activity on the West Bank and Gaza Strip, and cease all attempts at legislation intended to alter the status quo, because (a) The settlements constitute a precondition before negotiations; and just as we require the Arabs to sit down around the discussion table without prior conditions, so we must demand from ourselves a cessation of the settlements in the area under discussion in the negotiations. (b) The settlements are intended to create established facts, but they do not guarantee a better bargaining position; quite the reverse, they goad the other side into adopting even more extreme positions. (c) The settlements have an adverse effect on the peace process and on the stability of the peace with Egypt, and they testify to the Israeli government's intention to perpetuate Israeli sovereignty over the West Bank and to continue to exercise control over one and one-half million Arabs. (d) The settlements cause unrest among the inhabitants of the West Bank and the Gaza Strip and increase animosity. (e) The settlements cost billions of Israel pounds, an investment that damages Israel's security and its image instead of buttressing the society, the economy, and the army. A state with a shaky economy cannot maintain a modern army, and a state with a discontented population will also witness destructive trends in the army. (f) The settlements display haughtiness, immorality,

and a lack of integrity. (g) The settlements keep world Jewry aloof from Israel, cause a deterioration in Israel's foreign relations, and divide the nation.

5. The State of Israel paid a high price for the peace with Egypt. The Palestinian problem is the next stage in the process of creating peace, a stage during which lack of progress is liable to do harm to the stability of the existing peace with Egypt.

The Peace Now Movement has never demanded a return to the 1967 borders or the establishment of a Palestinian state. Since the chief consideration of the movement is the security of the State of Israel, we demanded and continue to demand that the government of Israel keep open any option for peace that does not negate Israel's security.

The government must investigate the following options: (a) the Jordanian option, which must be based on Resolution 242 [doc. 68], on the Camp David Accords [doc. 103], and on the principle of not endangering Israel's security; (b) a combination of the Jordanian option and the Palestinian option; (c) the Palestinian option, according to which the State of Israel must initiate a step that will break through the vicious circle of Israeli-Palestinian hostility and will advance the possibility of a solution. The State of Israel will hold negotiations with the Palestinians who will recognize the method of negotiation as the only way to find a solution to the conflict in the Middle East.

These negotiations must be based upon the following principles: (a) The Palestinians will recognize Israel's sovereign right to exist as a Jewish state within secure borders, and they will abandon the path of terror. For its part, Israel will recognize the rights of the Palestinians to a national existence, so long as this is not at odds with the security of the State of Israel. (b) Both parties will enter into negotiations with full cognizance of the fact that only by each side giving way on some of the political claims, based upon the historical rights of both nations, is there any likelihood of directing the region toward peace. (c) Israel will give way on its fundamental claims for sovereignty in the West Bank and the Gaza Strip, and will base her claims solely on considerations of security. During the course of the negotiations all settlement activity will come to a halt and also all legislation liable adversely to affect the peace process. Palestinian representatives will be given a status equal to that of the representatives of the other nations participating in finding a solution for their problem and the problem of the West Bank and the Gaza Strip.

The autonomy proposed in the Camp David Accords is simply an interim step on the way to a comprehensive solution for the Arab-Israeli conflict. The autonomy is linked to the peace-building process with Egypt and should be enforced in all the territories of the West Bank and the Gaza Strip. The negotiations between all parties who participate in the peace process will be conducted upon the basis of the Camp David Accords and Security Council Resolution 242. Israel will view the Palestinian question as the problem of a nationally distinct group and not merely as a question of refugees.

6. Jerusalem, the capital of Israel, will not be divided. Any proposal for a settlement will be discussed in detail in the framework of comprehensive negotiations.

7. The status of existing settlements will be discussed in the framework of negotiations for a permanent settlement regarding the West Bank and the Gaza Strip.

85

Asher Arian

The 1981 Elections

Fall 1981: Analysis

The elections of 1981, resulting in the second Likud government despite the Labor Party's improved performance over 1977, reflected the increasing polarization of Israeli politics. In the following article, Asher Arian, a professor of political science at Tel Aviv University who specializes in Israeli electoral politics, analyzes the processes that led to the Likud's second victory and the consequences of these elections for Israeli politics. The article appeared immediately after the elections in the Jerusalem Quarterly, *published in Jerusalem by the Middle East Institute.*

Israel's most bitter, violent and unsavory campaign ended on June 30, 1981, with the election of the Tenth Knesset, but it settled very little. It created a virtual tie between the two largest political groupings in the country—the Likud with 48 of the 120 Knesset seats and the Labor-Mapam Alignment with 47—and underscored the observation that the country was divided in an unprecedented manner.[1] The close elections retained for the religious parties the balance of political power which they had come to expect, although the National Religious Party (NRP), the largest component among them, lost half its previous strength by falling from twelve to six seats.

Elections determine the division of power in a political community and as such have far-reaching influence on the body politic. But the election results themselves are conditioned by a series of political, social, and economic factors, some objective and others subjective. The most striking characteristic to emerge from the 1981 elections was evidence of polarization in Israel along ethnic, social and political lines. These features were noted in the past; it was the degree of their intensity and the fact that these polarities tended to overlap which made the 1981 election campaign unique and its results disquieting.

Never before had the country been divided so evenly and so massively by the two major parties. Never before had the electorate of the two parties been so homogeneous in its ethnic composition. Never before had ethnicity been exploited as a campaign theme in such a barely implicit manner. Never before had violence in the campaign seemed so threatening and so immediate.

Competitiveness: Away from Dominance

The major party of the labor movement (first called Ahdut Haavodah, then Mapai, now Labor) had been dominant in Israeli politics for the first 29 years of independence and for a couple of decades before independence as well. In 1977 the pattern of dominance was broken when the Likud won the largest number of Knesset seats. The 1981 elections determined

---

Source: Asher Arian, "Elections 1981: Competitiveness and Polarization," *Jerusalem Quarterly,* no. 21 (Fall 1981): 3–27. Reprinted by permission.

beyond any doubt that the era of Labor dominance had ended, and not only temporarily suspended as some had thought. The system had become competitive, the former dominant party no longer being able to count on plurality support from most social groups of the electorate.

Never before in Israel's history had a more competitive election occurred, for this was the first time that both major parties considered the possibility that the other party might win. In the past, including the turnabout 1977 elections, the leaders of the Herut/Liberal Parties and coalitions (Gahal in 1969, the Likud since 1973) had been pretenders to victory but the Labor/Mapam leadership had always been confident—and correct until 1977—about remaining the biggest party and therefore the major component in the formation of the government coalition. The electorate was swept into the drama of a two-party race and many voters disappointed smaller contenders on the left, right and center by being sucked into the ranks of the two large parties.

The portion of the two-party vote was unprecedented, reaching 95 of the 120-member Knesset, or almost 80 percent. The previous high for the vote of the two largest parties was in 1973, when the Alignment and the Likud split 90 seats between them, 51 and 39 respectively. In 1981 the race was extremely close, the Likud winning 48 seats, the Alignment 47; between them they won almost a million and a half votes of the almost two million cast, but only 10,405 votes was the difference between them. Within the Jewish population the Likud was an even bigger winner, since Arabs accounted for 47,300 of the Alignment total.

There was a general feeling of disappointment with the election results within the two big parties. Inevitably, politicians deal with the relative and not the absolute. Therefore, objective indications of major achievements by both parties were overshadowed by the knowledge that the competitor did almost as well, or better. The Likud continued its steady growth and added more than 100,000 votes to its 1977 total. The Alignment was somewhat heartened by its 1981 showing since it bounced back from its 1977 trauma and grew by 50 percent. But comparing the 1981 results to the Alignment's more glorious past leads to the inevitable conclusion that it remains a party in decline despite the good 1981 showing. The difference between the 1969 and 1981 votes for the Alignment, for example, was a mere 75,000 votes, whereas the Likud in the same period added more than 375,000 votes to its total. The number of voting Israelis grew in that same period by more than half a million.

When looked at in terms of the two major parties, the growth of the Likud is clear. If present trends are projected into the future the Likud will continue to grow and the polarization of 1981 will be remembered as a momentary—and random—meeting of curves.

The size of the two-party vote in 1981 was unique; it is usually helpful in Israeli politics to think in terms of party blocs. Looked at in this way, it is also clear that political fortunes in Israel are steadily moving to the right. In 1981 Israeli politics was divided into two large camps, but over time the parties of the center and right grew and the parties left-of-center declined. Adding together the seats won by adjacent parties during the last four elections (1969, 1973, 1977 and 1981) provides the following breakdown for the center and right: 32, 39, 45, 51. For the left-of-center parties (including the Democratic Movement for Change [DMC] and the Arab parties affiliated with the Alignment) the trend line is 66, 62, 52 and 50. ([Moshe] Dayan's Telem was not included since he is hard to categorize.)

Images and Ideology

Images played a central role in the 1981 elections: the image of the Likud as an anti-establishment party representing the underprivileged in Israeli society, willing to use the "big lie" in portraying its policies in order to be re-elected; the image of the Alignment as the party of the bosses, anxious to return to the government to which their establishment status seemed to entitle them; the image of [Menahem] Begin as a self-confident leader expressing some of the deepest doubts of the Jewish people regarding the degree to which non-Jews could be trusted and the Israeli penchant for assertiveness even if cooler minds thought it dangerous at best, suicidal at worst; the image of Peres as an indecisive politician who would do almost anything to further his own career, whose smooth tongue sometimes appeared slick, and who was set on not missing the opportunity to be prime minister. Ideological differences between the parties were much less crucial in determining the election results. In a basic sense, this was a non-ideological election.

While emotions ran high and many found fault with both of the major contestants, this was not an "anti" election. Many voted for the party of their choice because they thought it was better, not only because the other was worse. There was no evidence of alienation from the political system or withdrawal from the election. The participation rate—78.5 percent in 1981—was similar to past elections.

Party Images

A social myth is a convenient way of ordering reality. While reality is usually complex, myths have a simplifying quality about them. They are easily grasped, widely accepted, able to convert masses of detail into an understandable whole.

Similarly, the image that a party or a leader has is no less important than his real opinion or personality. If [Shimon] Peres is thought of as insincere, or Begin as unstable, conflicting evidence can easily be put aside in favor of the popular image which allows us to grasp the essence of the man more easily.

In the 1981 election campaign the Alignment was perceived to be the establishment party even though it had been in opposition to the government for four years. The Alignment's negative image is also evidenced in that it was perceived to be the party more concerned about its own interests than those of the citizens', and not very honest. The Likud was closer to the ideal party image, perceived as a slightly stronger party, honest, one that could be trusted and a party more concerned with the citizens than with itself.

In politics, perceptions are as important, or more so, than reality. It may be that the sample's perceptions reflect reality, but it is certainly noteworthy that a party in opposition for four years still retains in the public mind many characteristics of an establishment, governing party. The Likud still benefited from its image of newness, of innocence, and was given credit for its efforts in undoing many of the difficult legacies it had inherited from the Alignment. In fact, 41 percent of a national sample reported that they thought that the argument "four years are not sufficient for the Likud to undo what the Alignment had destroyed in thirty years" was a convincing reason to vote for the Likud.

On other dimensions there were differences in the parties' images as well. For example, the Alignment was the opposite of the ideal on the young/old dimension, the ideal being young, the Alignment perceived as old. The Likud also had an older image, but much less extreme than that of the Alignment. While the ideal called for a progressive party, both parties were perceived as old-fashioned, but the Alignment more so than the Likud. A strong party was called for, and the Likud was perceived as slightly stronger than the Alignment. In fact, on almost every dimension, the Likud was closer to the ideal than the Alignment.

On class and ethnic dimensions the differences between the parties and their images were striking. The ideal party was almost evenly divided among those who preferred a middle-class party, those who preferred a working-class party and those in between. The Alignment was perceived to be close to that ideal, although more working-class, while the Likud was very far from the ideal with a high preponderance of middle-class responses. As we have seen, the workers tended to support the Likud and not the Alignment even though the Alignment is the labor party associated with the socialist movement.

The ethnic dimension also fits the pattern. The socialist label gave the Alignment claim to being the worker's party, but the Alignment was also overwhelmingly Ashkenazi, or European. As such, the Alignment had negative appeal for the Sephardi who tended to have lower education and lower status occupations. Both the Likud and the Alignment were led by Ashkenazi politicians, but the rejection of the Alignment was indicated by the fact that it was perceived to be so overwhelmingly Ashkenazi when in fact its leadership was no more Ashkenazi than the Likud's.

In the 1981 campaign, the Alignment was broadly perceived to be the party of the European, upper-middle-class bosses and the Likud the party of the Sephardi, lower-class workers. This image was heightened by a campaign which featured expressions of violence and political intolerance especially at Alignment rallies by individuals popularly portrayed as young Sephardi toughs inspired by Likud rhetoric. The ethnic tension was brought to a head during a huge Alignment rally held in Tel Aviv three days before the election, when a popular entertainer indulged in ethnic slurs against the Likud electorate, even evoking their relatively low army ranks in the supposedly egalitarian Israel Defense Forces. The polarization of the two parties and their respective ethnic supporters fortified the images which were already prevalent: the Alignment as the party of the bosses, running the Histadrut, the kibbutzim and other economic institutions which oversaw the dependency relations with which many of these individuals lived since arriving in Israel in the early fifties.

The images of the kibbutz had undergone a radical change since the years of independence when kibbutz membership was an ideal and the kibbutz member a folk-hero. The image of the kibbutz was now bifurcated: for the Alignment supporter, it was a preserve of socialist and idealist values and an example of economic success and social equality as well. The kibbutz member was seen as the Israeli landed gentry, loyal, affluent, and entitled to rule. For the Likud supporter, the kibbutz epitomized values perverted. In the name of non-exploitation, exploitation; in the name of equality, inequality. How else explain the kibbutz factories in outlying regions in which the kibbutz members were bosses and the workers Jews (and Arabs) from surrounding settlements? The most successful workers could never reach manager level since that was preserved for kibbutz members. The explanation was basic: since it was kibbutz capital which built the factory, it was only right for kibbutz members to manage the collective's property. Along with the disregard of socialist values, the tensions also overlapped the basic social data that the kibbutz members tended to be Ashkenazi, that they supported the Alignment overwhelmingly and had achieved positions of power and leadership in the Alignment, and hence in the country, above their proportion in the population, and that the workers in kibbutz factories were often Sephardi and Likud supporters.

The Likud was perceived as the party of the "Second Israel," the Jews from more "primitive" cultures, exotic music and spicy foods. They had been given so much by the state—education, housing, jobs—and yet they were basically ungrateful and, more than that, presented a serious threat to the continued strength of the state. Efforts at integration meant lower levels of schooling for the whole population. This brought about the popularization of mass culture and the weakening of the more ideological values of the past. Their social problems were associated with unruly behavior in the schools, on the buses and in the movie theaters, and now this was being expressed in the election campaign.

As in most social myths, there was some truth to these perceptions. Social problems were growing in Israel, the introduction of Sephardi at the highest level of social and economic élite groups was proceeding more slowly than full integration would require. Expressing the connection between myth and party almost openly accelerated the identification of the Ashkenazi with the Alignment and the Sephardi with the Likud. Yes, was the implication, Sephardi are violent, undemocratic, unsuited for governing. They must be defeated. Or, the other way: No! They have not learned the lesson, they have not changed. There, they are deciding who should be in which ministry, taking us for granted again. They'll use and exploit us as they always have. Besides, they can't even get along with each other.

The polarization was most evident in the campaign's rallies. The bases of support for Begin and the Likud overlapped: the young, Israeli-born, especially those of Asian and African origin, lower income and lower education groups supported him overwhelmingly. Peres and Alignment (and [Yitzhak] Rabin) support was centered in older, European, higher education and higher status groups. There was no important difference in the patterns of support between Peres and Rabin when running against Begin.

Begin's appeal to the crowd—some called it demagoguery—was as great as it had been during his fighting days in the opposition during the late forties and fifties. Calls of "Begin King of Israel" were widespread during the campaign, his supporters edging toward the frenzy of mass-hysteria frequent in other Middle Eastern settings. Peres' crowds were more polite, subdued—and smaller. Peres lacked the personal appeal which Begin enjoyed; an extraparty organization named Alef (Citizens for Peres) was set up to ensure his nomination and election by trying to improve his public image.

The tomatoes thrown at Peres during a Passover folk-festival of Moroccan Jews in Jerusalem was the first sign of violence in the campaign. It became fashionable to bait Peres among certain groups, almost like a seasonal sport. Whether the Likud actually had a hand in organizing the anti-Peres demonstrations (as the Alignment asserted) or not is beside the point; what is important is that the expression of anti-Peres feeling fed on deeply-held animosities and could easily be expanded much beyond the scope of the original group which began interfering at his rallies.

The reaction to the violence was immediate. It accelerated the "verbal violence" between the two parties which had already escalated in the campaign and it polarized the electorate along ethnic lines as never before. It made support for the small parties a luxury which many felt they could not afford since the elections were between two large forces. The stigmatization of the supporters of the Likud by the Alignment as unruly antidemocrats forced many—especially Sephardi—who had voted Likud in 1977, but were disappointed with its performance, to reconsider their decision. They saw in it a manifestation of the lengths to which the Alignment would go to regain (and by implication, to retain) power. They were offended by Peres' reference to "two cultures" (repeated by him in his stillborn victory speech on election night) which they took in an ethnic sense while he meant it in a political one.

The fear of being an embattled minority losing to the Sephardi hordes undoubtedly worked in the Alignment's favor. If the issue lost it some Sephardi votes, it won the Alignment many more Ashkenazi ones. It was also the first time in the long campaign that the Likud's momentum was broken. Everything had worked in the Likud's favor, from [Yoram] Aridor's economics to foreign policy crises such as the Syrian missiles in Lebanon,[2] Begin's verbal attacks on West Germany's Helmut Schmidt and the Israeli attack on the nuclear power installation in Baghdad. The Alignment floundered: its economic attacks were impotent and they were forced to play to Begin's strength in the field of foreign and security affairs. When the violent nature of the campaign became an issue working for the Alignment, its leaders exploited it to the full.

Israel had known violent political campaigns in the past and those familiar with Israel's education system, with the cases tried in its courts or even with Israel's soccer fans, know that violence is not unknown to this society. But instead of being an unpleasant feature of everyday life, in the 1981 campaign it became a focal issue. Partly because television is prohibited from showing candidates on the screen for the month prior to the elections, the television crews began covering the crowds. June was a hot month—and not only because it was summer.

Political Ideology

The heat of the campaign produced more noise than light. Policy questions were raised but the dominant tones of the election were the emotionally charged issues of Begin vs. Peres, democracy vs. fascism, political violence vs. political tolerance, continued progress with the Likud as opposed to going back to the old ways of the Alignment: the growers of the tomatoes against the throwers of tomatoes.

Because the positive pull of one party and the negative push of the other were so central to the 1981 elections, ideological differences between the parties were relegated to a secondary role. Of course, there is a basic sense in which all politics in Israel are ideological. Messages are packaged in ideological containers, code-words are frequently attached. The generation of political leadership active in the 1981 election campaign had grown up during the period when issues and phrases such as fascism, socialism, Revisionism and the basic values of the labor movement had intellectual content and emotional impact. For many of the voters in 1981, however, the ability of these words to evoke images of great events, men or battles or to arouse feelings of deep admiration or hatred, was limited. Yet the leadership persisted in its patterns of communication, talking of these things which meant little to most, as well as of the Holocaust and Zionism, which meant more to many.

The Israeli political system has the reputation of being ideological in character and indeed political communication is often presented in ideological terms. Policies are seen to flow from an overview of society and the nature of the Jewish state and it is important for political communicators to show how this action-oriented program fits in a general pattern of behavior and governing. Upon closer examination, however, it is clear that the style of political communication has overshadowed the importance of the substance. The public is conditioned to hear politicians explain, attack, plead or defend in ideological terms. One does not try to extend military control over parts of Lebanon or destroy Iraqi nuclear capacity, one prevents a holocaust for the Christians of Lebanon and the Jews of Israel, respectively. One does not merely oppose the Likud or try to win the elections, one tries to save the country from Revisionism and Beginism (a Peres phrase which seemed to be a cross between Khoumeinism and Fascism).

If ideology means a master-plan, a system of ideas based on social goals and phrased in terms of social and political action, then the campaign was non-ideological. In a campaign which saw the parties more competitive and the ethnic groups more polarized than ever before, it was not easy to mistake the elections as an ideological struggle over the nation's future. The 1981 elections centered on images and candidates, the frustrations of one ethnic group and the fears of the other.

There was no great debate in Israel over the future of the country or its policies in 1981. There was broad agreement—"national consensus" in the language of Israeli politics—regarding the continued existence of Israel as a Jewish state and with borders reaching from the Mediterranean to the Jordan. Only marginal groups consider pulling back to the pre-1967 borders or annexing all of them outright. In practical politics, the subtle variations between policies make all the difference, and it is basically on the tactics of holding on that the parties are divided. The Likud is not committed to the Camp David Accords [doc. 103] which provide for autonomy for the West Bank and Gaza populations, the Alignment to territorial concessions while the Jordan River is retained as a "defence border." Reality has forced the leaders of both parties to concentrate less on ideology and more on the tactics of continued security and existence.

There is no doubt about the fact that the country is moving to the right. When asked with which political tendency do you identify, more than a third say "right" today compared with 16 percent in 1969 and 8 percent in 1962. The "right" has become the largest single response category. But we must be careful not to mistake this with political ideology. While the "left-right" distinction is meaningful to most of the sample and widely used within the system, it is not a measure of ideology. What has happened in Israel is that the cues generated by the parties have become central in determining the left-right distribution, quite unrelated to attitudes or political ideology.

The literature on the subject would lead us to expect that as a society's ideological orientation shifts, so too should its positions on political issues. The fascinating finding about Israel is that, although the country has moved to the right politically, the distribution of attitudes on important matters has remained constant. Hardline stands on returning the territories are about as prevalent today as they were in 1969.

The picture is less static than it appears since changes have been taking place in the political context in which the question was asked. The 1973 question was asked before the Yom Kippur War, the 1981 question after most of Sinai had been returned. The samples are different and the distribution of responses is not identical. Still, what is striking is the relative stability of the attitude over time in the society. Ninety percent or more in both 1969 and 1981 favor returning none of the territories or only a small part.

This attitudinal stability even as the political continuum is moving to the right is even more astonishing since the population has not become more capitalistic in economic matters, as might be expected from the "right" label. Almost 60 percent favored socialism throughout the period. Government intervention is often decried and the economy has been liberalized, yet the movement to the right is not reflected in this important attitude. The stability of these attitudes over time forces us to consider the sense in which the system has changed.

What we have witnessed in Israel over the last few decades is a process of political change, not ideological change. The stability of attitudes and the shift of political power to the right has been made possible because ideology is not central to Israeli political life. The growth of the Likud and of the "right" must be understood as a reaction to the years of dominance of the Alignment and the "left." The terms are important as labels but not necessarily as instructors of ideological content. Likud means not only "right"—it also means non-Alignment and hence non-"left." High levels of response to the "left-right" question are artifacts of the passing of dominance and the emergence of competitiveness. The "right" and the Likud are increasing in strength over time and the "left" and Alignment are in decline. But when we look at the responses of only those who reported that they intend to vote for one of the two parties, the picture changes. Then the "right" and the Likud grow, but only the percentage of those who report they will vote Alignment is in decline. The portion of the Alignment voters who identify themselves as "left" is constant. The shrinkage of the "left" is a result of the decline of the Alignment; the growth of the "right" stems from the greater legitimacy and increasing power of the Likud.

That political labels should fill a function of veto by pointing out whom we want to avoid is not surprising to observers who know the nature of political communication in Israel. This function was filled by the "left" in the pre-state and early state era—the period of dominance—when the left was widely considered as the appropriate legitimate authority in the system. Now as that basic understanding is being overturned, the term "right" fills the role of identifying the bad guys (the "left") as much as it does of identifying the group with which one might wish to identify (the "right"). The prime motivator is the identification with one of the political parties; from that flows identification with one of the political labels. This in turn has been facilitated by the fact that the party system has become more competitive and less dominant.

The explanation for this topsy-turvy phenomenon is to be sought in Israel's political and social history. It was the parties of the left, and predominantly Ahdut Haavodah, and later Mapai, which developed the political institutions of the country and were instrumental in absorbing the immigrants who came later. If in Europe the leaders of socialism had to struggle to unite the workers to battle with the establishment of the right, in Israel the pattern was reversed. The establishment was of the left—and operated in the name of the workers. The newcomers were to be absorbed in existing socialist organizations; those who balked and tried to express their opposition to the establishment found a ready ally in the rightist Herut movement and the more centrist Liberal Party. The real proletariat of Israel was increasingly rejected by the establishment socialists and as their frustrations grew so too did their search for political outlets for their perceived deprivation.

That the growth of the "right" is a reaction to the "left" can be understood by contrasting the Israeli experience to that of Europe. In Europe, since the beginning of the century, the "left" worked and organized to replace the forces of the "right"—the establishment—in power. Now suppose that it is the "left" which is in power, which has privileged positions, which is associated with the faults of the existing system. The focus of identification for the outgroup in this case would be the "right" and not the "left." If we recall that these terms are relative, Israeli politics make much more sense. On May 5, 1789, the "left" emerged because the nobility took the place of honor to the King's right at the first joint meeting of the States-General in France, and the Third Estate was on the King's left. On July 20, 1981, the Likud was on the left of the Knesset chairman, because that provided better exposure to the television cameras covering the opening session of the Tenth Knesset. The Alignment, although members of the Socialist International, were on the chairman's right because the Likud had the majority in the committee that decided on such arrangements. Left and right in Israel are a product of the political party system and achieve their meaning by virtue of the parties and not from the ideological direction which they might provide.

Two factors which are closely related to the rise of the "right" are the political and demographic changes which have occurred in Israel since independence. Until 1967, Herut and Begin were ostracized by the Mapai establishment as being outside the system of consensus prior to the formation of the state. In 1967, in the period before the Six-Day War, Gahal (a combination of the Herut movement and the Liberal Party) joined the National Unity Government and Begin became a minister in the government of Israel. This legitimacy was enhanced by the fact that Gahal left the National Unity Government well before the 1973 Yom Kippur War which highlighted the process of decline of dominance of the Alignment. Not only were the political fortunes of the Likud and Begin picking up because the political fortunes of the Alignment were turning down, time was working in the Likud's favor. Twenty-five years after independence, a sizable portion of the electorate did not know of the stigma which Begin carried, let alone why. The intergroup fights of the past generation occupied older people and scholars but not the man on the street. His conceptual world of politics was different and with it the role of the "right" and the Likud.

The ascent of the right could be seen in the organizations of *both* parties. It was the Herut in the Likud and Rafi in the Alignment that were becoming dominant. The Liberal party and the other components of the Likud were hardly visible and certainly unimportant ideologically. In the Alignment, the dominant role of Mapai crumbled and the younger Rafi leaders (Peres, [Moshe] Dayan, [Yitzhak] Navon) became more influential. The ideological differences within the parties were often greater than those between parties.

Ethnic Polarization

The 1981 elections witnessed an unprecedented crystallization of ethnic differences in Israeli politics. There had always been undercurrents of ethnic politics in Israel's cacophonic symphony, but rather than remaining the counterpoint, in 1981 it became the dominant melody.

Every group develops rules of selection and rejection of members. Often-used criteria include race, religion, sex and—in the modern world—nationality. A group is partially defined by those who are excluded from its ranks. In the broadest sense, the most important ethnic difference in the Middle East as far as Israel is concerned is that between Jews and non-Jews. Jews are a small minority in the region, a majority in the state. Within the state, the non-Jewish groups (predominantly Arabs and Druse) are known in Israel as the "minorities"—a good example of a Hebrew concept with ideological loading. It is true that the Arabs and Druse are a numerical minority within the boundaries of pre–Six-Day War Israel of 1967; referring to them as minorities carries the clear political message that a Jewish state means a Jewish majority. Sometimes, though, it appears that this usage restricts the ability of the language to portray adequately their religious and cultural affinity to Arabs and Druse in the territories and in the neighboring countries.

When ethnic differences are discussed in Israel today, the likely connotation is to differences among Jewish groups and not between Jews and non-Jews. The major distinction among Jews is between Ashkenazi, who came to Israel from Europe and America, and Sephardi, who immigrated from countries of Asia and Africa. Scholars would find this distinction too simplistic and they would demand that finer distinctions be introduced. But for our purposes this basis distinction will suffice; it is popularly used in Israel and the Central Bureau of Statistics reports data based on place of birth and father's place of birth. There is a very high correlation between the European-American born and Ashkenazi and the Asian-African born and Sephardi. The original distinction between the groups relates to the patterns of sojourning of the various communities following different expulsions throughout history, but a useful gauge is the indigenous language once spoken in the community—Yiddish in the case of the Ashkenazi, Ladino by the Sephardi. This measure is only approximate since southern European Jews often spoke Ladino and not Yiddish and the Yemenites spoke neither.

Demographics

As our concern is with politics in Israel today and not with a definitive delineation of the various ethnic groups in Israel, we will not delve into the fascinating topic of intra-ethnic differences within the Jewish community. Suffice it to say that the differences between Iraqi and Moroccan Jews (both Sephardi) are as great or greater than the differences between Russian and German Jews (both Ashkenazi). The more recent interaction of these Jews with their host country varied their common heritage as Sephardi or Ashkenazi just as a more distant history varied the common heritage shared by all Jews as they were developing the rituals, traditions and language shared only by Ashkenazi or Sephardi.

For our discussion, these basic data are needed:

1. Jews constitute about 84 percent of Israel's population, Arabs and Druse living within the pre-1967 borders and in Jerusalem—but excluding those living in areas under Israeli military jurisdiction—make up the other 16 percent.
2. Of the fourteen and a half million Jews in the world, some 22 percent live in Israel. About 85 percent of the world's Jews are Ashkenazi, the other 15 percent Sephardi. About 10 percent of the world's Ashkenazi live in Israel compared with about two-thirds of the Sephardi. The Sephardi, however, make up about 55 percent of Israel's Jewish population, and the Ashkenazi about 45 percent.
3. The composition of the two ethnic groups in terms of place of birth is different. Of Israel's 3.2 million Jews at the beginning of 1981, more than 800,000 were born in Europe and America, almost 650,000 in Asia and Africa. The number of Israeli-born whose fathers were born in Europe and America was a little over 525,000, whereas the Israeli-born of Asian and African-born fathers numbered more than 800,000. An additional half million were born in Israel of fathers who were also born in Israel. At this stage of Israel's development—but not in fifteen or twenty years—it is safe to conclude that most of the last group are Ashkenazi, reflecting their earlier arrival in the country.
4. The reproduction rates of the various ethnic groups are also different, although increasingly less so.[3] The gross reproduction rate of Jewish mothers born in Asia and Africa was 1.48 in 1979 compared with 2.04 in 1969; for European and American born Jewish mothers it was 1.30 in 1979 compared with 1.32 in 1969. Part of this change is caused by the fact that the foreign-born population of both ethnic groups is aging and the largest fertile group now tends to be the Israeli-born. That group's rate has fallen too, from 1.43 in 1969 to 1.33 in 1979.[4]
5. Because the age structure and the growth rates of the groups differ, the impact on the political system through the composition of the electorate is not identical. European-American-born voters and their Israeli-born children comprised a majority of the electorate in 1981, as they did in past elections, but it is clear that they will soon be smaller in number than the Asian-African voters and their Israeli-born voting children. We have seen that the latter group is already a majority of the Jewish population and that their growth rates are higher than the Europeans'. In the 1981 elections the Ashkenazi had a voting potential of 52 Knesset seats, the Sephardi 48. The shrinking of the Ashkenazi base is evident when compared with their potential in the 1969 elections; 59 for the Ashkenazi, 43 for the Sephardi. The potential of the Sephardi will be more fully realized when their children who are under voting age (53.7 percent of the Asian-African children, 35.8 percent for the European-American children) begin voting, and when the Ashkenazi, who tend to be older and who have fewer children, make up an increasingly smaller percentage of the electorate. (Arabs and Druse constitute 10 percent of the electorate.)
6. Projecting these figures into the future and thereby calculating the composition of the electorate is risky since the population of Israel has known great fluctuations in the past and is likely to do so in the future. Israel is a country whose past was largely determined by immigrants and whose ideology is still based on the central concept of gathering in the exiled Jews of the world. The Jewish population in 1948 was made up of a little more than a third Israel-born; in 1980, about 55 percent were Israel-born. Population change in Israel is not simply a matter of fertility rates and life expectancies but is also determined directly by immigration—and of course by emigration.
7. Although we have stressed the importance of ethnic polarization in the 1981 elections,

the impression that this will be an important factor in future elections must be avoided. Much of Israel's future political life will turn on this very factor. At this point in the analysis it is important to stress that there is no deterministic force at work making it inevitable that ethnic differences will again be as salient in the future as they were in the 1981 elections. Things may be very different when the "desert generation" of Jews who immigrated to the country will no longer be dominant numerically, culturally and politically, and a new Israel-born generation emerges. The language gauge used before probably allows us a glimpse of the future: the young Israel-born generation speaks neither Yiddish nor Ladino (or Arabic)—all speak Hebrew.

Measures of ethnic integration abound but one will suffice. The rates of Jews marrying across ethnic lines rose from 12 percent in 1955 to 20 percent in 1978. Not only that, but the social acceptability of the behavior increased in the sense that the rates of inter-ethnic marriage of both grooms and brides became more nearly equal. In 1955 a little over a third of the marriages were between a groom from Asia-Africa and a European-American bride, with two-thirds the reverse pattern. In 1978 the Asian-African groom and the European-American bride combination accounted for almost half of the marriages, the reverse combination the other half. The fact that the two types of marriage are equally prevalent points to the increasing social acceptability of inter-ethnic Jewish marriages in Israel since, while both types of marriage are on the rise, it is the marriage of the high-status bride (European-American) with the lower-status groom (Asian-African) which is increasing faster.

The Political Dimension

The 1981 elections witnessed the two major parties clearly identified with ethnic groups—the Alignment with the Ashkenazi and the Likud with the Sephardi. This correlation with electoral behavior became more pronounced than in the past, although the general pattern was not a new one.

The Alignment had enjoyed the role of dominant party in the political system which it had founded and shaped. It was the major political force in the 1920s, in those early formative years of the British Mandate, when the major political institutions of the country, such as the Histadrut (the General Federation of Labor), were developed. Its leadership spoke for the young pioneers, newly arrived from Eastern Europe, anxious to fulfill the Zionist dream under very difficult economic and physical conditions. By the time the larger waves of immigration began coming in the period before the Second World War and immediately after the proclamation of independence, the forebears of the Labor party were firmly in position as leaders of the state soon to be proclaimed.

During this period Mapai (later Labor) and the Histadrut which it controlled, filled many functions and provided many services generally provided for by the modern state. Defense, education, housing, employment, culture, health, manufacturing and sport, among others, were activities which were sponsored and/or controlled by the party. It is no wonder then that new immigrants were often caught up in the web of the party. There may be no similar experience in a normal adult's life parallel to the dependency encountered after immigration to a foreign country. Certain features may ameliorate that dependency: for example, if the same language is spoken as in the home country or if one intermingles exclusively with compatriots from the country of origin. To be sure, some immigrants to Israel continued to speak German, Yiddish, English or Arabic and avoided some of the culture-shock of the new society. But for those who were forced to deal with the new reality, some special footing in the system was always helpful. Being affiliated with one of the parties was often such a footing and, since it was the biggest and most powerful of the parties, Mapai was successful in recruiting the largest number of immigrants.

Recruiting meant winning voters. The leaders of the labor movement realized that the ultimate test of their appeal was at the polls. The legitimacy accorded them by independence and sovereignty aided them mightily and some new immigrants could not easily distinguish between the state, the army, the party and Ben-Gurion.

The Irgun Zvai Leumi, the militia headed by Begin which later formed the core of the Herut Movement, was stigmatized as being an underground organization, outside the structure of the national institutions headed by Mapai. This was ironic since the activities of the Haganah and Palmah were equally illegal from the British point of view, but the power to define legitimate and illegitimate was held by the leaders of Mapai. Ben-Gurion placed them in the company of the other ostracized group when he declared that all parties were candidates for his coalition government except the Communists and Herut.

Mapai proved itself a model "party of democratic integration" by being flexible enough to attract large groups of voters and their leaders through changes in government and party policy and by revising ideological planks in its platform. It carried a large number of European votes since many of them had been oriented in youth groups abroad to the leadership and institutional arrangements which Mapai developed. Many of the new immigrant groups from non-European countries also supported Mapai for organizational, ideological and pragmatic reasons.

The important point to stress is that while an increasingly large share of the electorate was of Sephardi origin, Mapai maintained its dominant role as the largest plurality party and the leader of every government coalition. More than that, attempts to appeal to the Sephardi population at election time by lists set up by Sephardi themselves, largely failed. It was only before the mass immigration of the early fifties that representation to the Knesset was achieved by lists manifestly linking themselves with the Sephardi and Yemenites.

The point that must be clearly made was that neither of Israel's major political parties in 1981 was ethnic in the sense that neither had organized politically in order to further specific ethnic ends. The electoral support of both parties was largely ethnic-related, but that is another matter entirely. Both the Alignment and the Likud were run by Ashkenazi, as had always been the case with most parties in Israel. While the appeal to the ethnic vote characterized the 1981 elections, and the social bases of political support were more closely related to ethnicity than ever, the parties themselves were not ethnic.

In fact, the Alignment tried to deal with its problem of lacking appeal among Sephardi voters by placing Sephardi in places assured of election on its list. By any mechanical measure of representation, the Alignment did this more successfully than did the Likud. Of the members of Knesset elected by the two parties, the Alignment had fourteen Sephardi, the Likud nine. Both parties were led by men born in Poland, but both put Sephardi in the number-two slot. The Alignment had a Sephardi woman, Shoshanah Arbeli-Almozlino, as its number two on its list. She was born in Iraq and had been a very effective parliamentarian in the outgoing Knesset. The Likud made David Levi number-two. Minister of Housing and Immigrant Absorption and the Likud's candidate to head the Histadrut, Levi was born in Morocco and lived in Beit-Shean, a development town in northern Israel which is beset by many of the social and economic problems with which the underprivileged population must contend.

The Alignment may have been helped by having Arbeli-Almozlino in second place; the Likud was certainly not harmed by making Levi prominent. Everyone knows that the second place on the list has symbolic value only and no one thought that it promised anything about power or succession. In general, representation was not the issue. When asked what group you wanted to see better represented in the party list for which you intend to vote, only 11 percent mentioned an ethnic group while 34 percent wanted younger people, fresh faces. The Likud enjoyed the more favorable image; the number of its Sephardi candidates was irrelevant to the issue.

In the 1981 elections the term "ethnic party" was used often. It was supposed to portray the support of the Jews from Asian and African countries and their children for the Likud. The fact is that the Alignment was closer to being an "ethnic party" than was the Likud. The larger concentration of voters by ethnicity was to be found in the Alignment, with some 70 percent of its voters Ashkenazi. The percentage of the Likud voters who were Sephardi was 65. This had not always been the case. When dominant, the Alignment was heavily supported by Ashkenazi, but Sephardi also often voted for the Alignment. The bulk of the Likud's support also came from Ashkenazi in the past; after all, the Ashkenazi comprised a majority of the electorate. The Likud was set up in the seventies; its constituent parties in the fifties and sixties, the Herut Movement and the Liberal party, drew from either end of the social and ethnic spectrum. Herut was heavily supported by lower-class Sephardi, the Liberals by upper-class Ashkenazi.

Polls going back to the late 1960s indicate that then too about 70 percent of the Alignment vote was from Ashkenazi. What has been changing on the political map of Israel is the ethnic composition of the Likud vote and the relative size of the two parties. In the late sixties both parties were predominantly Ashkenazi; by 1981 the Alignment had stayed that way and the Likud had become predominantly Sephardi. The turning point seems to have occurred in 1977 when a majority of the Likud vote was Sephardi for the first time. Couple this with the growth of the Sephardi electorate and the abandonment of the Alignment by many Ashkenazi in favor of the DMC in 1977, and the enormity of the Alignment's problem becomes clearer. The period of incubation of the bitterness and frustrations felt against the ruling Alignment ended before the 1977 elections and expressed itself in the vote. In 1981 the Sephardi continued in their alienation from the Alignment; many Ashkenazi who had deserted in 1977 returned.

We have described the contribution of each ethnic group to the two parties, and have found that the portion of the Ashkenazi in the Alignment electorate had been high and consistent regardless of the fluctuations in the size of the Alignment vote, and that the Sephardi as a portion of the Likud vote has been growing and was, in 1981, slightly lower than the Ashkenazi portion of the Alignment vote. By turning the question around and asking how members of the two ethnic groups divided their votes in 1981 between the two large parties we get a mirror-image answer. About 60 percent of Ashkenazi voted Alignment, about 30 percent Likud. About 60 percent Sephardi voted Likud, about 30 percent Alignment.

The fortunes of the Likud and the misfortunes of the Alignment are evident along generational lines as well as the ethnic and demographic ones. The Likud does even better among the second generation of Sephardi than it does in the first. The Alignment's support is greater among Ashkenazi who immigrated than among their children who were born in Israel. The Likud has gained most in those groups which are youngest and growing fastest; the Alignment—gradually losing support within all groups—does best in that group which is oldest and shrinking most rapidly.

Neither the Likud nor the Alignment were "ethnic parties" in 1981. Neither of them organized along ethnic lines or carried an overt ethnic message. Almost a third of the "wrong" ethnic group voted for each party.

The Tami Phenomenon

There was one ethnic list in 1981 that was successful. That was Tami, former Minister of Religions Aharon Abuhazeira's party, which won three Knesset seats. Abuhazeira had been cleared of charges of bribery soon before the election and split from the National Religious Party [NRP] on the grounds that Sephardi were not adequately represented in the NRP and the other political parties. Abuhazeira managed to recruit a former Agriculture Minister from the Alignment, Aharon Uzan, who relinquished his place on the Alignment list in order to run on Tami's. Together with other leaders, they presented a Sephardi list with special appeal to Moroccan voters. The Moroccan Jews are the largest Sephardi group in the country and are disproportionally concentrated in its lower classes. The Moroccans who arrived in Israel in the early 1950s did not come as a complete community since many of the leadership preferred to emigrate to France. Unlike the Iraqi community which arrived with its political, economic and cultural leadership intact, the Moroccans were the slowest in achieving higher status and positions of influence. Lacking any other identifiable leadership, and with lower levels of skill, education and resources than other groups, some voters were receptive to Tami's arguments. Abuhazeira also capitalized on his being a scion of a prominent rabbinical family in Morocco and so for some his political plea turned into a religious appeal as well.

The emergence of lists trying to tap ethnic resentment is not new; what was special was its partial success in 1981 and its appearance during a campaign charged with ethnic tension. Tami's 45,000 votes were the clearest, most authentic expression of ethnic political organization to have appeared in these elections. But its appeal must also be measured against previous efforts. In the past two elections, ethnic lists had competed and, while they did not win representation, they came close. In 1973, the Black Panthers and Avner Shaki's list, which split from the NRP, received almost 25,000 votes between them and in 1977, [Mordechai] Ben-Porat's list (an Iraqi who was number two on Dayan's list in 1981) won almost 15,000 votes. With ethnic representation becoming more prevalent in the major parties, the likelihood of great success for ethnic lists in the future seems small. Despite Tami's gains, the rule remains that most voters—both Sephardi and Ashkenazi—tend to support the mainstream national lists.

Conclusion

The 1981 election results reflected deeper social processes. One of the most important of these was the clear emergence of social class politics in Israel. Ethnic polarization was the outward expression of the unrealized expectations of many Sephardi who had aspired to, and reached, the middle class but were stymied in their mobility, and the reaction of the Ashkenazi who were fearful that their privileged status was in jeopardy. It is fashionable to discuss the ethnic problem as if its focus was in the development towns of Israel and the underprivileged neighbourhoods of the big cities, but the statistical fact is that the Jews living in these places constitute a minority of the Sephardi community. Their problems are most acute and therefore most visible, but the bulk of the Sephardi voters have achieved middle to high levels of education and income to an extent greater than the stereotype of the slum-dweller permits. The feeling that the Alignment's vision of society meant the continued domination of Ashkenazi and the continued relegation of Sephardi to secondary levels of management, status and power, was as important a reason as any other for the massive support of the Likud by the Sephardi.

Another pressing issue, barely mentioned in the campaign, is the fundamental justification and goal of the State of Israel. Many Ashkenazi tend to accept the vision of Israel as a modern, liberal, Western state. The continued domination over a vast Arab population in the territories presents a problem for holders of this view. Another way of conceiving the Jewish state is that its legitimacy stems from basically religious sources. Whether God-given or not, the ties between the people, its history and the land are ultimately a matter of belief and therefore differ basically from the rationalist model of the modern state. Many Sephardi, who tend to be more traditional, respond to the logic of the religion-sanctioned state. Begin utilizes the symbols and language of religion masterfully; the Alignment, while attacking the religious parties and their disproportionate gains through coalition bargaining, appeared at times to be anti-religious.

Ethnicity is an extremely important factor in Israeli political life today, but its centrality is likely to prove transitory. Much more crucial in the long run are social cleavages based on class differences and divisions concerned with religion and religiosity. One of the reasons that the 1981 elections were so violent and polarized was that these cleavages overlapped. The upper-class secularist—who also tended to be Ashkenazi—voted Alignment. The lower-class traditionalist—who also tended to be Sephardi—voted Likud. The fact that these dimensions laced together accelerated the effect of each of them. Ethnicity will remain a central issue as long as the overlapping exists. But if the Alignment's practices and image change, and significant groups of the Sephardi community perceive it to be open to Sephardi leaders, aspirations and demands, the tension of the ethnic element will lessen in Israeli politics. But if the growing Sephardi population does not perceive such a change on the part of the Alignment, the Likud's fortunes are likely to continue to grow. It is useless to speculate here what effects changes of leadership in either party, international crises, massive immigration—to name but a few—might have on the equation. What is important to stress is that ethnic polarization is the symptom of a more fundamental cleavage within the Israeli society and polity.

There is an ideological consensus within Israeli society clearly establishing the norm of equality for all Jews as a direct extension of the notion of "gathering in the exiles." Ethnic political organization does not conform to this norm. There is of course no similar consensus regarding religion. That religious groups have organized politically and have always been successful in gaining at least some of their demands by being partners in the government coalitions has meant that the religious cleavage has been cushioned by being part of the legitimized struggle for power through the electoral and coalition processes. Organizing politically over ethnic differences, in contrast, has never been legitimized in the sense that most efforts have been unsuccessful. The norm being unity, the evidence of ethnic polarization in the 1981 elections was shocking. The unsettling—and even dangerous—features of the emergence of ethnicity is that it correlates so strongly with other indicators of social mobility. As long as the Alignment is perceived as denying opportunities for continued social advancement, the growing Sephardi community is unlikely to vote for it.

The Alignment did not use the power bases in its control—the Histadrut, the kibbutzim, the Sick Fund, the workers' councils—to restore its image as a worker's party. On the contrary, its elitist, Ashkenazi image was augmented over the years. The Likud benefited from the Alignment's stagnation, in part because of its popular policies, in part because of Begin's appeal.

The Likud capitalized on the Alignment's internal divisions and establishment image. As it becomes more comfortable in government power, the demands made on it are likely to grow. Simply castigating the Alignment's failures will no longer be enough. It must develop policies and a second generation of leadership equal to the expectations of the growing Sephardi electorate without alienating the large number of Ashkenazi who support it. The Likud will enjoy many of the advantages—and be exposed to the political dangers—which they won at the polls.

NOTES

1. Soon after the elections, Shulamit Aloni joined the Alignment, making the size of the Knesset delegations of the two largest groups equal (Arian's note).

2. In the spring of 1981 Syria placed sophisticated Soviet missiles in Lebanon. Israel considered this move provocative and a danger to its security and threatened a preemptive strike against these sites if Syria did not unilaterally remove the missiles. The United States restrained Israel from this move. Nevertheless, the situation in Lebanon deteriorated (see headnote to doc. 109).

3. The gross reproduction rate is the number of females born, per woman, given the age-specific fertility rates of the population. It is thus a measure of the extent to which a population reproduces itself.

4. The gross reproduction rates of the non-Jews is much higher, but it, too, is falling. For Muslim mothers it was 4.36 in 1969 and 3.22 in 1979; for Druze 3.59 in 1969 and 3.14 in 1979 (Arian's note).

Foreign Policy Issues

86

United Nations Security Council

Resolution 338

October 22, 1973

Israel's foreign relations following 1973 were dominated by the impact and consequences of the Yom Kippur (1973) War, primarily by the inauguration of the "peace process"—the efforts to settle the Arab-Israeli conflict through political means. Negotiations began with the agreements terminating the war itself. The following series of documents records the transition from the military hostilities to the process of peace-making.

On October 22, 1973, the United Nations Security Council adopted Resolution 338, which was based on the joint U.S.-Soviet draft proposal.

The Security Council,

1. *Calls upon* all parties to the present fighting to cease all firing and terminate all military activity immediately, no later than 12 hours after the moment of the adoption of this decision, in the positions they now occupy;

2. *Calls upon* the parties concerned to start immediately after the cease-fire the implementation of Security Council resolution 242 (1967) [doc. 68] in all of its parts;

3. *Decides that,* immediately and concurrently with the cease-fire, negotiations start between the parties concerned under appropriate auspices aimed at establishing a just and durable peace in the Middle East.

Source: United Nations, Official Documents System of the United Nations, http://daccessdds.un.org/doc/RESOLUTION/GEN/NRO/288/65/IMG/NRO28865.pdf.

87

Israeli Cabinet

Decision to Accept Resolution 338

October 22, 1973

Israel immediately accepted the draft proposal for U.N. Security Council Resolution 338 (doc. 86), and on the same day U.S. Secretary of State Henry Kissinger conferred with the Israeli prime minister and senior ministers, explaining the background for the resolution. Discussions resulted in the cease-fires of October 22 and 24 with Syria and Egypt respectively.

At its meeting this morning (Monday), the cabinet decided unanimously to accept the proposal of the U.S. government and President Nixon and to announce its readiness to agree to a cease-fire in accordance with the Security Council resolution following the joint U.S.-Soviet draft proposal.

Under the terms of this proposed resolution, the military forces will remain in the positions they occupy upon the coming into effect of the cease-fire. Israel will insist on an exchange of prisoners.

The implementation of the cease-fire is conditional upon reciprocity.

The cabinet decision will be brought to the notice of the Foreign Affairs and Defense Committee and of the Knesset. . . .

With regard to paragraph 2 of the proposed resolution [doc. 86], the cabinet has decided to instruct Israel's representative at the United Nations to include in his address to the Security Council a passage clarifying that Israel's agreement to this paragraph is given in the meaning defined by Israel when she decided, in August 1970, to accept the initiative of the U.S. government regarding the cease-fire as notified to the United Nations on August 4, 1970, and as announced by the prime minister, Mrs. Golda Meir, in the Knesset on the same date.

The minister of defense and the chief of staff reported on the situation on the battlefronts.

At 4 P.M. the government issued the following statement:

> The Government of Israel has been informed that the Government of Egypt has instructed the armed forced of Egypt to cease hostilities in accordance with the Security Council Resolution concerning the cease-fire.
>
> Following upon this, the Government of Israel has issued orders to the Israel Defense Forces on the Egyptian front to stop firing at 1850 hours Israel time today, October 22, provided it is confirmed that the Egyptians have indeed ceased hostilities.

Source: Meron Medzini, ed., *Israel's Foreign Relations: Selected Documents, 1947–74* (Jerusalem: Ministry of Foreign Affairs, 1976), 2:1053. Reprinted by permission of the director general, Ministry of Foreign Affairs, Jerusalem.

88

The Six-Point Agreement between Egypt and Israel

November 11, 1973

The cease-fire with Egypt left the Egyptian Third Army in the Sinai Peninsula completely surrounded by Israeli troops on the western bank of the Suez Canal. The Six-Point Agreement of November 11, 1973, reached through Henry Kissinger's mediation, was signed by Israeli and Egyptian military officers at Kilometer 101 on the Cairo-Suez road. It regulated some of the immediate problems threatening to undermine the fragile cease-fire.

---

1. Egypt and Israel agree to observe scrupulously the cease-fire called for by the U.N. Security Council.

2. Both sides agree that discussions between them will begin immediately to settle the question of the return to the October 22 positions in the framework of agreement on the disengagement and separation of forces under the auspices of the United Nations.

3. The town of Suez will receive daily supplies of food, water, and medicines. All wounded civilians in the town of Suez will be evacuated.

4. There shall be no impediment to the movement of nonmilitary supplies to the east bank of the Suez Canal.

5. The Israeli checkpoints on the Cairo-Suez road will be replaced by U.N. checkpoints. At the Suez end of the road, Israeli officers can participate with the U.N. in supervising the nonmilitary nature of the cargo at the bank of the Canal.

6. As soon as the U.N. checkpoints are established on the Cairo-Suez road, there will be an exchange of all prisoners of war, including wounded.

Source: Meron Medzini, ed., *Israel's Foreign Relations: Selected Documents, 1947–74* (Jerusalem: Ministry of Foreign Affairs, 1976), 2:1067. Reprinted by permission of the director general, Ministry of Foreign Affairs, Jerusalem.

89

League of Arab States

Sixth Arab Summit Conference, Algiers, Overview and Resolutions

November 28, 1973

The Sixth Arab Summit Conference, which met in Algiers in November 1973, formulated the new Arab consensus on the terms for a settlement of the Arab-Israeli conflict. This meeting enabled Egypt and Syria to sign the disengagement agreements of 1974, which led to troop withdrawals from the borders. Included with the official published text of the November 1973 summit meeting of the Arab League are the unpublished "secret" resolutions as they were reported in the Arabic-language Beirut newspaper, Al-Nahar.

The Arab world is passing through a decisive stage in its history. The struggle against Zionist invasion is a long-term historic responsibility which will require still further trials and sacrifices.

While the war of October 1973 showed the Arab nation's determination to liberate its occupied territories at all cost, the cease-fire in the field means in no way that the struggle has ended and that there can be imposed upon the Arab nation a solution not meeting its just goals.

So long as the causes of the war of aggression and expansion, which put the world on the edge of a generalized conflict, are not eliminated, there will be in the Middle East neither a lasting peace nor true security.

The October War, like those that took place earlier, is an unavoidable consequence of the policy of aggression and *fait accompli* pursued by Israel in defiance of principles and decisions by international organizations and of the law of nations. Since the spoliation of the Palestinian people and its expulsion from its fatherland, Israel has not ceased expanding, taking advantage of the active complicity and economic, technological and military support of the imperialist countries and above all of the United States.

This collusion came to light recently in the mobilization of unprecedented financial and material means, a massive use of specialized mercenaries and the unleashing of a political campaign pursued in union by all the enemies of the Third World's emancipation.

Beyond its policy of war and territorial expansion, Israel also aims, in the framework of the imperialist strategy, at destroying all the possibilities of development by the peoples in the area. At this juncture, marked by the rise of the movements of national liberation and decolonization, Zionism thus appears as a serious resurgence of the colonial system and its methods of domination and economic exploitation.

In spite of the complicity binding Israel and international imperialism, which puts at its disposal the most refined means for the pursuit of its aggressive designs, the Arab nation has never abandoned its national goals nor has it backed down before the imperatives of its

Source: Meron Medzini, ed., *Israel's Foreign Relations: Selected Documents, 1947–74* (Jerusalem: Ministry of Foreign Affairs, 1976), 2:1074–81. Reprinted by permission of the director general, Ministry of Foreign Affairs, Jerusalem.

struggle. Far from weakening its national will, the setback and trials have only stimulated and strengthened it.

In October 1973, the Egyptian and Syrian armed forces, together with the Palestinian resistance supported by other Arab forces, inflicted severe blows on the Israeli aggressors.

The Arab peoples and their governments gained in this fight a sharp awareness of their responsibilities and their material and human means. This awareness resulted in practical solidarity which showed its efficiency and which forms a new dimension in the process of Arab liberation.

The expansionist character of Israel policy has become clear to all. Israel's alleged friendship with the African peoples has been unmasked and alone in Africa, the colonialist and racist regimes of South Africa, Rhodesia, and Portugal lend it their support.

Israel's policy has likewise been openly condemned by other nonaligned nations.

The diplomatic isolation of Israel has today become a reality. It is significant in this respect that certain European governments, which traditionally have been won over to the Israeli viewpoint, are beginning to wonder about the foundations of an adventurous policy which has raised grave risks for international peace and cooperation.

The cease-fire, put into force more than a month ago, still keeps running into the Israeli side's manoeuvers and obstruction.

The cease-fire is not yet peace and peace presupposes, if it is to be achieved, a certain number of conditions. Among these are two which are paramount and unchangeable: (1) Evacuation by Israel of the occupied Arab territories and first of all Jerusalem; (2) reestablishment of full national rights for the Palestinian people.

So long as these two conditions have not been met, it will be illusory to expect in the Middle East anything but a continuation of unstable and explosive situations and new confrontations.

There is no doubt that the Arab nation will never agree to engage its future in an equivocal way with the sole basis being vague promises and secret dealings. . . .

Peace can be achieved only in full light, far from all manoeuvers and scheming and on the basis of the principles spelled out in this declaration. Thus the Arab countries, kings and chiefs of state believe that any serious and constructive coordination of their policies must take place on this basis.

If the conditions of a just peace are not available and if the Arab efforts in favour of peace run into refusal from Israel and its allies, the Arab countries will be forced to draw all the consequences and to continue, in the long-term perspective, their liberation struggle by all means and in all fields.

Determined to accomplish its duty, ready for sacrifices and abnegation, the Arab nation will not cease intensifying its struggle.

Secret Resolutions of the Algiers Summit Conference

The Current Goals of the Arab Nation

The conference resolves that the goals of the current phase of the common Arab struggle are:

1. The complete liberation of all the Arab territories conquered during the aggression of June 1967, with no concession or abandonment of any part of them, or detriment to national sovereignty over them.
2. Liberation of the Arab city of Jerusalem, and rejection of any situation that may be harmful to complete Arab sovereignty over the Holy City.
3. Commitment to restoration of the national rights of the Palestinian people, according to the decisions of the Palestine Liberation Organization, as the sole representative of the Palestine nation. (The Hashemite Kingdom of Jordan expressed reservations.)

4. The Palestine problem is the affair of all the Arabs, and no Arab party can possibly dissociate itself from this commitment, in the light of the resolutions of previous summit conferences.

Military

In view of the continuation of the struggle against the enemy until the goals of our nation are attained, the liberation of the occupied territories and the restoration of the national rights of the Palestinian people, the conference resolves:

1. Solidarity of all the Arab States with Egypt, Syria and the Palestinian nation, in the common struggle for attainment of the just goals of the Arabs.
2. Provision of all means of military and financial support to both fronts—Egyptian and Syrian—to strengthen their military capacity for embarking on the liberation campaign and standing fast in face of the tremendous amount of supplies and unlimited aid received by the enemy.
3. Support of Palestinian resistance by all possible measures, to ensure its active role in the campaign.

Economic

Considering the significance of the economy in the campaign against the enemy and the need to use every weapon at the disposal of the Arabs, as well as to concentrate all resources to enhance fighting capacity, the conference resolves:

1. To strengthen economic ties among the Arab states, and empower the Arab Economic Council to set up a plan of operations to that end.
2. To continue the use of oil as a weapon in the campaign, in view of the resolutions of the oil ministers and the link between the revocation of the ban on oil exports to any country and the commitment of that country to support the just cause of the Arabs. To establish a committee, subordinate to the oil Ministers, which will follow up the implementation of these resolutions and those of the oil ministers with regard to the percentage of the cut in oil supply, so as to arrive at coordination between this committee and the committee of Foreign ministers of the oil-producing countries in respect of the development of the positions of other countries vis-à-vis the Arab cause.
3. To strengthen, as is vital, the steadfast attitude within the occupied territories, and assure it.
4. To make good war-damages of the Arab states, and to heighten the spirit of struggle and the combat capacity of the countries involved in the confrontation.

Political

Political activity complements the military campaign, and is regarded as its continuation, all as part of our struggle against the enemy. As a direct result of the positions of foreign states toward the just struggle of the Arabs, the Conference resolves:

1. In Africa (a) to strengthen Arab-African cooperation in political affairs and enlarge Arab diplomatic representation in Africa; (b) to sever all the diplomatic, consular, economic, cultural and other relations with South Africa, Portugal and Rhodesia of those Arab states which have not yet done so.

90

William B. Quandt

Egyptian-Israeli Disengagement

December 1973–January 1974: Analysis

Following the Yom Kippur War, Egypt and Israel negotiated this separation-of-forces agreement. Though signed after the two-day Geneva Middle East Peace Conference in December 1973, much of the agreement's detail had been previously negotiated between Egyptian and Israeli generals (doc. 88). U.S. Secretary of State Henry Kissinger and Egyptian President Anwar Sadat wanted a public conference from which would flow an Israeli-Egyptian agreement. Kissinger wanted to demonstrate American dominance in Arab-Israeli negotiations, leaving the Soviet Union on the sideline; Sadat wanted a public conference to show to the Arab world that he was not undertaking a unilateral Arab policy of negotiating separate Egyptian interests with the Israelis. Syria stayed away from the conference because it believed the conference to be nothing more than a show for Egypt's interests; Jordan naively attended the conference, hoping that an Israeli-Jordanian disengagement agreement would be negotiated for the West Bank. The Geneva Conference provided the fig leaf that Sadat required. From it flowed military and political committee talks, but they, too, were only symbolic diplomatic mechanisms; the real negotiations were carried out by Kissinger in conjunction with Sadat and Israeli Prime Minister Golda Meir.

William B. Quandt, a senior fellow in the Foreign Policy Studies program at the Brookings Institution, participated in the policymaking process as a member of the National Security Council staff in both the Nixon and the Carter administrations.

Having successfully convened the Geneva conference, [Henry] Kissinger now faced the challenge of producing early results on the Egyptian-Israeli front. Several related problems stood in his way. The Syrians were on a high level of military alert in late December, and a resumption of fighting seemed possible. The oil embargo was continuing, and, equally important, the Organization of Petroleum Exporting Countries (OPEC) had decided to double oil prices on December 23. The fact that the shah of Iran played the leading role in the price rise did not make it any more palatable. More than ever, the energy crisis hung over the Arab-Israeli negotiations.

Apart from difficulties with Syria and the frustration of the continuing oil embargo, Kissinger had to confront again the fact that the positions of Egypt and Israel on disengagement were still far apart. In Israel on December 17 he had discussed disengagement with [Golda] Meir and her top aides. The Israeli

Source: William B. Quandt, *Peace Process: American Diplomacy and the Arab-Israeli Conflict since 1967* (Washington, D.C., and Berkeley, Calif.: Brookings Institution and University of California Press, 1993), pp. 197–200. Reprinted with permission.

position was that a small Egyptian force would be allowed to remain on the east bank of the canal up to a distance of ten kilometers. A lightly armed Israeli force would control the main north-south road beyond the Egyptian forces, and the Israeli main forces would be stationed east of the Mitla and Giddi passes, beyond Egyptian artillery range. Israel would not yield the passes in the disengagement phase. On other points there was less Israeli consensus. Some cabinet members felt Egypt should end the state of belligerency in return for the pullback of Israeli forces and should allow free passage for Israeli ships in the Suez Canal and at Bab al-Mandab. Some limits on Egyptian forces on both banks of the Suez Canal were also desired. Egypt should begin work on reopening the canal and rebuilding cities along it as a sign of peaceful intentions.

Egypt's position, as conveyed to Kissinger during his pre-Geneva talks in Cairo, began with the proposition that neither Egypt nor Israel should gain military advantage in the disengagement phase. In other words, any force limits would have to be mutual, as [Abdel Ghana] Gamasy had insisted at Kilometer 101 in November. Egypt would keep its forces east of the canal on existing lines in numbers not to exceed two divisions, a reduction of three divisions from current levels. No heavy artillery and no surface-to-air missiles would be placed across the canal. Israel would retain control of the eastern ends of the passes. A demilitarized zone would be established between the Egyptian and Israeli lines, to be patrolled by U.N. troops. Egypt would begin work on clearing the canal and would rebuild the cities once Israeli troops had withdrawn. Israeli cargoes would be allowed to pass through the canal after it reopened.

Two gaps separated the Egyptian and Israeli positions. Egypt wanted Israeli forces to withdraw east of the passes; Israel refused. Israel wanted only a token Egyptian force on the east bank; [Anwar] Sadat was thinking of two infantry divisions with 100 tanks each. It would be difficult for him publicly to accept substantial force limitations in territory returned to his control. Nonetheless, the conceptual underpinnings of the two sides' positions were not very far apart, and agreement seemed possible.

Israeli elections for the Knesset were held on December 31. The opposition to Prime Minister Meir's Labor Alignment coalition gained some strength, but not to the point of making a new cabinet and prime minister necessary. For the next six months, despite her own loss of popularity and the public disenchantment with her defense minister, Moshe Dayan, Meir carried the heavy burdens of government, fighting hard against American and domestic pressures in order to win agreements that protected Israel's vital interests. Kissinger found her to be tough and often emotional, and their talks were at times stormy, but the two nevertheless developed a genuine respect for each other during the difficult disengagement negotiations.

With Israeli elections out of the way, Dayan was sent to Washington for talks with Kissinger on January 4 and 5. He presented a five-zone concept for disengagement, in which each party would have two limited-force zones, separated by a U.N. buffer. He also specified the type of force limitations Israel could accept. Basically, each side's forces should be beyond the artillery range of the other side, and surface-to-air missiles should not be able to reach the other's aircraft. Also, the number of tanks in the limited zones should be kept very small.

During their talks Dayan urged Kissinger to return to the Middle East to aid in reaching an agreement. This idea proved to be acceptable to Sadat, and Kissinger left late on January 10. Kissinger originally expected to help establish the framework for an agreement, the details of which would be worked out by the parties at Geneva, but Sadat was anxious for results and asked Kissinger to stay in the region until an agreement was reached. Kissinger thus embarked on his first exercise in "shuttle diplomacy," flying between Egypt and Israel with proposals.

On January 13 the Israelis handed Kissinger a map of the proposed disengagement line and authorized him to show it to Sadat, which he did the next day. Sadat had already accepted, in his first talk with Kissinger, the idea of force limitations in three zones, and had promised to work for the end of the oil embargo once an agreement was reached. Now he also said he would accept Israeli forces west of the passes, but he had trouble with the extent of force limits.[1] To overcome Sadat's reservations, Kissinger suggested that the United States might take the responsibility for proposing the limitations on forces. Perhaps it would be easier for Sadat to accept an American plan than an Israeli one. And instead of publicly announcing the limits in the formal documents, these could be defined in letters exchanged by Sadat and [President Richard M.] Nixon. In addition, Sadat's private assurances on Israeli cargoes transiting the canal could be handled in a secret memo of understanding. Sadat agreed.

In Israel the next day, January 15, Prime Minister Meir dropped the demand for an end of belligerency as part of the disengagement agreement. A few changes in force levels and the line of disengagement were made, wherein Dayan played an especially constructive role. With a new map in hand Kissinger returned to Aswan to see Sadat on January 16, and Sadat agreed to scale down the Egyptian presence on the east bank to eight battalions and thirty tanks.[2] Kissinger then went back to Israel, and the next day, at 3:00 p.m., President Nixon announced that the two parties had reached an agreement on the disengagement of their military forces. The following day the chiefs of staff of Israel and Egypt signed the agreement at Kilometer 101.[3]

As part of the agreement, Israel and the United States signed a detailed ten-point memorandum of understanding.[4] The United States conveyed several Egyptian statements of intention concerning the Suez Canal and the demobilization of its armed forces. The United States promised that the completion of the disengagement agreement would take precedence over new steps at Geneva; that U.N. troops would not be withdrawn without the consent of both sides; that the United States regarded Bab al-Mandab as an international waterway; and that the United States would try to be responsive to Israel's defense needs on a continuing and long-term basis.

In letters exchanged with both Sadat and Meir, Nixon detailed the force limitations agreed upon. In the limited zones there would be no more than eight reinforced battalions with thirty tanks; no artillery above 122 mm would be allowed, and only six batteries of these weapons were permitted.[5] No weapons capable of interfering with reconnaissance flights over one's own zone were permitted; a maximum troop strength of seven thousand in the limited zone was set; and up to a distance of thirty kilometers from the Egyptian and Israeli lines, no weapons capable of reaching the other side would be allowed, nor would any surface-to-air missiles. Arrangements were specified whereby the United States would perform reconnaissance flights at regular intervals to monitor the agreement, and the results were to be made available to both sides.[6] Finally, a timetable for implementing the agreement was made part of the public text, and Sadat received a special guarantee from Nixon that the United States would use its influence to bring about the full implementation of Resolution 242 [doc. 68].

With the signing of the disengagement agreement on January 18 [see doc. 91], Nixon and Kissinger had entered into important and unprecedented commitments for the United States. American prestige in the Arab world was on the rise, and more than ever the United States seemed to hold the key cards. The Israelis might complain of excessive pressure, but the agreement was not bad for Israel and U.S. aid was still flowing in large quantities. A mood of optimism, a rare occurrence, could be sensed in much of the Middle East.

AUTHOR'S NOTES

1. Henry Kissinger, *Years of Upheaval* (Boston, 1982), pp. 821–29; and Marvin Kalb and Bernard Kalb, *Kissinger* (Boston, 1974), pp. 534–35.
2. Kalb and Kalb, *Kissinger*, p. 539.
3. The text and map appear in "The Agreement: New Deployment of Forces along the Suez Canal," *Jerusalem Post*, January 20, 1974, p. 1, and in Kissinger, *Years of Upheaval*, p. 839 (map) and p. 1250.
4. The memorandum of understanding is described in general terms in Bernard Gwertzman, "Congressmen Get Mideast Briefing," *New York Times*, January 22, 1974, p. 1.
5. Kissinger, *Years of Upheaval*, p. 1251, provides the text. The stipulation concerning six batteries of short-range artillery later became a source of controversy. In the Israeli army, a battery consisted of six guns; in the Egyptian army, it contained twelve. The first reconnaissance flights after the implementation of the disengagement agreement found seventy-two artillery pieces on the Egyptian side and thirty-six on the Israeli. After angry Israeli complaints in late March, Sadat agreed to reduce his forces to the Israeli level of thirty-six guns.
6. Ze'ev Schiff, "After Accord Signed on Friday, Separation of Forces Begins Next Sunday, Will End in 40 Days," *Jerusalem Post*, January 20, 1974, p. 1, contains a generally accurate account of the secret provisions of the agreement. See also "Secretary Kissinger's News Conference of January 22, 1974," *Department of State Bulletin*, vol. 70 (February 11, 1974), p. 137.

91

Memorandum of Understanding between the United States and Israel

January 18, 1974

The Egyptian-Israeli disengagement agreement was signed on January 18, 1974. It included limited force zones for both Egyptian and Israeli men and matériel and a U.N. buffer zone. The ten-point Memorandum of Understanding that accompanied the disengagement agreement was meant to assure Israel of American monitoring of the agreement. For Arab-Israeli negotiations this agreement was precedent setting because it made the United States witness to the agreement and assured Israel that the United States would see to it that provisions of the agreement were enforced. When the second Egyptian-Israeli Disengagement Agreement was signed in September 1975 (doc. 94), the U.S. again provided Israel with a memorandum of understanding, reaffirming America's policing role in implementing that agreement.

The United States informs Israel that Egypt's intentions are to clear and open the Suez Canal for normal operations, and to rehabilitate the cities and towns along the Canal and resume normal peacetime economic activities in that area, beginning as quickly as possible after the Disengagement Agreement is implemented.

The United States has received assurances from Egypt of its intention, upon completion of the implementation of the Agreement, to start reducing significantly its forces under mobilization if Israel gives a like indication to Egypt through the United States.

It is the policy of the United States that

Source: The Brookings Institution, *Towards Peace in the Middle East: Report of a Study Group* (Washington, DC: The Brookings Institution, 1975), pp. 1–3. Reprinted by permission.

implementation of the Disengagement Agreement and substantial steps by Egypt to implement its intentions in Paragraph 1 above should take precedence over the undertaking of new commitments by the parties related to subsequent phases of the Geneva Conference. The United States will do its best to help facilitate the Conference proceeding at a pace commensurate with this view.

The United States' position is that withdrawal of United Nations Emergency Forces[1] during the duration of the Disengagement Agreement requires the consent of both sides. Should the matter of the withdrawal come before the United Nations Security Council without the consent of Israel, the United States will vote against such withdrawal.

The United States will oppose supervision of Israeli-held areas by United Nations Observers from the Soviet Union, from other communist countries or from other countries which have no diplomatic relations with Israel. With respect to the deployment of forces in the United Nations Emergency Forces zone, the United States will approach the United Nations Secretary-General with a view to working out arrangements whereby no units or personnel of nations which do not have diplomatic relations with Israel will [a] be deployed adjacent to the Israeli line, or [b] participate in the inspection of the Israeli area of limited forces and armaments.

The United States has informed the Governments of Israel and Egypt that it will perform aerial reconnaissance missions over the areas covered by the Disengagement Agreement at a frequency of about one mission every ten days or two weeks, and will make photographs available to both Israel and Egypt.

The United States regards the Straits of Bab el-Mandeb[2] as an international waterway and will support and join with others to secure general recognition of the right of free and innocent passage through those Straits. The United States will strongly support free passage of Israeli ships and cargoes through the Straits. In the event of interference with such passage, the United States will consult with Israel on how best to assure the maintenance and exercise of such rights.

With regard to the Egyptian undertaking not to interfere with the free passage of Israeli ships or cargoes through the Straits of Bab el-Mandeb, the United States informs the Government of Israel that it is the United States' position that no notification in advance of the names of vessels passing through the Straits or any other prior communication to Egypt is required. The United States will immediately seek confirmation that this is also the Egyptian position.

Recognizing the defense responsibilities of the Government of Israel following redeployment of its forces under the Disengagement Agreement, the United States will make every effort to be fully responsive on a continuing and long-term basis to Israel's military equipment requirements.

In case of an Egyptian violation of any of the provisions of the Agreement or any of its attachments, the United States government and the Government of Israel will consult regarding the necessary reaction.

NOTES

1. The United Nations Emergency Forces were restationed in Sinai and on the west side of the Suez Canal immediately after the Yom Kippur War to monitor the U.N. cease-fire resolutions, assist in the exchange of war prisoners, and provide needed materials to stranded Egyptian soldiers.
2. The Straits of Bab el-Mandeb are located between Ethiopia and Saudi Arabia at the end of the Red Sea. Their control by any forces could deny access to Israel's southern port of Eilat, the Suez Canal, and cargoes coming to and from the Indian Ocean.

92

League of Arab States

Seventh Arab Summit Conference, Rabat Resolutions

October 29, 1974

The new Arab consensus in the wake of the Yom Kippur War was formulated at the Algiers Summit Conference in November 1973 (doc. 89). A year later the Arab position was reviewed and amended at Rabat. The most important resolution at Rabat installed the Palestine Liberation Organization as "the sole legitimate representative of the Palestinian people" and disqualified all others (namely Jordan) from reclaiming the West Bank, or parts of it, from Israel. The resolutions of the Seventh Arab Summit Conference were adopted on October 29, 1974. A summary, from the Lebanese newspaper al-Safir, *is reprinted below.*

The Seventh Arab Summit Conference—having reviewed the resolutions of the Sixth Arab Summit Conference in Algiers, the developments in the Arab and international situations, and the achievements of the combined Arab action in all fields, and after the discussion of the general situation in all its aspects and having noted the report of the Foreign Minister's Council and the reports of the director general of the Arab League, resolves as follows:

The Goal of the Arab Nation

The meeting confirms the following resolutions of the Sixth Arab Summit Conference:

1. Complete liberation of all Arab territories conquered in the aggressive action of June 1967, without surrendering or disregarding any part of the territories of the injury to the national sovereignty over them.
2. Liberation of the Arab city of Jerusalem and nonacceptance of any situation containing elements that adversely affect complete Arab sovereignty over the Holy City.
3. An undertaking to restore the national rights of the Palestinian people in accordance with the resolutions taken by the PLO [Palestine Liberation Organization] as the sole representative of the Palestinian people.
4. The problem of Palestine is the problem of all the Arabs, and no Arab party should give up this obligation as approved in the resolutions of the last Arab Summit conference.

Principles upon which Combined Arab Action Will Be Based

1. Strengthening the might of the Arab states, militarily, economically, and politically and continuing to build up the military strength of the forces for confrontation, and guaranteeing the means for this buildup.
2. Realizing the aim of efficient Arab political, military, and economic coordination that will effect the realization of Arab unity on all levels.
3. Nonacceptance of any attempt to obtain

Source: Al-Safir, November 30, 1977, reprinted in *Haaretz,* January 2, 1978, pp. 1–3. Reprinted by permission.

partial political settlements—this being based on the pan-Arab nature of the problem and its comprehensiveness.

4. Unswervingly maintaining the aim of all the Arab states of liberating all the conquered Arab territories and restoring the national rights of the Palestinian people.
5. Implementing a policy that will bring about Israel's isolation politically and economically and a cessation of the political, military, and economic aid she gets from any source in the world.
6. Refraining from Arab battles and contradictions, which are not central issues, so as to concentrate efforts against the Zionist enemy.

The Seventh Arab Summit Conference, following the detailed and exhaustive discussions held by the kings, presidents, and princes on the subject of the Arab situation, in general, and the Palestinian question, in particular, in its national and international senses; and having heard the announcements of King Hussein and Yasir Arafat and the pronouncements of the kings, presidents, and princes in a spirit of frankness, sincerity and full responsibility; and on the basis of the Arab leaders' assessment of the combined national responsibility that the present situation places upon them with regard to withstanding aggression and their obligations to liberate, which are a corollary of the oneness of the Arab problem and the oneness of the struggle for it; and because all understand the Zionists' attempts and plans that continue to be directed at negating the existence of a Palestinian entity and obliterating the Palestinian national entity; and because of a belief that these plans and attempts must be frustrated and reacted against by supporting this entity and that we must stand firm on our obligation to fulfill the requirements of its development and to increase its ability to restore the full rights of the Palestinian people and to shoulder its responsibility within the framework of the collective Arab commitment through close cooperation with their brothers; and basing itself upon the victories achieved by the Palestinian struggle against the Zionist enemy and on the Arab and international levels and in the United Nations, and owing to the necessity for a continuation of the combined Arab action to develop these victories and to put them into practical operation; and since everyone is convinced of all the above and of the conference's success in putting an end to the disputes between brothers by strengthening *Arab solidarity;* the Arab Summit Conference resolves as follows:

1. To confirm the right of the Palestinian people to return to its homeland and to dream of its future.
2. To confirm the right of the Palestinian people to establish an independent, national government under the leadership of the PLO as the sole legitimate representative of the Palestinian people, on all liberated Palestinian territory. The Arab states will assist this government when it is established in all fields and on all levels.
3. To assist the PLO to carry out its responsibility on the national and international levels within the framework of the Arab commitment.
4. To call upon Jordan, Syria, Egypt, and the PLO to decide upon a formula to improve the relations between them in the light of these resolutions and in order to implement them.
5. All the Arab States undertake to guard the Palestinian national unity and not to interfere in the internal affairs of Palestinian action. (The Iraqi delegation had reservations with respect to paragraphs 1–3 above.)

On the Political Level

Basing itself on the aims and principles determined by the Sixth Arab Summit Conference in Algiers, and persevering with political action that will serve the defined goals of the Arab struggle, and will direct the development of our foreign relations with the various world powers, the conference resolves as follows:

1. On the level of organizations and the international arena: (a) to make use of the United Nations and its bodies to expose Israel; to obtain further resolutions on the Palestinian issue and the Middle East that will isolate Israel, politically and propaganda-wise, in world opinion, to try to achieve more effective steps to expose Israel's maneuvers and her refusal to carry out the resolutions of international organizations and to make this apparent to the world and to lay at Israel's door the blame for frustrating the attempts to establish a just peace; (b) to consolidate the cooperation with the nonaligned nations and to take action to implement the resolutions of the Fourth Summit Conference of Nonaligned Nations and to raise the question of the introduction of sanctions mentioned in the seventh article of the U.N. Declaration against Israel and to demand that she be expelled from the United Nations. All this should take place at the Conference of Foreign Ministers of the Nonaligned Nations that will convene in summer 1975, prior to raising the issue at the 30th session of the U.N. General Assembly [doc. 96]; (c) to continue activity intended to consolidate the Arab cooperation with Islamic governments and peoples and to make further efforts among the Islamic nations having relations with Israel to persuade them to break off these relations and to make more effective efforts to increase the role played by the Islamic world in supporting the just Arab cause in the Arab-Zionist struggle; (d) to consolidate the cooperation between the Arab League and the Organization of African Unity in all areas of activity.

93
Palestine Liberation Organization
Political Program
June 9, 1974

The diplomatic offensive of the Palestine Liberation Organization and the Arab states (see docs. 89, 92) had its echo within the PLO itself. The political program adopted by the Palestine National Council on June 9, 1974, reflects the hard line that it could now take, having gained the support of much of the international community and established a "ministate" in Lebanon.

The Palestinian National Council,

On the basis of Palestinian National Charter and the Political Programme drawn up at the Eleventh Session, held from January 6–12, 1973 [doc. 72]; and from its belief that it is impossible for a permanent and just peace to be established in the area unless our Palestinian

Source: Yehoshafat Harkabi, *The Palestinian Covenant and Its Meaning* (London: Vallentine, Mitchell and Co., 1979), pp. 147–48.

people recover all their national rights and, first and foremost, their rights to return and to self-determination on the whole of the soil of their homeland; and in the light of a study of the new political circumstances that have come into existence in the period between the Council's last and present sessions, resolves the following:

1. To reaffirm the Palestine Liberation Organization's previous attitude to Resolution 242 [doc. 68], which obliterates the national right of our people and deals with the cause of our people as a problem of refugees. The Council therefore refuses to have anything to do with this resolution at any level, Arab or international, including the Geneva Conference.
2. The Liberation Organization will employ all means, and first and foremost armed struggle, to liberate Palestinian territory and to establish the independent combatant national authority for the people over every part of Palestinian territory that is liberated. This will require further changes being effected in the balance of power in favor of our people and their struggle.
3. The Liberation Organization will struggle against any proposal for a Palestinian entity the price of which is recognition, peace, secure frontiers, renunciation of national rights and the deprival of our people of their right to return and their right to self-determination on the soil of their homeland.
4. Any step taken towards liberation is a step toward the realisation of the Liberation Organization's strategy of establishing the democratic Palestinian state specified in the resolutions of previous Palestinian National Councils.
5. Struggle along with the Jordanian national forces to establish a Jordanian-Palestinian national front whose aim will be to set up in Jordan a democratic national authority in close contact with the Palestinian entity that is established through the struggle.
6. The Liberation Organization will struggle to establish unity in struggle between the two peoples and between all the forces of the Arab liberation movement that are in agreement on this programme.
7. In the light of this programme, the Liberation Organization will struggle to strengthen national unity and to raise it to the level where it will be able to perform its national duties and tasks.
8. Once it is established, the Palestinian national authority will strive to achieve a union of the confrontation countries, with the aim of completing the liberation of all Palestinian territory, and as a step along the road to comprehensive Arab unity.
9. The Liberation Organization will strive to strengthen its solidarity with the socialist countries, and with forces of liberation and progress throughout the world, with the aim of frustrating all the schemes of Zionism, reaction and imperialism.
10. In the light of this programme the leadership of the revolution will determine the tactics which will serve and make possible the realization of these objectives.

The Executive Committee of the Palestine Liberation Organization will make every effort to implement this programme, and should a situation arise affecting the destiny and the future of the Palestinian people, the National Council will be convened in extraordinary session.

94
Disengagement Agreement between Egypt and Israel
September 4, 1975

The cease-fires arranged by the United Nations and U.S. mediation and the direct negotiations between military offices at Kilometer 101—sixty-three miles from Cairo in Israeli-occupied territory—that resulted in the Six-Point Agreement (doc. 88) were only temporary steps to end the immediate problems of military hostilities in the Yom Kippur War. The United States and the Soviet Union, seeking a comprehensive settlement in the Middle East that would also maximize their own foreign policy goals, convened the Geneva Peace Conference with the United States, Soviet Union, Israel, Egypt, and Jordan as members; Syria was a member but did not attend. The conference met once, in December 1973, and failed to produce any results. On several occasions since then initiatives have been taken to reconvene it.

The talks at Kilometer 101, which were suspended in early December 1973, resumed to produce an interim separation-of-forces agreement on January 18, 1974 (docs. 90, 91). Israel left the west bank of the Suez Canal and pulled back about twelve miles from its positions on the east bank. Three narrow corridors were established on the east bank—an Egyptian and an Israeli limited force zone separated by a U.N. buffer zone. Egyptian forces along the entire eastern bank thereby controlled the canal itself. In a separate letter Egypt agreed to allow nonmilitary cargoes going to and from Israel to pass through the Suez Canal.

Meanwhile U.S. mediators were negotiating terms for a similar separation-of-forces agreement between Syria and Israel. On May 31, 1974, an agreement was reached—again establishing two limited force zones separated by a U.N. buffer zone. Israel withdrew to positions slightly west of the Purple Line, the pre-October 1973 cease-fire line. The disengagement of troops was completed three weeks after the agreement was signed in Geneva.

Following these agreements between Egypt and Israel and between Syria and Israel, Henry Kissinger sought to move to the next phase of the settlement process, but it proved extremely difficult to effect a second Egyptian-Israeli agreement. After a year of crisis-ridden negotiations what was in effect a trilateral American-Egyptian-Israeli agreement was reached. Again it established limited force zones separated by a U.N. buffer zone. Egyptian forces moved farther eastward into the Sinai, and Israeli forces moved back to the strategic Mitla Pass. This second separation-of-forces agreement, signed in September 1975, was secured by U.S. guarantees to Israel to provide for observation of Egyptian military activity to compensate for Israel's loss of early warning stations in the territory it evacuated. The September 1975 agreement resolved issues that had been outstanding since the Yom Kippur War, particularly the untenable position of Israeli and Egyptian troops near the canal. Hence it was also a step toward a resolution of the more fundamental conflict between the two states and set the stage for the 1979 Camp David Accords (doc. 103).

Source: "New Agreement between Egypt and Israel Negotiated through Secretary Kissinger during His Trip from August 20 to September 3," *U.S. Department of State Bulletin* 73, no. 1892 (September 29, 1975): 466–68.

The Government of the Arab Republic of Egypt and the Government of Israel have agreed that:

Article 1. The conflict between them and in the Middle East shall not be resolved by military force but by peaceful means.

The agreement concluded by the Parties on January 18, 1974, within the framework of the Geneva Peace Conference, constituted a first step toward a just and durable peace according to the provisions of Security Council Resolution 338 of October 22, 1973 [doc. 86].

They are determined to reach a final and just peace settlement by means of negotiations called for by Security Council Resolution 338, this Agreement being a significant step toward that end.

Article 2. The Parties hereby undertake not to resort to the threat or use of force or military blockade against each other.

Article 3. The Parties shall continue scrupulously to observe the cease-fire on land, sea and air and to refrain from all military or paramilitary actions against each other.

The Parties also confirm that the obligations contained in the Annex and, when concluded, the Protocol shall be an integral part of this Agreement.

Article 4.

1. The military forces of the Parties shall be deployed in accordance with the following principles [delineation of troop withdrawals].

2. The details concerning the new lines, the re-deployment of the forces and its timing, the limitation on armaments and forces, aerial reconnaissance, the operation of the early warning and surveillance installations and the use of the roads, the United Nations functions and other arrangements will all be in accordance with the provisions of the Annex and map which are an integral part of this Agreement and of the Protocol which is to result from negotiations pursuant to the Annex and which, when concluded, shall become an integral part of the Agreement.

Article 5. The United Nations Emergency Force is essential and shall continue its functions and its mandate shall be extended annually.

Article 6. The Parties hereby establish a Joint Commission for the duration of this Agreement. It will function under the aegis of the Chief Coordinator of the United Nations Peacekeeping Missions in the Middle East in order to consider any problem arising from this Agreement and to assist the United Nations Emergency Force in the execution of its mandate. The Joint Commission shall function in accordance with procedures established in the Protocol.

Article 7. Nonmilitary cargoes destined for or coming from Israel shall be permitted through the Suez Canal.

Article 8. This Agreement is regarded by the Parties as a significant step toward a just and lasting peace. It is not a final peace agreement.

The Parties shall continue their efforts to negotiate a final peace agreement within the framework of the Geneva Peace Conference in accordance with Security Council Resolution 338.

Article 9. This Agreement shall enter into force upon signature of the Protocol and remain in force until superseded by a new agreement.

95

Memorandum of Agreement between the United States and Israel regarding the Geneva Peace Conference

September 17, 1975

Subsequent to Israel's signing of the September 1975 Egyptian-Israeli Disengagement Agreement (doc. 94), Israel received assurances from the United States in letters and memoranda about future weapons acquisitions, financial assistance, and oil supplies, on the prospects of Israel retaining the Golan Heights in any future peace agreement with Syria and the future conduct of Arab-Israeli negotiations dealing with Geneva. These letters and memoranda were secret. With regard to the conduct of future negotiations, Israel received an iron-clad promise that Washington would neither recognize nor negotiate with the Palestine Liberation Organization until it recognized Israel's existence, refuted terrorism, and accepted U.N. Security Council Resolutions 242 (doc. 68) and 338 (doc. 86). This promise impeded official American negotiations with the PLO for the subsequent decade; only in 1988, when the PLO accepted the three premises in this memorandum, did the United States open a dialogue with the Palestine Liberation Organization. When the PLO was involved once again in a terror attack in 1990, the United States suspended talks with the PLO. Talks resumed in 1993 following the signing of the Oslo Accords (doc. 133).

---

1. The Geneva peace conference will be reconvened at a time coordinated between the United States and Israel.

2. The United States will continue to adhere to its present policy with respect to the Palestine Liberation Organization, whereby it will not recognize or negotiate with the Palestine Liberation Organization so long as the Palestine Liberation Organization does not recognize Israel's right to exist and does not accept Security Council Resolutions 242 and 338. The United States Government will consult fully and seek to concert its position and strategy at the Geneva peace conference on this issue with the Government of Israel. Similarly, the United States will consult fully and seek to concert its position and strategy with Israel with regard to the participation of any other additional states. It is understood that the participation at a subsequent phase of the conference of any possible additional state, group or organization will require the agreement of all the initial participants.

3. The United States will make every effort to insure at the conference that all the substantive negotiations will be on a bilateral basis.

4. The United States will oppose and, if necessary, vote against any initiative in the Security Council to alter adversely the terms of reference of the Geneva peace conference or to change Resolutions 242 and 338 in ways which are incompatible with their original purpose.

5. The United States will seek to insure that

Source: Yehuda Lukacs, ed., *The Israeli-Palestinian Conflict: A Documentary Record, 1967–1990* (New York: Cambridge University Press, 1992), pp. 60–61. Reprinted with the permission of Cambridge University Press.

the role of the co-sponsors will be consistent with what was agreed in the memorandum of understanding between the United States Government and the Government of Israel of December 20, 1973.

6. The United States and Israel will concert action to assure that the conference will be conducted in a manner consonant with the objectives of this document and with the declared purpose of the conference, namely the advancement of a negotiated peace between Israel and its neighbors.

96

United Nations General Assembly

Resolution 3379 (Anti-Zionist Resolution)

November 10, 1975

Emboldened by the Rabat Summit (doc. 92) and the initial success of the oil embargo, in the summer of 1975 the Arab states and the Palestine Liberation Organization launched a diplomatic offensive to condemn Israel and Zionism in international forums. The culmination of this effort occurred on November 10, 1975, when the U.N. General Assembly passed Resolution 3379, determining that Zionism is a form of racism and racial discrimination. The resolution, reprinted here, was repealed on December 16, 1991.

The General Assembly,

Recalling its resolution 1904 (XVIII) of 20 November 1963, proclaiming the United Nations Declaration on the Elimination of All Forms of Racial Discrimination, and in particular its affirmation that "any doctrine of racial differentiation or superiority is scientifically false, morally condemnable, socially unjust and dangerous" and its expression of alarm at "the manifestation of racial discrimination still in evidence in some areas in the world, some of which are imposed by certain Governments by means of legislative, administrative or other measures,"

Recalling also that, in its resolution 3151 G (XXVIII) of 14 December 1973, the General Assembly condemned, *inter alia,* the unholy alliance between South African racism and zionism,

Taking note of the Declaration of Mexico on the Equality of Women and Their Contribution to Development and Peace, 1975, proclaimed by the World Conference of the International Women's Year, held at Mexico City from 19 June to 2 July 1975, which promulgated the principle that "international co-operation and peace require the achievement of national liberation and independence, the elimination of colonialism and neo-colonialism, foreign occupation, zionism, *apartheid* and racial discrimination in all its forms, as well as the recognition of the dignity of peoples and their right to self-determination,"

Taking note also of resolution 77 (XII) adopted by the Assembly of Heads of State and

Source: United Nations Organization, General Assembly, *Resolutions of the Thirtieth Session*, pp. 83–84.

Government of the Organization of African Unity at its twelfth ordinary session, held at Kampala from 28 July to 1 August 1975, which considered "that the racist regime in occupied Palestine and the racist regimes in Zimbabwe and South Africa have a common imperialist origin, forming a whole and having the same racist structure and being organically linked in their policy aimed at repression of the dignity and integrity of the human being,"

Taking note also of the Political Declaration and Strategy To Strengthen International Peace and Security and To Intensify Solidarity and Mutual Assistance among Non-Aligned Countries, adopted at the Conference of Ministers for Foreign Affairs of Non-Aligned Countries held at Lima from 25 to 30 August 1975, which most severely condemned zionism as a threat to world peace and security and called upon all countries to oppose this racist and imperialist ideology,

Determines that Zionism is a form of racism and racial discrimination.

97
Chaim Herzog
Speech to the General Assembly on the Anti-Zionist Resolution
November 10, 1975

Chaim Herzog, Israeli ambassador to the United Nations, denounced Resolution 3379 (doc. 96) the same day it was passed. His tenure at the United Nations was marked by growing Israeli isolation as Arab, Muslim, and Third World states, often in alliance with the Soviet bloc, joined forces on Middle Eastern issues. A brother of Yaacov Herzog (see docs. 41, 42), Chaim Herzog had been a general in the Israeli army and later served as Israel's president from 1983 to 1993. He died in 1997.

It is symbolic that this debate, which may well prove to be a turning point in the fortunes of the United Nations and a decisive factor in the possible continued existence of this organization, should take place on November 10. Tonight, thirty-seven years ago, has gone down in history as Kristallnacht, the Night of the Crystals. This was the night in 1938 when Hitler's Nazi storm-troopers launched a coordinated attack on the Jewish community in Germany, burned the synagogues in all its cities and made bonfires in the streets of the Holy Books and the Scrolls of the Holy Law and Bible. It was the night when Jewish homes were attacked and heads of families taken away, many of them never to return. It was the night when the windows of all Jewish businesses and stores were smashed, covering the streets in the cities of

Source: Chaim Herzog, *Who Stands Accused? Israel Answers Its Critics* (New York: Random House, 1978), pp. 3–7. Reprinted by permission.

Germany with a film of broken glass which dissolved into the millions of crystals which gave that night its name. It was the night which led eventually to the crematoria and the gas chambers, Auschwitz, Birkenau, Dachau, Buchenwald, Teresienstadt and others. It was the night which led to the most terrifying holocaust in the history of man.

It is indeed befitting, Mr. President, that this debate, conceived in the desire to deflect the Middle East from its moves towards peace and born of a deep pervading feeling of anti-Semitism, should take place on the anniversary of this day. It is indeed befitting, Mr. President, that the United Nations, which began its life as an anti-Nazi alliance, should thirty years later find itself on its way to becoming the world center of anti-Semitism. Hitler would have felt at home on a number of occasions during the past year, listening to the proceedings in this forum, and above all to the proceedings during the debate on Zionism.

It is sobering to consider to what level this body has been dragged down if we are obliged today to contemplate an attack on Zionism. For this attack constitutes not only an anti-Israeli attack of the foulest type, but also an assault in the United Nations on Judaism—one of the oldest established religions in the world, a religion which has given the world the human values of the Bible, and from which two other great religions, Christianity and Islam, sprang. Is it not tragic to consider that we here at this meeting in the year 1975 are contemplating what is a scurrilous attack on a great and established religion which has given to the world the Bible with its Ten Commandments, the great prophets of old, Moses, Isaiah, Amos; the great thinkers of history, Maimonides, Spinoza, Marx, Einstein, many of the masters of the arts and as high a percentage of the Nobel Prizewinners in the world, in sciences, in the arts and in the humanities as has been achieved by any people on earth? . . .

The resolution against Zionism was originally one condemning racism and colonialism, a subject on which we could have achieved consensus, a consensus which is of great importance to all of us and to our African colleagues in particular. However, instead of permitting this to happen, a group of countries, drunk with the feeling of power inherent in the automatic majority and without regard to the importance of achieving a consensus on this issue, railroaded the U.N. in a contemptuous maneuver by the use of the automatic majority into bracketing Zionism with the subject under discussion.

I do not come to this rostrum to defend the moral and historical values of the Jewish people. They do not need to be defended. They speak for themselves. They have given to mankind much of what is great and eternal. They have done for the spirit of man more than can readily be appreciated by a forum such as this one.

I come here to denounce the two great evils which menace society in general and a society of nations in particular. These two evils are hatred and ignorance. These two evils are the motivating force behind the proponents of this resolution and their supporters. These two evils characterize those who would drag this world organization, the ideals of which were first conceived by the prophets of Israel, to the depths to which it has been dragged today.

The key to understanding Zionism is in its name. The easternmost of the two hills of ancient Jerusalem during the tenth century B.C.E. was called Zion. In fact, the name Zion, referring to Jerusalem, appears 152 times in the Old Testament. The name is overwhelmingly a poetic and prophetic designation. The religious and emotional qualities of the name arise from the importance of Jerusalem as the Royal City and the City of the Temple. "Mount Zion" is the place where God dwells. Jerusalem, or Zion, is a place where the Lord is King, and where He has installed His King, David.

King David made Jerusalem the capital of Israel almost three thousand years ago, and Jerusalem has remained the capital ever since. During the centuries the term "Zion" grew and expanded to mean the whole of Israel. The Israelites in exile could not forget Zion. The Hebrew Psalmist sat by the waters of Babylon and swore: "If I forget thee, O Jerusalem, let my right hand forget her cunning." This oath has been repeated for thousands of years by Jews throughout the world. It is an oath which was made over seven hundred years before the advent of Christianity and over twelve hundred years before the advent of Islam, and Zion came to mean the Jewish homeland, symbolic of Judaism, of Jewish national aspirations.

While praying to his God every Jew, wherever he is in the world, faces toward Jerusalem. For over two thousand years of exile these prayers have expressed the yearning of the Jewish people to return to their ancient homeland, Israel. In fact, a continuous Jewish presence, in larger or smaller numbers, has been maintained in the country over the centuries.

Zionism is the name of the national movement of the Jewish people and is the modern expression of the ancient Jewish heritage. The Zionist ideal, as set out in the Bible, has been, and is, an integral part of the Jewish religion.

Zionism is to the Jewish people what the liberation movements of Africa and Asia have been to their own people.

Zionism is one of the most dynamic and vibrant national movements in human history. Historically it is based on a unique and unbroken connection, extending some four thousand years, between the People of the Book and the Land of the Bible.

In modern times, in the late nineteenth century, spurred by the twin forces of anti-Semitic persecution and of nationalism, the Jewish people organized the Zionist movement in order to transform their dream into reality. Zionism as a political movement was the revolt of an oppressed nation against the depredation and wicked discrimination and oppression of the countries in which anti-Semitism flourished. It is no coincidence that the co-sponsors and supporters of this resolution include countries who are guilty of the horrible crimes of antisemitism and discrimination to this very day.

Support for the aim of Zionism was written into the League of Nations Mandate for Palestine and was again endorsed by the United Nations in 1947, when the General Assembly voted by overwhelming majority for the restoration of Jewish independence in our ancient land.

The re-establishment of Jewish independence in Israel, after centuries of struggle to overcome foreign conquest and exile, is a vindication of the fundamental concepts of the equality of nations and of self-determination. To question the Jewish people's right to national existence and freedom is not only to deny to the Jewish people the right accorded to every other people on this globe, but it is also to deny the central precepts of the United Nations.

98

Harold H. Saunders

The United States and the Palestinian Issue

December 1, 1975

Following the signing of the Egyptian-Israeli Disengagement Agreement on the Sinai in September 1975 (doc. 94), it became clear that U.S. Secretary of State Henry Kissinger's step-by-step approach to a Middle East settlement had exhausted itself. Kissinger began to contemplate what his critics had suggested—a comprehensive solution that would address the Palestinian issue as well.

Harold H. Saunders (b. 1930), a U.S. intelligence and foreign service officer, is a specialist in the Middle East. As deputy assistant secretary of state for Near Eastern and South Asia affairs, he accompanied Secretaries of State Kissinger and Cyrus Vance on all their Middle Eastern trips. Saunders's testimony before a subcommittee of the U.S. House of Representatives Committee on International Relations in November 1975 was an important signal of a potential change in U.S. policy.

A just and durable peace in the Middle East is a central objective of the United States. Both President [Gerald R.] Ford and Secretary [of State Henry] Kissinger have stated firmly on numerous occasions that the United States is determined to make every feasible effort to maintain the momentum of practical progress toward a peaceful settlement of the Arab-Israeli conflict.

We have also repeatedly stated that the legitimate interests of the Palestinian Arabs must be taken into account in the negotiation of an Arab-Israeli peace. In many ways, the Palestinian dimension of the Arab-Israeli conflict is the heart of that conflict. Final resolution of the problems arising from the partition of Palestine, the establishment of the State of Israel, and Arab opposition to those events will not be possible until agreement is reached defining a just and permanent status for the Arab peoples who consider themselves Palestinians.

The total number of Palestinian Arabs is estimated at a little more than 3 million. Of these, about 450,000 live in the area of Israel's pre-1967 borders; about 1 million are in the Israeli-occupied West Bank, East Jerusalem, and Gaza; something less than a million—about 900,000—are in Jordan; half a million are in Syria and Lebanon; and somewhat more than 200,000 or so are elsewhere, primarily in the gulf states.

Those in Israel are Israeli nationals. The great majority of those in the West Bank, East Jerusalem, and Jordan are Jordanian nationals. Palestinian refugees, who live outside of pre-1967 Israel and number 1.6 million, are eligible for food and/or services from the U.N. Relief and Works Agency (UNRWA); more than 650,000 of these live in camps.

Source: "Statement by Harold H. Saunders, Deputy Assistant Secretary of State for Near Eastern and South Asian Affairs Made before the Special Subcommittee on Investigations of the House Committee on International Relations on November 12," *U.S. Department of State Bulletin* 73, no. 1901 (December 1, 1975): 797–802.

The problem of the Palestinians was initially dealt with essentially as one involving displaced persons. The United States and other nations responded to the immediate humanitarian task of caring for a large number of refugees and trying to provide them with some hope in life.

In later years, there has been considerable attention given to the programs of UNRWA that help not only to sustain those people's lives but to lift the young people out of the refugee camps and to train them and give them an opportunity to lead productive lives. Many have taken advantage of this opportunity, and an unusually large number of them have completed secondary and university education. One finds Palestinians occupying leading positions throughout the Arab world as professionals and skilled workers in all fields.

The United States has provided some $620 million in assistance—about 62 percent of the total international support ($1 billion) for the Palestinian refugees over the past quarter of a century.

Today, however, we recognize that, in addition to meeting the human needs and responding to legitimate personal claims of the refugees, there is another interest that must be taken into account. It is a fact that many of the 3 million or so people who call themselves Palestinians today increasingly regard themselves as having their own identity as a people and desire a voice in determining their political status. As with any people in this situation, they have differences among themselves, but the Palestinians collectively are a political factor which must be dealt with if there is to be a peace between Israel and its neighbors.

The statement is often made in the Arab world that there will not be peace until the "rights of the Palestinians" are fulfilled; but there is no agreed definition of what is meant, and a variety of viewpoints have been expressed on what the legitimate objectives of the Palestinians are:

- Some Palestinian elements hold to the objective of a binational secular state in the area of the former mandate of Palestine. Realization of this objective would mean the end of the present State of Israel—a member of the United Nations—and its submergence in some larger entity. Some would be willing to accept merely as a first step toward this goal the establishment of a Palestinian state comprising the West Bank of the Jordan River and Gaza.
- Other elements of Palestinian opinion appear willing to accept an independent Palestinian state comprising the West Bank and Gaza, based on acceptance of Israel's right to exist as an independent state within roughly its pre-1967 borders.
- Some Palestinians and other Arabs envisage as a possible solution a unification of the West Bank and Gaza with Jordan. A variation of this which has been suggested would be the reconstitution of the country as a federated state, with the West Bank becoming an autonomous Palestinian province.
- Still others, including many Israelis, feel that with the West Bank returned to Jordan, and with the resulting existence of two communities—Palestinian and Jordanian—within Jordan, opportunities would be created thereby for the Palestinians to find self-expression.
- In the case of a solution which would rejoin the West Bank to Jordan or a solution involving a West Bank–Gaza state, there would still arise the property claims of those Palestinians who before 1948 resided in areas that became the State of Israel. These claims have been acknowledged as a serious problem by the international community ever since the adoption by the United Nations of Resolution 194 on this subject in 1948 [doc. 26], a resolution which the United Nations has repeatedly reaffirmed and which the United States has supported. A solution will be further complicated by the property claims against Arab states of the many Jews from those states who moved to Israel in its early years after achieving statehood.[1]

- In addition to property claims, some believe they should have the option of returning to their original homes under any settlement.
- Other Arab leaders, while pressing the importance of Palestinian involvement in a settlement, have taken the position that the definition of Palestinian interests is something for the Palestinian people themselves to sort out, and the view has been expressed by responsible Arab leaders that realization of Palestinian rights need not be inconsistent with the existence of Israel.

No one, therefore, seems in a position today to say exactly what Palestinian objectives are. Even the Palestine Liberation Organization (PLO), which is recognized by the Arab League and the U.N. General Assembly as the representative of the Palestinian people, has been ambivalent. Officially and publicly, its objective is described as a binational secular state, but there are some indications that coexistence between separate Palestinian and Israeli states might be considered.

When there is greater precision about those objectives, there can be clearer understanding about how to relate them to negotiations. There is the aspect of the future of the West Bank and Gaza—how those areas are to be defined and how they are to be governed. There is the aspect of the relationship between the Palestinians in the West Bank and Gaza to those Palestinians who are not living in those areas, in the context of a settlement.

What is needed as a first step is a diplomatic process which will help bring forth a reasonable definition of Palestinian interests—a position from which negotiations on a solution of the Palestinian aspects of the problem might begin. The issue is not whether Palestinian interests should be expressed in a final settlement, but how. There will be no peace unless an answer is found.

Another requirement is the development of a framework for negotiations—a statement of the objectives and the terms of reference. The framework for the negotiations that have taken place thus far and the agreements they have produced involving Israel, Syria, and Egypt has been provided by the U.N. Security Council Resolutions 242 and 338 [docs. 68, 86]. In accepting that framework, all of the parties to the negotiations have accepted that the objective of the negotiations is peace between them based on mutual recognition, territorial integrity, political independence, the right to live in peace within secure and recognized borders, and the resolution of the specific issues which comprise the Arab-Israeli conflict.

The major problem that must be resolved in establishing a framework for bringing issues of concern to the Palestinians into negotiation, therefore, is to find a common basis for the negotiation that Palestinians and Israelis can both accept. This could be achieved by common acceptance of the above-mentioned Security Council resolutions, although they do not deal with the political aspect of the Palestinian problem.

A particularly difficult aspect of the problem is the question of who negotiates for the Palestinians. It has been our belief that Jordan would be a logical negotiator for the Palestinian-related issues. The Rabat summit [doc. 92], however, recognized the Palestine Liberation Organization as "the sole legitimate representative of the Palestinian people."

The PLO was formed in 1964, when 400 delegates from Palestinian communities throughout the Arab world met in Jerusalem to create an organization to represent and speak for the Palestinian people. Its leadership was originally middle-class and relatively conservative, but by 1969 control had passed into the hands of the Palestinian *fedayeen*, or commando, movement, which had existed since the mid-1950s but had come into prominence only after the 1967 war. The PLO became an umbrella organization for six separate *fedayeen* groups: Fatah; the Syrian-backed Saiqa; the Popular Democratic Front for the Liberation of Palestine; the Popular Front for the Liberation of Palestine;

the General Command, a sub-group of the PFLP; and the Iraqi-backed Arab Liberation Front. Affiliated with the PLO are a number of "popular organizations"—labor and professional unions, student groups, women's groups, and so on. Fatah, the largest *fedayeen* group, also has a welfare apparatus to care for widows and orphans of deceased Fatah members.

However, the PLO does not accept the U.N. Security Council resolutions, does not recognize the existence of Israel, and has not stated its readiness to negotiate peace with Israel; Israel does not recognize the PLO or the idea of a separate Palestinian entity. Thus we do not at this point have the framework for a negotiation involving the PLO. We cannot envision or urge a negotiation between two parties as long as one professes to hold the objective of eliminating the other—rather than the objective of negotiating peace with it.

There is one other aspect to this problem. Elements of the PLO have used terrorism to gain attention for their cause. Some Americans as well as many Israelis and others have been killed by Palestinian terrorists. The international community cannot condone such practices, and it seems to us that there must be some assurance if Palestinians are drawn into the negotiating process that these practices will be curbed.

This is the problem which we now face. If the progress toward peace which has now begun is to continue, a solution to this question must be found. We have not devised an "American" solution, nor would it be appropriate for us to do so. This is the responsibility of the parties and the purpose of the negotiating process. But we have not closed our minds to any reasonable solution which can contribute to progress toward our overriding objective in the Middle East—an Arab-Israeli peace. The step-by-step approach to negotiations which we have pursued has been based partly on the understanding that issues in the Arab-Israeli conflict take time to mature. It is obvious that thinking on the Palestinian aspects of the problem must evolve on all sides. As it does, what is not possible today may become possible.

Our consultations on how to move the peace negotiations forward will recognize the need to deal with this subject. As Secretary Kissinger has said: "We are prepared to work with all the parties toward a solution of all the issues yet remaining—including the issue of the future of the Palestinians."

We will do so because the issues of concern to the Palestinians are important in themselves and because the Arab governments participating in the negotiations have made clear that progress in the overall negotiations will depend in part on progress on issues of concern to the Palestinians. We are prepared to consider any reasonable proposal from any quarter, and we will expect other parties to the negotiation to be equally open-minded.

NOTE

1. While Israel has acknowledged the legitimacy of property claims by Palestinian refugees from the War of Independence, and in fact released blocked bank accounts held by these refugees, it has always insisted that the final settlement take into account the property claims of Jews forced to flee Arab states in the aftermath of the war. More than 360,000 Jews went to Israel from Arab countries in these years, a large proportion of whom were forced to leave behind property. (Immigration figures, 1948–53, refer to all Jewish immigration from Asia and Africa. See Moshe Sicron, "Haaliyah LeIsrael, 1948–52" [The immigration to Israel, 1948–1953], in *Olim BeIsrael: Mikraah* [Immigrants in Israel: A Reader], ed. Moshe Lissak, Beverly Mizrahi, and Ofra Ben-David [Jerusalem: Akademon, 1969], p. 115).

99
Uri Lubrani
Yigal Allon in the Palace of the Shah
August 1976: Memoir

Until the Iranian revolution of late 1978 and early 1979, Israel had good diplomatic relations with Iran, which included the sale of Iranian oil to Israel. When the shah was deposed and the Ayatollah Khomeini rose to power, Iran severed diplomatic relations with Israel and openly articulated support for the Palestine Liberation Organization. One consequence of the Iranian monarchy's fall has been a series of revelations on the Iranian-Israeli relationship during the shah's reign. Uri Lubrani, former Israeli ambassador in Teheran, published this article in Davar, *at the time the daily newspaper of the Histadrut.*

At the time [Yigal] Allon was deputy prime minister and foreign minister, and the main purpose of his visit was to meet with the shah, Muhammad Reza Pahlavi.

I viewed the meetings between the Israeli leaders and the shah as important. In the first years of my service in Teheran, I was not given the opportunity of meeting him face to face. Only three and a half years after my arrival in Teheran, was the dam opened and I given the opportunity to meet him. Because of the centralized regime in the country and the many powers vested in the shah, it was important that he meet with Israeli leaders frequently in order to hear from them directly those things I was able to convey to him only through intermediaries. The latter included five or six of the persons closest to the shah. But I was never sure that what I wanted brought to the shah's notice was really conveyed to him accurately, just as I was never sure whether his reactions were faithfully relayed to me, without additional interpretations tacked on by the intermediaries. For this reason, the shah's meetings with Israeli leaders, which took place every few months, were important.

The Iranians agreed to these meetings only on condition—promised in advance—that they would not be publicized. For their part, the hosts took care of the physical safety of the guests from Israel, for it was clear that if an Israeli personality were injured, an international scandal would ensue and all efforts to preserve the secrecy of the visits would be foiled. From the Israeli point of view, there was no need to keep these visits secret. We were careful about this only because we knew that if one visit became public knowledge, the Iranians would be hesitant about allowing another. Arrangements were, therefore, made in Israel so that the absence of the Israeli leader would not be noticed and invite guesses. This was the reason why the visits usually took place on the Sabbath of festivals.

When the prime minister used to visit Iran, the pressures of security and the secrecy instructions were particularly stringent, and it was difficult to break through them. They

Source: Uri Lubrani, "Allon bearmon hashah" [Allon in the Palace of the Shah], *Davar,* April 20, 1980, pp. 3–4. Reprinted by permission.

made it necessary to minimize the length of the visit and the number of meetings. Allon's visit, too, had of course to be kept secret. But, at the same time, I was eager for Allon to meet not only with the Shah but also with some of his chief aides. . . .

. . . The visits of the Israeli leaders to Iran were usually planned with some matter of importance as the topic of discussion. The main subject on the agenda for this visit of Allon's was the character of the relations between Iran and Israel with respect to the supply of oil. In addition, the agenda included such subjects as a report on Israel's current political positions and particularly its attempts to find a way to a settlement with the Arab countries.

When the date of Allon's visit had been finalized, the detailed, practical planning of the visit began. For reasons of secrecy, only a handful of people in Israel knew about it. Even the top officials in the Foreign Ministry, except for the director general and the minister's closest aides, did not know about it. This made the staff work and preparation of the material more difficult, since I was not able to get assistance from the Foreign Ministry in Jerusalem. It meant that we had to make arrangements to brief the visitor from Israel upon his arrival in Teheran, before his visits with the Iranian leadership began.

The prime minister and other persons visiting Iran used to come on a special plane for reasons of secrecy and also because the El Al flight timetable would have introduced many restrictions. On this visit, Yigal Allon decided to make an effort to reduce expenses and to come on an El Al flight. In order to prevent recognition by the passengers, the foreign minister and his entourage were well made up. When I met him at Teheran airport between ten and eleven o'clock at night, I almost didn't recognize him. His hair was hidden under a wig. He was wearing strange glasses and a Tyrolean hat with a feather. Allon was accompanied by the head of his bureau, Haim Bar-On, who was also disguised, and a security man.

The Iranian services made sure that Allon did not have to go through a check, and he was taken to a guest room specially installed for visits like these. The official Iranian host who was waiting for him was the deputy prime minister, Ne'matollah Nasiri [executed after the revolution], who also headed the Savak, the Iranian Secret Service. The reception was very warm; we joked about the makeup and the disguise and without further delay we left for the guest house of the Prime Minister's Office. This guest house is situated in the northeastern part of Teheran, and, in order to reach it, we had to drive through the huge city of five million inhabitants for some forty-five minutes.

The absence of the Iranian foreign minister from the reception committee at the airport was not accidental. The foreign minister, ['Abbas 'Ali] Khal'atbari, was well known, and it was not desirable for questions to be asked about his presence at the airport. Furthermore, Nasiri was always the host for Israeli personalities. He had sole responsibility for their security, and since internal political considerations also played a role, he laid down rules that enabled him to be the first to meet important visitors from Israel. This gave him a special status in everything concerning relations with us, and he usually preferred to be the only one to receive the guest. Allon's other visits (he visited three times while I was in office) were not brought to the knowledge of the foreign minister, and it was my unpleasant task to inform Khal'atbari that his Israeli counterpart had visited Teheran and even met with the shah. I feared that the Iranian foreign minister would be insulted and suspect me of being involved in a plot against him. But eventually it was explained to me that, since every visit of an Israeli leader and all the arrangements are given the explicit approval of the shah, everyone accepted it as an unshakable command and even the foreign minister did not view it as a reason to feel insulted. But, this time, the Iranian foreign minister was included in the schedule of meetings with Allon, and he was waiting for us at the guest house of the Prime Minister's Office.

Khal'atbari was an experienced diplomat of the old school, educated and brought up in the West, a graduate of French universities, who had climbed up through the ranks of the Foreign Ministry. At the time, he had already been foreign minister for six or seven years. He was not garrulous, and it would be best to describe him as the shah's faithful retainer in the sphere of foreign policy. Khal'atbari did not initiate; he only carried out the shah's wishes with absolute loyalty. At the same time, he displayed a measure of politeness toward Israel as contrasted with the previous foreign minister, Ardashir Zahedi, the close friend of the shah and for a certain period even his son-in-law, who subsequently was the Iranian ambassador to Washington and was hostile to us, both as foreign minister and as ambassador.

Later that evening we reached the guest house where a few members of the embassy were waiting—the minister who is the ambassador's substitute and one or two of the senior staff. The others were not privy to the secret. After a few polite words, the foreign minister took his leave and Nasiri and the Israeli group were left alone with the guest house staff at our service.

This guest house is one of the most modern and luxurious buildings in Teheran. Much work had been put into designing it in a typical Iranian architectural style. Around the central building are auxiliary structures, and all the buildings are surrounded by a garden that stretches over tens of dunams, with lawns and trees, large pools, fountains, and artistic lighting, all of which create the feeling that the visitor is not in a real world but has suddenly found himself in the setting of an eastern fable.

It was the custom for the senior guest to be given a whole floor to himself in the central building which he and his bodyguard occupied. On the floor above, the ambassador and the guest's aides were housed. In this case, Haim Bar-On and the other members of the entourage resided in one of the adjacent buildings that are part of the guest house complex.

At first I thought that on that same evening we would hold a preparatory discussion for the meetings Allon was to have the next day. But I saw that Yigal was already tired, and I decided that it would be better to let him rest and to start the discussion on the morrow. The meeting with the shah was scheduled for 11 A.M., and Yigal had to leave the guest house at 10:35. The discussion was postponed until morning.

In this discussion, we reviewed the topics we were interested in having brought to the shah's attention. We also discussed Allon's possible reactions if the shah responded in this or that manner to the things he was told. During these talks we had to take into account the fact that the house had been equipped with the latest listening devices, and we, therefore, used to switch on a radio so as to prevent our talks from being recorded. As always, Yigal was a good listener, and he welcomed any idea or advice that gave him "ammunition" for his talk with the shah, which was always shrouded in tension. It must be recalled that, at that time, the shah was at the height of his power and influence in the international arena. Since the oil crisis following the Yom Kippur War, oil prices had risen dramatically and Iran had begun to enjoy royalties she had not dreamed of. Iran became a focal point of political and economic influence, and all the countries of Europe wished to cultivate her. The shah realized this and exploited it. He began to exhibit an aggressive stand toward the countries of the West and explained to them that he had no intention of continuing the old system whereby Iran supplied oil and the Western countries supplied her with equipment and services and thus the money they paid out for oil returned to them. The shah declared that it was his intention to turn Iran into a strong regional military and industrial power within fifteen years, a power that would not be dependent on the good will of countries or world blocs. In light of this, the delicate position of the Israelis on this visit to the shah must be understood, for our relationship with Iran was more complex and complicated than that of other states.

The main subject for this meeting between Allon and the shah was the attempt on the part of Iranian officials to change the relationship between the two countries with respect to the oil supply. Allon's intention was to persuade the shah to continue supplying oil, despite the proposals of his aides. Yigal digested the topic thoroughly in our talks before the meeting with the shah. It must be remembered that Allon was never very involved in the oil situation in Israel, while the shah was very well informed about everything concerning the Iranian oil setup. The confrontation with him was, therefore, no easy matter, particularly since the person facing him was not an oil man. But Yigal Allon was blessed with a flair for learning things quickly and thoroughly, and I was amazed that not only did he absorb the central issue but he developed a set of arguments to justify our position that had a touch of originality.

Yigal Allon also had to use this meeting with the shah to discuss, thoroughly, the political developments in the Middle East. For example, if my memory serves me, just prior to the date of the meeting we had discovered disturbing signs of a rapprochement between Syria and Iran, and Yigal wanted to investigate the nature of this development and also to get from the shah information and reactions to a wide variety of topics.

About half an hour before it was time to set out for the shah's palace, the Iranian foreign minister came to the guest house to hold a short meeting and to accompany Yigal Allon to the palace. We said farewell to Allon, who went with Khal'atbari in a car placed at his disposal by the Iranian authorities and accompanied by a guard. Allon went to the Niavaran Palace, the shah's new palace in northern Teheran where he resided most of the year and in which he had his private offices.

Visitors to the palace followed a fixed routine, and Allon did so too. He reached the central gate of the wall around the palace. The car was stopped, and the guards peered closely at the occupants even though they knew about the visit in advance and despite the fact that one of the occupants was the Iranian foreign minister. After this examination, an Iranian security officer entered Allon's car and rode with them for the few hundred meters to the palace entrance where the deputy chief of protocol of the palace awaited them. He was in charge of secret visits of this type and led Allon to a waiting room on the second floor of the building. On their way to the waiting room, the visitors passed objets d'art, priceless statues, and breathtaking carpets. After drinking the traditional glass of Persian tea, the moment came for Allon to enter the presence of the shah for a private conversation. According to the custom in the shah's court, the Iranian foreign minister had to remain outside, and it was an embarrassing moment when the Israeli guest went in to the meeting while his Iranian counterpart was forced to wait outside the door like an errand boy. I remember that Yigal Allon did not understand this arrangement and was distressed at the insult his colleague suffered. The custom of the shah's court epitomized the centralistic, authoritarian character of the regime. The shah, alone, was at the top, and subordinate to him were officials who received instructions from him and carried out his orders without really being part of the decision-making process.

Allon put all his powers of persuasion into the meeting with the shah in order to ensure that the relations between the two countries in regard to oil would continue along the same lines. Whoever meets the shah has to try to find the middle road between a cordial atmosphere that includes a desire to please the shah and an unwillingness to be obsequious and the necessity to bargain and argue convincingly against the claims and considerations of Iran, which we did not always find pleasant. Allon's argument was that a fundamental identity of interests between Iran and Israel made it essential to maintain the existing relationship. Allon explained that he would not allow the oil supply arrangement that had proved most convenient for Iran in the past to be interrupted at the recommendation of officials who took only economic considerations into account and were, perhaps, not always sufficiently aware of the real essence of common interests. To this end Yigal gave a well-informed lecture on the important role that, in his opinion, the cooperation between Iran and Israel had to play in the international arena. Allon even implied—and one must know how to hint to Orientals without insulting them—that the continuation of relations with Israel might be a bother to Iran now, but tomorrow the tables might be turned and so it was as well to base the relations between the two countries on firm principles rather than on a passing inference of events.

Since the conversation was held in private, we only learned about the dialogue later when, after the meeting was over, Allon reported what had taken place almost verbatim. There was no doubt that the entire conversation was recorded by the devices in the shah's palace. From Allon we learned that he had achieved his main objective: the shah told him that he did not intend to change the existing relations between the two countries with regard to the oil supply. This decision of the shah gave Yigal much personal satisfaction.

In meetings of this nature, it was customary for the shah to recite a monologue in which he presented his up-to-date interpretation of events in the international arena. In the conversation he would talk with some frankness about various aspects of Iran's foreign policy. Sometimes he would express serious complaints against the United States, which, he felt, did not understand the processes taking place on the international scene in general, and in the Middle East in particular. The shah would even express his evaluation of various statesmen, knowing that his words would not reach the wrong ears. During his talks with Allon, the shah made him privy to his worries about Iran's internal troubles, including her pace of development, but, at the same time, there was no hint that the shah sensed the signs of the earthquake that was to shake the foundations of his regime. The shah's talks with his Israeli visitors usually lasted sixty to seventy-five minutes, but the meeting with Allon took over two hours. As was customary, Allon presented the shah with a gift at the end of the meeting. It was usual to give the shah some antique object from the time of the Persian conquest of the Land of Israel. This time Allon had decided to give him something more modern—a statue of a Galilee leopard about to pounce, made by an artist from Safed. . . .

Allon returned to the guest house and after a short break continued on to the foreign minister's house where a luncheon was being given in his honor. A small group of senior Iranian officials was present at the meal. Allon had the opportunity to exert all his charm and talent for rhetoric. The people present were charmed by Allon's simple manner and his direct approach and by his experience and knowledge of international affairs. In his free-flowing style, Allon told about Israel's difficulties and about his home on [Kibbutz] Ginosar. I remember that the Iranian foreign minister was very impressed by his words and said that he very much wanted to visit Israel and see things for himself. And, indeed, he did come to Israel on a secret visit in March 1977 and was Yigal Allon's guest at Ginosar. Khal'atbari was accompanied by his wife and daughter, and he was the most senior Iranian representative to visit Israel while I was ambassador. A friendship sprang up between the two foreign ministers, and this later made my contact with Khal'atbari easier, for he paid closer attention to any message or request I brought him from Yigal Allon.

The conversation at the foreign minister's house was cut short because Allon was due at a meeting with the prime minister. This meeting took place due to the endeavors of Khal'atbari, who had a close relationship with Prime Minister ['Abbas] Hoveyda. We rushed off to the meeting at the Prime Minister's Office on Kakh Street in central Teheran. This time, we were driving in broad daylight in the court limousine with the companion car close to us. It was at the peak period of traffic, and we had to drive crazily and, at times, break the traffic regulations. I was afraid that someone would identify Allon, who was not disguised. We passed through bustling streets, and we sometimes stopped at junctions despite ourselves, and anyone could have looked in and seen who was sitting in the car. But I felt that Yigal Allon enjoyed this opportunity of rushing through the streets of Teheran and seeing something of the city and the human side of things. Perhaps he also enjoyed the drama in the situation, but for me, it was almost a traumatic experience.

Prime Minister Hoveyda was waiting for Allon in his luxurious office. He had already managed to fill himself in on the talks Allon had held with the shah and the foreign minister. Hoveyda was the most senior official in the Iranian government, and the meeting with him was important, not because I expected there to be any practical outcome but because I wanted Allon to have the opportunity to hear Hoveyda's views. Furthermore, it was obvious that this conversation would be reported to the shah, and it therefore gave Allon an opportunity to convey to the shah his complimentary impressions of the meeting with him.

Right from the very outset of the meeting, a feeling of intimacy was created—what is today called "chemistry"—between Allon and the prime minister. Amir 'Abbas Hoveyda, the scion of a Bahai family, was born in Acre. He moved up through the ranks of the Iranian bureaucracy after he began his service in the Foreign Ministry. He was then appointed to a senior post in the national oil company of Iran and finally became prime minister. Hoveyda was a highly educated man and at home with Western culture. He had a good command of English, French, German, and Arabic and was one of the few Iranian personalities who read widely. His well-endowed library was like that of a very cultured Western person. Hoveyda would follow events in the world not only in the political and economic sectors but was also conversant with trends in English, American, and French literature. During an evening at his home, one could also meet Iranian men of culture who were not part of the establishment. The conversation between Hoveyda and Allon ranged over a variety of topics. Hoveyda was not an Arab sympathizer. He told of meetings with prime ministers of foreign countries at which the issues of Israel and the Middle East were discussed. The talk moved on to affairs of culture and economics, and there was a feeling that it could have gone on and on. But Allon had to leave on the El Al plane, and it was clear that he and Hoveyda regretted having to part.

Once again, we rushed with Allon in the car from the Prime Minister's Office to the guest house in the north of the city and there we found the gifts from the shah and the prime minister, in reciprocation for the presents Allon had made them. Suitcases were hastily packed, and Allon once again looked like a tourist who had visited Teheran on a pleasure trip.

On the way to the airport, Allon was accompanied by his official host, Nasiri. The El Al passengers had already been on the plane for some time when the "strange tourist" and his two companions took their seats. The plane took off, and I heaved a sigh of relief that everything had gone off all right.

100

Anwar Sadat and Menahem Begin

Speeches to the Knesset

November 20, 1977

In November 1977, following an understanding reached through secret diplomacy, Egyptian President Anwar Sadat, speaking before the Egyptian People's Assembly, declared that he was willing to travel to Jerusalem if necessary to find a solution to the Arab-Israeli conflict. The Israeli government immediately picked up on this cue and sent Sadat an invitation to come to Jerusalem and address the Knesset. Sadat received the invitation on November 17, arrived in Israel on November 19, and on Sunday afternoon, November 20, spoke to the Israeli people. This special session of the Knesset was televised live throughout the world. Sadat spoke in Arabic, one of Israel's official languages. Israeli Prime Minister Menahem Begin replied in Hebrew and appeared to be speaking extemporaneously without a prepared text. Shimon Peres, leader of the Labor Party opposition, also spoke on that occasion.

Simultaneously, U.S. President Jimmy Carter was trying to reconvene the Geneva Peace Conference and bring the Soviet Union into the peace process. But the conference never reconvened, and Sadat's gambit effectively kept the Soviet Union out of the picture while beginning, after many years, direct negotiations between belligerents in the Arab-Israeli conflict. The ultimate results were the Camp David Accords of September 1978 (doc. 103), implemented by an Egyptian-Israeli peace treaty in 1979 (doc. 104).

Anwar Sadat, Speech to the Knesset, November 20, 1977

In the name of God, Mr. Speaker of the Knesset, ladies and gentlemen. Allow me first to thank the Speaker of the Knesset deeply for affording me this opportunity so that I may address you. And as I begin my address, I wish to say peace and the mercy of God Almighty be upon you, and may peace be for us all, God willing. Peace for us all, all the Arab lands and in Israel, as well as in every part of this big world, this world which is so complexed [*sic*] by its sanguinary conflicts, disturbed by its sharp contradictions, menaced now and then by costly wars launched by man to annihilate his fellow men. Amidst the ruins of what man has built, and the remains of the victims of mankind, there emerges neither victor nor vanquished. The only vanquished remains always a man—man, God's most sublime creation, man whom God has created as [Mohandas] Gandhi,[1] the apostle of peace, put it, to forge ahead, to mould a way of life, and to worship God Almighty.

I come to you today on solid ground to shape a new life and prepare a peace. Well, on this land, the land of God, we all—Muslims, Christians and Jews—we all worship God and no one but God. God's teaching and commandments are love, sincerity, purity and peace.

I do not blame all those who received my decision when I announced it to the entire world before the Egyptian People's Assembly—I say I do not blame them. I do not blame all

Sources: Colin Legum, Haim Shaked, and Daniel Dishon, eds., *Middle East Contemporary Survey, 1978–1979* (New York: Holmes and Meier Publishers, 1980), vol. 2, app. 1, pp. 134–39, 139–42. Reprinted by permission of the publisher.

those who received my decision with surprise and even with amazement. Some even, struck by violent surprise, believed that my decision was no more than verbal juggling to cater for world public opinion. Others still interpreted it as political tactics to camouflage my intention to launch a new war.

I would go as far as to tell you that one of my aides in the Presidential Office contacted me at the late hour following my return home from the People's Assembly and sounded worried as he asked me: "Mr. President, what would be our reaction if Israel should actually extend an invitation to you?" I replied calmly: "I would accept it immediately." I have declared that I would go to the end of the world. I would go to Israel, for I want to put before the people of Israel all the facts.

I can see the point of all those who were astounded by my decision, all those who had any doubts as to the sincerity of the intention behind the declaration of my decision. No one would ever have conceived that the President of the biggest Arab state, which bears the heaviest burden and the main responsibility pertaining to the cause of war and peace in the Middle East, could declare his readiness to go to the land of the adversary while we were still in a state of war. Rather we all are still bearing the consequences of four fierce wars waged within ten years [*sic*]. All this at a time when the families of the 1973 October War are still suffering the cruel pain of widowhood and bereavement of sons, fathers and brothers.

As I have already declared, I have not consulted, as far as this decision is concerned, with any of my colleagues or brothers, the Arab Heads of State, or the confrontation states. Those of them who contacted me following the declaration of this decision spoke of their objection because the feeling of opposite mission and absolute lack of confidence between the Arab states and the Palestinian people on the one hand, and Israel on the other, still surges in us all.

It is sufficient to say that many months within which peace could have been brought about have been wasted over differences and fruitless discussions of the process for the convocation of the Geneva conference, all showing utter suspicion and absolute lack of confidence. But, to be absolutely frank with you, I took this decision after long thinking, knowing that it constitutes a grave risk for, if God Almighty has made it my fate to assume responsibility on behalf of the Egyptian people and to share in the fate-determining responsibility of the Arab nation, the main duty dictated by this responsibility, is to exhaust every means in a bid to save my Arab people and the entire Arab nation the horrors of new, shocking and destructive wars, the dimensions of which are foreseen by no other than God Himself.

After long thinking, I was convinced that the obligation of responsibility before God and before the people makes it incumbent upon me that I should go to the farthest corners of the world, even to Jerusalem, to address members of the Knesset, the representatives of the people of Israel, and acquaint them with all the facts surging in me. Then I would leave you to decide for yourselves. Following this, may God Almighty determine our fate.

There are moments in the life of nations and peoples when it is incumbent for those known for their wisdom and clarity of vision to overlook the past with all its complexities and weighing memories in a bold drive toward new horizons. Those who, like us, are shouldering the same responsibilities entrusted to us, are the first who should have the courage to take fate-determining decisions which are in consonance with the circumstances. We must all rise above all forms of fanaticism, above all forms of self-deception and above all forms of obsolete theories of superiority. The most important thing is never to forget infallibility is the prerogative of God alone.

If I said that I wanted to avert from all the Arab people the horrors of shocking and destructive wars, I must sincerely declare before you that I have the same feelings and bear the same responsibility towards all and every man on earth, and certainly towards the Israel people. . . .

In light of these facts—which I've placed before you the way I see them—I would also wish, in all sincerity, *to warn you.* I warn you against some thought which could cross your minds. Frankness makes it incumbent upon me to tell you the following.

First, *I have not come here for a separate agreement between Egypt and Israel.* This is not part of the policy of Egypt. The problem is not that of Egypt and Israel. Any separate peace between Egypt and Israel, or between Arab confrontation states and Israel, will not bring permanent peace, based on justice, in the entire region. Rather, even if peace between all the confrontation states and Israel were achieved, in the absence of a just solution to the Palestinian problem, there would never be the durable and just peace upon which the entire world today insists.

Second, *I have not come to you to seek a partial peace*—namely, to terminate the state of belligerency at this stage, and put off the entire problem to a subsequent stage. This is not the radical solution that would steer us to permanent peace.

Equally, *I have not come to you for a third disengagement agreement in Sinai, or in the Golan and the West Bank,* for this would mean that we are merely delaying the ignition of the fuse. Rather, it would also mean that we are lacking the courage to face peace, that we are too weak to shoulder the burdens and responsibilities of a durable peace based on justice. I have *come to you so that together we can build* a durable peace based on justice, to avoid the shedding of one single drop of blood from either of the two parties.

It is for this reason that I have proclaimed my readiness to go to the farthest corner of the world. *Here I would go back to the big question: How can we achieve a durable peace based on justice?* In my opinion, and I declare it to the whole world from this forum, the answer is neither difficult, nor is it impossible, despite long years of feuds, vengeance, spite and hatred, and breeding generations on concepts of deep-rooted animosity. The answer is not difficult, nor is it impossible—if we sincerely and faithfully follow a straight line.

You want to live with us, in this part of the world. In all sincerity, I tell you we welcome you among us, with full security and safety. This in itself is a tremendous turning point, one of the landmarks of a decisive historic change.

We used to reject you. We had our reasons and our claims, yes. We refused to meet with you anywhere, yes. We used to brand you as "so-called Israel," yes. We were together in international conferences and organizations and our representatives did not—and still do not—exchange greetings with you, yes. This has happened and is still happening.

It is also true that we used to set, as a precondition for any negotiations with you, a mediator who would meet separately with each party, by this procedure the talks for the first and second disengagement agreements took place. Our delegates met in the first Geneva conference without exchanging a direct word, yes. This has happened.

Yet today *I tell you, and I declare it to the whole world, that we accept living with you in permanent peace based on justice.* We do not want to encircle you, or be encircled ourselves, by destructive missiles ready for launching, nor by the shells of grudges and hatred. *I have announced on more than one occasion that Israel has become a fait accompli, recognized by the world,* and that the two super-powers have undertaken the responsibility of its security and the defense of its existence.

As we really and truly seek peace, we really and truly welcome you to live among us in peace and security. There was a huge wall between us which you tried to build up over a quarter of a century, but it was destroyed in 1973. It was a wall of a continuously inflammable and escalating psychological warfare. It was a wall of fear of the force that could sweep the entire Arab nation. It was a wall of propaganda that we were a nation reduced to a motionless corpse. Some of you had gone as far as to say that even after 50 years the Arabs would not regain their strength. It was a wall that threatened always, with a long arm that could reach and strike anywhere. It was a wall that warned us against extermination and annihilation if we tried to use our legitimate right to liberate the occupied territories. Together we have to admit that the wall fell and collapsed in 1973.

Yet there remains another wall. This wall constitutes a psychological barrier between us. A barrier of suspicion. A barrier of rejection. A barrier of fear of deception. A barrier of hallucinations around any action, deed or decision. A barrier of cautious and erroneous interpretation of all and every event or statement. It is this psychological barrier which I described in official statements as constituting 70 percent of the whole problem. . . .

As I have told you, there is no happiness to the detriment of others. Direct confrontation and straight-forwardness are the short cuts, and the most successful way to reach a clear objective. Direct confrontation concerning the Palestinian problem and tackling it in one single language with a view to achieving a durable and just peace lie in the establishment of their state. With all the guarantees you demand, there should be no fear of a newly born state that needs the assistance of all countries of the world when the bells of peace ring, there will be no hands to beat the drums of war. Even if they existed, they would be soundless.

Conceive with me a peace agreement in Geneva that we would herald to a world thirsty for peace. A peace agreement based on the following points: (1) ending the Israeli occupation of the Arab territories occupied in 1967; (2) achievement of the fundamental right of the Palestinian people and their right to self-determination, including their right to establish their own state; (3) the right of all states in the area to live in peace, within their boundaries, their secure boundaries, which will be secured and guaranteed through procedures to be agreed upon, providing appropriate security for international boundaries, in addition to appropriate international guarantees; (4) commitment of all states in the region to administer the relations among them in accordance with the objectives and principles of the U.N. Charter, particularly the principles concerning the non-resort to force and the solutions to differences among them by peaceful means; (5) ending the state of belligerency in the region.

Peace is not a mere endorsement of written lines. Rather it is a rewriting of history. Peace is not a game of calling for peace to defend certain whims, or hide certain ambitions. Peace, in its essence, is a joint struggle against all and every ambition and whim. Perhaps the examples and experience taken from ancient and modern history teach us all that missiles, warships and nuclear weapons cannot establish security. Rather, they destroy what peace and security build, for the sake of our peoples, and for the sake of the civilization made by man, we have to defend men everywhere against the rule of the force of arms, so that we may endow the rule of humanity with all the power of the values and principles that promote the sublime position of mankind.

Allow me to address my call from this rostrum to the people of Israel. I address myself with true and sincere words to every man, woman and child in Israel. I tell them, from the Egyptian people who bless this sacred mission of peace; I convey to you the message of peace, the message of the Egyptian people, who do not know fanaticism and whose sons—Muslims, Christians and Jews—live together in a state of cordiality, love and tolerance.

This is Egypt, whose people have entrusted me with that sacred message—the message of security, safety and peace. To every man, woman and child in Israel, I say: encourage your leadership to struggle for peace. Let all endeavors be channelled towards building a huge edifice for peace, instead of strongholds and hideouts defended by destructive rockets. Introduce to the entire world the image of the new man in this area, so that we might set an example to the men of our age, the men of peace everywhere.

Be heroes to the sons. Tell them that past wars were the last of wars and the end of sorrows. Tell them that we are in for a new beginning to a new life—a life of love, prosperity, freedom and peace. You, bewailing mother; you, widowed wife, you, the son who lost a brother or a father; you, all victims of wars, fill the earth and space with recitals of peace. Fill bosoms and hearts with the aspirations of peace. Turn the song into a reality that blossoms and lives. Make hope a code of conduct and endeavour. The will of peoples is part of the will of God.

Before I came to this place, with every beat of my heart and with every sentiment, I prayed to God Almighty, while performing the 'Id al-Adha at the al-Aqsa Mosque and while visiting the Church of the Holy Sepulchre, I asked God Almighty to give me strength, and to confirm my belief that this visit may achieve the objective I look forward to for a happy present and a happier future.

I have chosen to set aside all precedents and traditions known by warring countries, in spite of the fact that occupation of the Arab territories still exists. Rather, the declaration of my readiness to proceed to Israel came as a great surprise that stirred many feelings and astounded many minds. Some even doubted its intent. Despite it all, the decision was inspired by all the clarity and purity of belief and with all the true expression of my people's will and intentions.

And I have chosen this difficult road, which is considered by many and in the opinion of many the most difficult road. I have chosen to come to you with an open heart and an open mind. I have chosen to give the great impetus to all international efforts exerted for peace. I have chosen to present to you and in your own home the realities devoid of any scheme or whim, not to manoeuvre or to win a round, but for us to win together the most dangerous of rounds and battles in modern history—the battle of permanent peace based on justice.

It is not my battle alone, nor is it the battle of the leadership in Israel alone. It is the battle of all and every citizen in all our territories, whose right it is to live in peace. It is the commitment of conscience and responsibility in the hearts of millions.

When I put forward this initiative, many asked, what is it that I conceive as possible to achieve during this visit and what my expectations were. And, as I answered the questioners, I announce before you that I have not thought of carrying out this initiative from the concept of what could be achieved during this visit.

But I have come here to deliver a message. I have delivered the message and may God be my witness.

I repeat with Zachariah, "Love right and justice." From the Holy Koran I quote the following verses: "We believe in God and in what has been revealed to us and in what was revealed to Abraham, Ismael, Isaac, Jacob and the tribes and in the books given to Moses, Jesus and the Prophet from their Lord. We make no distinction between one and another among them, and to God's will we submit."

Peace be upon you.

Menahem Begin, Speech to the Knesset, November 20, 1977

Mr. Speaker, Mr. President of the State of Israel, Mr. President of the Arab Republic of Egypt, ladies and gentlemen, members of the Knesset: We send our greetings to the President, to all the people of the Islamic religion in our country, and wherever they may be, on this occasion of the feast of the festival of the sacrifice 'Id al-Adha. This feast reminds us of the binding of Isaac. This was the way in which the Creator of the World tested our forefather Abraham, our common forefather, to test his faith, and Abraham passed this test. However, from the moral aspect and the advancement of humanity, it was forbidden to sacrifice human beings. Our two peoples in their ancient traditions know and taught what the Lord, blessed be He, taught while peoples around us still sacrificed human beings to their gods. Thus, we contributed, the people of Israel and the Arab people, to the progress of mankind, and thus we are continuing to contribute to human culture to this day.

I greet and welcome the President of Egypt for coming to our country and on participating in the Knesset session. The flight time between Cairo and Jerusalem is short, but the distance between Cairo and Jerusalem was until last night almost endless. President Sadat crossed this distance courageously. We, the Jews, know how to appreciate such courage, and we know how to appreciate it in our guest, because it is with courage that we are here, and this is how we continue to exist, and we shall continue to exist.

Mr. Speaker, this small nation, the remaining refuge of the Jewish people who returned to their historic homeland, has always wanted peace, and since the dawn of our independence, on 14 May 1948 (5 Iyar Tashah), in the declaration of independence in the founding scroll of our national freedom [doc. 21], David Ben-Gurion said: "We offer peace and amity to all the neighboring states and their peoples and invite them to cooperate with the independent Jewish nation for the common good of all." One year earlier, even from the underground, when we were in the midst of the fateful struggle for the liberation of the country and the redemption of the people, we called on our neighbors in these terms: "In this country we will live together and we will live lives of freedom and happiness. Our Arab neighbors, do not reject the hand stretched out to you in peace."

But it is my bounden duty, Mr. Speaker, and not only my right, not to pass over the truth that our hand outstretched for peace was not grasped and one day after we had renewed our independence, as was our right, our eternal right, which cannot be disputed, we were attacked on three fronts, and we stood almost without arms, the few against many, the weak against the strong, while an attempt was made, one day after the declaration of independence, to strangle it at birth, to put an end to the last hope of the Jewish people, the yearning renewed after the years of destruction and holocaust. No, we do not believe in might and we have never based our attitude toward the Arab people on might. Quite the contrary, force was used against us. Over all the years of this generation we have never stopped being attacked by might, of the strong arm stretched out to exterminate our people, to destroy our independence, to deny our rights. We defended ourselves, it is true. We defended our rights, our existence, our honor, our women, and our children, against these repeated and recurring attempts to crush us through the force of arms, and not only on one front. That, too, is true. With the help of God Almighty, we overcame the forces of aggression, and we have guaranteed existence for our nation. Not only for this generation, but for the coming generations. Yet we do not believe in might, we believe only in right. And therefore our aspiration, from the bottom of our hearts, has always been to this very day, for peace.

Mr. President, Mr. President of Egypt, the commanders of the underground Hebrew fighting organizations are sitting in this democratic house. They had to conduct a campaign of the few against the many, against a huge, a world power. Here are sitting the veteran commanders and captains who had to go forth into battle because it was forced upon them and forward to victory, which was unavoidable because they were defending their rights. They belong to different parties. They have different views, but I am sure, Mr. President, that I am expressing the views of everyone, with no exceptions, that we have one aspiration in our hearts, one desire in our souls, and all of us are united in these aspirations and desires—to bring peace, peace for our nation, which has not known peace for even one day since we started returning to Zion, and peace for our neighbors, whom we wish all the best, and we believe that if we make peace, real peace we will be able to help our neighbors, in all walks of life, and a new era will open in the Middle East, an era of blossoming and growth, development and expansion of the economy, its growth as it was in the past.

Therefore, permit me today to set forth the peace program as we understand it. We want full, real peace with complete reconciliation between the Jews and the Arab peoples. I do not wish to dwell on the memories of the past, but there have been wars: there has been blood spilt: wonderful young people have been killed on both sides. We will live all our life with the memories of our heroes who gave their lives so this day would arrive, this day, too, would come, and we respect the bravery of a rival, and we honor all the members of the younger generation among the Arab people who also fell.

I do not wish to dwell on memories of the past, although they be bitter memories. We will bury them; we will worry about the future, about our people, our children, our joint and common future. For it is true indeed that we will have to live in this area, all of us together will live here, for generations upon generations: The great Arab people in their various states and countries, and the Jewish people in their country, Eretz Israel. Therefore, we must determine what peace means.

Let us conduct negotiations, Mr. President, as free negotiating partners for a peace treaty, and, with the aid of the Lord, we fully believe the day will come when we can sign it with mutual respect, and we will then know that the era of wars is over, that hands have been extended between friends, that each has shaken the hand of his brother and the future will be shining for all the peoples of this area. The beginning of wisdom in a peace treaty is the abolition of the state of war. I agree, Mr. President, that you did not come here, we did not invite you to our country in order, as has been said in recent days, to divide the Arab peoples. Somebody quoted an ancient Roman saying, Divide and rule. Israel does not want to rule and therefore does not need to divide. We want peace with all our neighbors: with Egypt, with Jordan, with Syria and with Lebanon. We would like to negotiate peace treaties. . . .

And there is no need to distinguish between a peace treaty and an abolition of the state of war. Quite the contrary, we are not proposing this nor are we asking for it. The first clause of a peace treaty is cessation of the state of war, forever. We want to establish normal relations between us, as they exist between all nations, even after wars. We have learned from history, Mr. President, that war is avoidable, peace is unavoidable. Many nations have waged war among themselves, and sometimes they used the tragic term perennial enemy. There are no perennial enemies. And after all the wars, the inevitable comes—peace. And so we want to establish, in a peace treaty, diplomatic relations as is the custom among civilized nations.

Today two flags are flying over Jerusalem: the Egyptian flag and the Israeli flag. And we saw together, Mr. President, little children waving both the flags. Let us sign a peace treaty and let us establish this situation forever, both in Jerusalem and in Cairo, and I hope the day will come when the Egyptian children wave the Israeli flag and the Egyptian flag, just as the children of Israel waved both these flags in Jerusalem.

And you, Mr. President, will have a loyal ambassador in Jerusalem and we will have an ambassador in Cairo. And even if differences of opinion arise between us, we will clarify them like civilized peoples through our authorized envoys.

We are proposing economic cooperation for the development of our countries. There are wonderful countries in the Middle East. The Lord created it thus: oases in the deserts as well and we can make them flourish. Let us cooperate in this field. Let us develop our countries. Let us eliminate poverty, hunger, the lack of shelter. Let us raise our peoples to the level of developed countries and let them not call us "developing countries."

And with all due respect, I am willing to confirm the words of his majesty the King of

Morocco, who said—in public too—that if peace arises in the Middle East, the combination of Arab genius and Jewish genius together can turn this area into a paradise on earth.

Let us open our countries to free traffic. You come to our country and we will visit yours. I am ready to announce, Mr. Speaker, this day that our country is open to the citizens of Egypt and I make no conditions on our part. I think it is only proper and just that there should be a joint announcement on this matter. But, just as there are Egyptian flags in our streets, and there is also an honored delegation from Egypt in our capital and in our country, let the number of visitors increase; our border will be open to you, and also all the other borders.

And as I pointed out, we want this in the south and in the north and in the east. And so I am renewing my invitation to the President of Syria to follow in your footsteps, Mr. President, and come to us to open negotiations for achieving peace between Israel and Syria and to sign a peace treaty between us. I am sorry to say but there is not justification for the mourning they have declared beyond our northern border. Quite the contrary such visits, such links, such clarifications can and must be days of joy, days of lifting spirits for all peoples. I invite King Hussein to come to us to discuss all the problems which need to be discussed between us, and also genuine representatives of the Arabs of Eretz Israel, I invite them to come and hold talks with us to clarify our common future, to guarantee the freedom of man, social justice, peace, mutual respect. And if they invite us to go to their capitals, we will go to those capitals in order to hold negotiations with them there. We do not want to divide. We want real peace with all our neighbors, to be expressed in peace treaties whose contents I have already made clear.

Mr. Speaker, it is my duty today to tell our guest and the peoples watching us and listening to our words about the link between our people and this country. The President recalled the Balfour Declaration [doc. 7]. No, sir, we did not take over any strange land; we returned to our homeland. The link between our people and this country is eternal. It arose in the earliest days of the history of humanity and has never been disrupted. In this country we developed our civilization, we had our prophets here, and their sacred words stand to this day. Here the kings of Judah and Israel knelt before their gods. This is where we became a people; here we established our kingdom. And when we were expelled from our land because of force which was used against us, the farther we went from our land, we never forgot this country for even a single day. We prayed for it, we longed for it, we believed in our return to it from the day the words were spoken: "When the Lord restores the fortunes of Zion, we will be like dreamers. Our mouths will be filled with laughter, and our tongues will speak with shouts of joy." These verses apply to all our exiles and our sufferings, giving the consolation that the return to Zion would come.

This, our right, was recognized. The Balfour Declaration was included in the mandate laid down by the nations of the world, including the United States, and the preface to this recognized international document says: "Whereas recognition has the Bible given to the historical connection of the Jewish people with Palestine and to the grounds for reconstituting their national home in that country"—the historic connection between the Jewish people and Palestine—or, in Hebrew, Eretz Israel, was given reconfirmation, reconfirmation as the national homeland in that country, that is, in Eretz Israel.

In 1919 we also won recognition of this right by the spokesman of the Arab people and the agreement of 3 January 1919, which was signed by Emir Faisal and Chaim Weizmann. It reads: [in English] Mindful of the racial kinship and ancient bonds existing between the Arabs and the Jewish people, and realizing that the surest means of working out the consummation of the national aspirations in the closest possible collaboration in the development of the Arab state and of Palestine [ends English]. And afterward come all the clauses about co-operation between the Arab state and Eretz Yisrael. This is our right. The existence—truthful existence.

What happened to us when our homeland was taken from us? I accompanied you this morning, Mr. President, to Yad Vashem. With your own eyes you saw the fate of our people when this homeland was taken from it. It cannot be told. Both of us agreed, Mr. President, that anyone who has not seen with his own eyes everything there is in Yad Vashem cannot understand what happened to this people when it was without a homeland, when its own homeland was taken from it. And both of us read a document dated 30 January 1939, where the word "Vernichtung"—annihilation—appears. If war breaks out, the Jewish race in Europe will be exterminated. Then, too, we were told that we should not pay attention to the racists. The whole world heard. Nobody came to save us. Not during the nine fateful, decisive months after the announcement was made, the like of which had not been seen since the Lord created man and man created the Devil.

And during those six years, too, when millions of our people, among them 1.5m of the little children of Israel who were burned on all the strange beds [*sic*], nobody came to save them, not from the East nor from the West. And because of this, we took a solemn oath, this entire generation, the generation of extermination and revival, that we would never again put our people in danger, that we would never again put our women and our children, whom it is our duty to defend—if there is a need for this, even at the cost of our lives—in the hell of the exterminating fire of an enemy. Since then, it has been our duty for generations to come to remember that certain things said about our people must be taken with complete seriousness. And we must not, heaven forbid, for the sake of the future of our people, take any advice whatsoever against taking these things seriously.

President al-Sādāt knows, and he knew from us before he came to Jerusalem, that we have a different position from his with regard to the permanent borders between us and our neighbours. However, I say to the President of Egypt and to all our neighbours: Do not say, there is not negotiation, there will not be negotiations about any particular issue. I propose, with the agreement of the decisive majority of this parliament, that everything be open to negotiation. Anyone who says, with reference to relations between the Arab people, or the Arab peoples around us, and the State of Israel, that there are things which should be omitted from negotiations is taking upon himself a grave responsibility. Everything can be negotiated.

No side will say the contrary. No side will present prior conditions. We will conduct the negotiations honourably. If there are differences of opinion between us, this is not unusual. Anyone who has studied the histories of wars and the signing of peace treaties knows that all negotiations over a peace treaty began with differences of opinion between the sides. And in the course of the negotiations they reached an agreement which permitted the signing of peace treaties and agreement. And this is the road which we propose to take.

And we will conduct the negotiations as equals. There are no vanquished and there are no victors. All the peoples of the area are equal and all should treat each other with due respect. In this spirit of openness, of willingness to listen to each other, to hear the facts and the reasoning and the explanations, accepting all the experience of human persuasion, let us conduct the negotiations as I have asked and am proposing, open them and carry them out, carry them on constantly until we reach the longed-for hour of the signing of a peace treaty between us.

We are not only ready to sit with the representatives of Egypt, and also with the representatives of Jordan and Syria and Lebanon. If it is ready, we are ready to sit together at a peace conference in Geneva. We propose that the Geneva conference be renewed, on the basis of the two Security Council Resolutions: 242 and 338. If there are problems between us, by convening the Geneva conference we will be able to clarify them. And if the President of Egypt wants to continue clarifying them in Cairo, I am for it. If in a neutral place, there is no objection. Let us clarify anywhere, even before the Geneva conference convenes, the problem which should be clarified before it is convened. And our eyes will be open and our ears will listen to all proposals.

Permit me to say a word about Jerusalem. Mr. President, you prayed today in the house of prayer sacred to the Islamic religion, and from there you went to the Church of the Holy Sepulchre. You realized, as those coming from all over the world have realized, that ever since this city was unified, there has been completely free access, without interference and without any obstacle, for the members of every religion to the places sacred to them. This positive phenomenon did not exist for 19 years. It has existed for about 11 years, and we can promise the Muslim world and Christian world, all the peoples, that there will always be free access to the sacred places of every religion. We will defend this right to free access, for we believe in it. We believe in equal rights for all men and citizens and respect for every faith.

Mr. Speaker, this is a special day for our legislative chamber, and certainly this day will be remembered for many years in the history of our nation, and perhaps also in the history of the Egyptian nation, maybe in the history of all nations. And this day, with your agreement, ladies and gentlemen, members of the Knesset, let us pray that the God of our fathers, our common fathers, will give us the wisdom needed to overcome difficulties and obstacles, calumnies and slander, incitement and attacks. And with the help of God, may we arrive at the longed-for-day for which all our people pray—peace. For it is indeed true that the sweet singer of Israel [King David] said: "Righteousness and peace will kiss each other," and the Prophet Zachariah said: "Love, truth and peace."

NOTE

1. Mohandas Gandhi (1869–1948), spiritual leader of the Indian nationalist and anticolonial movement. Gandhi's philosophy of militant passive resistance and nonviolence has had a great impact on political movements throughout the world. His followers called him Mahatma (Great Soul).

101

Government of Israel

Autonomy Plan

December 28, 1977

The Autonomy Plan represents Menahem Begin's attempt to cope with the Palestinian issue in the context of seeking to make peace with Egypt. Egypt refused to sign a document that would look like a separate peace with Israel. Begin was committed to his ideology of "Greater Israel." By offering the Palestinians self-rule without sovereignty he was trying to adhere to his ideological stance while securing an agreement with Cairo.

Source: U.S. Department of State, *The Camp David Summit, September 1978*, Department of State publication 8954, Near East and South Asia ser. 88 (Washington, D.C.: Government Printing Office, September 1978), pp. 6–15.

1. The administration of the Military Government in Judaea, Samaria and the Gaza district will be abolished.

2. In Judaea, Samaria and the Gaza district, administrative autonomy of the residents, by and for them, will be established.

3. The residents of Judaea, Samaria and the Gaza district will elect an Administrative Council composed of eleven members. The Administrative Council will operate in accordance with the principles laid down in this paper.

4. Any resident, eighteen years old and above, without distinction of citizenship, or if stateless, will be entitled to vote in the elections to the Administrative Council.

5. Any resident whose name is included in the list of candidates for the Administrative Council and who, on the day the list is submitted, is 25 years old or above, will be entitled to be elected to the Council.

6. The Administrative Council will be elected by general, direct, personal, equal and secret ballot.

7. The period of office of the Administrative Council will be four years from the day of its election.

8. The Administrative Council will sit in Bethlehem.

9. All the administrative affairs relating to the Arab residents of the areas of Judea, Samaria, and the Gaza district will be under the direction and within the competence of the Administrative Council.

10. The Administrative Council will operate the following Departments: education; religious affairs; finance; transportation; construction and housing; industry, commerce and tourism; agriculture; health, labor and social welfare; rehabilitation of refugees; and the administration of justice and the supervision of local police forces; and promulgate regulations relating to the operation of these Departments.

11. Security and public order in the areas of Judaea, Samaria and the Gaza district will be the responsibility of the Israeli authorities.

12. The Administrative Council will elect its own chairman.

13. The first session of the Administrative Council will be convened thirty days after the publication of the election results.

14. Residents of Judaea, Samaria and the Gaza district, without distinction of citizenship, or if stateless, will be granted free choice (option) of either Israeli or Jordanian citizenship.

15. A resident of the areas of Judaea, Samaria and the Gaza district who requests Israeli citizenship will be granted such citizenship in accordance with the citizenship law of the state.

16. Residents of Judaea, Samaria and the Gaza district who, in accordance with the right of free option, choose Israeli citizenship, will be entitled to vote for, and be elected to, the Knesset in accordance with the election law.

17. Residents of Judaea, Samaria and the Gaza district who are citizens of Jordan or who, in accordance with the right of free option will become citizens of Jordan, will elect and be eligible for election to the Parliament of the Hashemite Kingdom of Jordan in accordance with the election law of that country.

18. Questions arising from the vote to the Jordanian Parliament by residents of Judaea, Samaria and the Gaza district will be clarified in negotiations between Israel and Jordan.

19. A committee will be established of representatives of Israel, Jordan, and the Administrative Council to examine existing legislation in Judaea, Samaria and the Gaza district, and to determine which legislation will continue in force, which will be abolished, and what will be the competence of the Administrative Council to promulgate regulations. The rulings of the committee will be adopted by unanimous decision.

20. Residents of Israel will be entitled to acquire land and settle in the areas of Judaea, Samaria and the Gaza district. Arabs, residents of Judaea, Samaria and the Gaza district who, in accordance with the free option granted them, will become Israeli citizens, will be entitled to acquire land and settle in Israel.

21. A committee will be established of representatives of Israel, Jordan and the Administrative Council to determine norms of immigration to the areas of Judaea, Samaria and the Gaza district. The committee will determine the norms whereby Arab refugees residing outside Judaea, Samaria and the Gaza district will be permitted to immigrate to these areas in reasonable numbers. The rulings of the committee will be adopted by unanimous decision.

22. Residents of Israel and residents of Judaea, Samaria and the Gaza district will be assured freedom of movement and freedom of economic activity in Israel, Judaea, Samaria and the Gaza district.

23. The Administrative Council will appoint one of its members to represent the Council before the Government of Israel for deliberation on matters of common interest, and one of its members to represent the Council before the Government of Jordan for deliberation on matters of common interest.

24. Israel stands by its right and its claim of sovereignty to Judea, Samaria and the Gaza district. In the knowledge that other claims exist, it proposes, for the sake of the agreement and the peace, that the question of sovereignty in these areas be left open.

25. With regard to the administration of the holy places of the three religions in Jerusalem, a special proposal will be drawn up and submitted that will include the guarantee of freedom of access to members of all the faiths to the shrines holy to them.

26. These principles will be subject to review after a five-year period.

102

United Nations Security Council

Resolutions 425 and 426

March 19, 1978

After it was expelled from Jordan in 1970, the Palestine Liberation Organization made Lebanon the base for numerous attacks against Israel. On March 14, 1978, Israeli forces entered southern Lebanon (Operation Litani) in response to a deadly PLO attack on a bus near Tel Aviv in which thirty-five Israeli civilians were killed. The Israel Defense Forces gained control of the southern part of Lebanon up to the Litani River and lost eighteen soldiers in the operation.

On March 19, the United Nations Security Council adopted resolutions 425 and 426, which called for Israeli withdrawal and the establishment of a U.N. force in southern Lebanon. On March 21, 1978, Israel accepted the call for a cease-fire and began to withdraw from the region.

In 1982, following an assassination attempt on the life of the Israeli ambassador in London, Shlomo Argov, Israeli forces reentered Lebanon, this time all the way to Lebanon's capital, Beirut. Though Israel performed a partial withdrawal in 1985, Israeli forces remained in a self-declared security zone in the south of Lebanon until

Source: UN online, Official Documents System of the United Nations, March 19, 1978, www.yale.edu/lawweb/avalon/un/un425.htm, www.yale.edu/lawweb/avalon/un/un426.htm (accessed May 21, 2007).

2000 in order to defend northern Israel from attacks by the Shiite terror group, Hezbollah. During this period, U.N. Security Council Resolutions 425 and 426 served as the basis for Arab calls for Israeli withdrawal.

On April 1, 1998, Israel accepted U.N. Security Council Resolution 425, but with lack of appropriate security arrangements the actual withdrawal was carried out only in May 2000, following Prime Minister Ehud Barak's election promise in 1999 to do so. The U.N. Interim Force in Lebanon (UNIFIL) that was established for an "interim" period in 1978 by these resolutions continued in southern Lebanon and was expanded following the war in 2006.

Resolution 425

The Security Council,

Taking note of the letters from the Permanent Representative of Lebanon and from the Permanent Representative of Israel, Having heard the statement of the Permanent Representatives of Lebanon and Israel, Gravely concerned at the deterioration of the situation in the Middle East and its consequences to the maintenance of international peace, Convinced that the present situation impedes the achievement of a just peace in the Middle East,

1. *Calls for* strict respect for the territorial integrity, sovereignty and political independence of Lebanon within its internationally recognized boundaries;
2. *Calls upon* Israel *immediately* to cease its military action against Lebanese territorial integrity and withdraw forthwith its forces from all Lebanese territory;
3. *Decides,* in the light of the request of the Government of Lebanon, to establish *immediately* under its authority a United Nations interim force for Southern Lebanon for the purpose of confirming the withdrawal of Israeli forces, restoring international peace and security and assisting the Government of Lebanon in ensuring the return of its effective authority in the area, the Force to be composed of personnel drawn from Member States;
4. *Requests* the Secretary-General to report to the Council *within twenty-four hours* on the implementation of the present resolution.

Resolution 426

The Security Council,

1. *Approves* the report of the Secretary-General on the implementation of Security Council resolution 425 (1978), contained in document S/12611 of 19 March 1978,
2. *Decides* that the United Nations Interim Force in Lebanon shall be established in accordance with the above-mentioned report for an initial period of six months, and that it shall continue in operation thereafter if required, provided the Security Council so decides.

103
Camp David Accords
September 17, 1978

Following Anwar Sadat's historic trip to Jerusalem, Menahem Begin and Sadat met together in Ismailia on December 26, 1977. In early January 1978 Jimmy Carter and Sadat met at Aswan. Sadat visited the United States, February 3–8, and from February 9 to 13 he met European leaders. But Arab leaders and the Palestine Liberation Organization were seeking to frustrate the peace negotiations, and while Begin was in Washington, March 21–22, the negotiations began to reach an impasse. Israel had staged Operation Litani in southern Lebanon in March, as the positions of both the Egyptians and the Israelis hardened. On July 19, after Egyptian and Israeli foreign ministers met in England, Egypt stated that further talks were futile. Israel recalled its ten-man mission from Alexandria.

As the Egyptian-Israeli negotiations came to a standstill, Carter launched his "personal diplomacy" and arranged for a summit meeting at Camp David, a presidential retreat near Washington, D.C. On August 8, 1978, the White House announced the two heads of state accepted the president's offer for a meeting that would "seek a framework for peace in the Middle East." The meeting opened on September 5, 1978, without a specified time limit. The accords were signed two weeks later, in a historic ceremony at the White House. An exchange of letters among Carter, Sadat, and Begin, clarifying the accords, is printed at the end of the official document.

A Framework for Peace in the Middle East

Muhammed Anwar al-Sadat, President of the Arab Republic of Egypt, and Menahem Begin, Prime Minister of Israel, met with Jimmy Carter, President of the United States of America, at Camp David from September 5 to September 17, 1978, and have agreed on the following framework for peace in the Middle East. They invite other parties to the Arab-Israeli conflict to adhere to it.

Preamble

The search for peace in the Middle East must be guided by the following:

The agreed basis for a peaceful settlement of the conflict between Israel and its neighbors is United Nations Security Council Resolution 242 [doc. 68] in all its parts.

After four wars during thirty years, despite intensive human efforts, the Middle East, which is the cradle of civilization and the birthplace of three great religions, does not yet enjoy the blessings of peace. The people of the Middle East yearn for peace, so that the vast human and natural resources of the region can be turned to the pursuits of peace and so that this area can become a model for coexistence and cooperation among nations. . . .

The provisions of the Charter of the United Nations and the other accepted norms of international law and legitimacy now provide accepted standards for the conduct of relations among all states.

Source: U.S. Department of State, *The Camp David Summit, September 1978*, Department of State publication 8954, Near East and South Asia ser. 88 (Washington, D.C.: Government Printing Office, September 1978), pp. 6–15.

To achieve a relationship of peace, in the spirit of Article 2 of the United Nations Charter,[1] future negotiations between Israel and any neighbor prepared to negotiate peace and security with it, are necessary for the purpose of carrying out all the provisions and principles of Resolutions 242 and 338 [doc. 86].

Peace requires respect for the sovereignty, territorial integrity and political independence of every state in the area and their right to live in peace within secure and recognized boundaries free from threats or acts of force. Progress toward that goal can accelerate movement toward a new era of reconciliation in the Middle East marked by cooperation in promoting economic development, in maintaining stability and in assuring security.

Security is enhanced by a relationship of peace and by cooperation between nations which enjoy normal relations. In addition, under the terms of peace treaties, the parties can, on the basis of reciprocity, agree to special security arrangements such as demilitarized zones, limited armaments areas, early warning stations, the presence of international forces, liaison, agreed measures for monitoring, and other arrangements that they agree are useful.

Framework

Taking these factors into account, the parties are determined to reach a just, comprehensive, and durable settlement of the Middle East conflict through the conclusion of peace treaties based on Security Council Resolutions 242 and 338 in all their parts. Their purpose is to achieve peace and good neighborly relations. They recognize that, for peace to endure, it must involve all those who have been most deeply affected by the conflict. They therefore agree that this framework as appropriate is intended by them to constitute a basis for peace not only between Egypt and Israel, but also between Israel and each of its other neighbors which is prepared to negotiate peace with Israel on this basis. With that objective in mind, they have agreed to proceed as follows:

A. West Bank and Gaza

1. Egypt, Israel, Jordan and the representatives of the Palestinian people should participate in negotiations on the resolution of the Palestinian problem in all its aspects. To achieve that objective, negotiations relating to the West Bank and Gaza should proceed in three stages:

(a) Egypt and Israel agree that, in order to ensure a peaceful and orderly transfer of authority, and taking into account the security concerns of all the parties, there should be transitional arrangements for the West Bank and Gaza for a period not exceeding five years. In order to provide full autonomy to the inhabitants, under these arrangements the Israeli military government and its civilian administration will be withdrawn as soon as a self-governing authority has been freely elected by the inhabitants of these areas to replace the existing military government. To negotiate the details of a transitional arrangement, the government of Jordan will be invited to join the negotiations on the basis of this framework. These new arrangements should give due consideration both to the principle of self-government by the inhabitants of these territories and to the legitimate security concerns of the parties involved.

(b) Egypt, Israel, and Jordan will agree on the modalities for establishing the elected self-governing authority in the West Bank and Gaza. The delegations of Egypt and Jordan may include Palestinians from the West Bank and Gaza or other Palestinians as mutually agreed. The parties will negotiate an agreement which will define the powers and responsibilities of the self-governing authority to be exercised in the West Bank and Gaza. A withdrawal of Israeli armed forces will take place and there will be a redeployment of the remaining Israeli forces into specified security locations. The agreement will also include arrangements for assuring internal and external security and public order. A strong local police force will be established, which may include Jordanian citizens. In addition, Israeli and Jordanian forces will participate in joint patrols and in the manning of control posts to assure the security of the borders.

(c) When the self-governing authority (administrative council) in the West Bank and Gaza is established and inaugurated, the transitional period of five years will begin. As soon as possible, but not later than the third year after the beginning of the transitional period, negotiations will take place to determine the final status of the West Bank and Gaza and its relationship with its neighbors, and to conclude a peace treaty between Israel and Jordan by the end of the transitional period. These negotiations will be conducted among Egypt, Israel, Jordan, and the elected representatives of the inhabitants of the West Bank and Gaza. Two separate but related committees will be convened, one committee, consisting of representatives of the four parties which will negotiate and agree on the final status of the West Bank and Gaza, and its relationship with its neighbors, and the second committee, consisting of representatives of Israel and representatives of Jordan to be joined by the elected representatives of the inhabitants of the West Bank and Gaza, to negotiate the peace treaty between Israel and Jordan, taking into account the agreement reached on the final status of the West Bank and Gaza. The negotiations shall be based on all the provisions and principles of U.N. Security Council Resolution 242. The negotiation will resolve, among other matters, the location of the boundaries and the nature of the security arrangements. The solution from the negotiations must also recognize the legitimate rights of the Palestinian people and their just requirements. In this way, the Palestinians will participate in the determination of their own future through: (i) the negotiations among Egypt, Israel, Jordan and the representatives of the inhabitants of the West Bank and Gaza to agree on the final status of the West Bank and Gaza and other outstanding issues by the end of the transitional period; (ii) submitting their agreement to a vote by the elected representatives of the inhabitants of the West Bank and Gaza; (iii) providing for the elected representatives of the inhabitants of the West Bank and Gaza to decide how they shall govern themselves consistent with the provisions of their agreement; (iv) participating as stated above in the work of the committee negotiating the peace treaty between Israel and Jordan.

2. All necessary measures will be taken and provisions made to assure the security of Israel and its neighbors during the transitional period and beyond. To assist in providing such security, a strong local police force will be constituted by the self-governing authority. It will be composed of inhabitants of the West Bank and Gaza. The police will maintain continuing liaison on internal security matters with the designated Israeli, Jordanian, and Egyptian officers.

3. During the transitional period, representatives of Egypt, Israel, Jordan, and the self-governing authority will constitute a continuing committee to decide by agreement on the modalities of admission of persons displaced from the West Bank and Gaza in 1967, together with necessary measures to prevent disruption and disorder. Other matters of common concern may also be dealt with by this committee.

4. Egypt and Israel will work with each other and with other interested parties to establish agreed procedures for a prompt, just and permanent implementation of the resolution of the refugee problem.

B. EGYPT-ISRAEL

1. Egypt and Israel undertake not to resort to the threat or the use of force to settle disputes. Any disputes shall be settled by peaceful means in accordance with the provisions of Article 33 of the Charter of the United Nations.[2]

2. In order to achieve peace between them, the parties agree to negotiate in good faith with a goal of concluding within three months from the signing of this Framework a peace treaty between them, while inviting the other parties to the conflict to proceed simultaneously

to negotiate and conclude similar peace treaties with a view to achieving a comprehensive peace in the area. The Framework for the Conclusion of a Peace Treaty between Egypt and Israel will govern the peace negotiations between them. The parties will agree on the modalities and the timetable for the implementation of their obligations under the treaty.

C. ASSOCIATED PRINCIPLES

1. Egypt and Israel state that the principles and provisions described below should apply to peace treaties between Israel and each of its neighbors—Egypt, Jordan, Syria and Lebanon.

2. Signatories shall establish among themselves relationships normal to states at peace with one another. To this end, they should undertake to abide by all the provisions of the Charter of the United Nations. Steps to be taken in this report include: (a) full recognition; (b) abolishing economic boycotts; (c) guaranteeing that under their jurisdiction the citizens of the other parties shall enjoy the protection of the due process of law.

3. Signatories should explore possibilities for economic development in the context of final peace treaties, with the objective of contributing to the atmosphere of peace, cooperation and friendship which is their common goal.

4. Claims Commissions may be established for the mutual settlement of all financial claims.

5. The United States shall be invited to participate in the talks on matters related to the modalities of the implementation of the agreements and working out the timetable for the carrying out of the obligations of the parties.

6. The United Nations Security Council shall be requested to endorse the peace treaties and ensure that their provisions shall not be violated. The permanent members of the Security Council shall be requested to underwrite the peace treaties and ensure respect for their provisions. They shall also be requested to conform their policies and actions with the undertakings contained in this Framework.

Framework for the Conclusion of a Peace Treaty between Egypt and Israel

In order to achieve peace between them, Israel and Egypt agree to negotiate in good faith with a goal of concluding within three months of the signing of this framework a peace treaty between them:

It is agreed that:

The site of the negotiations will be under a United Nations flag at a location or locations to be mutually agreed.

All of the principles of U.N. Resolution 242 will apply in this resolution of the dispute between Israel and Egypt.

Unless otherwise mutually agreed, terms of the peace treaty will be implemented between two and three years after the peace treaty is signed.

The following matters are agreed between the parties: (1) the full exercise of Egyptian sovereignty up to the internationally recognized border between Egypt and mandated Palestine; (2) the withdrawal of Israeli armed forces from the Sinai; (3) the use of airfields left by the Israelis near al-Arish, Rafah, Ras en-Naqb, and Sharm el-Sheikh for civilian purposes only, including possible commercial use by all nations; (4) the right of free passage by ships of Israel through the Gulf of Suez and the Suez Canal on the basis of the Constantinople Convention of 1888[3] applying to all nations; the Strait of Tiran and the Gulf of Aqaba are international waterways to be open to all nations for unimpeded and nonsuspendable freedom of navigation and overflight; (5) the construction of a highway between the Sinai and Jordan near Eilat with guaranteed free and peaceful passage by Egypt and Jordan; and (6) the stationing of military forces listed below.

Stationing of Forces

No more than one division (mechanized or infantry) of Egyptian armed forces will be stationed within an area lying approximately 50 km [30 miles] east of the Gulf of Suez and the Suez Canal.

Only United Nations forces and civil police equipped with light weapons to perform normal police functions will be stationed within an area lying west of the international border and the Gulf of Aqaba, varying in width from 20 km [12 miles] to 40 km [24 miles].

In the area within 3 km [1.8 miles] east of the international border there will be Israeli limited military forces not to exceed four infantry battalions and United Nations observers.

Border patrol units, not to exceed three battalions, will supplement the civil police in maintaining order in the area not included above.

The exact demarcation of the above areas will be as decided during the peace negotiations.

Early warning stations may exist to insure compliance with the terms of the agreement.

United Nations forces will be stationed: (1) in part of the area in the Sinai lying within about 20 km of the Mediterranean Sea and adjacent to the international border, and (2) in the Sharm el-Sheikh area to ensure freedom of passage through the Strait of Tiran; and these forces will not be removed unless such removal is approved by the Security Council of the United Nations with a unanimous vote of the five permanent members.

After a peace treaty is signed, and after the interim withdrawal is complete, normal relations will be established between Egypt and Israel, including full recognition, including diplomatic, economic and cultural relations; termination of economic boycotts and barriers to the free movement of goods and people; and mutual protection of citizens by the due process of law.

Interim Withdrawal

Between three months and nine months after the signing of the peace treaty, all Israeli forces will withdraw east of a line extending from a point east of al-Arish to Ras Muhammad, the exact location of this line to be determined by mutual agreement.

Exchange of Letters Accompanying the Camp David Accords

Prime Minister Menahem Begin to President Jimmy Carter, September 17, 1978

I have the honor to inform you that during two weeks after my return home, I will submit a motion before Israel's parliament (the Knesset) to decide on the following question: "If during the negotiations to conclude a peace treaty between Israel and Egypt all outstanding issues are agreed upon, 'are you in favor of the removal of the Israeli settlers from the northern and southern Sinai areas or are you in favor of keeping the aforementioned settlers in those areas?'"

The vote, Mr. President, on this issue will be completely free from the usual parliamentary party discipline to the effect that although the coalition is being now supported by 70 members out of 120, every member of the Knesset, as I believe, both of the government and the opposition benches will be enabled to vote in accordance with his own conscience.

President Carter to President Anwar Sadat, September 22, 1978

I transmit herewith a copy of a letter to me from Prime Minister Begin setting forth how he proposes to present the issue of the Sinai settlements to the Knesset for the latter's decision.

In this connection, I understand from your letter that Knesset approval to withdraw all Israeli settlers from Sinai according to a timetable within the period specified for the implementation of the peace treaty is a prerequisite to any negotiations on a peace treaty between Egypt and Israel.

President Sadat to President Carter, September 17, 1978

In connection with the "Framework for a Settlement in Sinai" to be signed tonight, I would like to reaffirm the position of the Arab Republic of Egypt with respect to the settlements:

1. All Israeli settlers must be withdrawn from Sinai according to a timetable within the period specified for the implementation of the peace treaty.
2. Agreement by the Israeli Government and its constitutional institutions to this basic principle is therefore a prerequisite to starting peace negotiations for concluding a peace treaty.
3. If Israel fails to meet this commitment, the "framework" shall be void and invalid.

President Sadat to President Carter, September 17, 1978

I am writing you to reaffirm the position of the Arab Republic of Egypt with respect to Jerusalem:

1. Arab Jerusalem is an integral part of the West Bank. Legal and historical Arab rights in the city must be respected and restored.
2. Arab Jerusalem should be under Arab sovereignty.
3. The Palestinian inhabitants of Arab Jerusalem are entitled to exercise their legitimate national rights, being part of the Palestinian People in the West Bank.
4. Relevant Security Council Resolutions, particularly Resolutions 242 and 267,[4] must be applied with regard to Jerusalem. All the measures taken by Israel to alter the status of the city are null and void and should be rescinded.
5. All peoples must have free access to the City and enjoy the free exercise of worship and the right to visit and transit to the holy places without distinction or discrimination.
6. The holy places of each faith may be placed under the administration and control of their representatives.
7. Essential functions in the city should be undivided and a joint municipal council composed of an equal number of Arab and Israeli members can supervise the carrying out of these functions. In this way, the city shall be undivided.

Prime Minister Begin to President Carter, September 17, 1978

I have the honor to inform you, Mr. President, that on 28 June 1967, Israel's parliament (the Knesset) promulgated and adopted a law to the effect: "The Government is empowered by a decree to apply the law, the jurisdiction and administration of the State to any part of the Eretz Israel (land of Israel—Palestine), as stated in that decree."

On the basis of this law, the Government of Israel decreed in July 1967 that Jerusalem is one city indivisible, the Capital of the State of Israel.

President Carter to President Sadat, September 17, 1978

I have received your letter of 17 September 1978, setting forth the Egyptian position on Jerusalem. I am transmitting a copy of that letter to Prime Minister Begin for his information.

The position of the United States on Jerusalem remains as stated by [U.S.] Ambassador [Arthur] Goldberg in the United Nations General Assembly on July 14, 1967, and subsequently by Ambassador [Charles] Yost in the United Nations Security Council on July 1, 1969.

President Sadat to President Carter, September 17, 1978

In connection with the "Framework for Peace in the Middle East," I am writing you this letter to inform you of the position of the Arab Republic of Egypt, with respect to the implementation of the comprehensive settlement.

To ensure the implementation of the provisions related to the West Bank and Gaza and in order to safeguard the legitimate rights of the Palestinian people, Egypt will be prepared to assume the Arab role emanating from these provisions, following consultations with Jordan and the representatives of the Palestinian people.

President Carter to Prime Minister Begin, September 22, 1978

I hereby acknowledge that you have informed me as follows:

1. In each paragraph of the Agreed Framework Document the expressions "Palestinians" or "Palestinian People" are being and will be construed and understood by you as "Palestinian Arabs."

2. In each paragraph in which the expression "West Bank" appears, it is being, and will be, understood by the Government of Israel as Judaea and Samaria.

Harold Brown, U.S. Secretary of Defense, to Ezer Weizman, Israeli Defense Minister, September 29, 1978

The United States understands that, in connection with carrying out the agreements reached at Camp David, Israel intends to build two military airbases at appropriate sites in the Negev to replace the airbases at Eitam and Ezion which will be evacuated by Israel in accordance with the peace treaty to be concluded between Egypt and Israel. We also understand the special urgency and priority which Israel attaches to preparing the new bases in light of its conviction that it cannot safely leave the Sinai airbases until the new ones are operational.

I suggest that our two governments consult on the scope and costs of the two new airbases as well as on related forms of assistance which the United States might appropriately provide in light of the special problems which might be presented by carrying out such a project on an urgent basis.

The President is prepared to seek the necessary Congressional approvals for such assistance as may be agreed upon by the U.S. side as a result of such consultations.

NOTES

1. Article 2 of the U.N. Charter reads:

The Organization and its Members, in pursuit of the Purposes stated in Article 1, shall act in accordance with the following Principles.

1. The Organization is based on the principle of the sovereign equality of all its Members.

2. All Members, in order to ensure to all of them the rights and benefits resulting from membership, shall fulfil in good faith the obligations assumed by them in accordance with the present Charter.

3. All Members shall settle their international disputes by peaceful means in such a manner that international peace and security, and justice, are not endangered.

4. All Members shall refrain in their international relations from the threat or use of force against the territorial integrity or political independence of any state, or in any other manner inconsistent with the Purposes of the United Nations.

5. All Members shall give the United Nations every assistance in any action it takes in accordance with the present Charter, and shall refrain from giving assistance to any state against which the United Nations is taking preventive or enforcement action.

6. The Organization shall ensure that states which are not Members of the United Nations act in accordance with these Principles so far as may be necessary for the maintenance of international peace and security.

7. Nothing contained in the present Charter shall authorize the United Nations to intervene in matters which are essentially within the domestic jurisdiction of any state or shall require the Members to submit such matters to settlement under the present Charter; but this principle shall not prejudice the application of enforcement measures under Chapter VII.

2. Article 33 of the U.N. Charter reads:

1. The parties to any dispute, the continuance of which is likely to endanger the maintenance of international peace and security, shall, first of all, seek a solution by negotiation, enquiry, mediation, conciliation, arbitration, judicial settlement, resort to regional agencies or arrangements, or other peaceful means of their own choice.

2. The Security Council shall, when it deems necessary, call upon the parties to settle their dispute by such means.

3. The convention among Great Britain, Austria-Hungary, France, Germany, Italy, the Netherlands, Russia, Spain, and Turkey, respecting the free navigation of the Suez Maritime Canal, signed in Constantinople, October 29, 1888, has guided public international law ever since. Article 1 reads: "The Suez Maritime Canal shall always be free and open, in time of war as in time of peace, to every vessel of commerce or of war, without distinction of flag. Consequently the High Contracting Parties agree not in any way to interfere with the free use of the Canal, in time of war as in time of Peace. The Canal shall never be subject to the exercise of the blockade." Following the nationalization of the canal and the Sinai Campaign, Egypt issued the Declaration on the Suez Canal and the Arrangements for Its Operation on April 24, 1957, in which it reaffirmed its commitment "to respect the terms and the spirit of the Constantinople Convention of 1888 and the rights and obligations arising therefrom" (R. R. Baxter, *The Law of International Waterways, With Particular Regard to Interoceanic Canals* [Cambridge, Mass.: Harvard University Press, 1964], pp. 119–23).

4. Resolution 267, July 3, 1969, "censures in the strongest terms all measures taken to change the status of the City of Jerusalem; confirms that all legislative and administrative measures and actions taken by Israel with purport to alter the status of Jerusalem, including expropriation of land and properties thereon, are invalid and cannot change that status."

104
Peace Treaty between Israel and Egypt
March 26, 1979

On March 26, 1979, Israel and Egypt signed the peace treaty, below, that ended thirty-one years of conflict between the two nations and five major wars in the following years: 1948–49, 1956, 1967, 1968–70, and 1973. The treaty also included mutual recognition between the two. Israel agreed to withdraw from the Sinai Peninsula and removed thousands of settlers from that area. Egypt committed to demilitarization of the Sinai, and a multinational force of observers (MFO) was stationed there to supervise the implementation of the Egyptian commitment as well as other security provisions stipulated in the agreement.

The Israeli-Egyptian rapprochement of the late 1970s was launched with the surprise visit made by Egyptian President Anwar Sadat to Israel on November 19, 1977 (doc. 100). It further reflected Israel's long-held desire to gain acceptance and recognition from the Arab countries that surround it, and its willingness to concede territory in return. The treaty came on the heels of the Camp David Accords (doc. 103), one of two framework agreements that Israel and Egypt signed with the active involvement of U.S. President Jimmy Carter.

The Government of the Arab Republic of Egypt and the Government of the State of Israel:

Convinced of the urgent necessity of the establishment of a just, comprehensive and lasting

Source: Israel Foreign Ministry online, www.mfa.gov.il (accessed August 28, 2006).

peace in the Middle East in accordance with Security Council Resolutions 242 [doc. 68] and 338 [doc. 86];

Reaffirming their adherence to the "Framework for Peace in the Middle East Agreed at Camp David," dated September 17, 1978 [doc. 103];

Noting that the aforementioned Framework as appropriate is intended to constitute a basis for peace not only between Egypt and Israel but also between Israel and each of its other Arab neighbors which is prepared to negotiate peace with it on this basis;

Desiring to bring to an end the state of war between them and to establish a peace in which every state in the area can live in security;

Convinced that the conclusion of a Treaty of Peace between Egypt and Isreal is an important step in the search for comprehensive peace in the area and for the attainment of settlement of the Arab-Israeli conflict in all its aspects;

Inviting the other Arab parties to this dispute to join the peace process with Israel guided by and based on the principles of the aforementioned Framework;

Desiring as well to develop friendly relations and cooperation between themselves in accordance with the United Nations Charter and the principles of international law governing international relations in times of peace;

Agree to the following provisions in the free exercise of their sovereignty, in order to implement the "Framework for the Conclusion of a Peace Treaty Between Egypt and Israel":

Article 1

1. The state of war between the Parties will be terminated and peace will be established between them upon the exchange of instruments of ratification of this Treaty.
2. Israel will withdraw all its armed forces and civilians from the Sinai behind the international boundary between Egypt and mandated Palestine, as provided in the annexed protocol (Annex 1), and Egypt will resume the exercise of its full sovereignty over the Sinai.
3. Upon completion of the interim withdrawal provided for in Annex 1, the parties will establish normal and friendly relations, in accordance with Article 3 (3).

Article 2

The permanent boundary between Egypt and Israel is the recognized international boundary between Egypt and the former mandated territory of Palestine, as shown on the map at Annex 2, without prejudice to the issue of the status of the Gaza Strip. The Parties recognize this boundary as inviolable. Each will respect the territorial integrity of the other, including their territorial waters and airspace.

Article 3

1. The Parties will apply between them the provisions of the Charter of the United Nations and the principles of international law governing relations among states in times of peace. In particular:
   a. They recognize and will respect each other's sovereignty, territorial integrity and political independence;
   b. They recognize and will respect each other's right to live in peace within their secure and recognized boundaries;
   c. They will refrain from the threat or use of force, directly or indirectly, against each other and will settle all disputes between them by peaceful means.
2. Each Party undertakes to ensure that acts or threats of belligerency, hostility, or violence do not originate from and are not committed from within its territory, or by any forces subject to its control or by any other forces stationed on its territory, against the population, citizens or property of the other Party. Each Party also undertakes to refrain from organizing, instigating, inciting, assisting or participating in acts or threats of belligerency, hostility, subversion or violence against the other Party, anywhere, and undertakes to ensure that perpetrators of such acts are brought to justice.

3. The Parties agree that the normal relationship established between them will include full recognition, diplomatic, economic and cultural relations, termination of economic boycotts and discriminatory barriers to the free movement of people and goods, and will guarantee the mutual enjoyment by citizens of the due process of law. The process by which they undertake to achieve such a relationship parallel to the implementation of other provisions of this Treaty is set out in the annexed protocol (Annex 3).

Article 4

1. In order to provide maximum security for both Parties on the basis of reciprocity, agreed security arrangements will be established including limited force zones in Egyptian and Israeli territory, and United Nations forces and observers, described in detail as to nature and timing in Annex 1, and other security arrangements the Parties may agree upon.
2. The Parties agree to the stationing of United Nations personnel in areas described in Annex 1. The Parties agree not to request withdrawal of the United Nations personnel and that these personnel will not be removed unless such removal is approved by the Security Council of the United Nations, with the affirmative vote of the five Permanent Members, unless the Parties otherwise agree.
3. A Joint Commission will be established to facilitate the implementation of the Treaty, as provided for in Annex 1.
4. The security arrangements provided for in paragraphs 1 and 2 of this Article may at the request of either party be reviewed and amended by mutual agreement of the Parties.

Article 5

1. Ships of Israel, and cargoes destined for or coming from Israel, shall enjoy the right of free passage through the Suez Canal and its approaches through the Gulf of Suez and the Mediterranean Sea on the basis of the Constantinople Convention of 1888, applying to all nations. Israeli nationals, vessels and cargoes, as well as persons, vessels and cargoes destined for or coming from Israel, shall be accorded non-discriminatory treatment in all matters connected with usage of the canal.
2. The Parties consider the Strait of Tiran and the Gulf of Aqaba to be international waterways open to all nations for unimpeded and non-suspendable freedom of navigation and overflight. The parties will respect each other's right to navigation and overflight for access to either country through the Strait of Tiran and the Gulf of Aqaba.

105
Yigal Allon
The West Bank and Gaza within the Framework of a Middle East Peace Settlement
1948–1979: Analysis

Yigal Allon, who died in 1980, held during his political career such positions as deputy prime minister and minister of foreign affairs. At the end of the Six-Day War he constructed the Allon Plan (map 4) for a territorial compromise in the West Bank. In 1976, while minister of foreign affairs, he used the prestigious journal Foreign Affairs *to present his own personal perspective regarding the Arab-Israeli conflict and preferred paths toward its settlement. In the following article he re-analyzes the conflict and discusses the Camp David Accords (doc. 103) in light of competing peace proposals.*

Now that a peace treaty has been signed between Egypt and Israel and the reality of peace between the two peoples is slowly evolving, the unraveling of the remainder of the Middle East knot depends, to a very large extent, on a judicious settlement for Samaria, Judaea and the Gaza District.

These three regions, which had formed part of the Palestine Mandate were, for various reasons, not regions of intensive Jewish settlement prior to the departure of the British from the country, except for the Gush Ezion area (which fell into Arab hands in the 1948 fighting). Due to their predominantly Arab populations these regions were allotted to the Arab Palestinian state which was supposed to emerge following the U.N. Partition Plan of November 29th, 1947. However, the Palestinian Arabs rejected the opportunity offered them to establish their own state in 1948. Following the British evacuation of Palestine on May 15th, 1948, Samaria and Judaea were occupied and later annexed by Jordan, and came to be known as the West Bank within the Hashemite Kingdom of Jordan, while the Gaza Strip was occupied by Egypt.

Many Israelis, myself included, found it difficult to come to terms with the partition of Palestine in 1948, believing as we did in the absolute historical right of the People of Israel to the Land of Israel. In the course of the 1948–49 Israeli War of Independence I had also become concerned with the problem of defensible boundaries and in particular with the "soft underbelly" of Israel's defense system that resulted from the fact that Samaria and Judaea remained in the hostile hands of the Jordanian Arab Legion.

The outcome of the Six-Day War, the third war imposed upon the State of Israel in twenty years, appeared, on the surface, to have made our dreams of an undivided Eretz Israel come true. Yet, even while the guns were still roaring doubts began to creep into my mind as to the wisdom of fulfilling the dream and utilizing our right.

Source: Yigal Allon, "The West Bank and Gaza within the Framework of a Middle East Peace Settlement," *Middle East Review* 12, no. 2 (Winter 1979–80): 15–18. Reprinted by permission of Transaction Publishers. Copyright © 1979–80 by Transaction Publishers.

Until the establishment of the State of Israel in 1948, I had believed that once the gates of the country were opened to free Jewish immigration the ancient messianic dream of a mass return by the dispersed Jewish people would materialize. I believed that if the majority of the Jewish people would return to the western half of the Land of Israel there would be no reason why a substantial Arab minority could not continue to live in our midst, with full minority rights and its own cultural heritage, religion and traditions fully respected.

However, the rate of Jewish immigration which followed the establishment of the State of Israel proved to be much lower than expected and the Jewish birth rate in the country did not exceed that of the indigenous Arab population, or even keep up with it for that matter, and so the dream of the Jewish people rapidly becoming a solid majority within an undivided Eretz Israel, *without* an exodus of the Palestinian Arab population, vanished into thin air. The military victory of 1967 did not change an iota of this basic demographic reality despite a temporary rise in Jewish immigration figures which followed the Six-Day War.

Though the outcome of the War seemed to open up many new possibilities for resolving the Middle East tangle in a manner favorable to Israel, actually the situation in 1967 was less favorable, from an Israeli point of view, than that which had existed in 1949. For one thing, the Palestinian problem had become more acute after twenty years of festering without any real effort having been made to resolve it and the political exploitation of the plight of the refugees by the Arab States and extremist Palestinian elements. Secondly, the international atmosphere was less sympathetic than it had been when the Holocaust was still fresh in peoples' minds and the Zionist enterprise was the object of great admiration as demonstrating both the vitality of the wounded Jewish people and the development possibilities of a land which had suffered the ravages of centuries of neglect. In 1948 both Superpowers had given their blessing to the newly born Jewish State, and there was as yet no independent Third World emotionally inclined towards the Arab position in the Middle East conflict. By 1967 the international arena had become much less congenial.

Since Israel wished to preserve her Jewish, democratic and progressive character and avoid complete international isolation both demographic and international realities dictated Israeli withdrawal from *most* of the territories occupied in the West Bank and Gaza in the course of the War. However, though the repartitioning of Eretz Israel seemed inevitable, it became of great importance for Israel to use the military gains made during the War to ensure that two major issues be confronted and tackled *before* her withdrawal: (a) Israel's security would have to be protected more effectively than under the 1949 Armistice Lines; (b) the various aspects of the problem of the Arab Palestinians would have to be satisfactorily resolved once and for all.

In the plan which eventually came to bear my name I attempted to offer practical and just solutions to both problems. I proposed to return the densely populated territories of the West Bank and Gaza to Arab sovereignty while ensuring that certain desolate and unpopulated zones vital for Israel's security—particularly the Jordan Valley Rift, the first mountain range west of it and several other locations of strategic importance to Israel in the deserts of Judaea and Samaria—should remain under Israeli control.

This plan advocated that those areas of the West Bank and Gaza which were to be returned to Arab sovereignty should not be constituted into a separate state but should merge with the Kingdom of Jordan either in the form of a federation or some other constitutional arrangement that would enable the population of either side of the River Jordan to maintain their separate identities that had evolved after 1922.

The proposal of uniting the West Bank and Gaza with Jordan is not as far-fetched as some observers might protest, and for the following reasons: (a) The West Bank and Gaza are territorially too small to form a viable state capable of offering homes, land and jobs to all the Arab Palestinians who might wish to live in a Palestinian Arab state. (b) Transjordan is part of historical Palestine which was arbitrarily cut off from the rest of the country by the British in order to provide the Emir Abdullah with a realm. (c) The Arab population on either side of the River Jordan forms part of the same ethnic group.

Though this plan was never adopted as the official policy of the Israel Labor Party when it was in power, successive Labor Governments saw to it that Jewish settlement in the Administered Territories took place within the parameters of the plan, and with the exception of East Jerusalem which was reunited with its western half, refrained from extending Israeli sovereignty to the Administered Territories.

In fact all options were left open. The West Bank and Gaza remained under an Israeli Military Government, enforcing the Jordanian and British Mandatory laws respectively, while their economy was allowed to develop with a dual orientation: one towards the Israeli economy which allowed for the free movement of labor and goods across the "Green Line" [Israel's pre-1967 borders] and the other towards Jordan and beyond by means of the "open bridges" policy which encouraged the maintenance of trade and personal contacts between the populations of the two banks of the Jordan River.

In the latter part of 1974, following the signature of disengagement agreements between Israel, Egypt and Syria, there was a real chance for a partial interim agreement between Israel and Jordan on the basis of the "Jericho Plan"[1] which might well have acted as a first step towards the realization of peace on the basis of the plan outlined above. Unfortunately, the Rabat Conference [doc. 92] prevented Jordan from taking this positive step by unequivocally stating that the PLO alone could act as the representative of the Palestinian people to negotiate the future of the West Bank and Gaza.

The "political unheaval" of May 1977 brought the Likud Party to power in Israel, and with it a concept that maintained that Samaria, Judaea and Gaza, as part of the ancient homeland of the Jewish people, should never pass from Israeli sovereignty. Though Mr. Begin's Government has so far taken no legal steps to annex the West Bank and Gaza to Israel, its settlement policy in the Administered Territories and its official declarations, not least of all in regard to the proposed Autonomy Plan [doc. 101] now being negotiated, point in this direction.

The Labor Alignment rejects this policy of the Likud Government not because there is no link between the Jewish people and the whole of Eretz Israel, not because there is no legal basis for a continued Israeli presence in the West Bank and Gaza, not because there are no security reasons for Israel's occupation of the Administered Territories, but despite these considerations. We reject this policy because we want Israel to remain a democratic, progressive Jewish state following a realistic policy, and because we want to see the Palestinian issue satisfactorily resolved.

At the outset I stated that now that a peace treaty had been signed between Egypt and Israel the next problem on the peace agenda was working out a settlement concerning the status of the West Bank and Gaza. In fact, Egypt made the signing of the Peace Treaty conditional on progress on the Palestinian issue; the Camp David Agreements of September 1978 [doc. 103] unfolded a basic plan for the establishment of autonomy for the inhabitants of the West Bank and Gaza as an interim arrangement towards the negotiation of a permanent settlement—a settlement that would determine the status of these territories, the future of the Palestinian Arabs, the nature of the peace between Israel and her eastern neighbor and provisions for the security needs of Israel.

The Likud Government has viewed the whole autonomy concept as presented in the Camp David Agreements as a means for perpetuating Israeli control over the West Bank and Gaza while giving their Arab inhabitants a measure of self-rule in the form of *personal* autonomy.

The Labor Alignment, on the other hand, true to the letter and spirit of the Camp David Agreements, sees Autonomy, a *territorially* based autonomy, as an interim arrangement paving the way for a permanent settlement. Such a settlement must *prevent* the establishment of a third state in addition to Israel and Jordan in the territory of historical Palestine, should not include the continuation of Israeli control over the territories inhabited by Arabs in the West Bank and Gaza and must ensure that Israel would remain in control of certain locations and zones vital for her long run security. In conformity with this concept the Labor Party Center decided that Autonomy must apply to the territories densely inhabited by Arabs in the West Bank and Gaza while the Israel Defense Forces should be redeployed into the Jordan Valley Rift, the Gush Ezion area, a minute buffer zone in the southern tip of the Gaza Strip, and several other minor locations of vital importance.

Though the Camp David Agreement deliberately left many details concerning the proposed Autonomy Plan vague, in order to paper-over some fundamental differences of approach between the Egyptian and Israeli Governments, and thus left much to be desired with regard to the basic frame of reference for the Autonomy's establishment, the Labor Party accepted it as a constructive step in the direction of a comprehensive peace settlement in the Middle East.

In particular the plan makes the following three important contributions towards attaining this goal by providing for: (a) the election of an Administrative Council which will form the first democratically elected representation of the Arab Palestinian community in the West Bank and Gaza. This Administrative Council will gain five years of experience in self-government within the Autonomy Plan and will be able to participate alongside with Egypt, Jordan and Israel in working out a permanent settlement; (b) the involvement of Jordan in the process of establishing the Autonomy Plan and the negotiations which are to follow its establishment; (c) the determination of security locations into which the Israel Defense Forces are to withdraw once the Autonomy Plan is established—security locations which should be designed to take into account Israel's long run security needs.

Though the Jordanian Government and the Palestinian Arab community in the West Bank and Gaza have so far opted not to be involved in the Autonomy negotiations, whether due to pressure from the Arab Rejectionist Front or because of concrete objections to the Camp David formula, at present the Autonomy Plan is the *only* key to opening further gates on the path leading to an overall peace. Unless the Jordanians and representatives of the Palestinian Arabs from the West Bank and Gaza join the negotiations this key may be lost. Such a situation would lead to a dangerous stalemate which would not only prevent further progress on the road to peace but would endanger the stability of the peace between Egypt and Israel.

On the basis of informal and unpublished discussions which I have had with various important personalities from the Administered Territories I can state that I am not pessimistic with regard to the prospect of Palestinian spokesmen from the Territories and of Jordanian representatives joining the Autonomy negotiations, if not while the Likud is in power then once it is replaced by a Labor government.

NOTE

1. The Jericho Plan (Jericho Corridor Plan) was outlined in 1974 for an initial Jordanian settlement based on the return of the Jericho region to Jordanian control. It was integrated into the Allon Plan (see map 4).

106

Moshe Zak

A Survey of Israel's Contacts with Jordan

April 25, 1980: Analysis

Israel has always viewed relations with Jordan as a key toward a permanent peace, and its contacts with Jordan and King Hussein were a well-known but unadvertised secret (see docs. 20, 34). In 1980, as part of the debate in Israel over the feasibility of a Jordanian-Israeli settlement in the West Bank, many details concerning these contacts were revealed. Prime Minister Menahem Begin's public reference to past contacts served to embarrass Hussein in the Arab world, which had proclaimed the Palestine Liberation Organization to be the only legitimate voice regarding any such negotiations. In the following article, Moshe Zak, then editor of the Israeli independent daily newspaper Maariv, *surveys Israel's contacts with Hussein on the basis of the newly revealed information.*

"Relations in our region are cyclical," said King Hussein during one of his meetings "somewhere in Israel." "We build and develop," his deep voice continued, "and then comes the war and destroys our achievements. Again we turn to development, rehabilitation, and again there is war. How long will we be caught up in this vicious cycle?"

His emotional appeal came in the middle of a discussion of Israeli proposals to Jordan for cooperative irrigation and transportation development projects. In one of the meetings, Israel offered Hussein a "free area" in the Kishon port. Israel went even further, suggesting that Jordan might keep a battalion of soldiers to guard this free area in the vicinity of Haifa, as well as guarantee the road for the transfer of merchandise to and from Jordan via the port.

Israel's offers were very generous, but when the time for decisions came, Hussein explained that he could not sign any agreement that granted him less than a complete Israeli withdrawal to the June 4, 1967, lines. "If you want to give less, go to the PLO [Palestine Liberation Organization]. They can agree to less, I can't. I'm ready to sign a full peace agreement, without reservations—but only in return for full withdrawal."

The talks with Hussein began in September 1960, a few days after the murder of Jordan's premier, Haz'a al-Majali. The Syrians had planted explosives in the parliament of the Jordanian government, and the prime minister and several of his cabinet were killed. At first Hussein had considered a reprisal action in Syria, but the Syrians were quicker and concentrated troops on the Jordanian border. At that time, Hussein turned to Israel for guarantees of quiet on his "back" border, while his army was busy on the Syrian front.

Exactly ten years later, in September 1970, Hussein appealed to Israel, via the Americans,

---

Source: Moshe Zak, "Kol hapgishot im Hussein" [All the Meetings with Hussein], *Maariv,* April 25, 1980, pp. 13–14. Reprinted by permission of Moshe Zak.

to enlist its support in resisting the Syrian invasion of Jordan; that time the initiative was Syria's. But in September 1960, when he planned his acts of reprisal in Syria, he did not want to involve the Americans. He simply requested guarantees that Israel would not take advantage of the situation, and that the Israel Defense Forces [IDF] would not take action even if border skirmishes should occur.

And so the cyclical pattern was established. In September 1960, as in September 1970, Hussein turned to Israel in connection with the Jordanian-Syrian dispute. Anyone troubling to search for signs of the cyclical pattern need only recall that in September 1950 the American Embassy reported to the State Department in Washington that David Ben-Gurion and Moshe Sharett were "adamant in their determination not to allow the incident to prevent the planned meeting" (between Israeli representatives and King Abdullah).

The incident referred to was a serious one, in which four Israeli soldiers were killed by a mine planted in the vicinity of Beit Guvrin by terrorists who had come from Jordan. In a meeting between Dr. Walter Eytan and the king, Abdullah announced "that he intended to dismiss the existing Jordanian cabinet and appoint another, which would renew relations with Israel which had been severed some months earlier, and also, perhaps, to sign a nonaggression treaty for five years."

That was in 1950. Hussein's request in 1960 was more modest: not an agreement, but silent consent. He sent the head of his office to confer with an Israeli representative. The request was referred via the Israeli officer to the Armistice Committee. The government sent General Chaim Herzog to the meeting; the head of the king's office delivered to Herzog the king's request that Israel should not harm Jordan while the Jordanian army was involved on the Syrian front. Israel's promise was given.

Later this meeting aroused a debate in the top levels. One person felt that Chaim Herzog should not have met with the head of the king's office, lest this meeting lead to the cancellation of another meeting he had planned—between David Ben-Gurion and King Hussein, in Teheran, at the shah's invitation.

This plan was nearing realization, but meanwhile Hussein was under pressure to guarantee quiet on his "back" border with Israel, while he was busy on the Syrian border.

Anyone who examines all the links of the Israeli-Jordanian dialogue can't help but be impressed by the extent to which the Syrian question provided a bridge upon which the talks between Hussein and Israel developed.

This was in 1960, in the wake of the attempt to instigate a revolution in Jordan. The Syrian bomb planted in the parliament of the Jordanian government was intended as a sign for revolt; actually, even when Hussein forsook the line of talks with Israel, at the time when he aligned himself with Hafez al-Assad, the Syrian question continued to be brought up in the Jordanian-Israeli talks.

Although the Jordanian front was not active in the 1973 War, the Jordanian army was beaten in that war: the Jordanian division which Hussein had no choice but to dispatch to the Golan front, in order to assist the Syrians, suffered heavy losses (as Jordan did when Hussein was drawn by the enthusiasm of May 1967 into the Six-Day War). Hussein learned from his own experience that any military confrontation in the region drags both him and his army with it; therefore he feared a Syrian-Israeli confrontation in Lebanon.

The rapprochement between Hussein and Assad is based on their shared opposition to Sadat's policies. Hussein considered himself tricked by Sadat at the Rabat Conference in 1974 [doc. 92], and Assad considered himself tricked by Sadat at the time of the signing of the Sinai Agreement in 1975 [doc. 94]. But while Hussein continued to meet and discuss with Israeli representatives, Assad talked of "Sadat's betrayal." Yet, though Assad knew of the "hidden connection" between the king of Jordan and Israel, he did not sever ties with him.

At that time both Kissinger and Hussein thought that the Syrian involvement in Lebanon might lead directly to the beginning of a Syrian-Israeli rapprochement. The military necessity for a Red Line[1] to prevent confrontation might, in [Henry] Kissinger's opinion, lead to the achievement of other partial arrangements. The Red Line would merely be the first step. But Operation Litani cancelled the need for Syrian-Israeli talks about the Red Line because the Red Line was replaced by UNIFIL [United Nations Interim Force in Lebanon; see doc. 102].

Hussein's first change of attitude toward Syria after his bitter experiences with that neighbor in 1960 and 1970 occurred, as a matter of fact, on the eve of the Yom Kippur War. Shortly before the war, Amman renewed its diplomatic relations with Damascus, and this in itself should have been sufficient warning to Israel that the reconciliation between Jordan and Syria was similar to that which took place between Amman and Cairo just before the Six-Day War [doc. 60].

Only later was it understood that the renewal of diplomatic relations was merely an external sign of a much broader understanding. Even Kissinger did not read the signs from Amman; the day before the outbreak of the Yom Kippur War, when Israel notified him that war was imminent, he turned to Hussein (and to Faisal), and asked them to exert their influence on Egypt and Syria to refrain from war. The two kings didn't even bother to answer him. The war broke out before there was time for answers.

Today it is clear that Hussein was not happy about this war either. He was dragged into it. Damascus asked him to open up a "third front," but since he had been so badly burned in the Six-Day War, he did all in his power to avoid becoming embroiled in another war, or more correctly, to avoid exposing himself to IDF actions on his border.

In the past, when the need arose to move soldiers from the Jordanian-Israeli border, Hussein tried to make contact with Israel so that it would not "take advantage of the situation." So it was in 1960, and again in 1970, when he planned his army's offensive against the Fatah strongholds. In both cases he appealed to Israel not to attack him at this opportune moment, when his forces were thinned.

In October 1973, when the Syrians demanded that he send Jordanian army units to fight Israel on the Golan front, the situation was not quite the same. The problem was more an Israeli one; the IDF had its hands full with two fronts—the Egyptian and the Syrian—and it was Israel that wanted to know how much strength it had to allot for the "quiet front" on the Jordan. The chief of staff, Commanding General David Elazar, estimated correctly that Hussein would not open up a "third front," while Defense Minister Moshe Dayan, who had until then avoided meeting with Hussein, was concerned—he had been mistaken in his estimate of Amman just prior to the outbreak of the war—and now tried to be overly careful.

Elazar took the chance, and only afterwards did confirmation come that Jordan was sending an armed force to the Golan front. By some trick of fate it was the Jordanian division, which advanced slowly, not rushing into battle, that was most heavily beaten by the IDF.

After the war, when the meetings between Hussein and the Israeli representatives were resumed, the king did not spare his criticism of the government of Israel for not relating correctly to his estimates on the eve of the war. Hussein returned to this subject in five meetings, and warned the Israeli ministers not to be deaf to his estimations, as they had been prior to the Yom Kippur War.

Hussein kept returning to this subject, hoping to reap benefits. Why not a "separation agreement" between Israel and Jordan, like the one between Israel and Egypt, and between Israel and Syria, he asked. "Is it because I didn't open fire during the war, and didn't tie your troops up on the Jordanian front?"

Hussein's suggestion was very simple: he asked for a 12 km-wide Israeli withdrawal along the whole length of the Jordan. The Israeli government could not agree to this, because such a separation agreement would have meant the uprooting of the Jordan Valley settlements and denial of the government program that regarded the Jordan River as Israel's security border.

Israel suggested a political interim agreement: the transfer of civil government in some parts of Judaea and Samaria, even without being granted, in return, the end of the state of war. But Hussein was not prepared for any partial political agreement and simply repeated over and over again that he was ready to sign a full peace treaty in return for full withdrawal, but he was also prepared to accept the model of a "separation agreement" like that between Israel and Egypt and between Israel and Syria; in other words, a military withdrawal without any salient political components.

This was the background on which Yigal Allon thought up the Jericho Corridor Plan [see doc. 105]. It was an interim period, and there were no National Religious Party ministers in the government; therefore there was no need to uphold the obligation not to withdraw under any circumstances from Judaea and Samaria without first asking the nation.

In any case, Yigal Allon was prepared to take a chance on new elections on this issue while Yitzhak Rabin preferred that the elections be centered on a real agreement with Jordan, and not on a "separation agreement" with no political components. But the two didn't argue the matter for long, because both Kissinger and Hussein feared that the Jericho Corridor Plan, with its hint of the Allon Plan, might create problems for Hussein at the Rabat Conference.

Shulamit Aloni, who in October was still a member of Yitzhak Rabin's government, wrote to me that she remembers Rabin rejecting Kissinger's suggestion regarding the Jericho Corridor. But Rabin vehemently denies that the American or Hussein presented Israel with such a plan.

There are others who were ministers in Yitzhak Rabin's government who confirm that there was no discussion of an American proposal for a Jericho Corridor. What some of the [Labor] Alignment ministers do recall is a discussion among a team of ministers about Yigal Allon's suggestion, and that Yitzhak Rabin said that it was not worth calling new elections on the question of Jericho. But, as mentioned above, this plan wasn't given a chance because Kissinger was afraid to jeopardize Hussein's position in Rabat by any sort of agreement between him and Israel. Kissinger was worried that the PLO might use such an agreement to pull the rug out from under Hussein's feet, whereas if Hussein himself went to Rabat, an agreement with Sadat in his hand, Hussein was sure that the Arab Summit Conference would accept the formula of a Jordanian-Palestinian Federation under his leadership just as he was certain of Sadat's support against the PLO stand. This explains Hussein's disappointment after Rabat, and this is the reason he abandoned Sadat and joined with Assad.

Unlike the situation during the days of [Dean] Rusk and [William] Rogers, Kissinger requested reports about the Hussein-Israel meetings from both sides as soon as he took over the position of secretary of state. He followed every detail of the long talks carefully. Once, when Israel was one day late in sending a report on a meeting with Hussein, Kissinger unhesitatingly remarked, "What happened to the Israelis? Hussein has already reported, and no word from them."

That was why Kissinger did not make a fuss about Hussein befriending Assad after Sadat signed the Sinai Agreement. He knew Hussein's position and considered that in this way he was preserving a connection with Assad for the United States. Kissinger learned the "Hussein subject" from the detailed reports he received from both Hussein and Rabin about their eight meetings, and also from face-to-face meetings with Hussein. He knew, as did the Israeli ministers, to respect Hussein's analytical ability and not simply his courage. For that reason, at the last stage, during President [Gerald] Ford's leadership, Kissinger approached Israel with the suggestion of a partial agreement in return for a conclusion of the state of war; he was aware that Hussein had told the Israelis he could not make full peace without full withdrawal and that Israel could never agree to such a withdrawal.

Meanwhile, however, there was a change of power in Washington. Ford and Kissinger stepped down, and were replaced by [Jimmy] Carter and [Zbigniew] Brzezinski. And not only Israel but Hussein as well immediately noticed President Carter's new coin—"the Palestinian homeland." . . . The new administration did not encourage the continuation of talks between the Israelis and Hussein.

At the time of the Camp David talks, Washington left the job of inviting Hussein to the conference, or even to a postconference report meeting, up to Sadat. Carter did not show any sensitivity to Hussein's lack of trust in Sadat. And when Hussein later requested an audience with Carter, the president of the United States gave a reception at the White House for Hussein to meet with Robert Strauss, at that time the special ambassador to the autonomy talks.

Hussein, insulted, did not come to Washington. . . .

The long-term talks between the Israelis and Hussein raised many ideas, and examined many possibilities, though no agreement was reached.

And yet the talks created an atmosphere which was useful for both sides. Pinhas Sapir was able to meet with the heir to the Jordanian throne, the king's brother, and arrange practical matters with him, but this same brother of Hussein refused to meet with Yigael Yadin, even when the Americans initiated such a move because Moshe Dayan had no patience for the dialogue. When Hussein came and told him that nothing less than full withdrawal would do, Dayan backed out of the talks. Dayan had no time for "symposiums"; he rushed to the practical negotiations with Egypt, but because of that there was no way to hold the Yadin-Hussein talk, and for that reason contact was entirely cut off.

NOTE

1. The Red Line was a line Israel drew in southern Lebanon, roughly parallel to the Litani River, below which it would not accept the presence of Syrian or PLO troops. In 1978 Israeli troops engaged in Operation Litani to enforce this policy and remove the military threat growing on its border (see doc. 109).

107

Ronald Reagan

The Reagan Peace Plan

September 1, 1982

The Israeli invasion of Lebanon on June 6, 1982, created a new window of opportunity for revamping peace efforts in the Middle East. The Palestine Liberation Organization and Syria—Israel's fierce rivals—were defeated in the war. The PLO, whose control of southern Lebanon was deemed a serious security threat by Israel prior to the invasion, was evacuated altogether from Lebanon by September 1, 1982. The Palestinian leadership was

Source: "Address to the Nation on United States Policy for Peace in the Middle East," Ronald Reagan Presidential Library, *The Public Papers of President Ronald W. Reagan*, http://www.reagan.utexas.edu/archives/speeches/1982/90182d.htm.

redeployed in Tunisia, thousands of miles away. Finally, the election of a new president in Lebanon, Bashir Jumayyil, on August 23, 1982, raised hopes in Jerusalem and Washington that an Israeli-Lebanese peace treaty would follow shortly.

In the summer of 1982, American officials completed a new plan—the Reagan Plan—that was intended to seize the moment. The plan was presented privately to Israeli Prime Minister Menahem Begin on August 28, 1982, and was introduced by President Ronald Reagan on television on the last day of the PLO's evacuation from Lebanon—September 1, 1982.

The plan was rejected by the Israeli cabinet the next day. In its decision, the cabinet declared that the plan contradicted the 1978 Camp David Accords (doc. 103). Prime Minister Begin was further offended that Israel—which had just assisted the United States by defeating Syria and the PLO, two local Soviet allies—was not consulted when the plan was formulated by the U.S. administration.

The Arab world responded by adopting the Fez Plan on September 8, 1982, as part of the Twelfth Summit of Arab leaders. While the Fez Plan did not mention the Reagan Plan specifically, some of its core tenets, such as a call for an independent Palestinian state, contradicted Reagan's framework.

With this unfavorable response from both parties, the Reagan Plan never gained traction, despite U.S. efforts. The plan's failure, alongside the U.S. withdrawal from Lebanon in the wake of a deadly attack on U.S. marines in Beirut on October 23, 1982, led the administration to decrease the level of U.S. involvement in resolving the Arab-Israeli conflict. The plan thus quietly joined a long list of unimplemented international initiatives to bring peace to the region.

Today has been a day that should make all of us proud. It marked the end of the successful evacuation of the PLO [Palestine Liberation Organization] from Beirut, Lebanon. This peaceful step could never have been taken without the good offices of the United States and, especially, the truly heroic work of a great American diplomat, Ambassador Philip Habib. Thanks to his efforts, I am happy to announce that the U.S. Marine contingent helping to supervise the evacuation has accomplished its mission. Our young men should be out of Lebanon within two weeks. They, too, have served the cause of peace with distinction and we can all be very proud of them.

But the situation in Lebanon is only part of the overall problem of conflict in the Middle East. So, over the past two weeks, while events in Beirut dominated the front page, America was engaged in a quiet, behind-the-scenes effort to lay the groundwork for a broader peace in the region. For once, there were no premature leaks as U.S. diplomatic missions traveled to Mideast capitals and I met here at home with a wide range of experts to map out an American peace initiative for the long-suffering peoples of the Middle East, Arab and Israeli alike.

It seemed to me that, with the agreement in Lebanon, we had an opportunity for a more far-reaching peace effort in the region and I was determined to seize that moment. In the words of the scripture, the time had come to "follow after the things which make for peace." Tonight, I want to report to you on the steps we have taken, and the prospects they can open up for a just and lasting peace in the Middle East.

America has long been committed to bringing peace to this troubled region. For more than a generation, successive U.S. administrations have endeavored to develop a fair and workable process that could lead to a true and lasting Arab-Israeli peace. Our involvement in the search for Mideast peace is not a matter of preference, it is a moral imperative. The strategic importance of the region to the U.S. is well known.

But our policy is motivated by more than strategic interests. We also have an irreversible commitment to the survival and territorial integrity of friendly states. Nor can we ignore the fact that the well-being of much of the world's economy is tied to stability in the strife-torn Middle East. Finally, our traditional humanitarian concerns dictate a continuing effort to peacefully resolve conflicts.

When our administration assumed office in January 1981, I decided that the general framework for our Middle East policy should follow the broad guidelines laid down by my predecessors.

There were two basic issues we had to address. First, there was the strategic threat to the region posed by the Soviet Union and its surrogates, best demonstrated by the brutal war in Afghanistan; and, second, the peace process between Israel and its Arab neighbors. With regard to the Soviet threat, we have strengthened our efforts to develop with our friends and allies a joint policy to deter the Soviets and their surrogates from further expansion in the region, and, if necessary, to defend against it. With respect to the Arab-Israeli conflict, we have embraced the Camp David framework [doc. 103] as the only way to proceed. We have also recognized, however, that solving the Arab-Israeli conflict, in and of itself, cannot assure peace throughout a region as vast and troubled as the Middle East.

Our first objective under the Camp David process was to insure the successful fulfillment of the Egyptian-Israeli peace treaty [doc. 104]. This was achieved with the peaceful return of the Sinai to Egypt in April 1982. To accomplish this, we worked hard with our Egyptian and Israeli friends, and eventually with other friendly countries, to create the multinational force which now operated in the Sinai.

Throughout this period of difficult and time-consuming negotiations, we never lost sight of the next step of Camp David—autonomy talks to pave the way for permitting the Palestinian people to exercise their legitimate rights. However, owing to the tragic assassination of President [Anwar] Sadat and other crises in the area, it was not until January 1982 that we were able to make a major effort to renew these talks. Secretary of State [Alexander] Haig and Ambassador [Richard] Fairbanks made three visits to Israel and Egypt this year to pursue the autonomy talks. Considerable progress was made in developing the basic outline of an American approach which was to be presented to Egypt and Israel after April.

The successful completion of Israel's withdrawal from Sinai and the courage shown on this occasion by Prime Minister [Menahem] Begin and President [Hosni] Mubarak in living up to their agreements convinced me the time had come for a new American policy to try to bridge the remaining differences between Egypt and Israel on the autonomy process. So, in May, I called for specific measures and a timetable for consultations with the Governments of Egypt and Israel on the next steps in the peace process. However, before this effort could be launched, the conflict in Lebanon pre-empted our efforts. The autonomy talks were basically put on hold while we sought to untangle the parties in Lebanon and still the guns of war.

The Lebanon war, tragic as it was, has left us with a new opportunity for Middle East peace. We must seize it now and bring peace to this troubled area so vital to world stability while there is still time. It was with this strong conviction that over a month ago, before the present negotiations in Beirut had been completed, I directed Secretary of State [George] Shultz to again review our policy and to consult a wide range of outstanding Americans on the best ways to strengthen chances for peace in the Middle East.

We have consulted with many of the officials who were historically involved in the process, with members of the Congress, and with individuals from the private sector, and I have held extensive consultations with my own advisers on the principles I will outline to you tonight.

The evacuation of the PLO from Beirut is now complete. And we can help the Lebanese to rebuild their war-torn country. We owe it to ourselves, and to posterity, to move quickly to build upon this achievement. A stable and revived Lebanon is essential to our hopes for peace in the region. The people of Lebanon deserve the best efforts of the international community to turn the nightmares of the past several years into a new dawn of hope.

But the opportunities for peace in the Middle East do not begin and end in Lebanon. As we help Lebanon rebuild, we must also move to resolve the root causes of conflict between Arabs and Israelis.

The War in Lebanon has demonstrated many things, but two consequences are key to the peace process:

First, the military losses of the PLO have not diminished the yearning of the Palestinian people for a just solution of their claims; and second, while Israel's military successes in Lebanon have demonstrated that its armed forces are second to none in the region, they alone cannot bring just and lasting peace to Israel and her neighbors.

The question now is how to reconcile Israel's legitimate security concerns with the legitimate rights of the Palestinians. And that answer can only come at the negotiating table. Each party must recognize that the outcome must be acceptable to all and that true peace will require compromises by all.

So, tonight I am calling for a fresh start. This is the moment for all those directly concerned to get involved—or lend their support—to a workable basis for peace. The Camp David agreement remains the foundation of our policy. Its language provides all parties with the leeway they need for successful negotiations.

I call on Israel to make clear that the security for which she yearns can only be achieved through genuine peace, a peace requiring magnaminity, vision, and courage. I call on the Palestinian people to recognize that their own political aspirations are inextricably bound to recognition of Israel's right to a secure future.

And I call on the Arab states to accept the reality of Israel, and the reality that peace and justice are to be gained only through hard, fair, direct negotiation. In making these calls upon others, I recognize that the United States has a special responsibility. No other nation is in a position to deal with the key parties to the conflict on the basis of trust and reliability.

The time has come for a new realism on the part of all the peoples of the Middle East. The State of Israel is an accomplished fact; it deserves unchallenged legitimacy within the community of nations. But Israel's legitimacy has thus far been recognized by too few countries, and has been denied by every Arab state except Egypt. Israel exists; it has a right to demand of its neighbors that they recognize those facts.

The War in Lebanon has demonstrated another reality in the region. The departure of the Palestinians from Beirut dramatizes more than ever the homelessness of the Palestinian people. Palestinians feel strongly that their cause is more than a question of refugees. I agree. The Camp David agreement recognized that fact when it spoke of the legitimate rights of the Palestinian people and their just requirements. For peace to endure, it must involve all those who have been most deeply affected by the conflict. Only through broader participation in the peace process, most immediately by Jordan and by the Palestinians, will Israel be able to rest confident in the knowledge that its security and integrity will be respected by its neighbors. Only through the process of negotiation can all the nations of the Middle East achieve a secure peace.

These then are our general goals. What are the specific new American positions, and why are we taking them?

In the Camp David talks thus far, both Israel and Egypt have felt free to express openly their views as to what the outcome should be. Understandably, their views have differed on many points.

The United States has thus far sought to play the role of mediator. We have avoided public comment on the key issues. We have always recognized, and continue to recognize, that only the voluntary agreement of those parties most directly involved in the conflict can provide an enduring solution. But it has become evident to me that some clearer sense of America's position on the key issues is necessary to encourage wider support for the peace process.

First, as outlined in the Camp David Accords, there must be a period of time during which the Palestinian inhabitants of the West Bank and Gaza will have full autonomy over their own affairs. Due consideration must be given to the principle of self-government by the inhabitants of the territories and to the legitimate security concerns of the parties involved.

The purpose of the five-year period of transition which would begin after free elections for a self-governing Palestinian authority is to prove to the Palestinians that they can run their own affairs, and that such Palestinian autonomy poses no threat to Israel's security.

The United States will not support the use of any additional land for the purpose of settlements during the transition period. Indeed, the immediate adoption of a settlement freeze by Israel, more than any other action, could create the confidence needed for wider participation in these talks. Further settlement activity is in no way necessary for the security of Israel and only diminishes the confidence of the Arabs that a final outcome can be freely and fairly negotiated.

I want to make the American position clearly understood. The purpose of this transition period is the peaceful and orderly transfer of domestic authority from Israel to the Palestinian inhabitants of the West Bank and Gaza. At the same time, such a transfer must not interfere with Israel's security requirements.

Beyond the transition period, as we look to the future of the West Bank and Gaza, it is clear to me that peace cannot be achieved by the formation of an independent Palestinian state in those territories. Nor is it achievable on the basis of Israeli sovereignty or permanent control over the West Bank and Gaza.

So the United States will not support the establishment of an independent Palestinian state in the West Bank and Gaza, and we will not support annexation of permanent control by Israel.

There is, however, another way to peace. The final status of these lands must, of course, be reached through the give-and-take of negotiations. But it is the firm view of the United States that self-government by the Palestinians of the West Bank and Gaza in association with Jordan offers the best chance for a durable, just, and lasting peace.

We base our approach squarely on the principle that the Arab-Israeli conflict should be resolved through negotiations involving an exchange of territory for peace. This exchange is enshrined in the United Nations Security Council Resolution 242 [doc. 68], which is, in turn, incorporated in all its parts in the Camp David agreements. U.N. Resolution 242 remains wholly valid as the foundation stone of America's Middle East peace effort.

It is the United States' position that—in return for peace—the withdrawal provision of Resolution 242 applies to all fronts, including the West Bank and Gaza.

When the border is negotiated between Jordan and Israel, our view on the extent to which Israel should be asked to give up territory will be heavily affected by the extent of true peace and normalization and the security arrangements offered in return.

Finally, we remain convinced that Jerusalem must remain undivided, but its final status should be decided through negotiations.

In the course of the negotiations to come, the United States will support positions that seem to us fair and reasonable compromise, and likely to promote a sound agreement. We will also put forward our own detailed proposals when we believe they can be helpful. And, make no mistake, the United States will oppose any proposal—from any party and at any point in the negotiating process—that threatens the security of Israel. America's commitment to the security of Israel is ironclad.

During the past few days, our ambassadors in Israel, Egypt, Jordan, and Saudi Arabia have presented to their host governments the proposals in full detail that I have outlined here tonight.

I am convinced that these proposals can bring justice, bring security, and bring durability to an Arab-Israeli peace. The United States will stand by these principles with total dedication. They are fully consistent with Israel's security requirements and the aspirations of the Palestinians. We will work hard to broaden participation at the peace table as envisaged by the Camp David Accords. And I fervently hope that the Palestinians and Jordan, with the support of their Arab colleagues, will accept this opportunity.

Tragic turmoil in the Middle East runs back to the dawn of history. In our modern day, conflict after conflict has taken its brutal toll there. In an age of nuclear challenge and economic interdependence, such conflicts are a threat to all the people of the world, not just the Middle East itself. It is time for us all, in the Middle East and around the world, to call a halt to conflict, hatred, and prejudice; it is time for us all to launch a common effort for reconstruction, peace, and progress.

It has often been said—and regrettably too often been true—that the story of the search for peace and justice in the Middle East is a tragedy of opportunities missed.

In the aftermath of the settlement in Lebanon, we now face an opportunity for a broader peace. This time we must not let it slip from our grasp. We must look beyond the difficulties and obstacle of the present and move with fairness and resolve toward a brighter future. We owe it to ourselves, and to posterity, to do no less. For if we miss this chance to make a fresh start, we may look back on this moment from some later vantage point and realize how much that failure cost us all.

These, then, are the principles upon which American policy towards the Arab-Israeli conflict will be based. I have made a personal commitment to see that they endure and, God willing, that they will come to be seen by all reasonable, compassionate people as fair, achievable, and in the interests of all who wish to see peace in the Middle East.

Tonight, on the eve of what can be a dawning of new hope for the people of the troubled Middle East—and for all the world's people who dream of a just and peaceful future—I ask you, my fellow Americans, for your support and your prayers in this great undertaking.

108

Ariel Sharon

The War in Lebanon

Summer 1982: Memoir

The controversial War in Lebanon (also called Operation Peace for the Galilee) led to unprecedented disobedience in the ranks of the Israel Defense Forces. A career army colonel, Eli Geva, resigned his command in protest

Source: This address by Ariel Sharon was delivered August 11, 1987, at the Center for Strategic Studies at Tel Aviv University.

during the war, and three thousand reserve soldiers refused to take part in it; more than 150 were jailed for their refusal. For the war's immediate background, see the headnote for document 109 (Kahan Commission Report).

In the following document, Minister of Defense Ariel Sharon defends the war's aims and conduct, responding to three main critiques leveled against him in the Israeli public sphere since 1982.

First, it was suggested that Sharon misled the Israeli government about the war's goals. Rather than the limited operation that Sharon presented to the cabinet, he had in fact ordered a wider operation aiming to occupy Lebanon's capital and secure the election of a pro-Israel president. Second, many had argued that the war contradicted Israeli security strategy. Rather than limiting the use of force to defensive purposes, in the War in Lebanon Israel used force for far-reaching goals that included political change in a neighboring country. Third, it was suggested that the war included an unnecessary engagement with the Syrian forces stationed in Lebanon.

When some of these critiques persisted into the 1990s, Sharon responded to them. He also brought a libel suit (Sharon v. Benziman) *against the journalist who tried to substantiate the first accusation against him—that he misled the cabinet. Sharon lost the case in 1997 and lost an appeal to the Israeli Supreme Court in 2001, shortly after he was elected prime minister.*

The war that was fought in Lebanon in the summer of 1982 was markedly different from previous Arab-Israeli wars in several important respects. It was a long war lasting almost three months—as compared to four days in 1956, six days in 1967, and nineteen days in 1973. It was the first war since the early part of the 1948–49 War of Independence fought primarily between Israel and Palestinian forces. (There was a Syrian-Israeli dimension to the war whose outcome had a decisive influence on its course, but it was brief, limited, and controlled.) Except for the 1956 Sinai Campaign, it was the only Arab-Israeli war whose timing and scope were determined by Israel. Like the Sinai Campaign, but in a more comprehensive and ambitious fashion, it was a war designed to achieve political aims and to implement a political plan. It was also Israel's most anticipated war: predictions of its imminence and fairly prescient speculations about its course abounded in the Middle Eastern and international media during the six months which preceded it.

The controversy which had surrounded the war from its outset derived to a large extent from some of these elements, but it was exacerbated by several other factors: the conduct of war in densely populated urban areas; the close scrutiny by the international media (much of it in a critical, not to say unfriendly, fashion); the dissension in Israel over the aims of conduct of the war; and the disagreement of most of the international community not just with the war aims, but also with the underlying policies.[1]

From every conceivable aspect, Operation Peace for the Galilee was a just and warranted act of war, not less so than any of our wars in the past and, from most points of view, more so than most of them.

We should explore how and why this operation became our most maligned war, not only in order to set the historic record straight—an important task in its own right—but first and foremost because the significance of denouncing Operation Peace for the Galilee and everything that was included in it and emanated from it goes well beyond the specific issue of securing the Galilee against the PLO [Palestine Liberation Organization] in 1982.

From Security First to Now-ism

In June 1982, the practical process of destroying the traditional, accepted concept of national security (or the historic Zionist consensus)—which is the bedrock of Israel's existence as the independent state of the Jewish people—was launched in a strident fashion. Something happened between the beginning of the operation and the massacre in Sabra and Shatila and the completion of the PLO's uprooting from Beirut and its practical elimination as a military factor and as a principal Arab victim building up its strength—at our expense—in the international arena. The Zionist Left and the Labor Party as its leader and principal component turned against this historic security consensus. In its stead, they adopted a counter, contradictory concept which can be dubbed Now-ism: peace—now, concessions—now, withdrawal—now, without any connection to the difficult reality within which we have lived and acted during the previous hundred years.

Now-ism means a leftist world view, that of the non-Zionist Left and the "lunatic fringes" of the Zionist Left, a doctrine born out of the ideological stem that has hosted Jewish leftism for a long time now, a mix of cosmopolitanism and communism with Jewish self-hate that reaches the level of "Jewish anti-Semitism." . . .

The explanation for this about-face (Labor's relinquishing of the traditional security consensus) is painful but simple: the Labor Party (the historic Mapai) is, as its own leaders and intellectuals testify, a political and economic apparatus, created in order to obtain power and hold it forever. Its leaders, functionaries, and various constituents do not see themselves as capable of surviving over time out of power. . . . For Mapai and its apparatus, certainly today, power is an objective in its own right. The leadership and functionaries of the Left sensed, correctly, that the road to power leads through Operation Peace for the Galilee—its success would consolidate the Likud's story for many years—and it therefore became crucial for them that the operation, as the Likud's War, end in failure or that it could at least be presented and condemned as a superfluous, failed war. . . .

The Objectives Were Known and Transparent in Advance

Operation Peace for the Galilee was the first (Israeli) war whose declared objectives were known to everybody fully and precisely. Its potential objectives and security and policy advantages were clear to everybody. He who claims that he was "declined" (I am not a fool or out of touch with the media and from the reality of Israel) is simply not speaking the truth, be it a member of the cabinet or an opposition leader in those days, a man on the street or a reserve soldier. . . .

Operation Peace for the Galilee had one single aim: "to take all residents of the Galilee out of the range of fire of the terrorists concentrated, they, their commands and buses, in Lebanon." Had the terrorists ceased fire after the operation's first phase, when the IDF [Israel Defense Forces] settled on the 40-kilometer line under Beirut, fighting would have ceased on that line. The terrorists failed to end the fighting and explicitly rejected the proposed cease-fire. . . . We could not conceivably stay on the 40-kilometer line with the bulk of the PLO's state, its infrastructure and military force alive and active, conducting against us an ever-intensifying war of attrition . . . further progression until the destruction of the PLO's state was our only reasonable option. . . .

The Fighting against the Syrians

Fighting against the Syrians was deliberately limited to the level required by the need to eliminate the terrorist agent. This is why the IDF was stopped by the political level upon reaching the 40-kilometer line in the Behaa Valley. Our advance in the central sector was initially designed to create a threat against the Syrians, so as to induce them to withdraw from the Behaa internal fighting. Later, we ordered the "military" toward the Beirut-Damascus road, since cutting it off was necessary in order to cut Beirut off, namely in order to accomplish the goal of eliminating the terrorists. We planned successfully to refrain from and avoid a full-fledged war with the Syrians. . . .

"The new order in Lebanon," or obtaining a peace treaty, was not the objective for which the IDF was disputed "to kill and get killed."

NOTE

1. In the aftermath of the massacre of Palestinians by the Lebanese forces militia in Sabra and Shatila, the Kahan Commission ordered Sharon's dismissal from the Ministry of Defense.

109

Kahan Commission

Report on the 1982 War in Lebanon

February 7, 1983

The 1982 War in Lebanon (also called Operation Peace for the Galilee) was Israel's most controversial war to date. Prior to the 1975–76 civil war in Lebanon, Israel had had a comfortable relationship with a state only marginally involved in the Arab-Israeli conflict. But the civil war changed all that, confronting Israel with the possibility of Syrian or another form of Arab domination of Lebanon and the strong presence of terrorist operatives of the Palestine Liberation Organization in southern Lebanon. In the late 1970s, Israel's involvement in the Lebanese crisis deepened with the growth of a proto-Palestinian state in the southern half of Lebanon and the consolidation of Syria's grip over the country. In 1981 a series of developments occurred that a year later led to the launching of a full-fledged war: (1) the introduction of Syrian ground-to-air missiles in Lebanon; (2) the Palestinian-Israeli artillery duel of July 1981, which demonstrated the PLO's ability to shell most of northern Israel from southern Lebanon; (3) the Likud's electoral victory of June 1981, and the formation of the second government under Menahem Begin with Ariel Sharon as defense minister; (4) the preparations for a new phase in the Arab-Israeli settlement process, focusing this time on the West Bank and the Gaza Strip, following the completion of Israel's withdrawal from the Sinai in April 1982; (5) the change in the U.S. outlook on the Lebanese crisis as the Reagan administration decided to support a solution based on the reconstruction of the Lebanese state and a reduction of Syria's and the PLO's roles (see doc. 107).

In 1982 the Begin government formulated a plan that, through a large-scale military operation, sought to achieve four aims: (1) to destroy the PLO's military infrastructure and presence in southern Lebanon and to create an effective security zone there; (2) to diminish—if not eliminate—the hold of Syria and the PLO over the Lebanese state and to facilitate its reconstruction under the presidency of Bashir Jumayyil, leader of the Phalange, the predominantly Christian party; (3) to preempt the possibility of a Syrian-Israeli war; (4) to guarantee a better bargaining position for Israel in the new phase of negotiations on the continuation of the settlement process.

The expected clash finally erupted in June 1982 (see Map 5). Officially, Israel stated that when it launched Operation Peace for the Galilee it was retaliating against the assassination attempt on its ambassador in

Source: Commission of Inquiry into the Events at the Refugee Camps in Beirut, 1983, *Final Report* (Jerusalem: Government Printer, February 8, 1983).

London. The initial thrust into Lebanon and the military campaigns against the PLO and the Syrian forces and missile system were conducted swiftly and successfully. Israel then opted for the siege of Beirut, which lasted ten weeks. The PLO finally evacuated Beirut, but the lengthy siege and bombardment of parts of the city were the principal factors in turning the War in Lebanon into Israel's most controversial war, at home and abroad.

Israel's ally, Jumayyil, was elected president of Lebanon in August, and in the first half of September it looked like most of the war's aims had been accomplished. But Jumayyil was assassinated, prompting the Israeli government to dispatch the Israel Defense Forces into West Beirut. In this context, the Israeli army authorized and facilitated the entry of Phalange militiamen into Beirut to "mop up" the Palestinian camps, or neighborhoods of Sabra and Shatila, where, according to its information, PLO combatants were still positioned. The result was a massacre that, aside from its tragic human dimensions, had important bearings on Israel's domestic politics and on its standing in Lebanon.

The public outcry in Israel forced the government to form a judicial commission of inquiry on September 28, 1982, despite Prime Minister Begin's initial vehement opposition. It was chaired by Yitzhak Kahan, president of the Supreme Court. The two other appointees were Aharon Barak, justice of the Supreme Court, and Maj. Gen. (Res.) Yonah Efrat. Although most of the Kahan Commission's hearings were closed, due to the security and national defense information that was scrutinized, many hearings were open. Similarly, when the commission completed its work in February 1983, a portion of its report was not published. The most important immediate outcome of the report was the resignation of Defense Minister Ariel Sharon, the architect of the War in Lebanon. But it also sheds an important light on the War in Lebanon and its broader context.

Introduction

The commission's task, as stipulated by the cabinet's resolution [of September 28, 1982] is "to investigate all the facts and factors connected with the atrocity which was carried out by a unit of the Lebanese Forces against the civilian population of the Shatila and Sabra camps." These acts were perpetrated between Thursday, September 16, 1982, and Saturday, September 18, 1982. The establishment of the facts and the conclusions in this report relate only to the facts and factors connected with the acts perpetrated in the aforementioned time frame, and the commission did not deliberate or investigate matters whose connection with the aforementioned acts is indirect or remote. The commission refrained, therefore, from drawing conclusions with regard to various issues connected with activities during the war that took place in Lebanon from June 6, 1982, onward or with regard to policy decisions taken by the government before or after the war, unless these activities or decisions were directly related to the events that are the subject of this investigation. . . .

In one area we have found it necessary to deviate somewhat from the stipulation of the cabinet's resolution, which represents the commission's terms of reference. The resolution speaks of atrocities carried out by "a unit of the Lebanese Forces." The expression "Lebanese Forces" refers to an armed force known by the name "Phalanges" or "Keta'ib." It is our opinion that we would not be properly fulfilling our task if we did not look into the question of whether the atrocities spoken of in the cabinet's resolution were indeed perpetrated by the Phalanges, and this question will indeed be treated in the course of this report.

The commission's deliberations can be divided into two stages. In the first stage, the commission heard witnesses who had been

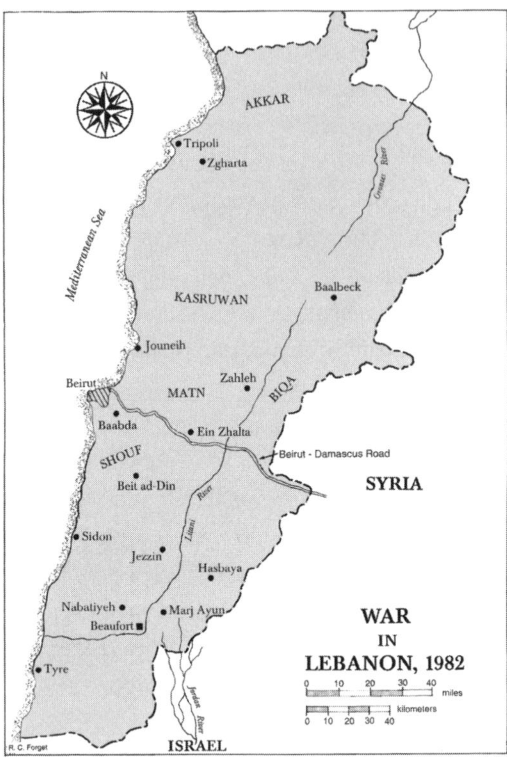

MAP 5. THE WAR IN LEBANON, 1982

summoned by it as well as witnesses who had expressed the desire to appear before it.[1] . . . When this stage terminated, the commission issued a resolution in accordance with [the Commissions of Inquiry Law of 1968], concerning the harm that might be caused certain people as a result of the investigation or its results; this was done in order to enable these people to study the material to appear before the commission and to testify. . . . The chairman of the commission sent notices to nine people; the notices detailed how each one of them might be harmed.[2] The material in the commission's possession was placed at the disposal of those receiving the notices and of the attorneys representing them. During the second stage of the deliberations we heard witnesses who had been summoned at the request of the lawyers, and thus some of the witnesses who had testified during the first stage were cross-examined.

Afterwards, written summations were submitted, and the opportunity to supplement these summations by presenting oral arguments was given. . . .

When we resolved to issue . . . notices about harm to the nine people, we were not oblivious to the fact that during the course of the investigation, facts were uncovered that could be the *prima facie* basis for results that might cause harm to other persons as well. Our consideration in limiting the notices about possible harm to only nine persons was based on [the conception] that it is our duty as a public judicial commission dealing with an extremely important issue—one which had raised a furor among the general public in Israel and other nations—to deliberate and reach findings and conclusions with regard to the major and important things connected with the aforementioned events, and to the question of the responsibility of those persons whose decisions and actions could have decisively influenced the course of events. We felt that with regard to the other people who were involved in one way or another in the events we are investigating, but whose role was secondary, it would be better that the clarification or investigation, if deemed necessary, be carried out in another manner, and not before this commission, viz., before the military authorities, in accordance with the relevant stipulations of the military legal code and other legislation. We chose this path so that the matters under investigation would not expand and become overly complicated and so that we could complete our task in not too long a time.

In the course of the investigation, not a few contradictions came out regarding various facts about which we had heard testimony. In those cases where the contradictions referred to facts important for establishing findings and drawing subsequent conclusions, we shall decide between the variant versions in accordance with the usual criteria in judicial and quasi-judicial tribunals. Our procedures are not those of a criminal court; and therefore the criterion of criminal courts that stipulates that in order to convict someone his guilt must be proven beyond a reasonable doubt, does not apply in this case. Nevertheless, since we are aware that our findings and conclusions are liable to be of significant influence from a social and ethical standpoint, and to harm also in other ways persons involved in our deliberations, no finding of significant harm was established with regard to any one of those to whom notices were sent, unless convincing evidence on which to base such a finding was found, and we shall not be satisfied with evidence that leaves room for real doubt. We shall not pretend to find a solution to all the contradictions in testimony. . . .

A Description of the Events: The Period before the Events in Beirut

In 1975, civil war broke out in Lebanon. This war began with clashes in Sidon between the Christians and Palestinian terrorists and subsequently widened in a manner to encompass many diverse armed forces—under the auspices of ethnic groups, political parties, and various organizations—that were active in Lebanon. In its early stages, this war was waged primarily between the Christian organizations on the one hand, and Palestinian terrorists, Lebanese leftist organizations, and Muslim and Druze organizations of various factions on the other. In the course of the civil war, Syrian army forces entered Lebanon and took part in the war, for a certain period of time on the side of the Christian forces, and subsequently on the side of the terrorists and the Lebanese leftist organizations. During the early years of the war, massacres on a large scale were perpetrated by the fighting forces against the civilian population. The Christian city of Damour was captured and destroyed by Palestinian terrorists in January 1976. The Christian residents fled the city and the conquering forces carried out acts of slaughter that cost the lives of many Christians. In August 1976, the Christian forces captured the Tel Za'atar refugee camp in Beirut, where Palestinian terrorists had dug in, and thousands of Palestinian refugees were massacred. Each massacre brought in its wake acts of revenge of a similar nature. The number of victims of the civil war has been estimated at close to 100,000 killed, including a large number of civilians, among them women and children.

The Palestinians' armed forces organized in camps inhabited by refugees who had arrived in Lebanon in various waves, beginning in 1948. There are various estimates as to the number of Palestinian refugees who were living in Lebanon in 1982. According to the figures of UNRWA (the United National Relief and Works Agency), the Palestinian refugees numbered approximately 270,000. On the other hand, the leaders of the Christian armed forces estimated the number of Palestinian refugees at approximately 500,000 or more. This estimate is probably exaggerated, and the more realistic estimate is the one that puts the number of Palestinian refugees at approximately 300,000—and in any case not more than 400,000.

The main Christian armed force that took part in the civil war consisted mainly of Maronite Christians,[3] though a small number of Shi'ites[4] joined them. This force comprised several armed Christian organizations, the largest among them being the organizations under the leadership of the Chamoun family and of the Jumayyil family. The head of the Jumayyil family, Mr. Pierre Jumayyil, founded the Phalange;[5] and the leader of this organization in recent years was Pierre's son, Bashir Jumayyil. In the course of time, the Phalange became the central element in the Christian forces; in 1982 the Phalange ruled the Christian armed forces. Even though the "Lebanese Forces" formally comprised several Christian organizations, the dominant and primary force in this organization at the time under our scrutiny was the Phalange led by the Jumayyil family.

When the war broke out in Lebanon in June 1982, the Phalange force included a nucleus of approximately 2,000 full-time recruited soldiers. In addition, the Phalange had a reserve armed force—that is, men who served part time in their free hours or when they were called up for special service. When fully mobilized the number of Phalange soldiers reached 5,000. Similarly, the Phalange had militias in the villages. There were not ranks in this military force, but it was organized along military lines with Bashir Jumayyil as the military and political leader who enjoyed unimpeachable authority. The Phalange had a general staff comprised of several commanders. At the head of this general staff was a commander named Fadi Frem; at the head of the Phalange's intelligence division was a commander by the name of Elie Hobeika.

The link between the Christian forces and the State of Israel was formed shortly after the start of the civil war. In the course of time, this link grew stronger, from both political and military standpoints. The Christian forces were promised that if their existence were to become endangered, Israel would come to their aid. Israel extended significant aid to the Christian armed forces, supplying arms, uniforms, etc. and also training and instruction. Over the course of time, a considerable number of meetings were held between leaders of the Phalange and representatives of the Government of Israel and the IDF [Israel Defense Forces]. In the course of these meetings the ties between the leaders of the two sides grew stronger. The Institute for Intelligence and Special Assignments (henceforth, the Mossad) was made responsible for the link with the Phalange; and representatives of the Mossad maintained—at various times, and in various ways—a rather close connection with the Phalange leadership. In the course of these meetings, the Phalange leaders brought up various plans for strengthening the Christian forces' position as well as various ways of bringing about the end of the civil war in Lebanon and restoring the independence of that nation, while (simultaneously) buttressing the status of the Phalange and those allied with it in a regime that would be established in Lebanon. Israel's representatives expressed reservations with regard to these plans and Israel's involvement in their realization.

A separate armed force is the military force in southern Lebanon—the Army of Free Lebanon under the command of Major [Saad] Haddad. This force comprises several hundred full-time soldiers. In addition, there is in southern Lebanon a National Guard, which, under the command of local officers, does guard duty in the villages. Relations between the Phalange and Haddad's men are not particularly close, for various reasons, and there were points of tension between these two forces. In 1982, soldiers of both Major Haddad and the Phalange wore uniforms provided by Israel—and similar to those worn by the IDF. The Phalange's uniforms bore an emblem consisting of the inscription "Keta'ib Lubnaniyeh" and the drawing of a cedar, embroidered over the shirt pocket. Major Haddad's soldiers had an emblem on the epaulet inscribed with the words "Army of Free Lebanon" in Arabic and the drawing of a cedar. During the war, Haddad's force advanced and reached the Awali River. Pursuant to IDF orders, Haddad's army did not proceed north of the Awali River.

The subject of the Palestinian population in Lebanon, from among whom the terrorist organizations sprang up and in the midst of whom their military infrastructure was entrenched, came up more than once in meetings between Phalange leaders and Israeli representatives. The position of the Phalange leaders, as reflected in various pronouncements of these leaders, was, in general, that no unified and independent Lebanese state could be established without a solution being found to the problem of the Palestinian refugees, who, according to the Phalange's estimates, numbered half a million people. In the opinion of the Phalange, that number of refugees, for the most part Muslims, endangered (both) the demographic balance between the Christians and Muslims in Lebanon and (from other standpoints as well) the stability of the State of Lebanon and the status of the Christians in that country. Therefore, Phalange leaders proposed removing a large portion of the Palestinian refugees from

Lebanese soil, whether by methods of persuasion or other means of pressure. They did not conceal their opinion that it would be necessary to resort to acts of violence in order to cause the exodus of many Palestinian refugees from Lebanon.

As we have said, the Mossad was the organization that actually handled the relations between the Phalange and Israel, and its representatives maintained close contacts with Phalange leadership. In addition, the Intelligence Branch of the IDF (henceforth Military Intelligence) participated, albeit in a more limited capacity, in the contacts with the Phalangists; and it, by virtue of its job, was to issue a not insignificant number of evaluation papers on the Phalange, its leaders, aims, fighting ability, etc. The division of labor between the Mossad and Military Intelligence with regard to the Phalange was spelled out in a document. While this division of duties left room for misunderstandings and also duplication in various areas, there is no room for doubt that both the Mossad and Military Intelligence specifically dealt with drawing up evaluations on the Phalange, and each one of them was obligated to bring these evaluations to the attention of all interested parties. Neither the head of the Mossad nor the director of Military Intelligence disagreed with this in his testimony before us.

From the documents submitted to us and the testimony we heard, it emerges that there were differences of opinion between the Mossad and Military Intelligence with regard to the relations with the Phalange. The Mossad, to a not inconsiderable extent under the influence of constant and close contact with Phalange elite, felt positively about strengthening relations with that organization, though not ignoring its faults and weaknesses. This approach of the Mossad came out clearly in the testimony we heard from the person who was in charge of the Mossad's contacts with the Phalange. The head of the Mossad, in his testimony before us on December 27, 1982, said, *inter alia,* that "the Mossad tried, to the best of its ability, throughout this period, to present and approach the subject as objectively as possible; but since it was in charge of the contacts, I accept as an assumption that subjective, and not only objective, relations also emerged. I must accept that in contacts, when you talk to people, relationships are formed." In contrast, Military Intelligence was to emphasize in its evaluations the danger in the link with the Phalange, primarily because of this organization's lack of reliability, its military weakness, and other reasons we need not specify here. A characteristic expression of the difference in approach between these two agencies, whose responsibility it was to provide evaluations on the Phalange and the desirability of relations with them, can be found in the exchange of documents when one of the intelligence officers who served as a liaison officer on behalf of Military Intelligence in the Mossad's representation at Phalangist headquarters at the beginning of the war submitted an assessment on cooperation with the Phalange. The Military Intelligence officer rendered a negative evaluation, from Israel's standpoint, of the Phalange policy during the war and its aims for the future. This criticism was vigorously rejected by the Mossad.

The "Peace for the Galilee" War (henceforth, the war) began on June 6, 1982. On June 12–14, IDF forces took over the suburbs of Beirut and linked up with the Christian forces who controlled East Beirut. On June 25 the encirclement of West Beirut was completed, and IDF forces were in control of the Beirut-Damascus road. There followed a period of approximately one and a half months of negotiations on the evacuation of the terrorists and the Syrian forces from West Beirut, and during this time various targets in West Beirut were occasionally shelled and bombed by the IDF's Air Force and artillery. On August 19, 1982, the negotiations on the evacuation of the terrorists and the Syrian forces from West Beirut were completed. On August 23, 1982, Bashir Jumayyil was elected president of Lebanon. His term of office was supposed to begin on September 23, 1982.

On August 21–26, a multinational force arrived in Beirut, and the evacuation of the terrorists and the Syrian forces began. The evacuation was completed on September 1; however, according to information from various sources, the terrorists did not fulfill their obligation to evacuate all their forces from West Beirut and hand their weapons over to the Lebanese army but left in West Beirut, according to various estimates, approximately 2,000 fighters, as well as many arms caches, some of which were handed over by the terrorists to the Lebanese leftist militia Mourabitoun. This militia numbered approximately 7,000 men in West Beirut, and it cooperated with the terrorists. After the evacuation was completed, the multinational force left Lebanon (September 10–12, 1982).

At the beginning of the war, the chief of staff [Lt. Gen. Rafael Eitan] told the Phalange that it should refrain from all fighting. This order was issued because of the fear that if the Phalange force got into trouble while fighting, the IDF would be forced to come to its aid, thereby disrupting the IDF's plan of action. Even after IDF forces reached the Damour-Shouf line, the IDF's orders were that the Phalangists would not participate in fighting. After IDF forces reached the area under Christian control, the Phalangist commanders suggested that a company of theirs of approximately three hundred men set up a training base at a place called Beit ad-Din, a site of historical importance in Lebanon. The chief of staff agreed to this, but made his agreement conditional on the Phalange forces' exercising restraint and discipline, as the area was Druze. At first this condition was honored; afterwards there were outbursts of hostilities between the Phalange and the Druze in Beit ad-Din. The Druze committed some murders, and the Phalange took revenge; a small IDF force was stationed in the area in order to prevent such actions. In the early stages of the war there were also some acts of revenge and looting on the part of the Christians in Sidon; these were stopped by the IDF.

When IDF forces were fighting in the suburbs of Beirut and along the Beirut-Damascus road, the Phalange was asked to cooperate with the IDF's actions by identifying terrorists, a task at which the Phalange's expertise was greater than that of the Israeli security forces. During these actions there were generally no acts of vengeance or violence against the Palestinian civilian population by the Phalanges who were operating with the IDF. Another action of the Phalange's military force was the capture of the technical college in Reihan, a large building in Beirut not located in a built-up area. The Phalangists captured this place from the armed Shi'ite organization Amal. One day after the place was taken, the Phalange turned the building over to the IDF and left the site.

The fighting actions of the Phalangists during that time were few, and in effect the fighting was all done by IDF forces alone. This state of affairs aroused criticism and negative reactions from the Israeli public, and among IDF soldiers as well. This dissatisfaction was expressed in various ways; and in the political echelon, as well as in the media, there was amazement that the Phalange was not participating in the fighting, even though the war was its battle as well, and it was only right that it should be taking part in it. The feeling among the Israeli public was that the IDF was "pulling the chestnuts out of the fire" for the Phalange. As the number of IDF casualties mounted, public pressure for the Phalange to participate in real fighting increased. The plan formulated in mid-June 1982, when it was still uncertain whether the terrorists would agree to leave West Beirut, was that the Christian forces would fight to take control of West Beirut; the IDF would not take part in that operation; and only in the event that it became necessary would the IDF help out the Phalange with long-range artillery fire. This plan was discussed in the cabinet meeting of June 15, 1982, where it was proposed by the Prime Minister, and his proposal was adopted by the cabinet, namely, that IDF forces would not enter West Beirut, and this job was to be done by other forces (meaning the Phalange) with help it would be given by the IDF. Even after his resolution, no real fighting was done by the Phalange for the purpose of extending control over West Beirut; and, as we have said, eventually the terrorists were evacuated as the result of a political agreement, after the IDF had shelled various targets in West Beirut.

NOTES

1. The commission had previously published notices in the press and other media inviting anyone who wished to testify or to submit material in any form to do so. A special effort was made to collect testimony from foreigners, including provision of transportation, etc. There was little response from abroad.

2. Prime Minister Menahem Begin was chastised for his lack of involvement in the decisions regarding using the Phalange, and his indirect responsibility was noted.

Defense Minister Ariel Sharon was chastised for having disregarded the danger of using the Phalange and for not ordering measures to prevent or reduce the danger of a massacre. The commission recommended that he resign or be removed from his position. The cabinet subsequently forced him to resign as defense minister and appointed him minister without portfolio.

Foreign Minister Yitzhak Shamir's indirect responsibility was noted. He erred in not immediately reporting information he received from Communications Minister Mordekhai Zippori regarding the Phalange's actions.

The chief of staff, General Rafael Eitan, was chastised for his inaction in preventing the massacre and for issuing an order to provide the Phalange with a tractor. The commission noted that since he was due to retire in April and would not be reappointed, no purpose would be served in recommending his dismissal.

The commission recommended the dismissal of the director of military intelligence, Major General Yehoshua Saguy.

The commission noted that the inaction by the head of the Mossad was not serious. (For security reasons, the name of the head of the Mossad is rarely revealed publicly.)

The commission noted the indirect responsibility of general operations commander of the Northern Area, Major General Amir Drori.

The commission recommended that division commander Brigadier General Amos Yaron not serve as a field commander for at least three years.

The commission was unable to determine whether the personal aide to the defense minister, Avi Dudai, had failed to pass on information in a timely manner.

3. The Maronites are the largest Christian community in Lebanon, constituting about 25 percent of the total population or roughly the same size as the Sunni Muslim community. The Maronites are a Uniate church, i.e., tied to the Vatican.

4. Shiites are nominally the second largest Muslim community in Lebanon but in fact the largest. Shi'i Muslims are part of the sect of the Matawilah who believe that only Muhammad's son-in-law, Ali, and his descendants, are true successors to the Prophet Muhammad.

5. Phalange (or Keta'ib Party) is the dominant Christian force in Lebanon. The followers of Camille Chamoun took a more uncompromising stand against the Syrian presence in Lebanon.

CHAPTER 6

From War in Lebanon to Hope for Peace in Madrid, 1982–1991

1983
Menahem Begin resigns, and Yitzhak Shamir becomes prime minister

1984
Shimon Peres becomes prime minister of a National Unity government

Operation Moses begins; it will eventually bring seven thousand Ethiopian Jews to Israel

1985
Israel Defense Forces withdraw from Lebanon to a security zone in the southern part of the country

1986
Yitzhak Shamir becomes prime minister for a second time, as part of the National Unity government rotation agreement

1987
The Palestinian uprising (*intifada*) begins in the West Bank and Gaza Strip

1989
With the beginning of the collapse of the Soviet Union, Jewish immigration increases dramatically

1991
In the Persian Gulf War, a coalition of allies led by the United States removes Iraqi troops from Kuwait; Israel is attacked by Iraqi Scud missiles

In Operation Solomon, Israel airlifts fourteen thousand Ethiopian Jews for settlement in Israel

By attending the Middle East Peace Conference in Madrid, Arab states tacitly acknowledge that Israel exists and Israel negotiates bilaterally with its Arab neighbors

Domestic Issues

110

Amos Oz

On Behalf of Pluralism

December 1982

Amos Oz (b. 1939), one of Israel's finest novelists, is also a leading spokesman of the Israeli moderate Left and a critic of radical Jewish nationalism and of the growing militarization of Israeli society. These excerpts from a discussion he had in December 1982 with the people of Ofrah, a Jewish settlement in the West Bank, illustrate the major differences between two leading world views in Israeli society. In this discussion, Oz criticizes the Gush Emunim's perception of Judaism (see doc. 81) and tries to portray his own opposing world view.

I do not suppose that I will change anybody's opinion or creed in Ofrah. But it seems to me that of late, particularly during the last few months, we have all reached very high emotional strident tones and I have a moral and personal stake in preventing the difficult, bitter controversy from crossing the borderline between controversy and hatred. And such danger does exist in my opinion. In the course of the evening, I will say a few things that you will find hard to hear. I will not obfuscate positions for the sake of peaceful atmosphere. It has been said, "You should love truth and peace," in this order. If I wanted to jump directly to the bottom line and to formulate that line in the most dramatic fashion, I would have put it in the following fashion: Most of you, perhaps all of you, believe that giving up Judaea and Samaria constitutes an existential threat to the State of Israel. I think that the annexation of Judaea and Samaria poses an existential threat to the State of Israel. This is a difficult and bitter contrast that cannot be blurred. But this is merely the tip of the iceberg. The root of the controversy is a matter of principle and spirit, it concerns beliefs and could reach the proportions of a theological controversy. You may be surprised to hear this term used by a secular person like myself. It is in fact difficult to reach agreement on the very purpose of the Zionist enterprise.

Source: Amos Oz, *In Your Ears: The Real Now-ists,* Nekuda, no. 53 (January 1983): 16–19, 21–24. Reprinted by permission of Amos Oz.

Zionism, according to a definition that I have used on several occasions, is "a surname" without a "first name." And we are looking at a divided family. I know it includes several brothers-in-law and cousins that would have been delighted to throw me out of the family, if they only could; and I confess that I, too, feel uncomfortable with my family relationship with some of its members. But I believe that it is a primary duty to grind our teeth and accept the fact that Zionism is a surname and not a first name and not to succumb to an attitude of boycotting and pushing beyond the pale even when encountering Zionist positions which seem to us rigid, dangerous, groundless or even peripheral. This approach does not derive from the quest to integrate diverse groups but is essential. . . . We have to live with that pluralism whether it pleases us or not. Personally, I am pleased by it; not as a temporary state until we all gather around the one single truth, but as a permanent state. To my mind, an abundance of currents, attitudes, traditions and, yes, "imported goods" too produce a fertile spiritual tension that leads to a life of creativity. They are also a potential source of a bitter internecine conflict that could even lead to a civil war. But this depends on us: how will we accept this pluralism. . . .

. . . My friends and I left Mapai in 1962 and since then we have not found a political home. . . . There is a group of people, whose scope I do not know, that has its roots in the labor movement, but feels uncomfortable with it on grounds of both politics and values. This group has had an ambivalent relationship with the political mechanisms of the labor movement for the past two decades. . . .

. . . You would now say that this group should or could have been a national interlocutor for the first activist generation of the graduates of the Bnei Akiva Yeshivot[1]. . . . What was it that obstructed, prevented and postponed such a dialogue for years? I learned the reason also through my discussion with Israel Harel and other friends here. In the past—this was mainly in the 1980s—the members of Bnei Akiva looked up to Labor's youth movements. The feeling then was that Bnei Akiva was some kind of a marginal correction, modest, lower than the grass, looking with admiration at the spirit and values of the Palmach [see docs. 22, 24] and so forth. With time, your confidence increased and our first confrontation occurred in the immediate aftermath of the Six-Day War. . . .

. . . We were used to being the leading elite, the one which sets the tone . . . and lo and behold, this crown was stolen from us . . . and stolen by people who pretended to be us—more our mind-breakers, adopted our story, now on the hills carrying wireless equipment. Then even stole the tenets of our founding fathers: they misled Yaackov Hazan, Yitzhak Tabenkin and Nathan Alterman[2] into believing that they were the real successors to that pioneering spirit that had allegedly been extinguished. The legitimate son was pushed away by the pretender. . . .

. . . This is not an easy experience, but it is fully egocentric, it is entirely concerned with lost honor . . . what really hurt was the profound contempt directed by Gush Emunim at us. . . . We were depicted and possibly seen by you as a superficial mix of Dizengoff Street,[3] Now-ism, fatigue, greed, foreign influence, peaceniks, nihilism. . . .

I do not know whether the veterans among you realize the depth of the damage caused at that time. . . . We viewed the obstune to the moral issues raised by us, heavy handed, complacent and arrogant, physical, drunken with power, full of rhetoric alien to me and to my friends, messianic, ethnocentric, apocalyptic, in one word—not human. Our interlocutors were not concerned with human beings; they were concerned with ideas and sites. . . .

We, from our Jewish vantage point, saw this as an interpretation of the spirit of Judaism that was alien to us . . . from a Jewish point of view, we saw this as a superficial, fundamentalist, simple minded and primarily a monistic concept which reduces Judaism to one issue—Greater Israel. . . .

. . . I view Judaism as a civilization, one of the few civilizations that had shaped mankind; a civilization in which religion constitutes a central and decisive part, but cannot be based on religion alone. . . . I view myself as one of the legitimate heirs of this civilization: not a stepson, not an inferior son, not a sinful son, not a disobedient son, but a legitimate heir.

NOTES

1. Bnei Akiva Yeshivot, religious educational institutions closely aligned with the National Religious Party and its predecessors, that offered a combination of religious and national education for teenagers and young adults.
2. All three, though identified with the left-wing Labor-led Israel of the 1940s to 1970s, nevertheless were among the early supporters of the settlement project in the West Bank, which came to be identified with Israel's right-wing flank.
3. Dizengoff Street, a central commercial street in Tel Aviv, represented for many Israelis from the 1950s to 1980s a materialistic and hedonistic lifestyle.

111

Benny Morris

The New Historiography: Israel Confronts Its Past

Autumn 1988: Analysis of 1947–1949

In the late 1980s and early 1990s, a fierce debate erupted between a group of revisionist Israeli historians and their critics. Drawing on only recently opened Israeli archives and writings of prospective critics of Israeli and contemporary Arab policies, members of this group challenged some of the most fundamental assumptions and arguments of the traditional historians of Israel's birth and early years. Other Israeli historians responded angrily. In the following text, historian Benny Morris, whom many labeled as a "new historian," describes the differences between the two approaches.

The treatment of the Lydda-Ramle affair[1] by past Israeli historians is illustrative of what can be called, for want of a better term, the "old" or "official" history. That history has shaped the way Israelis and Diaspora Jews—or, at least, Diaspora Zionists—have seen and, in large measure, still see Israel's past; and it has also held sway over the way Gentile Europeans and Americans (and their governments) see that past. This understanding of the past, in turn, has significantly influenced the attitudes of Diaspora Jews, as well as the attitude of European and American non-Jews, toward present-day Israel—which affects government policies concerning the Israeli-Arab conflict.

The essence of the old history is that Zionism was a beneficent and well-meaning progressive national movement; that Israel was

Source: Tikkun 3, no. 3 (Autumn 1988): 20–21. Reprinted by permission of *Tikkun: A Bimonthly Jewish Critique of Politics, Culture and Society*, www.tikkun.org.

born pure into an uncharitable, predatory world; that Zionist efforts at compromise and conciliation were rejected by the Arabs; and in their wake, the surrounding Arab states, for reasons of innate selfishness, xenophobia, and downright cussedness, refused to accede to the burgeoning Zionist presence and in 1947 to 1949 launched a war to extirpate the foreign plant. The Arabs, so goes the old history, were politically and militarily assisted in their efforts by the British, but they nonetheless lost the war. Poorly armed and outnumbered, the Jewish community in Palestine, called the Yishuv, fought valiantly, suppressed the Palestinian "gangs" (*knufiyot* in Israeli parlance), and repelled the five invading Arab armies. In the course of that war, says the old history—which at this point becomes indistinguishable from Israeli propaganda—Arab states and leaders, in order to blacken Israel's image and facilitate the invasion of Palestine, called upon/ordered Palestine's Arabs to quit their homes and the "Zionist areas"—to which they were expected to return once the Arab armies had proved victorious. Thus was triggered the Palestinian Arab exodus which led to the now forty-year-old Palestinian refugee problem.

The old history makes the further claim that, in the latter stages of the 1948 war and in the years immediately thereafter, Israel desperately sought to make peace with all or any of its neighbors, but the Arabs, obdurate and ungenerous, refused all overtures, remaining hell-bent on destroying Israel.

The old historians offered a simplistic and consciously pro-Israeli interpretation of the past, and they deliberately avoided mentioning anything that would reflect badly on Israel. People argued that since the conflict with the Arabs was still raging, and since it was a political as well as a military struggle, it necessarily involved propaganda, the goodwill (or ill will) of governments in the West, and the hearts and minds of Christians and Diaspora Jews. Blackening Israel's image, it was argued, would ultimately weaken Israel in its ongoing war for survival. In short, *raisons d'etat* often took precedence over telling the truth.

The past few years have witnessed the emergence of a new generation of Israeli scholars and a "new" history. These historians, some of them living abroad, have looked and are looking afresh at the Israeli historical experience, and their conclusions, by and large, are at odds with those of the old historians.

Two factors are involved in the emergence of this history—one relating to materials, the other to personae. Thanks to Israel's Archives Law (passed in 1955, amended in 1964 and 1981), and particularly to the law's key "thirty-year rule," starting in the early 1980s, a large number (hundreds of thousands, perhaps millions) of state papers were opened to researchers. Almost all the foreign ministry's papers from 1947 to 1956, as well as a large number of documents—correspondence, memoranda, and minutes—from other ministries, including the prime minister's office (though excluding the defense ministry and the IDF [Israel Defense Forces]), have been released. Similarly, large collections of private papers and political party papers from this period have been opened. Therefore, for the first time, historians have been able to write studies of the period on the basis of a large collection of contemporary source material. (The old history was written largely on the basis of interviews and memoirs, and, at best, it made use of select batches of documents, many of them censored, such as those from the IDF archive.)

The second factor is the nature of the new historians. Most of them were born around 1948 and have matured in a more open, doubting, and self-critical Israel than the pre-Lebanon War Israel in which the old historians grew up. The old historians had lived through 1948 as highly committed adult participants in the epic, glorious rebirth of the Jewish commonwealth. They were unable to separate their lives from this historical event, unable to regard impartially and objectively the facts and processes that they later wrote about. Indeed, they admit as much. The new historians, by contrast, are able to be more impartial.

Inevitably, the new historians focused their attention, at least initially, on 1948, because the documents were available and because that was the central, natal, revolutionary event in Israeli history. How one perceives 1948 bears heavily on how one perceives the whole Zionist/Israeli experience. If Israel, the haven of a much-persecuted people, was born pure and innocent, then it was worthy of the grace, material assistance, and political support showered upon it by the West over the past forty years—and worthy of more of the same in years to come. If, on the other hand, Israel was born tarnished, besmirched by original sin, then it was no more deserving of that grace and assistance than were its neighbors.

NOTE

1. In what was known as the Lydda-Ramle Affair, Israelis removed some Palestinians from the towns of Lod (Lydda) and Ramle.

112

Anita Shapira

The "New Historians": The Past Is Not a Foreign Country

1988–1996: Analysis

In this excerpt from her 1999 article published in the New Republic, *Israeli historian Anita Shapira, the former head of the Weizmann Institute for Zionist Research at Tel Aviv University and an "old historian" according to some "new historians," casts doubts over the contribution and methodology used by the latter.*

In the fall of 1988, the journal *Tikkun* published an article called "The New Historiography: Israel Confronts Its Past." Its author was a relatively unknown historian named Benny Morris. A year before, Morris had brought out *The Birth of the Palestinian Refugee Problem, 1947–1949*, a richly and rigorously detailed book that had not yet made much of a splash. His *Tikkun* article would fix that. In his article, Morris described himself and three of his confederates (Avi Shlaim and Ilan Pappe from academia, and Simha Flappan from political journalism) as "new historians," arguing that they had together undertaken to expose the skeletons in Zionism's closet, to declare war on the dogmas of Israeli history. The label stuck and soon the Israeli media was abuzz about the "new historians," who were catapulted into notoriety.

Morris also accused Israel of creating the Palestinian refugee problem, a charge that he had not leveled in his book. In his view, Israel bore a terrible burden of guilt. The vehemence

Source: The New Republic, November 29, 1999, pp. 26–37. Reprinted by permission of The New Republic © 1999, The New Republic, LLC.

of his accusations, and the moralizing tone in which they were delivered, fell on receptive ears: Morris was writing in the inflamed days of the Intifada. It is unlikely that the scholarly tomes of Morris and his fellow revisionists had many readers, but many Israelis were exposed to their heterodoxies in the media, which relish positions that are brief and barbed. And in this respect, the "new historians" certainly delivered the goods. Suddenly an argument raged over the true nature of what Israelis call the War of Independence, or what Palestinians call *al-naqba* or the Catastrophe, or what historians call, more neutrally, the 1948 War. That war furnished the founding myth of the state of Israel; and it is but a short step from questioning its justice to doubting Israel's very right to exist.

In fact, the ideas advanced by Benny Morris, Avi Shlaim, and Ilan Pappe, the vanguard of the "new historians," were nothing new. An anti-narrative of Zionism, counterposed to the Zionist (and Israeli) narrative of Zionism, had existed since the very inception of the Zionist movement. Opponents of the movement, Jewish and non-Jewish, had created an entire literature explaining what was foul in Zionism and why Zionism was destined to fail, and later why the state of Israel was an illegitimate and unjust construct that had to be resisted. The Soviet propaganda machine excelled in developing this anti-narrative, and in proliferating it. Arab propaganda also did its work. And at the margins of the Israeli left, there had always been groups and currents that doubted the right of Israel to exist and stressed the wrongs that were perpetrated against the Arabs. Yet those heretical elements remained marginal in Israeli politics and culture, and failed to gain wide public support. The advent of the "new historians" changed all that. These views now gained a certain legitimacy, since they appeared in the context of a debate between ostensibly objective scholars.

Revision in history is salutary. A critical look at premises refreshes historical inquiry and helps to generate new understanding. Every generation reexamines the present and the past under the impact of changing realities. Sometimes revisionism is the result of a generational shift among historians, and sometimes it springs from dramatic historical developments that throw an unexpected light on the past. The Vietnam War led American historians to reconsider certain accepted accounts of the cold war. Forty years after the end of World War II, a heated debate flared among historians in Germany about how to interpret the Nazi era: was it a rupture in Germany's past, or evidence of its continuity? Some British historians have responded to the belligerence of Thatcherism by attempting to rehabilitate Chamberlain and the Munich agreement. To be sure, not all revisions are laudable; the denial of the Holocaust is also a variety of revisionism. But historical revisionism does not take place in a vacuum. It is surrounded by politics. The revisionist scholar feels obligated to a particular political purpose, and proceeds with his research, and sometimes with his ready conclusions, to substantiate that purpose.

The "new historians" of Israel have not exactly pioneered fresh critical approaches in Israeli historiography. Already in the 1970s, scholars had begun to develop new and sophisticated views of Jewish-British relations under the mandate, of Zionism's relation to the Arab problem, of the rise of the Arab nationalist movement, of the nature of Zionism as the national liberation movement of the Jewish people. There was a tense and constant dialogue between collective memory and historical scholarship, as the new approaches slowly penetrated into the educational system and public consciousness. Since the advent of the "new historians," however, a new polarization has set in. The "new historians" dismissed all previous historiography as apologetic. Whoever dares to oppose or to criticize the pronouncements of these self-styled iconoclasts is savagely maligned.

In 1996, for example, when the historian Ephraim Karsh charged that Benny Morris had falsified certain documents, Morris did not even deign to reply; instead he asserted that Karsh's article on "rewriting Israel's history" was replete with distortions and half-truths, and he went on to add: "His piece contains more than fifty footnotes but is based almost entirely on references to and quotations from secondary works, many of them of dubious value." A look at Karsh's notes indicates that thirty of his references actually refer to writings by Shlaim and Morris, and fifteen others cite primary sources, and the rest refer to studies by major historians such as Avraham Selah and to several books by journalists that Morris himself now adduces in his new book. Of dubious value, indeed.

The revisionist dispute quickly spilled over from history into sociology and cultural studies, as new topics and new heresies were added to those that treated the War of Independence and the relation to the Palestinians: the pre-state Jewish community in Palestine and its conduct during the Holocaust, the absorption of Holocaust survivors and Oriental Jewish immigrants, and so on. No longer were particular Zionist or Israeli figures impugned; Zionist ideology as a whole was now the real culprit. Several of the new school's devotees labeled themselves "post-Zionist," and charged that the "lunatic" ambition of Jews to transform themselves into a people with a state of their own was senseless, and opposed to the natural inclinations of the Jews. They claimed that the Jews had never been a people until the Zionists muddled their thinking, and had no desire for nationhood. Post-Zionism turned out to be a peculiar form of anti-Zionism. In contrast with the anti-Zionism of an earlier era, the post-Zionists made their peace with Israel's existence as a state. (It is hard to argue with success.) But they sought to undermine the state's moral and philosophical foundations, to dismantle the Jewish identity of the state and reconfigure it as a state of "all its citizens."

Academic disputes tend to thrive on their own momentum, even when the realities that gave rise to them have changed. The controversy about "the new historians" began during Yitzhak Shamir's tenure as prime minister, while the Intifada raged and Israeli politics was gridlocked. The debate fumed on during the Gulf War, when some Israelis with post-Zionist sympathies felt compassion for the embattled Iraqi ruler. It continued into the years of Rabin's premiership, as a kind of atonal accompaniment to the Oslo Accords [doc. 133]. But [Yitzhak] Rabin's assassination in 1995 took the wind out of the confrontation over the new historiography; and it is beginning to seem a little stale.

113

Yair Tzaban

The Quandaries of an Israeli Minister of Absorption

1989–1994: Memoir

Between 1989 and 2003, more than 1 million people made Israel their new home. These new immigrants—the majority of whom came from the former Soviet Union—now account for about 16 percent of Israel's population. In the following text, Yair Tzaban (b. 1930), Israel's absorption minister from 1992 to 1996, describes the contribution this group of immigrants has made and some challenges they have faced.

In the years 1989 until the end of 1994, we absorbed 635,000 new immigrants, 545,000 of them from the USSR/FSU [former Soviet Union]. The vast immigration of 1990 and 1991 presented the previous government with an enormous challenge and the legacy it left us was no less prodigious and sometimes even more complex. Since I have been in office (as of July 1992) we, in the ministry, have made a tremendous effort to improve the absorption process. I believe that in every one of the areas in which we have been involved positive and important changes have taken place. At the same time, unfortunately, these changes have not been powerful enough to instill, in the newcomers and in Israeli society in general, the feeling that a basic, sweeping turnabout has occurred in absorption policy. We have had to pay a heavy price for the absence of this feeling among the *olim* [immigrants to Israel]—in the way they relate both to the Israeli establishment and to society.

The years between the two large waves of *aliyah* from the FSU, the first in the 1970s and the second at the beginning of the 1990s, were characterized by very meager immigration. Between 1980 and 1988, only 17,000 *olim* arrived from the Soviet Union. In fact, the total *aliyah* in the 1980s (1980–88 inclusive) was the lowest for any decade since the establishment of the state—130,000. In 1989–90, a new absorption policy was developed, called "direct absorption." In place of a system of services that helped the newcomers deal with their problems, they were given a number of grants as part of an "absorption basket." Instead of the government handling their housing needs, they were given a housing aid package, containing mainly mortgages and rent subsidies.

Even confirmed believers in the market economy, however, have to admit that there are situations in which a country and a society cannot allow market forces alone to solve problems. The impressive achievement of partially freeing immigrants from some of the bureaucratic intricacies that existed previously could not by itself provide the ultimate solution. It might have been possible to justify this policy when applied to about 70 percent of the *olim*; but what about the aged, the infirm and single-parent families?

About 55,000 engineers came to Israel between 1989 and 1994, as against some 30,000

Source: Noah Lewin-Epstein, Yaacov Roi, and Paul Ritterband, eds., *Russian Jews on Three Continents* (London: Frank Cass Publishers, 1997). Reprinted by permission.

Israeli engineers who were here before. Only about 30 percent of them found work in their fields. We offered professional retraining courses to many of these engineers, but beyond that we left their absorption mainly to market forces.

As against approximately 15,000 Israeli scientists who lived here before the new *aliyah,* 10,400 scientists arrived from the USSR/FSU in the years 1989–94. We succeeded in finding provisional positions for 7,000 newcomers in one field of science or another. Foreign observers are amazed at this achievement and we enjoy receiving their praise. But what will happen in three or four years, when the number of those leaving the system will increase?

In medicine, the situation is even more complicated. It is well known that even before the recent wave of immigration, Israel was one of the world's leaders with respect to the ratio of physicians per thousand population—about three per thousand. But, among the immigrants, the ratio is eight times greater: over 24 per thousand. In short, today we see the partial realization of the dream of the Russian *yiddishe mama* at the beginning of the century: the eldest son will become a doctor and the second son a lawyer—partially, because when then Bolshevik Revolution occurred in October 1917, the *yiddishe mama* was forced to rethink her plans. The eldest son would still be a doctor, but the younger—why should he be a lawyer when there was now a system of ultimate justice? He must become an engineer. And, since the future of the first two was ensured, the third could allow himself the luxury of becoming an artist—a musician, for example. This is in fact the family structure of the Russian *olim.*

We tend to talk about culture shock as part of the immigration experience. One of its characteristics is the identity crisis, which the *oleh* experiences. He is no longer Russian, but he is also not yet Israeli. His Jewish background is usually non-existent or minimal. Moreover, as if this is not enough, he is deprived of his profession—and in today's world, one of the most important components of a person's identity is his profession. The Soviet Jew, in particular, tended to define his identity not only, or not so much, according to his name, country of origin, nationality and religion, but above all according to his profession, which was his main source of pride. Yet, here in Israel, many newcomers have been unable to realize their professional identity. This crisis becomes particularly acute for those who have been prevented from practicing their professions over long periods of time.

An identity crisis is dangerous. It can cause a person to lose his self-respect, which is possibly the key to good absorption: giving a person esteem, honoring his personality, his education and culture, and recognizing his profession and his ability to contribute.

How do we deal with such a crisis? Perhaps we should begin by providing employment in general, and professional employment in particular for an increasing number of *olim.* For them, this is an existential problem as well as a solution to emotional stress and a partial answer to the question of identity.

Simultaneously with the study of Hebrew, we must help *olim* get to know our Jewish heritage. We can do this pluralistically, giving credit to all streams of Judaism. If we use indoctrination, we will only lose them. We must involve them in the Israeli experience through social and cultural integration in schools and universities, at the workplace and in the community. At the same time, we must not rush to cut them off from their Russian cultural roots. We must give full legitimization to their Russian background, especially in schools when dealing with the absorption of adolescents.

114

Micha Feldman

The Ethiopian Emigration

May 1991: Memoir

During the 1980s and 1990s Israel made extraordinary efforts to bring Ethiopian Jews into the country. The complicated politics and logistics of these missions required the involvement of a number of Israeli government agencies, the U.S. government, the Jewish Agency, and numerous non-Israeli Jewish organizations and individuals. They had to coordinate the Ethiopian Jews' journey out of Ethiopia, through the Sudan and Europe, and finally to Israel. Between November 1984 and January 1985, in a mission called Operation Moses, Israel transported about 7,000 people from Ethiopia to Israel; in May 1991, Israel airlifted 14,000 Ethiopian Jews within thirty-six hours in a mission known as Operation Solomon. In the following memoir, Micha Feldman of the Jewish Agency describes the tremendous complexities of the Israeli operations.

A week ago, a high level meeting took place at the Intercontinental Hotel in Geneva. The meeting was initiated by a person who was still concealed behind the scene, a person who had been responsible for the operations that had transported directly from Sudan or through intermediary stations in Europe 80 percent of the 6,649 Ethiopian Jews who had arrived in Israel, a person whose identity must not be disclosed.

. . . The dominant figure in the meeting was undoubtedly Jerry Weaver, the man in charge of the refugee issue at the U.S. Embassy in Khartoum. Jerry's nickname in the diplomatic community in Khartoum was "The Crazy American," since, unlike the other diplomats who spent their time in cocktail parties or in sports, he used to spend most of his time with the Sudanese, whom he liked.

Jerry is a tall broad-shouldered man who looks more like an athlete than a strictly dressed diplomat. For nearly two years he had been monitoring the Israeli's activities in Sudan and reported to the State Department that the Sudanese were familiar with this activity. This report reached us, too, at a later stage through our own embassy in Washington. Weaver supported the idea of getting the Ethiopian refugees out of Sudan; he criticized the State Department's leadership for daring too little in this regard, while commending Israel's activity.

During the past few months Jerry had paid numerous visits to the area of Gadarif getting as far as Umm-Ruqala. In the Geneva meeting he presented a very grim picture. He reported that of the more than 10,000 Jews who had arrived in Sudan during the previous five months, dozens were dying daily. All suffered from malnutrition and their survival prospects were dim. He compared the Jews in Umm-Ruqala to those discovered by the American liberators who entered Bergen-Belsen, Dachau, and Sachsenhausen.[1]

Having heard this description, the Israeli members of the group asked that medical and financial help be sent immediately to the Jews suffering in those camps. Weaver objected, fearing that the Israelis would settle on such help and would fail to proceed swiftly with a rescue mission. When Weaver managed to persuade the

---

Source: Micha Feldman, *Out of Ethiopia* (Jerusalem: The Jewish Agency, 1998).

Israelis that the Sudanese would agree to a swift evacuation, it was agreed that a working session would be held in which Weaver, Kreger (formerly in charge of refugee affairs at the State Department), [Yehuda] Dominitz (director of the department of immigration in the Jewish Agency), and the mysterious Israeli will take part.

The four men met during the late afternoon and Weaver presented his plan, according to which the Jews would be flown out of Khartoum's international airport with the knowledge and consent of the Sudanese authorities. Ostensibly, they would be flown to the U.S. and Europe, but in fact it was known to everybody that Israel would be their real destination. Weaver undertook to coordinate the plan with the Sudanese. That evening he met with his Sudanese friend and liaison who approved the plan, provided that no Israelis be present on the ground.

The next day, Weaver reported that all Jewish refugees could be evacuated within five or six weeks by gathering them in the Gadarif region, busing them to Khartoum by special buses, flying them from Khartoum Airport to Europe and then to Israel. Weaver communicated to his Israeli interlocutors the only condition raised by the Sudanese—that the Israelis not take an active role in the operation. In a subsequent meeting with Weaver's Sudanese liaison, it was agreed that "in order to identify the Falasha one black person be present." The Sudanese liaison did not view this as a problem, even though it was clear that such a person would be a member of the community who would be flown for this purpose from Israel to Sudan.

At the end of the discussion it was clear that the Israelis would take responsibility for the financial issue including the acquisition of buses and small cars, several tons of fuel and communication equipment. It was understood that all these items will remain in the hands of the Sudanese when the operation was over. The organization of the flights was also left to the Israelis. Neil Kutz (head of the UJA [United Jewish Appeal] office in Israel) immediately called New York and arranged for the necessary sum of money while the mysterious man's assistants set about finding an airline that would be acceptable to the Sudanese and would agree to fly the 10,000 Jews—this was the estimate—from Khartoum to Europe and on to Israel.

In their final working session, Weaver and the Israelis agreed that they would refrain from direct communication but would communicate by cable through Washington. In a telephone report from Geneva to Jerusalem, Weaver summed up by commenting that "the Jews had no choice but to decide to deposit the fate of the Falasha into the hands of an American they did not know and in the hands of the Sudanese whom they did not trust."

Weaver returned to Khartoum carrying in his suitcase a quarter of a million dollars that he had been given by the Israelis. Upon arrival he began with the practical preparations for the operation. He rented cars, built straw cabins in Tueta, rented houses in Khartoum and sent money to Gadarif. A few days later he was left with some thirty thousand dollars. He sent a cable to Washington asking them to inform Israel that additional money was needed for purchasing buses and medical equipment.

According to press reports outside Israel, the Israelis, while searching for a suitable airline, stumbled upon a Belgian Jew, George Gitelman, the owner of TEA—Trans European Airlines—which ran a large number of flights in the region including flights by Muslim pilgrims from Sudan and other Arab countries to the holy Muslim places in Saudi Arabia.

In meetings held in Geneva it was agreed that the operation of transferring the Ethiopian Jews from Sudan will begin within a month and will be completed within less than six weeks.

NOTE

1. These Nazi death camps were liberated toward the end of World War II.

Foreign Policy Issues

115

Hezbollah

The Hezbollah Program: An Open Letter

February 16, 1985

Hezbollah is a Lebanese military militia, social movement, political party, and terrorist organization that emerged in the wake of the 1979 Iranian revolution and the 1982 Israeli invasion of Lebanon. The organization holds a Shi'a fundamentalist Islamic ideology and is closely associated with the Islamic Republic of Iran while also enjoying support from the secular regime in Syria.

Western intelligence agencies believe that Hezbollah is responsible for numerous terrorist attacks around the world, such as the March 17, 1992, attack on the Israeli Embassy in Argentina, killing twenty-nine people, and the July 18, 1994, attack on the headquarters of the Argentinian Jewish community (AMIA), killing eighty-five people. Indeed, the organization is on the designated Foreign Terrorist Organizations list published by the U.S. State Department.

The organization's roots are also closely related to mass terror attacks. Western intelligence agencies suggest that factions that later became a part of Hezbollah were behind the October 23, 1983, attack on U.S. Marines in Beirut. The attack killed 241 U.S. servicemen and is the deadliest of its kind on Americans overseas since the Second World War.

The organization fought Israeli forces in Lebanon since the mid-1980s, and continued to do so even after Israel left Lebanon in May 2000. In the summer of 2006 Israel and Hezbollah collided in a one-month-long war that left some 158 Israelis and more than one thousand Lebanese dead. Hezbollah's position in Lebanon is an important component of Iran's current quest for regional hegemony in the Middle East.

Source: Jerusalem Quarterly, no. 48 (Fall 1988), a slightly abridged translation of "Nass al-Risala al-Maftuha allati wajahaha Hizballah ila-l-Mustad'afin fi Lubnan wa-l-Alam," published February 16, 1985, in *al-Safir* (Beirut). The full version here is from www.ict.org.il (accessed November 3, 2006).

The following is a text of the "open letter" of February 16, 1985, that marks the official launch of the organization. It was presented by a spokesperson for the organization and was also published in the Lebanese paper al-Safir *as well as in a publicly available brochure. The text offers the core beliefs of the organization, a reflection of its self-image, and a list of its goals including the destruction of the State of Israel.*

Our Identity

We are often asked: Who are we, the Hezbollah, and what is our identity? We are the sons of the *umma* (Muslim community)—the party of God (Hizb Allah) the vanguard of which was made victorious by God in Iran. There the vanguard succeeded to lay down the bases of a Muslim state which plays a central role in the world. We obey the orders of one leader, wise and just, that of our tutor and *faqih* (jurist) who fulfills all the necessary conditions: Ruhollah Musawai Khomeini. God save him!

By virtue of the above, we do not constitute an organized and closed party in Lebanon, nor are we a tight political cadre. We are an *umma* linked to the Muslims of the whole world by the solid doctrinal and religious connection of Islam, whose message God wanted to be fulfilled by the Seal of the Prophets, i.e., Muhammad. This is why whatever touches or strikes the Muslims in Afghanistan, Iraq, the Philippines and elsewhere reverberates throughout the whole Muslim *umma* of which we are an integral part. Our behavior is dictated to us by legal principles laid down by the light of an overall political conception defined by the leading jurist (*wilayat al-faqih*).

As for our culture, it is based on the Holy Koran, the Sunna and the legal rulings of the *faqih* who is our source of imitation (*marja'al-taqlid*). Our culture is crystal clear. It is not complicated and is accessible to all.

No one can imagine the importance of our military potential as our military apparatus is not separate from our overall social fabric. Each of us is a fighting soldier. And when it becomes necessary to carry out the Holy War, each of us takes up his assignment in the fight in accordance with the injunctions of the Law, and that in the framework of the mission carried out under the tutelage of the Commanding Jurist.

Our Fight

The U.S. has tried, through its local agents, to persuade the people that those who crushed their arrogance in Lebanon and frustrated their conspiracy against the oppressed (*mustad'afin*) were nothing but a bunch of fanatic terrorists whose whole aim is to dynamite bars and destroy slot machines. Such suggestions cannot and will not mislead our *umma*, for the whole world knows that whoever wishes to oppose the U.S., that arrogant superpower, cannot indulge in marginal acts which may make it deviate from its major objective. We combat abomination and we shall tear out its very roots, its primary roots, which are the U.S. All attempts made to drive us into marginal actions will fail, especially as our determination to fight the U.S. is solid.

We declare openly and loudly that we are an *umma* which fears God only and is by no means ready to tolerate injustice, aggression and humiliation. America, its Atlantic Pact allies, and the Zionist entity in the holy land of Palestine, attacked us and continue to do so without respite. Their aim is to make us eat dust continually. This is why we are, more and more, in a state of permanent alert in order to repel aggression and defend our religion, our existence, our dignity. They invaded our country, destroyed our villages, slit the throats of our children, violated our sanctuaries and appointed masters over our people who committed the worst massacres against our *umma.* They do not cease to give support to these allies of Israel, and do not enable us to decide our future according to our own wishes.

In a single night the Israelis and the Phalangists executed thousands of our sons, women and children in Sabra and Shatilla.[1] No international organization protested or denounced this ferocious massacre in an effective manner, a massacre perpetrated with the tacit accord of America's European allies, which had retreated a few days, maybe even a few hours earlier, from the Palestinian camps. The Lebanese defeatists accepted putting the camps under the protection of that crafty fox, the U.S. envoy Philip Habib.

We have no alternative but to confront aggression by sacrifice. The coordination between the Phalangists and Israel continues and develops. A hundred thousand victims—this is the approximate balance sheet of crimes committed by them and by the U.S. against us. Almost half a million Muslims were forced to leave their homes. Their quarters were virtually totally destroyed in Nab'a, my own Beirut suburb, as well as in Burj Hammud, Dekonaneh, Tel Zaatar, Sinbay, Ghawarina and Jubeil—all in areas controlled today by the "Lebanese Forces." The Zionist occupation then launched its usurpatory invasion of Lebanon in full and open collusion with the Phalanges. The latter condemned all attempts to resist the invading forces. They participated in the implementation of certain Israeli plans in order to accomplish its Lebanese dream and acceded to all Israeli requests in order to gain power.

And this is, in fact, what happened. Bashir Jumayyil, that butcher, seized power with the help also of OPEC [Organization of Petroleum Exporting Countries] countries and the Jumayyil family. Bashir tried to improve his ugly image by joining the six-member Committee of Public Safety presided over by former President Ellias Sarkis, which was nothing but an American-Israeli bridge borrowed by the Phalangists in order to control the oppressed. Our people could not tolerate humiliation any more. It destroyed the oppressors, the invaders and their lackeys. But the U.S. persisted in its folly and installed Amin Jumayyil to replace his brother. Some of his first so-called achievements were to destroy the homes of refugees and other displaced persons, attack mosques, and order the army to bombard the southern suburbs of Beirut, where the oppressed people resided. He invited European troops to help him against us and signed the May 17th, [1984] accord with Israel making Lebanon an American protectorate.

Our people could not bear any more treachery. It decided to oppose infidelity—be it French, American or Israeli—by striking at their headquarters and launching a veritable war of resistance against the Occupation forces. Finally, the enemy had to decide to retreat by stages.

Our Objectives

Let us put it truthfully: the sons of Hezbollah know who are their major enemies in the Middle East—the Phalanges, Israel, France and the U.S. The sons of our *umma* are now in a state of growing confrontation with them, and will remain so until the realization of the following three objectives:

(a) to expel the Americans, the French and their allies definitely from Lebanon, putting an end to any colonialist entity on our land;
(b) to submit the Phalanges to a just power and bring them all to justice for the crimes they have perpetrated against Muslims and Christians;
(c) to permit all the sons of our people to determine their future and to choose in all the liberty the form of government they desire. We call upon all of them to pick the option of Islamic government which, alone, is capable of guaranteeing justice and liberty for

all. Only an Islamic regime can stop any further tentative attempts of imperialistic infiltration into our country.

These are Lebanon's objectives; those are its enemies. As for our friends, they are all the world's oppressed peoples. Our friends are also those who combat our enemies and who defend us from their evil. Towards these friends, individuals as well as organizations, we turn and say:

Friends, wherever you are in Lebanon . . . we are in agreement with you on the great and necessary objectives: destroying American hegemony in our land; putting an end to the burdensome Israeli Occupation; beating back all the Phalangists' attempts to monopolize power and administration.

Even though we have, friends, quite different viewpoints as to the means of the struggle, on the levels upon which it must be carried out, we should surmount these tiny divergencies and consolidate cooperation between us in view of the grand design.

We are an *umma* which adheres to the message of Islam. We want all the oppressed to be able to study the divine message in order to bring justice, peace and tranquility to the world. This is why we don't want to impose Islam upon anybody, as much as we [don't want] that others impose upon us their convictions and their political systems. We don't want Islam to reign in Lebanon by force as is the case with the Maronites today. This is the minimum that we can accept in order to be able to accede by legal means to realize our ambitions, to save Lebanon from its dependence upon East and West, to put an end to foreign occupation and to adopt a regime freely wanted by the people of Lebanon.

This is our perception of the present state of affairs. This is the Lebanon we envision. In the light of our conceptions, our opposition to the present system is the function of two factors; (1) the present regime is the product of an arrogance so unjust that no reform or modification can remedy it. It should be changed radically, and (2) World Imperialism which is hostile to Islam.

We consider that all opposition in Lebanon voiced in the name of reform can only profit, ultimately, the present system. All such opposition which operates within the framework of the conservation and safeguarding of the present constitution without demanding changes at the level of the very foundation of the regime is, hence, an opposition of pure formality which cannot satisfy the interests of the oppressed masses. Likewise, any opposition which confronts the present regime but within the limits fixed by it, is an illusory opposition which renders a great service to the Jumayyil system. Moreover, we cannot be concerned by any proposition of political reform which accepts the rotten system actually in effect. We could not care less about the creation of this or that government coalition or about the participation of this or that political personality in some ministerial post, which is but a part of this unjust regime.

The politics followed by the chiefs of political Maronism through the "Lebanese Front" and the "Lebanese Forces" cannot guarantee peace and tranquility for the Christians of Lebanon, whereas it is predicated upon *'asabiyya* (narrow-minded particularism), on confessional privileges and on the alliance with colonialism. The Lebanese crisis has proven that confessional privileges are one of the principal causes of the great explosion which ravaged the country. It also proved that outside help was of no use to the Christians of Lebanon, just when they need it most. The bell tolled for the fanatic Christians to rid themselves of denominational allegiance and of illusion deriving from the monopolization of privileges to the detriment of other communities. The Christians should answer the appeal from heaven and have recourse to reason instead of arms, to persuasion instead of confessionalism.

To the Christians

If you, Christians, cannot tolerate that Muslims share with you certain domains of government, Allah has also made it intolerable for Muslims to participate in an unjust regime, unjust for you and for us, in a regime which is not predicated upon the prescriptions (*ahkam*) of religion and upon the basis of the Law (the *Shari'a*) as laid down by Muhammad, the Seal of the Prophets. If you search for justice, who is more just than Allah? It is He who sent down from the sky the message of Islam through his successive prophets in order that they judge the people and give everyone his rights. If you were deceived and misled into believing that we anticipate vengeance against you—your fears are unjustified. For those of you who are peaceful, continue to live in our midst without anybody even thinking to trouble you.

We don't wish you evil. We call upon you to embrace Islam so that you can be happy in this world and the next. If you refuse to adhere to Islam, maintain your ties with the Muslims and don't take part in any activity against them. Free yourselves from the consequences of hateful confessionalism. Banish from your hearts all fanaticism and parochialism. Open your hearts to our Call (*da'wa*) which we address to you. Open yourselves up to Islam where you'll find salvation and happiness upon earth and in the hereafter. We extend this invitation also to all the oppressed among the non-Muslims. As for those who belong to Islam only formally, we exhort them to adhere to Islam in religious practice and to renounce all fanaticisms which are rejected by our religion.

World Scene

We reject both the USSR and the U.S., both Capitalism and Communism, for both are incapable of laying the foundations for a just society.

With special vehemence we reject UNIFIL [United Nations Interim Force in Lebanon], as they were sent by world arrogance to occupy areas evacuated by Israel and serve for the latter as a buffer zone. They should be treated much like the Zionists. All should know that the goals of the Phalangists regime do not carry any weight with the Combatants of the Holy War, i.e., the Islamic resistance. This is the quagmire which awaits all foreign intervention.

There, then, are our conceptions and our objectives which serve as our basis and inspire our march. Those who accept them should know that all rights belong to Allah and He bestows them. Those who reject them, we'll be patient with them, till Allah decides between us and the people of injustice.

The Necessity for the Destruction of Israel

We see in Israel the vanguard of the United States in our Islamic world.[2] It is the hated enemy that must be fought until the hated ones get what they deserve. This enemy is the greatest danger to our future generations and to the destiny of our lands, particularly as it glorifies the ideas of settlement and expansion, initiated in Palestine, and yearning outward to the extension of the Great Israel, from the Euphrates to the Nile.

Our primary assumption in our fight against Israel states that the Zionist entity is aggressive from its inception, and built on lands wrested from their owners, at the expense of the rights of the Muslim people. Therefore our struggle will end only when this entity is obliterated. We recognize no treaty with it, no cease fire, and no peace agreements, whether separate or consolidated.

We vigorously condemn all plans for negotiation with Israel, and regard all negotiators as enemies, for the reason that such negotiation is nothing but the recognition of the legitimacy of the Zionist occupation of Palestine. Therefore we oppose and reject the Camp David Agreements [doc. 103], the proposals of King Fahd, the Fez and Reagan plan [doc. 107], [Leonid] Brezhnev's and the French-Egyptian proposals, and all other programs that include the recognition (even the implied recognition) of the Zionist entity.

NOTES

1. On September 16–18, 1982, Lebanese-Christian forces massacred hundreds of Palestinians in the Sabra and Shatilla refugee camps in Beirut, Lebanon, in response to the assassination of Lebanon's Christian President Bashir Jumayyil on September 14, 1982. The massacre shocked the Israeli public as Israeli forces controlled the outskirts of the camps and authorized the Christians' entry into the camps. An Israeli commission of inquiry concluded that Israel was not involved in the killing in any way, but that it did bear indirect responsibility for the events. See doc. 109.

2. This paragraph did not appear in the original translation published by the *Jerusalem Quarterly*. It is possible that this omission is due to the fact that the source (*al-Safir*) for the translation did not include this text, which appears in the original Hezbollah Program. The original program was published on 16 February 1985. The organization's spokesman, Sheikh Ibrahim al-Amin, read the program at the al-Ouzai Mosque in west Beirut and afterwards it was published as an open letter "to all the Oppressed in Lebanon and the World." It should be emphasized that none of Hezbollah's web sites have published the full text of the organization's program, and they prefer to publish the 1996 electoral program which was intended for the specific propaganda campaign before the Lebanese parliamentary elections in 1996. (Institute for Counter-Terrorism note)

116

The London Agreement between Jordan and Israel

April 11, 1987

The Labor Party's partial return to power in 1984, as part of a National Unity government, reinvigorated the secret talks between Israeli leaders and Jordan's King Hussein. As part of the talks, Israel allowed Jordan to try to revive its diminishing stature in the West Bank through such moves as allowing it to open banks in the Israeli-controlled territories. The most important product of these talks was the April 1987 London Agreement presented below. The agreement, signed by King Hussein of Jordan, and Israel's Foreign Minister Shimon Peres, offered general principles for an international conference between Israel and the Arabs that, it was hoped, would lead to peace. The agreement also contained the Palestinian issue within a joint Jordanian-Palestinian delegation and, in effect, gave Jordan the lead role in any peace arrangement regarding the future of the territories. The agreement came on the heels of Hussein's failure (1986) to reach an understanding with the Palestine Liberation Organization about possible Jordanian-Palestinian joint control of the territories, should Israel withdraw from them in the future.

The agreement was not approved by Israeli Prime Minister Yitzhak Shamir, who resisted an international conference as a mechanism for resolving the Arab-Israeli conflict and instead offered direct Israeli-Jordanian talks, an offer refused by King Hussein. Shortly afterward, in December 1987, the Palestinians launched an uprising (intifada) *against Israel—the First Intifada—which led King Hussein in July 1988 to publicly cede all claims to the territories, thus paving the way to an independent Palestinian role as later reflected in the 1993 Oslo Accords (doc. 133).*

Source: Maariv, January 1, 1988; reprinted in *Foreign Broadcast Information Service—Near East and South Asia,* January 4, 1988.

Accord between the Government of Jordan, which has confirmed it to the Government of the United States, and the Foreign Minister of Israel, pending the approval of the Government of Israel. Parts "a" and "b," which will be made public upon agreement of the parties, will be treated as proposals of the United States to which Jordan and Israel have agreed. Part "c" is to be treated with great confidentiality, as commitments to the United States from the Government of Jordan to be transmitted to the Government of Israel.

A. THREE-PART UNDERSTANDING BETWEEN JORDAN AND ISRAEL:

a. Invitation by the U.N. secretary-general: The U.N. secretary-general will send invitations to the five permanent members of the Security Council and to the parties involved in the Israeli-Arab conflict to negotiate an agreement by peaceful means based on U.N. Resolutions 242 [doc. 68] and 338 [doc. 86] with the purpose of attaining comprehensive peace in the region and security for the countries in the area, and granting the Palestinian people their legitimate rights.
b. Decisions of the international conference: The participants in the conference agree that the purpose of the negotiations is to attain by peaceful means an agreement about all the aspects of the Palestinian problem. The conference invites the sides to set up regional bilateral committees to negotiate bilateral issues.
c. Nature of the agreement between Jordan and Israel: Israel and Jordan agree that: (1) the international conference will not impose a solution and will not veto any agreement reached by the sides; (2) the negotiations will be conducted in bilateral committees in a direct manner; (3) the Palestinian issue will be discussed in a meeting of the Jordanian, Palestinian, and Israeli delegations; (4) the representatives of the Palestinians will be included in the Jordanian-Palestinian delegation; (5) participation in the conference will be based on acceptance of U.N. Resolutions 242 and 338 by the sides and the renunciation of violence and terror; (6) each committee will conduct negotiations independently; and (7) other issues will be resolved through mutual agreement between Jordan and Israel.

This document of understanding is pending approval of the incumbent Governments of Israel and Jordan. The content of this document will be presented and proposed to the United States.

117

Hamas

The Covenant of the Islamic Resistance Movement

August 18, 1988

Hamas is a Palestinian Islamist organization that was established in 1987 in Gaza as an offshoot of the Egyptian Muslim Brotherhood. The organization's creation marked the transformation of an Islamic network of social activists and clerics, active since the 1970s, into a political and military force that challenged Israel as well as the dominance of the secular Fatah leadership in the Palestinian national movement.

The organization opposed the Oslo Accords (doc. 133) and refused to recognize the Palestinian Authority (PA) that emerged out of them (see doc. 136). Hamas launched a series of deadly suicide attacks in Israel in order to undermine Israeli-Palestinian rapprochement and benefited from the PA's inability to hinder its activities, or lack of interest in interfering. The organization continued its deadly attacks in Israel in the Second Intifada (beginning in September 2000) and lost some of its leaders in Israeli retaliatory actions.

On January 25, 2006, Hamas won the parliamentary elections in the Palestinian Authority and subsequently formed a government. Power was split between the new government and the chair of the Palestinian Authority, Mahmoud Abbas, Yasir Arafat's successor and a representative of the Old Guard of the Fatah movement. Hamas's victory marked both the end of an era and the beginning of a new phase in Palestinian history and politics. This trend was reinforced by Hamas's military takeober of the Gaza Strip in 2007. One of the major issues at stake is the tension between the organization's ideology and platform and the constraints of governance. The following excerpts from the Hamas Charter, published in 1988, illustrate the severity of this tension.

Preamble

"Israel will exist and will continue to exist until Islam will obliterate it, just as it obliterated others before it" (The Martyr, Imam Hassan al-Banna, of blessed memory).

Introduction

O People:

Out of the midst of troubles and the sea of suffering, out of the palpitations of faithful hearts and cleansed arms; out of the sense of duty, and in response to Allah's command, the call has gone out rallying people together and making them follow the ways of Allah, leading them to have determined will in order to fulfill their role in life, to overcome all obstacles, and surmount the difficulties on the way. Constant preparation has continued and so has the readiness to sacrifice life and all that is precious for the sake of Allah. . . .

When the idea was ripe, the seed grew and the plant struck root in the soil of reality, away

Source: Mideastweb.org; excerpts selected by Dr. Meir Litvak.

from passing emotions, and hateful haste. The Islamic Resistance Movement emerged to carry out its role through striving for the sake of its Creator, its arms intertwined with those of all the fighters for the liberation of Palestine. The spirits of the fighters meet with the spirits of all the fighters who have sacrificed their lives on the soil of Palestine, ever since it was conquered by the companions of the Prophet, Allah bless him and grand him salvation until this day.

This Covenant of the Islamic Resistance Movement (HAMAS), clarifies its picture, reveals its identity, outlines its stand, explains its aims, speaks about its hopes, and calls for its support, adoption and joining its ranks. Our struggle against the Jews is very great and very serious. It needs all sincere efforts. It is a step that inevitably should be followed by other steps. The Movement is but one squadron that should be supported by more and more squadrons from this vast Arab and Islamic world, until the enemy is vanquished and Allah's victory is realized.

Article 1. The Islamic Resistance Movement: The Movement's programme is Islam. From it, it draws its ideas, ways of thinking and understanding of the universe, life and man. It resorts to it for judgment in all its conduct, and it is inspired by it for guidance of its steps.

The Islamic Resistance Movement's Relation with the Muslim Brotherhood Group

Article 2. The Islamic Resistance Movement is one of the wings of Muslim Brotherhood in Palestine. Muslim Brotherhood Movement is a universal organization which constitutes the largest Islamic movement in modern times. . . .

Article 5. Time extent of the Islamic Resistance Movement: By adopting Islam as its way of life, the Movement goes back to the time of the birth of the Islamic message, of the righteous ancestor, for Allah is its target, the Prophet is its example and the Koran is its constitution. Its extent in place is anywhere that there are Muslims who embrace Islam as their way of life everywhere in the globe. This being so, it extends to the depth of the earth and reaches out to the heaven.

Article 6. The Islamic Resistance Movement is a distinguished Palestinian movement, whose allegiance is to Allah, and whose way of life is Islam. It strives to raise the banner of Allah over every inch of Palestine, for under the wing of Islam followers of all religions can coexist in security and safety where their lives, possessions and rights are concerned. In the absence of Islam, strife will be rife, oppression spreads, evil prevails and schisms and wars will break out.

Article 7. As a result of the fact that those Muslims who adhere to the ways of the Islamic Resistance Movement spread all over the world, rally support for it and its stands, strive towards enhancing its struggle, the Movement is a universal one. It is well-equipped for that because of the clarity of its ideology, the nobility of its aim and the loftiness of its objectives. . . .

The Islamic Resistance Movement is one of the links in the chain of the struggle against the Zionist invaders. It goes back to 1939, to the emergence of the martyr Izz al-Din al Kissam and his brethren the fighters, members of Muslim Brotherhood. It goes on to reach out and become one with another chain that includes the struggle of the Palestinians and Muslim Brotherhood in the 1948 war and the *jihad* operations of the Muslim Brotherhood in 1968 and after.

Moreover, if the links have been distant from each other and if obstacles, placed by those who are the lackeys of Zionism in the way of the fighters, obstructed the continuation of the struggle, the Islamic Resistance Movement aspires to the realization of Allah's promise, no matter how long that should take. The Prophet, Allah bless him and grant him salvation, has said: "The Day of Judgment will not come about until Muslims fight the Jews (killing the Jews), when the Jew will hide behind stones and trees. The stones and trees will say O Muslims, O Abdulla, there is a Jew behind me, come and kill him. Only the Gharkad tree [evidently a certain kind of tree] would not do that because it is one of the trees of the Jews."

Article 8. Allah is its target, the Prophet is its model, the Koran its constitution: *jihad* is its path and death for the sake of Allah is the loftiest of its wishes.

Article 9. The Islamic Resistance Movement found itself at a time when Islam has disappeared from life. Thus rules shook, concepts were upset, values changed and evil people took control, oppression and darkness prevailed, cowards became like tigers: homelands were usurped, people were scattered and were caused to wander all over the world, the state of justice disappeared and the state of falsehood replaced it. Nothing remained in its right place. Thus, when Islam is absent from the arena, everything changes. From this state of affairs the incentives are drawn.

As for the objectives: They are the fighting against the false, defeating it and vanquishing it so that justice could prevail, homelands be retrieved and from its mosques would the voice of the *mu'azen* [announcer of daily prayers] emerge declaring the establishment of the state of Islam, so that people and things would return each to their right places and Allah is our helper. . . .

Article 11. The Islamic Resistance Movement believes that the land of Palestine is an Islamic *waqf* consecrated for future Muslim generations until Judgment Day. It, or any part of it, should not be squandered: it, or any part of it, should not be given up. Neither a single Arab country nor all Arab countries, neither any king or president, nor all the kings and presidents, neither any organization nor all of them, be they Palestinian or Arab, possess the right to do that. Palestine is an Islamic *waqf* land consecrated for Muslim generations until Judgment Day. This being so, who could claim to have the right to represent Muslim generations till Judgment Day?

This is the law governing the land of Palestine in the Islamic Sharia [law] and the same goes for any land the Muslims have conquered by force, because during the times of (Islamic) conquests, the Muslims consecrated these lands to Muslim generations till the Day of Judgment.

Article 12. Nationalism, from the point of view of the Islamic Resistance Movement, is part of the religious creed. Nothing in nationalism is more significant or deeper than in the case when an enemy should tread Muslim land. Resisting and quelling the enemy become the individual duty of every Muslim, male or female. A woman can go out to fight the enemy without her husband's permission, and so does the slave: without his master's permission. Nothing of the sort is to be found in any other regime. This is an undisputed fact. If other nationalist movements are connected with materialistic, human or regional causes, nationalism of the Islamic Resistance Movement has all these elements as well as the more important elements that give it soul and life. It is connected to the source of spirit and the granter of life, hoisting in the sky of the homeland the heavenly banner that joins earth and heaven with a strong bond.

Article 13. Initiatives, and so-called peaceful solutions and international conferences, are in contradiction to the principles of the Islamic Resistance Movement. Abusing any part of Palestine is abuse directed against part of religion. Nationalism of the Islamic Resistance Movement is part of its religion. Its members have been fed on that. For the sake of hoisting the banner of Allah over their homeland they fight. "Allah will be prominent, but most people do not know." Now and then the call goes out for the convening of an international conference to look for ways of solving the [Palestinian] Question. Some accept, others reject the idea, for this or other reason, with one stipulation or more for consent to convening the conference and participating in it. Knowing the parties constituting the conference, their past and present attitudes towards Muslim problems, the Islamic Resistance Movement does not consider these conferences capable of realizing the demands, restoring the rights or doing justice to the oppressed. These conferences are only ways of setting the infidels in the land of the Muslims as arbitrators. When did the infidels do justice to the believers?

"But the Jews will not be pleased with thee, neither the Christians, until thou follow their religion; say, The direction of Allah is the true direction. And verily if thou follow their desires, after the knowledge which hath been given thee, thou shalt find no patron or protector against Allah" (The Cow, verse 120).

There is no solution for the Palestinian question except through *jihad.* Initiatives, proposals and international conferences are all a waste of time and vain endeavors. The Palestinian people know better than to consent to having their future, rights and fate toyed with.

Article 14. The question of the liberation of Palestine is bound to three circles: the Palestinian circle, the Arab circle and the Islamic circle. Each of these circles has its role in the struggle against Zionism. Each has its duties, and it is a horrible mistake and a sign of deep ignorance to overlook any of these circles. Palestine is an Islamic land which has the first of the two *kiblahs* [direction to which Muslims turn in praying], the third of the holy (Islamic) sanctuaries, and the point of departure for Muhammad's midnight journey to the seven heavens [i.e., Jerusalem].

"Praise be unto him who transported his servant by night, from the sacred temple of Mecca to the farther temple of Jerusalem, the circuit of which we have blessed, that we might show him some of our signs; for Allah is he who heareth, and seeth." (The Night-Journey, verse 1).

Since this is the case, liberation of Palestine is then an individual duty for every Muslim wherever he may be. On this basis, the problem should be viewed.

This should be realized by every Muslim.

The day the problem is dealt with on this basis, when the three circles mobilize their capabilities, the present state of affairs will change and the day of liberation will come nearer.

Article 15. The day that enemies usurp part of Muslim land, *jihad* becomes the individual duty of every Muslim. In face of the Jews' usurpation of Palestine, it is compulsory that the banner of *jihad* be raised. To do this requires the diffusion of Islamic consciousness among the masses, both on the regional, Arab and Islamic levels. It is necessary to instill the spirit of *jihad* in the heart of the nation so that they would confront the enemies and join the ranks of the fighters.

It is necessary that scientists, educators and teachers, information and media people, as well as the educated masses, especially the youth and sheikhs of the Islamic movements, should take part in the operation of awakening [the masses]. It is important that basic changes be made in the school curriculum, to cleanse it of the traces of ideological invasion that affected it as a result of the orientalists and missionaries who infiltrated the region following the defeat of the Crusaders at the hands of Salah el-Din [Saladin]. . . .

It is necessary to instill in the minds of the Muslim generations that the Palestinian problem is a religious problem, and should be dealt with on this basis. Palestine contains Islamic holy sites. In it there is al-Aqsa Mosque which is bound to the great Mosque in Mecca in an inseparable bond as long as heaven and earth speak of Isra' [Muhammad's midnight journey to the seven heavens] and Mi'ra [Muhammad's ascension to the seven heavens from Jerusalem].

The Role of the Muslim Woman

Article 17. The Muslim woman has a role no less important than that of the Muslim man in the battle of liberation. She is the maker of men. Her role in guiding and educating the new generations is great. The enemies have realized the importance of her role. They consider that if they are able to direct and bring her up the way they wish, far from Islam, they would have won the battle. That is why you find them giving these attempts constant attention through information campaigns, films, and the school curriculum, using for that purpose their lackeys who are infiltrated through Zionist organizations under various names and shapes, such as Freemasons, Rotary Clubs, espionage groups and others, which are all nothing more than cells of subversion and saboteurs. These organizations have ample resources that enable them to play their role in societies for the purpose of achieving the Zionist targets and to deepen the concepts that would serve the enemy. These organizations operate in the absence of Islam and its estrangement among its people. The Islamic peoples should perform their role in confronting the conspiracies of these saboteurs. The day Islam is in control of guiding the affairs of life, these organizations, hostile to humanity and Islam, will be obliterated.

Article 18. Woman in the home of the fighting family, whether she is a mother or a sister plays the most important role in looking after the family, rearing the children and imbuing them with moral values and thoughts derived from Islam. She has to teach them to perform the religious duties in preparation for the role of fighting awaiting them. . . .

Article 20. Muslim society is a mutually responsible society. The Prophet, prayers and greetings be unto him, said: "Blessed are the generous, whether they were in town or on a journey, who have collected all that they had and shared it equally among themselves."

The Islamic spirit is what should prevail in every Muslim society. The society that confronts a vicious enemy which acts in a way similar to Nazism, making no differentiation between man and woman, between children and old people—such a society is entitled to this Islamic spirit. Our enemy relies on the methods of collective punishment. He has deprived people of their homeland and properties, pursued them in their places of exile and gathering, breaking bones, shooting at women, children and old people, with or without a reason. The enemy has opened detention camps where thousands and thousands of people are thrown and kept under subhuman conditions. Added to this, are the demolition of houses, rendering children orphans, meting out cruel sentences against thousands of young people, and causing them to spend the best years of their lives in the dungeons of prisons.

In their Nazi treatment, the Jews made no exception for women or children. Their policy of striking fear in the heart is meant for all. They attack people where their breadwinning is concerned, extorting their money and threatening their honour. They deal with people as if they were the worst war criminals. Deportation from the homeland is a kind of murder. . . .

Article 22. For a long time, the enemies have been planning, skillfully and with precision, for the achievement of what they have attained. They took into consideration the causes affecting the current of events. They strived to amass great and substantive wealth which they devoted to the realization of their dream. With their money, they took control of the world media, news agencies, the press, publishing houses, broadcasting stations, and others. With their money they stirred revolutions in various parts of the world with the purpose of achieving their interests and reaping the fruit therein. They were behind the French Revolution, the Communist revolution and most of the revolutions we heard and hear about, here and there. With their money they formed secret societies, such as Freemasons, Rotary Clubs, the Lions and others in different parts of the world for the purpose of sabotaging societies and achieving Zionist interests. With their money they were able to control imperialistic countries and instigate them to colonize many countries in order to enable them to exploit their resources and spread corruption there. You may speak as much as you want about regional and world wars. They were behind World War I, when they were able to destroy the Islamic Caliphate, making financial gains and controlling resources. They obtained the Balfour Declaration, formed the League of Nations through which they could rule the world. They were behind World War II, through which they made huge financial gains by trading in armaments, and paved the way for the establishment of their state. It was they who instigated the replacement of the League of Nations with the United Nations and the Security Council to enable them to rule the world through them. There is no war going on anywhere, without having their finger in it. . . .

Article 27. The Palestinian Liberation Organization is the closest to the heart of the Islamic Resistance Movement. It contains the father and the brother, the next of kin and the friend. The Muslim does not estrange himself from his father, brother, next of kin or friend. Our homeland is one, our situation is one, our fate is one and the enemy is a joint enemy to all of us.

Because of the situations surrounding the formation of the Organization, of the ideological confusion prevailing in the Arab world as a result of the ideological invasion under whose influence the Arab world has fallen since the defeat of the Crusaders and which was, and still is, intensified through orientalists, missionaries and imperialists, the Organization adopted the idea of the secular state. And that is how we view it.

Secularism completely contradicts religious ideology. Attitudes, conduct and decisions stem from ideologies.

That is why, with all our appreciation for the Palestinian Liberation Organization—and what it can develop into—and without belittling its role in the Arab-Israeli conflict, we are unable to exchange the present or future Islamic Palestine with the secular idea. The Islamic nature of Palestine is part of our religion and whoever takes his religion lightly is a loser.

The day the Palestinian Liberation Organization adopts Islam as its way of life, we will become its soldiers, and fuel for its fire that will burn the enemies. Until such a day, and we pray to Allah that it will be soon, the Islamic Resistance Movement's stand towards the PLO is that of the son towards his father, the brother towards his brother, and the relative to relative, suffers his pain and supports him in confronting the enemies, wishing him to be wise and well-guided.

Article 28. The Zionist invasion is a vicious invasion. It does not refrain from resorting to all methods, using all evil and contemptible ways to achieve its end. It relies greatly in its infiltration and espionage operations on the secret organizations it gave rise to, such as the Freemasons, the Rotary and Lions clubs, and other sabotage groups. All these organizations, whether secret or open, work in the interest of Zionism and according to its instructions. They aim at undermining societies, destroying values, corrupting consciences, deteriorating character and annihilating Islam. It is behind the drug trade and alcoholism in all its kinds so as to facilitate its control and expansion. Arab countries surrounding Israel are asked to open their borders before the fighters from among the Arab and Islamic nations so that they could consolidate their efforts with those of their Muslim brethren in Palestine. As for the other Arab and Islamic countries, they are asked to facilitate the movement of the fighters from and to it, and this is the least thing they could do.

We should not forget to remind every Muslim that when the Jews conquered the Holy City in 1967, they stood on the threshold of the Aqsa Mosque and proclaimed that "Mohammed is dead, and his descendants are all women." Israel, Judaism and Jews challenge Islam and the Muslim people. "May the cowards never sleep." . . .

Article 31. The Islamic Resistance Movement is a humanistic movement. It takes care of human rights and is guided by Islamic tolerance when dealing with the followers of other religions. It does not antagonize anyone of them except if it is antagonized by it or stands in its way to hamper its moves and waste its efforts.

Under the wing of Islam, it is possible for the followers of the three religions—Islam, Christianity and Judaism—to coexist in peace and quiet with each other. Peace and quiet would not be possible except under the wing of Islam. Past and present history are the best witness to that.

It is the duty of the followers of other religions to stop disputing the sovereignty of Islam in this region, because the day these followers should take over there will be nothing but carnage, displacement and terror. Everyone of them is at variance with his fellow-religionists, not to speak about followers of other religionists. Past and present history are full of examples to prove this fact.

Article 32. World Zionism, together with imperialistic powers, try through a studied plan and an intelligent strategy to remove one Arab state after another from the circle of struggle against Zionism, in order to have it finally face the Palestinian people only. Egypt was, to a great extent, removed from the circle of the struggle, through the treacherous Camp David Agreement [doc. 103]. They are trying to draw other Arab countries into similar agreements and to bring them outside the circle of struggle.

The Islamic Resistance Movement calls on Arab and Islamic nations to take up the line of serious and persevering action to prevent the success of this horrendous plan, to warn the people of the danger emanating from leaving the circle of struggle against Zionism. Today it is Palestine, tomorrow it will be one country or another. The Zionist plan is limitless. After Palestine, the Zionists aspire to expand from the Nile to the Euphrates. When they will have digested the region they overtook, they will aspire to further expansion, and so on. Their plan is embodied in the "Protocols of the Elders of Zion,"[1] and their present conducts is the best proof of what we are saying.

The Islamic Resistance Movement considers itself to be the spearhead of the circle of struggle with world Zionism and a step on the road. The Movement adds its efforts to the efforts of all those who are active in the Palestinian arena. Arab and Islamic Peoples should augment by further steps on their part; Islamic groupings all over the Arab world should also do the same, since all of these are the best-equipped for the future role in the fight with warmongering Jews. . . .

Article 34. Palestine is the navel of the globe and the crossroad of the continents. Since the dawn of history, it has been the target of expansionists. The Prophet, Allah bless him and grant him salvation, had himself pointed to this fact in the noble Hadith in which he called on his honourable companion, Ma'adh ben-Jabal, saying: "O Ma'adh, Allah throw open before you, when I am gone, Syria, from Al-Arish to the Euphrates. Its men, women and slaves will stay firmly there till the Day of Judgment. Whoever of you should choose one of the Syrian shores, or the Holy Land, he will be in constant struggle till the Day of Judgment."

Article 35. The Islamic Resistance Movement views seriously the defeat of the Crusaders at the hands of Salah ed-Din al-Ayyubi and the rescuing of Palestine from their hands, as well as the defeat of the Tatars at Ein Galot, breaking their power at the hands of Qataz and al-Dhaher Bivers and saving the Arab world from the Tatar onslaught which aimed at the destruction of every meaning of human civilization. The Movement draws lessons and examples from all this. The present Zionist onslaught has also been preceded by Crusading raids from the West and other Tatar raids from the East. Just as the Muslims faced those raids and planned fighting and defeating them, they should be able to confront the Zionist invasion and defeat it. This is indeed no problem for the almighty Allah, provided that the intentions are pure, the determination is true and that Muslims have benefited from past experiences, rid themselves of the effects of ideological invasion and followed the customs of their ancestors.

NOTE

1. *The Protocols of the Elders of Zion* is an antisemitic literary hoax aimed at showing the existence of an international Jewish conspiracy bent on world dominance. The *Protocols* were almost certainly concocted in Paris in the last decade of the nineteenth century. Although first published in Russia at the beginning of the twentieth century, the *Protocols* were translated into numerous languages after World War I.

118

James A. Baker

The Madrid Middle East Peace Conference

October 30–November 2, 1991: Memoir

In the wake of the 1991 Gulf War, which dislodged Iraqi President Saddam Hussein's forces from his brutal effort to take over Kuwait, the stature of the United States rose among most Middle Eastern Arab states. Converting that prominence into support for Arab-Israeli diplomacy and regional security was part of the vision that U.S. President George H. W. Bush articulated after the war. In eight diplomatic shuttle missions to the region after Iraq's defeat, U.S. Secretary of State James A. Baker III persevered in convincing Israel and its Arab neighbors to convene a Middle East Peace Conference in Madrid on October 31, 1991.

The U.S. role in repelling Saddam Hussein's aggression in itself was insufficient to convene an Arab-Israeli peace conference. A confluence of other factors made the Madrid Middle East Peace Conference possible. A reluctant Arab admission existed that Israel's military and economic strength made it immovable from the Middle East. Second, in the absence of a major patron to provide international political support and military aid, the Arab world lacked a military option to dislodge Israel from the region. Third, despite its public fears of going to a conference where Arab states would align uniformly against it, Israel accepted the conference format where that possibility was prohibited. Eagerly, Israel was prepared to negotiate bilaterally with Arab neighbors because its military superiority was unchallenged. Moreover, the Israeli public was weary of controlling the Palestinian population and wanted to find a suitable accommodation in which Israelis could separate their lives from governing the Palestinians who resided in East Jerusalem, the Gaza Strip, and the West Bank. Finally, both Israel and the Arab world placed their faith in American diplomatic choreography. For Israel, the United States remained its most dependable ally. Arab state acquiescence to the U.S. request to support the conference came especially because those in the oil-producing regions found that their territorial integrity, sovereignty, and political longevity were dependent upon a strong and long-term military relationship with the United States. Since the conference legitimized its

Source: James A. Baker III, *The Politics of Diplomacy: Revolution, War and Peace, 1989–1992* (New York: G. P. Putnam's Sons, 1995), pp. 511–13. Copyright © 1995 by James A. Baker III. Used by permission of G. P. Putnam's Sons, a division of Penguin Group (USA) Inc., and the author.

earlier peace treaty with Israel, Egypt warmly endorsed the conference concept and supported the American effort for its convocation.

The three-day conference in Madrid was precedent setting. Not only were Arab states willing to meet with Israel in a conference format; they were willing to use the conference's ceremonial beginning as an opening to engage in direct bilateral talks with Israel. Unlike all previous efforts at Arab-Israeli conference diplomacy, the conference did not take place in the aftermath of a prolonged period of communal violence or state-to-state conflict between Israel and its Arab neighbors. Rather, it came after the longest period of prenegotiations. Political, not military, issues were the main items on the negotiating agenda.

Each delegation came to the conference with the objective of fulfilling different purposes. In general, the Arab delegations came to Madrid to negotiate, and Israel came open to the negotiating process. But neither negotiated in front of the media nor negotiated except in a bilateral manner. Jordan's imperative was to let the Palestinians in the territories be the engine of negotiations and thereby diminish, if possible, the role of Yasir Arafat and the Palestine Liberation Organization. A joint Jordanian-Palestinian delegation allowed Amman to remain harnessed to progress in the Palestinian-Jordanian theater while letting the Palestinians determine the procedural agenda. The Palestinians, seeking parity with Israel, used the international forum to give them a much desired spotlight. The Syrians were the most antagonistic of Arab states toward Israel. Syria's extreme tones put the Palestinians, Jordanians, and Egyptians in a comparatively more moderate light. Syria's fear was isolation from an Arab support system; its worst fear was that progress on the Israeli-Jordanian-Palestinian front would proceed at a pace that would leave Syria to negotiate alone without an Arab umbrella to help protect its interests. Lebanon's presentation was noticeably restrained, leaving even the untrained ear to understand that Syria would decide Lebanon's negotiation options. Egypt used the conference to promote additional agreements between Israel and Arab delegations in order to justify its earlier peace treaty with Israel (doc. 104) and thereby continue the process of Cairo's complete and total return to the world of inter-Arab politics.

Madrid was planned by Americans; the Soviets played only a supporting role. The conference's formulation, conduct, and diplomatic aftermath reaffirmed the preeminent role of the United States over the Soviet Union in the region. U.S. Secretary of State James A. Baker was the diplomatic maestro. All sides looked to the United States to nurture the process, break logjams, and keep the negotiating ball in play. Out of the conference came bilateral talks between Israel and a Jordanian-Palestinian delegation and between Syria and Israel. Multilateral working groups emerged from the conference, which included discussions on arms control, economic development, the environment, refugees, and water. These were important discussions because they included Middle Eastern states—those outside the region—that had until then cool or no diplomatic relations with Israel.

The following account comes from U.S. Secretary of State James A. Baker.

Organizing this first-ever multilateral Arab-Israeli peace conference[1] proved to be an enormous logistical challenge. In addition to arrangements ensuring proper security and accommodations for both delegations and the press, we had to determine nearly every aspect of the actual meeting—such details as the length and order of speeches, the design of the table (which we had specially built), where representatives would be seated (which was the subject of extensive squabbling among the parties), and the amount of space allotted to each delegation. . . .

Except for a vivid painting of Charles V slaughtering the Moors, hurriedly warehoused for obvious reasons, Madrid's Royal Palace proved a splendid setting for the peace conference. Beneath eight stunning chandeliers in the ornate Hall of Columns, representatives of Israel, Syria, Egypt, Jordan, Lebanon, and the Palestinians warily convened around a T-shaped table on the morning of October 30, 1991. The opening ceremonies were hosted by Presidents [George H. W.] Bush and Mikhail Gorbachev [of the Soviet Union], whose eloquent remarks contributed to the sense of high drama and spectacle.

The scene exuded all the warmth of an arranged courtship, which in fact it was. Delegates appraised one another furtively, shunning direct eye contact, and taking pains to avoid even a perfunctory handshake. Except for the co-sponsors, national flags were banned from the ceremonies in deference to Israel's refusal to sit with a Palestinian delegation under the multi-colored banner of the PLO [Palestine Liberation Organization]. I cannot remember any meeting so devoid of diplomatic trappings.

Yet by every reasonable barometer, Madrid was a resounding triumph. Its enduring legacy was simply that it happened at all. After forty-three years of bloody conflict, the ancient taboo against Arabs talking with Israelis had in a space of one carefully choreographed hour been dramatically consigned to the benches of history. Like the walls of Jericho, the psychological barriers of a half-century came tumbling down with resounding finality that clear fall morning.

None of us, swept up in the satisfaction of the moment, harbored any illusions about the travails ahead. As I told reporters afterward, "We have to crawl before we walk, and we have to walk before we run, and today I think we all began to crawl." As I write these words over three years later, the peace process has matured to the point where these ancient adversaries are walking and may even learn to run. I'm hopeful that in my lifetime we'll see a splendid sprint toward a lasting peace. And I hope it doesn't sound arrogant to say that I'm proud to have contributed to a process which has begun to replace hatred with hope, and fear with friendship.

Some of my advisers said later they'd never seen me so serene. After eight months of grueling and often times exasperating diplomacy, I suspect they simply confused serenity with sheer exhaustion. But in truth, I knew the President and I had accomplished something significant in the search for peace, and I hope to be forgiven some measure of self-satisfaction in that regard.

During a break in the opening session, I spotted Eytan Bentsur in the last row of the Israeli delegation. A career Foreign Service officer, Bentsur was a senior aide to David Levy, who, like his boss, was one of the few members of [Yitzhak] Shamir's government I felt wholeheartedly supported the peace process. As early as September 1990, in fact, in a meeting with Dennis Ross at a New York delicatessen, he'd proposed the two-track formula that later became the centerpiece for the U.S. initiative. I grasped his hand warmly, then he enveloped me in a giant bear hug. "We did it, Mr. Secretary, we did it," he said, with quiet emotion so infectious that it overpowered my usual reserve. "You're right, Eytan," I said. "We did it."

NOTE

1. In writing his memoir, James A. Baker was either unaware or discounted previous Arab-Zionist or Arab-Israeli conferences, notably those held in London in February 1939, in Lausanne in 1949, and in Geneva in 1973.

CHAPTER 7

A Decade of Hope, 1991–2000

1992
Yitzhak Rabin of the Labor Party becomes prime minister for the second time

1993
Oslo Accords between Israel and the Palestine Liberation Organization indicate a resolve to terminate their conflict through compromise

1994
Israel and Jordan sign a peace treaty

1995
After Rabin is assassinated by a Jewish right-wing activist, Shimon Peres becomes prime minister for the third time

Alice Miller v. Minister of Defense opens the Air Force's pilots' course to women

United Mizrahi Bank v. Migdal Cooperative Village establishes the Supreme Court's power of judicial review

1996
Benjamin Netanyahu of the Likud becomes prime minister

1999
Ehud Barak of the Labor Party becomes prime minister

Israel completes its withdrawal from Lebanon

2000
Israeli-Palestinian peace conference at Camp David fails

An uprising of violence in the territories warrants the label of the Second Intifada

Domestic Issues

119

Meimad

Position Papers

1988

The original Meimad (acronym in Hebrew for "Jewish state, democratic state") was a political party that sought, but did not gain, representation in the Knesset elected in 1988. After right-wing supernationalists gained control of the National Religious Party (NRP) in 1987, political centrists like Rabbi Yehuda Amital, Rabbi Aaron Lichtenstein, and NRP activist Yitzchak Yaeger and attorney Yishayahu Privas felt the need for a firmly religious but politically moderate movement within the Religious Zionist community. As Rabbi Amital was quoted at the time, "What is being presented as Torah today is so militant, that I don't recognize it as coming from inside the Beit Midrash! . . . *I hear rabbis saying, 'Our religion obligates us to go out and start wars to conquer more land.'* Gevalt! *This is base ignorance."*

A few months before the scheduled elections of 1988, Rabbi Amital, Hebrew University professor Shalom Rosenberg, and Rabbi Dr. Daniel Tropper, founder of Gesher (Bridge), an organization promoting a better understanding between secular and religious Jews, scrambled to form a new political movement that would demonstrate that dedication to Torah does not necessarily dictate extreme political or social positions. Although the moderate political positions of this movement—Meimad—attracted the most media attention, its leaders also stressed the danger of internal disunity and emphasized the rift between religious and nonreligious Israelis as the greatest danger to Israel. In 1999 and 2003 Meimad ran again, but this time as a bloc with the Labor Party.

The first excerpt, taken from the 1988 campaign literature, is indicative of the party's focus at the time. The second excerpt deals with the Conversion Bill, which would have recognized only Orthodox conversions to Judaism. Few issues in Israel have raised the ire of American Jews as much as the debate over the this bill, which was charged with delegitimizing Reform and Conservative Jews in the Diaspora. Others have considered this charge an exaggeration but realize that the attitude of observant Jews in Israel toward Reform and Conservative Judaism has been called into question. As a movement made up almost completely of Jews committed to the halakhah (Jewish religious law), Meimad has been asked how the State of Israel should relate to

---

Source: Meimad—Position Papers and Social/Religious Initiatives, 1988.

Reform and Conservative Judaism. In this excerpt, Rabbi Amital and others emerge as staunchly Orthodox, in fundamental disagreement with the theological bases and ideology of Reform Judaism. They also recognize both the democratic Right and the educational advantages of allowing Reform Jews greater participation in religious life in Israel.

Meimad's Positions at a Glance

- Jewish tradition must play a central role in Israeli life for both the religious and secular communities, lest Israel lose its basic identity as a Jewish state. Meimad will, therefore, provide opportunities for increased Jewish education in both the general and religious school systems.
- The ways of Torah, however, are the ways of peace. Coercive legislation is not the way to advance religious observance. Meimad, therefore, will not support "religious legislation" that lacks a clear national consensus or that threatens the unity of the Jewish people.
- Meimad rejects the stale, political sloganism used by both right and left to mask the complexity of our situation.
- Meimad is committed to the principle that the peace, welfare, and preservation of the Jewish people and the State of Israel take precedence over political control of every inch of the Land of Israel. We make no apologies for the legitimate claim of the Jewish people to Eretz Israel. Nevertheless, our primary political responsibility is to preserve Israel's security, to bring an end to the cycle of war and bloodshed, and to maintain the Jewish character of the State.
- Forced expulsion of the Arab population as a means of solving our demographic or political problems is morally repugnant and politically self-destructive.
- Meimad supports the full integration of women in public and political life, including in the elected leadership of Meimad itself. The State of Israel should present to the world the finest possible example of advanced health and social services. The religious community should regard this as no less important a political goal than preserving the sanctity of Shabbat in public life or advancing the interests of religious education.
- Holding a political office should be seen as performing a public service in the true sense of the word. Meimad will demand the highest level of accountability of its and all other political representatives, and will work against the blight of patronage at all levels of public and religious life, including within the Jewish Agency. Meimad will work to halt the current practice of allocating public funds on the basis of political affiliation.
- Meimad will call upon the religious-Zionist community of Israel to become a new force that will unite the Jews of Israel, that will uphold the principles of Religious Zionism, and that will bring honor to the Torah.

Rabbi Yehuda Amital, "Meimad's Position on Reform Judaism in Israel"

When we consider Reform Judaism today, we have to consider it in the context of what is happening in the Jewish world in general, and we have to understand the particular historic circumstances we are living in. Before we begin, let's remember that there is a difference between the Reform and Conservative Movements, and what I say here applies to the Reform Movement only. We can talk about the Conservative Movement at some other time. It is also important to remember that there are different positions within the Reform Movement. Now, keeping all that in mind, we can see if there is a chance to reach some kind of understanding with them.

At the moment, what most religious Israelis think about Reform Judaism is based on an inadequate understanding of what is going on in the Jewish world. We cannot blame the Reform Movement in the United States if so many Jews there do not observe the *mitzvot* [religious commandments]. We are talking about a community that lost its belief in a God-given Torah two or three generations ago, and without that belief you cannot expect them to observe *mitzvot.* And we cannot keep faulting Reform Jews for some kind of historic opposition to Zionism. That is a thing of the past. Let there be no mistake, however. We utterly reject many theological premises of Reform Judaism. We are especially disturbed by what we consider its distortion of original Judaism. In this sense, Reform Judaism is worse than secular Judaism, and we have the most serious criticism of Reform Judaism's departure from the central elements of historic and traditional Judaism.

Moreover, there are three or four major errors of Reform Judaism that we do not think can be excused: (1) that they sanction intermarriage by performing supposedly religious wedding ceremonies when one of the couple is not Jewish; (2) that they co-officiate with non-Jewish clergymen at such mixed marriages; and (3) that they perform what is construed to be a religious ceremony at the "wedding" of homosexuals. And the fourth, which cannot be forgiven: that they have tried to re-define Jewish identity by recognizing patrilineal descent. This is especially grave because it will split the Jewish people into two groups that will never be able to unite again. Nonetheless, when it comes to the individual, I surely prefer that a Jew has some kind of belief in God—even if he belongs to a movement I do not approve of—rather than be a complete atheist.

To be frank, I don't think that the Reform Movement today is much of a threat to religious [Orthodox] Judaism in Israel. What is enticing religious Jews away from observance is complete secularism, not what most here consider a watered-down version of authentic Judaism. And those secular Jews who are searching for a way back to Judaism are not going to find what they want in Reform Judaism. When the time comes, some may prefer a Reform wedding ceremony to an Orthodox one, or a Reform burial to the *chevra kadisha* [burial society], but that does not make them practicing Reform Jews. Neither are the anti-religious politicians in Israel who have found a certain common cause with Reform Judaism here, really what one would call Reform Jews. They have the same enemy, the religious establishment, but they are not Reform Jews, and we should not mistake the media attention they command as a true indication of the strength of Reform Judaism. Too many people in Israel have to be reminded that assimilation is Diaspora Judaism's greatest enemy, and it is spreading like wildfire, wiping out whole communities. It is assimilation that world Jewry must devote all its energies to combat, and to do so we must strengthen every ounce of Jewish awareness and identity that any individual Jew may have. The Reform Movement has made an undeniably positive contribution in that struggle. Unlike in the past, the Reform Movement is no longer a way station on the road from religious observance to complete assimilation. Today, the gates to assimilation are open so wide that one who wants to leave the world of Torah and *mitzvot* doesn't need the Reform Movement to give him/her legitimization. Both on principle and because it is in our national interest, we want every Jew—even if he/she has no religious affiliation—to preserve some kind of Jewish awareness. By belonging to the Reform Movement, hundreds of thousands of Diaspora Jews declare that they consider themselves Jews, and the activities of the Reform Movement are thus an important element in the Jewish people's struggle for survival.

When we in Israel make decisions that affect the entire Jewish world, we must remember that an affinity with the State of Israel is an important factor in the Jewish identity of Reform Jews and that Reform Jews constitute a significant part of American Jewry. It is, therefore, of great value that they be able to identify with what we are doing here in Israel, and we would do well to keep this in mind at every step of our way. I think it crucial that the masses of Reform Jews in America not be alienated or made to feel rejected by the actions of the State of Israel and its institutions.

The situation in Israel, however, is radically different. Here, virtually every citizen feels identified with the State no matter what. Here, one would expect Reform Judaism to invest its energies in advancing Jewish culture, and in combating materialism and simplistic atheism, those remnants of the Enlightenment and Marxism. We would expect to hear it fostering a greater awareness of the moral foundations of Judaism. But unfortunately, that is not what is being done. So far, the main efforts of the Reform Movement in Israel have been devoted to fighting the Orthodox establishment and to gaining official recognition from state authorities.

I have already expressed my opinion that in accordance with democratic principles we should allow Reform Judaism to express itself in public matters. I mean that Reform Jews should have a say, in proportion to their numbers in the general population, in matters having to do with local synagogues, etc. What I oppose is the artificial manipulation of Reform Judaism by secular politicians to enhance their efforts to separate the Jewish religion from the State of Israel. I think that by allowing democratic principles to determine the degree of influence of Reform Jews in religious matters in Israel, no drastic changes will take place in representation, yet we would see a much needed revamping of religious services in general and of the religious councils in particular. And assuming that doing so would have a positive Jewish influence on many secular Israelis, I would also say that Reform Jews should be involved in educational activities here.

On the other hand, I am strongly opposed to giving legal standing to Reform weddings. I know that we can't just continue the situation as it is, both because of the problems created by the influx of new immigrants who are not halakhically Jewish, and also because of the growing number of Israelis who need some alternative kind of wedding. Up until now I supported civil marriages only for those who (by halakhah) cannot be married in a religious ceremony, but today I think that we must allow civil marriages for anyone who so requests. I am convinced that only a small minority of Israelis who can have a religious ceremony would choose a civil one. So I do not think that allowing them the possibility would be a major blow to the Jewish character of life here. On the contrary, many of those who make the effort to have a civil ceremony do so on principle to express their resentment of the coercion of the religious establishment. I might even hope that if couples didn't feel like they were being forced into a kind of ceremony they didn't choose, and with the welcome numbers of young rabbis who are now willing to take the sensitivities of secular Israelis into account when planning the ceremony, it could even be that the number of civil ceremonies in Israel would, in fact, decrease if they were made legal.

In spite of my suggestion that the state recognize civil marriages, I want to emphasize again my opposition to the recognition of Reform weddings as religious ceremonies. To extend that recognition would be to recognize the legitimacy of sects within Judaism. Giving validity to such marriages, as if they were marriages *k'dat Moshe v'Yisrael* (according to the rites of Moses and Israel) would be tantamount to recognizing a sect within Judaism. I suggest that the State allow civil marriages, not Reform marriages, for all couples who might want them, on condition that those who elect to have a religious ceremony be required to go to a Rabbinic court if they later want a divorce. It stands to reason that whoever chooses a civil marriage will have the right to a private ceremony if they so desire. Thus, the State of Israel will not be called upon to recognize non-halakhic weddings as religiously Jewish weddings.

It is an open secret that many of the *dayanim* [judges in the rabbinic courts] support the option of a civil ceremony, since it simplifies solutions to many complex halakhic situations that could arise among people who do not live their lives according to halakhah.

If we do not prepare the way in due time, we are liable to find ourselves confronting social, political, and family situations that will make things extremely difficult for us in the future. It has happened before.

120

Yitzhak Rabin

Speech to the Knesset on the 1992 Elections

July 13, 1992

The election of Yitzhak Rabin as prime minister in June 1992 and the formation of the new government in July were turning points in Israel's relations with its Arab neighbors. Determined to move forward with the peace negotiations that began at the Madrid Peace Conference in October 1991 (doc. 118), Rabin called on Arab leaders to follow the example of Egypt and come to Jerusalem. This, his inaugural speech to the Knesset, was followed by a series of decisions and actions that galvanized the peace process.

Members of the Knesset, please take note that this government is determined to expend all the energy to take any path, to do everything necessary, possible, and more for the sake of national and personal security, to achieve peace and prevent war, to do away with unemployment, for the sake of immigration and absorption, for economic growth, to strengthen the foundations of democracy and the rule of law, to ensure equality for all citizens and to protect human rights. We are going to change the national order of priorities. We know very well that obstacles will stand in our path. Crises will erupt; there will be disappointments, tears, and pain. But after it all, once we have traveled this road, we shall have a strong state, a good state, a state in which we will be proud to be citizens and partners in the great effort: A concerted, stubborn, and eternal effort of a thousand arms. "Will it succeed in rolling the stone off the mouth of the well?" asked the poetess Rahel. The answer is within us; the answer is us, ourselves.

Mr. Speaker, members of the Knesset, in the last decade of the twentieth century, the atlases, history and geography books no longer present an up-to-date picture of the world. Walls of enmity have fallen, borders have disappeared,

Source: Israeli Knesset online, July 13, 1993, http://www/knesset.gov.il/Tql//mark01/h0003891.html#TQL (accessed March 1, 2005).

powers have crumbled and ideologies collapsed, states have been born, states have died, and the gates of emigration have been flung open. And it is our duty, to ourselves and to our children, to see the new world as it is now—to discern its dangers, explore its prospects, and do everything possible so that the State of Israel will fit into this world whose face is changing. No longer are we necessarily "a people that dwells alone," and no longer is it true that "the whole world is against us." We must overcome the sense of isolation that has held us in its thrall for almost half a century. We must join the international movement toward peace, reconciliation, and cooperation that is spreading over the entire globe these days—lest we be the last to remain, all alone, in the station.

The new government has accordingly made it a prime goal to promote the making of peace and take vigorous steps that will lead to the conclusion of the Israeli-Arab conflict. We shall do so based on the recognition by the Arab countries, and the Palestinians, that Israel is a sovereign state with a right to live in peace and security. We believe wholeheartedly that peace is possible, that it is imperative, and that it will ensue.

The government will propose to the Arab states and the Palestinians the continuation of the peace talks based upon the framework forged at the Madrid conference. As a first step toward a permanent solution, we shall discuss the institution of autonomy in Judaea, Samaria, and the Gaza District. We do not intend to lose precious time. The government's first directive to the negotiating teams will be to step up the talks and hold continuous discussions between the sides. Within a short time we shall renew the talks in order to diminish the flame of enmity between the Palestinians and the State of Israel.

Come to Jerusalem

As a first step, to illustrate our sincerity and good will, I wish to invite the Jordanian-Palestinian delegation to an informal talk, here in Jerusalem, so that we can hear their views, make ours heard, and create an appropriate atmosphere for neighborly relations.

To you, the Palestinians in the territories, our foes today and partners to peaceful coexistence tomorrow, I wish to say: We have been fated to live together on the same patch of land, in the same country. We lead our lives with you. Beside you, and against you. You have failed in the war against us. One hundred years of your bloodshed and terror against us have brought you only suffering, humiliation, bereavement, and pain. You have lost thousands of your sons and daughters, and you are losing ground all the time. For forty-four years now, you have been living under a delusion. Your leaders have led you through lies and deceit. They have missed every opportunity, rejected all our proposals for a settlement, and taken you from one tragedy to another.

You who live in the wretched poverty of Gaza and Khan Yunis, in the refugee camps of Hebron and Shechem, you who have never known a single day of freedom and joy in your lives, listen to us, if only this once. We offer you the fairest and most viable proposal from our standpoint today: autonomy, with all its advantages and limitations. You will not get everything you want. Neither will we. So once and for all, take your destiny in your hands. Don't lose this opportunity that may never return. Take our proposal seriously—to avoid further suffering, humiliation, and grief; to end the shedding of tears and of blood. The new government urges the Palestinians in the territories to give peace a chance—and to cease all violent and terrorist activity for the duration of autonomy negotiations. If you reject this proposal, we shall go on talking but treat the territories as though there were no dialog on autonomy going on between us.

Instead of extending a friendly hand, we will employ every possible means to prevent terror and violence. The choice, in this case, is yours.

No Knife Will Stop Us

Members of the Knesset, we shall continue to fight for our right to live here in peace and tranquility. No knife or stone, no firebomb or landmine will stop us. The government presented here today sees itself as responsible for the security of every one of Israel's citizens, Jews and Arabs, within the state of Israel, in Judaea, in Samaria, and in the Gaza District. We shall strike hard, without flinching, at terrorists and those who abet them. There will be no compromise in the war against terror. The IDF and the other security forces will prove to the agents of bloodshed that our lives are not for the taking. We shall act to contain the hostile activities as much as possible and maintain the personal security of the inhabitants of Israel and the territories while both upholding the law and guarding the rights of the individual.

Allow me to take this opportunity, on your behalf as well as my own, members of the Knesset, to express gratitude and appreciation to the soldiers and officers of the IDF [Israel Defense Forces], to the secret soldiers of the Security Service, to the policemen of the Border Police and the Israel Police for the nights spent in ambushes and manhunts, for the days spent on guard, and for their watchful eyes. I shake your hands in the name of us all.

Members of the Knesset, the plan to apply self-government to the Palestinians in Judaea, Samaria, and Gaza—the autonomy of the Camp David Accords [doc. 103]—is an interim settlement for a period of five years. No later than three years after the institution of autonomy, discussions will begin on the permanent solution. It is only natural that the holding of talks on autonomy creates concern among those who have chosen to settle in Judaea, Samaria, and the Gaza District. At the same time, the government will refrain from any steps and activities that would disrupt the proper conduct of the negotiations.

We see the need to stress that the government will continue to enhance and strengthen Jewish settlement along the lines of confrontation, due to their importance for security, and in Greater Jerusalem.

This government, like all of its predecessors, believes there is no disagreement in this House about Jerusalem as the eternal capital of Israel. United Jerusalem has been and will forever be the capital of the Jewish people, under Israeli sovereignty, a focus of the dreams and longings of every Jew. The government is firm in its resolve that Jerusalem will not be open to negotiation.

The Winds of Peace

Mr. Speaker, members of the Knesset, the winds of peace have lately been blowing from Moscow to Washington, from Berlin to Beijing. The voluntary liquidation of weapons of mass destruction and the abrogation of military pacts have lessened the risk of war in the Middle East as well. And yet this region with Syria and Jordan, Iraq and Lebanon, is still fraught with danger. Thus when it comes to security, we will concede not a thing. From our vantage, security takes preference even over peace.

A number of countries in our region have recently stepped up the efforts to develop and produce nuclear weapons. According to published information, Iraq was very close to attaining nuclear arms. Fortunately, its nuclear capability was discovered in time and, according to various testimonies, was damaged during and following the Gulf War. The possibility that nuclear weapons will be introduced into the Middle East in the coming years is a very grave and negative development from Israel's standpoint.

The government, from its very outset—and possibly in collaboration with other countries—will address itself to thwarting any possibility that one of Israel's enemies will possess nuclear weapons. Israel has long been prepared to face the threat of nuclear arms in the Middle East. At the same time, this situation requires us to give further thought to the urgent need to end the Israeli-Arab conflict and live in peace with our Arab partners.

Members of the Knesset, from this moment forward the concept of "peace process" is outdated. From now on we shall not speak of a "process" but of making peace. In that peacemaking we wish to call upon the aid of Egypt, whose late leader, President Anwar Sadat, exhibited such courage and was able to bequeath to his people—and to us—the first peace agreement. The government will seek further ways of improving neighborly relations and strengthening ties with Egypt and its President Hosni Mubarak.

I call upon the leaders of the Arab countries to follow the lead of Egypt and its president and take the step that will bring us—and them—peace: I invite the king of Jordan and the presidents of Syria and Lebanon to this rostrum in Israel's Knesset, here in Jerusalem, for the purpose of talking peace. In the service of peace, I am prepared to travel to Amman, Damascus, and Beirut today, tomorrow. For there is no greater victory than the victory of peace. Wars have their victors and their vanquished, but everyone is a victor in peace.

Mr. Speaker, members of the Knesset, security is not only the tank, the plane, and the missile boat. Security is also, and perhaps above all, the man: the Israeli citizen. Security is a man's education; it is his home, his school, his street and neighborhood, the society that has fostered him. Security is also a man's hope. It is the peace of mind and livelihood of the immigrant from Leningrad, the roof over the head of the immigrant from Gondar, in Ethiopia, the factory that employs a demobilized soldier, a young native son. It means merging into our way of life and culture; that, too, is security.

New National Priorities

You ask how we're going to ensure it? We're going to change the national order to priorities and the allocation of financial resources from the state budget and from funds mobilized abroad. Preference will be given to the war on unemployment and to strengthening the economic and social systems.

- We intend to increase the rate of economic growth, to create places of work for the hundreds of thousands of new immigrants and natives of this country who will enter the job market in the coming years. We shall do this by retooling the economy for open management free of administrative restrictions and superfluous government involvement. There's too much paperwork—and not enough production.
- We shall promote the sale of state-owned firms and privatization, and we shall do so in collaboration with the workers, so that they will suffer no harm. A free world demands a free economy.
- We shall invest in basic necessary projects so as to attract entrepreneurs to build enterprises. We shall allocate funds for the infrastructure—transportation, electricity, water and sewerage, high-tech industries, research and development. That is the government's job.
- We shall decrease the government's involvement in the capital market and open a market for venture capital.
- We shall encourage the creation of small businesses.
- We shall establish a basket of social services to be provided, by law, to all citizens covering education, health, welfare and housing.
- We want the new immigrants and our sons and daughters to find work, a livelihood and a future in this country. We don't want Israel's main export to be our children.

The government that embarks on its journey today sees the health of its citizens as one of its highest priorities. "May you enjoy a full recovery" is not just a wish for good health; it will be the right of the ailing according to a national health law. That law will establish the public funding necessary to maintain a high-level public-health system that ensures equality for all. Every citizen in Israel will benefit from health insurance through public health funds.

Closing Minority Gaps

Members of the Knesset, it is proper to admit that for years we have erred in our treatment of Israel's Arab and Druse citizens. Today, almost forty-five years after the establishment of the state, there are substantial gaps between the Jewish and Arab communities in a number of spheres.

On behalf of the new government, I see it as fitting to promise the Arab, Druse, and Bedouin population that we shall do everything possible to close those gaps. We shall try to make the great leap that will enhance the welfare of the minorities that have tied their fate to our own.

The Jewish heritage has kept the Jewish people alive through all its wanderings and dispersions, and we see it as a duty to preserve the tie between the State of Israel and the Jewish heritage. Safeguarding the unity of the people requires tolerance and the creation of conditions for religious and secular to live together in mutual respect. We shall see to it that all Jewish children are educated in the light of Jewish values.

The government will refrain from any religious or anti-religious coercion and will provide for the public religious needs of the country's citizens regardless of political affiliation.

- All special funding will be canceled.
- The minister of defense will appoint a team, under his auspices, to investigate and determine the criteria for exempting yeshiva citizens from army service, so as to prevent the abuse of existing arrangements.

I believe that these steps, taken in full collaboration with the religious and *haredi* [Ultra-Orthodox] parties, will help mitigate the polarization of our society and bring the people of Israel closer together.

121

Israel Supreme Court

Alice Miller v. Minister of Defense

November 8, 1995

In 1994 an Israeli Air Force officer, Alice Miller, petitioned the Supreme Court, contesting the Air Force's policy of not allowing women to apply for the pilot training course. The course is probably the most prestigious one offered in the Israeli armed forces, but for most of Israel's history (with the exception of the early years of the state) women could not participate. The court rejected the state's arguments and ruled that women should not be discriminated against. While Miller did not enjoy the new ruling (she did not pass the preliminary exam required for the course), the case made it possible for women to enter Israel's most prestigious military track.

Source: Alice Miller v. Minister of Defense (1995) 49(iv) P.D. 94, as translated in *Israel Law Review* 32 (1998): 170–75. Legal footnotes have been omitted.

In June 2001 the first woman, Second Lieutenant Roni (the granddaughter of the Warsaw Ghetto Rebellion second in command; her last name was not publicized in accordance with military censorship) graduated the course as a fighter pilot.

Justice Dahlia Dorner

. . . In the State of Israel, as in other democratic countries, the principle of non-discrimination against women because of their sex is gaining force as a legal fundamental principle. Legal discourse is being translated into reality [citing the relevant provisions from the Declaration of Independence; the Women's Equal Rights Law, 1951; the Male and Female Workers (Equal Pay) Law, 1964; the Equal Opportunity in Employment Law, 1988]. The case law added its contribution by establishing a substantive-interpretative principle according to which, absent statutory provisions that establish otherwise, government bodies (and in some cases, even individuals and private bodies) are forbidden to discriminate against women because of their sex, and the laws must be interpreted—as far as possible—in keeping with this proscription.

The Basic Law: Human Dignity and Liberty (hereinafter: the Basic Law) granted a constitutional—supra-statutory—status to the prohibition of discrimination against women. This status derives from the following two factors:

Firstly, sec. 1 of the Basic Law (which also appears as sec. 1 in the Basic Law: Freedom of Occupation) provides that:

> Fundamental human rights in Israel are founded upon recognition of the value of the human being, the sanctity of human life, and the principle that all persons are free; these rights shall be upheld in the spirit of the principles set forth in the Declaration of the Establishment of the State of Israel.

This provision establishes, at the very least, that the fundamental rights must be respected in the spirit of the principles of the Declaration of Independence, among them, equality between citizens without regard to sex. Therefore, for example, one may not discriminate against women in relation to their property rights (sec. 3 of the Basic Law) or in relation to their freedom of occupation (sec. 3, Basic Law: Freedom of Occupation).

Secondly, the prohibition of discrimination against women is included in the right to human dignity, safeguarded in secs. 2 and 4 of the Basic Law.

The question whether the general principle of equality is included in the right to human dignity, as guaranteed in the Basic Law, has been raised *obiter dictum* in many decisions of this Court.

The legislative history of the Basic Law teaches that the failure to entrench the principle of equality in the Basic Law was intentional. In the Knesset's discussion of the Bill of the Basic Law, the Knesset Members Shulamit Aloni and Moshe Shahal argued against the failure to include in the Basic Law a provision regarding the right to equality. And in his reply to these claims, the presenter of the Bill, Knesset Member Amnon Rubinstein, said the following:

> There is no provision of general equality. Indeed, this general provision of equality was a stumbling block, which made it impossible to pass the Bill in its entirety.

In these circumstances, I doubt whether it is possible—or in any event, whether it is prudent—

to establish by means of interpretation that the objective of the Basic Law is to afford protection to the general principle of equality! The clear intention of the legislator, as revealed by the preparatory work, was precisely not to secure in the Basic Law this general principle. The preparatory work of a law carries weight when determining its objective. It is true that the weight of the preparatory work—which reveals the intention of the Knesset members in enacting the law—is lessened as the time since the law's enactment increases, and there have been shifts in policy or social or legal changes that are likely to justify the departure from this intention. However, only a few years intervene between the day of the enactment of the Basic Law and the present, and it would appear that the Basic Law may not be interpreted in a way that conflicts with its objective as revealed in the preparatory work.

Nonetheless, there can be no doubt that the objective of the Basic Law is to protect the human being from degradation. The degradation of a human being harms his human dignity. There is no sensible way to interpret the right to human dignity, as established in the Basic Law, such that the degradation of a human being will not be considered a violation of that right.

Indeed, not every infringement of equality is of sufficient magnitude to be considered degradation, and hence not every violation of equality violates human dignity. Thus, for example, it has been decided that the discrimination of small [political] parties as opposed to large parties, or new parties as opposed to veteran parties constitutes a violation of the needs of women. The interest of upholding the dignity and standing of women, on the one hand, and the continued existence of society and the raising of children, on the other hand, requires—as far as possible—not expropriating from women the possibility of realizing their potential and their aspirations simply because of their special natural functions, which would result in discrimination against them. The social institutions—including the legal regulations—must be adapted to the woman's needs.

This intermediary model, according to which every employer is required to take into account the fact that a woman's performance is liable to be interrupted because of pregnancy, nursing and looking after children, is entrenched in Israel in labour legislation. So, for example, the Employment of Women Law, 1954, establishes a woman's right to maternity leave (sec. 6(a)), the right to be absent from work during the period of the pregnancy, if there is a medical need (sec. 7(c)1), and the right to return to work after the birth following an absence of no longer than twelve months (sec. 7(d)(1)).

Naturally, the institution of the intermediary model costs money and encumbers the organization. These expenses must be carried—sometimes with the participation of Social Security—by the private employer. How much more so does this obligation apply to the State.

The need to consider the special needs of women is similar to the requirement to take into account a person's religious belief. Such a requirement is accepted by the United States. In the Elitzur case, Kister J. wrote that we must adopt the approach of the American case law. . . .

It is worth mentioning that in 1981 the Hours of Work and Rest Law, 1951, was amended and according to sec. 9C(a) an employer is forbidden to refuse to employ a person solely because the latter is not prepared to work during the weekly days of rest according to the commandment of his religion (para. 16).

122

Israel Law Review

United Mizrahi Bank v. Migdal Cooperative Village

November 9, 1995

In 1992 the Israeli Knesset added two new laws to the emerging Israeli constitution. The laws were Basic Law: Human Dignity and Liberty, and Basic Law: Freedom of Occupation. The laws offered, for the first time in Israeli history, a legislated (as opposed to judicial) constitutional defense of human rights. However, in the three years between the legislation of these laws and the Mizrahi Case, it was unclear whether these laws could be used by the Supreme Court to perform judicial review of other Knesset legislation. The 1995 Mizrahi Case brought this issue to the forefront, when creditors of a number of agricultural communities contested the constitutionality of 1993 legislation that forced them to forgive some of the debt they were owed. While the court did not grant the creditors their request and did not annul Knesset legislation, it nevertheless used the case to clarify the normative hierarchy between the different laws. Relying heavily on the American model, and in particular Marbury v. Madison *(1803), the court ruled that it indeed had the power to perform judicial review and annul Knesset laws that contradict the two new Knesset Basic Laws. In 1997 the court used the new powers for the first time, and annulled a section of a Knesset law.*

The Arrangements in the Family Agricultural Sector Law (the Gal Law) was part of an attempt to rehabilitate the agricultural sector following a severe economic crisis. It provided for the establishment of a special body called "HaMeshakem" (the Rehabilitator) which was granted broad powers, including the power to cancel part of a debt. The creditors of a cancelled debt, including the United Mizrahi Bank and the other appellants, applied to the District Court to annul the Gal Law on the grounds that it violated their property rights. The District Court accepted their petition, holding that the amendment violated sec. 3 of the Basic Law: Human Dignity and Liberty, and should be annulled. The matter was appealed before the Supreme Court, which overturned the District Court decision. Each of the nine judges wrote a separate opinion.

Editorial Commentary

The *Gal* decision marks a turning point in Israeli constitutional law. In this decision, the Supreme Court of Israel confronts a number of major constitutional dilemmas for the first time. Most importantly, the decision gives recognition to the existence of substantive judicial review of legislation in the Israeli legal system. In order to understand the case, a brief explanation of Israeli constitutional law is warranted.

Israel has no comprehensive document known as the "Constitution" or the "Bill of Rights." This absence may be attributed mainly to the traditional coalition system which developed in the Israeli politic, with the major

Source: Editorial commentary on *United Mizrahi Bank PLC. v. Migdal Cooperative Village* (1995) 49(iv) P.D 221, as translated in *Israel Law Review* 31 (1997): 765–70. Legal footnotes have been omitted.

opposition issuing forth from the religious parties and the military. In the past, the Supreme Court dealt with this situation by identifying a list of judicially recognized fundamental rights. However, these principles were not considered binding on the legislative powers of the Israeli parliament (the Knesset). Such supra-statutory norms could not be instated by the judiciary. Finally, what may be viewed as a political compromise was reached within the Knesset: on the understanding that the enactment of a general bill of rights was a political impossibility, it was decided to enact legislation that would cover those rights that were less politically controversial. This was achieved in 1992 in the form of two "Basic Laws."

These two laws were not the first to earn the title "Basic Law"; however, two differences supported their claim to increased normative status. Firstly, these laws deal, as mentioned above, with fundamental civil rights, in particular, "Freedom of Occupation" and "Human Dignity and Liberty." Secondly, the rights included in these two laws enjoy not only formal entrenchment (only by a certain majority may they be amended or infringed); they are also safeguarded by a limitation clause that constitutes substantive entrenchment. In other words, from now on the Knesset may not enact a law that contradicts the principles set out in the Basic Laws, unless it meets the substantive conditions set out in the limitation clause. The District Court decision, the subject of the present case, marked the first time that an Israeli court had ever overturned a law for the reason that it was substantively repugnant to fundamental human rights as set out in the Basic Law. Not surprisingly, the matter was appealed before the Supreme Court. Thus, the cardinal issue of the competence of Israel's judiciary to revoke a law of the Knesset on the basis of its substantive unconstitutionality was brought before the Supreme Court. An unusually large panel of nine justices was convened to meet the occasion.

The first question posed by the Court was whether the Basic Laws enacted by the Knesset may be considered supra-statutory constitutional legislation. In deciding the issue, the Court had to consider whether or not the Knesset had the authority to frame a constitution, thus limiting its own future legislative power. Eight of the nine justices concluded (Cheshin dissenting) that the Knesset did indeed have authority to frame a constitution for Israel. The Court's primary approaches were proposed by Justice Barak, with whom the majority of justices concurred, and Past President Shamgar.

Justice Barak bases the Knesset's authority to enact constitutional legislation on the doctrine of constituent authority. The Knesset acts in two capacities: generally it functions as a (regular) legislature. However, on special occasions it functions as a constituent assembly and exercises its constituent authority by enacting constitutional Basic Laws. According to Justice Barak, the Knesset derives its constituent authority from the constitutional continuity that began with the Declaration of Independence, which expressly provided for the framing of a Constitution by a Constituent Assembly, and may be traced until the existing Knesset. Barak bases his decision, in part, on the Harari Resolution according to which the Constitution would be drawn up in the form of chapters or Basic Laws that together would finally be consolidated into the Constitution. Hence, the Knesset's constituent authority is finite, and will terminate when the Knesset, as a Constituent Assembly, declares that it has completed the process of framing the Constitution. The Constitution will set out the process for future amendment. Barak also bases his decision on the "broad national consensus," namely, today, nearly fifty years later, the Knesset is perceived in the Israeli national consciousness as having the authority to frame a Constitution for the State of Israel.

President Shamgar, on the other hand, bases the Knesset's constituent authority on the theory of the Knesset's unlimited sovereignty. According to this approach, the Knesset's sovereignty allows it to enact any law, including constitutional legislation. Thus, the principle of the sovereignty of parliament includes the ability to limit its own power and that of future Knessets. No member of the court concurred with Shamgar in this approach.

In his dissenting opinion, Justice Cheshin holds that although the First Knesset was authorized to frame a constitution, this power was not transferable and was not transferred to subsequent Knessets. According to Cheshin, constituent authority must be clear and unequivocal, and here it is not: the first Knesset did not establish a Constitution because it was unclear whether the people wanted one. Since then, there has been no clear statement by the public as a whole regarding either its desire for a Constitution, or the Knesset's authority to frame one. The Basic Laws were not always passed by an overwhelming consensus. Even those concerning fundamental human rights were passed when attendance was sparse. In addition, Cheshin suggests that most of the Knesset members failed to perceive the significance of enacting a central chapter to the Israeli Constitution. Justice Bach emphasizes that the present case did not require that the Court determine the issue of the source of the Knesset's constituent authority, and the discussion may actually be classified as *obiter dictum.* Be that as it may, the fact that eight of the nine judges held that the Knesset has the constituent authority to pass constitutional laws means that the Court is entitled to regard the Basic Law under discussion as a superior norm, against which to examine the constitutionality of a "regular" law that infringes a fundamental right entrenched therein.

How may one controvert a Basic Law? The Court emphasises that the distinction must be made between "amending" and "violating" a Basic Law. Regarding the first, both Barak and Shamgar point out that while previously it was held that a Basic Law can be amended by a regular law, that ruling must now be reversed. In the future, every amendment to a Basic Law must be made in a Basic Law—the change must be consonant with the normative level of the object of that change. Regarding the second, a "regular" law passed by the Knesset (by whatever majority) cannot "violate" a human right safeguarded in the Basic Law, unless it meets the conditions established in the limitation clause. According to the majority, if the "regular" law does not meet these conditions, it is unconstitutional, whether it states explicitly its intention to violate a fundamental right protected by the Basic Law (Justice Cheshin's view), or whether the violation is implicit. What we have here then, is the recognition by the Supreme Court that the Israeli judiciary has the authority to exercise substantive judicial review regarding the constitutionality of a law. Moreover, if the Court reaches the conclusion that the protected right has been impaired and that the conditions of the limitation clause have not been met, it is empowered to grant constitutional remedies, among them the declaration of the law (or part of it) invalid. Although not included in the decision, this conclusion may still be considered a breakthrough in Israeli constitutional law in light of the fact that the Basic Law includes no express remedy. However, the Court does not state whether this power should reside in all courts, or in the Supreme Court alone, in accordance with Justice Cheshin's view.

The most important thing to remember about the *Gal* judgment, however, is that most of the discussion included in its few hundred pages, although interesting and even groundbreaking, is purely academic. As evidenced by the excerpts given in this note, the *ratio* of the case is considerably narrower because ultimately the District Court's decision was overturned and the Gal Law was held to be constitutional. The Basic Law: Human Dignity and Liberty expressly prohibits "the infringement of a person's property." Thus, in order to decide on the validity of the law in *Gal,* the Court was required to analyse the meaning and scope of the right to "property" as it appears in the Basic Law. Despite the differences in their approach to the question of property rights, all the judges conclude that the Gal Law Amendment, which resulted in creditors losing part of their money, infringed the creditors' property rights. Thus the Law had to be examined in light of the limitation clause and it is here that it made its claim to validity. While all nine judges agreed that the creditors' property rights had been violated, they also agreed that the amendment met the conditions of the limitation clause; it was in keeping with the values of the State of Israel, and served the legitimate purpose of preventing the collapse of an important branch of the Israeli economy. The justices also concluded that the violation of the creditors' property rights did not violate the principle of proportionality since it did not exceed what was necessary and that no effective alternative arrangements, which would be less injurious to the creditors' property rights, were available. (However, several of the judges questioned whether it would have been more appropriate to remand the case to the District Court on this point.)

The Court expanded on the requirement of the limitation clause that the law violates the human right "to a degree that does not exceed what is necessary"—the test of proportionality. According to Justice Barak the test defines a "limitations zone." The choice among different options within the zone lies with the legislature alone. The court will not test whether the law is ideal, good, effective or justified, but only if it is constitutional and falls within the "limitation clause." Consequently, the District Court's decision to overturn the Gal Law Amendment was reversed.

Regarding the future implications of this decision, we must note that the Gal Law, and its Amendment, are fiscal laws. Here, the Court gives the impression that while it has the authority to overturn unconstitutional laws, it will not do so lightly, particularly when the claim is that its unconstitutionality derives from an infringement of property rights. Only time will tell how the Court will decide when called upon to review a law that cannot be defined as fiscal.

Finally, it should be noted that the constitutional impact of the Basic Law: Human Dignity and Liberty is, for the time being, prospective, that is, binding only as regards later legislation. In *Gal* the Supreme Court was called upon to review what was actually an amendment to the original Gal Law, the latter being immune from scrutiny, having come into force "prior to the commencement of the Basic Law." However, both the District Court and the Supreme Court concluded that an amendment should be viewed not merely as part of the pre-existing law, but as a new law that could itself be constitutionally reviewed.

123

Shamgar Commission

Report on Yitzhak Rabin's Assassination

1996

On the evening of November 4, 1995, as he was leaving a peace rally in Tel Aviv, Israeli Prime Minister Yitzhak Rabin was shot and killed. The assassin, Yigal Amir, was a religious right-wing activist hoping to stop the peace process that Rabin's government and the Palestinians were in the midst of implementing. Amir's act was a violent

Source: Israel Ministry of Justice, http://www.justice.gov.il/MOJHeb/Sifria/Dochot (accessed August 28, 2006).

reflection of how deeply divided Israeli society had become over the land-for-peace deal that the government had made with the Palestinians in 1993, and it showed the tremendous danger such divisions could pose to Israel's democratic system of government. The assassination also brought into painfully sharp focus the differences between the Zionist visions—and methods—of the murderer and the victim. Yitzhak Rabin was in many ways the ultimate exemplar of the secular Zionist revolution. He followed in the footsteps of previous Labor leaders like David Ben-Gurion, adopting a pragmatic approach to attaining a vision of a secure, modern, just, and prosperous Israel. For Yigal Amir and the segment of ultra-right-wing religious extremists who would champion his actions, the goals and the means, and their own personal experiences, were radically different. Rabin grew up during Israel's struggle for independence and survival and, through a long and dedicated career in his nation's service as a soldier and a statesman, realized not only the importance and complexity of constructing military might but also its limits. Amir was born into an Israel that had not only secured its existence but already controlled the territories. His religious vision of Israel's future was inextricably linked to retaining that control, not as a means of ensuring Israel's security but to fulfill a religious calling. For Amir, that vision justified any action—including a direct attack on the Jewish state and the murder of one of its most ardent defenders.

Introduction

In the aftermath of the assassination of the Prime Minister, Mr. Yitzhak Rabin, of blessed memory, on Saturday, November 4, 1995, the Cabinet decided on November 8, to appoint a commission of inquiry, according to paragraph 1 of the Law on Commissions of Inquiry 1968.

The Commission's task was defined as follows:

> The Commission will investigate and establish findings and conclusions in all matters concerning the security and intelligence deployment and in everything concerning the protection of (senior) persons in general and particularly so in the rally in which the assassination occurred.

The President of the Supreme Court, Aharon Barak, determined on November 9, 1995, on the strength of his authority according to the Law on Commissions of Inquiry, that the members of the commission would be the retired president of the Supreme Court, Justice Meir Shamgar, who will act as Chairman, and retired General Zvi Zamir and Professor Ariel Rosen Zvi as members.

The legal proceedings against the assassin were conducted in the district court in Tel Aviv–Jafo.

The Assassin—Yigal Amir

(1) Yigal Amir (identity card number 0-2779008-8) was born on May 23, 1970, single, lives in the Neve Amal section of Herzeliyya, 56 Borochov Street, at the home of his parents, Geula and Shlomo. He has three brothers and four sisters. In the past he lived briefly in the settlement of Shavey Shomron in Judaea and Samaria.

He grew up in Herzeliyya. His father is an ultra-Orthodox man. His mother is a kindergarten teacher by profession. In his youth he was not a member of a youth movement. He studied five years in an ultra-Orthodox Yeshiva in Tel Aviv. Later he transferred to a *yeshivat-hesder* (combining religious scholarship with military service) and studied in this framework in the Keren BeYavne Yeshiva.

Yigal Amir performed his active military

service as a rifleman in the Golani brigade. Later, when he was still in the non-military part of his special service period, he was sent to Estonia by the Foreign Ministry's liaison office and spent three months organizing Jewish youth and teaching service. Upon the completion of his mandatory service in 1993, he was admitted into Bar-Ilan University's Law Faculty and Kotel (a type of yeshiva). At the outset, he studied criminology as well and later shifted to computer studies. At the time of the assassination, he was in his third year at the Faculty of Law.

(2) Amir was active in organizing demonstrations by Bar-Ilan students and participated also in other demonstrations including the one which took place in Givat Hadagnan. He was the organizer and the leader in student gatherings in various settlements in Judaea and Samaria and in the Gaza Strip . . . and acted in this vein together with Avishai Raviv who was at that time connected to the General Security Service.

He was described by his acquaintances as extreme in his views. He was not affiliated with Kach[1] but according to Avishai Raviv, Amir supported Dr. Baruch Goldstein's act.[2]

As he told the researchers of this commission, his latent intention was to organize among the participants at the students' weekend gatherings groups of people who would be willing to defend settlements with weapons in the event of the area's evacuation by the IDF [Israel Defense Forces].

Persons close to him among the student weekend organizers, including Avishai Raviv, heard him more than once stating that the retribution for "persecution" applied to Yitzhak Rabin and that the latter should be killed. Avishai Raviv himself used the same language and according to various testimonies was even more vociferous in this matter.

(3) According to Yigal Amir's own explanation, the idea of the assassination matured slowly in his mind through lengthy reflection and soul searching.

These are some of his explanations during his interrogation by the GSS [General Security Service]:

> Without my belief in the Almighty, I would not have had the strength to do it—namely belief in the next world. During the last three years, I understood that Rabin was not a leader fit to lead the people . . . he abandoned Jews, he lied, he had a lust for power. He brainwashed people and the media. He raised ideas such as (that of) a Palestinian state. He received the Nobel Prize together with Arafat, the killer, but overlooked his own people. He divided the nation. He left the settlers on the sidelines and did not take them into consideration. I had to save the people because the people failed to understand that real situation; this is why I acted. He kept using the term "victims of peace." Soldiers were killed in Lebanon and Israel did not respond because a peace process was unfolding. . . .
>
> Without a religious opinion or the verdict of "persecutor" that was applied to Rabin by a number of rabbis that I know of, I would have had a hard time performing an assassination. Such an assassination requires backing. Had I not had backing and had I not had numerous additional people behind me, I would not have acted.

In his interrogation by the researchers of this committee (Amir) raised an additional version: that the media disregarded the protests and demonstrations by the right-wingers. This produced the desperation which led him to take the action that would trigger a shock. He went so far as to state that had the protest activities been covered by the media, he may not have assassinated Rabin.

In his interrogation by the researchers, he denied having been influenced by a rabbinical verdict or opinion. He planned, according to his own decision and consideration, an act that would cause shock and stoppage of the government's political moves.

He stated that he had tried to hit the prime minister on a number of previous occasions, but in the event the circumstance proved to be unsuitable, or the prime minister failed to show up . . . or Amir failed to arrive on time so as to implement his scheme. . . .

There is no need to add details with regard to the assassin's motives and considerations, particularly since his criminal case is being heard and these issues are in the court's purview. And yet in this context, we cannot refrain from expressing our concern and disgust with the fact that a Jewish student, who is no more than an arrogant fool, had descended to the low level and cruelty which manifested themselves in the act of assassination whose circumstances we are exploring. In this he caused the social and psychological break in our public, caused by the historic stain he put on our society.

NOTES

1. Kach was a radical right-wing movement that was outlawed in Israel in the 1990s.
2. The reference is to a massacre of twenty-nine Palestinians in Hebron by Jewish radical Baruch Goldstein.

124

Aryeh Dayan

Arye Deri's Speech of April 23, 1997

Analysis

Israeli political history witnessed numerous attempts by Sephardi Jews (Jews of Middle Eastern origin) to politically organize and secure representation in the Knesset that would reflect their own agenda. But it was not until the emergence of Shas in the mid-1980s that these efforts led to the creation of a lasting and successful Sephardi party. Shas's accomplishment was not only its extraordinary electoral gains (by 1999, it grew to become the third largest party in the Knesset) but also the scope of its message. Shas moved beyond merely representing the Sephardi vote into offering a new vision of the Jewish state as a whole. Shas was further effective in reaching its electoral base by creating a network of grass-roots social organizations, such as day schools, farmers associations, and women's clubs. Much of the party's success was due to the charismatic character of its two leaders: Rabbi Ovadia Yossef and Arye Deri. Rabbi Yossef, a much-revered former chief Sephardi rabbi, provided spiritual leadership to the party while controlling it behind the scenes. Arye Deri, the actual political leader of the party for most of its years, combined charisma with a cunning political ability. His speech on April 23, 1997, to a Shas rally in Jerusalem prompted the following comments and analysis by Aryeh Dayan, an Israeli journalist. The speech was given a few weeks after Deri was investigated by the police for corruption. Following his conviction for corruption in 1999, Deri was forced to leave the party leadership.

Source: Aryeh Dayan, *Hamaayan hamitgaber: Sipurah shel tnuat Shas* (Jerusalem: Keter Publishing House, 1999), pp. 9–12. Translated for the 2nd ed. of *Israel in the Middle East.*

If anyone present had any doubts about David Yosef's remark about the "revolution," the speech [Arye] Deri gave a few minutes later eliminated them. The speech Deri gave at the convention was entirely different from all the hundreds and thousands of speeches given by him and his friends in the Shas leadership up to that time and since then. It was an ideological and programmatic speech, which with great clarity set forth the outlines of the transformation Shas had been effecting in Israeli society during the fourteen years that had passed since its founding. Deri's speech afforded a rare and quick—indeed, a one-time-only—glance into his spiritual world and the true motives of the movement he was leading. The main message coming out of it was indeed revolutionary: The mission of Shas was to change the secular character of the State of Israel—Shas was striving to turn Israel into a religious state.

Deri's speech was surprising mainly because he spoke using concepts and phraseology he had absorbed in his youth, while a student in the Ashkenazi/Lithuanian-origin yeshiva. From the time he graduated from Jerusalem's Hevron yeshiva up to his speech at the center of the University Stadium, some fifteen years had passed, years full of events in which he managed to become the right-hand man of Rabbi Ovadia Yossef, to found Shas and to march it to the center of the political stage in Israel. During all that time he rarely expressed himself in public in terms drawn from the conceptual world of the *haredim* (Ultra-Orthodox) and Ashkenazim. Yet in the course of the Passover of 1997, it became clear to him that out of all those involved in the gigantic scam he alone would be indicted; suddenly it seemed as though all of secular society and all its institutions—the police, the court system, the parties, and the media—were uniting to wipe out him and the creation he had toiled over since leaving the Hevron yeshiva. It was then that Deri went back to openly display his connection to the world that he had grown up in, that in fact he had never left.

Zionism, so he learned in the Hevron yeshiva, strove to create a new Jew in the Land of Israel, a Jew who isn't a Jew. The aspiration to preserve the ancient religious fundamentals passed down from generation to generation, he was taught, is replaced in the soul of the Zionist by the desire to create a state that would be integrated into the family of nations, that is, a hope that the Jewish people would become "a nation like every other nation." To that end the Zionist leaders, virtually all of them Ashkenazim, needed to make every effort to cut the Eastern Jews off from their religious roots. They, the Ashkenazi Zionists, understood that they could not realize their Zionist vision without converting the immigrants from the East from Jews into Israelis. The Ashkenazi *haredim,* he was told already in the Hevron yeshiva, wanted to turn this around and convert the Israelis, and mainly the Mizrahim [Jews of Middle Eastern descent] among them, back into Jews. "To restore the crown as of yore"—so Rabbi Ovadia Yossef was later to call it.

"Zionism," said Deri in the University Stadium when the frantic crowd finally let him speak, "Zionism is a heretical movement that wants to create a new Judaism." Zionism, he added, tried to "get rid of the Torah, to get rid of religion and to get rid of Sephardi culture." The juxtaposition of the old effort to wipe out religion with the current effort to wipe out Shas was natural and self-evident: "It is clear to me why it is this holy movement in particular they are persecuting. This is not political persecution. This is religious and ethnic persecution. They are afraid the Shasniks will change the secular character of the State of Israel, after they saw that with all their great Zionist vision they weren't able to wipe us out.

"The true Zionists, that's us—the Sephardi observant Jews, which the Establishment calls 'primitives.' They treated us like we were from outer space, but the more they humiliated us the more our power grew," he concluded in an assertion that hinted also at the promise of the future; and pointing past the road leading to the stadium, toward the site of the Prime Minister's office, the Knesset and the Supreme Court building—the three symbols of the sovereignty of the secular state—he added: "You may break us physically, but you will never break our spirit. This melody can never be stopped. For every indictment and every inquiry—we will build more Talmud Torah schools and more synagogues."

When Shas was founded, on the eve of the municipal elections of November 1983, it was no more than a tiny protest movement that tried to moderate the prejudice and mistreatment that were the lot of the few Mizrahim who sought to be integrated into *haredi* society; within a decade it had become the central axis around which the entire political system revolved. Shas is the third largest party in the Knesset, and it represents the new ideological spirit that is gradually pushing Israeli secularism out of the positions of control—cultural, social, and governmental—it has held since the establishment of the State.

It may seem as if there's been no real change in Israel's political structure during the years of Shas's existence. The political stalemate between the "Left camp" and the "Right camp," first formed during the elections of 1981, was maintained in all the elections from that time up until 1996. Both in 1981 and in 1996 the Right beat out the Left by a narrow majority of votes. But the feeling that nothing had changed was just an illusion: over these years a deep change had taken place in Israeli society. Most, if not all, of this change occurred in the "Right half" of the society.

The "Left half" slightly radicalized its positions, but continued to stick to the liberal and secular principles that guided it in 1981, whereas the "Right half" changed its character almost completely. In 1981, the secularist Likud won with forty-eight mandates; the religious parties, its partners in the rightist block, won thirteen seats. Fifteen years later the power of the secular Right shrank to only thirty-two seats; the power of the religious parties, conversely, rose to twenty-three mandates. The significance of these figures and of the trend implicit in them was that the religious public, which in 1981 was still the junior partner of the secularists in the camp of the Right, would within a few years become the power that leads the Right. At that time the secular Right will have turned into the junior partner of the religious Right.

This process still has not been fully realized at the parliamentary level, but it is quite conspicuous in the extra-parliamentary political activities. Anyone who watched the Right-wing demonstrations of the 1990s could not help noticing that there were virtually no bareheaded demonstrators to be seen in them. The process is quite noticeable on the ideological level, too. The Israeli Right, which in the early 1980s commonly justified its positions using political, strategic and security arguments, in the Nineties was sounding mainly religious arguments. "The sanctity of the Land of Israel," one of the fundamental principles of Jewish fundamentalism, has supplanted the "need for secure borders." Shas filled a central role in the process that led to this change: the "sanctity of the Land," and "the right of Jews to live anywhere in the Land of Israel" has a place in its ideology no less prominent than in the ideology of the National Religious Party.

The tens of thousands of people who cheered Deri on at the stadium of the Hebrew University are the most authentic representatives of the new breed sprouted by Zionism in the last two decades—*haredi* Zionism. In the State's first years the *haredim* felt like a persecuted minority. They rarely identified with its struggles and its goals, and up to the 1970s were content merely to defend their rights as a minority. At the end of the 1990s the relation of the *haredim* to the State changed—also because of the dissolution of secular Zionist ideology: they take an unambiguous stand in all the political battles involving the future of the Land of Israel and determining the State's borders, and also strive to be full partners in shaping the cultural and spiritual character of society.

The place of the vision of David Ben-Gurion and his colleagues in the Zionist Labor movement—the establishment of a secular Jewish state and the invention of a new Jew whose soul and person would be filled by nationalism instead of religion—was supplanted by another vision. At its core too there is a Jewish state, but its form and the form of the Jew in it are quite different from the one described in the old vision.

The new *haredi* Zionism, of which Ovadia Yossef and Arye Deri are the prime movers, sees itself precisely as its Socialist predecessor did: as a supremely righteous movement seeking to correct a historic injustice. The injustice that the *haredi* Zionism of Shas seeks to correct is the injustice caused by the Socialist Zionism of David Ben-Gurion to vast numbers of Jews, both Ashkenazim and Mizrahim, when it cut them off from the sources of their religious faith. "In the Kibbutzim they made Goyim of us," shouted Minister Yitzhak Peretz, when he was leader of Shas, from the Knesset podium toward the benches of the Labor Party.

The rise of *haredi* Zionism was made possible, in a somewhat ironic manner, thanks to twenty years of rule by another branch of Zionism—Revisionist Zionism. This branch, from which both the Herut movement and the Likud stemmed, sought to mold the State of Israel into a secular and liberal country in the form of Western Europe. Its attitude toward religion and its values was more considerate and sympathetic than the attitude of the Labor movement, but it too sought to create in Israel a new breed of secular Jew. The *haredim* and Mizrahim did not view the leaders of the Herut movement and the Likud, or their leader Menahem Begin, as ruthless rivals—both because of their views and because in the first year of the State they were in the opposition to the Labor movement's government.

It seems that at the end of the 1990s the rule of Revisionist Zionism—which began with the victory of the Likud in the 1977 elections and at the time seemed an alternative to Socialist Zionism—is about to clear its place on the ideological map in favor of *haredi* Zionism. The years of rule by the Likud have readied the ground for the emergence of *haredi* Zionism as a genuine political force, which threatens to undermine the traditional support enjoyed by the Likud among half of Israeli society. The process began in the period of Begin, who because of his favorable attitude toward religion and tradition and for tactical political reasons granted the *haredim* the full legitimacy that had been denied them by the Labor Party. Begin's regime also restored some pride to the hundreds of thousands of non-*haredi* Mizrahim which the labor movement's regime and the Labor Party had marginalized. Begin drew the *haredim* into the core of the government and made them his trusted junior partners. In the period of [Benjamin] Netanyahu, Begin's successor as leader of the Likud, the Likud has become the junior partner of the *haredim.*

It was no accident that Shas, with its amalgam of Mizrahi-ism and *haredi*-ism, was born once Begin descended from the stage of history.

125
Neeman Commission
Report on the Conversion Law
January 22, 1998

The mass immigration from the former Soviet Union and the slow emergence of Reform and Conservative Judaism in Israel in the 1990s forced the Israeli government to try to resolve the issue of non-Orthodox conversions to Judaism. While the Israeli Orthodox rabbinical authorities enjoy a state-sponsored monopoly over issues of Jewish marriages and divorces, the question of state recognition of Reform and Conservative conversions was less clear and was brought before the Supreme Court a number of times in the 1990s. In 1997 the government of Benjamin Netanyahu appointed a committee, led by the finance minister, Professor Yaakov Neeman, to resolve the issue. In its recommendations from 1998, which appear below and were approved by a government decision and a Knesset resolution (but not legislation), the committee suggested leaving the final decision over conversions to the Orthodox authorities (through conversion courts). The committee also recommended creating an Institute for Jewish Studies that would offer future converts a comprehensive outlook on Judaism and would reflect the views of all three major Jewish denominations.

By 2003, more than nine thousand people had attended the Institute for Jewish Studies, which attracts not only future converts but also interested Jews, who constituted 40 percent of the students and alumni. About 20 percent of the students began conversion proceedings, and about 8 percent of the total number of students were converted by 2003. In the meantime, the Supreme Court ordered the executive branch in 2002 to accept, for purposes of registration in an Israeli ID card, any conversion—Reform, Conservative, or Orthodox—as valid.

The discussion and debate about the conversion issue is not confined to Israel; it is affected by the country's close relations with the American Jewish community, where Reform and Conservative Judaism are much more prevalent than in Israel.

Part One—Introduction

1. Selection of the Committee

On 27 June 1997, the Prime Minister appointed a committee to develop ideas and proposals regarding the issue of religious conversion in Israel (hereafter: the Committee). . . .

The members of the Committee took account of the legal situation in existence in this matter since establishment of the State, and also the acute problem facing the large numbers of immigrants from the members of the world community, who immigrated to Israel under the Law of Return [doc. 29] and have been integrated into the educational system, the Israel Defense Forces, the public and private sector, the towns and villages throughout the country, and are not Jews according to halakhah [Jewish

Source: Israeli Knesset online, The Neeman Report on the Conversion Law, January 22, 1998, http://www.knesset.gov.il/docs/heb/neeman.htm (accessed April 2, 2005).

religious law]. These immigrants have been precluded from fully integrating into Israeli society because, in part, they are prohibited from marrying Jews in Israel.

The problem of conversion in Israel is a difficult humanitarian problem—personal and national—that urgently requires a suitable solution.

2. The Committee Hearings

The Committee held fifty meetings, heard the testimony of almost eighty witnesses involved in conversion matters . . . , and received extensive written material. . . . The Committee's members reached unanimous agreement that, beyond the question of the dispute between the streams of Judaism, a consensual solution must be found in the matter of conversion.

The committee reached—after debate and profound and penetrating elucidation of the matter—an agreed-upon proposal that will lead to the arrangement described later in this document. It is emphasized that, although the debate was intense and dealt with the basic principles, it was amicable, each participant respecting the other and believing that it was desirable and possible to reach understanding and agreement. This jointly-held understanding is particularly important because the subject involved is so emotionally charged that it has created a feeling of polarity and division among the public. The comments of Rabbi Zvi Yehuda HaCohen Kook, Zaddik of Blessed Memory, in his article, *It Is My Brother I Seek*, published in the Israeli press in September 1949, are particularly appropriate in this matter.

> My brother and my sister, throughout our people, in all the political parties and all the organizations, known and unknown, revealed and unrevealed, and those who are not in political parties or in organizations—I beg all of you. Take pity on your souls and on the soul of all our people. Let us not ignore, even for a moment, the gravity of our responsibility concerning the dimension of the destruction and of the building that we are undertaking at this fearsome and exalted time, and do not let us desecrate the Lord, Heaven forbid. Let us not individually decide, each political party and organization and parts thereof, for we certainly all want the good of our people and the establishment of our country, that for only with Him lies all truth and justice. Let no one desire or imagine, being faced with the terrible situation in which we find ourselves, to impose his opinion on his neighbor; let us not forget, from the excitement of the holy ideal, that opinion cannot be imposed and will not be realized, but rather will become mixed, softened, and then vanish. Let us not disturb our public freedom in opinions and thoughts, in ambitions and plans, in elucidating and handling them, by transferring the boundaries of the use of physical force and rooting the hate and contempt of the heart. Let us recall that "He who raises his hand on his fellow is called an evil person," and that the negative relationship multiplies mutually and unceasingly between individuals and brothers. Let us reduce our written and verbal disagreements in public and prevent their realization, and let us not descend to the level of the incivility of the fist and the venom of negativity. Let us recall the intention of the ideal justice that is in each one of us, and let us find the correct and proper path to put the relationship between us in order and temper our tendencies. "Truth and justice of peace reigned at your gates, and do not think evil of your fellow in your heart." As we objected to physical force and nurturing the contrast, having preferred that which unites and joins us, which is decisive and greater than that which separates and disperses us, as we heeded and directed ourselves in the channel of our public activities, the possibility of mutual understanding and cooperation of

discourse among us will increase, peace among us will increase, and our success and glory of our people will increase.

3. The Sole Method of Conversion in Accordance with Halakhah

The order of the day is that we strive to achieve unity, cooperation, and mutual respect. It is accepted and agreed that there should be a unified governmental conversion procedure—according to the law of Torah—that will be recognized by all of Israel. In this way it will be possible to ensure the unity of the Jewish people.

The proposed method for conversion is intended to ensure, to the extent possible, within the framework of halakhah, that the numerous current constraints and human distress be given maximum consideration.

4. The Institute for Jewish Studies

Ms. Irah Dashevski, in her impressive and convincing comments to the Committee, described the ideal of the immigrants to integrate totally into Israeli-Jewish society, so that they will be recognized for every purpose. She described the activity of the organization Mahanayim and its approach regarding immigrants. Committee members approve of the organization's approach, which enables immigrants who are not Jews—where possible, together with their Jewish family members—to learn about the world of Judaism in an open manner, without any obligation on their part. For this reason, and because immigrants are dispersed throughout Israel, it is extremely important that the Institute for Jewish Studies—established in the manner recommended by the Committee and discussed below—operate in various locations throughout Israel, giving special emphasis to those areas where concentrations of immigrants are found, and provide suitable accessibility and programs of study to meet the needs of each person wanting to learn about Judaism's values.

The composition of the Committee, which included, among others, a representative of the Reform movement and a representative of the Conservative movement, reflects a trend of cooperation among the streams of Judaism and toward unity of the Jewish people, a trend that is to be maintained. In implementing the recommendations of the Committee regarding the nature and activity of the Institute of Jewish Studies, this trend will become manifest. The Institute, intended to be a learning stage preceding the conversion process, and rooted in it, will reflect the entire Jewish population in Israel, in its variations and streams. It will include a variety of courses that will teach the student about Judaism. The curriculum will emphasize the uniqueness of the Jewish people and its Torah, and what unites the Jewish people in its variations and streams. The program is intended to teach, prepare, and qualify the students—if they wish—for the conversion process conducted by special rabbinical courts for conversion.

5. Rabbinical Conversion Courts

The Chief Rabbis of Israel, as heads of the Jewish religious denomination for the purposes of the Religious Denomination (Conversion) Ordinance, as mentioned in HCJ 1031/93, *Pasaro Goldstein v. Minister of the Interior* (Piskei Din 30(4)661), and pursuant to their functions set forth in the Chief Rabbi of Israel Law, 5740–1980, will establish special rabbinical courts for conversion and will appoint the courts' members. The court will consist of three judges, in accordance with halakhah, as required for conversion (Shulkhan Arukh, Yore Deah, chap. 388, secs. 3–4). The court will not be competent to adjudicate pursuant to the Rabbinical Judges Law, 5715–1955. Such conversion—being accepted by the Jewish people—will contribute to the unity of the Jewish people.

The desire to establish a standard and consensual process is understandable. Prior to its execution, during the period of the studies or upon their conclusion, each student can come to an educated decision as to whether he or she wants to apply to the Court to undergo the conversion process.

It is assumed that the aforementioned does not limit the discretion of the court, which will convert, according to halakhah, those whom it considers to have accepted the obligation of obeying the commandments.

A candidate for conversion "is taught the essentials of the religion, which is that the Lord is One and that idolatry is forbidden. This matter is further taught, and the candidate is instructed about some of the lesser commandments and some of the more serious commandments, but these are not taught at length," all as stated by Maimonides in Chapter 14 of *Hilkhot Isurei Bi'ah* [Laws of Cohabitation]—". . . do not be strict with him lest it bother him and cause him to stray from the good to the bad path already at the start, and do not draw him to you other than through soft and acceptable words. . . ."

6. Necessity of Disclosure

These "soft and acceptable words" must be embodied in each of the partners—when giving advice and in their actions—to the complex structure being devised in accordance with the Committee's recommendations. The "together" and the contact are necessary. The words of Rabbi Yehonatan Eybeschutz, Zaddik of Blessed Memory, in his commentary, *Tiferet Yehonatan* to Genesis, chap. 37, v. 4, are appropriate to our subject. That verse speaks about Joseph's brothers who hated him, and "could not speak peaceably unto him." What prevented one from speaking peaceably with the other?

> When a person feels a complaint in his heart and disaffection toward his fellow, the hate increases daily, but where he speaks to his fellow . . . the peace returns, and if the tribes could speak with him, it would have brought peace among them. . . .

It cannot be denied: in matters dealing with faith and philosophy, there have been and still are disputes. The Committee does not purport to settle these disputes, but rather to propose an arrangement that will comprise an agreed, practical framework for conversions in Israel.

We were given the task of finding a way to live together in mutual respect despite different world views, and as a road that Rabbi Avraham Yitzhak HaCohen Kook, Zaddik of Blessed Memory, wrote of in 1933 in his article, *Trip of the Camps:*

> . . . And we must decide that there is a latent power leading toward the good in each of the camps and in each of the heads of the nation, and in the unification of all of these that the general value of the Jewish people and its hope are dear. Each person shall come to know his brother by the general name Israel, not by the name of the party or camp.
>
> Know that in each camp, we have much to mend and much to receive from the light and the good of each other, that will result in a general supreme light from which we shall attain everlasting salvation. The holiest prayer of the Holy of Holies will dwell within us, and we shall express it with all our soul "and unite us into one group to do Your will with a faithful heart."

126

Azmi Bishara

Arab Citizens of Palestine: Little to Celebrate

1998: Analysis

Azmi Bishara, born in Nazareth in 1956, was a professor of philosophy at Birzeit University in the West Bank until elected to the Israeli Knesset on May 29, 1996. Bishara is a part of the National Democratic Assembly (NDA), a party advocating cultural autonomy and civil rights of Palestinian citizens of Israel. In 1999 Bishara presented his candidacy for prime minister. He did so to demonstrate to the Arab and Jewish populations of Israel that the Arab population was not necessarily in Labor's hands. He withdrew forty-eight hours before the elections. One of the most important Arab intellectuals in Israel, Dr. Bishara has written six books on political philosophy, religion, and the state. In November 2001 the Knesset removed his parliamentary immunity at the request of the attorney general, who wanted to prosecute him for incitement to terrorism following statements he made in Syria in support of Hezbollah. In April 2007 he left the Knesset following another police investigation and left Israel in order to avoid investigation and likely indictment for espionage. The following article was published in 1998, during the Yovel (fiftieth) celebrations for the establishment of the State of Israel.

There's not much for Israeli Arabs to celebrate as they face the fiftieth anniversary of 1948. What happened in 1948 were the establishment of a Jewish State and the disintegration of a Palestinian reality in this land. Palestinian society was dispersed and destroyed, so you can't really expect us to look back on that moment with nostalgia or fondness or a celebratory mode regardless of how one feels about the Israel that subsequently developed. Arabs in Israel are part of the Palestinian people and the Arab nation, sharing Arab culture, religion, and language; they had this Arabic identity long before the State of Israel. Israel was not founded at Israeli Arabs' choice or in coexistence with them, though they remained in Israel and eventually were allowed to become citizens unlike their brothers, sisters, cousins, and friends on the West Bank, in Gaza, and in the refugee camps of the Palestinian Diaspora. They remained, but what did not remain was any independent Palestinian economy or any Palestinian city. Except for education, no realm of Israeli Arabs' lives remained autonomous. They had a right to speak and write in Arabic, but in every other respect they were marginalized onto the sidelines of dominant Israeli society. In the early years they lived under Israeli military rule, and were only allowed to vote in Israeli elections beginning in 1967. In this same year, 1967, the rest of the Palestinian people came under military rule without becoming citizens, living under military rule just as had Israeli Arabs until that year.

But even when these Israeli Arabs were allowed to vote, it was as part of a Jewish communitarian democracy, a democracy unified not by

Source: *Tikkun* 13, no. 4 (Summer 1998): 14. Reprinted by permission of *Tikkun: A Bimonthly Jewish Critique of Politics, Culture and Society*, www.tikkun.org.

its Israeliness but by its Jewishness. The Israeli Supreme Court ruled that Israel was a State that was Jewish in its essence and democratic in its character. Israeli Arabs then, even today, are part of the form but not part of the essence of the State in which they are citizens. It is not citizenship, but Jewishness, which regulates the relationship between individual and state.

Everything changed for Israel in 1967. Suddenly, worldwide Jewish investment in the State dramatically mushroomed. So did military aid: in one year, 1968, Israel received as much aid from the United States as it had in the entire nineteen previous years of its existence. The implications of 1967 became clear in the 1970s: a rise in investments, a rise in living standards which led to an expanded middle class, the privatization of social services, competition between political parties, the rise of the right political bloc, and a loosening of the hold of the Labor Party and agricultural militarism in politics (a phenomenon manifested by the decline of the kibbutzim).

In response to these changes, Israeli Arabs went through two phases: from 1967 to the mid-1970s, they rediscovered their Palestinian identity through their encounter with West Bank and Gaza, an identity which previously had been repressed through military occupation-generated fear. This phase also marked the development of a new Arab middle class and intelligentsia that would become the repository of Palestinian nationalist consciousness in the face of the defeat of Arab nationalism as represented by [Egyptian president Gamal Abdul] Nasser. After Land Day, March 30, 1976 (the first one-day general strike by the Palestinian people protesting the Israeli confiscation of their land—the first time that Arabs in Israel used civil disobedience), Palestinians began to realize that they were torn between demanding equality in Israeli civil society and demanding an independent national identity. So the second phase, a phase of compromise, began: we began to demand equality in Israel and to demand a Palestinian state in the West Bank and Gaza (a state which we will not become part of).

127

Anna Isakova

A Russian Immigrant Looks at Israeli (or Jewish?) Culture

1998: Analysis

Anna Isakova, born in Lithuania, came to Israel in 1971 and worked as a physician in two major hospitals. She also published articles and stories in Israeli newspapers in the Russian language and served as adviser to Prime Minister Ehud Barak (1999–2000) for immigrant integration. Isakova can be seen as representative of an important part of the 1970s Russian emigration—young intellectuals who, after a comparatively smooth initial absorption, found themselves in a state of cultural alienation.

Source: Anna Isakova, "The Gold Fish and the Jewish State," *Alpayim* 16 (Tel Aviv, 1998): 192–213. Reprinted by permission of the author.

Some of my best friends are liberal Israelis. We are not divided over issues of principle but three issues generate constant arguments: the first is my gold fish, its violent behavior and my right to punish it; the second is the ostracization of smokers in modern society, their evolution into a minority, and the ways available to this minority for defending itself against the majority; and the third issue: the cultural discrimination in Israel. . . .

. . . The third issue is the most difficult. Most of the state's inhabitants, myself included, do not regard the dominant Hebrew culture as their own representative culture and do not wish to operate within its orbit or to be amongst its active consumers. Most of my liberal Israeli friends belong to this very culture and have no wish to discuss this issue with me. They do agree that culture is a salad that should be made up of all the cultural parts in this country. Up to this point, I am in agreement with them. But they also see no wrong in having a cook prepare this salad and they assign this role to themselves. From this point on, our paths part. As soon as the cook shows up, freedom comes to an end, as does productive activity. As a rule, the debate is doomed at the point in which it reaches the cook's arrival. This is the reason for my writing this essay. I would like to make my full statement even just once and then debate would cease to elude us and would finally begin. . . .

. . . I had imagined that the Jewish experience was at the heart of the cultural activity in the state of Israel. I had thought that the state came into being in order to preserve Judaism through both its cultural and national manifestation and to endow both with a statelike seal of approval.

How could I envisage that here of all places there would be no demand for an expression of Jewish culture and contents? That of all places, in the Jewish state Bavel, Mandelstam, Ehrenburg, and Falk would be unknown and regarded as an alien element? That if the Museum would ever be opened, it would happen, of all places, in Moscow, and that Isaac Marcus would be transformed in Israel from a well known Jewish writer into a forgotten Jewish teacher.

And the question is raised, whether there was a point to liquidating the Jewish community in Lithuania for the sake of having all of its past cultural efforts forgotten in Israel. And who is more right—the Jews who stayed in Moscow and built the Jewish university in Moscow, where an effort is being made to collect, preserve, and revive the remnants of the Russian Jewish culture, or the Russian Jewish intellectuals who arrived in this country and became bank clerks?

I believe that the mass immigration of the Russian Jewish intellectual stratum to Israel was a mistake, as was the immigration of the intellectual elite from any other diaspora. Israel has no intention of forming a comprehensive, contemporary Jewish culture. It is trying to create something else which I regard as senseless. It is creating an independent Israeli culture which is limited by a discriminatory cultural doctrine. This Hebrew Israeli culture has from the outset placed the Jewish content outside the pale. An attempt was made here to leap from Massada to Tel Aviv over the head of two thousand years of cultural activity in exile. A decision was made to erase the exotic Jew and in his place what is defined as a void but in reality was full of fantastic energy. It was decided to grow a synthetic product—the Israeli.

. . . The image of the new Jew was composed of the absolute opposite of the anti-Semitic fantasy. The same components that had characterized the Jew in the anti-Semitic joke and cartoon were taken out and replaced by their absolute opposites. This is how the new Aryan Jew was born—the Israeli. For him, Jewish culture was not only superfluous, it became untouchable.

In my view, here is where the roots of Israeli xenophobia lie. The humiliating attitude to Middle Eastern Jews, for instance, originates in the same mind set and not in the European Ashkenazi myth. In fact, Ashkenazi culture had died out by the early twentieth century. Hitler's ovens destroyed its last residues. If European Jews are (presently) creating an independent, distinct culture they are doing so in the framework of the dominant culture in their countries of origin. . . .

. . . When the Oriental Jews complain that Israel had suppressed their distinctive culture, the following should be borne in mind—Israel had done the same with regard to the distinct culture of all groups from the diaspora that had settled in it. Only the figure of the "Polish Mother" was left of the Polish Jewry's rich culture and the glorious German community turned into a segregated group of "Yekes."

The new Jew, the Aryan, was not fond of his past and of his Jewish looks. The Oriental Jews with their traditional Jewish culture and distinctive Jewish looks served as a constant reminder of his historic roots and he did not like it.

In time, when the new American liberalism served as a sweeping model for the Israeli intelligentsia, a change occurred in the desirable external qualities. The American liberal suffered from guilt feelings toward the black man. The dark pigmentation became "in." In Israel, the American liberal doctrine was translated literally. The role of the Afro-Americans was filled by the Arabs and, to a lesser extent, by the Oriental Jews. The Aryan look was replaced by the Semitic look but the cultural doctrine and the attendant cultural doctrine and xenophobia were left intact. . . .

. . . Complaints about "Ghettoization" of "the Russians" are very common. It should be remembered that the "Ghetto" is always built on both sides of the surrounding wall—the isolationists use those who had been isolated. This brings us to describe another quality of Israeli culture, which is essentially anti-Jewish, the concept of the self as an ideal type. . . .

. . . Many Israelis take joy in emphasizing the differences between the veteran, Zionist immigrants who had arrived in the 1970s and the newer, greedy immigrants who have arrived in recent years. This perspective reflects a basic lack of understanding . . . the real line separating the (recent) immigrants from the former Soviet Union from the immigrants of the 1970s is not their attitude to Zionism but rather their attitude toward the Soviet regime. The supporters and opponents of that regime are separated by a deep gap, while the relationship between the more Zionist and the less Zionist can, at most, be chilly.

In the 1970s, those who left the Soviet Union were the regime's strident opponents. In the 1990s, the disintegrating power was left also by those who had deep bonds to the Soviet regime. At the time, tension was created between them and the veteran immigrants, but that tension had evaporated a long time ago. The Soviet Union no longer exists and the ideological difference between the two groups is vanishing accordingly. Whoever believes that there exists here two separate communities of veterans and new immigrants is wrong. The community has long been united. . . .

. . . But the worst mistake is probably dubbing this ethnos Russian. It is the Soviet ethnos which unites the new immigrants with the old ones, those who came from Georgia with those who came from Ukraine, the university graduates with the common people. . . .

. . . Still something unique and interesting happened here. Since the 1970s, a unique culture developed among the immigrants in the Russian language. This culture comprises Israeli experiences and is the product of a thought process that is not solely predicated in Russian culture and includes Jewish and Russian Jewish elements. The heroes of this culture are well integrated with the circles of Russian dissident culture that had developed in the centers of immigration in the West.

128

Reuven Y. Hazan

The 1996 and 1999 Elections in Israel

1996, 1999: Analysis

The 1996 and 1999 elections in Israel were the only ones in which the Israeli population was given two ballots: one for the prime minister and one for the Knesset, Israel's parliament. This essay concentrates on two aspects of these elections: first, the electoral dynamics, i.e., the convergence toward the center in both the executive and the legislative elections; and second, the election results, i.e., the decimation of the two main parties and the rise of sectarian parties. The most significant ramifications, therefore, of the implementation of the direct popular election of the prime minister have been a dramatic change in the competitive electoral orientation of the Israeli party system and a significant shift in the electoral strength of the parties. Dr. Reuven Y. Hazan is a senior lecturer in the Political Science Department of the Hebrew University of Jerusalem.

Electoral Convergence

The Prime Ministerial Campaigns

In the wake of the assassination of Prime Minister Yitzhak Rabin in November of 1995, his successor Shimon Peres enjoyed massive popular support and called for early elections in May 1996. Only two candidates for the prime ministership presented themselves on election day, Prime Minister Peres, and the leader of the Likud Party, Benjamin Netanyahu.

The 1999 elections, on the other hand, did see more than two candidates in the race for prime minister, but not in the election itself. After the collapse of the Netanyahu government, early elections were called for in May of 1999. Prime Minister Netanyahu and the leader of the Labor Party, Ehud Barak, were the two front runners. The other candidates were: on the extreme left, Azmi Bishara, an Arab; on the extreme right, Benjamin Begin, who had split from the Likud Party; and, in the middle, Yitzhak Mordechai, the former defense minister. As election day neared, the polls showed that Barak had pulled ahead of Netanyahu and could likely win the required majority already in the first round. This situation created a domino effect of disappearing candidates in the thirty-six hours prior to the election. On election day, only two candidates remained in the race for prime minister, Netanyahu and Barak (see table 1).

Prior to both the 1996 and 1999 elections, Israel's two major parties, Labor and Likud, created two election headquarters; one for the prime ministerial election and one for the Knesset election. Despite a series of struggles within each party concerning the prevalence of one campaign over the other—and on which issues emphasis should be placed—the result was the same in both parties: There was only one comprehensive campaign, not two, and the race for prime minister prevailed.

Source: Written for the 2nd ed. of *Israel in the Middle East.*

TABLE 1. ELECTION RESULTS FOR PRIME MINISTER, 1996 AND 1999

	MAY 29, 1996			MAY 17, 1999	
Eligible Voters	3,933,250			4,285,428	
Voters	3,121,270	(79.4 %)		3,372, 952	(78.7 %)
Valid Votes	2,972,589	(95.2 %)		3,193,494	(94.7 %)
Invalid Votes	148,681	(4.8 %)		179,458	(5.3 %)
CANDIDATE	**NUMBER VOTES**	**PERCENT**	**CANDIDATE**	**NUMBER VOTES**	**PERCENT**
Benjamin Netanyahu	1,501,023	50.5	Ehud Barak	1,791,020	56.1
Shimon Peres	1,471,566	49.5	Benjamin Netanyahu	1,402,474	43.9

Moreover, the Knesset race was not only relegated to a lower level of importance; it was largely absent in the campaign of the two largest parties. Both parties thought, correctly, that whoever won the contest for prime minister would be able to form a supporting majority coalition in the Knesset. However, in order for either of the two equally sized camps to win the necessary majority, their candidates had to capture the undecided voters. The candidates, and their parties, decided that the best way to achieve this goal was to converge on the center.

In 1996, the movement of the Labor Party and its candidate for prime minister into the center can be seen in a series of actions taken by the party and its leader on the dominant dimension of electoral competition in Israel—the peace process—during the campaign. For example, Labor's move into the center in the 1996 elections was exemplified by the inclusion of new articles in the party's platform that were meant to attract the floating voters, while other articles that might have repelled many of these voters were eliminated from the platform. In 1999, the Labor Party moved even more toward the center. Barak, the new Labor leader, was a former chief of staff and decorated war hero, characteristics upon which much of his campaign was based.

The Likud party's shift to the center in 1996 was, to an extent, a reaction to Labor's strategy. Since the peace process was supported by a majority of the Israeli public, Netanyahu, the party leader and candidate for prime minister, toned down his rhetoric and opposition to the peace process. For example, when Netanyahu announced his policy guidelines, he repeated his opposition to the Oslo Peace Accords [doc. 133], but stated that the reality was that these agreements exist, and thus they could not be ignored. As a result, Netanyahu concluded that it was necessary to negotiate with the Palestinian Authority, which he had previously refused to recognize. Netanyahu's 1999 campaign continued along this trend. After he was brought down by the extreme right because he signed the Wye River Accords [doc. 139], which called for a transfer of land to the Palestinian Authority, his campaign focused on the continuation of the peace process and reciprocity with the Palestinians.

Despite a basic gap on the most fundamental principles between Labor and Likud—or Peres/Barak and Netanyahu—in both the 1996 and 1999 elections, it is clear that both sides decided to blur their differences in order to attract the undecided voters, with whom victory rested in the more important prime ministerial race.

In the 1999 elections, a new center party was created that also presented a viable candidate for prime minister. This candidate, Mordechai, stated that neither side could truly bridge the gap that divided Israeli society, a gap that had resulted in electoral deadlocks. Only a center candidate could move the peace process ahead with the support of a clear majority and based on a national consensus. In short, this campaign was anchored squarely in the center of the Israeli political map.

With the overall convergence of the two parties in the center—particularly their candidates for prime minister—along with the appearance of a center party and its own prime ministerial aspirant, the floating voters were left few means of differentiation. The result was that ideology and principles took a back seat in the race for prime minister, while individual attributes, such as credibility, rose to the forefront.

At the same time, the smaller parties concentrated on the proportional Knesset election, and were expected to adhere to their traditional polarized and ideological campaign strategy. Such a strategy would not only make them appear different from the main parties and from each other, but had long been the convention in Israeli politics. However, in the 1996 and the 1999 elections this was no longer the case.

The Knesset Campaigns

In previous Knesset elections, there was an incentive for new parties to emerge because of the insignificant threshold of only 1.5 percent. Due to the polarized nature of Israeli politics, these parties appeared primarily at the extremes rather than in the center. In the 1996 Knesset election, however, the direction of this trend was reversed. The two new parties that succeeded in winning seats were located in the center, rather than at the extremes, of the party spectrum.

In 1999, new parties appeared all over the party system—partly as a reaction to the explicit centripetal dynamics of the previous elections—but numerically the convergence on the center intensified. The relative success of the extreme Right in 1999, compared to 1996, is thus misleading. In 1996, the extreme Right was composed of one party, Moledet, which won only two seats. In 1999, there were two parties—National Unity (Ha-Ihud Haleumi) and Israel Our Home (Yisrael Beitenu)—with eight seats, an apparent increase. However, one of these parties, National Unity, was comprised of members of Knesset who split from several of the right-wing parties, based on a joint opposition to further concessions to the Palestinians. These splits brought together no less than eight legislators into this one new party. The other party, Israel Our Home, also incorporated a split of two extremist legislators from the Yisrael B'Aliyah Party (Ascending [to] Israel). Yet, despite their having ten legislators between them prior to the elections, *both* parties on the extreme right won only eight seats. In other words, compared to the pre-election constellation in the Knesset on the extreme Right, rather than the 1996 election results, the 1999 elections show that this group of parties actually lost seats. The extreme Left, on the other hand, also saw a new party appear in the 1999 elections, but this was an existing list that had run in partnership with another list in 1996. Moreover, even after this split, the extreme Left showed a gain of only one seat in the 1999 elections (see table 2).

Both the 1996 and the 1999 elections saw two new center parties—and quite successful ones. The two new center parties in 1996, Israel Baliyah and the Third Way (Hadereh Hashlishit), together won eleven seats in a center that had been vacant. In 1999, one of these parties failed to pass the legal threshold but was replaced by two new center parties, the Center (Mercaz) and Change (Shinui) Parties. Thus, in the 1999 elections, the center grew to 18 seats—an increase of 64 percent.

The center, therefore, became a very crowded area in the 1996 and 1999 elections. Two new, successful parties appeared at each election—while still others tried to occupy the same location but

TABLE 2. ELECTION RESULTS FOR THE KNESSET

	MAY 29, 1996		MAY 17, 1999	
Eligible Voters	3,933,250		4,285,428	
Voters	3,119,832	(79.3 %)	3,373,748	(78.7 %)
Valid Votes	3,052,130	(97.8 %)	3,309,416	(98.1 %)
Invalid Votes	67,702	(2.2 %)	64,332	(1.9 %)

failed to win representation—together with the two main parties and their candidates for prime minister in 1996, and all these plus the third candidate for prime minister in 1999. Some of the religious parties also tried to locate themselves closer to the center, somewhat reversing their right-leaning tendencies and opening themselves up to the possibility of joining a Labor coalition. Even the extreme Right and the extreme Left converged toward the center by attempting to open a dialogue with the "other" prime ministerial candidate.

We must keep in mind that we have so far seen only two examples of the centrifugal dynamics that have resulted from the electoral reforms, and thus their endurance is far from certain. It is quite possible that coalition dynamics will move in the opposite direction from electoral dynamics—which is precisely what happened in 1998 and brought about the collapse of the Netanyahu coalition government. Responsiveness to the public during elections could be undermined by responsiveness to the party and the coalition during governance. Electoral dynamics themselves could shift in future elections. However, in light of the 1996 and the 1999 elections, the consequences of the new electoral system in Israel for the direction of electoral competition are both clear and significant.

Representative Divergence

The results of the 1996 and the 1999 Knesset elections, which for the first time permitted split-ticket voting, increased the multiparty composition of the Knesset, while the two main parties were decimated.

Ballot-splitting decreased the size of the two major parties (Labor and Likud) from 76 to 56 seats in the 1996 elections, a reduction of over 25 percent,[1] and then to 45 seats in the 1999 elections, a further reduction of 20 percent. The sectarian parties—those representing a particular subgroup in society—increased their representation from 21 to 39 seats in the 1996 elections, a growth of 86 percent, and to 47 seats in the 1999 elections, a further increase of 21 percent. These parties included the religious parties, which represent the orthodox religious Jewish minority and whose seats increased from 16 to 23 in the 1996 elections and to 27 in the 1999 elections; the Arab parties, who represent the national minority in Israel and whose seats rose from 5 to 9 in 1996 and to 10 in 1999; and the immigrants' parties, which represent the Russian ethnic minority and won 7 seats for the first time in 1996, and 10 in 1999.

In other words, not only did ballot-splitting increase fragmentation in the Israeli party system, with a subsequent impact on legislative representation; it also reduced the strength of all of the main ideological and aggregating parties while exacerbating sectarian tensions along the three main contentious cleavages in Israeli society: religious and secular Jews; Arabs and Jews; and natives and immigrants.

The results of the two implementations of separate executive and legislative elections are, therefore, dramatic. The largest party list in the Knesset has been reduced to its lowest point ever, while the parties representing the three

LIST NAME	VOTES		SEATS		LIST NAME	VOTES		SEATS	
Labor	818,741	(26.8%)	34	(28.3%)	One Israel [1]†	670,484	(20.3%)	26	(21.7%)
Likud-Gesher-Tsomet‡	767,401	(25.1%)	32	(26.9%)	Likud[2]	468,103	(14.2%)	19	(15.8%)
Shas‡	259,796	(8.5%)	10	(8.3%)	Shas†	430,676	(13.0%)	17	(14.2%)
Meretz	226,275	(7.4%)	9	(7.5%)	Meretz†	253,525	(7.7%)	10	(8.3%)
Yisrael B'aliyah‡	174,994	(5.7%)	7	(5.8%)	Yisrael B'aliyah†	171,705	(5.2%)	6	(5.0%)
					Shinui[3]	167,748	(5.1%)	6	(5.0%)
					Center†	165,622	(5.0%)	6	(5.0%)
NRP‡	240,271	(7.9%)	9	(7.5%)	NRP†	140,307	(4.2%)	5	(4.2%)
Yadadut HaTorah‡	98,657	(3.2%)	4	(3.3%)	Yahadut HaTorah†	125,741	(3.8%)	5	(4.2%)
Ra'am	89,514	(2.9%)	4	(3.3%)	Ra'am	114,810	(3.5%)	5	(4.2%)
Moledet	72,001	(2.4%)	2	(1.7%)	National Unity[4]	100,181	(3.0%)	4	(3.3%)
					Israel Our Home	86,153	(2.6%)	4	(3.3%)
Hadash	129,455	(4.2%)	5	(4.2%)	Hadash	87,022	(2.6%)	4	(3.3%)
					Balad[5]	66,103	(2.0%)	2	(1.7%)
					One People	64,143	(1.9%)	2	(1.7%)
Third Way‡	96,474	(3.2%)	4	(3.3%)	Third Way	26,290	(0.8%)	—	—
Others	78,550	(2.7%)	—	—	Others	170,803	(5.1%)	—	—

1. In 1999, Labor joined with Gesher and Meimad to form a joint list called One Israel.

2. In 1996, Likud ran on a joint list with Gesher and Tsomet. In 1999, Likud ran alone.

3. In 1996, Shinui was part of the Meretz alliance.

4. In 1999 the newly formed National Unity party was based on splits from the Likud and the National Religious party, and incorporated the Moledet party.

5. In 1996, the newly formed Balad ran together with Hadash.

‡ Parties forming the 1996 coalition government headed by Prime Minister Benjamin Netanyahu.

† Parties forming the 1999 coalition government headed by Prime Minister Ehud Barak.

subcultural minorities in Israeli society—Orthodox Jews, Arabs, and immigrants—together control more seats than the two largest parties in the Israeli party system. The two largest parties together now hold only 45 seats—38 percent of the total number of seats—which is the lowest number of seats they have ever won. In the 1999 elections, the main party on the Right, Likud, and the main party on the Left, Labor, each won their lowest number of seats ever.

The implications for governability in light of this decline, and the simultaneous upsurge in sectarian representation, are clear. While the first two directly elected prime ministers were able to create a coalition relatively easily, they each confronted the increasingly difficult tasks of keeping the coalition intact and sustaining its legislative discipline. The reason for this is that ballot-splitting eroded the size of the two major parties and benefited the necessary coalition partners in terms of both size and number, thereby undermining the nucleus of support for either prime ministerial candidate. For example, the Likud Party in 1996 and the Labor Party in 1999, which headed the two coalition governments, were each actually a minority within the coalition (22 of 66 legislators in 1996, and 26 of 75 in 1999), the first two times this situation has occurred in Israeli history.[2]

On the voter level, the availability of two ballots allowed each voter not only to split the ballot but also to create a hierarchy of voting intentions for each ballot based on different motivations. Since the two prime ministerial candidates competed primarily on the dominant dimension of Israeli politics of foreign affairs and security, the voters adopted this dimension as the criterion for choosing one candidate over the other. At the Knesset level, where parties presented much more particular appeals, the voters could now express a more specific identity.

The voters were thus able to express both a national interest and a rather narrow social identity, or distinct ideological stand, by selecting from a multidimensional menu of parties on two distinct ballots. The prime ministerial elections became the arena for general ideas, while the political parties in the Knesset that either gained entrance (except for the single case of the Center Party in 1999) or enlarged their representation were the less aggregative ones that sought a more specific social or ideological voter base.

Conclusion

The comprehensive trend of convergence toward the center, which has come to characterize the entire Israeli party system, along with the loss of almost one-half of the seats by the two main parties and the dramatic increase in the representation of sectarian parties, created a multidimensional party system with centrifugal social pressures alongside the centripetal security issue. The already overloaded Israeli political system thus became even more overloaded after the 1996 and 1999 elections. The consequences of the electoral reform are the breakdown and Balkanization of the Israeli party system. Instead of social groups being represented *within* parties, they are represented *by* parties. Incentives for negotiation and compromise between social groups have also decreased, due to the enhanced reflection of social cleavages in the party system.

AUTHOR'S NOTES

1. The decrease can also be seen as one from 84 down to 66, a decline of 26 percent, if Likud and Tsomet are combined for the 1992 elections and the joint Likud-Gesher-Tsomet list is counted as one party for the 1996 elections.
2. This description does not include the deviant case of National Unity (grand) coalitions, in which neither of the two major parties, by itself, constituted a majority within the coalition.

129

Avirama Golan

Between the Lines of the Election Results

May 24, 1999

The 1999 elections brought the Labor Party back to power following three years in opposition. The elections were also a great success for Shas, a party representing traditional Jews of Middle Eastern origin (see doc. 124). The following excerpt, from an editorial of the Israeli daily Haaretz, *offers a penetrating analysis of the election results.*

The 1999 elections were the first to be conducted separately for the Knesset and the prime ministership. In the race for the prime ministry the result was a decisive victory for Ehud Barak, defeating Prime Minister [Benjamin] Netanyahu by 56.08 percent to 43.92 percent. Within less than an hour of the TV exit polls, Netanyahu announced his resignation as leader of the Likud, paving the way for the nomination of Ariel Sharon as head of the party.

However, that is not the whole picture. The 1999 elections shattered, even if only partially, the oft-repeated socio-economic explanation of Shas's electoral successes. In seeking reasons for the party's achievements in the polls, we can no longer cite fresh rolls and chocolate milk, or cheaper day care centers, or busing services to and from Shas schools, when we consider the support for Shas in voting returns from kibbutzim and moshavim: 2.3 percent in Kfar Tavor, 2.1 in Ma'aleh Gilboa, 0.8 in Kibbutz Negba, and 2.2 in Ein Gedi. Do the Ein Gedi kibbutzniks who voted for Shas feel socioeconomically deprived? Do they feel the lack of a long school day? Has the disintegrating welfare state robbed them of their children's bowl of soup at school?

Even in Kochav Ya'ir, where [Ehud] Barak won 71.8 percent of the ballots, 1 percent of the voters cast a ballot for Shas. In Kfar Havradim, 2.2 percent voted Shas, while in Savyon, 79.7 percent voted Barak and 1.5 voted Shas. No superbly organized public education system and no sophisticated social network can separate the voters in these affluent communities from the warm hearth and cultural bond Shas offers them. Nor do amulets explain Shas's dramatic surge forward in the polls, although in this election campaign, the party's leaders were prepared to use any means to attain their end. Even Arye Deri's "J'accuse" videocassette was a form of black magic [see doc. 124].

It is absurd to label Shas's 400,000 voters as "enemies of the people" or as "enemies of law and order." Even the collapse of Israel's two largest parties and the direct election method cannot explain the complex voter returns. The worldwide trend toward religious fundamentalism is not an adequate reason, and Tommy Lapid's destructive political debut is only part of the jigsaw puzzle. More time and serious and innovative thought will be needed to discover why this traditionalist party, which is constantly moving toward religious extremism,

---

Source: Haaretz, May 24, 1999. Copyright © *Haaretz.* Reprinted by permission of *Haaretz.*

has developed so vigorously, strengthening its electoral stature, while its leader's popularity increases as the date of his expected imprisonment nears. Shas's 17 Knesset seats are clearly the writing on the wall,[1] and we should read the words courageously. This reading comprehension exercise is essential for Barak, who chose "to continue to the bitter end in the campaign over social issues," as his advisers now proudly report. If this was his electoral strategy, Barak can already begin to count the months remaining until his defeat in the next election. Hopefully, Barak and his One Israel colleagues will grasp the fact that, in the major repair job they are proposing for Israel's crumbling society, they must continue the process of atonement and promote a social covenant and social partnership.

We need more than a long school day, university scholarships, or housing loans. We need a profound answer to the craving for identity and for a sense of belonging, commodities that cannot be articulated through partisan activity alone. Quite the contrary, they belong primarily to the social field. Secular culture must be reinforced, amended and made more flexible, and the school system should have a multicultural and universal message, as in the United States. The tens of thousands of Shas voters who placed a ballot for Barak and the tens of thousands who last week cheered the rabbis who dubbed Barak "our flesh and blood" now feel besieged in the face of the cacophonous secular vote, which defines itself solely in terms of hatred of the "other" and in the face of the competing Russian vote. Author Amos Oz, the symbol of Israeli secularism, boldly declared over the weekend that he had given up on the hope of "converting others to think like me" and proposed an era of tolerance for the cultural aspirations of the "other." The responsibility for this change in direction will fall largely on Barak's shoulders. He can outline the parameters of the change in our school system, in his government's guidelines, and in the conciliating dialectic he has already begun. However, some responsibility must also be borne by secular groups like the Sephardi Democratic Rainbow[2] and Dor Shalem.[3] If they are offering an alternative, they must define and expand it. The time for doing so is now.

NOTES

1. It seems the writer thinks that the vote for Shas is a way for traditional Jews of Middle Eastern origin to defy the state apparatus, including the courts, which Shas voters view as hostile.
2. The Sephardi Democratic Rainbow is a social movement of Israeli intellectual Jews of Middle Eastern origin that holds a critical perspective of Israeli society. The movement has a complex set of goals that include, among others, the strengthening of Mizrahi/Sephardi sense of identity, redistributing land resources, advancing a multicultural agenda, changing common stereotypes of Mizrahi/Sephardi persons, and feminist goals.
3. Dor Shalom was a short-lived social movement turned political party, established in the aftermath of the assassination of Prime Minister Yitzhak Rabin in 1995. The movement advanced a Center-Left agenda coupled with a limited social justice platform centered around education. In 1999 it assisted Ehud Barak in his successful bid for prime minister and won a number of seats in some Israeli municipalities. By 2006, the movement was no longer active.

130

Orr Commission

Report on Clashes between the Security Forces and Israeli Citizens in October 2000

September 1, 2003

Following the eruption of violence in the territories—the Second Intifada—in late September 2000, Israeli Arabs and security forces clashed in a number of places across Israel. In the course of this short burst of violence (it all subsided by October 10, 2000), thirteen Israeli Arabs and one Israeli Jew were killed. On November 8, the Israeli government appointed an inquiry commission headed by Supreme Court Justice Theodor Orr to investigate the events. The following excerpt from the commission's report analyzes the background to the violence and provides an overview of relations between Israel and its Arab citizens.

The Basic Problem

The relations of minorities and majorities are problematic everywhere, and especially in a state that defines itself in terms of the nationality of the majority. In practice, there are no perfect solutions to the dilemmas that arise in such a state, and there are those who contend that there is a significant conflict between the principles of a majoritarian nation-state and those of liberal democracy. In any event, establishing reasonable harmony in minority-majority relations is a difficult task, which falls to all sectors of society. This task requires special effort on the part of the state institutions that express the majority's hegemony, to counterbalance the injury to the minority resulting from its structural and numerical inferiority and its inferior influence. Failure to engage in such an effort, or engaging in it unsatisfactorily, creates within the minority the sense and the reality of deprivation, which are apt to worsen over time. These characteristics apply as well to the situation of the Arab minority in the State of Israel, which is in many respects the subject of adverse discrimination. Moreover, in the case of the Arab citizens of Israel, there are several unique factors that further magnify the problematic nature of their sociopolitical status in the state.

First, the Arab minority population in Israel is a native population, which sees itself subject to the hegemony of a majority population that is not. In the customary distinction in professional literature between "native minorities" and "migration minorities," the Arab minority in Israel falls clearly into the former category.[1] Generally, the native character of a minority magnifies its self-consciousness and the strength of its demands considerably beyond those of minorities that arise, for example, from the arrival in well-to-do societies of immigrants seeking to improve their lot. This applies to the case of the Arab minority in Israel. The value called *sumud,* i.e., determined possession of ancestral lands in face of the challenges presented by the Jewish majority, which

Source: Chapter 1, Processes of Escalation in the Arab Sector in the Background of the Eruption of Rioting, Judicial Authority online, August 2003, http://or.barak.net.il/inside_index.htm (accessed April 1, 2005). Translated by Harvey N. Bock for the 2nd ed. of *Israel in the Middle East.*

is perceived as an immigrant community, occupies a lofty position in the Arabs' world view. This formula, of a "native" minority opposed to an "immigrant" majority, carries the potential for growing tension.

Second, the Arab minority in Israel is the metamorphosis of a majority population. In contrast to other minorities in the region, which have occupied minority status for centuries, the Arab sector in Israel became a minority only in recent times. It carries the heritage, and the viewpoints and expectations, of those who were always members of a majority community (at least the Muslims among them) and who were twice as many in number as the Jews even with the expansion of the Jewish Yishuv (settlement) during the Mandate. The dramatic turnabout that made them a minority of less than 20 percent of the state's population was not easy to internalize. Their rebellion against it was expressed by, among other things, a refusal to accept the label "minority members" in the language of state institutions. Their consciousness of being a branch of a large human collective, constituting a majority of the Middle East, fed their displeasure at being defined as a minority.

Third, this turnabout was the result of the difficult defeat that the Arabs suffered in their war against the Jewish Yishuv. The state in which they found themselves in minority status represents, by its very existence, a chronic reminder of their still smarting downfall; or, in the words of one of their leaders, "The state arose on the ruins of the Palestinian community." The establishment of the State of Israel, which the Jewish people celebrated as the realization of a longstanding dream, is bound in their historical memory with the most difficult collective trauma in their history—the *naqba* (catastrophe). Even if they do not mention it constantly, the gestation and birth of the state are inseparably bound up with a polar confrontation between two national movements that engendered a long, bloody conflict. The content and symbols of the state, which are legislatively grounded and which trumpet its victories in this conflict, signify in the eyes of the Arab minority their own defeat, and it is doubtful whether true identification with this content and these symbols is possible. Time can perhaps reduce the pain, but as national consciousness increases, so does the Arabs' consciousness of this problem, which accompanies the very establishment of the state.

Fourth, the victory that the Zionist movement achieved in the struggle over the establishment of the state had a continuing dynamic dimension. The Zionist ideals of settlement and ingathering of exiles became organizing principles in the life of the Jewish state. The application of this policy in practice meant control over most of the land in the state and clearing space for the large numbers of immigrants. The Jewish majority saw in such plans as Yihud Hagalil[2] legitimate objectives for the State of Israel. The Arab minority, which found itself in a reality of land expropriation, "in-place absentees," and building restrictions, saw the state as representing interests that infringed its own rights. It also found it difficult to accept the theory and practice of the definition of Israel as the state of the entire Jewish people, entitling Jewish immigrants and new citizens to rights that the Arab minority did not itself enjoy. This state of affairs fed the sense that Israeli democracy is not democratic toward Arabs to the same degree that it is toward Jews (or that it was, as it was referred to in intellectual discourse, an "ethnic democracy" or "ethnocracy"). This led to increasing protests by the Arabs against the inferiority of their status.

Fifth, from a national perspective, the Arab minority in Israel belongs to the Palestinian people (defined narrowly) and to the Arab nation (defined broadly), while the State of Israel is engaged in a difficult conflict with both. While it is true that during the six wars that Israel fought against Arab states, the Arabs in Israel refrained from attacks against law and order, it is unquestionable that many of them felt sympathy for the national aspirations represented by the Arab regimes. The peace treaties that Israel signed with two of its neighbors reduced the polarity in which the Arab minority finds itself, but the continuation of the conflict with the rest of the Arab states, and the consequent threats of war, prevented the complete elimination of that polarity. The rift caused by the continuation of the Israeli-Palestinian struggle is even more difficult. Since the establishment of the state, Israel has faced *fedayeen* incursions, attacks by the Palestine Liberation Organization's constituent organizations, and the clashes of the *intifada*. Many on both sides were killed in these many confrontations, and much suffering was caused. The sense of the Arab citizens of Israel, whose ties to the Palestinians beyond the border and the Green Line are not only national but also social and familial, was expressed by the famous statement of Abd Al-Aziz Al-Zuabi, "My state is in a state of war with the members of my people." This does not mean that the Arab sector in its entirety supports all of the Palestinians' means of struggle. A decisive majority consistently supports the peace process. But at the same time, it identifies absolutely with the aspiration of establishing a Palestinian state and sees Israeli policy as the principal obstacle to achieving that goal.

This fundamental contradiction has given rise to a downward spiral that has left its mark on the status of the Arab minority in Israel. Because of the Arab citizens' ties to the state's rivals, they stirred within the majority—to differing degrees, as well, among different Jews—a sense of potential threat. The senses of threat led to the implementation of a system of oversight of the Arab sector. In the early years of the state, this system was principally embodied in military rule, but even after its cancellation in 1966 oversight continued, by overt or covert means, through the security apparatuses. It was natural that the Arab citizens felt themselves injured by what they called the "securitist" approach toward them, which led to the implementation of means of oversight and manipulation that are inconsistent, they argue, with civil rights. This situation exacerbated the feelings of alienation within the minority, and these in turn increased the majority's suspiciousness.

Recently, the status of the Arab minority in Israel has been characterized and weakened by the fact that this minority lacks substantial collective rights. The State of Israel clearly established full civil rights for all members of the Arab minority, but only as individuals. Unlike states whose constitutional arrangements establish collective rights for their minorities, Israel has never granted such rights to the Arab minority. In practice, it is true, the Arab sector has enjoyed a number of rights of a collective nature. Particularly prominent are the recognition of Arabic as an official language and the implementation of special educational programs for Arabs; similarly, there are collective rights granted to the Arab minority on the basis of communal affiliation, such as a religious court system for matters of personal status and the opportunity for days of rest on a religious basis. However, these arrangements were established largely based on practical considerations, on a case-by-case basis, and were not grounded in a fundamental recognition of the rights of Arabs to collective rights as the members of a different people. The state recognized the separate existence of the Arab sector as a community that is not expected to be assimilated into the majority society. However, it has not given this separate existence a binding legal foundation. This attitude toward the Arab citizens has given rise to the accusation that the state regards them as only a "demographic" group and not as a national minority. This sense increased their feeling of injury and deprivation. This sense was also fed by the prominent existence of collective rights for the Jewish majority. Those rights were expressed in the Law of Return [doc. 29] and the citizenship laws; in normative definitions of the educational, media, and judicial systems; and in unique institutions for the Jewish community, such as the Jewish National Fund and the Jewish Agency. They were also expressed in the very fact of the legal definition of the state as a Jewish state, making it possible for the majority to legislatively enforce the implications of this definition upon the minority. Regarding the absence of collective rights for the Arab sector, it has been said that "the principle of equality, which requires equal law for Jews and for non-Jews, applies at the level of individual rights. It apparently does not apply at the level of collective rights."[3]

Processes of Intensification Approaching October 2000

The problematic nature of the status of the Arab minority, including all the intricate aspects surveyed to this point, is not new; it has been a structural feature of the situation of the Arab sector for more than fifty years. Why did the issue of the status of this sector in the State of Israel become so acute toward the end of the century, to the point that it led to political unrest in the Arab sector on the eve of the events of October 2000? Naturally, this development was not the result of a single, isolated cause, but the accumulation of a variety of processes and factors. These will be dealt with individually in the following portions of this chapter. Here they will be noted only in outline, in the specific context of the emergence of discussion of the question of the status of the Arab minority in the state.

First and foremost, it should be noted that difficult problems that are not dealt with properly increase in severity over time. This was the case for the fundamental problems of the Arab minority. Beyond the inherent weight of this problem, its centrality was also enhanced by a series of changes that occurred within the Arab sector. The Arab community at the close of the twentieth century was very different from the community at mid-century. In place of the weakness, disintegration, and demoralization that characterized the survivors of the 1948 war, a dynamism and vitality now became apparent in the Arab sector and led it to present its demands with determination. A population that had been traditional and rural in the main increasingly took on an urban coloration. A dramatic change occurred in the occupational structure of the Arab community, and it became markedly stronger economically. The Arab sector, which numbered some 150,000 in 1948, reached nearly 1,200,000 by the end of the century. Even if its proportion of the population did not change significantly, it was now a critical mass, which also gave it a sense of confidence. Accordingly, the willingness of the Arab citizens to accept the inferior status in which they found themselves declined, and their desire to examine thoroughly the basic assumptions regarding their status in the state increased.

The political consciousness of the Arab citizens increased to a large degree as the result of an increasing level of education and of greater exposure to the media—both media within the sector itself and media from Arab countries. In the Arab sector, a layer of intelligentsia developed that was largely bilingual. In Israeli universities, Arab scholars appeared who specialized in the study of the Arab community in Israel and examined, with new paradigms, the bases of its status in the state. Against the background of the strengthening of civil society and processes of liberalization in the political and judicial life of Israel society generally, political activity in the Arab sector expanded in the final quarter of the century. This activity was expressed in political parties, ideological movements and NGOs (nongovernmental organizations], which became increasingly numerous. Familiarity with the Israeli political system improved, and more effective methods of activity were learned. Countrywide associations and not-for-profit organizations arose that sought to represent various interests of the Arab sector, and there was a turnabout in their activity—from a position of defensiveness to a tactic of initiative-taking. Independent Arab parties pushed aside the "satellite parties" that were affiliated with the Zionist parties. A layer of radical political activists developed who challenged the authorities' policies toward the Arab sector and objected to the principles defining its status. Their activity expressed feelings within their public and in turn further empowered these feelings. This activity gained encouragement from intellectual and political circles in the Jewish sector, as well, which were motivated by a variety of ideological orientations—from liberalism to post-Zionism (and, indirectly, by ideological trends that gained currency in Western countries in the postcolonial era). Against this background, there arose in the 1990s a call to correct the status of the Arab minority by altering the very definition of the state and changing it to "a state for all its citizens." Within this movement, which was led by the BaLaD (National Democratic Alliance) Party, a tendency to give priority to this demand for redefinition was seen, even ahead of traditional demands for equality in the allocation of resources and for relations of harmonious coexistence between the two communities.

Parallel to the rise of this trend, whose basic assumption was secular, the Islamic trend also rose. As this movement imbibed from the world of Islamic concepts and symbols, it had the potential for broad popular recruitment. And it did indeed gain considerable strength during the 1990s. This trend, whose significant exponents organized themselves in the Islamic movement, attacked the problems of the status of the Arab sector from a different angle. The movement's adherents declared that they recognize the State of Israel, operate within its framework, and obey its laws. Nonetheless, at the level of consciousness it was difficult to distinguish completely between their belief system and that of the radical Islamic movements that are widespread in all the Islamic countries (and that absolutely reject the State of Israel's legitimacy and the very situation of Muslims' being a minority in a Jewish state). The movement's spokesmen, especially its most radical faction, explained that while they accept the State of Israel, it was at the same time difficult for them to accept a state that is defined as Jewish or any state that is, in their words, "an exploitative state." In contrast to the secular trend, which sought to be integrated into the state on the basis of a new conception of citizenship, tendencies toward segregation and aspirations to autarchy for the Arab sector were visible in the radical faction. What the two trends shared was that at the close of the century, they became skeptical about the possibility of meaningful improvements in the situation of the Arab citizens as long as no substantial change was made in the state's framework and in the status of the Arab sector within it.

Other developments that put the problem of the Arab minority in Israel on the public agenda with great intensity appeared in the field of Palestinian-Israeli control of the entire land, from the Mediterranean to the Jordan, changed the context of the Palestinian problem, and many believed that it "reopened the files of 1948." The Oslo Accords (doc. 129) which were based on the concept of two states for two peoples, led the Arabs in Israel to ponder their status in the new reality that was about to be created. The Palestinian leadership, which after many years of alienation began to show an interest in the Arabs who were citizens of Israel, did not offer solutions to the question of their status in the Jewish state. The establishment of the institutions of the Palestinian Authority, with all of their indicia of sovereignty, inspired the Arabs in Israel and strengthened their Palestinian national identification. The Palestinian component of Israeli Arabs' sense of identification increased particularly during the *intifada* period, when the rebellion and sacrifices of the Palestinians in the territories aroused deep feelings of solidarity within the Arab sector. The consolidation of a majority in the Arab sector in Israel that defines its nationality as Palestinian nourished the stance that Israeli society is bi-national and that the status of the Arab minority and the character of the state must be redefined accordingly.

The unrest around the issue of their status in the state was also increased by the fact that the problem of discrimination by state institutions remained in force at the end of the twentieth century. While some gaps gradually narrowed, with respect to the main topics the changes were either too slow or nonexistent. Against this background, friction and confrontation between the members of the Arab sector and the authorities multiplied. They multiplied particularly around the issues that express the very heart of the problem of Arabs in the state: that is, the issues relating to land ownership and to rights of construction and residence. Land Day in 1967 marked the beginning of the path of escalation in confrontations surrounding these issues. The members of the Arab public, whose political consciousness and sensitivity were now more developed, tended to direct their protests against the state's very relationship to them. Accusations of state "racism" became widespread among their spokesmen. Inequality in the distribution of resources changed from a quantitative question to a substantive question of status and rights. It thus became a more profound and critical problem, and it contributed, on the eve of the events of October 2000, to the atmosphere of embitterment and unrest.

NOTES

1. It had been suggested that the Palestinian society as a whole emerged out of waves of immigration from neighboring countries in the nineteenth century and during the British Mandate era. This argument, even if it was true, has no bearing on the Palestinians' own image as natives of the land since time immemorial. It is this self-perception that matters for the discussion above. (commission note)
2. Yihud Hagalil was a plan devised by the Israeli government in the 1970s to encourage Jews to settle in the Upper Galilee.
3. Itzhak Zamir, *The Administrative Authority* (Jerusalem, 1966) 44. See also the opinion of Justice Cheshin in H.C 4112/99, *Adalah v. the City of Tel-Aviv,* Dinim Eliyon 62, p. 271. (commission note)

131

Ehud Eiran

Revolution and Counterrevolution: The Israel Supreme Court from the 1980s Onward

1980–2004: Analysis

The Israel Supreme Court has gone through a dramatic transformation since the proclamation of the State of Israel in 1948. While at first it kept a cautious and formalist approach to intervention in public issues, by the 1990s it had adopted an activist value-based approach and had become a significant actor in shaping Israeli public policy. In the following article, Ehud Eiran, an Israeli lawyer and scholar, describes the process and places it in broader institutional, historical, and cultural contexts.

Source: Written for the 2nd ed. of *Israel in the Middle East.*

The 1980s and 1990s are perhaps the most dramatic years in the history of the Israel Supreme Court. Under the leadership of Chief Justice Aharon Barak, the court followed a two-track strategy: strengthening itself institutionally by introducing substantial judicial review in 1997, as well as promoting a stronger than ever before liberal-democratic agenda that clashed, in some cases, with long-held norms in Israeli society. The court's new active posture exposed it to attempts to curb the newly acquired powers. This "counterrevolutionary" effort led the court to change some of its policies in order to maintain public legitimacy. The following describes the transformation of the court from a restrained formalist institution to an active actor in shaping Israeli public policy.

The Israel Supreme Court had always enjoyed, but not always utilized, the institutional tools that enabled it to play a significant role in shaping public life in Israel. The court's power draws on three main sources. First, it is the court of last resort of almost all legal conflicts in the land. The court not only heads the institutional hierarchy of the regular court system, where most civil and criminal matters are decided, but also assumed authority over the parallel legal systems (military, labor, and religious courts) through a special procedure described below. Second, the court serves also as the High Court of Justice (Beit Hadin Hagavoha Letzedek or Bagatz), which is the first instance for almost all claims against any Israeli administrative entity. It is this power that allowed the Supreme Court to serve, in effect, as the court of last resort regarding decisions taken by the last instance of the parallel court systems. Third, the court traditionally enjoyed significant support in public opinion and broad legitimacy from large sectors of Israeli society.

However, for at least the first three decades since Israel proclaimed its independence, the court followed a cautious and non-interventionist approach. This limited role for judicial intervention in political questions was a result of the British heritage, a strong executive, and a communitarian-Zionist ethos.

The British left the young Jewish state with a legal system that awarded great discretion to the executive and a legal doctrine—formalism—in which the court followed closely the letter of the law, as opposed to a substantial model in which the court enjoys much discretion. The executive branch during Israel's early decades enjoyed great powers and did not volunteer to assist the court's (successful) effort to secure its independence. In at least one case *(Atzlan v. the Commander and Governor of the Galilee)*, the executive outright ignored a court ruling, and until 1953 the judges' independence was not secured through legislation but rather through a thinly defined constitutional tradition. The young Israel, especially in the decade following the State's proclamation, had a communitarian ethos with Zionism, and, to a lesser extent, socialism, at its core. This ethos contributed to the court's reluctance to challenge the executive and the legislative branches.

By the 1980s those institutional and cultural attributes were severely eroded. In 1977 the Labor Party, once the centerpiece of communitarian Zionism, lost its political hegemony and both the executive and the legislature were weakened by the political deadlock in the decade that followed. The economic crisis that peaked in the 1980s pushed Israel to transform its economy from a centralized socialist model to an open neo-liberal one. During this decade the court became more and more active and slowly moved away from the formalist legal doctrine it employed earlier on. This shift was especially evident in the area of public law. Through the mechanism of Bagatz, the court awarded itself more power to review the actions of other branches of government while using a two-pronged approach: First, the court developed legal doctrines that allowed it to hear more and more cases. For example, the court waived the need for a personal interest by the person who petitioned the court opposing an action taken by an administrative action. Second, the court further developed new criteria in reviewing the actions of the other branches and moved away from strict formalism toward a substantial review which was at least partly based on the court's liberal-democratic values. While the effect of this development was largely felt in the public realm, it also permeated to the court's role as the final resort in criminal and civil cases. For example, the court made extensive use of "Good Faith" doctrine as a tool of interpretation in contract law. These doctrinal innovations provided the court a sound platform for judicial control of the other branches and paved the way for a substantial role for the Supreme Court in public policy. The court was now ruling over public policy matters such as political agreements between parties *(Zarzevski v. the Prime Minister)*, retirement age for women *(Nevo v. the National Labor Court)*, and the attorney general's discretion in prosecuting criminal issues *(Ganor v. the Attorney General)*.

The 1992 Knesset legislation of two Basic Laws (Human Dignity and Liberty, and Freedom of Occupation) provided the court the ultimate tool for judicial review. Though the laws did not say so literally, the court interpreted them as giving it the power of judicial review: disqualifying laws passed by the legislature, based on the court's normative judgments. The court was cautious in using this new self-awarded authority and prepared the public and the political system for a while before it indeed used this power. In 1995, while relying heavily on the American model *(Marbury v. Madison)* the court declared for the first time *(United Mizrahi Bank v. Migdal Cooperative Village)* [doc. 122] that it has the powers of judicial review. It took another two years until the court used this power and canceled one section of a law *(Chamber of Financial Consultants v. Finance Ministry)*. During that decade the court became the most active tool in safeguarding and promoting the liberal-democratic agenda in Israel. In doing so, it directly conflicted with long-held norms in Israeli society, including aspects of Israel's Zionist ethos. During the 1990s the court forced the military to allow women into the prestigious all-male pilot course *(Alice Miller v. Minister of Defense)*[doc. 121]; equalized the rights of gay men in receiving benefits from the national air carrier with the rights of heterosexual couples *(El Al v. Danilowitz)*; and prevented the state from allocating land to the Jewish Agency if the latter would use it for settlements that were for "Jews only" *(Kaadan v. Israel Land Authority)*.

However, the court's forceful entry into the arena of public policy in the 1980s and 1990s made it also vulnerable to attacks by those who objected to the policies the court promoted. In arguments that sound familiar to the American ear, opponents of the court asserted that it was not an elected body and therefore lacked legitimacy in shaping public policy. These arguments were made mostly by proponents of a stronger Jewish character for Israel, such as some religious circles. At least, it was suggested, judges should be appointed through a politically controlled method rather than the current system in which the court itself is the dominant force in appointing judges. Other critiques of the court focused on the way it was using its discretion. Most notably, it was suggested that the court adopted liberalism not only as a political theory, but also as an economic approach, avoiding any intervention in defending social and economic rights. By 2001, the court was almost fully dragged into the political arena: politicians felt comfortable mounting crashing attacks against it, parties arranged rallies in front of the court, and the Knesset was searching for ways to curb the power of the justices by creating a constitutional court that would override the Supreme Court.

Faced with mounting public pressure and early signs of loss of legitimacy among widening circles in Israeli society, the court changed some of its policies but retained the liberal core of its project. In 2001, the Court was receptive to public criticism of the way in which judges are selected and was central in appointing a committee that would evaluate that process. The committee, headed by a former justice, agreed to some extent with the public critique about lack of diversity among its members and recommended that future judges "reflect the various sectors of Israeli society." Similarly, the court moved in 2003 and 2004 toward wider recognition of social and economic rights. In 2003 Chief Justice Barak called upon the Knesset to legislate a basic law that would guarantee those rights, and in early 2004, the court intervened in the executive budgetary process and asked the state *(Mehuyavot Le'Shloam v. Minister of Finance)* to clearly define what is "dignified minimal sustenance" in a petition against the curbing of social security benefits.

As these lines are written in 2004, the court's struggle in the political arena is far from being determined. While it was able to deflect some of the pressure it faced, by conceding to a limited number of the critiques, it is the liberal and activist nature of the court from the 1980s onward that brought about the pressure on the court. Therefore, as long as the court remains actively involved in shaping public policy, it is bound to be involved in a struggle.

Foreign Policy Issues

132

Itamar Rabinovich

The Israeli-Syrian Negotiations

August 1993: Analysis

The 1993–96 Israeli-Syrian talks were the first significant attempt for both parties to negotiate directly for a land-for-peace deal. In the following excerpt, Professor Itamar Rabinovich, the chief Israeli negotiator (and co-editor of this collection) shares his perspective on one of the central legacies of that attempt: the conditional commitment Prime Minister Yitzhak Rabin made to the Syrians, through the good services of U.S. Secretary of State Warren Christopher.

[Warren] Christopher's trip to the region was constructed so as to enable him to meet first with [Yitzhak] Rabin, listen to his positions and questions, then meet with [Bashar al-] Assad and get his reactions to them. The secretary of state departed on August 1 to Cairo and arrived in Israel on the 2nd for a morning meeting with Rabin on the 3rd. The meeting was divided, like most such meetings, into two parts: a smaller meeting in Rabin's office and a larger meeting in the adjacent conference room. Structuring meetings in this fashion, whether in Washington or in Jerusalem, was a perpetual source of tension and aggravation, but there was no escaping it. On more than one occasion, there was no real difference between the smaller and larger meetings, but on August 3, 1993, the difference was stark.

In addition to Rabin and Christopher, the smaller meeting was attended by [Dennis] Ross and myself as note-takers. Rabin wasted no time and went directly into the heart of the matter. Israel could not move forward on two tracks simultaneously, so that progress in the peace process would have to be phased. Rabin's own preference was to move first with Syria and Lebanon, and to settle on a limited simultaneous progress with the Palestinians (on the scale of the "Gaza first" plan). Rabin saw two alternatives for dealing with Syria and Lebanon. One was to deal with Lebanon "as a pilot." If the Lebanese army were to deploy along the

---

Source: Itamar Rabinovich, *The Brink of Peace: The Israeli-Syrian Negotiations* (Princeton: Princeton University Press, 1998), pp. 104–6.

security zone and provide six months of quiet, Rabin was willing to sign a peace treaty and withdraw to the international border. Israel's security concerns and her commitments to her allies and partners in the security zone would also have to be addressed. But Rabin was doubtful whether Syria would agree to this plan.

The second alternative was to deal with Syria and Lebanon together. In order to find out whether this alternative was feasible, Rabin asked Christopher to explore with Assad, on the assumption that his own demand would be satisfied, first whether Syria would be willing to sign a peace treaty with Israel without linkage to the pace of progress with others; second, whether Syria was ready for a real peace including normalization, diplomatic relations, and the other paraphernalia of real peace; and third, whether Syria was ready to offer elements of peace before the completion of withdrawal. Rabin explained to Christopher that he saw the whole process completed in five years, and that given the fact that Israel was asked to give tangibles, in return for intangibles, he wanted tangible proofs of peace before going through a significant withdrawal. What he had in mind was the Israeli-Egyptian precedent, when Sadat agreed to the establishment of embassies after the first phase of withdrawal.

In addition to the three questions to Assad, Rabin raised four other points. First, the security arrangements were as important as the other issues. In addition to the security arrangements with Syria, he expected U.S. participation in the post-settlement security regime (I added that on the basis of what we saw in the Washington talks, particularly the Syrian demand for "equal footing" in the security arrangements, stiff Syrian opposition could be expected in this matter). Second, he emphasized that he was speaking of "an assumption." Third, he insisted on the absolute confidentiality of the exercise we were about to engage in. And fourth, he explained to the secretary of state that there would have to be a referendum in Israel before he could sign an agreement with Syria.

After clarifying some of these issues, the secretary of state wanted to know whether Jericho would be part of the concomitant "limited agreement" with the Palestinians that Rabin had in mind. (This was clearly an echo of the parallel negotiation with the Palestinians, with which the secretary of state was familiar at least in general terms.) Rabin's answer was that in the event of an agreement with Syria the agreement with the Palestinians would have to be limited to Gaza, but if the first agreement were to be made with the Palestinians, both Gaza and Jericho would be included.

Before we moved on to the large meeting, I said to Ross that the wings of history could be heard in the room. Rabin's gambit took me by surprise, but it was clear to me that by being willing to engage in the "hypothetical approach" he opened the door wide for Assad. If Assad were to respond appropriately, we could soon find ourselves in the midst of a real negotiation with Syria. Before we all departed, Rabin told me again that the details of the meeting in his office must remain secret. He would update whomever needed to know about it in the Israeli government (by which he meant, first and foremost, Foreign Minister [Shimon] Peres).

Christopher and Ross saw Assad in Damascus on the 4th and returned to Israel to report to Rabin on the 5th. They then traveled back to Damascus with Rabin's response. I was briefed by Ross on the second meeting on August 8th after we had both returned to Washington. Soon thereafter both Christopher and Ross left for their planned family vacations in California.

While Christopher and Ross saw Assad's response as positive in that he accepted "the basic equation," Rabin saw it as disappointing. Assad was willing to offer formal contractual peace for full withdrawal and was, in principle, willing to view the agreement as "standing on its own two feet," but then came a long list of "ifs and buts." Most significantly, Assad did not accept Rabin's demand that the agreement be implemented in a fashion that would offer Israel at the outset a large measure of normalization for a limited withdrawal. Nor did he accept a five-year time frame and offered instead a six-month period for implementing the agreement.

Assad's response on the issue of linkage to the other tracks, while positive in principle, was not clear. Rabin knew that Syria would insist on full linkage to the Lebanese track, and understood well that Assad needed a measure of progress with the Palestinians in order to legitimize his own move, but it was not clear what that measure was. Assad agreed to a full-fledged peace, but he told Christopher that he had difficulties with the very term "normalization." He rejected Rabin's idea of establishing a direct discreet channel; the most he agreed to were meetings between both [Mowaffak] Allaf and [Walid] Mu'allim and myself, attended also by an American representative. The whole issue of security arrangements was not discussed in any detail (at least as reported to us), and Rabin's insistence that without significant Syrian investment in public diplomacy he would lack a political basis for moving on fell on deaf ears.

133

Oslo Accords between Israel and the Palestine Liberation Organization

September 13, 1993

The Israeli-Palestinian agreements of August–September 1993 were the single most important set of events in the evolution of the Madrid peace process and a crucial turning point in the evolution of Arab-Israeli relations. While falling far short of offering a resolution of the Israeli-Palestinian conflict, they represented the parties' resolve to terminate the conflict through compromise. They also provided a framework and a course for resolution and formalized the mutual recognition of enemies who had demonized and boycotted each other for many years. Although the agreements collapsed in 2000, the mutual recognition as well as public support on both sides for a two-state solution remained as an enduring heritage of the Oslo process.

The Oslo Accords were the product of a secret negotiation that had been conducted for several months in Oslo parallel to the formal Israeli-Palestinian track of the Washington talks. The draft agreement reached in Oslo in August 1993 was presented later that month to the Clinton administration. The latter, despite the priority it had assigned to the Israeli-Syrian track, decided to endorse, consolidate, and magnify the Oslo Accords by converting it into the September 13 signing ceremony on the White House lawn.

The text of the agreement, initialed in Oslo on August 20, was signed at the White House following the Israeli-PLO mutual recognition by Israeli Foreign Minister Shimon Peres and PLO Executive Committee member Mahmoud Abbas (Abu Mazen) in the presence of Israeli Prime Minister Yitzhak Rabin and PLO Chairman

Source: Israel Ministry of Foreign Affairs, www.mfa.gov.il/MFA/Peace%20Process/Guide%20to%20the%20Peace%20Process/Declaration%20of%20Principles (accessed May 21, 2007).

Yasir Arafat. The final agreement is identical to the draft except for one change, added just before the ceremony: in the preamble, the words "the Palestinian team" were changed to read "the PLO team (in the Jordanian-Palestinian delegation to the Middle East peace conference: the "Palestinian Delegation")." The annexes referred to in the document below are not included in this excerpt.

The Government of the State of Israel and the PLO team (in the Jordanian-Palestinian delegation to the Middle East Peace Conference, "the Palestinian delegation"), representing the Palestinian people, agree that it is time to put an end to decades of confrontation and conflict, recognize their mutual legitimate and political rights, and strive to live in peaceful coexistence and mutual dignity and security to achieve a just, lasting, and comprehensive peace settlement and historic reconciliation through the agreed political process. Accordingly, the two sides agree to the following principles.

Article 1. Aim of the Negotiations. The aim of the Israeli-Palestinian negotiations within the current Middle East peace process is, among other things, to establish a Palestinian Interim Self-Government Authority, the elected Council (the "Council") for the Palestinian people in the West Bank and the Gaza Strip, for a transitional period not exceeding five years, leading to a permanent settlement based on Security Council Resolutions 242 [doc. 68] and 338 [doc. 86].

It is understood that the interim arrangements are an integral part of the whole peace process and that the negotiations on the permanent status will lead to the implementation of Security Council Resolutions 242 and 338.

Article 2. Framework for the Interim Period. The agreed framework for the interim period is set forth in this Declaration of Principles.

Article 3. Elections.

1. In order that the Palestinian people in the West Bank and Gaza Strip may govern themselves according to democratic principles, direct, free and general political elections will be held for the Council under agreed supervision and international observation, while the Palestinian police will insure public order.

2. An agreement will be concluded on the exact mode and conditions of the elections in accordance with the protocol attached as Annex I, with the goal of holding the elections not later than nine months after the entry into force of this Declaration of Principles.

3. These elections will constitute a significant interim preparatory step toward the realization of the legitimate rights of the Palestinian people and their just requirements.

Article 4. Jurisdiction. Jurisdiction of the Council will cover West Bank and Gaza Strip territory, except for issues that will be negotiated in the permanent status negotiations. The two sides view the West Bank and Gaza Strip as a single territorial unit, whose integrity will be preserved during the interim period.

Article 5. Transitional Period and Permanent Status Negotiations.

1. The five-year transitional period will begin upon the withdrawal from Gaza Strip and Jericho area.

2. Permanent status negotiations will commence as soon as possible, but not later than the beginning of the third year of the interim period between the Government of Israel and the Palestinian people representatives.

3. It is understood that these negotiations shall cover remaining issues, including: Jerusalem, refugees, settlements, security arrangements, borders, relations and cooperation with other neighbors, and other issues of common interest.

4. The two parties agree that the outcome of the permanent status negotiations should not be prejudiced or preempted by agreements reached for the interim period.

Article 6. Preparatory Transfer of Powers and Responsibilities.

1. Upon the entry into force of this Declaration of Principles and the withdrawal from the Gaza Strip and the Jericho area, a transfer of authority from the Israeli military government and its Civil Administration to the authorized Palestinians for this task, as detailed herein, will commence. This transfer of authority will be of preparatory nature until the inauguration of the Council.

2. Immediately after the entry into force of this Declaration of Principles and the withdrawal from the Gaza Strip and Jericho area, with the view to promoting economic development in the West Bank and Gaza Strip, authority will be transferred to the Palestinians on the following spheres: education and culture, health, social welfare, direct taxation, and tourism. The Palestinian side will commence in building the Palestinian police force, as agreed upon. Pending the inauguration of the Council, the two parties may negotiate the transfer of additional powers and responsibilities, as agreed upon.

Article 7. Interim Agreement.

1. The Israeli and Palestinian delegations will negotiate an agreement on the interim period (the "Interim Agreement").

2. The Interim Agreement shall specify, among other things, the structure of the Council, the number of its members, and the transfer of powers and responsibilities from the Israeli military government and its Civil Administration to the Council. The Interim Agreement shall also specify the Council's executive authority, legislative authority in accordance with Article 9 below, and the independent Palestinian judicial organs.

3. The Interim Agreement shall include arrangements, to be implemented upon the inauguration of the Council, for the assumption by the Council of all of the powers and responsibilities transferred previously in accordance with Article VI above.

4. In order to enable the Council to promote economic growth, upon its inauguration, the Council will establish, among other things, a Palestinian Electricity Authority, a Gaza Sea Port Authority, a Palestinian Development Bank, a Palestinian Export Promotion Board, a Palestinian Environmental Authority, a Palestinian Land Authority, and a Palestinian Water Administration Authority, and any other authorities agreed upon, in accordance with the Interim Agreement that will specify their powers and responsibilities.

5. After the inauguration of the Council, the Civil Administration will be dissolved, and the Israeli military government will be withdrawn.

Article 8. Public Order and Security. In order to guarantee public order and internal security for the Palestinians of the West Bank and the Gaza Strip, the Council will establish a strong police force, while Israel will continue to carry the responsibility for defending against external threats, as well as the responsibility for overall security of Israelis for the purpose of safeguarding their internal security and public order.

Article 9. Laws and Military Orders.

1. The Council will be empowered to legislate, in accordance with the Interim Agreement, within all authorities transferred to it.

2. Both parties will review jointly laws and military orders presently in force in remaining spheres.

Article 10. Joint Israeli-Palestinian Liaison Committee. In order to provide for a smooth implementation of this Declaration of Principles and any subsequent agreements pertaining to the interim period upon the entry into force of this Declaration of Principles, a Joint Israeli-Palestinian Liaison Committee will be established in order to deal with issues requiring coordination, other issues of common interest, and disputes.

Article 11. Israeli-Palestinian Cooperation in Economic Fields. Recognizing the mutual benefit of cooperation in promoting the development of the West Bank, the Gaza Strip, and Israel, upon the entry into force of this Declaration of Principles, an Israeli-Palestinian Economic cooperation committee will be established in order to develop and implement in a cooperative manner the programs identified in the protocols attached as Annex III and Annex IV.

Article 12. Liaison and Cooperation with Jordan and Egypt. The two parties will invite the Governments of Jordan and Egypt to participate in establishing further liaison and cooperation arrangements between the Government of Israel and the Palestinian representatives, on one hand, and the Governments of Jordan and Egypt, on the other hand, to promote cooperation between them. These arrangements will include the constitution of a Continuing Committee that will decide by agreement on the modalities of admission of persons displaced from the West Bank and Gaza Strip in 1967, together with necessary measures to prevent disruption and disorder. Other matters of common concern will be dealt with by this Committee.

Article 13. Redeployment of Israeli Forces.

1. After entry into force of this Declaration of Principles, and not later than the eve of elections for the Council, a redeployment of Israeli military forces in the West Bank and Gaza Strip will take place, in addition to withdrawal of Israeli forces carried out in accordance with Article 14.

2. In redeploying its military forces, Israel will be guided by the principle that its military forces should be redeployed outside populated areas.

3. Further redeployments to specified locations will be gradually implemented commensurate with the assumption of responsibility for public order and internal security by the Palestinian police force pursuant to Article 8 above.

Article 14. Israeli Withdrawal from the Gaza Strip and Jericho Area. Israel will withdraw from the Gaza Strip and Jericho area, as detailed in the protocol attached as Annex II.

Article 15. Resolution of Disputes.

1. Disputes arising out of the application or interpretation of this Declaration of Principles, or any subsequent agreements pertaining to the interim period, shall be resolved by negotiations through the Joint Liaison Committee to be established pursuant to Article 10 above.

2. Disputes which cannot be settled by negotiations may be resolved by a mechanism of conciliation to be agreed upon by the parties.

3. The parties may agree to submit to arbitration disputes relating to the interim period which cannot be settled through reconciliation. To this end, upon the agreement of both parties, the parties will establish an Arbitration Committee.

Article 16. Israeli-Palestinian Cooperation Concerning Regional Programs. Both parties view the multilateral working groups as an appropriate instrument for promoting a "Marshall Plan," the regional programs and other programs, including special programs for the West Bank and Gaza Strip, as indicated in the protocol attached as Annex IV.

Article 17. Miscellaneous Provisions.

1. This Declaration of Principles will enter into force one month after its signing.

2. All protocols annexed to this Declaration of Principles and Agreed Minutes pertaining thereto shall be regarded as an integral part hereof.

134

Peace Treaty between Jordan and Israel

October 26, 1994

The Israeli-Jordanian Peace Treaty of October 1994 is a culmination of six decades of Zionist-Hashemite and Israeli-Hashemite secret diplomacy and the product of the policies pursued by Yitzhak Rabin's government for the previous fifteen months. King Abdullah, the Hashemite Kingdom's founder, and his grandson, King Hussein, came several times to the "brink of peace" with Israel but never achieved it. Ironically, it was the signing of the Oslo Accords (doc. 133) in August and September 1993 that finally moved King Hussein to sign this treaty. The Oslo Accords, which the Jordanian monarch resented, had a dual effect on his policies: they persuaded him to fully join the diplomatic effort in order to monitor the Palestinian issue, and they legitimized his own peacemaking with Israel.

The annexes referred to in the document below are not included in this excerpt.

Article 1. Establishment of Peace. Peace is hereby established between the State of Israel and the Hashemite Kingdom of Jordan (the "Parties") effective from the exchange of the instruments of ratification of this treaty.

Article 2. General Principles. The Parties will apply between them the provisions of the Charter of the United Nations and the principles of international law governing relations among states in times of peace. In particular:

1. They recognize and will respect each other's sovereignty, territorial integrity and political independence;

2. They recognize and will respect each other's right to live in peace with secure and recognized boundaries;

3. They will develop good neighborly relations of cooperation between them to ensure lasting security, will refrain from the threat or use of force against each other and will settle all disputes between them by peaceful means;

4. They respect and recognize the sovereignty, territorial integrity and political independence of every state in the region;

5. They respect and recognize the pivotal role of human development and dignity in regional and bilateral relationships;

6. They further believe that within their control, involuntary movements of persons in such a way as to adversely prejudice the security of either Party should not be permitted.

Article 3. International Boundary

1. The international boundary between Israel and Jordan is delimited with reference to the boundary definition under the Mandate as is shown in Annex 1(a) on the mapping materials attached thereto and co-ordinates specified therein.

Article 4. Security Cooperation. Mutual understanding and co-operation in security-related matters will form a significant part of relations. The Parties recognize the achievements of the European Union in developing the

Source: *Journal of Palestine Studies* 24, no. 2 (Winter 1995): 126–32.

Conference on Security and Co-operation in Europe (CSCE) and commit themselves to the creation, in the Middle East, of a CSCME (Conference on Security and Co-operation in the Middle East). The Parties commit themselves to refrain from the threat or use of force or weapons, conventional, nonconventional or of any other kind, and to combat terrorism of all kinds.

Article 5. Diplomatic and Other Bilateral Relations

1. The Parties agree to establish full diplomatic and consular relations and to exchange resident ambassadors within one month of the exchange of the instruments of ratification of this Treaty.

2. The Parties agree that the normal relationship between them will further include economic and cultural relations.

Article 6. Water. With the view to achieving a comprehensive and lasting settlement of all the water problems between them:

1. The Parties agree mutually to recognize the rightful allocations of both of them in Jordan River and Yarmouk River waters and Arava ground water in accordance with the agreed acceptable principles, quantities, and quality as set out in Annex II, which shall be fully respected and complied with.

2. The Parties, recognizing the necessity to find a practical, just and agreed solution to their water problems and with the view that the subject of water can form the basis for the advancement of cooperation between them, jointly undertake to ensure that the management and development of their water resources do not, in any way, harm the water resources of the other Party.

3. The Parties recognize that their water resources are not sufficient to meet their needs. More water should be supplied for their use through various methods, including projects of regional and international cooperation.

4. In light of paragraph 3 of this Article, with the understanding that cooperation in water-related subjects would be to the benefit of both Parties, and will help alleviate their water shortages, and that water issues along their entire boundary must be dealt with in their totality, including the possibility of trans-boundary water transfers, the Parties agree to search for ways to alleviate water shortage and to cooperate in the following fields:

a. development of existing and new water resources, increasing the water availability including cooperation on a regional basis as appropriate, and minimizing wastage of water resources through the chain of their uses;
b. prevention of contamination of water resources;
c. mutual assistance in the alleviation of water shortages;
d. transfer of information and joint research and development in water-related subjects, and review of the potentials for enhancement of water resources development and use.

5. The implementation of both Parties' undertakings under this Article is detailed in Annex II. . . .

Article 8. Refugees and Displaced Persons

1. Recognizing the massive human problems caused to both Parties by the conflict in the Middle East, as well as the contribution made by them toward the alleviation of human suffering, the Parties will seek to further alleviate those problems arising on a bilateral level.

2. Recognizing that the above human problems caused by the conflict in the Middle East cannot be fully resolved on the bilateral level, the Parties will seek to resolve them in appropriate forums, in accordance with international law, including the following:

a. in the case of displaced persons, in a quadripartite committee with Egypt and the Palestinians;
b. in the case of refugees,
   1. in the framework of the Multilateral Working Group on Refugees;

2. in negotiations, in a framework to be agreed, bilateral or otherwise, in conjunction with and at the same time as the permanent status negotiations pertaining to the territories referred to in Article 3 of this Treaty;

c. through the implementation of agreed United Nations programs and other agreed international economic programs concerning refugees and displaced persons, including assistance to their settlement.

Article 9. Places of Historical and Religious Significance

1. Each party will provide freedom of access to places of religious and historical significance.
2. In this regard, in accordance with the Washington Declaration, Israel respects the present special role of the Hashemite Kingdom of Jordan in Muslim Holy shrines in Jerusalem. When negotiations on the permanent status take place, Israel will give high priority to the Jordanian historic role in these shrines.
3. The Parties will act to promote interfaith relations among the three monotheistic religions, with the aim of working toward religious understanding, moral commitment, freedom of religious worship, and tolerance and peace.

Article 10. Cultural and Scientific Exchanges. The Parties, wishing to remove biases developed through periods of conflict, recognize the desirability of cultural and scientific exchanges in all fields, and agree to establish normal cultural relations between them. Thus, they shall, as soon as possible and not later than 9 months from the exchange of the instruments of ratification of this Treaty, conclude the negotiations on cultural and scientific agreements. . . .

Article 16. Posts and Telecommunications. The Parties take note of the opening between them, in accordance with the Washington Declaration, of direct telephone and facsimile lines. Postal links, the negotiations on which having been concluded, will be activated upon the signature of this Treaty. The Parties further agree that normal wireless and cable communications and television relay services by cable, radio, and satellite, will be established between them, in accordance with all relevant international conventions and regulations. The negotiations on this subject will be concluded not later than 9 months from the exchange of the instruments of ratification of this Treaty.

Article 17. Tourism. The Parties affirm their mutual desire to promote cooperation between them in the field of tourism. In order to accomplish this goal, the Parties—taking note of the understandings reached between them concerning tourism—agree to negotiate, as soon as possible, and to conclude not later than three months from the exchange of the instruments of ratification of this Treaty, an agreement to facilitate and encourage mutual tourism and tourism from third countries.

135

William Jefferson Clinton

Speech to the Knesset

October 27, 1994

U.S. President William Jefferson Clinton's speech to the Knesset in the aftermath of the signing of the Israeli-Jordanian peace treaty in October 1994 (doc. 134) reflected the immensely close relationship between President Clinton and Israeli Prime Minister Yitzhak Rabin and their governments. Rabin's adoption of a policy seeking Israeli-Arab accommodation based on compromise removed the acrimony that had previously permeated the U.S. relationship with Israel. The United States had reaped large diplomatic benefits from its conduct of the post-1973 Israeli-Arab peace process. But that role involved a measure of friction with several Israeli prime ministers willing to make peace but reluctant to make concessions.

The Oslo Accords (doc. 133) negotiated by Israel with its former archenemy, the Palestine Liberation Organization, and the subsequent peace treaty with Jordan provided the Clinton administration with two of its most prominent foreign policy achievements and facilitated its role as a superpower dealing with both Israelis and Arabs. Against this backdrop, the special bilateral relationship between the United States and Israel could flourish and unfold smoothly.

Mr. President, Mr. Prime Minister, Mr. Speaker, Mr. [Benjamin] Netanyahu, Ladies and Gentlemen of the Knesset. Let me begin by thanking the Prime Minister and the people of Israel for welcoming me to your wonderful country and thanking all of you for giving me the opportunity to address this great democratic body where clearly people of all different views are welcome to express their convictions. I felt right at home.

Yesterday Israel took a great stride toward fulfilling the ancient dream of the Jewish people, the Patriarch's dream of a strong and plentiful people living freely in their own land, enjoying the fruits of peace with their neighbors.

Nearly seventeen years after President Sadat came to this chamber to seek peace and Prime Minister Begin reached out in reconciliation [doc. 100] and just over a year after Israel and the PLO declared a pathway to peace on the South Lawn of the White House [doc. 133], Israel and Jordan have now written a new chapter. Tonight we praise the courage of the leaders who have given life to this treaty, Prime Minister [Yitzhak] Rabin and Foreign Minister [Shimon] Peres. They have shown the vision and the tenacity of other leaders of Israel's past whose names will be remembered always for their devotion to your cause and your people—[David] Ben-Gurion, [Golda] Meir, [Menahem] Begin.

In your life, Prime Minister, we see the life of your country. As a youth you wished to fulfill the commandment to farm the land of Israel but instead you had to answer the call to defend the people of Israel. You have devoted your life to cultivating strength so that others can till the soil in safety. You have fought many battles and

Source: *Divrei haknesset* [Protocols of the Knesset], October 4, 1994, pp. 913–15.

won many victories in war. Now in strength you are fighting and winning battles for peace.

Indeed, you have shown your people that they can free themselves from the siege, that for the first time they can make real a peace for the generations.

For the American people too this peace is a blessing. For decades, as Israel has struggled to survive, we have rejoiced in your triumphs and shared in your agonies. In the years since Israel was founded, Americans of every faith have admired and supported you. Like your country, ours is a land that welcomes exiles, a nation of hope, a nation of refuge. From the Orient and Europe and now from the former Soviet Union, your people have come—Ashkenazim and Sephardim, Yemenites and Ethiopians—all of you committed to living free, to building a common home.

One in every four citizens of this country is an Arab, something very few people know beyond the borders. Even without the blessings of secure borders, you have secured for your own people the blessings of democracy. With all of its turmoil and debate, it is still the best of all systems.

In times of war and times of peace, every President of the United States since Harry Truman and every Congress has understood the importance of Israel. The survival of Israel is important not only to our interests but to every single value we hold dear as a people. Our role in war has been to help you to defend yourself by yourself. That is what you have asked. Now that you are taking risks for peace, our role is to help you to minimize the risks of peace.

I am committed to working with our Congress to maintain the current levels of military and economic assistance. We have taken concrete steps to strengthen Israel's qualitative edge. The U.S.-Israel Science and Technology Commission, unprecedented Israeli access to the U.S. high technology market and acquisition of advanced computers—all these keep Israel in the forefront of global advances and competitive and global markets.

I have also taken steps to enhance Israel's military and your capacity to address possible threats not only to yourselves but to the region. F-15 aircraft are being provided and F-16s transferred out of U.S. stocks. We work closely with you to develop the Arrow missile, to protect against the threat of ballistic missiles.

As we help to overcome the risks of peace, we are also helping to build a peace that will bring with it the safety and security Israel deserves.

That peace must be real, based on treaty commitments arrived at directly by the parties, not imposed from outside. It must be secure. Israel must always be able to defend itself by itself.

And it must be comprehensive. We have worked hard to end the Arab boycott and we've had some success, but we will not stop until it is completely lifted.

There is a treaty with Jordan and an agreement with the PLO, but we must keep going until Syria and Lebanon close the circle of states entering into peace and the other nations of the Arab world normalize their relations with Israel.

This morning in Damascus, I discussed peace with President [Hafez al-] Assad. He repeated at our press conference what he had earlier said to his own Parliament. Syria has made a strategic choice for peace with Israel. He also explained that Syria is ready to commit itself to the requirements of peace through the establishment of normal peaceful relations with Israel. His hope, as he articulated it, is to transform the region from a state of war to a state of peace that enables both Arabs and Israelis to live in security, stability, and prosperity.

We have been urging President Assad to speak to you in a language of peace that you can understand. Today, we began to do so. Of course, it will take more than words, much more than words. Yet, I believe something is changing in Syria. Its leaders understand that it is time to make peace. There will still be a good deal of hard bargaining before a breakthrough, but they are serious about proceeding.

Just as we have worked with you from Camp David to Wadi Arava to bring peace with security to your people, so too we will walk with you on the road to Damascus for peace and security.

There are those who see peace still as all too distant. Surely they include the families of those buried in the rubble of the community center in Buenos Aires, those in the basement of New York's World Trade Center, the loved ones of the passengers on bus number 5 and, of course, two people who, as has been noted, are in this chamber with us tonight and we honor their presence, the parents of Corporal Nachshon Wachsman, a son of your nation and I proudly say a citizen of ours.

We grieve with the families of those who are lost and with all the people of Israel. So long as Jews are murdered just because they are Jews or just because they are citizens of Israel, the plague of antisemitism lives and we must stand against it.

We must stand against terror as strongly as we stand for peace. For without an end to terror there can be no peace. The forces of terror and extremism still threaten us all. Sometimes they pretend to act in the name of God and country, but their deeds violate their own religious faith and make a mockery of any notion of honorable patriotism.

As I said last night to the Parliament in Jordan, we respect Islam. Millions of American citizens every day answer the Muslim call to prayer, but we know that the real fight is not about religion or culture. It is about a worldwide conflict between those who believe in peace and those who believe in terror, those who believe in hope and those who believe in fear. Those who stoke the fires of violence and seek to destroy the peace, make no mistake about it, have one great goal. Their goal is to make the people of Israel, who have defeated all odds on the field of battle, give up inside on the peace by giving in to the doubts that terror brings to every one of us.

But having come so far, you cannot give up or give in. Your future must lie in the words of a survivor of the carnage of bus number 5 who said, "I want the peace process to continue. I want to live in peace. I want my children to live in peace."

So, let us say to the merchants of terror once again, you cannot succeed, you must not succeed, you will not succeed. You are the past, not the future. The peacemakers are the future.

I say to you, my friends, in spite of all the dangers and difficulties that still surround you, the circle of your enemies is shrinking. Their time has passed. Their increasing isolation is reflected in the desperation of their disgusting deeds. Once in this area you were shunned. Now, more and more you are embraced.

As you share the waters of the River Jordan and work with your neighbors, new crops will emerge where the soil is now barren. As you join together to mine the Dead Sea for its minerals, you will bring prosperity to all your people. As you roll up the barbed wire and cross the desert of the Arava, the sands will yield new life to you. As you dock in each other's ports along the Gulf of Aqaba, more and more people will have the chance to experience the wonders of both your lands, and more and more children will share the joys of youth and not the dread of war.

This is the great promise of peace. It is the promise of making sure that all those who have sacrificed their lives did not die in vain. The promise of a Sabbath afternoon not violated by gunfire, a drive across the plains to the mountains of Moab where Moses died and Ruth was born, a Yom Kippur of pure prayer without the rumble of tanks, voices of fear or rumors of war. After all the bloodshed and all your tears, you are now far closer to the day when the clash of arms is heard no more and all the children of Abraham, the children of Isaac, and the children of Israel will live side by side in peace.

This was, after all, the message the Prophet Mohammed himself brought to the peoples of the faith when he said, "There is no argument between us and you. God will bring us together and unto Him is the homecoming." And this was the message that Moses spoke to the Children of Israel when, for the last time, he spoke to them as they gathered to cross the River Jordan into the promised land, when he said, "I have set before you life and death, blessings and curses; choose life so that you and your descendants may live."

This week once again the people of Israel made a homecoming. Once, you chose life. Once again, America was proud to walk with you.

The Prime Minister mentioned a story in his remarks that he never asked me about. Wouldn't it be embarrassing if it weren't true? The truth is that the only time my wife and I ever came to Israel before today was thirteen years ago with my pastor on a religious mission. I was then out of office. I was the youngest former governor in the history of the United States. No one thought I would ever be here. Perhaps my mother. No one else.

We visited the holy sites. I relived the history of the Bible, of your scriptures and mine, and I formed a bond with my pastor. Later, when he became desperately ill, he said he thought I might one day become president and he said, more bluntly than the Prime Minister did, if you abandon Israel, God will never forgive you.

He said that it is God's will that Israel, the biblical home of the people of Israel, continue forever and ever.

So I say to you tonight, my friends, one of our presidents, John Kennedy, reminded us that here on earth God's will must truly be our own. It is for us to make the homecoming, for us to choose life, for us to work for peace. But until we achieve a comprehensive peace in the Middle East, and then after we achieve a comprehensive peace in the Middle East, know this: your journey is our journey and America will stand with you now and always.

Thank you and God bless you.

136

Hamas

Opposition to Any Accommodation with Israel

1992, 1994, 1997, 1999

The most significant Palestinian opposition to the Oslo process came from Hamas, the Islamic fundamentalist movement. The movement's military arm, currently known as Izz al-Din al-Qassam Battalions, began its activities in 1988 (see doc. 117) and launched its first attack in December of 1989.

Hamas was the first Palestinian organization to carry out suicide bombings, and it launched a significant number of such attacks in 1994–96, mostly against civilians in territorial Israel in an effort to derail the peace process. The collapse of the Oslo process and the resumption of violence in 2000 led other Palestinian organizations to adopt Hamas's tactics of suicide bombings and brought about an increase in public support for the organization that objected to a peaceful arrangement with Israel all along, exemplified by the following collection of statements by Hamas leaders and spokesmen. In 2005 Hamas won the elections for the Palestinian Authority.

Ibrahim Ghawshah, head of Hamas in Gaza, *Keyhan* (Teheran), October 31, 1992

I agree with you that there is a dangerous plot under way that threatens the entire region; that is, the plot to have the Arab, Islamic fold accept the Zionists. If, God forbid, this materializes and Arab-Israeli relations improve, . . . it would engulf all aspects including the political, cultural and social spheres. In this way Israel would be able to attain its strategic objectives of a Greater Israel without fighting. True peace can only be attained by returning the Palestinians to their homeland and returning the Zionist aggressors to the countries from where they have come.

Mahmud al-Zahhar, Hamas leader in Gaza, *La Vanguardia* (Barcelona), March 6, 1994

This is no peace process. It [the Oslo Accords, doc. 133] is an agreement between the PLO and Israel. The occupation will be more legal from the international viewpoint. Israel will be the dominant force and the center of authority in Tel Aviv, and will give us Palestinians the right to self-control. That is what autonomy means; the same as the Kurds in Iraq. The central government—the master of the land—will give self-determination to a minority national group. With the signing of this agreement Arafat is saying that Israel is the master of all Palestine and that it is giving us the opportunity to set up an autonomous entity. This is the most dangerous point in the agreement signed in the so-called peace talks.

al-Quds (Palestinian Arab Radio), October 14, 1994, quoted in Foreign Broadcast Information Service–Near East and South Asia (FBIS-NESA), *Daily Report,* October 14, 1994

The principles of Hamas are genuine and are determined by two things. First, the Islamic faith and principles to which it adheres and which are derived from the Holy Koran; and second, the interests of the Palestinian people alone. Hamas's organization, power, and leadership are inside the occupied territories. Undoubtedly, the battle against the Zionists is a cultural one. Hamas now represents the first phase of that war and we are certain that the Muslims and Arabs will sooner or later join us and liberate this area, just as it was liberated by Salah-al-Din more than eight centuries ago.

'Abd-al-'Aziz al-Rantisi, Hamas spokesman in Gaza, *al-Sabil* (Amman), September 30, 1997, p. 16, quoted in FBIS-NESA, *Daily Report,* October 2, 1997

Our aim is to carry out jihad for the sake of God. [We are] . . . determined to continue along this path until the liberation of the last inch of Palestine. Hamas's approach is religious. I believe that political dialogue with the PA [Palestine Authority] is useless and a waste of time, because each of us has his own political program. Hamas will not be harmed by maintaining its perspective and political program for as long as it takes. We will not give up our principles for which we have sacrificed. This is the crystal clear stance of Hamas.

'Abd al-'Aziz Rantisi, Hamas spokesman in Gaza, *al-Quds al-Arabi,* and *al-Hayat,* April 22, 1997, quoted in FBIS-NESA, *Daily Report,* April 24, 1997

Islam does not permit giving up one inch of Palestine and states that Palestine belongs to the Muslims, belongs to the Palestinian people, not to the Jews. This is the Islamic position, which says that if one inch of the Muslims' land is occupied they must liberate it. When they (Arafat and the PLO) speak of Oslo, they speak of a Palestinian state in the West Bank and Gaza with [East] Jerusalem as its capital while giving up the rest of Palestine. Oslo boils down to relinquishing Palestine, . . . bartering land for land to which I am entitled is not liberation and is not permissible in Islam.

Khalid Mishal, Hamas leader in Jordan, *al-Istiqlal* (Gaza), January 29, 1999, quoted in FBIS-NESA, *Daily Report,* February 2, 1999

First, the suspension of the Wye River [October 1999] agreement [doc. 139]was the result of Israeli differences over the implementation of the agreement. Second, the next five months or more after the elections and the formation of a new coalition will witness complete and real suspension of negotiations on the Palestinian track. In spite of this Zionist procrastination, the PA [Palestinian Authority] merely waits and watches and this certainly confirms its incapacity and that it is captive and forcibly linked to the internal Israeli political bandwagon and to U.S. pressures. Third, regardless of which political side wins in Israel—whether the Likud, Labor, or so-called centrists—extremism would prevail.

Furthermore, the stands of the main parties on the major final status issues such as Jerusalem, the settlements, borders, refugees, and other difficult and complicated issues are similar to a great extent. Thus, we conclude that it would be a kind of delusion to pin any optimism or hopes on the outcome of the [May 1999] Israeli elections. Instead of wasting another year of fumbling and waiting, therefore, the PA should look for new options, reconsider its rash positions on negotiations, and be biased in favor of our people and their aspirations and options.

137

Oslo II Accords between Israel and the Palestine Liberation Organization

September 28, 1995

Signed on September 28, 1995, the Israeli-Palestinian Interim Agreement on the West Bank and the Gaza Strip (also known as Oslo II), stipulated the major structural arrangements of the Palestinian Authority to be, as well as various arrangements between the Palestinian Authority and Israel such as security and economic relations, as well as Israeli transfer of powers. The agreement concluded the first phase of Israeli-Palestinian negotiations, the phase dealing with the interim period, and expanded the authority granted to the Palestinians in the previous interim phase agreements.

As part of the peace process begun in the Madrid conference in October 1991 [doc. 118], the Israeli Government and the PLO [Palestine Liberation Organization], the representative of the Palestinian people, reaffirm their resolute decision to put an end to the decades-long conflict and to coexist in peace . . . and their recognition of the political and legitimate rights of each side and their wish to attain a comprehensive permanent and just peace . . . recognize the fact that the peace process is irreversible and that the purpose of the Israeli-Palestinian negotiations is to

Source: *Maariv,* September 20, 1995.

establish a Palestinian self-rule authority for the interim period; namely, an elected council and an elected *ra'is* [president or leader] for the Palestinian people in the West Bank and the Gaza Strip for the interim period, which will not exceed five years from the day the Gaza-Jericho agreement was signed on 4 May 1994, which led to a permanent arrangement based on U.N. Security Council Resolutions 242 [doc. 68] and 338 [doc. 86].

Both sides reaffirm their understanding that the self-government arrangements for the interim period included in this agreement are an integral part of the entire peace process and that the negotiations on the permanent arrangement, which will begin no later than 4 May 1996, will lead to the implementation of Security Council Resolutions 242 and 338. Both sides agree that the elections of the Palestinian council and the *ra'is* will be a preliminary and significant interim step toward the realization of the legitimate rights of the Palestinian people and its just demands and will provide a democratic basis for the establishment of Palestinian institutions. Both sides reaffirm their mutual commitment to take immediate, efficient, and effective action against terror activities or threats, violence, and incitement by either Palestinians or Israelis.

Security Appendix

The first stage of the IDF [Israel Defense Forces] redeployment includes populated areas in the West Bank: cities, villages, refugee camps, etc., as detailed in the security appendix, and it will be completed twenty-two days before the elections to the Palestinian council. The rest of the redeployment will be effected gradually after the establishment of the Council, and will be completed within eighteen months from the day the Council is established. The Palestinian Police will deploy and be responsible for public order and internal security among the Palestinians. Israel will continue to bear responsibility for external security, as well as for the overall security of the Israelis.

Upon the signing of the agreement, an Israel-Palestinian cooperation and coordination mechanism on security issues will be formed. It will be headed by a joint committee for coordination and cooperation which will meet on a biweekly basis. Two regional security committees (in Gaza and the West Bank) will be subordinate to it. All these bodies will determine their modus operandi on their own. The regional coordination offices will be informed about any development in the field which might affect one of the sides, such as terror actions, blocking of roads, and hospitalization of Israelis in Palestinian hospitals (and vice versa). The same offices will also be responsible for the joint patrols.

While in the cities, responsibility for security will lie with the Palestinians alone, Israel proposes that in the villages and small towns the Palestinian Police see to law and order among the Palestinians, while the Israeli forces defend Israeli citizens from terrorist actions. The Palestinian Authority [PA] will be in charge of security in the Jewish Holy Sites, but a motorized unit (a type of joint patrol) will operate nearby. Israel also wants plain-clothes Israeli policemen to be present in those places.

As for the roads: Israel will provide a safe passage through its territory between both parts of the PA at least ten hours a day. At the same time, Israel retains the right to prevent free passage from anybody abusing this right. Those not allowed to enter Israel will be transported in police-escorted buses twice a week.

Israeli vehicles driving in the West Bank will be stopped only for documentation checks, and only by a joint patrol. On other roads, the Palestinian Police will be allowed to stop Israeli cars for identification only. The Palestinians will not be allowed to stop or incarcerate Israelis under any circumstances whatsoever, but they will be allowed to detain Israelis who violate the law, while seeing to their safety until the arrival of the joint patrol.

Legal Appendix

The Palestinian Council's criminal jurisdiction will apply to any offense committed by Palestinians and/or non-Israelis in all areas of the PA, excluding settlements, army bases, and Area C. It will also apply to offenses involving Palestinians and their visitors outside the PA's boundaries, excluding issues pertaining to Israel's security, as well as to offenses committed by Israelis doing continuing business within the boundaries of the PA, including Israeli-owned firms. Israel retains the right to arrest suspects who commit offenses cited in the Israeli penal code within the boundaries of the PA when the offender is an Israeli. In the event of an offense within the boundaries of the PA against Israel or Israelis, the Palestinian Council will inform Israel about the outcome of the investigation and the legal proceedings. In addition to that, Israel retains its criminal jurisdiction with regard to offenses committed within the boundaries of the PA against Israel or Israelis. Tourists who commit offenses within the boundaries of the PA will be detained by the Palestinians until the arrival of the Israeli forces, who will deal with them from that point onward.

Israel demands that the PA hand over to it without any delay any offender suspected of having committed any offense which falls within Israel's exclusive jurisdiction. For its part, Israel proposes to extradite to the Palestinians any non-Israeli charged with an offense which falls within the Palestinian Council's jurisdiction, on condition that it is not a security-related offense. Both sides will prevent people sought by the other side from leaving their territory.

The Palestinians are entitled to request the extradition of wanted non-Israelis, while Israel is entitled to request the extradition of an offender encountered within the boundaries of the PA. The extradition request must include a court-issued arrest warrant. A person facing a death sentence will not be extradited under any circumstances, unless the side requesting the extradition pledges not to sentence him to death.

Civilian Appendix

The civilian appendix defines the various powers that will be transferred to the PA and the way in which they will be transferred. A joint Israeli-Palestinian coordination and cooperation committee will decide on civilian issues pertaining to both sides. In the area of agriculture, the Palestinians will receive very broad powers, including the authority to issue licenses and to oversee the marketing of agricultural products (including imports and exports), veterinary services, irrigation, etc., archeology, banking and finances, civil administration workers, trade and industry, employment, gas, oil, and fuel, land and real estate. In addition the agreement covers all areas of administration: health, insurance, internal affairs, labor issues, land registration, judicial administration, local government, nature reserves, parks, regional and industrial planning, population registry and identification, postal services, public works and construction, quarries, minerals, land mining, religious affairs, social welfare, statistics, telecommunications, tourism, transportation, treasury, water, and sewage.

Economic Appendix

Mutual tax exemptions will go into effect as soon as the IDF redeployment is completed; namely, no later than twenty-two days before the Palestinian elections. At the same time, Israel is prepared to take the PA's needs into consideration and in the two months after the signing of the agreement transfer to it 50 percent of the tax revenues on goods shipped to the West Bank and on fuel purchased by the Palestinians for the West Bank, as well as 100 percent of the tax revenues collected between the last transfer and the aforementioned date. Israel will also transfer to the PA 15 million shekels as an advance payment on the surplus budget of the Civil Administration, and 12 million shekels to cover the expenses of the eight powers which were handed over to the PA as of 1 September

1995. Israel will deduct 3 percent from each transfer of import taxes and other indirect taxes to cover collection expenses.

Elections Appendix

Pursuant to Chapter 3 of the Declaration of Principles [DOP] and in accordance with the stipulations in this appendix, direct, free, and general elections to the council and the job of *ra'is* will be held simultaneously. The right to vote will be general, regardless of gender, race, religion, opinion, social background, education, or status. Every eligible voter will be entitled to register. In order to enter the voter registry, eligible voters must be Palestinian, over the age of 17, reside in the voting area where they are registered, and appear in the population registry of the PA or the Israeli authorities. The election process will be open to international supervision, in accordance with accepted international norms. A certain number of Palestinians in Jerusalem will vote in post offices in Jerusalem. The elections will be held as soon as possible after the IDF redeployment.

The council and the *ra'is* will be elected directly and simultaneously by the Palestinian people in the West Bank, Jerusalem, and Gaza for an interim period that will not exceed five years from the signing of the Gaza-Jericho Agreement on 4 May 1994. The council, in its executive role, will be responsible for the operation of the offices, services, and departments that will be handed over to it and will decide on its modus operandi and decision-making process. A committee that will serve as an executive authority will be set up within the council. The *ra'is* will be an ex-officio member of the executive authority. All other members of the executive authority will be members of the council. They will be chosen by the *ra'is,* who will submit them to the council for approval. The *ra'is* will be entitled to appoint several members who will not be members of the council—these will not exceed 20 percent of the total number of members of the executive authority—to jobs in the executive authority. These members will not be allowed to vote in the council's sessions. Members of the executive authority not elected to the council must have a residence address within the boundaries of the PA. The president of the council will also be the president of the executive authority and will assign portfolios to members of the executive authority. The powers and jurisdiction of the executive authority: The council will have legislative and executive powers. The executive powers will apply to all the issues within its boundaries according to the agreement, including the power to formulate and conduct a Palestinian policy and responsibility for its implementation.

According to the DOP, the council will have no powers or responsibility over foreign relations, including the establishment of embassies, consulates, or any other type of foreign diplomatic legations abroad, or to permit their establishment in the West Bank or the Gaza Strip. At the same time, the PLO will be entitled to conduct negotiations and sign agreements with countries or international bodies on behalf of the council, such as: economic accords; agreements with donor countries; agreements on the execution of development projects in the region; as well as cultural, scientific, and educational agreements. Within its boundaries, the council will have an independent judicial system of Palestinian courts and tribunals.

Cooperation Appendix

The main areas of cooperation planned are: preservation of the environment, economy, science and technology, culture, and education. This cooperation will consist of joint economic enterprises, transfer of agricultural know-how, development and implementation of methods for the handling of toxic and dangerous materials, and the development of environmental-friendly energy sources. A permanent cooperation committee will be established to that end, which will decide on its working procedures on its own.

138

Palestinian Authority

Amendment to the Palestine National Charter

May 4, 1996

On April 24, 1996, the Palestinian National Council amended the Palestine National Charter (doc. 69), omitting those sections that contradicted the Israeli-Palestinian peace accords (docs. 133, 137) signed earlier that decade. The amendment was a fulfillment of a commitment the Palestine Liberation Organization undertook in a September 9, 1993, letter from Chairman Yasir Arafat to Israeli Prime Minister Yitzhak Rabin, which was sent alongside the Declaration of Principles the two sides signed on the same day. However, it took considerable Israeli and American pressure on the Palestinians to secure the changes. Moreover, the United States and Israel argued that the general language did not suffice, and under further U.S. pressure (and an impending visit to Gaza by U.S. President Bill Clinton), the Palestinians undertook a number of clarifiations. On January 22, 1998, Arafat sent a letter to Clinton outlining the implications of the council's decision. On December 7, 1998, the Executive Committee of the PLO reaffirmed Arafat's letter. Three days later, the PLO's Central Council also reaffirmed it.

Letter from Palestinian Authority President Yasir Arafat to Prime Minister Shimon Peres

May 4, 1996

Mr. Shimon Peres
Prime Minister of Israel

Dear Mr. Peres,

I convey my best wishes to your excellency, and I would like to convey to you the recent historical resolution adopted by the Palestinian National Council [PNC] at its 21st session held in Gaza City.

As part of our commitment to the peace process, and in adhering to the mutual recognition between the Palestinian Liberation Organization and the Government of Israel, the PNC was held in Gaza City between 22 of April 1996, and in an extraordinary session decided that the Palestine National Charter is hereby amended by cancelling the provisions that are contrary to the letters exchanged between the PLO and the government of Israel on 9/10 Sept. 1993.

Please find enclosed copies of the official Arabic and English texts of the PNC's resolutions.

We remain committed to the peace process.

Yasir Arafat
Chairman of the Executive Committee of
Palestine Liberation Organization
President of the Palestinian National Authority

Source: Permanent Observer Mission of the PLO to the United Nations, http://www.palestine-un.org/plo/pna_one.html (accessed September 11, 2006).

Official Translation

The Palestinian National Council, at its 21st session held in the city of Gaza,

Emanating from the declaration of independence and the political statement adopted at its 19th session held in Algiers on Nov. 15, 1988, which affirmed the resolution of conflicts by peaceful means and accepted the two states solution,

And based on the introduction of the Declaration of Principles signed in Washington D.C. on 13 September 1993 [doc. 133], which included the agreement of both sides to put an end to decades of confrontation and conflict and to live in peaceful coexistence, mutual dignity and security, while recognizing their mutual legitimate and political right,

And reaffirming their desire to achieve a just and comprehensive peace settlement and historic reconciliation through the agreed political process,

And based on international legitimacy represented by the United Nations Resolutions relevant to the Palestinian question, including those relating to Jerusalem, Refugees and Settlements, and the other issues of the permanent status and the implementation of Security Council Resolutions 242 and 338,

And affirming the adherence of the Palestine Liberation Organization to its commitments deriving from the DOP [Declaration of Principles] (Oslo 1), the provisional Cairo Agreement, the letter of mutual recognition signed on 9 and 10 September 1993, the Israeli-Palestinian Interim Agreement on the West Bank and the Gaza Strip (Oslo 2) signed in Washington D.C. on 28 September 1995, and reconfirm the resolution of the central Council of the PLO adopted in October 1993, which approved the Oslo Agreement and all its annexes,

And based on the principles which constituted the foundation of the Madrid Peace Conference and the Washington negotiations, decides:

1. The Palestinian National Charter is hereby amended by canceling the articles that are contrary to the letters exchanged between the PLO and the Government of Israel 9–10 September 1993.
2. Assigns its legal committee with the task of redrafting the Palestinian National Charter in order to present it at the first session of the Palestinian central council.

139

Wye River Memorandum between Israel and the Palestine Liberation Organization

October 23, 1998

Signed on October 23, 1998, the Wye River Memorandum was one of a few Israeli-Palestinian agreements that dealt with implementing the already agreed upon interim phase. These were needed as the sides lost trust in each other. Wye River, named after the venue of the talks in Maryland, was one of the few agreements from the Oslo era that was signed by a Likud-led government.

Source: *Mideast Mirror*, October 26, 1998. Copyright © *Mideast Mirror*. Reprinted by permission.

By negotiating with the Palestinians and signing an accord with them, as was done in this memorandum, Israeli Prime Minister Benjamin Netanyahu contributed to public legitimacy of the controversial peace process with the Palestinians and moved his party, Likud, to a more centrist political position. The memorandum also reflected both sides' interest in a growing American role and it included provisions that assigned U.S. Central Intelligence Agency personnel to verification roles.

The following are steps to facilitate implementation of the Interim Agreement on the West Bank and Gaza Strip of September 28, 1995 [doc. 137] (the "Interim Agreement"), and other related agreements including the Note for the Record of January 17, 1997 (hereinafter referred to as "the prior agreements"), so that the Israeli and Palestinian sides can more effectively carry out their reciprocal responsibilities, including those relating to further redeployments and security respectively.

These steps are to be carried out in a parallel phased approach in accordance with this Memorandum and the attached time line. They are subject to the relevant terms and conditions of the prior agreements and do not supersede their other requirements.

I. Further Redeployments [FRDs]

A. Phase One and Two Further Redeployments

1. Pursuant to the Interim Agreement and subsequent agreements, the Israeli side's implementation of the first and second FRD will consist of the transfer to the Palestinian side of 13 percent from Area C as follows:
—1 percent to Area (A)
—12 percent to Area (B). . . .
2. As part of the foregoing implementation of the first and second FRD, 14.2 percent from Area (B) will become Area (A).

B. Third Phase of Further Redeployments
With regard to the terms of the Interim Agreement and of Secretary [of State Warren] Christopher's letters to the two sides of January 17, 1997, relating to the further redeployment process, there will be a committee to address this question. The United States will be briefed regularly.

II. Security

In the provisions on security arrangements of the Interim Agreement, the Palestinian side agreed to take all measures necessary in order to prevent acts of terrorism, crime and hostilities directed against the Israeli side, against individuals falling under the Israeli side's authority and against their property, just as the Israeli side agreed to take all measures necessary in order to prevent acts of terrorism, crime and hostilities directed against the Palestinian side, against individuals falling under the Palestinian side's authority and against their property. The two sides also agreed to take legal measures against offenders within their jurisdiction and to prevent incitement against each other by any organization, groups or individuals within their jurisdiction.

Both sides recognize that it is in their vital interests to combat terrorism and fight violence in accordance with Annex I of the Interim Agreement and the Note for the Record. They also recognize that the struggle against terror and violence must be comprehensive in that it deals with terrorists, the terror support structure, and the environment conducive to the support of terror. It must be continuous and constant over a long term, in that there can be no pauses in the work against terrorists and their structure. It must be cooperative in that no effort can be fully effective without Israeli-Palestinian cooperation and the continuous exchange of information, concepts, and actions.

Pursuant to the prior agreements, the Palestinian side's implementation of its responsibilities for security, security cooperation, and other issues will be as detailed below during the time periods specified in the attached time line:

A. Security Actions

1. Outlawing and Combating Terrorist Organizations
   - (a) The Palestinian side will make known its policy of zero tolerance for terror and violence against both sides.
   - (b) A work plan developed by the Palestinian side will be shared with the U.S. and thereafter implementation will begin immediately to ensure the systematic and effective combat of terrorist organizations and their infrastructure.
   - (c) In addition to the bilateral Israeli-Palestinian security cooperation, a U.S.-Palestinian committee will meet biweekly to review the steps being taken to eliminate terrorist cells and the support structure that plans, finances, supplies, and abets terror. In these meetings, the Palestinian side will inform the U.S. fully of the actions it has taken to outlaw all organizations (or wings of organizations, as appropriate) of a military, terrorist or violent character and their support structure and to prevent them from operating in areas under its jurisdiction.
   - (d) The Palestinian side will apprehend the specific individuals suspected of perpetrating acts of violence and terror for the purpose of further investigation, and prosecution and punishment of all persons involved in acts of violence and terror.
   - (e) A U.S.-Palestinian committee will meet to review and evaluate information pertinent to the decisions on prosecution, punishment or other legal measures which affect the status of individuals suspected of abetting or perpetrating acts of violence and terror.
2. Prohibiting Illegal Weapons
   - (a) The Palestinian side will ensure an effective legal framework is in place to criminalize, in conformity with the prior agreements, any importation, manufacturing or unlicensed sale, acquisition or possession of firearms, ammunition or weapons in areas under Palestinian jurisdiction.
   - (b) In addition, the Palestinian side will establish and vigorously and continuously implement a systematic program for the collection and appropriate handling of all such illegal items in accordance with the prior agreements. The U.S. has agreed to assist in carrying out this program.
   - (c) A U.S.-Palestinian-Israeli committee will be established to assist and enhance cooperation in preventing the smuggling or other unauthorized introduction of weapons or explosive materials into areas under Palestinian jurisdiction.
3. Prevention Incitement
   - (a) Drawing on relevant international practice and pursuant to Article XXII (1) of the Interim Agreement and the Note for the Record, the Palestinian side will issue a decree prohibiting all forms of incitement to violence or terror, and establishing mechanisms for acting systematically against all expressions or

threats of violence or terror. This decree will be comparable to the existing Israeli legislation which deals with the same subject.

(b) A U.S.-Palestinian-Israeli committee will meet on a regular basis to monitor cases of possible incitement to violence or terror and to make recommendations and reports on how to prevent such incitement. The Israeli, Palestinian and U.S. sides will each appoint a media specialist, a law enforcement representative, an educational specialist, and a current or former elected official to the committee.

B. Security Cooperation

The two sides agree that their security cooperation will be based on a spirit of partnership and will include, among other things, the following steps:

1. Bilateral Cooperation. There will be full bilateral security cooperation between the two sides which will be continuous, intensive, and comprehensive.
2. Forensic Cooperation. There will be an exchange of forensic expertise, training, and other assistance.
3. Trilateral Committee. In addition to the bilateral Israeli-Palestinian security cooperation, a high-ranking U.S.-Palestinian-Israeli committee will meet as required and not less than biweekly to assess current threats, deal with any impediments to effective security cooperation and coordination, and address the steps being taken to combat terror and terrorist organizations. The committee will also serve as a forum to address the issue of external support for terror. In these meetings, the Palestinian side will fully inform the members of the committee of the results of its investigations concerning terrorist suspects already in custody and the participants will exchange additional relevant information. The committee will report regularly to the leaders of the two sides on the status of cooperation, the results of the meetings and its recommendations.

C. Other Issues

1. Palestinian Police Force
   (a) The Palestinian side will provide a list of its policemen to the Israeli side in conformity with the prior agreements.
   (b) Should the Palestinian side request technical assistance, the U.S. has indicated its willingness to help meet those needs in cooperation with other donors.
   (c) The Monitoring and Steering Committee will, as part of its functions, monitor the implementation of this provision and brief the U.S.
2. PLO Charter. The Executive Committee of the Palestine Liberation Organization and the Palestinian Central Council will reaffirm the letter of 22 January 1998 from PLO Chairman Yasir Arafat to President [William] Clinton concerning the nullification of the Palestinian National Charter provisions that are inconsistent with the letters exchanged between the PLO and the Government of Israel on 9–10 September 1993. PLO Chairman Arafat, the Speaker of the Palestine National Council [PNC], and the Speaker of the Palestinian Council will invite the members of the PNC, as well as the members of the Central Council, the Council, and the Palestinian Heads of Ministries to a meeting to be addressed by President Clinton to reaffirm their support for the peace process and the aforementioned decisions of the Executive Committee and the Central Council.

3. Legal Assistance in Criminal Matters. Among other forms of legal assistance in criminal matters, the requests for arrest and transfer of suspects and defendants pursuant to Article II (7) of Annex IV of the Interim Agreement will be submitted (or resubmitted) through the mechanism of the Joint Israeli-Palestinian Legal Committee and will be responded to in conformity with Article II (7) (f) of Annex IV of the Interim Agreement within the twelve-week period. Requests submitted after the eighth week will be responded to in conformity with Article II (7) (f) within four weeks of their submission. The United States has been requested by the sides to report on a regular basis on the steps being taken to respond to the above requests.
4. Human Rights and the Rule of Law. Pursuant to Article XI (1) of Annex I of the Interim Agreement, and without derogating from the above, the Palestinian Police will exercise powers and responsibilities to implement this Memorandum with due regard to internationally accepted norms of human rights and the rule of law, and will be guided by the need to protect the public, respect human dignity, and avoid harassment.

III. Interim Committees and Economic Issues

1. The Israeli and Palestinian sides reaffirm their commitment to enhancing their relationship and agree on the need actively to promote economic development in the West Bank and Gaza. In this regard, the parties agree to continue or to reactivate all standing committees established by the Interim Agreement, including the Monitoring and Steering Committee, the Joint Economic Committee (JEC), the Civil Affairs Committee (CAC), the Legal Committee, and the Standing Cooperation Committee.
2. The Israeli and Palestinian sides have agreed on arrangements which will permit the timely opening of the Gaza Industrial Estate. They also have concluded a "Protocol Regarding the Establishment and Operation of the International Airport in the Gaza Strip During the Interim Period."
3. Both sides will renew negotiations on Safe Passage immediately. As regards the southern route, the sides will make best efforts to conclude the agreement within a week of the entry into force of this Memorandum. Operation of the southern route will start as soon as possible thereafter. As regards the northern route, negotiations will continue with the goal of reaching agreement as soon as possible. Implementation will take place expeditiously thereafter.
4. The Israeli and Palestinian sides acknowledge the great importance of the Port of Gaza for the development of the Palestinian economy, and the expansion of Palestinian trade. They commit themselves to proceeding without delay to conclude an agreement to allow the construction and operation of the port in accordance with the prior agreements. The Israeli-Palestinian Committee will reactivate its work immediately with a goal of concluding the protocol within sixty days, which will allow the commencement of the construction of the port.
5. The two sides recognize that unresolved legal issues adversely affect the relationship between the two peoples. They therefore will accelerate efforts through the Legal Committee to address outstanding legal issues and to

implement solutions to these issues in the shortest possible period. The Palestinian side will provide to the Israeli side copies of all of its laws in effect.

6. The Israeli and Palestinian sides also will launch a strategic economic dialogue to enhance their economic relationship. They will establish within the framework of the JEC an Ad Hoc Committee for this purpose.
   The committee will review the following four issues:
   (1) Israeli purchase taxes;
   (2) cooperation in combating vehicle theft;
   (3) dealing with unpaid Palestinian debts; and
   (4) the impact of Israeli standards as barriers to trade and the expansion of the A1 and A2 lists. The committee will submit an interim report within three weeks of the entry into force of this Memorandum, and within six weeks will submit its conclusions and recommendations to be implemented.
7. The two sides agree on the importance of continued international donor assistance to facilitate implementation by both sides of agreements reached. They also recognize the need for enhanced donor support for economic development in the West Bank and Gaza. They agree to jointly approach the donor community to organize a Ministerial Conference before the end of 1998 to seek pledges for enhanced levels of assistance.

IV. Permanent Status Negotiations

The two sides will immediately resume permanent status negotiations on an accelerated basis and will make a determined effort to achieve the mutual goal of reaching an agreement by May 4, 1999. The negotiations will be continuous and without interruption. The United States has expressed its willingness to facilitate these negotiations.

V. Unilateral Actions

Recognizing the necessity to create a positive environment for the negotiations, neither side shall initiate or take any step that will change the status of the West Bank and the Gaza Strip in accordance with the Interim Agreement. . . .

Time Line

Parenthetical references below are to paragraphs in "The Wye River Memorandum" to which this time line is an integral attachment. Topics not included in the time line follow the schedule provided for in the text of the memorandum.

1. Upon Entry into Force of the Memorandum:
   - Third further redeployment committee starts (I (B))
   - Palestinian security work plan shared with the U.S. (II(A)(1)(b))
   - Full bilateral security cooperation (II (B)(1))
   - Trilateral security cooperation committee starts (II (B)(3))
   - Interim committees resume and continue; Ad Hoc Economic Committee starts (III)
   - Accelerated permanent status negotiations start (IV)
2. Entry into Force—Week 2:
   - Security work plan implementation begins (II (A)(1)(b)); (II (A)(1)(c)) committee starts
   - Illegal weapons framework in place (II (A)(2)(a)); Palestinian implementation report (II (A)(2)(b);
   - Anti-incitement committee starts (II (A)(3)(b)); decree issued (II (A)(3)(a))
   - PLO Executive Committee reaffirms Charter letter (II (C)(2))
   - Stage 1 of F.R.D. implementation: 2

percent C to B, 7.1 percent B. to A. Israeli officials acquaint their Palestinian counterparts as required with areas; F.R.D. carried out; report on F.R.D. implementation (I(A))

3. Week 2–6:
   - Palestinian Central Council reaffirms Charter letter (weeks two to four) (II (C))2))
   - PNC and other PLO organizations reaffirm Charter letter (weeks four to six) (II (C)(2))
   - Establishment of weapons collection program (II (A)(2)(b)) and collection stage (II (A)(2)(c)); committee starts and reports on activities
   - Anti-incitement committee report (II (A)(3)(b))
   - Ad Hoc Economic Committee: interim report at week three; final report at week six (III)
   - Policemen list (II (C)(1)(a)), Monitoring and Steering Committee review starts (II (C)(1)(c))
   - Stage 2 of F.R.D. implementation: 5 percent C to B. Israeli officials acquaint their Palestinian counterparts as required with areas; F.R.D. carried out; report on F.R.D. implementation (I (A))
4. Week 6–12:
   - Weapons collection stage (II (A)(2)(b)); (II (A)(2)(c)) committee report on its activities.
   - Anti-Incitement committees report (II (A)(3)(b))
   - Monitoring and Steering Committee briefs U.S. on policemen list (II (C)(1)(c))
   - Stage 3 of F.R.D. implementation: 5 percent C to B, 1 percent C to A, 7.1 percent B to A
   - Israeli officials acquaint Palestinian counterparts as required with areas; F.R.D. carried out; report on F.R.D. implementation (I (A))
5. After Week 12:
   Activities described in the Memorandum continue as appropriate and if necessary, including;
   - Trilaterial security cooperation committee (II (B)(3))
   - (II (A)(1)(c)) committee
   - (II (A)(1)(e)) committee
   - Anti-incitement committee (II (A)(3)(b))
   - Third Phase F.R.D. Committee (I (B))—Interim Committees (III)
   - Accelerated permanent status negotiations (IV)

140
Mahmoud Darwish
The Appeal of the Palestinian People on the Fiftieth Anniversary of *al-Naqba*
1948–1998

Mahmoud Darwish is perhaps the best-known Palestinian poet of our times. Born in 1942, Darwish grew up in Israel and left the country in 1971 in order to work for the Palestine Liberation Organization in Beirut. In 1987 he was made a member of the PLO's executive, but he resigned in 1993 in a protest against the Oslo Accords [doc. 133].

The following text was written by Darwish as part of the fiftieth anniversary of the 1948–49 War of Independence, known to Palestinians as al-naqba *(the Catastrophe). The text was broadcast on Radio Palestine on May 14, 1998.*

We, the Palestinian offspring of this sacred land, advocates of universal values, seekers of peace and freedom, the living testament of endurance and human dignity in the face of adversity, victims of half a century of perpetual night of occupation and dispersion—Declare our resounding presence in time and place, despite all attempts to uproot us from the land which has borne our name from the beginning of time. Not emerging from the darkness of myth or legend, we were born in the pristine daylight of history on this land which gave birth to the most ancient of civilizations. On this land humanity found its way to building its first home, to planting its first wheat grain, to creating its first alphabet. From the hills of Jerusalem, the first prayers of gratitude rose to the Creator. Our land, modest in size, hosted vast cultures and civilizations, both in conflict and in harmony, our own culture emerging from the fullness of this diverse and rich heritage. Our human history began with the history of humanity. Our Arab history began with the history of the Arabs. The consciousness of our national history began with our resistance to conquest and greed, which beset our land.

Today, as we confront half a century of *naqba* and resistance, pained at the continuing tragedy of our recent past, we cast our sights to the future that we are molding in hope and in the promise of freedom and justice. For we have vanquished all attempts at our obliteration and denial and at the eradication of the name of Palestine from the map of Palestine. On the fiftieth anniversary of one of the greatest crimes of the age, committed against the gentle people and land of Palestine, we stand in reverence in the sight of the martyrs who had offered their lives as a libation to the continuity of the land and its immortal name, in defense of our identity and sovereign existence on our land—a land infused with the words of God to humanity as with our ancestral blood.

From the bereavement of mothers, to the captivity of prisoners, to the exile of generations,

Source: Written by Mahmoud Darwish, and delivered on May 14, 1998, http://www.arabicnews.com/ansub/Daily/Day/1980514/1998051435.html.

we stand in awe at the heroism of the ordinary individual and the collective will to endure, both Palestinian and Arab. Victims of a myth "A land without a people for a people without a land," we dared to intrude on the course of history and expose the falsehood that sought our denial. Slated for national obliteration and severance from the land, we have affirmed our identity and ties to our homeland, snatching our reality from the jaws of oblivion.

Four hundred and eighteen living and thriving Palestinian villages were razed to the ground in 1948 by the Zionist perpetrators of the myth and the crime. Terrorized, massacred, and expelled, most of the Palestinian nation was reduced to the status of refugees and stateless persons at the mercy of various host countries. Bereft of their birthright, the Palestinian refugees carried Palestine in their hearts along with their land deeds and the keys to their homes. Both the topography and demography of our reality remain alive in our collective memory and continuity. We have refused to adopt their distorted version of our history and we remain advocates and witnesses of the authentic narrative of Palestinian endurance and the will to live.

From revolution, to *intifada,* to nation building, we have extracted recognition from the world. The dual injustice of exile and occupation could not break the will of a people bent on achieving freedom, dignity, and the redemption of history. Thus, it was the PLO [Palestine Liberation Organization] which first offered the olive branch as a genuine alternative to the gun. Peace was in sight, but not appeasement or capitulation. The PLO, the embodiment of our collective national identity, the guardian of the integrity of our past and the vehicle to the fulfillment of our future, has ensured the independence of our utterance and our will and has shaped the course of our destiny. It obtained recognition from the international community for the Palestinian people's right to self-determination and the right of return as anchors to secure us against the gales of loss and denial. Above all, Jerusalem, more than a right, is the soul of our being and the essence of harmony.

Our commitment to democracy and the politics of inclusion were expressed in the PLO's historic proposal of a secular, pluralistic, democratic state in Palestine. While Zionism insisted on a racist exclusivity which denied the humanity and rights of the other, we sought to affirm tolerance and celebrate diversity. The inclusive sharing of the historical land of Palestine having been denied by the Israeli drive for exclusive possession, we formulated the alternative of sharing the land on the basis of the two state solution. Such a solution would meet the imperative of international legality as defined by U.N. Resolution 181 [doc. 19], and would grant the Palestinian people relative justice on their land. It would also grant reprieve for tortured Jerusalem to be celebrated as an eternal city and our eternal capital.

The transition from the historical memory of Palestine as a homeland to the collective endeavor to establish Palestine as a geo-political state on part of historical Palestine, signals a painful and difficult transformation in the political discourse as well as in the national ethos of the Palestinian people. While it demands recognition as a conciliatory compromise of historical magnitude, it must not be misconstrued as self-negation or weakness. Rather, it demands an immediate and unequivocal recognition of our legitimacy and right to sovereignty as a nation among equals. The vision, courage, and moral magnanimity of the victim reaching out to the oppressor must not be met with further rejection, denial, and victimization.

The world now is called upon to undertake not only a recognition of guilt and admission of culpability in relation to the Palestinian people, but also to undertake an active and massive process of rectification to secure the implementation of Palestinian rights. The international community is called upon to intervene effectively to rescue the peace process in the face of current Israeli extremism and politics of threat, intimidation, and power, rather that succumbing to Israeli demands, pressures, and unilateral policies and measures. In pursuing a policy of colonization and land confiscation, reneging on signed agreements, negating the terms of reference to the peace process, violating the timetable and denying the agenda of permanent status talks, while continuing the imposition of collective punitive measures on the Palestinian people, Israel is not only attempting to derail the peace process but also to destroy any prospects of peace in the future. In reviving fundamentalism, hostility, and distrust, Israel is also drawing the whole region outside the course of contemporary history and into an anachronistic future of conflict and violence.

True stability, security, and prosperity can emanate only from a genuine peace which incorporates the basic principle of justice. Such is the Palestinian vision and the Palestinian collective endeavor. No amount of pain or suffering can justify the victimization and infliction of injustice on others. While we extend a compassionate recognition of the unspeakable Jewish suffering during the horror of the Holocaust, we find it unconscionable that the suffering of our people be denied or even rationalized. As victims, we seek to prevent the recurrence of pain, regardless of the identity of the perpetrator or the recipient. No country or nation must pretend to be, or must be perceived to be, above the law or beyond accountability. If Israel seeks recognition and legitimacy then it must comply with the norms and laws that govern the behavior of civilized nations. The arrogance of power may prevail, but only temporarily. Only a just peace can lay claim to durability and permanence.

We do not seek to be captives of history or victims of the past. The Palestinian people have launched a redemptive journey to the future. From the ashes of our sorrow and loss, we are resurrecting a nation celebrating life and hope. We will not surrender. Nor will we lose faith in a just and genuine peace that will enable us to exercise our right to independence and sovereignty. Fifty years since the Nakba were not spent in grief over a painful memory. The past has not entirely departed, nor has the future entirely arrived yet. The present is an open potential to struggle. For fifty years, Palestinian history has stood witness to epics of perseverance and resistance, to confronting the implications, consequences, and injustices of the Nakba. For half a century Palestinian history became a living pledge to future generations for their right to a life of freedom and dignity on their own land. We have begun painstakingly the nation-building process, to ensure a free homeland for a free people. The state of Palestine is returning to contemporary history after fifty years of forced eviction, a state embodying the principles and practice of democracy, separation of powers, human rights, gender equality, accountability, and the rule of law. Despite the present constraints of geography and transition, our vision remains expansive and unfettered. For we thrive on the spirit of resistance and the longing for freedom, motivated by that will which produced the luminous flame of the Intifada. Born in Palestine, no other land gave us birth. No other can claim our future. Nor can Jerusalem be replaced as our capital or extracted from our land and our being: It is the home of our souls and the soul of our homeland, forever.

141

Government of Israel

Resolution on Withdrawal from Lebanon

March 5, 2000

While the bulk of Israeli forces withdrew from Lebanon in 1985, Israel kept a self-declared security zone in the southern part of the country where Israeli forces remained deployed to thwart attacks by the Shiite organization Hezbollah. As the Israeli death toll rose as a result of Hezbollah's increased attacks in the late 1990s, more and more Israelis became skeptical of the security necessity of holding on to the region. In 1998 the Israeli government adopted Security Council Resolution 425 (doc. 102), and in 1999 the Labor candidate for prime minister, Ehud Barak, committed to leaving Lebanon within the first year of his administration. Once elected, Barak was hoping to carry out the withdrawal as part of a peace agreement with Syria, which, in effect, controlled Lebanon. However, once Israel realized in March 2000 that a peace agreement with Syria was unlikely, it moved ahead with a unilateral withdrawal, which was completed on May 24, 2000. On June 16, 2000, the secretary-general of the United Nations reported to the Security Council that he endorsed a Lebanese government report confirming that Israel had indeed completed its withdrawal. Nevertheless, Hezbollah argued that a tiny piece of land under Israeli control, the Shaba Farms, was in fact Lebanese. The organization continued, therefore, to carry out a limited military confrontation with Israel, mostly in a restricted part of the Israeli-Lebanese border, that led to the deaths of twenty Israelis between May 2000 and June 2006, and ultimately to the Second Lebanon War in 2006.

The internal Israeli debate about the continuing presence in Lebanon brought to the forefront, for the first time in Israel's history, women's groups that lobbied for a security-related policy. A leader of the most dominant women's group, Four Mothers, even participated in the official military press conference following the withdrawal's completion.

The withdrawal, in essence, as a result of Hezbollah's military pressure on the security zone, is considered by some analysts as contributing to the Palestinian choice to turn to violence in September 2000, with the collapse of the Oslo process. Barak's decision to withdraw unilaterally and his own and Ariel Sharon's responses to Hezbollah attacks between May 2000 and July 2006 are now part of the Israeli debate over the war in 2006.

Decided, In accordance with the government's commitment on the basis of its guidelines and the announcement by the Prime Minister and Minister of Defense:

a. The Israel Defense Forces [IDF] will deploy on the border with Lebanon by July 2000, and from there will secure the safety of the northern towns and villages.
b. The government will act to ensure that this deployment will be carried out in the framework of an agreement.
c. In the event that conditions will not be conducive to IDF deployment in the framework

Source: Israel Ministry of Foreign Affairs online, March 5, 2000, http://www.mfa.gov.il/MFA/Government/Communiques/2000/Government%20of%20Israel%20Resolution%20-%2005-Mar-2000 (accessed April 1, 2005).

of an agreement, the government will convene, at an appropriate time, to discuss the method of implementation of the abovementioned decision.

d. Israel will honor its commitment toward the South Lebanese Army and the civil aid forces in Southern Lebanon.

e. The government will act to strengthen the frontline towns and villages in both the security and the socio-economic aspects.

142

William Jefferson Clinton

Proposal for Israeli-Palestinian Peace

December 23, 2000

The collapse of the Camp David summit in July 2000, the renewal of violence between Israelis and Palestinians in September 2000, and even Prime Minister Ehud Barak's weakening grip on power and eventual call for new elections, did not stop the efforts to reach a peace agreement between Israel and the Palestinians in autumn 2000 and the early winter of 2001. Following dozens of meetings in the region, and a concentrated effort between Israeli and Palestinian negotiators at Bolling Air Force Base in Washington, D.C., in December 2000, President William Jefferson Clinton presented the following ideas regarding the shape of a peace treaty between the parties. On December 27, 2000, Israel agreed to accept Clinton's ideas as a basis for negotiations, if the Palestinian side adopted a similar position. Israel also forwarded to President Clinton a memo with its substantial comments regarding his ideas.

Clinton's ideas did not lead to a peace agreement. The failure was a consequence of his waning political power in his last days in office, the uncertainty of upcoming elections in Israel, and the continuation of violence between Israelis and Palestinians. However, as no other serious blueprint was offered by any of the parties involved in the years that followed, President Clinton's proposal remained, some analysts contend, a good approximation of a future agreement or, at the least, a baseline that neither Israelis nor Palestinians would ignore when they again sit to negotiate the nature of a peace treaty.

After reading the text below to the Israeli and Palestinian delegates in the Roosevelt Room of the White House, President Clinton left the room. His aides went over the text subsequently to ensure that each side had copied the points accurately. No written text was presented. This version is derived from that published in Haaretz *(English), January 8, 2001, and a slightly more complete version issued by the Jerusalem Media and Communication Center.*

Source: Haaretz, January 8, 2001. Reprinted by permission. Jerusalem Media and Communication Center, www.jmcc.org/documents/clintonprop.htm (accessed May 21, 2007).

Territory

Based on what I heard, I believe that the solution should be in the mid-90 percents, between 94–96 percent of the West Bank territory of the Palestinian State.

The land annexed by Israel should be compensated by a land swap of 1–3 percent in addition to territorial arrangements such as a permanent safe passage.

The Parties also should consider the swap of leased land to meet their respective needs. There are creative ways of doing this that should address Palestinian and Israeli needs and concerns.

The parties should develop a map consistent with the following criteria:

- 80 percent of settlers in blocks.
- Contiguity.
- Minimize annexed areas.
- Minimize the number of Palestinians affected.

Security

The key lies in an international presence that can only be withdrawn by mutual consent. This presence will also monitor the implementation of the agreement between both sides.

My best judgment is that the Israeli presence would remain in fixed locations in the Jordan Valley under the authority of the international force for another thirty-six months. This period could be reduced in the event of favorable regional developments that diminish the threats to Israel.

On early warning stations, Israel should maintain three facilities in the West Bank with a Palestinian liaison presence. The stations will be subject to review every ten years with any changes in the status to be mutually agreed.

Regarding emergency developments, I understand that you will still have to develop a map of the relevant areas and routes. But in defining what is an emergency, I propose the following definition: Imminent and demonstrable threat to Israel's national security of a military nature that requires the activation of a national state emergency.

Of course, the international forces will need to be notified of any such determination.

On airspace, I suggest that the state of Palestine will have sovereignty over its airspace but that the two sides should work out special arrangements for Israeli training and operational needs.

I understand that the Israeli position is that Palestine should be defined as a "demilitarized state" while the Palestinian side proposes "a state with limited arms." As a compromise, I suggest calling it a "non-militarized state."

This will be consistent with the fact that in addition to strong Palestinian security forces, Palestine will have an international force for border security and deterrent purposes.

Jerusalem and Refugees

I have a sense that the remaining gaps have more to do with formulations than practical realities.

Jerusalem

The general principle is that Arab areas are Palestinian and Jewish ones are Israeli. This would apply to the Old City as well. I urge the two sides to work on maps to create maximum contiguity for both sides.

Regarding the Haram/Temple Mount, I believe that the gaps are not related to practical administration but to the symbolic issues of sovereignty and to finding a way to accord respect to the religious beliefs of both sides.

I know you have been discussing a number of formulations, and you can agree on one of these. I add to these two additional formulations guaranteeing Palestinian effective control over the Haram while respecting the conviction of the Jewish people.

Regarding either one of these two formulations will be international monitoring to provide mutual confidence.

1. Palestinian sovereignty over the Haram, and Israeli sovereignty over (a) the Western Wall and the space sacred to Judaism of which it is a part; (b) the Western Wall and the Holy of Holies of which it is a part.

   There will be a firm commitment by both not to excavate beneath the Haram or behind the Wall.
2. Palestinian sovereignty over the Haram and Israeli sovereignty over the Western Wall and shared functional sovereignty over the issue of excavation under the Haram and behind the Wall such that mutual consent would be requested before any excavation can take place.

Refugees

I sense that the differences are more relating to formulations and less to what will happen on a practical level.

I believe that Israel is prepared to acknowledge the moral and material suffering caused to the Palestinian people as a result of the 1948 war and the need to assist the international community in addressing the problem.

An international commission should be established to implement all the aspects that flow from your agreement: compensation, resettlement, rehabilitation, etc.

The United States is prepared to lead an international effort to help the refugees.

The fundamental gap is on how to handle the concept of the right of return. I know the history of the issue and how hard it will be for the Palestinian leadership to appear to be abandoning this principle.

The Israeli side could not accept any reference to a right of return that would imply a right to immigrate to Israel in defiance of Israel's sovereign policies and admission or that would threaten the Jewish character of the state.

Any solution must address both needs.

The solution will have to be consistent with the two-state approach that both sides have accepted as a way to end the Palestinian-Israeli conflict: the state of Palestine as the homeland of the Palestinian people and the state of Israel as the homeland of the Jewish people.

Under the two-state solution, the guiding principle should be that the Palestinian state would be the focal point for Palestinians who choose to return to the area without ruling out that Israel will accept some of these refugees.

I believe that we need to adopt a formulation on the right of return that will make clear that there is no specific right of return to Israel itself but that does not negate the aspiration of the Palestinian people to return to the area.

In light of the above, I propose two alternatives:

1. Both sides recognize the right of Palestinian refugees to return to historic Palestine, or,
2. Both sides recognize the right of Palestinian refugees to return to their homeland.

The agreement will define the implementation of this general right in a way that is consistent with the two-state solution. It would list the five possible homes for the refugees:

1. The state of Palestine.
2. Areas in Israel being transferred to Palestine in the land swap.
3. Rehabilitation in host country.
4. Resettlement in third country.
5. Admission to Israel.

In listing these options, the agreement will make clear that the return to the West Bank, Gaza Strip, and areas acquired in the land swap would be the right of all Palestinian refugees, while rehabilitation in host countries, resettlement in third countries and absorption into Israel will depend upon the policies of those countries.

Israel could indicate in the agreement that it intends to establish a policy so that some of the refugees would be absorbed into Israel consistent with Israel's sovereign decision.

I believe that priority should be given to the refugee population in Lebanon.

The parties would agree that this implements Resolution 194 [doc. 26].

The End of Conflict

I propose that the agreement clearly mark the end of the conflict and its implementation put an end to all claims. This could be implemented through a U.N. Security Council Resolution that notes that Resolutions 242 [doc. 68] and 338 [doc. 86] have been implemented and through the release of Palestinian prisoners.

Concluding Remarks

I believe that this is the outline of a fair and lasting agreement.

It gives the Palestinian people the ability to determine their future on their own land, a sovereign and viable state recognized by the international community, Al-Quds as its capital, sovereignty over the Haram, and new lives for the refugees.

It gives the people of Israel a genuine end to the conflict, real security, the preservation of sacred religious ties, the incorporation of 80 percent of the settlers into Israel, and the largest Jewish Jerusalem in history recognized by all as its capital.

This is the best that I can do. Brief your leaders and tell me if they are prepared to come for discussions based on these ideas. If so, I would meet them next week separately. If not, I have taken this as far as I can.

These are my ideas. If they are not accepted, they are not just off the table, they also go with me when I leave office.

143

Martin Indyk

Evolution of Palestinian-Israeli Negotiations

2000–2001: Analysis

Martin Indyk played an important role in shaping American policy toward the Middle East in the 1990s and especially regarding the peace process. He was responsible for Middle Eastern issues in the National Security Council, 1993–95, ambassador to Israel, 1995–97, 1999–2001, and assistant secretary for Near Eastern affairs in the State Department, 1997–99. In the following interview, granted to the Israeli daily Maariv *shortly before he left Israel, Indyk analyzes the collapse of the Oslo process in the aftermath of the 2000 Camp David conference.*

Source: Maariv, July 13, 2001.

You [Israel] may not realize it yet, but once the fog lifts you will discover that you have won. You have, quite simply, won. The fact that the Palestinians accepted the Mitchell[1] and Tenet[2] proposals means that the *intifada* is over. The violence is continuing, but the Intifada, as a Palestinian war of independence aimed at achieving their objectives by violence, has failed. The Palestinians lost the Israeli public, got [Ariel] Sharon, lost the American public, missed out on the [William] Clinton opportunity and instead got the [George W.] Bush administration which, given the circumstances, is focusing on managing the crisis, not resolving it. Their economy is in ruins, their international support has weakened, and all this because of the violence. The bottom line is: Violence doesn't pay.

I fear that the Middle East will be swept up in a new war before the sides return to the negotiating table. It has happened before. But even in this respect I am more of an optimist than a pessimist, because the Intifada was unable to shake up the region. Your Arab neighbors, led by President [Hosni] Mubarak, King Abdullah, the Saudi crown prince, and even Bashar al-Assad, in his own Syrian way, continue to maintain that peace is the only strategic option. They refuse to support negative elements such as Nasrallah [leader of the Hezbollah in Lebanon], the Iranians, and the Iraqis. They refuse to return to the military option, and that is very important.

We came here, my wife and I, to try to complete the task that was begun by Yitzhak Rabin and was stopped short by his murder. It was clear to us that this could be done in the time that remained to the Clinton administration. We dedicated ourselves to it, but it did not succeed, and I am disappointed. I feel regret, but I will continue to adhere to Winston Churchill's motto: Never, never surrender. The effort for peace is alive, and it is the only way.

[On Israeli Prime Minister Ariel Sharon, elected in February 2001] I am greatly impressed by him. He is in a difficult situation—violence on the one hand and political pressure on the other—and I am impressed by the road he has chosen and the manner in which he conducts his relations with the U.S. Administration. His way, the policy of restraint, is the correct way, despite the enormous pressure on him. We have had many good and serious talks. He is a man who listens with understanding, and I admire that very much.

[On former Israeli Prime Minister Ehud Barak] I believe that he came to Camp David genuinely prepared to achieve a breakthrough. He has faithfully followed his path since his service in an elite army unit, and he was prepared for both possibilities. I don't believe the theory that he planned everything and that all he wanted was to unmask Arafat. As a responsible leader and as prime minister, he could not have raised such historic and dramatic proposals as the division of the Old City of Jerusalem merely to isolate Arafat. According to his calculations, the Israelis were prepared to pay for peace, and he went all the way with that. True, things might have been better if he had talked with Arafat and conducted the negotiations in a more personal manner. That may have been a factor, but it was not the real cause. On the table were the fateful, historical problems of this conflict. Barak spotted a window of opportunity that was about to close and took a calculated risk. He was the antithesis of a politician; each time, he did exactly the opposite of what should have been done in order to survive. When a right turn was called for, he made a left, and vice versa. He wanted to exploit this attempt to the fullest, and that was more important to him than being reelected.

[On the Camp David Summit] I think it collapsed mainly because of Jerusalem. We could have reached an agreement on the territorial issue, including the security arrangements. That was supposed to be our contingency plan, but it did not coincide with the interests of the sides. Some people say that Camp David [doc. 103] was not prepared properly, and that is a fair criticism. Preparations for the summit could have been better. But you must take the circumstances into account: There was a prior secret negotiating channel in Stockholm. The moment this was revealed, everything got bogged down and progress became impossible. Time was running out, and there was no alternative.

[On Yasir Arafat] I am no mind reader, particularly where his mind is concerned. He must be judged by his actions. I don't think he has given up violence as a tool to gain objectives, but that does not mean that the conclusions of Israel's right wing are correct. I believe that his goal is not to destroy Israel but to establish a Palestinian state within the 1967 borders, with East Jerusalem as its capital, and to resolve the refugee problem. Arafat is the leader of the Palestinians, and there is no alternative to him. The best thing to do would be to increase the pressure on him to meet his obligations. That is the only logical way to extricate ourselves from the situation we are in. We have had a great deal of experience with Arafat. Eight years have elapsed since Oslo [doc. 133]. We know how he operates, how he reacts, and we are familiar with his considerations. He signed, he committed himself, and now he must execute. He has taken some action, but a great deal still remains to be done. I don't think that he has made a 100-percent effort yet.

[On waning U.S. involvement] We are not running away. Ambassador Daniel Kurtzer will replace me, and he is an experienced man. We presented a plan for a way out of the crisis, and both sides signed it. It is time that we treated the sides as adults who must abide by their commitments. We cannot do anything in your stead. Now it is your turn to meet your obligations. Arafat needs to halt the violence; Israel needs to totally freeze the settlements and to cease the initiated activity inside Area A (see map 6). That's all.

[On who is to blame] The three sides are equally to blame. After Camp David, we engaged in intense contacts with the sides. The President was supposed to submit a detailed proposal for an overall agenda. And then, just before the proposal was to have been submitted, the riots broke out. In the wake of Camp David, I feel that all three sides should have focused on an effort to prevent a conflagration and restore confidence instead of resorting to mudslinging and attempting to isolate one another. That is what brought us to this point.

NOTES

1. The Mitchell proposal was a plan offered by an international panel, led by former U.S. Senator George Mitchell, on April 30, 2001, to end the renewed Israeli-Palestinian violence (the Second Intifada) and to resume the peace process. The panel was appointed under the auspices of the U.S. president as part of a conference in Sharm El-Sheikh that met on October 17, 2000. The plan was part of a broader fact finding effort to discern the reasons for the new round of Israeli-Palestinian violence (see doc. 144).

2. The Tenet plan was proposed by CIA director George Tenet on June 13, 2001, to end Israeli-Palestinian violence. It was later integrated into the broader Roadmap for Peace proposed by U.S. President George W. Bush on April 30, 2003 (doc. 147).

144

Sharm el-Sheikh Fact-Finding Committee

Mitchell Report

May 4, 2001

The failure of the 2000 Camp David Israeli-Palestinian summit was followed in September of that year by the eruption of Palestinian violence, later to be named the Al-Aqsa Intifada, which brought to an end the seven-year endeavor of the Oslo peace process. In an effort to stop the violence and resume the talks, representatives of Israel, Egypt, the Palestinians, Jordan, the European Union, the United Nations, and the United States met in Sharm el-Sheikh, Egypt, on October 17, 2000. Most of the decisions adopted by the parties in the summit were never executed, but the summit did lead to the creation of an international fact-finding committee that was mandated to determine how the violence began and what could be done to end it. The committee, an international panel headed by former U.S. Senator George Mitchell, published its findings on May 4, 2001. The findings and the recommendations were in effect, and the position about the path to be taken served as part of the basis for the subsequent U.S. policy statement and initiatives.

Despite their long history and close proximity, some Israelis and Palestinians seem not to fully appreciate each other's concerns. Some Israelis appear not to comprehend the humiliation and frustration that Palestinians must endure every day as a result of living with the continuing effects of occupation, sustained by the presence of Israeli military forces and settlements in their midst, or the determination of the Palestinians to achieve independence and genuine self-determination. Some Palestinians appear not to comprehend the extent to which terrorism creates fear among the Israeli people and undermines their belief in the possibility of co-existence, or the determination of the GOI (Government of Israel) to do whatever is necessary to protect its people. Fear, hate, anger, and frustration have risen on both sides. The greatest danger of all is that the culture of peace, nurtured over the past decade, is being shattered. In its place there is a growing sense of futility and despair, and a growing resort to violence.

Two proud people share a land and a destiny. Their competing claims and religious differences have led to a grinding, demoralizing, dehumanizing conflict. They can continue in conflict or they can negotiate to find a way to live side-by-side in peace.

So much has been achieved. So much is at risk. If the parties are to succeed in completing their journey to their common destination, agreed commitments must be implemented, international law respected, and human rights protected. We encourage them to return to negotiation, however difficult. It is the only path to peace, justice and security. The relevance and impact of our work, in the end, will be measured by the recommendations we make concerning the following: Ending the Violence, Rebuilding Confidence, and Resuming Negotiations.

Source: Haaretz, May 8, 2001.

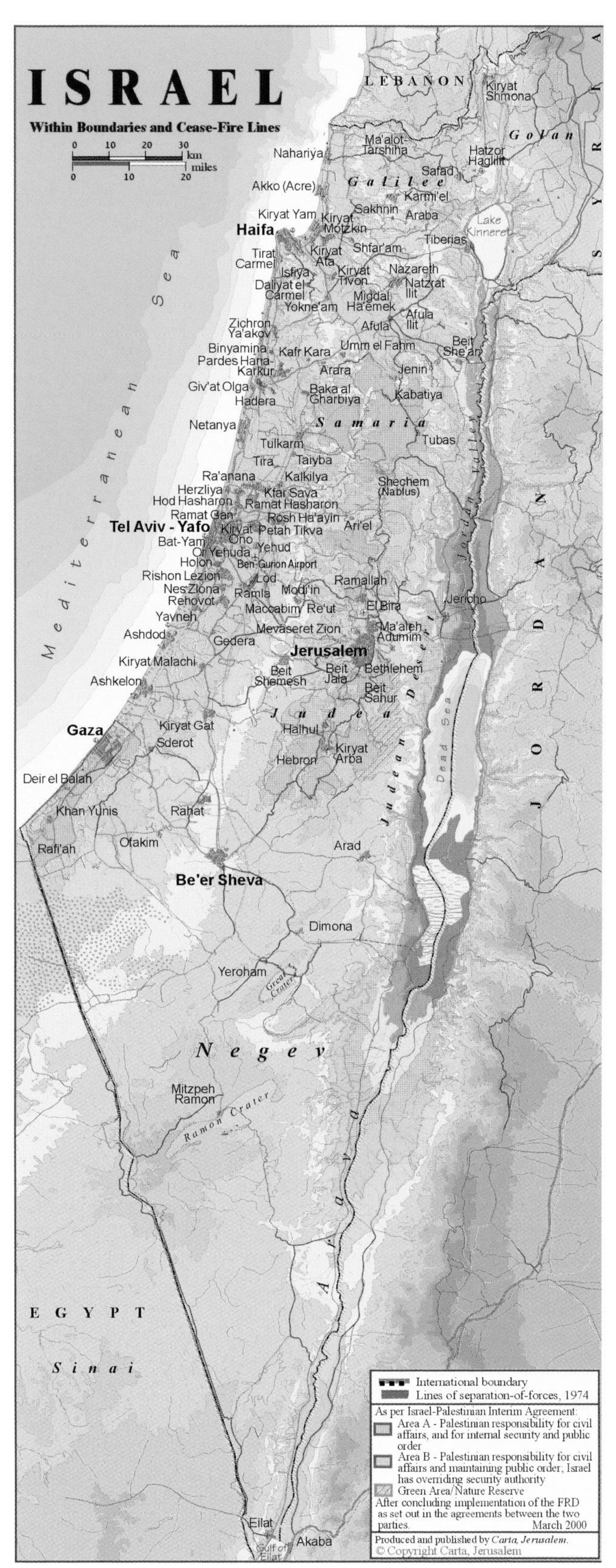

MAP 6. ISRAEL AND THE PALESTINIAN AUTHORITY, MARCH 2000.

What Happened?

We are not a tribunal. We complied with the request that we not determine the guilt or innocence of individuals or of the parties. . . . In late September 2000, Israeli, Palestinian, and other officials received reports that Member of the Knesset (now Prime Minister) Ariel Sharon was planning a visit to the Haram al-Sharif/Temple Mount in Jerusalem. Mr. Sharon made the visit on September 28. . . . Palestinians saw it as highly provocative to them. On the following day, in the same place, a large number of unarmed Palestinian demonstrators and a large Israeli police contingent confronted each other.

Thus began what has become known as the "Al-Aqsa Intifada" (Al-Aqsa being a mosque at the Haram al-Sharif/Temple Mount). The GOI asserts that the immediate catalyst for the violence was the breakdown of the Camp David negotiations on July 25, 2000, and the "widespread appreciation in the international community of Palestinian responsibility for the impasse." In this view, Palestinian violence was planned by the PA (Palestinian Authority) leadership, and was aimed at "provoking and incurring Palestinian casualties as a means of regaining the diplomatic initiative."

The Palestine Liberation Organization (PLO) denies the allegation that the Intifada was planned. It claims, however, that "Camp David represented nothing less than an attempt by Israel to extend the force it exercises on the ground to negotiations." From the perspective of the PLO, Israel responded to the disturbances with excessive and illegal use of deadly force against demonstrators; behavior which, in the PLO's view, reflected Israel's contempt for the lives and safety of Palestinians.

What began as a series of confrontations between Palestinian demonstrators and Israeli security forces, which resulted in the GOI's initial restrictions of the movement of people and goods in the West Bank and Gaza Strip (closures), has since evolved into a wider array of violent actions and responses. In their submissions, the parties traded allegations about the motivation and degree of control exercised by the other. However, we were provided with no persuasive evidence that the Sharon visit was anything other than an internal political act; neither were we provided with persuasive evidence that the PA planned the uprising.

Accordingly, we have no basis on which to conclude that there was a deliberate plan by the PA to initiate a campaign of violence at the first opportunity; or to conclude that there was a deliberate plan by the GOI to respond with lethal force. However, there is also no evidence on which to conclude that the PA made a consistent effort to contain the demonstrations and control the violence once it began; or that the GOI made a consistent effort to use non-lethal means to control demonstrations of unarmed Palestinians. Amid rising anger, fear, and mistrust, each side assumed the worst about the other and acted accordingly. The Sharon visit did not cause the "Al-Aqsa Intifada." But it was poorly timed and the provocative effect should have been foreseen; indeed, it was foreseen by those who urged that the visit be prohibited.

Why Did It Happen?

The roots of the current violence extend much deeper than an inconclusive summit conference. Both sides have made clear a profound disillusionment with the behavior of the other in failing to meet the expectations arising from the peace process.

DIVERGENT EXPECTATIONS

We are struck by the divergent expectations expressed by the parties in relating to the implementation of the Oslo process. Results achieved from this process were unthinkable less than ten years ago. During the latest round of negotiations the parties were closer to a permanent settlement than ever before.

Nonetheless, Palestinians and Israelis alike told us that the premise on which the Oslo process is based—that tackling the hard "permanent status" issues be deferred to the end of the process—has gradually come under serious pressure.

The GOI has placed primacy on moving toward a Permanent Status Agreement in a nonviolent atmosphere, consistent with commitments contained in the agreements between the parties.

The PLO view is that delays in the process have been the result of an Israeli attempt to prolong and solidify the occupation. . . . "In sum, Israel's proposals at Camp David provided for Israel's annexation of the best Palestinian lands, the perpetuation of Israeli control over East Jerusalem, a continued military presence on Palestinian territory, Israeli control over Palestinian natural resources, airspace and borders, and the return of fewer than 1% of refugees to their homes."

Both sides see the lack of full compliance with agreements reached since the opening of the peace process as evidence of a lack of good faith. This conclusion led to an erosion of trust even before the permanent status negotiations began. During the last seven months, these views have hardened into divergent realities. Each side views the other as having acted in bad faith; as having turned the optimism of Oslo into suffering and grief of victims and their loved ones. In their statements and actions, each side demonstrates a perspective that fails to recognize any truth in the perspective of the other.

End the Violence

With widespread violence, both sides have resorted to portrayals of each other in hostile stereotypes. This cycle cannot easily be broken. Without considerable determination and readiness to compromise, the rebuilding of trust will be impossible.

CESSATION OF VIOLENCE

Since 1991, the parties have consistently committed themselves, in all their agreements, to the path of nonviolence. To stop the violence now, the PA and GOI need not "reinvent the wheel." Rather, they should take immediate steps to end the violence, reaffirm their mutual commitments, and resume negotiations.

RESUMPTION OF SECURITY COOPERATION

Palestinian security officials told us that it would take some time for the PA to reassert full control over armed elements nominally under its command and to exert decisive influence over other armed elements operating in Palestinian areas. Israeli security officials have not disputed these assertions. What is important is that the PA make an all-out effort to enforce a complete cessation of violence and that it be clearly seen by the GOI as doing so. The GOI must likewise exercise a 100 percent effort to ensure that potential friction points, where Palestinians come into contact with armed Israelis, do not become stages for renewed hostilities.

Rebuild Confidence

The historic handshake between Chairman [Yasir] Arafat and the late Prime Minister [Yitzhak] Rabin at the White House in September 1993 symbolized the expectation of both parties that the door to the peaceful resolution of differences had been opened. Despite the current violence and mutual loss of trust, both communities have repeatedly expressed a desire for peace. Channeling this desire into substantive progress has proved difficult. The restoration of trust is essential, and the parties should take affirmative steps to this end. Given the high level of hostility and mistrust, the timing and sequence of these steps are obviously crucial. This can be decided only by the parties. We urge them to begin the process of decision immediately.

TERRORISM

In the September 1999 Sharm el-Sheikh Memorandum, the parties pledged to take action against "any threat or act of terrorism, violence, or incitement." Terrorism involves the deliberate killing and injuring of randomly selected noncombatants for political ends. It seeks to promote a political outcome by spreading terror and demoralization throughout a population. We believe that the PA has a responsibility to help rebuild confidence by making it clear to both communities that terrorism is reprehensible and unacceptable, and by taking all measures to prevent terrorist operations and to punish perpetrators. This effort should include immediate steps to apprehend and incarcerate terrorists operating within the PA's jurisdiction.

SETTLEMENTS

The GOI also has a responsibility to help rebuild confidence. A cessation of Palestinian-Israeli violence will be particularly hard to sustain unless the GOI freezes all settlement construction activity. Settlement activities must not be allowed to undermine the restoration of calm and the resumption of negotiations. Palestinians contend that there is no distinction between "new" and "expanded" settlements; and that, except for a brief freeze during the tenure of Prime Minister Yitzhak Rabin, there has been a continuing, aggressive effort by Israel to increase the number and size of settlements.

REDUCING TENSION

We were told by both Palestinians and Israelis that emotions generated by the many recent deaths and funerals have fueled additional confrontations, and, in effect, maintained the cycle of violence. Both sides must make clear that violent demonstrations will not be tolerated. We can and do urge that both sides exhibit a greater respect for human life when demonstrators confront security personnel.

We are deeply concerned about the public safety implications of exchanges of fire between populated areas. Palestinian gunmen have directed small arms fire at Israeli settlements and at nearby IDF [Israel Defense Forces] positions from within or adjacent to civilian dwellings in Palestinian areas, thus endangering innocent Israeli and Palestinian civilians alike. We condemn the positioning of gunmen within or near civilian dwellings. . . . We urge that such provocations cease and that the IDF exercise maximum restraint in its responses if they do occur. Inappropriate or excessive uses of force often lead to escalation. On the Palestinian side there are disturbing ambiguities in the basic areas of responsibility and accountability. We urge the PA to take all necessary steps to establish a clear and unchallenged chain of command for armed personnel operating under its authority.

INCITEMENT

In their submissions and briefings to the Committee, both sides expressed concerns about hateful language and images emanating from the other. . . . We call on the parties to renew their formal commitments to foster mutual understanding and tolerance and to abstain from incitement and hostile propaganda.

ECONOMIC AND SOCIAL IMPACT OF VIOLENCE

Further restrictions on the movement of people and goods have been imposed by Israel on the West Bank and the Gaza Strip. These closures . . . have disrupted the lives of hundreds of thousands of Palestinians. Of particular concern to the PA has been the destruction by Israeli security forces and settlers of tens of thousands of olive and fruit trees and other agricultural property. The closures have also had other adverse effects.

We acknowledge Israel's security concerns. We believe, however, that the GOI should lift closures, transfer to the PA all revenues owed, and permit Palestinians who have been employed in Israel to return to their jobs. Closure policies play into the hands of extremists seeking to expand their constituencies and thereby contribute to escalation. The PA should resume cooperation with Israeli security agencies to ensure that Palestinian workers employed within

Israel are fully vetted and free of connections to terrorist organizations.

HOLY PLACES

It is particularly regrettable that the places such as the Temple Mount/Haram al-Sharif in Jerusalem, Joseph's Tomb in Nablus, and Rachel's Tomb in Bethlehem have been the scenes of violence, death, and injury. These are places of peace, prayer and reflection which must be accessible to all believers. Places deemed holy by Muslims, Jews, and Christians merit respect, protection, and preservation.

INTERNATIONAL FORCE

One of the most controversial subjects raised during our inquiry was the issue of deploying an international force to the Palestinian areas. The PA is strongly in favor of having such a force to protect Palestinian civilians and their property. . . . The GOI is just as adamantly opposed to an "international protection force," believing it would prove unresponsive to Israeli security concerns and interfere with bilateral negotiations to settle the conflict. We believe that to be effective such a force would need the support of both parties.

Resume Negotiations

Israeli leaders do not wish to be perceived as "rewarding violence." Palestinian leaders do not wish to be perceived as "rewarding occupation." We appreciate the political constraints on leaders of both sides. Nevertheless, if the cycle of violence is to be broken and the search for peace resumed, there needs to be a new bilateral relationship incorporating both security cooperation and negotiations.

We cannot prescribe to the parties how best to pursue their political objectives. Yet the construction of a new bilateral relationship solidifying and transcending an agreed cessation of violence requires intelligent risk-taking. It requires, in the first instance, that each party again be willing to regard the other as a partner.

To define a starting point is for the parties to decide. Both parties have stated that they remain committed to their mutual agreements and undertakings. It is time to explore further implementation. The parties should declare their intention to meet on this basis, in order to resume full and meaningful negotiations, in the spirit of their undertakings at Sharm el-Sheikh in 1999 and 2000.

Recommendations

The GOI and the PA must act swiftly and decisively to halt the violence. Their immediate objectives then should be to rebuild confidence and resume negotiations.

End the Violence

The GOI and the PA should reaffirm their commitment to existing agreements and undertakings and should immediately implement an unconditional cessation of violence.

The GOI and PA should immediately resume security cooperation.

Effective bilateral cooperation aimed at preventing violence will encourage the resumption of negotiations. . . . We believe that the security cooperation cannot long be sustained if meaningful negotiations are unreasonably deferred, if security measures "on the ground" are seen as hostile, or if steps are taken that are perceived as provocative or as prejudicing the outcome of negotiations.

Rebuild Confidence

The PA and GOI should work together to establish a meaningful "cooling off period" and implement additional confidence building measures.

The PA and GOI should resume their efforts to identify, condemn and discourage incitement in all its forms.

The PA should make clear through concrete action to Palestinians and Israelis alike that terrorism is reprehensible and unacceptable, and that the PA will make a 100 percent effort to prevent terrorist operations and to punish perpetrators. This effort should include immediate steps to apprehend and incarcerate terrorists operating within the PA's jurisdiction.

The GOI should freeze all settlement activity, including the "natural growth" of existing settlements. The kind of security cooperation desired by the GOI cannot for long co-exist with settlement activity.

The GOI should give careful consideration to whether settlements which are the focal points for substantial friction are valuable bargaining chips for future negotiations or provocations likely to preclude the onset of productive talks.

The GOI may wish to make it clear to the PA that a future peace would pose no threat to the territorial contiguity of a Palestinian state to be established in the West Bank and Gaza Strip.

The IDF should consider withdrawing to positions held before September 28, 2000, which would reduce the number of friction points and the potential for violent confrontations.

The GOI should ensure that the IDF adopt and enforce policies and procedures encouraging non-lethal responses to unarmed demonstrators, with a view to minimizing casualties and friction between the two communities.

The GOI should lift closures, transfer to the PA all tax revenues owed, and permit Palestinians who have been employed in Israel to return to their jobs; and should ensure that security forces and settlers refrain from the destruction of homes and roads, as well as trees and other agricultural property in Palestinian areas.

The PA should renew cooperation with Israeli security agencies to ensure, to the maximum extent possible, that Palestinian workers employed within Israel are fully vetted and free of connections to organizations and individuals engaged in terrorism.

The PA should prevent gunmen from using Palestinian populated areas to fire upon Israeli populated areas and IDF positions. This tactic places civilians on both sides at unnecessary risk.

The GOI and IDF should adopt and enforce policies and procedures designed to ensure that the response to any gunfire emanating from Palestinian populated areas minimizes the danger to the lives and property of civilians, bearing in mind that it is probably the objective of the gunmen to elicit an excessive IDF response.

Resume Negotiations

We reiterate our belief that a 100 percent effort to stop the violence, an immediate resumption of security cooperation and an exchange of confidence building measures are all important for the resumption of negotiations. Yet none of these steps will long be sustained absent a return to serious negotiations.

It is not within our mandate to prescribe the venue, the basis or the agenda of negotiations. However, in order to provide an effective political context for practical cooperation between the parties, negotiations must not be unreasonably deferred and they must, in our view, manifest a spirit of compromise, reconciliation and partnership, notwithstanding the events of the past seven months.

Postscript, after 2000

2001
Ariel Sharon is elected prime minister

2002
U.S. President George W. Bush outlines the Roadmap for Peace

2003
Ariel Sharon is reelected prime minister

2005
Israel withdraws from Gaza and removes all settlements in Gaza, as well as four settlements in the northern West Bank

2006
Ehud Olmert is appointed acting prime minister following Ariel Sharon's illness and is later elected prime minister

Following Hamas's abduction of two Israeli soldiers patrolling the Israeli-Lebanese border and the attack on northern Israel, Israel invades Lebanon

A few weeks later U.N. Security Council Resolution 1701 ends the full-fledged confrontation

145

League of Arab States

The Arab Peace Initiative (Beirut Declaration)

March 28, 2002

On March 28, 2002, the Arab League adopted the peace plan presented below. The plan, which was initiated by the Saudi Crown Prince Abdullah Bin Abdulaziz, offered Israel normal relations with the Arab world in return for full withdrawal from all the territories it gained in 1967. Though the plan was perhaps the boldest commitment by the Arab League in its willingness to pursue a peaceful path with Israel, it did not create any momentum. Its timing, in the midst of a bloody wave of suicide bombings in Israel and just before an Israeli response that brought Israel back in control of the territories, left the initiative little chance of success. Furthermore, the general language of the declaration, which omitted issues that both sides felt are crucial, such as Israel's demand for an end to Palestinian terror and the Palestinian insistence on the right of return, weakened its support base. Some, especially in official Israel, were also suspicious of the Saudi motives in launching the peace proposal, during a time of strained U.S.-Saudi relations, following the terrorist attacks in the United States on September 11, 2001. In March 2007, however, Israel changed its approach and Prime Minister Ehud Olmert declared that there were some positive aspects to the plan in its modified version.

The Council of the League of Arab States at the Summit Level, at its 14th Ordinary Session, reaffirming the resolution taken in June 1996 at the Cairo extraordinary Arab Summit that a just and comprehensive peace in the Middle East is the strategic option of the Arab countries, to be achieved in accordance with international legality, and which would require a comparable commitment on the part of the Israeli Government.

Having listened to the statement made by His Royal Highness Prince Abdullah Bin Abdulaziz, the Crown Prince of the Kingdom of Saudi Arabia, in which His Highness presented his initiative, calling for full Israeli withdrawal from all the Arab territories occupied since June 1967, in implementation of Security Council Resolutions 242 [doc. 68] and 338 [doc. 86], reaffirmed by the Madrid Conference of 1991 [doc. 118] and the land-for-peace principle; and for Israel's acceptance of an independent Palestinian State, with East Jerusalem as its capital, in return for the establishment of normal relations in the context of a comprehensive peace with Israel.

Emanating from the conviction of the Arab countries that a military solution to the conflict will not achieve peace or provide security for the parties, the Council:

1. Requests Israel to reconsider its policies and declare that a just peace is its strategic option as well.
2. Further calls upon Israel to affirm:
   a. Full Israeli withdrawal from all the territories occupied since 1967, including the

Source: Israel Ministry of Foreign Affairs online, March 28, 2002, www.mfa.gov.il/MFA/Peace+Process/Guide+to+the+Peace+Process/Beirut+Declaration+on+Saudi+Peace+Initiative+-+28-.htm (accessed May 21, 2007).

Syrian Golan Heights to the lines of June 4, 1967, as well as the remaining occupied Lebanese territories in the south of Lebanon.

b. Achievement of a just solution to the Palestinian Refugee problem to be agreed upon in accordance with U.N. General Assembly Resolution 194 [doc. 26].

c. The acceptance of the establishment of a Sovereign Independent Palestinian State on the Palestinian territories occupied since the 4th of June 1967 in the West Bank and Gaza Strip, with East Jerusalem as its capital.

3. Consequently, the Arab Countries affirm the following:
   a. Consider the Arab-Israeli conflict ended, and enter into a peace agreement with Israel, and provide security for all the states of the region.
   b. Establishes normal relations with Israel in the context of this comprehensive peace.
4. Assures the rejection of all forms of Palestinian patriation which conflict with the special circumstances of the Arab host countries.
5. Calls upon the Government of Israel and all Israelis to accept this initiative in order to safeguard the prospects for peace and stop the further shedding of blood, enabling the Arab countries and Israel to live in peace and good neighborliness and provide future generations with security, stability, and prosperity.
6. Invites the international community and all countries and organizations to support this initiative.
7. Requests the Chairman of the Summit to form a special committee composed of some of its concerned member states and the Secretary General of the League of Arab States to pursue the necessary contacts to gain support for this initiative at all levels, particularly from the United Nations, the Security Council, the United States of America, the Russian Federation, the Muslim States and the European Union.

146

George W. Bush

Remarks on the Middle East

June 24, 2002

On June 24, 2002, U.S. President George W. Bush delivered the speech presented below. The speech outlined the policy that Bush was to follow in the subsequent year, and it was his first clear policy statement placing the Israeli-Palestinian issue in the context of the U.S. War on Terrorism following the terrorist attacks on September 11, 2001. The speech was also the first step in an American effort that followed to weaken the leadership of Palestine Liberation Organization chairman Yasir Arafat and that led to the appointment of Prime Minister Mahmoud Abbas in the Palestinian Authority.

Source: White House online, June 24, 2002, http://www.whitehouse.gov/news/releases/2002/06/20020624-3.html (accessed April 1, 2005).

For too long, the citizens of the Middle East have lived in the midst of death and fear. The hatred of a few holds the hopes of many hostage. The forces of extremism and terror are attempting to kill progress and peace by killing the innocent. And this casts a dark shadow over the entire region.

For the sake of all humanity, things must change in the Middle East. . . .

My vision is two states, living side by side, in peace and security. There is simply no way to achieve that peace until all parties fight terror. . . .

Peace requires a new and different Palestinian leadership, so that a Palestinian state can be born. I call on the Palestinian people to elect new leaders, leaders not compromised by terror.

I call upon them to build a practicing democracy based on tolerance and liberty.

If the Palestinian people actively pursue these goals, America and the world will actively support their efforts. . . .

And when the Palestinian people have new leaders, new institutions and new security arrangements with their neighbors, the United States of America will support the creation of a Palestinian state, whose borders and certain aspects of its sovereignty will be provisional until resolved as part of a final settlement in the Middle East.

A Palestinian state will never be created by terror. It will be built through reform. And reform must be more than cosmetic change or a veiled attempt to preserve the status quo. True reform will require entirely new political and economic institutions based on democracy, market economics and action against terrorism.

Today the elected Palestinian legislature has no authority and power is concentrated in the hands of an unaccountable few. A Palestinian state can only serve its citizens with a new constitution which separates the powers of government.

The Palestinian parliament should have the full authority of a legislative body. Local officials and government ministers need authority of their own and the independence to govern effectively.

Today, the Palestinian people lack effective courts of law and have no means to defend and vindicate their rights. A Palestinian state will require a system of reliable justice to punish those who prey on the innocent. The United States and members of the international community stand ready to work with Palestinian leaders to establish, finance and monitor a truly independent judiciary.

Today, Palestinian authorities are encouraging, not opposing terrorism. This is unacceptable. And the United States will not support the establishment of a Palestinian state until its leaders engage in a sustained fight against the terrorists and dismantle their infrastructure.

This will require an externally supervised effort to rebuild and reform the Palestinian security services. The security system must have clear lines of authority and accountability and a unified chain of command.

I've said in the past that nations are either with us or against us in the War on Terror. To be counted on the side of peace, nations must act. Every leader actually committed to peace will end incitement to violence in official media and publicly denounce homicide bombings. Every nation actually committed to peace will stop the flow of money, equipment and recruits to terrorist groups seeking the destruction of Israel, including Hamas, Islamic *jihad* and Hezbollah.

Every nation actually committed to peace must block the shipment of Iranian supplies to these groups and oppose regimes that promote terror, like Iraq.

And Syria must choose the right side in the war on terror by closing terrorist camps and expelling terrorist organizations.

Leaders who want to be included in the peace process must show by their deeds an undivided support for peace.

And as we move toward a peaceful solution, Arab states will be expected to build closer ties of diplomacy and commerce with Israel, leading to full normalization of relations between Israel and the entire Arab world.

Israel also has a large stake in the success of a democratic Palestine. Permanent occupation threatens Israel's identity and democracy. A stable, peaceful Palestinian state is necessary to achieve the security that Israel longs for.

So I challenge Israel to take concrete steps to support the emergence of a viable, credible Palestinian state.

As we make progress toward security, Israeli forces need to withdraw fully to positions they held prior to September 28, 2000. And consistent with the recommendations of the Mitchell committee [doc. 144], Israeli settlement activity in the occupied territories must stop.

The Palestinian economy must be allowed to develop. As violence subsides, freedom of movement should be restored, permitting innocent Palestinians to resume work and normal life. Palestinian legislators and officials, humanitarian and international workers, must be allowed to go about the business of building a better future. And Israel should release frozen Palestinian revenues into honest, accountable hands.

Ultimately, Israelis and Palestinians must address the core issues that divide them if there is to be a real peace, resolving all claims and ending the conflict between them.

This means that the Israeli occupation that began in 1967 will be ended through a settlement negotiated between the parties, based on U.N. Resolutions 242 [doc. 68] and 338 [doc. 86], with Israeli withdrawal to secure and recognized borders.

We must also resolve questions concerning Jerusalem, the plight and future of Palestinian refugees, and a final peace between Israel and Lebanon and Israel and a Syria that supports peace and fights terror.

All who are familiar with the history of the Middle East realize that there may be setbacks in this process. Trained and determined killers, as we have seen, want to stop it. Yet the Egyptian and Jordanian peace treaties with Israel remind us that, with determined and responsible leadership, progress can come quickly.

As new Palestinian institutions and new leaders emerge, demonstrating real performance on security and reform, I expect Israel to respond and work toward a final status agreement.

With intensive effort by all of us, agreement could be reached within three years from now. And I and my country will actively lead toward that goal.

I can understand the deep anger and anguish of the Israeli people. You've lived too long with fear and funerals, having to avoid markets and public transportation, and forced to put armed guards in kindergarten classrooms. The Palestinian Authority has rejected your offered hand and trafficked with terrorists. You have a right to a normal life. You have a right to security. And I deeply believe that you need a reformed, responsible Palestinian partner to achieve that security.

I can understand the deep anger and despair of the Palestinian people. For decades you've been treated as pawns in the Middle East conflict. Your interests have been held hostage to a comprehensive peace agreement that never seems to come, as your lives get worse year by year.

You deserve democracy and the rule of law. You deserve an open society and a thriving economy. You deserve a life of hope for your children.

An end to occupation and a peaceful democratic Palestinian state may seem distant, but America and our partners throughout the world stand ready to help, help you make them possible as soon as possible.

Prosperity and freedom and dignity are not just American hopes or Western hopes, they are universal human hopes. And even in the violence and turmoil of the Middle East, America believes those hopes have the power to transform lives and nations.

This moment is both an opportunity and a test for all parties in the Middle East: an opportunity to lay the foundations for future peace, a test to show who's serious about peace and who is not.

The choice here is stark and simple, the Bible says, "I have set before you life and death, therefore choose life." The time has arrived for everyone in this conflict to choose peace and hope—and life.

147

Government of the United States

A Performance-Based Roadmap to a Permanent Two-State Solution to the Israeli-Palestinian Conflict

April 30, 2003

*On April 30, 2003, the Quartet—the United States, the European Union, Russia, and the United Nations—released a three-phased plan for a two-state solution also known as the Roadmap for Peace. A draft of the document had been prepared in December 2002, but elections in Israel on January 28, 2003, delayed its public presentation. On May 25, 2003, the Israeli government adopted the plan, with fourteen reservations, and following that the United States launched a diplomatic effort in the Arab world to garner support for the plan. The renewed U.S. effort led by June 2003 to a three-month cease-fire (*Hudna*) between Israelis and Palestinians. But the full plan was never implemented, with Palestinians and Israelis each blaming the other for failing to fulfill their obligations.*

The following is a performance-based and goal-driven roadmap, with clear phases, timelines, target dates, and benchmarks aiming at progress through reciprocal steps by the two parties in the political, security, economic, humanitarian, and institution-building fields, under the auspices of the Quartet [the United States, European Union, United Nations, and Russia]. The destination is a final and comprehensive settlement of the Israel-Palestinian conflict by 2005, as presented in President Bush's speech of June 24 [doc. 146], and welcomed by the E.U., Russia and the U.N. in the July 16 and September 17 Quartet Ministerial statements.

A two-state solution to the Israeli-Palestinian conflict will only be achieved through an end to violence and terrorism, when the Palestinian people have a leadership acting decisively against terror and willing and able to build a practicing democracy based on tolerance and liberty, and through Israel's readiness to do what is necessary for a democratic Palestinian state to be established, and a clear, unambiguous acceptance by both parties of the goal of a negotiated settlement as described below. The Quartet will assist and facilitate implementation of the plan, starting in Phase I, including direct discussions between the parties as required. The plan establishes a realistic timeline for implementation. However, as a performance-based plan, progress will require and depend upon the good faith efforts of the parties, and their compliance with each of the obligations outlined below. Should the parties perform their obligations rapidly, progress within and through the phases may come sooner than indicated in the plan. Non-compliance with obligations will impede progress.

A settlement, negotiated between the parties, will result in the emergence of an independent, democratic, and viable Palestinian state living side by side in peace and security with

---

Source: U.S. Department of State online, April 30, 2003, http://www.state.gov/r/pa/prs/ps/2003/20062.htm (accessed April 1, 2005).

Israel and its other neighbors. The settlement will resolve the Israel-Palestinian conflict, and end the occupation that began in 1967, based on the foundations of the Madrid Conference [doc. 118], the principle of land-for-peace, UNSCRs 242 [doc. 68], 338 [doc. 86] and 1397, agreements previously reached by the parties, and the initiative of Saudi Crown Prince Abdullah—endorsed by the Beirut Arab League Summit [doc. 145]—calling for acceptance of Israel as a neighbor living in peace and security, in the context of a comprehensive settlement. This initiative is a vital element of international efforts to promote a comprehensive peace on all tracks, including the Syrian-Israeli and Lebanese-Israeli tracks.

The Quartet will meet regularly at senior levels to evaluate the parties' performance on implementation of the plan. In each phase, the parties are expected to perform their obligations in parallel, unless otherwise indicated.

Phase I: Ending Terror and Violence, Normalizing Palestinian Life, and Building Palestinian Institutions, Present to May 2003

In Phase I, the Palestinians immediately undertake an unconditional cessation of violence according to the steps outlined below; such action should be accompanied by supportive measures undertaken by Israel. Palestinians and Israelis resume security cooperation based on the Tenet work plan to end violence, terrorism, and incitement through restructured and effective Palestinian security services. Palestinians undertake comprehensive political reform in preparation for statehood, including drafting a Palestinian constitution, and free, fair and open elections upon the basis of those measures. Israel takes all necessary steps to help normalize Palestinian life. Israel withdraws from Palestinian areas occupied from September 28, 2000 and the two sides restore the status quo that existed at that time, as security performance and cooperation progress. Israel also freezes all settlement activity, consistent with the Mitchell report [doc. 144].

At the outset of Phase I:

- Palestinian leadership issues unequivocal statement reiterating Israel's right to exist in peace and security and calling for an immediate and unconditional cease-fire to end armed activity and all acts of violence against Israelis anywhere. All official Palestinian institutions end incitement against Israel.
- Israeli leadership issues unequivocal statement affirming its commitment to the two-state vision of an independent, viable, sovereign Palestinian state living in peace and security alongside Israel, as expressed by President Bush, and calling for an immediate end to violence against Palestinians everywhere. All official Israeli institutions end incitement against Palestinians.

Security

- Palestinians declare an unequivocal end to violence and terrorism and undertake visible efforts on the ground to arrest, disrupt, and restrain individuals and groups conducting and planning violent attacks on Israelis anywhere.
- Rebuilt and refocused Palestinian Authority [PA] security apparatus begins sustained, targeted and effective operations aimed at confronting all those engaged in terror and dismantlement of terrorist capabilities and infrastructure. This includes commencing confiscation of illegal weapons and consolidation of security authority, free of association with terror and corruption.
- GOI takes no actions undermining trust, including deportations; attacks on civilians; confiscation and/or demolition of Palestinian homes and property, as a punitive measure or to facilitate Israeli construction; destruction of Palestinian institutions and infrastructure; and other measures specified in the Tenet work plan.

- Relying on existing mechanisms and on-the-ground resources, Quartet representatives begin informal monitoring and consult with the parties on establishment of a formal monitoring mechanism and its implementation.
- Implementation, as previously agreed, of U.S. rebuilding, training and resumed security cooperation plan in collaboration with outside oversight board (United States–Egypt–Jordan). Quartet support for efforts to achieve a lasting, comprehensive cease-fire.
- All Palestinian security organizations are consolidated into three services reporting to an empowered Interior Minister.
- Restructured/retrained Palestinian security forces and IDF [Israel Defense Forces] counterparts progressively resume security cooperation and other undertakings in implementation of the Tenet work plan, including regular senior-level meetings, with the participation of U.S. security officials.
- Arab states cut off public and private funding and all other forms of support for groups supporting and engaging in violence and terror.
- All donors providing budgetary support for the Palestinians channel these funds through the Palestinian Ministry of Finance's Single Treasury Account.
- As comprehensive security performance moves forward, IDF withdraws progressively from areas occupied since September 28, 2000, and the two sides restore the status quo that existed prior to September 28, 2000. Palestinian security forces redeploy to areas vacated by IDF.

Palestinian Institution-Building

- Immediate action on credible process to produce draft constitution for Palestinian statehood. As rapidly as possible, constitutional committee circulates draft Palestinian constitution, based on strong parliamentary democracy and cabinet with empowered prime minister, for public comment/debate. Constitutional committee proposes draft document for submission after elections for approval by appropriate Palestinian institutions.
- Appointment of interim prime minister or cabinet with empowered executive authority/decision-making body.
- GOI fully facilitates travel of Palestinian officials for PLC [Palestine Legislative Council] and Cabinet sessions, internationally supervised security retraining, electoral and other reform activity, and other supportive measures related to the reform efforts.
- Continued appointment of Palestinian ministers empowered to undertake fundamental reform. Completion of further steps to achieve genuine separation of powers, including any necessary Palestinian legal reforms for this purpose.
- Establishment of independent Palestinian election commission. PLC reviews and revises election law.
- Palestinian performance on judicial, administrative, and economic benchmarks, as established by the International Task Force on Palestinian Reform.
- As early as possible, and based upon the above measures and in the context of open debate and transparent candidate selection/electoral campaign based on a free, multi-party process, Palestinians hold free, open, and fair elections.
- GOI facilitates Task Force election assistance, registration of voters, movement of candidates and voting officials. Support for NGOs [nongovernmental organizations] involved in the election process.
- GOI reopens Palestinian Chamber of Commerce and other closed Palestinian institutions in East Jerusalem based on a commitment that these institutions operate strictly in accordance with prior agreements between the parties.

Humanitarian Response

- Israel takes measures to improve the humanitarian situation. Israel and Palestinians implement in full all recommendations of the Bertini report to improve humanitarian conditions, lifting curfews and easing restrictions on movement of persons and goods, and allowing full, safe, and unfettered access of international and humanitarian personnel.
- AHLC [Ad-hoc Liaison Committee] reviews the humanitarian situation and prospects for economic development in the West Bank and Gaza and launches a major donor assistance effort, including to the reform effort.
- GOI and PA continue revenue clearance process and transfer of funds, including arrears, in accordance with agreed, transparent monitoring mechanism.

Civil Society

- Continued donor support, including increased funding through PVOs [private voluntary organizations]/NGOs, for people to people programs, private sector development and civil society initiatives.

Settlements

- GOI immediately dismantles settlement outposts erected since March 2001.
- Consistent with the Mitchell Report, GOI freezes all settlement activity (including natural growth of settlements).

Phase II: Transition, June 2003–December 2003

In the second phase, efforts are focused on the option of creating an independent Palestinian state with provisional borders and attributes of sovereignty, based on the new constitution, as a way station to a permanent status settlement. As has been noted, this goal can be achieved when the Palestinian people have a leadership acting decisively against terror, willing and able to build a practicing democracy based on tolerance and liberty. With such a leadership, reformed civil institutions and security structures, the Palestinians will have the active support of the Quartet and the broader international community in establishing an independent, viable, state.

Progress into Phase II will be based upon the consensus judgment of the Quartet of whether conditions are appropriate to proceed, taking into account performance of both parties. Furthering and sustaining efforts to normalize Palestinian lives and build Palestinian institutions, Phase II starts after Palestinian elections and ends with possible creation of an independent Palestinian state with provisional borders in 2003. Its primary goals are continued comprehensive security performance and effective security cooperation, continued normalization of Palestinian life and institution-building, further building on and sustaining of the goals outlined in Phase I, ratification of a democratic Palestinian constitution, formal establishment of office of prime minister, consolidation of political reform, and the creation of a Palestinian state with provisional borders.

- International Conference: Convened by the Quartet, in consultation with the parties, immediately after the successful conclusion of Palestinian elections, to support Palestinian economic recovery and launch a process leading to establishment of an independent Palestinian state with provisional borders.
- Such a meeting would be inclusive, based on the goal of a comprehensive Middle East peace (including between Israel and Syria, and Israel and Lebanon), and based on the principles described in the preamble to this document.
- Arab states restore pre-Intifada links to Israel (trade offices, etc.).
- Revival of multilateral engagement on issues including regional water resources,

environment, economic development, refugees, and arms control issues.

- New constitution for democratic, independent Palestinian state is finalized and approved by appropriate Palestinian institutions. Further elections, if required, should follow approval of the new constitution.
- Empowered reform cabinet with office of prime minister formally established, consistent with draft constitution.
- Continued comprehensive security performance, including effective security cooperation on the bases laid out in Phase I.
- Creation of an independent Palestinian state with provisional borders through a process of Israeli-Palestinian engagement, launched by the international conference. As part of this process, implementation of prior agreements, to enhance maximum territorial contiguity, including further action on settlements in conjunction with establishment of a Palestinian state with provisional borders.
- Enhanced international role in monitoring transition, with the active, sustained, and operational support of the Quartet.
- Quartet members promote international recognition of Palestinian state, including possible U.N. membership.

Phase III: Permanent Status Agreement and End of the Israeli-Palestinian Conflict, 2004–2005

Progress into Phase III, based on consensus judgment of Quartet and taking into account actions of both parties and Quartet monitoring. Phase III objectives are consolidation of reform and stabilization of Palestinian institutions, sustained, effective Palestinian security performance, and Israeli-Palestinian negotiations aimed at a permanent status agreement in 2005.

- Second International Conference: Convened by Quartet, in consultation with the parties, at beginning of 2004 to endorse agreement reached on an independent Palestinian state with provisional borders and formally to launch a process with the active, sustained, and operational support of the Quartet, leading to a final, permanent status resolution in 2005, including on borders, Jerusalem, refugees, settlements; and, to support progress toward a comprehensive Middle East settlement between Israel and Lebanon and Israel and Syria, to be achieved as soon as possible.
- Continued comprehensive, effective progress on the reform agenda laid out by the Task Force in preparation for final status agreement.
- Continued sustained and effective security performance, and sustained, effective security cooperation on the bases laid out in Phase I.
- International efforts to facilitate reform and stabilize Palestinian institutions and the Palestinian economy, in preparation for final status agreement.
- Parties reach final and comprehensive permanent status agreement that ends the Israel-Palestinian conflict in 2005, through a settlement negotiated between the parties based on UNSCR 242, 338, and 1397, that ends the occupation that began in 1967, and includes an agreed, just, fair, and realistic solution to the refugee issue, and a negotiated resolution on the status of Jerusalem that takes into account the political and religious concerns of both sides, and protects the religious interests of Jews, Christians, and Muslims worldwide, and fulfills the vision of two states, Israel and sovereign, independent, democratic and viable Palestine, living side-by-side in peace and security.
- Arab state acceptance of full normal relations with Israel and security for all the states of the region in the context of a comprehensive Arab-Israeli peace.

148
Gal Luft
Israel and Iraq after the Fall of Saddam Hussein
March 2004

In the immediate aftermath of the U.S. invasion of Iraq—code-named Operation Iraqi Freedom—national security experts argued, with a practical consensus, that Israel's national security was dramatically improved. The following excerpt from a study by the Israeli expert Dr. Gal Luft, sponsored by the Saban Center in Washington, D.C., reflects some of the issues raised in the debate over the repercussions of the Iraq War for Israel's security. The argument that Operation Iraqi Freedom made Israel more secure has since been weakened by the continuing insurgency in Iraq.

Throughout the decades of the Arab-Israeli conflict, Iraq has always been one of the most hostile and militant of Israel's neighbors. The threat of a combined attack from the east by a Syrian force in the Golan Heights and Iraq, Jordan and possibly Saudi Arabia along the 150 mile Jordanian-Israeli border, has been a nightmare scenario for Israeli defense planners. To prevent such a contingency the Israel Defense Forces (IDF) has always prepared to deploy heavy forces along the Jordan River Valley in order to destroy enemy forces on their own territory. Consequently, with the exception of the government headed by Ehud Barak, all Israeli governments held that permanent control over the Jordan River Valley is essential to Israel's security and should not be ceded even in the framework of a permanent peace agreement with the Palestinians. Operation Iraqi Freedom and the destruction of Saddam Hussein's military defused this threat. With no Iraqi military that can attack from the east, Israel's defense doctrine requires reevaluation.

This paper analyzes the changes in the Arab-Israeli military balance in light of the disintegration of the Iraqi military, outlining the conventional and non-conventional threats potentially facing Israel. It assesses the prospects and viability of a conventional attack on the eastern front in both the short and long run. It then revisits the concept of secure borders along Israel's eastern front, examining whether Israel's rationale for control of the Valley is consistent with the changes in its strategic environment.

The paper concludes that with the decline of the Iraqi military the Arab-Israeli military balance has shifted in favor of Israel and that in the short run the threat of an eastern front no longer exists. But despite the improvement in Israel's strategic posture, it is premature to assume that the threat from the east has been permanently removed and that the Valley is no longer essential to Israel's security. There are still several unknowns including the nature of the new Iraqi regime and the changes, if any, that may take place in Jordan and Syria, as well

---

Source: "All Quiet on the Eastern Front?" Saban Center for Middle East Policy at the Brookings Institution, Analysis Paper 2, March 2004. Reprinted by permission.

as the impact of *Pax Americana* in the Middle East on the behavior of the Palestinians and countries like Iran, Syria, Libya, Saudi Arabia and Lebanon.

The Jordan River Valley has an additional role no less important than preventing and deterring an attack from the east. The Valley separates the future Palestinian state from Jordan in case the Palestinians ever try to undermine and topple the Jordanian monarchy. Therefore, Israeli presence along the Jordan River is of critical importance to the security and stability of the Hashemite regime. Additionally, a joint Jordanian-Palestinian border and Palestinian control over the bridges of the Jordan River would deny Israel the ability to monitor those entering and exiting the area and allow the Palestinians to import heavy weapons, terrorists, and military reinforcements from abroad.

Nevertheless, if and when progress toward a permanent agreement resumes, Israel would surely be expected to alter its approach to deploying forces in the Jordan Valley. It will be required to articulate a new rationale for its insistence on continuous control of this territory. Adherence to the old mantra that the Valley is a buffer against an eastern front is not likely to resonate even with many of Israel's friends in the United States. On the other hand, to legitimize the Valley's role as a buffer between Jordan and the West Bank, Israel will have to make a strong case why destabilization of Jordan is likely and why this could significantly undermine Israel's security. Furthermore, such a claim could only be accepted if Jordan supports it either publicly or privately.

If Israel were required to relinquish control over the Valley as part of a final status agreement, such a withdrawal should include a test period of at least a decade before complete hand-over of the Valley takes place. In the interim period, Israel and the Palestinians can agree on certain security arrangements regarding the future of the Valley that would address Israel's security concerns without infringing on Palestinian sovereignty in the Valley.

A withdrawal would have significant ramifications for Israel's defense doctrine and force structure. Without full control of the Valley it will be more difficult for Israel to shift the battleground into neighboring territory and achieve a rapid victory the way it has done in previous wars. Without heavy forces near the bridges Israel would have to rely mostly on its airpower in order to prevent enemy forces from moving west of the Jordan River. Israel will need to develop a much more robust strategic branch capable of using long range weapons to deal with over-the-horizon threats. Currently, Israel's strategic forces are primarily designed for deterrence and defensive purposes. But were it to relinquish control of the Valley, Israel would have to significantly increase its arsenal of high-precision conventional surface-to-surface missiles capable of hitting distant enemy targets at great accuracy.

149

Government of Israel

Resolution regarding the Disengagement Plan

June 6, 2004

Following three years of Israeli-Palestinian violence, and with no prospects for negotiation, Israeli Prime Minister Ariel Sharon declared on December 18, 2003, that Israel should "unilaterally disengage" from some occupied areas that were presently under Israeli control. Sharon made clear in what became known as the Herzliya Speech that this policy would require the relocation of some Israeli settlements in the West Bank and Gaza. The prime minister asked the Israeli National Security Council to initiate a governmental process to plan for relocation. The Ministry of Justice was assigned the task of drafting legislation to authorize the evacuation and provide for compensation for those settlers who would be required to move.

Though Sharon faced substantial resistance among his coalition partners and, indeed, within his own party, he was able to pass the resolution below in the Israeli cabinet on June 6, 2004, and supporting legislation on October 25, 2004. Consequently, Sharon formed a new government with the Labor Party in January 2005. In the summer of 2005 the plan was implemented, and 9,400 settlers were relocated.

I. Background: Political and Security Implications

The State of Israel is committed to the peace process and aspires to reach an agreed resolution of the conflict based upon the vision of U.S. President George Bush.

The State of Israel believes that it must act to improve the current situation. The State of Israel has come to the conclusion that there is currently no reliable Palestinian partner with which it can make progress in a two-sided peace process. Accordingly, it has developed a plan of revised disengagement (hereinafter, the plan), based on the following considerations:

1. The stalemate dictated by the current situation is harmful. In order to break out of this stalemate, the State of Israel is required to initiate moves not dependent on Palestinian cooperation.

2. The purpose of the plan is to lead to a better security, political, economic, and demographic situation.

3. In any future permanent status arrangement, there will be no Israeli towns and villages in the Gaza Strip. On the other hand, it is clear that in the West Bank, there are areas which will be part of the State of Israel, including major Israeli population centers, cities, towns, and villages, security areas, and other places of special interest to Israel.

4. The State of Israel supports the efforts of the United States, operating alongside the international community, to promote the reform process, the construction of institutions, and the improvement of the economy and welfare

---

Source: Israel Office of the Prime Minister online, June 6, 2004, http://www.israel-mfa.gov.il/Peace+Process/Reference+Documents/Revised+Disengagement+Plan+6-June-2004.htm (accessed May 21, 2007).

of the Palestinian residents, in order that a new Palestinian leadership will emerge and prove itself capable of fulfilling its commitments under the Roadmap.

5. Relocation from the Gaza Strip and from an area in Northern Samaria should reduce friction with the Palestinian population.

6. The completion of the plan will serve to dispel the claims regarding Israel's responsibility for the Palestinians in the Gaza Strip.

7. The process set forth in the plan is without prejudice to the relevant agreements between the State of Israel and the Palestinians. Relevant arrangements shall continue to apply.

8. International support for this plan is widespread and important. This support is essential in order to bring the Palestinians to implement in practice their obligations to combat terrorism and effect reforms as required by the Roadmap [doc. 147], thus enabling the parties to return to the path of negotiation.

II. Main Elements

A. The process: The required preparatory work for the implementation of the plan will be carried out (including staff work to determine criteria, definitions, evaluations, and preparations for required legislation).

Immediately upon completion of the preparatory work, a discussion will be held by the Government in order to make a decision concerning the relocation of settlements, taking into consideration the circumstances prevailing at that time—whether or not to relocate, and which settlements.

The towns and villages will be classified into four groups, as follows:

(1) Group A: Morag, Netzarim, Kfar Darom
(2) Group B: the villages of Northern Samaria (Ganim, Kadim, Sa-Nur and Homesh)
(3) Group C: the towns and villages of Gush Katif
(4) Group D: the villages of the Northern Gaza Strip (Elei Sinai, Dudit, and Nissanit)

It is clarified that, following the completion of the aforementioned preparations, the Government will convene periodically in order to decide separately on the question of whether or not to relocate, with respect to each of the aforementioned groups.

150

Mahmoud Ahmadinejad

Speech to the World without Zionism Conference, Teheran

October 28, 2005

Following the Iranian Revolution of 1979 and the emergence of the Ayatollahs' regime, Iran has turned from being Israel's ally into being a declared enemy. There have been ups and downs in the new regime's hostility

Source: Middle East Media Research Institute, Special Dispatch Series 1013, http://www.memri.org. The Iranian Students News Agency (ISNA) published the full text of Ahmadinejad's speech. The following is a translation of excerpts from ISNA's report and from the speech, published by MEMRI.

to Israel, but in 2005–2006 matters came to a head over two main developments: Iran's quest for nuclear weapons and Israel's opposition to it, and the election of Mahmoud Ahmadinejad as Iran's president. Ahmadinejad introduced a new level of rhetoric calling for Israel's destruction, denying the Holocaust and presenting Israel and the Jews as Iran's archenemies. This rhetoric accompanied a persistent drive for Iranian hegemony in the Middle East.

We must see what the real story of Palestine is. . . . The establishment of the regime that is occupying Jerusalem was a very grave move by the hegemonic and arrogant system against the Islamic world. We are in the process of a historical war between the World of Arrogance and the Islamic world, and this war has been going on for hundreds of years.

In this historical war, the situation at the fronts has changed many times. During some periods, the Muslims were the victors and were very active, and looked forward, and the World of Arrogance was in retreat.

Unfortunately, in the past three hundred years, the Islamic world has been in retreat vis-à-vis the World of Arrogance. . . . During the period of the last one hundred years, the [walls of the] world of Islam were destroyed and the World of Arrogance turned the regime occupying Jerusalem into a bridge for its dominance over the Islamic world. . . .

This occupying country [Israel] is in fact a front of the World of Arrogance in the heart of the Islamic world. They have in fact built a bastion [Israel] from which they can expand their rule to the entire Islamic world. . . . This means that the current war in Palestine is the front line of the Islamic world against the World of Arrogance, and will determine the fate of Palestine for centuries to come.

Today the Palestinian nation stands against the hegemonic system as the representative of the Islamic *ummah* [nation]. Thanks to God, since the Palestinian people adopted the Islamic war and the Islamic goals, and since their struggle has become Islamic in its attitude and orientation, we have been witnessing the progress and success of the Palestinian people.

The issue of this [World without Zionism] conference is very valuable. In this very grave war, many people are trying to scatter grains of desperation and hopelessness regarding the struggle between the Islamic world and the front of the infidels, and in their hearts they want to empty the Islamic world. . . .

They [ask]: "Is it possible for us to witness a world without America and Zionism?" But you had best know that this slogan and this goal are attainable, and surely can be achieved. . . .

When the dear Imam [Khomeini] said that [the shah's] regime[1] must go, and that we demand a world without dependent governments, many people who claimed to have political and other knowledge [asked], "Is it possible [that the shah's regime can be toppled]?"

That day, when Imam [Khomeini] began his movement, all the powers supported [the shah's] corrupt regime . . . and said it was not possible. However, our nation stood firm, and by now we have, for twenty-seven years, been living without a government dependent on America. Imam [Khomeini] said: "The rule of the East [Soviet Union] and of the West [United States] should be ended." But the weak people who saw only the tiny world near them did not believe it.

Nobody believed that we would one day witness the collapse of the Eastern Imperialism [Soviet Union], and said it was an iron regime. But in our short lifetime we have witnessed how this regime collapsed in such a way that we must look for it in libraries, and we can find no literature about it.

Imam [Khomeini] said that Saddam [Hussein] must go, and that he would be humiliated in a way that was unprecedented. And what do you see today? A man who, ten years ago, spoke as proudly as if he would live for eternity is today chained by the feet, and is now being tried in his own country. . . .

Imam [Khomeini] said: "This regime that is occupying Qods [Jerusalem] must be eliminated from the pages of history." This sentence is very wise. The issue of Palestine is not an issue on which we can compromise.

Is it possible that an [Islamic] front allows another front [i.e., country] to arise in its [own] heart? This means defeat, and he who accepts the existence of this regime [Israel] in fact signs the defeat of the Islamic world.

In his battle against the World of Arrogance, our dear Imam [Khomeini] set the regime occupying Qods as the target of his fight.

I do not doubt that the new wave which has begun in our dear Palestine and which today we are also witnessing in the Islamic world is a wave of morality which has spread all over the Islamic world. Very soon, this stain of disgrace [Israel] will be purged from the center of the Islamic world—and this is attainable.

But we must be wary of *fitna* [civil war]. For more than fifty years, the World of Arrogance has tried to give recognition to the existence of this falsified regime [Israel]. With its first steps, and then with further steps, it has tried hard in this direction to stabilize it.

Regrettably, twenty-seven or twenty-eight years ago . . . one of the countries of the first line [Egypt] made this failure [of recognizing Israel]—and we still hope that it will correct it.

Lately we have new *fitna* under way. . . . With the forced evacuation [of Gaza] that was imposed by the Palestinian people, they [the Israelis] evacuated only a corner. [Israel] declared this as the final victory and, on the pretext of evacuating Gaza and establishing a Palestinian government, tried to put an end to the hopes of the Palestinians.

Today [Israel] seeks, satanically and deceitfully, to gain control of the front of war. It is trying to influence the Palestinian groups in Palestine so as to preoccupy them with political issues and jobs—so that they relinquish the Palestinian cause that determines their destiny, and come into conflict with each other.

On the pretext of goodwill, it [Israel] intended, by evacuating the Gaza Strip, to gain recognition of its corrupt regime by some Islamic states. I very much hope, and ask God, that the Palestinian people and the dear Palestinian groups will be wary of this *fitna*.

The issue of Palestine is by no means over, and will end only when all of Palestine will have a government belonging to the Palestinian people. The refugees must return to their homes, and there must be a government that has come to power by the will of the [Palestinian] people. And, of course those [the Jews] who came to this country from far away to plunder it have no right to decide anything for the [Palestinian] people.

I hope that the Palestinians will maintain their wariness and intelligence, much as they have pursued their battles in the past ten years. This will be a short period, and if we pass through it successfully, the process of the elimination of the Zionist regime will be smooth and simple.

I warn all the leaders of the Islamic world to be wary of *fitna*: if someone is under the pressure of hegemonic power [the West] and understands that something is wrong, or he is naïve, or he is an egotist and his hedonism leads him to recognize the Zionist regime—he should know that he will burn in the fire of the Islamic *ummah*. . . .

The people who sit in closed rooms cannot decide on this matter. The Islamic people cannot allow this historical enemy to exist in the heart of the Islamic world.

Oh dear people, look at this global arena. By whom are we confronted? We have to understand the depth of the disgrace of the enemy, until our holy hatred expands continuously and strikes like a wave.

151

Bashar al-Assad

Speech to the Arab Lawyers Union Annual Convention

January 21, 2006

In June 2000, Hafez al-Assad, Syria's ruler since 1970, passed away. Assad had built the Syrian state and turned it into an important regional and occasionally international actor. He was succeeded by his son Bashar. Bashar al-Assad's first years in power were far from smooth, and his ability to govern Syria effectively has been questioned by numerous observers inside and outside Syria. In 2005 he found himself on a collision course with the United States over his opposition to Washington's policies in Iraq and the assassination of Lebanon's former Prime Minister Ziad al-Hariri. Following are excerpts from a speech Bashar al-Assad delivered in Damascus to defend his conduct and to project a resolute image to his subjects and to the international community.

Before I start my speech . . . when I met with some foreign officials in Syria, they criticized Syrian stances and accused her of being hardliner. . . . They said that the speech of President Bashar al-Assad was hardliner and the like. . . . They accused Syria's stances of being radical, and criticized the speeches of President Bashar al-Assad in their meetings with me. I used to tell them: you should not figure out a picture of the situation through your meetings with us as officials. . . . On the contrary we are very quiet, . . . the street is boiling and we are quiet. I'm happy about what I heard because they will have the opportunity now on the TV screen to make a comparison with the difference between the stances of man on the street and recognize that concerning official stance we stand behind, not before, the stances of man on the street. Today I will be quiet, so that the picture will be completely clear and the contrast obvious.

Dear Sisters and Brothers Members of the General Conference of the Arab Lawyers' Ladies and Gentlemen. . . . It's great happiness to meet you in this conference, which you chose to be held in Damascus expressing solidarity with your country Syria. It's a great opportunity to extend to you most sincere thanks for your kind initiative for holding your conference as an expression of solidarity with your brothers in Syria, and to express my own appreciation for the honest efforts you exercise in the field of work and struggle for the victory of right and in defense of the Arab nation's issue and protect her against the dangers that threaten her. It's natural the nation calls upon her sons at times of need, . . . It's a thing taken for granted that the sons stick to their nation at hard times. . . . But in addition to that, this stage through which our nation passes requires a high degree of sense of belonging and readiness to exert more sincere efforts at work coupled with the purity of insight and the clear direction. . . . It's not a ceremonial to underscore your important role. . . .

Source: Campaign for Good Governance in Lebanon Center for Democracy and the Rule of Law, http://www.cggl.org/scripts/document.asp?id=46253 (accessed May 21, 2007).

Dear Arab lawyers, as you work for your nation's issues, I would like to focus on your exceptional role in this exceptional stage. . . . You are—by virtue of your work and proficiency, by dealing with issues of everyday life, by general activities and sticking to the issues of virtue and justice—closer than others to recognizing the nature of the accelerating ever-changing events in today's world in which the concepts of right and justice turn into mere goods for bargaining and dealings on the existing international scene, and in which conflicts of interests, powers, ideologies, and ideas clash with each other, and where concepts are sacrificed through a systematic course to deface the main aspects of conflict. In such a situation, right and virtue turn into null and void concepts, legitimate rights of peoples are denied for the interest of those who seize them. My talk with you today is therefore of particular meaning as it's addressed to professional figures who enjoy huge roles and responsibilities in the life of people and defense of their rights, . . . to lawyers who actually defend the nation and her rights, . . . to those active and important people who have their distinguished status in the lives of their countries and societies.

Dear sisters and brothers, we all follow up the current events. All of us recognize these events and the surrounding circumstances as well as their direct and indirect consequences [that] are not the product of today but rather date back to past decades. . . . But they have intensified in recent years . . . where the Arab people paid a dear price because of serious Western political projects which are strange to this region. . . . They paid the debts of others from their own blood and their stability without having any interest or role in what is going on. And while we thought that the political changes in the 1990s would lead to finding reasonable solutions to the chronic problems in our region as promised by the New World Order and its dreams, we found out that these problems had become more complicated and more confused. . . . All pledges were only illusions or daydreams. . . . We call this the New World Disorder. . . . It's only a name, but the real content is the new world disorder because there is no order at all. At the same time new problems, not less dangerous than those previous, had emerged. . . . They had rather been accumulated with them or resulted from them. . . . New spots of tension, not less than the previous in terms of heat and inflammability had come to light, and their consequences started to spread everywhere, causing problems to our Arab people. . . . And so the Palestinian issue moved nowhere. . . . Instead it retreated a step backward if we take into consideration the actual circumstances surrounding our Palestinian people and the extent of repression Israel has been practicing against this people. . . . Israel has blocked all the roads to the Middle East peace process, not only because of the rejection by Israeli successive governments to respond to the peace requirement and continued denial of Arab basic rights but also because the current international situation and influential powers are not ready to push the peace process forward, as well as for the backing down of the international community to meet their obligation toward the peace process and stability in the region. Besides, Arab actual retreat of support to the Palestinian issue as a result of continued pressures practiced for the benefit of Israel had also played a role in that retreat. The Palestinian track was not different from the Syrian-Lebanese track; added to that are the Israeli violations of Lebanese airspace and land before the eyes of a silent international community. Of course the international community is silent in such cases. . . . When it comes to a simple statement that disturbs Israel a little bit, . . . here the international community turns into an active and influential society with a tongue to speak and some times this tongue becomes fierce. . . . But when it comes to a statement by an Israeli rabbi accusing the Arabs of being serpents that must be eliminated . . . or when [the] U.S. Congress says that there is an Arab country which must be po[u]nd[ed] with a nuclear weapon to eliminate, . . . then this society keeps silent. The Iraqi issue emerged in our current political life to cause a political, pan-Arab, and moral earthquake that has created a new reality in the Middle East and whose tragic features have begun to appear on the structure of the Arab society and check up convections of people and their national and pan-Arab belonging. In addition to that, the phenomena of terrorism has begun to spread painfully, threatening the national and social structure of the countries in the region. . . . This is because of a set of factors, particularly regional, international wrong and reckless policies toward the Arab nation's heritage and issues. . . . In addition, the exploitation of this phenomena, namely terrorism, is a tool in the hands of some powers which claim [they are] fighting terrorism in order to intimidate and terrorize the others and attack their cultures [and] identities and intervene in their internal affairs.

Therefore, the developments of the Lebanese situation had emerged as one of the consequences of the new international situation since the issuing of resolution 1559 until the killing of Premier Hariri and the formation of the investigation committee and the subsequent new international resolutions, which seek to harm Syria and its stances. If some analysis said that some of the consequences of events in Lebanon were meant to cover up the failure of the occupation troops in Iraq, as their project failed there in making Iraq as its main gate—and that's right—then it's fully right to say that this is meant to target Syria and Lebanon as part of an integrated project to undermine the region's identity and reshape it under different names that finally meet Israel's ambitions to dominate the region and its resources. It's wrong to use the idiom of targeting Syria, Syria and Lebanon as brother Sameh Ashour said, . . . not in defense of Syria against Lebanon . . . as they are both targeted, . . . but what is targeted is the Arabs and the Islamic nation. . . . The targeted is wider than that. . . . But now we are talking about targeting the Arab nation. . . . What is happening now is part of a big conspiracy as Iraq is part of this conspiracy, . . . and as Gaza First[1] also was . . . and as Oslo [doc. 133] was. . . . We don't want to go back to the older parts in order not to raise some sensitivities. Gaza First was a part that failed since the very first days. . . . It aimed at causing sedition among the Palestinians. . . . Oslo was foiled by the Intifada at the beginning of its eruption. . . . The Iraqi project is now failing before the eyes of the whole world. . . . The project of the Syrian-Palestinian part will also fail. . . . But to foil this part we have to deal with the elements as one project or one conspiracy and subsequently we have to recognize that behind each conspiracy lies another conspiracy and after each part there is another part. . . . There is an interlink among these parts. The issue is not Syria and Lebanon, it is bigger than that. . . . We're not worried. . . . We feel worry over the general situation, over the Arab nation . . . so we have to know the whole dimensions of conspiracy so that we can deal with each part of it. Of course they will say now that Arabs have always [had] a psychological complex, which is the complex of conspiracy. If we go back to the past century from Sykes-Picot[2] to the occupation of Palestine in 1948 to the invasion of Lebanon in 1982 and the occupation of Iraq and the intervening events and what is happening now with Syria and Iraq, . . . maybe they don't consider these events as a conspiracy, . . . maybe they consider them as part of durable developments for the region or part of charity actions and we have to send them a cable of gratitude. As obvious in this context, Syria had been the focal point of this event, not only for its geographical site, political, social, and human link to the main conflict areas, but also for her role, status, and history. Besides, those who stand behind this conspiracy considered Syria as a main block to the establishment of their aims. In light of that, Syria had to face successive waves of challenges, and had to set out in each stance depending on her national and pan-Arab responsibilities and her strategic interests and keenness on her independence and sovereignty. . . . But this was not accepted by some international powers as well as by some Arab forces and figures who introduce themselves as agents to those powers or as a tool to carry out their plots. There is a problem with some big powers toward the Arabs and Muslims, and as I said with many or maybe with most countries of the world. We recognize this problem continuously through their statements and our meetings and discussions with them. They don't want us to commit to anything. . . . Their problem is not only the pan-Arabism or Islam. . . . They don't want all those to commit to any principle or religious, national, or even economic doctrine. They want to turn the peoples and the world into a set of computers in which they insert information and operation systems and program them in their own way to use as they like whenever they want for their own interests. And when we agree on this, then we are described as nationalist, wise, realistic, and democrats; otherwise, we are either terrorist or terrorism sponsors. . . . And this terrorism has names that change with the circumstances and interests. . . . We call this real fashion. We used to hear for decades about Palestinian terrorism then they began to talk about Lebanese terrorism during the civil war in Lebanon. . . . Today they are talking about Islamic terrorism. . . . Don't be astonished if they put soon a new idiom called sovereign terrorism which is now actually being applied to countries which seek to establish its sovereignty. In fact it is being applied, and it is only a matter of time to find out the suitable idiom. . . . This is not an exaggeration as there are now dialogues in the United Nations and the Security Council corridors by some known international powers to discuss the principle of the national sovereignty to cancel this principle under different pretexts, . . . human rights corrupt regimes, corruption and other excuses, they are searching for now. So this speech is real, but they always present idioms and we as Arabs don't go to the depth of these idioms.

As for the Arab-Israeli peace issue, we announced our desire to establish the just and comprehensive peace on the basis of U.N. resolutions, and on the basis of these resolutions we committed ourselves to the Arab Peace Initiative of Arab Summit in Beirut 2002 [doc. 145], which nobody talks about any more today. This initiative calls upon Israel to work for peace and confirms Arab readiness for peace, . . . but Israel responded to all this by ignoring peace initiatives and by more massacres and assassinations against our people under unlimited support by the United States and total silence by the other international powers. In addition to the massacres committed by Israel, particularly after the Arab initiative, it invaded Jenin and Nablus and the many systematic and premeditated assassinations, the most dangerous of which was assassination of President Yasir Arafat,[3] and I am happy because you mentioned that before the eyes of the world . . . no country dared to issue a statement or a stance towards this issue . . . as if nothing had happened in this region. Brother Colonel Muamar al-Qaddafi presented an initiative about two months ago to the current presidency of the Arab Summit represented by Algeria calling for forming an international committee to investigate into this issue. . . . Syria of course has immediately supported this initiative in writing, and I think that you as Arab lawyers and specialized in legal issues can reach a technical detailed study on this issue as a complete plan that could be presented to the next Arab Summit within months so that it could be adopted by the summit and then an Arab united move could be taken about it.

NOTES

1. In this context, the term refers to the complete Israeli withdrawal from the Gaza Strip on September 11, 2005. The same term was used a decade earlier to denote Israel's limited withdrawal from Gaza under the Oslo Accords.

2. A British-French agreement to divide the Middle East between them in the post–World War I era. The

agreement was signed in secret on May 16, 1916, and was later expanded to include Italy and Russia. The agreement includes a "border" demarcation between the British and French areas. This line determined some of the region's borders for generations to come.

3. Arafat died on November 11, 2004, in a hospital in France, from an unidentified disease. Some in the Arab world believed, however, that Israel clandestinely infected the Palestinian leader and caused his death.

152

Ehud Olmert

Speech to the Knesset on Israel's New Government

May 4, 2006

The early months of 2006 saw a series of dramatic events in Israeli politics: Ariel Sharon's decision to leave the Likud and form a new party (Kadimah), his subsequent illness and incapacitation, his succession by Ehud Olmert and Olmert's electoral victory. The impact of these events was enhanced by the changes within the Labor Party, primarily Amir Peretz's takeover and Shimon Peres's departure. The outcome of the elections held on March 28 produced a coalition resting primarily on partnership between Kadimah and the Labor Party.

On May 4, 2006, Ehud Olmert presented his new government to the Knesset and outlined its platform. The central issue governing the elections campaign and the coalition formation was Ehud Olmert's determination to continue the policy begun by Ariel Sharon when he disengaged from Gaza. The following excerpt from the speech addresses this issue.

From its birth, the State of Israel advocated two founding bases—the Jewish base and the democratic base: the supreme value of a "Jewish state," at the same time with the uncompromising demand that the democratic state of Israel will provide "complete social and political equality to all its citizens, regardless of religion, race or gender." These two bases embody the core values of the renewed Jewish sovereignty in the Land of Israel. If you take one and disconnect it from the state, it is as if you cut off its lifeline.

Therefore, those wishing to look directly into our past, see the reality of our lives and look to the future, must do so with both eyes open—the Jewish eye and the democratic eye. Only then, with both eyes open, do the colors of Israeli society come together into one clear, vivid and meaningful picture.

I, like many others, also dreamed and yearned that we would be able to keep the entire Land of Israel, and that the day would never come when we would have to relinquish parts of our land. Only those who have the Land of Israel burning in their souls know the pain of relinquishing and parting with the land of our forefathers. I personally continue to advocate

Source: JTA (Global News Service of the Jewish People), jta.org.

the idea of the entire land as a heart's desire. I believe with all my heart in the people of Israel's eternal historic right to the entire land of Israel. However, dreams and recognition of this right do not constitute a political program. Even if the Jewish eye cries, and even if our hearts are broken, we must preserve the essence. We must preserve a stable and solid Jewish majority in our State.

Therefore, we must focus on the area in which a Jewish majority is secured and ensured. The disengagement from the Gaza Strip and Northern Samaria was an essential first step in this direction, but the main part is still ahead. The continued dispersed settlement throughout Judaea and Samaria creates an inseparable mixture of populations which will endanger the existence of the State of Israel as a Jewish state. It is those who believe, as I do, in [Zeev] Jabotinsky's teachings and in full civil equality between Jews and Arabs, who must understand that partition of the land for the purpose of guaranteeing a Jewish majority is the lifeline of Zionism. I know how hard it is, especially for the settlers and those faithful to Eretz Israel, but I am convinced, with all my heart, that it is necessary and that we must do it with dialogue, internal reconciliation, and broad consensus.

This does not mean that the settlement enterprise was entirely in vain. On the contrary. The achievements of the settlement movement in its major centers will forever be an inseparable part of the sovereign State of Israel, with Jerusalem as our united capital. Let us come together around this consensus and turn it into a uniting political and moral fact.

The strength of this nation is in its unity. I will not help those wishing to cause a rift among the sectors of our nation. It is my intention to take all future steps through continuous dialogue with the wonderful settlers in Judaea and Samaria. We are brothers and we will remain brothers.

From this podium, I again address the elected President of the Palestinian Authority, Mr. Mahmoud Abbas. The Government of Israel under my leadership prefers negotiations with a Palestinian Authority committed to the principles of the Roadmap [doc. 147], which fights terror, dismantles terrorist organizations, abides by the rules of democracy, and upholds, practically and thoroughly, all agreements which have thus far been signed with the State of Israel. Negotiation with such an Authority is the most stable and desired basis for the political process, which can lead to an agreement which will bring peace. This is what we desire. The guidelines of this Government propose this. The parliamentary majority which will back the Government policy is committed to this process. These conditions cannot be blurred. We will not, under any circumstances, relinquish these demands as a basis for negotiation. The Palestinian Authority must make fundamental changes in its patterns of behavior, its reactions and its commitments to the principles which are the basis for any future negotiations.

A Palestinian Government led by terrorist factions will not be a partner for negotiation, and we will not have any practical or day-to-day relations.

The State of Israel is prepared to wait for this necessary change in the Palestinian Authority. We will closely follow the conduct of the Authority. We will continue to strike at terror and terrorists. We will not hesitate to reach terrorists, their dispatchers and operators anywhere—I repeat—anywhere, but we will give the Authority an opportunity to prove that it is aware of its responsibilities and willing to change.

That said, we will not wait forever. The State of Israel does not want, nor can it suspend the fateful decisions regarding its future—until the Palestinian Authority succeeds in implementing the commitments it undertook in the past. If we reach the conclusion that the Authority is dawdling and is not planning to engage in serious, substantial, and fair negotiation—we will act in other ways.

We will also act without an agreement with the Palestinians to create an understanding which will, first and foremost, be founded on a correct definition of the desired borders for the State of Israel.

These borders must be defensible, and ensure a solid Jewish majority. The Security Fence will be adjusted to the borders formulated east and west. The operational range of the security forces will not be limited, and will be in accordance with the security reality with which we have to deal.

The State of Israel will invest its resources in areas which will be an organic part of it. The borders of Israel, which will be defined in the coming years, will be significantly different from the areas controlled by the State of Israel today.

This is the Government's plan, it is the basis for its existence, it is the commitment made to the Israeli electorate whose trust we asked for—and received.

The agreement to which we aspire to shape the Middle East is based on consensus, broad consensus first and foremost within ourselves, and thereafter with our friends around the world.

No political process, certainly not one as fundamentally decisive and comprehensive as the one for which we are preparing, can be realized without the understanding of many officials in the international community. We have no intention of acting alone. We will consult, discuss, talk, and I am certain that we will reach understandings which will create a broad base of international backing for these steps, first and foremost with our ally and close friend, the United States led by President George Bush, and also with our friends in Europe. Israel strives to improve the understandings and agreements with the countries of Europe. Today's European leaders better understand the complexity of the situation in the Middle East. They understand that there are no simple solutions, certainly given the upswing in fundamentalist religious fanaticism in various countries in the Middle East, and the ascendancy of the pro-Iranian Hamas to the Palestinian Authority. We will deepen dialogue with Europe and strive to include its leaders in the dialogue process with the United States. I aspire to deepen the ties with Arab countries. Egypt and Jordan, countries with which we have peaceful relations, have leaders who are inspirational. President [Hosni] Mubarak and King Abdullah the Second are welcome, credible, and responsible partners—for those goals which I defined. I will do all that I can so that our relations with Egypt and the Jordanian Kingdom will continue to strengthen, and serve as a basis for diplomatic and open relations with additional Arab countries.

153

Ehud Olmert

Speech to the Knesset on the Israeli-Hezbollah Summer War

July 17, 2006

On July 12, 2006, a war in Lebanon erupted unexpectedly. On the morning of that day, Hezbollah attacked an Israel Defense Forces patrol, abducted two soldiers, and killed three. Another five Israeli soldiers were killed when an Israeli tank entered Lebanese territory in a futile attempt to bring back the abducted soldiers. At the

Source: Israel Office of the Prime Minister, Communications Department, http://www.pmo.gov.il/PMOEng/Communication/PMSpeaks/speechknesset170706.htm (accessed May 1, 2007).

same time Hezbollah shelled a number of Israeli villages as a diversion. This attack came shortly after Hamas staged a similar attack on an Israeli tank in Israel's territory close to the fence separating the Gaza Strip from Israel. These two attacks confronted Ehud Olmert's government with a severe challenge. It tested the credibility of a new prime minister, a new minister of defense, and a relatively new chief of staff of the IDF, who was the first air force general to be appointed to that post.

More broadly, given Israel's unilateral withdrawal from Lebanon in May 2000 and the disengagement from Gaza Strip in the summer of 2005, the two guiding notions of the Olmert government's policies—unilateralism and separation—were put into question. Within hours, the cabinet decided on a massive military response, fully aware of the certainty of a missile attack on northern Israel by Hezbollah. Thus a full-fledged confrontation developed. It was concluded a few weeks later by U.N. Security Council Resolution 1701 [doc. 164].

In this speech to the Knesset, Olmert provides the initial definition of the war aims. However, when the war ended on August 12, 2006, many Israelis felt that its goals were not achieved. Moreover, the government's inability to halt Hezbollah's shelling of Israel's northern sector and to appropriately assist those affected by the attacks added to the sense of failure. On September 17, 2006, in the face of public pressure, the goverment appointed an inquiry commission headed by retired Judge Eliyahu Vinograd. The commission was authorized to analyze and present findings with regard to political, civil, and military aspects of the war. On April 30, 2007, the commission submitted an interim report that was highly critical of the decision-making process prior to and during the war, within both the cabinet and the armed forces. The commission pointed to long-standing institutional weaknesses and placed much of the blame on Prime Minister Ehud Olmert and then Chief of Staff General Dan Halutz.

Madam Speaker,
Ladies and gentlemen,
Members of the Knesset,

At the outset, I offer condolences, on my behalf and on behalf of the Government, the Knesset and the entire nation, to the families of the victims—both civilian and Israel Defense Forces. I also send best wishes for recovery to the wounded, and a huge embrace for the families of those kidnapped and the boys themselves.

Over the past few weeks, our enemies have challenged the sovereignty of the State of Israel and the safety of its residents—first in the southern sector, then on the northern border, and deeper into the home front.

Israel did not seek these confrontations. On the contrary. We have done a lot to prevent them. We returned to the borders of the State of Israel recognized by the entire international community. There were those who misconstrued our desire for peace—for us and our neighbors—as a sign of frailty. Our enemies misinterpreted our willingness to exercise restraint as a sign of weakness.

They were wrong!

Madam Speaker, Members of Knesset,

The State of Israel has no territorial conflict, neither on our southern border nor on our northern one.

In these two areas, we are sitting on the recognized international border—both vis-à-vis the Palestinian Authority in the Gaza Strip, and in Lebanon.

We have no intention of interfering in their internal affairs. On the contrary, stability and tranquility in Lebanon, free of the rule of foreign powers, and in the Palestinian Authority, are in Israel's interest.

We yearn for the day when peace will prevail between us, for the mutual benefit of our peoples from both sides of our common border.

The campaign we are engaged in these days is against the terror organizations operating from Lebanon and Gaza. These organizations are nothing but "subcontractors" operating under the inspiration, permission, instigation, and financing of the terror-sponsoring and peace-rejecting regimes, on the Axis of Evil[1] which stretches from Tehran to Damascus.

Lebanon has suffered heavily in the past, when it allowed foreign powers to gamble on its fate.

Iran and Syria still continue to meddle, from afar, in the affairs of Lebanon and the Palestinian Authority, through Hezbollah and the Hamas.

Even if last Wednesday's criminal attack against an IDF patrol was carried out without the consent of the Lebanese government and without the assistance of its military, this does not absolve it of full responsibility for the attack which emanated from its sovereign territory. Just as the fact that the Chairman of the Palestinian Authority opposes terrorism against Israel does not relieve him and the Palestinian Authority of their responsibility for the attack carried out from their territory against our soldiers in Kerem Shalom. They are both fully responsible for the safety of our soldiers who were taken hostage.

Radical, terrorist, and violent elements are sabotaging the life of the entire region and placing its stability at risk. The region in which we live is threatened by these murderous terror groups.

It is a regional—as well as global—interest to take control and terminate their activity.

We can all see how the majority of the international community supports our battle against the terror organizations and our efforts to remove this threat from the Middle East.

We intend to do this. We will continue to operate in full force until we achieve this. On the Palestinian front, we will conduct a relentless battle until terror ceases, Gilad Shalit is returned home safely, and the shooting of Qassam missiles stops.

And in Lebanon, we will insist on compliance with the terms stipulated long ago by the international community, as unequivocally expressed only yesterday in the resolution by the eight leading countries of the world:

- the return of the hostages, Ehud (Udi) Goldwasser and Eldad Regev;
- a complete cease-fire;
- deployment of the Lebanese army in all of southern Lebanon;
- expulsion of Hezbollah from the area, and fulfillment of United Nations Resolution 1559.[2]

We will not suspend our actions.

On both fronts we are exercising self-defense in the most basic and essential sense. In both cases, it is a matter whose importance and significance go far beyond the size of the military units involved.

We are at a national moment of truth. Will we consent to living under the threat of this Axis of Evil, or will we mobilize our inner strength and show determination and equanimity?

Our answer is clear to every Israeli, and it echoes today throughout the entire region.

NOTES

1. A term used by President George W. Bush in his State of the Union address on January 29, 2002, to denote nations that threaten "the peace of the world" through the acquisition of weapons of mass destruction and the support of terrorism. President Bush named North Korea, Iran, and Iraq as members of the "Axis of Evil."
2. This U.N. Security Council resolution dated September 2, 2004, called for Syrian withdrawal from Lebanon and the disbanding of all militias operating in Lebanon.

154
United Nations Security Council
Resolution 1701
August 11, 2006

U.N. Security Council Resolution 1701 ended the Israeli-Hezbollah summer war of 2006 (July 12–August 15). During the fighting, Hezbollah fired about four thousand rockets into Israel and fought against Israeli forces in southern Lebanon. Israel bombed various targets in Lebanon and its ground forces entered southern Lebanon, while the navy blockaded Lebanese seaports. Israel suffered 158 deaths (mostly soldiers), and about a thousand Lebanese were killed.

The Security Council,

Recalling all its previous resolutions on Lebanon, . . .

Expressing its utmost concern at the continuing escalation of hostilities in Lebanon and in Israel since Hezbollah's attack on Israel on 12 July 2006, which has already caused hundreds of deaths and injuries on both sides, extensive damage to civilian infrastructure, and hundreds of thousands of internally displaced persons,

Emphasizing the need for an end of violence, but at the same time *emphasizing* the need to address urgently the causes that have given rise to the current crisis, including by the unconditional release of the abducted Israeli soldiers,

Mindful of the sensitivity of the issue of prisoners and *encouraging* the efforts aimed at urgently settling the issue of the Lebanese prisoners detained in Israel,

Welcoming the efforts of the Lebanese Prime Minister and the commitment of the Government of Lebanon, in its seven-point plan, to extend its authority over its territory, through its own legitimate armed forces, such that there will be no weapons without the consent of the Government of Lebanon and no authority other than that of the Government of Lebanon, *welcoming also* its commitment to a United Nations force that is supplemented and enhanced in numbers, equipment, mandate, and scope of operation, and *bearing in mind* its request in this plan for an immediate withdrawal of the Israeli forces from southern Lebanon,

Determined to act for this withdrawal to happen at the earliest,

Taking due note of the proposals made in the seven-point plan regarding the Shebaa farms area,

Welcoming the unanimous decision by the Government of Lebanon on 7 August 2006 to deploy a Lebanese armed force of 15,000 troops in South Lebanon as the Israeli army withdraws behind the Blue Line[1] and to request the assistance of additional forces from the United Nations Interim Force in Lebanon (UNIFIL) as needed, to facilitate the entry of the Lebanese armed forces into the region and to restate its intention to strengthen the Lebanese armed forces with material as needed to enable it to perform its duties,

---

Source: United Nations, Official Documents System of the United Nations, http://www.un.org/News/Press/docs/2006/sc8808.doc.htm (accessed May 21, 2007).

Sources:
Israel 1:500000 - Survey of Israel 1950
Israel 1:500000 - Survey of Israel 1975
Israel 1:250000 - Survey of Israel 2006

MAP 7. ISRAEL'S BOUNDARIES, 1949–2007

Aware of its responsibilities to help secure a permanent cease-fire and a long-term solution to the conflict,

Determining that the situation in Lebanon constitutes a threat to international peace and security,

1. *Calls for* a full cessation of hostilities based upon, in particular, the immediate cessation by Hezbollah of all attacks and the immediate cessation by Israel of all offensive military operations;

2. Upon full cessation of hostilities, *calls upon* the Government of Lebanon and UNIFIL as authorized by paragraph 11 to deploy their forces together throughout the South and *calls upon* the Government of Israel, as that deployment begins, to withdraw all of its forces from southern Lebanon in parallel;

3. *Emphasizes* the importance of the extension of the control of the Government of Lebanon over all Lebanese territory in accordance with the provisions of resolution 1559 (2004) and resolution 1680 (2006), and of the relevant provisions of the Taif Accords,[2] for it to exercise its full sovereignty, so that there will be no weapons without the consent of the Government of Lebanon and no authority other than that of the Government of Lebanon;

4. *Reiterates* its strong support for full respect for the Blue Line;

5. *Also reiterates* its strong support, as recalled in all its previous relevant resolutions, for the territorial integrity, sovereignty, and political independence of Lebanon within its internationally recognized borders, as contemplated by the Israeli–Lebanese General Armistice Agreement of 23 March 1949;

6. *Calls on* the international community to take immediate steps to extend its financial and humanitarian assistance to the Lebanese people, including through facilitating the safe return of displaced persons and, under the authority of the Government of Lebanon, reopening airports and harbours, consistent with paragraphs 14 and 15, and *calls on* it also to

consider further assistance in the future to contribute to the reconstruction and development of Lebanon;

7. *Affirms* that all parties are responsible for ensuring that no action is taken contrary to paragraph 1 that might adversely affect the search for a long-term solution, humanitarian access to civilian populations, including safe passage for humanitarian convoys, or the voluntary and safe return of displaced persons, and *calls on* all parties to comply with this responsibility and to cooperate with the Security Council;

8. *Calls for* Israel and Lebanon to support a permanent ceasefire and a long-term solution based on the following principles and elements:

- full respect for the Blue Line by both parties;
- security arrangements to prevent the resumption of hostilities, including the establishment between the Blue Line and the Litani River of an area free of any armed personnel, assets and weapons other than those of the Government of Lebanon and of UNIFIL as authorized in paragraph 11, deployed in this area;
- full implementation of the relevant provisions of the Taif Accords, and of resolutions 1559 (2004) and 1680 (2006), that require the disarmament of all armed groups in Lebanon, so that, pursuant to the Lebanese cabinet decision of 27 July 2006, there will be no weapons or authority in Lebanon other than that of the Lebanese State;
- no foreign forces in Lebanon without the consent of its Government;
- no sales or supply of arms and related materiel to Lebanon except as authorized by its Government;
- provision to the United Nations of all remaining maps of landmines in Lebanon in Israel's possession;

9. *Invites* the Secretary-General to support efforts to secure as soon as possible agreements in principle from the Government of Lebanon and the Government of Israel to the principles and elements for a long-term solution as set forth in paragraph 8, and *expresses* its intention to be actively involved;

10. *Requests* the Secretary-General to develop, in liaison with relevant international actors and the concerned parties, proposals to implement the relevant provisions of the Taif Accords, and resolutions 1559 (2004) and 1680 (2006), including disarmament, and for delineation of the international borders of Lebanon, especially in those areas where the border is disputed or uncertain, including by dealing with the Shebaa farms area, and to present to the Security Council those proposals within thirty days;

11. *Decides,* in order to supplement and enhance the force in numbers, equipment, mandate, and scope of operations, to authorize an increase in the force strength of UNIFIL to a maximum of 15,000 troops, and that the force shall, in addition to carrying out its mandate under resolutions 425 and 426 (1978) [doc. 102]:

(a) Monitor the cessation of hostilities:

(b) Accompany and support the Lebanese armed forces as they deploy throughout the South, including along the Blue Line, as Israel withdraws its armed forces from Lebanon as provided in paragraph 2;

(c) Coordinate its activities related to paragraph 11 (b) with the Government of Lebanon and the Government of Israel;

(d) Extend its assistance to help ensure humanitarian access to civilian populations and the voluntary and safe return of displaced persons;

(e) Assist the Lebanese armed forces in taking steps towards the establishment of the area as referred to in paragraph 8;

(f) Assist the Government of Lebanon, at its request, to implement paragraph 14;

12. Acting in support of a request from the Government of Lebanon to deploy an international force to assist it to exercise its authority throughout the territory, *authorizes* UNIFIL to take all necessary action in areas of deployment

of its forces and as it deems within its capabilities, to ensure that its area of operations is not utilized for hostile activities of any kind, to resist attempts by forceful means to prevent it from discharging its duties under the mandate of the Security Council, and to protect United Nations personnel, facilities, installations, and equipment, ensure the security and freedom of movement of United Nations personnel, humanitarian workers, and, without prejudice to the responsibility of the Government of Lebanon, to protect civilians under imminent threat of physical violence;

13. *Requests* the Secretary-General urgently to put in place measures to ensure UNIFIL is able to carry out the functions envisaged in this resolution, *urges* Member States to consider making appropriate contributions to UNIFIL and to respond positively to requests for assistance from the Force, and *expresses* its strong appreciation to those who have contributed to UNIFIL in the past;

14. *Calls upon* the Government of Lebanon to secure its borders and other entry points to prevent the entry in Lebanon without its consent of arms or related materiel and *requests* UNIFIL as authorized in paragraph 11 to assist the Government of Lebanon at its request;

15. *Decides* further that all States shall take the necessary measures to prevent, by their nationals or from their territories or using their flag vessels or aircraft:

(a) The sale or supply to any entity or individual in Lebanon of arms and related materiel of all types, including weapons and ammunition, military vehicles and equipment, paramilitary equipment, and spare parts for the aforementioned, whether or not originating in their territories; and

(b) The provisions to any entity or individual in Lebanon of any technical training or assistance related to the provision, manufacture, maintenance, or use of the items listed in subparagraph (a) above;

except that these prohibitions shall not apply to arms, related material, training, or assistance authorized by the Government of Lebanon or by UNIFIL, as authorized in paragraph 11;

16. *Decides* to extend the mandate of UNIFIL until 31 August 2007, and *expresses its intention* to consider in a later resolution further enhancements to the mandate and other steps to contribute to the implementation of a permanent cease-fire and a long-term solution;

17. *Requests* the Secretary-General to report to the Council within one week on the implementation of this resolution and subsequently on a regular basis;

18. *Stresses* the importance of, and the need to achieve, a comprehensive, just and lasting peace in the Middle East, based on all its relevant resolutions including its resolutions 242 (1967) [doc. 68] of 22 November 1967, 338 (1973) [doc. 86] of 22 October 1973 and 1515 (2003) of 19 November 2003;

19. *Decides* to remain actively seized of the matter.

NOTES

1. The Israeli-Lebanese border, as marked by United Nations experts when Israel withdrew from Lebanon in 2000.
2. Also known as the "National Reconciliation Charter," the Taif Accords are an intra-Lebanese agreement that ended that country's fourteen-year civil war, signed on October 22, 1989, in Taif, Saudi Arabia.

155
David Grossman
Speech at the Rabin Memorial Ceremony, Tel Aviv
November 4, 2006

David Grossman (b. 1954) is an acclaimed Israeli author. On November 4, 2006, he was the keynote speaker in a memorial gathering in Tel Aviv, marking the eleventh anniversary of the assassination of Prime Minister Yitzhak Rabin. In his speech, Grossman echoed the growing discontent of Israelis with their leadership following the second Lebanon war, a war in which Grossman lost his son, Uri.

A number of separate developments converged into a broad sense of gloom in the autumn of 2006. First, the war in Lebanon eroded the public's confidence in the executive's ability to deal with the challenges the country was facing. The erosion was mostly a result of the war's inconclusive military outcome as well as the flaws it exposed in the military and civilian decision-making processes and policy implementation.

Second, the war further highlighted questions about national solidarity and the role of the state in providing for its citizens. The state was ill equipped to support the thousands of Israelis who took shelter from Hezbollah's shelling of the north.

Third, the war led the government, in effect, to abandon its plan for further withdrawal from the West Bank. As the convergence plan (which called for further withdrawals) was the only significant item on the cabinet's agenda, the decision left Israelis wondering what vision their government held in respect to the Palestinian challenge.

Fourth, Israelis' self-confidence was challenged as the year drew to a close, as it became clear that Iran was advancing its plan to acquire a nuclear device. Combined with statements by Iranian President Mahmoud Ahmadinejad about the collapse of the Israeli state, or its being wiped off the map, the prospect of an Iranian nuclear capability seemed especially threatening (see doc. 150).

Finally, the Israeli public was disappointed to discover that a number of its leaders, including the prime minister, the president, and the minister of justice, were all being investigated for—or were engaged in—personal misconduct.

Most of all, then, Grossman's speech points to what seems like a serious gap between the challenges the country was facing, and the actual performance and quality of its leadership.

At the annual memorial ceremony for Yitzhak Rabin, we pause to remember Yitzhak Rabin the man, and the leader. We also look at ourselves, at Israeli society, at its leadership, at the state of the national spirit, at the state of the peace process, and at our place, as individuals, within these great national developments.

This year, it is not easy to look at ourselves.

Source: Yediot Aharonoth, http://vnet.co.il/articles/0,7340,L-3323594.00.html. Translated by Haim Watzman. Reprinted by permission of the author.

We had a war. Israel brandished its huge military biceps, but at its back its reach proved all too short, and brittle. We realized that our military might alone cannot, when push comes to shove, defend us. In particular, we discovered that Israel faces a profound crisis, much more profound than we imagined, in almost every part of our collective lives.

I speak here, this evening, as one whose love for this land is tough and complicated, but nevertheless unequivocal. And as one for whom the covenant he always had with this land has become, to my misfortune, a covenant of blood. I am a man entirely without religious faith, but nevertheless, for me, the establishment, and very existence, of the state of Israel is something of a miracle that happened to us as a people—a political, national, human miracle. I never forget that, even for a single moment. Even when many things in the reality of our lives enrage and depress me, even when the miracle disintegrates into tiny fragments of routine and wretchedness, of corruption and cynicism, even when the country looks like a bad parody of that miracle, I remember the miracle always.

That sentiment lies at the foundation of what I will say tonight.

"See, land, that we were most wasteful," the poet Shaul Tchernichowski wrote in 1938. He grieved that in the bosom of the earth, in the land of Israel, we have interred, time after time, young people in the prime of their lives. The death of young people is a horrible, outrageous waste. But no less horrible is the feeling that the state of Israel has, for many years now, criminally wasted not only the lives of its sons and daughters, but also wasted the miracle that occurred here—the great and rare opportunity that history granted it, the opportunity to create an enlightened, properly functioning democratic state that would act in accordance with Jewish and universal values. A country that would be a national home and refuge, but not only a refuge. It would also be a place that gives new meaning to Jewish existence. A country in which an important, essential part of its Jewish identity, of its Jewish ethos, would be full equality and respect for its non-Jewish citizens.

Look what happened.

Look what happened to this young, bold country, so full of passion and soul. How in a process of accelerated senescence Israel aged through infancy, childhood and youth, into a permanent state of irritability and flaccidity and missed opportunities. How did it happen? When did we lose even the hope that we might some day be able to live different, better lives? More than that—how is it that we continue today to stand aside and watch, mesmerized, as madness and vulgarity, violence and racism take control of our home?

And I ask you, how can it be that a people with our powers of creativity and regeneration, a nation that has known how to pick itself up out of the dust time and again, finds itself today—precisely when it has such great military power—in such a feeble, helpless state? A state in which it is again a victim, but now a victim of itself, of its fears and despair, of its own shortsightedness?

One of the harsh things that this last war sharpened for us was the feeling that in these times there is no king in Israel. That our leadership is hollow, both our political and military leadership. I am not speaking now of the obvious fiascos in the conduct of the war, or of the way the rear was left to its own devices.[1] Nor am I speaking of our current corruption scandals, great and small.[2] My intention is that the people who today lead Israel are unable to connect Israelis with their identity, and certainly not with the healthy, sustaining, inspiring parts of Jewish identity. I mean those constitutive parts of identity and memory and values that can give us strength and hope, that can serve as antidotes to the attenuation of mutual responsibility and of our connection to the land, that can grant meaning to our exhausting, desperate struggle for survival.

Today, Israel's leadership fills the husk of its regime primarily with fears and intimidations, with the allure of power and the winks of the backroom deal, with haggling over all that is dear to us. In this sense, they are not real leaders. They are certainly not the leaders that a people in such a complicated, disoriented state need. Sometimes, it seems that the sound box of their thinking, of their historical memory, of their vision, of what really is important to them, fills only the tiny space between two newspaper headlines. Or between two police investigations.

Look at those who lead us. Not at all of them, of course, but all too many of them. Look at the way they act—terrified, suspicious, sweaty, legalistic, deceptive. It's ridiculous to even hope that the Law will come forth from them, that they can produce a vision, or even an original, truly creative, bold, momentous idea. When was the last time that the prime minister suggested or made a move that could open a single new horizon for Israelis? A better future? When did he take a social, cultural, or ethical initiative, rather than just react frantically to the actions of others?

Mr. Prime Minister, I do not say these things out of anger or vengeance. I have waited long enough; I am not speaking on the impulse of a moment. You cannot dismiss my words tonight by saying "a man should not be held to what he says when he is mourning." Of course I am mourning. But more than I am in pain, I hurt. This country, and what you and your colleagues are doing to it, pains me. In all sincerity, it is important to me that you succeed. Because our future depends on your ability to rise up and act. Yitzhak Rabin turned to the path of peace with the Palestinians[3] not because he was fond of them or their leaders. Then also, if you remember, the common wisdom was that we had no partner among the Palestinians, and that there was nothing for us to talk about with them. Rabin decided to act, because he detected, with great astuteness, that Israeli society could not long continue in a state of unresolved conflict. He understood, before many people understood, that life in a constant climate of violence, of occupation, of terror and fear and hopelessness, comes at a price that Israel cannot afford to pay.

All this is true today as well, and much more sharply. In a bit we'll talk about the partner that we do or don't have, but first let's look at ourselves.

For more than a hundred years we have lived in a conflict. We, the citizens of that conflict, were born into a war, we were educated within it, and in a sense we were educated for it. Perhaps for that reason we sometimes think that this madness that we've been living in for a century now is the only true thing, that it is the life we are destined for, and that we have no way, even no right, to aspire to a different kind of life. We will live and die by the sword, and the sword shall devour forever.

Maybe that explains the apathy with which we accept the total cessation of the peace process, a moratorium that has lasted for years now, and has cost ever more casualties. That can also explain how most of us have failed to respond to the brutal kick democracy received when Avigdor Lieberman was appointed a senior cabinet minister. It's the appointment of a compulsive pyromaniac to head the country's firefighters.[4]

And these are some of the reasons that, in an amazingly short time, Israel has degenerated into heartlessness, real cruelty toward the weak, the poor, and the suffering. Israel displays indifference to the hungry, the elderly, the sick, and the handicapped, equanimity in the face of, for example, trafficking in women, or the exploitation of foreign workers in conditions of slave labor; and in the face of profound, institutionalized racism toward its Arab minority. When all this happens as if it were perfectly natural, without outrage and without protest, I begin to fear that even if peace comes tomorrow, even if we eventually return to some sort of normality, it may be too late to heal us completely.

The calamity that my family and I suffered, when my son Uri fell in the war last summer, does not give me any special privileges in our national debate. But it seems to me that facing death and loss brings with it a kind of sobriety and clarity, at least when it comes to distinguishing the wheat from the chaff, between what can and cannot be achieved. Between reality and fantasy.

Every thinking person in Israel—and, I will add, in Palestine as well—knows today precisely the outline of a possible solution to the conflict between the two peoples. All thinking people, in Israel and in Palestine, know deep in their hearts the difference between, on the one hand, their dreams and wishes, and on the other, what they can get at the end of the negotiations. Those who don't know that, whether Jews or Arabs, are already not part of the dialogue. Such people are trapped in their hermetic fanaticism, so they are not partners. Let's look for a minute at our potential partners. The Palestinians have placed Hamas in their leadership, and Hamas refuses to negotiate with us, refuses even to recognize us. What can we do in such a situation? What more can we do? Tighten the noose even more? Continue to kill hundreds of Palestinians in the Gaza Strip, the great majority of them innocent civilians, like us?

Appeal to the Palestinians, Mr. Olmert. Appeal to them over Hamas's head. Appeal to the moderates among them, to those who, like you and me, oppose Hamas and its ideology. Appeal to the Palestinian people. Speak to their deepest wound, acknowledge their unending suffering. You won't lose anything, and Israel's position in any future negotiation will not be compromised. But hearts will open a bit to each other, and that opening has great power. Simple human compassion has the power of a force of nature, precisely in a situation of stagnation and hostility.

Look at them, just once, not through a rifle's sights and not through a road block. You will see a people no less tortured than we are. A conquered, persecuted, hopeless people. Of course the Palestinians are also guilty of the dead end we've reached. Of course they bear part of the blame for the failure of the peace process. But look at them for a moment in a different way. Not just at their extremists. Not just at those who have an alliance of mutual interest with our own extremists. Look at the great majority of this wretched nation, whose fate is bound up with ours, like it or not.

Go to the Palestinians, Mr. Olmert. Don't look for reasons not to talk to them. You've given up on unilateral disengagement. And that's good. But don't leave a vacuum. It will fill up immediately with violence and destruction. Talk to them. Make them an offer that their moderates can accept (there are far more of them than the media shows us). Make them an offer, so that they will have to decide whether to accept it, or instead remain hostages to fanatical Islam. Go to them with the boldest, most serious plan that Israel is able to put forward. A plan that all Israelis and Palestinians with eyes in their heads will know is the limit of refusal and concession, ours and theirs. If you hesitate, we'll soon be longing for the days when Palestinian terrorism was an amateur affair. We will pound ourselves on our heads and shout, why did we not use all our flexibility, all our Israeli creativity, to extricate our enemy from the trap in which he ensnared himself?

Just as there is unavoidable war, there is also unavoidable peace. Because we no longer have any choice. We have no choice, and they have no choice. And we need to set out towards this unavoidable peace with the same determination and creativity with which we set out to an unavoidable war. Anyone who thinks there is an alternative, that time is on our side, does not grasp the profound, dangerous process that is now well underway.

Perhaps, Mr. Prime Minister, I need to remind you, that if any Arab leader sends out signals of peace, even the slightest, most hesitant ones, you must respond. You must immediately test his sincerity and seriousness. You have no moral right not to respond. You must do so for the sake of those who will be expected to sacrifice their lives if another war breaks out.

So if President Assad says that Syria wants peace, even if you don't believe him—and we're all suspicious—you must propose a meeting that very same day. Don't wait a single day longer. After all, when you set out on the last war you didn't wait for even an hour. You charged in with all our might. With every weapon we have. With all our power to destroy. Why, when there is some sort of flicker of peace, do you immediately reject it, dismiss it? What do you have to lose? Are you suspicious of the Syrian president? Go offer him terms that will reveal his trickery. Offer him a peace process lasting several years, only at the end of which, if he meets all the conditions, lives up to all the restrictions, will he get the Golan Heights. Force him into a process of ongoing dialogue. Act so that his people will be made aware of the possibility, help the moderates, who must exist there as well. Try to shape reality, not to be its collaborator. That's why you were elected. Precisely for that reason.

And in conclusion. Of course not everything depends on what we do. There are great and strong forces acting in this region and in the world, and some of them, like Iran, like radical Islam, wish us ill. Nevertheless, so much does depend on what we do, and what we will be. The differences between right and left are not that great today. The decisive majority of Israel's citizens now understand—of course, some of them without enthusiasm—what the shape of a peaceful solution will look like. Most of us understand that the land will be divided, that there will be a Palestinian state. Why, then do we continue to sap ourselves with the internal bickering that has gone on now for almost forty years? Why does our political leadership continue to reflect the positions of the extremists and not of the majority? After all, we'll be much better off if we reach this national consensus on our own, before circumstances—external pressures, or a new Palestinian uprising, or another war—force us to do so. If we do it, we will save ourselves years of erosion and error, years in which we will shout again and again, "See, land, that we were most wasteful."

From where I stand at this moment, I request, call out to all those listening—to young people who came back from the war, who know that they are the ones who will have to pay the price of the next war; to Jewish and Arab citizens, to the people of the right and the people of the left: stop for a moment. Look over the edge of the abyss, and consider how close we are to losing what we have created here. Ask yourselves if the time has not arrived for us to come to our senses, to break out of our paralysis, to demand for ourselves, finally, the lives that we deserve to live.

NOTES

1. Grossman refers to the limited state support to the thousands of Israelis who remained in shelters in northern Israel during the summer war.
2. These included a police investigation into sexual misconduct by the president and the minister of justice and a number of other investigations into the prime minister's conduct in some financial matters.
3. Grossman is referring to Yitzhak Rabin's 1993 decision to negotiate with the PLO.
4. Avigdor Lieberman (b. 1958) was appointed on October 30, 2006, to serve as minister for strategic affairs and deputy prime minister. Grossman is critical of the appointment as Lieberman had made a number of controversial and hawkish statements prior to his appointment.

Appendices

APPENDIX 1. PRESIDENTS OF THE STATE OF ISRAEL, 1949–2007

NAME	TERM
Chaim Weizmann	February 1949–November 1952[a]
Yitzhak Ben-Zvi	December 1952–April 1963[a]
Zalman Shazar	May 1963–May 1973
Efraim Kaztir	May 1973–May 1978
Yitzhak Navon	May 1978–May 1983
Chaim Herzog	May 1983–May 1993
Ezer Weizman	May 1993–July 2000[b]
Moshe Katzav	August 2000–July 2007[b]
Shimon Peres	July 2007–

a. Died in office.
b. Resigned.

APPENDIX 2. CHIEFS OF STAFF OF THE ISRAEL DEFENSE FORCES, 1939–2007

NAME	TERM
Yaacov Dori	1939–1945
Yaacov Dori	1947–1948 (Haganah)
Yaacov Dori	1948–1949
Yigael Yadin	1949–1952
Mordechai Makleff	1952–1953
Moshe Dayan	1953–1958
Haim Laskov	1958–1961
Zvi Zur	1961–1964
Yizhak Rabin	1964–1968
Haim Bar-Lev	1968–1972
David Elazar	1972–1974
Mordechai Gur	1974–1978
Rafael Eytan	1978–1983
Moshe Levi	1983–1987
Dan Shomron	1987–1991
Ehud Barak	1991–1995
Amnon Lipkin-Shahak	1995–1998
Shaul Mofaz	1998–2002
Moshe Ya'alon	2002–2005
Dan Halutz	2005–2007
Gabi Ashkenazi	2007–

APPENDIX 3. GOVERNMENTS OF ISRAEL, 1948–2006

KNESSET	PROV. GOV.	1		2				3		4		5		6		7	8		9	10		11		12		13	14	15	16		17
	5/14/1948	3/7/1949	11/1/1950	10/8/1951	12/22/1952	1/26/1954	6/29/1955	11/3/1955	1/7/1958	12/17/1959	11/2/1961	6/24/1963	12/22/1964	1/12/1966	3/17/1969	12/15/1969	3/10/1974	6/3/1974	6/20/1977	8/7/1981	10/10/1983	9/14/1984	8/26/1986	12/22/1988	6/11/1990	7/13/1992	6/18/1996	7/7/1999	3/7/2000	2/28/2003	5/4/2006
Mapai	▲	▲	▲	▲	▲	▲	▲	▲	▲	▲	▲	▲	▲	▲																	
P. Miz	▲	▲	▲	▲	▲	▲	▲	▲																							
Mapam								▲	▲	▲				▲	▲	▲	▲	▲													
Gen. Zion																															
Progr.	▲	▲	▲		▲	▲	▲	▲	▲	▲																					
Sephardim																															
Mizrahi	▲	▲	▲																												
Agudah	▲	▲	▲	▲																											
NRP						▲	▲	▲	▲	▲	▲	▲	▲	▲	▲	▲	▲	▲	▲	▲	▲	▲	▲	▲	▲		▲	▲	▲	▲	
Ahdut Avodah								▲	▲	▲	▲	▲	▲	▲																	
Rafi														▲																	
ILP [a]														▲	▲	▲	▲	▲												▲	▲
Ind. Lib.														▲	▲	▲	▲	▲													
Gahal														▲	▲	▲															
CRM																	▲														
Lik-Herut																		▲	▲	▲											
DMC																		▲													
Lik-Lib																		▲	▲	▲											
Shlomzion																		▲													
Lik-Laam																		▲	▲	▲											
Hatehiyah																			▲	▲											
Tami																			▲	▲											
Telem																			▲												
ILP/One Israel [b]																					▲	▲	▲			▲		▲	▲		
Likud [c, d]																					▲	▲	▲	▲		▲		▲	▲		

Ometz	▲									
Shas	▲	▲	▲		▲	▲	▲	▲		▲
Shinui	▲								▲	
Morasha	▲									
Yahad	▲									
Tsomet					▲					
Meretz[e]								▲		
The Third Way									▲	
UTJ									▲	▲
Yisrael Beitenu										▲
Yisrael Ba'aliya									▲	
Kadimah[f]									▲	▲
Ihud Leumi [g]										▲
Gil										▲

Source: Israel Government Year Book, 1950–1965, 1968–1972, 1981, 1982, 1984, 1986, 1988, 1990, 1992, 1996, 1999; official website of the Knesset, www.knesset.gov.il.

a. Joined in January 2005.
b. Includes ILP, Gesher, and Meimad.
c. Includes Likud, Gesher, and Tsomet.
d. Includes Yisrael Ba'aliya.
e. Includes Ratz, Mapam, and Shinui.
f. Founded during the sixteenth Knesset.
g. Includes Yisrael Beitenu, Tkumah, and Moledet.

Political Party Abbreviations

Agudah	Agudat Israel
Ahdut Avodah	Ahdut Haavodah
CRM	Civil Rights Movement
DMC	Democratic Movement for Change
Gen. Zion	General Zionists
Gil	Gimlaai Israel Laknesset (Pensioners' Party, founded 2006)
Ihud Le'eumi	(includes Yisrael Beitenu, Tkuma, and Mopedet)
ILP	Israel Labor Party
Ind. Lib.	Independent Liberals
Kadimah	Founded in November 2005 by Ariel Sharon, who left the Likud
Lik-Herut	Herut Faction of the Likud
Lik-Laam	Laam Faction of the Likud
Lik-Lib	Liberal Faction of the Likud
Mizrahi	Hamizrahi
NRP	National Religious Party (Mafdal)
P. Agudah	Poalei Agudat Israel
P. Miz	Hapoel Hamizrahi
Progr.	Progressive Party
Ratz	Hatnuah Lezkhuyot Haezrah Veshalom (Movement for Civil Rights and Peace)
Shinui	Tnuah Leshinui Veyozmah (Change)
Tami	Tnuah Mesortit Israelit (Israeli Traditional Movement)
UTJ	United Torah Judaism

APPENDIX 4. VALID VOTES FOR PRIME MINISTER ELECTIONS, 1996, 1999, 2001

	PERCENT	ABSOLUTE NUMBERS
5/29/1996		
Total Voters		3,121,270
Valid Votes		2,972,589
Benjamin Netanyahu	50.49	1,501,023
Shimon Peres	49.51	1,471,566
5/17/1999		
Total Voters		3,372,952
Valid Votes		3,193,494
Ehud Barak	56.08	1,791,020
Benjamin Netanyahu	43.92	1,402,474
6/2/2001		
Total Voters		2,805,938
Valid Votes		2,722,021
Ehud Barak	37.62	1,012,944
Ariel Sharon	62.38	1,698,077

Source: Central Bureau of Statistics, *Statistical Abstract of Israel, 1999* (Jerusalem, 1999) table 20.4; *Statistical Abstract of Israel, 2002* (Jerusalem, 2002), table 20.4; *Statistical Abstract of Israel, 2005* (Jerusalem, 2005), table 20.4.

APPENDIX 5. JEWISH AND NON-JEWISH POPULATION OF PALESTINE-ISRAEL, 1517–2004

YEAR	GRAND TOTAL	JEWS	NON-JEWS	NON-JEWISH PERCENTAGE
1517	300,000 est.	5,000	295,000	98.3
1882	300,000	24,000	276,000	92.0
1918	660,000	60,000	600,000	90.9
1931	1,035,821	174,610	861,211	83.1
1936	1,366,692	384,078	982,614	71.9
1946	1,810,037	543,000	1,267,037	70.0
1948[a]	872,700	716,700	156,000	17.9
1949	1,173,900	1,013,900	160,000	13.6
1950	1,370,100	1,203,000	167,100	12.2
1951	1,577,800	1,404,400	173,400	11.0
1952	1,629,500	1,450,200	179,300	11.0
1953	1,669,400	1,483,600	185,800	11.1
1954	1,717,800	1,526,000	191,800	11.1
1955	1,789,100	1,590,500	198,600	11.1
1956	1,872,400	1,667,500	204,900	10.9
1957	1,976,000	1,762,800	213,200	10.7
1958	2,031,700	1,810,200	221,500	10.9
1959	2,088,700	1,858,800	229,900	11.0
1960	2,150,400	1,911,300	239,100	11.1
1961	2,234,200	1,981,700	252,500	11.3
1962	2,331,800	2,068,900	262,900	11.2
1963	2,430,100	2,155,600	274,500	11.3
1964	2,525,600	2,239,200	286,400	11.3
1965	2,598,400	2,299,100	299,300	11.5
1966	2,657,400	2,344,900	312,500	11.7
1967	2,776,300	2,383,600	392,700	14.1
1968	2,841,100	2,434,800	406,300	14.3
1969	2,929,500	2,506,800	422,700	14.4
1970	3,022,100	2,582,000	440,100	14.5
1971	3,120,700	2,662,000	458,700	14.7
1972	3,225,000	2,752,700	472,300	14.6
1973	3,338,200	2,845,000	493,200	14.8
1974	3,421,600	2,906,900	514,700	15.0
1975	3,493,200	2,959,400	533,800	15.3
1976	3,575,400	3,020,400	555,000	15.5
1977	3,653,200	3,077,300	575,900	15.7
1978	3,737,600	3,141,200	596,400	15.9
1979	3,836,200	3,218,400	617,800	16.1

APPENDIX 5. JEWISH AND NON-JEWISH POPULATION *(CONTINUED)*

YEAR	GRAND TOTAL	JEWS	NON-JEWS	NON-JEWISH PERCENTAGE
1980	3,921,700	3,282,700	639,000	16.3
1981	3,977,700	3,320,300	657,400	16.5
1982	4,063,600	3,373,200	690,400	17.0
1983	4,118,600	3,412,500	706,100	17.1
1984	4,199,700	3,471,700	728,000	17.3
1985	4,266,200	3,517,200	749,000	17.5
1986	4,331,300	3,561,400	769,900	17.7
1987	4,406,500	3,612,900	793,600	18.0
1988	4,476,800	3,659,000	817,800	18.2
1989	4,559,600	3,717,100	842,500	18.4
1990	4,821,700	3,946,700	875,000	18.1
1991	5,058,800	4,144,600	914,200	18.0
1992	5,195,900	4,242,500	953,400	18.3
1993	5,327,600	4,335,200	992,400	18.6
1994	5,471,500	4,441,100	1,030,400	18.8
1995	5,612,300	4,522,300	1,090,000	19.4
1996	5,757,900	4,616,100	1,141,800	19.8
1997	5,900,000	4,701,600	1,198,400	20.3
1998	6,041,400	4,785,100	1,256,300	20.8
1999	6,209,100	4,872,800	1,336,300	21.5
2000	6,369,300	4,955,400	1,413,900	22.2
2001[b]	6,508,800	5,025,000	1,483,800	22.8
2002	6,631,100	5,094,200	1,536,900	23.2
2003	6,748,400	5,165,400	1,583,300	23.4
2004	6,869,500	5,237,600	1,631,900	23.7

Source: Central Bureau of Statistics, *Statistical Abstract of Israel, 1999* (Jerusalem, 1999), table 2.1; *Statistical Abstract of Israel, 2002* (Jerusalem, 2002), table 2.1; *Statistical Abstract of Israel, 2005* (Jerusalem, 2005), table 2.1.

a. Majority Arab [non-Jewish] population displaced by Israel's establishment.

b. The data do not include about 150,000 guest workers.

APPENDIX 6. JEWISH SETTLEMENTS ESTABLISHED IN PALESTINE, ISRAEL, AND THE ADMINISTERED TERRITORIES BY REGION AND PERIOD OF SETTLEMENT, BEFORE 1870–1997 (MEASURED IN TERMS OF SERVICE OF WORLD ZIONIST CONGRESSES)

FROM CONGRESS TO CONGRESS	PERIOD	TOTAL	GALILEE MTNS.	NORTHERN REGION	CENTRAL REGION	NEGEV & ARAVA	WEST BANK	JORDAN VALLEY	GOLAN HEIGHTS	GAZA REGION
Old Settlement	Established before 1870	8	1	3	3	1	—	—	—	—
Up to First Zionist Congress	1870–1896	14	—	6	8	—	—	—	—	—
1–5	1897–1900	—	—	—	—	—	—	—	—	—
5–8	1901–1906	7	—	6	1	—	—	—	—	—
8–11	1907–1912	8	—	6	2	—	—	—	—	—
11–14	1913–1924	32	—	22	10	—	—	—	—	—
14–17	1925–1930	28	—	13	15	—	—	—	—	—
17–20	1931–1936	64	1	20	43	—	—	—	—	—
20–22	1937–1947	125	7	65	36	17	—	—	—	—
22–23	1948–1950	261	27	62	130	42	—	—	—	—
23–24	1951–1955	122	4	22	51	45	—	—	—	—
24–25	1956–1960	41	6	9	11	15	—	—	—	—
25–26	1961–1963	9	1	3	1	4	—	—	—	—
26–27	1964–1966	13	5	—	5	3	—	—	—	—
27–28	1967–1971	33	—	—	4	3	4	9	12	1
28–29	1972–1976	32	—	2	2	7	6	5	9	1

APPENDIX 6. JEWISH SETTLEMENTS ESTABLISHED IN PALESTINE, ISRAEL, AND THE ADMINISTERED TERRITORIES BY REGION AND PERIOD OF SETTLEMENT, BEFORE 1870–1997 (MEASURED IN TERMS OF SERVICE OF WORLD ZIONIST CONGRESSES) *(CONTINUED)*

FROM CONGRESS TO CONGRESS	PERIOD	TOTAL	GALILEE MTNS.	NORTHERN REGION	CENTRAL REGION	NEGEV & ARAVA	WEST BANK	JORDAN VALLEY	GOLAN HEIGHTS	GAZA REGION
29–30	1977–1982	205	64	4	6	29	62	17	14	9
30–31	1983–1988	65	13	4	1	10	28	3	2	4
31–32	1989–1992	15	2	—	—	1	9	—	1	2
32–33	1993–1997	14	1	—	7	2	3	—	1	—
Grand Total		1096	132	247	336	179	112	34	39	17
Been Approved		25	3	1	—	2	15	2	1	1

Source: "Map of Settlements of Eretz Israel," presented by the Settlement Division of the Jewish Agency and the Settlement Division of the Zionist Organization, September 1997.

Note: This table includes the following types of settlements: kibbutzim, moshavim shitufim, moshavim, villages, moshavot (farm communities), rural/industrial centers, nahal settlements intended for conversion into civilian settlements, community villages/settlements (planned housing projects in the West Bank, usually for about 300 families, with closed membership and nominally cooperative structure for the provision of municipal, welfare, and cultural services and economic activity), agricultural institutions, and schools and urban settlements.

Settlements that have undergone ideological schisms subsequent to their initial establishment and hence have divided into two settlements affiliated with different movements are treated according to the date of initial settlement. Similarly, settlements that have been abandoned and subsequently resettled are treated according to the date of first settlement.

APPENDIX 7. IMMIGRATION TO ISRAEL, 1948–2004

YEAR	NUMBER OF IMMIGRANTS[a]
1948–99	2,971,827
1948[b]	101,821
1949	239,954
1950	170,563
1951	175,279
1952	24,610
1953	11,575
1954	18,491
1955	37,258
1956	56,330
1957	72,634
1958	27,290
1959	23,988
1960	24,692
1961	47,735
1962	61,533
1963	64,489
1964	55,036
1965	31,115
1966	15,957
1967	14,469
1968	20,703
1969	38,111
1970	36,750
1971	41,930
1972	55,888
1973	54,886
1974	31,981
1975	20,028
1976	19,754
1977	21,429
1978	26,394
1979	37,222
1980	20,428
1981	12,599
1982	13,723
1983	16,906
1984	19,981
1985	10,642
1986	9,505
1987	12,965
1988	13,034

APPENDIX 7. IMMIGRATION TO ISRAEL, 1948–2004 *(CONTINUED)*

YEAR	NUMBER OF IMMIGRANTS[a]
1989	24,050
1990	199,516
1991	176,100
1992	77,057
1993	76,805
1994	79,844
1995	76,361
1996	70,919
1997	66,221
1998	56,722
1999	76,766
2000	60,192
2001	43,580
2002	33,567
2003	23,268
2004	20,898

Source: Central Bureau of Statistics, *Statistical Abstract of Israel, 1999* (Jerusalem, 1999), table 5.1; *Statistical Abstract of Israel, 2005* (Jerusalem, 2005), table 4.4.

a. Number includes tourists who change their status and potential immigrants from 1969, but excludes immigrating citizens.

b. From May 15, 1948.

APPENDIX 8. IMMIGRANTS TO ISRAEL FROM ARAB COUNTRIES, 1948–2004

COUNTRY[a]	1948–51	1952–60	1961–64	1965–71	1972–79	1980–89	1990–2001	2003	2004
Lebanon	235	846	150	2,058	564	179	99	—	9
Syria	2,678	1,870	1,251	887	842	995	1,664	4	—
Iraq	123,371	2,989	520	1,609	939	111	1,325	26	19
Yemen[b]	48,315	1,170	732	334	51	17	686	4	12
Libya	30,972	2,079	318	2,148	219	66	94	—	5
Egypt, Sudan	16,024	17,521	1,233	1,730	535	352	202	15	14
Morocco	28,263	95,945	100,354	30,153	7,780	3,809	3,276	283	251
Algeria	3,810	3,433	9,680	3,177	2,137	1,830	1,682	180	238
Tunisia	13,293	23,569	3,813	7,753	2,148	1,942	1,607	263	228

Source: Central Bureau of Statistics, *Statistical Abstract of Israel, 2005* (Jerusalem, 2005), table 4.4.

a. Country of birth.

b. Includes South Yemen.

APPENDIX 9. AMERICAN IMMIGRATION TO ISRAEL, 1948–2004

YEAR	NUMBER OF IMMIGRANTS
1948–99	77,654
1948–51	1,711
1952–60	1,553
1961–64	2,102
1965–71	16,569
1972–79	20,963
1980–89	18,904
1990–97	12,925
1998	1,604
1999	1,323
2000	492
2001	1250
2002	1536
2003	1688
2004	1891

Source: Central Bureau of Statistics, *Statistical Abstract of Israel, 1999* (Jerusalem, 1999), table 5. 1; *Statistical Abstract of Israel, 2002* (Jerusalem, 2002), table 4.4; *Statistical Abstract of Israel, 2005* (Jerusalem, 2005), table 4.4.

Note: This table includes all immigrants and potential immigrants whose last country of residence was the United States.

APPENDIX 10. JEWISH IMMIGRATION TO ISRAEL FROM THE SOVIET UNION AND FORMER SOVIET UNION, 1968–2004

YEAR	NUMBER LEAVING	NUMBER IMMIGRATING TO ISRAEL
1968	231	231
1969	3,033	3,033
1970	999	999
1971	12,897	12, 839
1972	31,903	31,652
1973	34,733	33,277
1974	20,767	16,888
1975	13,363	8,435
1976	14,254	7,250
1977	16,833	8,350
1978	28,956	12,090
1979	51,331	17,278
1980	21,648	7,570
1981	9,448	1,762
1982	2,692	731
1983	1,314	861
1984	896	340
1985	1,140	348
1986	904	201
1987	8,155	2,072
1988	18,961	2,173
1989	71,005	12,117
1990	228,400	183,400
1991	187,500	147,520
1992	122,398	64,145
1993	101,887	66,145
1994	100,830	68,079
1995		64,847
1996		59,043
1997		54,591
1998		46,033
1999		66,848
2000		50,817
2001		33,600
2002		18,525
2003		12,423
2004		10,130

Source: Noah Lewin-Epstein and Yaacov Ro'i, eds., *Russian Jews on Three Continents* (London, 1997), p. 19; Central Bureau of Statistics, *Statistical Abstract of Israel, 1996* (Jerusalem, 1996), table 5.4; *Statistical Abstract of Israel, 1997* (Jerusalem, 1997), table 5.3; *Statistical Abstract of Israel, 1998* (Jerusalem, 1998), table 5.3; *Statistical Abstract of Israel, 1999* (Jerusalem, 1999), table 5.3; *Statistical Abstract of Israel, 2000* (Jerusalem, 2000), table 5.3; *Statistical Abstract of Israel, 2001* (Jerusalem, 2001), table 4.4, table 5.4; *Statistical Abstract of Israel, 2002* (Jerusalem, 2002), table 4.4; *Statistical Abstract of Israel, 2003* (Jerusalem, 2003), table 4.4; *Statistical Abstract of Israel, 2004* (Jerusalem, 2004), table 4.4; *Statistical Abstract of Israel, 2005* (Jerusalem, 2005), table 4.4.

Note: Statistics on numbers leaving the Soviet Union and former Soviet Union, 1995–2004, were not readily available.

APPENDIX 11. CHANGE IN LEVEL OF CONSUMER PRICE INDICES, 1973–2005

YEAR	CONSUMER PRICE INDEX
1973	20.0
1974	39.7
1975	39.3
1976	31.3
1977	34.6
1978	50.6
1979	78.3
1980	131.0
1981	116.8
1982	120.3
1983	145.7
1984	373.8
1985	304.6
1986	48.1
1987	19.9
1988	16.3
1989	20.2
1990	17.2
1991	19.0
1992	12.0
1993	11.0
1994	12.3
1995	10.1
1996	11.3
1997	9.0
1998	5.4
1999	5.2
2000	1.1
2001	1.1
2002	5.6
2003	0.7
2004	−0.4
2005	1.3

Source: Central Bureau of Statistics. *Statistical Abstract of Israel, 1999* (Jerusalem, 1999), table 10.1; *Statistical Abstract of Israel, 2005* (Jerusalem, 2005), table 13.1.

APPENDIX 12. NUMBER OF INSTITUTIONS AND STUDENTS IN THE EDUCATIONAL SYSTEM, 1948–2005

	1948–49	1959–60	1969–70	1979–80	1989–90	1999–2000	2003–4	2004–5
Number of Institutions in the Educational System, Jewish Education								
Primary	467	1,501	1,519	1,475	1,392	1,880	1,972	1,960
Post-primary	98	353	545	521	620	1,137	1,292	1,292
Intermediate	—	—	32	248	304	481	504	500
Secondary (total, one- and multi-track)	98	353	544	478	538	992	1,162	1,156
General (secondary)	39	113	219	232	340	569	733	727
Continuation classes	33	95	109	59	50	—	—	—
Vocational (secondary)	26	60	258	310	313	102	106	109
Agricultural (secondary)	—	30	30	27	24	2	2	2
Teacher Training	—	—	40	53	27	40	54	54
Universities[a]	3	5	6	7	7	7	7	7
Total (primary, intermediate, and secondary)	565	1,854	2,064	1,996	2,012	2,957	3,131	3,114
Grand Total (Jews and Arabs, primary, intermediate, and secondary)	611	2,000	2,320	2,367	2,432	3,539	3,805	3,007

Source: Central Bureau of Statistics, *Statistical Abstract of Israel, 2005* (Jerusalem, 2005), table 8.10.

a. Excludes the Open University.

Note: In this and the following tables, schools in which studies are held at more than one level (such as primary and intermediate, or intermediate and secondary) are counted at each level, but in the "total" they are counted only once. Institutions defined as "other" include special schools, centers for juvenile offenders, and, in the Jewish sector, certain religious schools with curricula not controlled by the Ministry of Education. Enrollment figures for the universities include all students, including non-Jews. Through 1970, over 98 percent of the university students were Jews. In 1978–79, 96.7 percent of all university students were Jews (and 94.6 percent of all students were studying for their first degree).

APPENDIX 12. NUMBER OF INSTITUTIONS AND STUDENTS IN THE EDUCATIONAL SYSTEM, 1948–2005 (*CONTINUED*)

	1948–49	1959–60	1969–70	1979–80	1999–2000	2003–4	2004–5
Number of Students, Jews							
Kindergarten	25,406	75,699	107,668	246,600	294,384	306,193	310,000
Primary	91,133	375,054	394,354	436,387	558,640	569,068	573,225
Post-primary	10,218	55,142	129,436	143,810	272,267	286,623	284,284
Intermediate	—	—	7,908	72,792	195,024	190,095	188,906
General (secondary)	7,168	32,894	63,731	61,583	153,405	172,776	174,718
Continuation (secondary)	1,048	7,065	8,508	6,438	—	—	—
Vocational (secondary)	2,002	10,167	49,556	70,681	115,224	110,252	105,672
Agricultural (secondary)	—	5,016	7,641	5,108	2,892	2,965	3,227
Teacher Training	—	—	4,994	11,285	28,442	31,104	31,144
Post-secondary Institutions	1,296	5,801	11,894	25,341	47,211	54,946	55,000
Non-university Institutions for Higher Education	—	—	—	—	53,809	73,168	77,738
Universities (Jews and Arabs)	1,635	9,275	35,374	54,480	113,010	124,805	124,430
Other Institutions	—	10,952	26,300	44,000	40,305	36,054	36,000
Total	129,688	531,923	712,954	1,023,410	1,573,930	1,640,952	1,649,583
Grand Total (Jews and Arabs)	140,817	578,003	823,491	1,200,636	1,911,427	2,059,740	2,080,900

Source: Central Bureau of Statistics, *Statistical Abstract of Israel, 2005* (Jerusalem, 2005), table 8.12.

APPENDIX 12. NUMBER OF INSTITUTIONS AND STUDENTS IN THE EDUCATIONAL SYSTEM, 1948–2005 (*CONTINUED*)

	1948–49	1959–60	1969–70	1979–80	1989–90	1999–2000	2003–4	2004–5
Number of Institutions in the Educational System, Arab Education								
Primary	45	139	219	312	330	401	442	454
Post-primary	1	7	37	59	90	194	257	267
Intermediate	—	—	4	43	69	106	132	138
Secondary (total, one and multi-track)	1	7	35	49	93	136	186	185
General (secondary)	1	5	18	51	80	74	105	103
Vocational (secondary)	—	—	16	31	43	4	22	23
Agricultural (secondary)	—	1	1	2	2	—	—	—
Teacher Training	—	—	1	2	2	3	4	4
Universities (primary, intermediate, and secondary)	0	0	0	0	0	0	0	0
Total	46	146	256	371	420	582	674	693
Grand Total (Jews and Arabs, primary, intermediate, and secondary)	611	2,000	2,320	2,367	2,432	3,539	3,805	3,007

Source: Central Bureau of Statistics, *Statistical Abstract of Israel, 2005* (Jerusalem, 2005), table 8.10.

APPENDIX 12. NUMBER OF INSTITUTIONS AND STUDENTS IN THE EDUCATIONAL SYSTEM, 1948–2005 (*CONTINUED*)

	1948–49	1959–60	1969–70	1979–80	1999–2000	2003–4	2004–5
Number of Students, Arabs							
Kindergarten	1,124	7,274	14,211	17,344	55,480	83,305	84,000
Primary	9,991	36,729	85,449	121,985	181,640	208,695	211,917
Post-primary	14	1,956	8,050	22,473	49,543	60,471	64,873
Intermediate	—	—	2,457	14,803	47,844	63,414	67,927
General (secondary)	14	1,933	6,198	19,034	35,615	38,623	40, 147
Vocational (secondary)	—	—	1,462	2,645	13,333	21,546	23,986
Agricultural (secondary)	—	23	390	794	568	15	448
Teacher Training	—	121	370	485	2,621	3,633	4,074
Post-secondary Institutions	—	121	370	621	2,990	2,903	2,600
Universities (Jews and Arabs)	1,635	9,275	35,374	54,480	113,010	124,805	124,340
Total	11,129	46,080	110,537	177,226	337,497	418,788	431,317
Grand Total (Jews and Arabs)	140,817	578,003	823,491	1,200,636	1,911,427	2,059,740	2,080,900

Source: Central Bureau of Statistics, *Statistical Abstract of Israel, 2005* (Jerusalem, 2005), table 8.12.

Glossary

Abuhazeira, Aharon (b. 1938): former minister in both Menahem Begin cabinets and mayor of Ramle, 1971–77.

Ahdut Haavodah (Unity of Labor): Socialist Zionist Party, although this name is used to refer to two separate political parties. Ahdut Haavodah was founded in 1919. In 1930 it merged with Hapoel Hazair to form Mapai. Hapoel Hazair (Young Worker; full name Histadrut Hapoalim Hazeirim Beeretz Israel, or Organization of Young Workers in Eretz Israel) was a Social-Democratic Zionist Party active in Palestine, 1919–30.

In the 1930s Siah Bet (Faction B), a leftist faction within Mapai, opposed many of Ben-Gurion's compromises with the Revisionists and with the non-Socialist Zionists. This faction was based in the settlements of Hakibbutz Hameuhad, which had been politically aligned with the previous Ahdut Haavodah and the Tel Aviv Labor Council. In 1942 Mapai decided to prohibit organized factions within the party. In 1944 Siah Bet left Mapai and formed a new party, Hatnuah Leahdut Haavodah (Movement for the Unity of Labor).

In 1946 Poalei Zion Smol (Leftist Labor Zionists) joined this party to form Hatnuah Leahdut Haavodah–Poalei Zion. In 1947–48 Hatnuah Leahdut Haavodah-Poel Zion merged with Hashomer Hatzair to form Mapam, but this merger lasted only until 1954, when Ahdut Haavodah reconstituted itself as a separate party. In 1968 Ahdut Haavodah joined in the formation of the Labor Party.

Ahmadinejad, Mahmoud (b. 1956): sixth president of the Islamic Republic of Iran. Ahmadinejad is known for his confrontational style—from denying the Holocaust to vowing to destroy Israel—and his support for Hezbollah.

Alliance Israélite Universelle (est. 1860): first modern international Jewish organization, centered in Paris. Among its most significant activities was the establishment of many schools for Jewish children in the French colonies, which facilitated their "modernization."

Allon (Feikovitz), Yigal (1918–1980): leader of Ahdut Haavodah and a leading figure in the Labor Party. Allon was commander in chief of the Palmach from 1946 until its dissolution in 1948. He entered the government for the first time in 1961. After the formation of the Labor Party he emerged as one of the major political figures in Israel, serving as deputy prime minister and minister of foreign affairs.

Aloni, Shulamit (b. 1928): Israeli lawyer who left the Labor Party in 1973 to form the Civil Rights Movement (CRM). Aloni was minister without portfolio in the Yitzhak Rabin government until November 1974, when her party joined the opposition. Aloni was head of the Meretz Party in 1992 and served as minister of education under Rabin, 1992–93.

Alterman, Nathan (1910–1970): a leading Israeli poet, writer, and translator who was one of the most influential public intellectuals from the 1940s until his death.

American Jewish Committee (est. 1906): oldest Jewish defense organization in the United States. Originally an elitist organization of prominent Jews, it has broadened its membership and organizational base. In the early 1950s it cooperated, to a limited extent, with other Jewish organizations.

American Jewish Congress (est. 1922): organization with a broad membership base and a democratic structure that seeks to act on behalf of the desires and interests of American Jewry.

American Jewish Joint Distribution Committee (est. November 27, 1914, as the Joint Distribution Committee of American Funds for the Relief of Jewish War Sufferers; frequently called "The Joint"): major relief organization of American Jewry. It coordinated American Jewish philanthropic efforts to aid European Jewry during and after the Holocaust.

Arafat, Yasir (1929–2004): chairman of al-Fatah, 1968–2004, and of the Palestine Liberation Organization, 1969–2004. An engineer by profession, Arafat served as a reserve officer in the Egyptian army in the late 1950s and was chairman of the Palestinian Student Union in Gaza, 1957. By 1958 he had emerged as one of the foremost leaders of al-Fatah and became its spokesman in February 1968. When Palestinian groups led by al-Fatah took over the PLO the following year, Arafat assumed its chairmanship as well. In September 1970 he became commander in chief of all Palestinian guerrilla forces. In 1994 Arafat shared the Nobel Peace Prize with Shimon Peres and Yitzhak Rabin for achieving the Oslo Accords. In 1990 Arafat was elected chairman of the Palestinian Authority, a position he held until his death in 2004.

Aranne (Aronowicz), Zalman (1899–1970): leader of Mapai and its secretary general, 1948–41. Aranne entered the cabinet for the first time in 1954 and twice served as minister of education and culture, 1955–60, 1963–69.

Aridor, Yoram (b. 1933): Israeli minister of finance, 1981–83, and Israeli ambassador to the United Nations, 1990–92.

Assad, Hafez al- (1930–2000): leader of the Syrian Ba'ath Party and Syrian head of state, 1970–2000. Assad was minister of defense, commander of the Syrian Air Force, 1966–70, and a member of the Allawite minority. In October 1970 he led a coup and became prime minister and minister of defense. He was elected president in 1971 and held that position until his death in 2000, after which his son, Bashar, was appointed president.

Avidar, Yosef (1906–1995): prominent figure in Mapai and the Labor movement. Avidar joined the Haganah in the late 1920s and worked his way up through the defense establishment and later into the leading circles of the ministry of foreign affairs. He was ambassador to the Soviet Union, 1955–58, and to Argentina, 1961–65. He was also director general of the ministry of labor, 1959–60, and comptroller of the Histadrut, 1968–71.

Avriel, Ehud (1917–1980): protegé of Ben-Gurion and leading figure in the Israeli Ministry of Foreign Affairs. As ambassador to Czechoslovakia and Hungary in 1948, Avriel was involved in arms procurement. As deputy director general in charge of African affairs and international cooperation and ambassador to Ghana in the 1960s, he was one of the architects of Israel's African policy.

Azaniah, Baruch (1904–1995): member of Knesset, 1949–69. Azaniah was a lawyer turned kibbutz teacher.

Aziz, Faisal Ibn Abd al- (c. 1905–1975): king of Saudi Arabia, 1964–75. Faisal was the second son of Abd al-Aziz, the first monarch of Saudi Arabia. Faisal's ability to establish order and his good fiscal management eventually led to his rise to power. In March 1964, the ministerial committee stripped his brother, King Saud (r. 1963–64), of power in the midst of the crisis caused by the Yemen civil war and the conflict with Egypt; Faisal became king. He was assassinated by a nephew in March 1975 and was immediately succeeded by his half-brother, crown prince and deputy prime minister Khalid Ibn Abd-al-Aziz Al Saud (1913–1982).

Bader, Yohanan (1901–1994): one of the chief leaders of the Herut movement and a longtime active member of the Knesset, 1949–77. Bader was an economist and a lawyer by profession.

Bar-Lev, Haim (1924–1994): deputy chief of staff during the Six-Day War and chief of staff, 1968–72. Like two of his predecessors in the Israel Defense Forces' top position—Moshe Dayan and Yitzhak Rabin—Bar-Lev began his military career in the Palmach. After his tenure as chief of staff, Bar-Lev entered the cabinet and was later secretary general of the Labor Party, 1978–84; member of the Knesset, 1977–92; minister of trade and industry, 1972–77; and minister of police, 1984–90.

Bar-Rav-Hai, David (1894–1977): lawyer who represented Mapai in the first five Knessets, 1949–65.

Barkatt (Burstein), Reuven (1906–1972): head of the International Department of the Histadrut, 1950–60. Later Barkatt was secretary general of Mapai, 1962–66, and speaker of the Knesset, 1969–72.

Barou, Noah (1889–1955): economist and Labor Zionist who settled in Britain and became chairman of the British and European sections of the World Jewish Congress.

Begin, Menahem (1913–1992): Israeli prime minister, 1977–83, and leader of the Herut movement (later Gahal) and later the Likud Party. Begin joined the Revisionist youth movement, Beitar, in interwar Poland and quickly became one of the leaders of the Revisionist movement in Europe. He was imprisoned in the Soviet Union for his activities and spent time in a Soviet labor camp. Upon his release, he left for Palestine and in December 1943 became the commander of Etzel. With the founding of the State of Israel, Begin reorganized the Revisionists into a political party—the Herut movement—and thus he remained the leader of the Israeli Labor movement's chief political rival. He led his party for twenty-eight years. As an opposition leader he was given a position in the National Unity cabinet of June 1967. Elected prime minister in 1977 and serving for six years, Begin signed Israel's first peace accord with an Arab country (Egypt, 1979) and authorized the 1982 War in Lebanon.

Ben Eliezer, Aryeh (1913–1970): member of the Knesset, 1949–70, representing the Herut (later Gahal and later Likud) Party.

Ben-Gurion, David (1886–1973): Israel's first prime minister. Ben-Gurion led the campaign toward Jewish statehood and enforced the decisions to accept the partition plan and Jewish statehood in the territory assigned to it. During his long career Ben-Gurion left his mark on practically every aspect of pre-state Israel and on the new State of Israel. He was leader of the Histadrut, the Federation of Workers in Israel, and of the Jewish Agency. He built Israel's defense establishment and laid the foundations for pro-Israeli political organization in the United States. He was a dominant figure in the life of the country until his second and final resignation as prime minister in 1970.

Ben-Porat, Mordechai (b. 1923): minister without portfolio in the second and third Likud cabinets. Ben-Porat, who was a member of Mapai, Rafi, and the Labor Party, left the Labor Party to lead the Zionist and Social Renewal Party in

1977. In the 1981 elections he joined Moshe Dayan's Telem. With the death of Dayan, the party ceased to be a coherent political organization, and in the summer of 1982 the remnant of Telem joined the Likud coalition in return for Ben-Porat's ministerial appointment, which was confirmed by the Knesset on July 5, 1982. During the War of Independence, Ben-Porat was sent back to his birthplace, Iraq, to organize Operation Ezra and Nehemiah, the underground organization of immigration to Israel of Iraqi Jews.

Ben-Zvi, Yitzhak (Shimshelevitz) (1884–1963): second president of the State of Israel, 1952–1963. Ben-Zvi was an early leader of the Socialist Zionist movement in Russia and Palestine and a co-founder of the Hashomer movement.

Berlin, Isaiah (1909–1997): noted British historian and philosopher who was active in public life and Jewish and Zionist affairs.

Bernadotte, Folke (1895–1948): Swedish diplomat appointed by the U.N. General Assembly on May 20, 1948, as the mediator in the War of Independence. He was effective in securing two cease-fires between the warring sides. His solutions, however, were unacceptable to Jewish extremists. On September 17, 1948, he and his assistant were assassinated in Jerusalem. In response, the Israeli government disbanded Lehi, the organization to which the killers belonged. In 1995 Israel's foreign minister apologized to the Bernadotte family.

Bernstein, Perez (1890–1971): member of the Knesset, 1949–65. Bernstein served as minister of trade and industry, 1948–49, 1953–55.

B'nai B'rith (est. 1843): world's oldest and largest Jewish service and fraternal organization.

Board of Deputies of British Jews (est. 1760): representative organization of British Jewry.

Boumedienne, Houari (pseud. of Muhammed Ben Brahim Boukharrouba) (1923–1978): president of Algeria, 1965–78. Colonel Boumedienne joined forces with Ahmed Ben-Bella to stage the civilian-military coup of 1962, then became commander of the National People's Army and, in late September 1962, independent Algeria's first minister of defense. For almost three years Ben-Bella and Boumedienne shared power, until Boumedienne led a coup in May 1965.

Brezhnev, Leonid (1906–1982): secretary general of the Communist Party of the Soviet Union. In 1964 Brezhnev and Aleksey Kosygin replaced Nikita Khrushchev as head of the Soviet government and Communist Party. Brezhnev was succeeded by Yuri Andropov.

Brzezinski, Zbigniew (b. 1928): national security adviser to President Jimmy Carter, 1977–81, who like his predecessor, Henry Kissinger, had an academic career.

Bunche, Ralph Johnson (1904–1971): American diplomat who accompanied Folke Bernadotte on his mission to the Middle East and succeeded him as mediator. Bunche was successful in arranging a cease-fire and the subsequent Rhodes armistice negotiations. For this work he was awarded the 1950 Nobel Peace Prize, the first of several individuals to receive the award for peace efforts in this war-ravaged area. After the Suez crisis Bunche directed U.N. operations, including the U.N. Emergency Force, in the Middle East. A brilliant scholar, Bunche was the first African American to earn a PhD in government from Harvard (1934). Following his work in the Middle East, he was appointed under secretary general of the United Nations in 1955.

Bush, George Herbert Walker (b. 1924): president of the United States, 1989–93. Bush was president during the 1991 Persian Gulf War.

Bush, George Walker (b. 1946): president of the United States beginning in 2001.

Carter, James (Jimmy) Earl (b. 1924): president of the United States, 1977–81. In the early years of his presidency Carter seemed to favor improving U.S. relations with the Palestine Liberation Organization and (in order to promote a U.S.-Soviet détente) including the Soviet Union in peace negotiations. Following Anwar Sadat's visit to Jerusalem in 1977, however, Carter dropped these policies and was instrumental in achieving the Camp David Accords. In 2002 he was awarded the Nobel Peace Prize for his humanitarian work.

Chamoun, Camille (1900–1986): Christian president of Lebanon, 1952–58, and leader of the National Liberal Party. In the 1950s Chamoun advocated close relations with the United States. His attempt to run for another term in 1958 was one of the causes of U.S. military intervention in Lebanon that year. Afterward he opposed Syria's presence in Lebanon, and his party and forces were reduced to a secondary role within Lebanon's Christian community.

Chou En-Lai (Zhou Enlai) (1898–1976): first prime minister of the People's Republic of China, from 1949 until his death. Chou was also minister of foreign affairs. He played a major role in the Bandung Conference and in early efforts to promote Third World interests, especially opposition to the two great powers, the United States and the Soviet Union.

Christopher, Warren (b. 1925): American lawyer and diplomat. Christopher served as secretary of state, 1993–97, during President William Jefferson Clinton's first term.

Clinton, William Jefferson (b. 1946): president of the United States, 1993–2001.

Cohen-Kagen, Rachel (1888–1982): member of the Knesset, 1949–51, 1961–65, first representing the WIZO Women's Party and later representing the Liberals and Independent Liberals.

Danin, Ezra (1903–1984): leading Arab affairs expert in the Jewish Agency's Political Department. After independence, Danin served for twenty years as a senior official in the Ministry of Foreign Affairs.

Dayan, Moshe (1915–1981): Israeli military and political leader. Dayan received his early military experience in the Haganah and British forces. During the War of Independence he held several different commands. From 1956 to 1958 he was chief of staff of the Israel Defense Forces. In 1957 he became active in Mapai. He was a member of the Knesset, 1959–81. As one of David Ben-Gurion's young protégés being groomed for future leadership, Dayan was appointed minister of agriculture, 1959–64. Dayan resigned in October 1964 as a result of his conflict with Prime Minister Levi Eshkol, and the next year he left Mapai to join Ben-Gurion in Rafi. During the May 1967 crisis Dayan was asked to serve as defense minister and remained in that position until 1974. After that his political career was uneven. He was elected to the Knesset in 1977 on the Labor Party list. After the elections he left the Labor Party and joined Menahem Begin's government, where he served as minister of foreign affairs, 1977–79, playing an important and constructive role in the Israeli-Egyptian negotiations. He left Begin's government because he was denied the role of chief negotiator for Israel in the autonomy talks relating to policy in the West Bank. In the 1981 elections he gained a seat in the Knesset by forming his own new party, Telem.

De Gaulle, Charles (1890–1970): leader of the French Resistance during World War II, founder of the Fifth Republic, and president of France, 1959–69. During the last years of the Fourth Republic, de Gaulle remained aloof from the political squabbles and conflicts. Nevertheless, he still commanded great influence and loyalty among many French politicians and citizens. After the Six-Day War, de Gaulle accused Israel of aggression, criticized Israeli policy, and called for an immediate withdrawal of Israeli troops from the conquered territory.

Democratic Movement for Change (DMC; also called by its acronym, Dash): movement and political party formed in 1976 when the Shinui (Change) movement (a liberal protest movement arising after the Yom Kippur War and led by Tel Aviv University law professor Amnon Rubinstein; see doc. 63) merged with Yigael Yadin's Democratic list. Later that year the DMC also attracted the Zionist Panthers (a faction of the former Black Panthers; see doc. 64) and Shmuel Tamir's faction of the Merkaz Hofshi. It thus expanded its base but also sowed the seeds of its own destruction. In the 1977 elections the DMC won fifteen seats and became the third largest party. Apparently it attracted many intellectuals and middle-class Ashkenazim who were disgruntled with the Labor Party. Following the elections it joined the Likud government, and Yadin became the deputy prime minister after some protracted negotiations that split the party.

Dulles, John Foster (1888–1959): American statesman who served as U.S. secretary of state, 1953–59.

Dulzhin, Aryeh (1913–1987): chairman of the Jewish Agency, 1978–87. Born in Belarus, Dulzhin immigrated to Mexico (1928) and then to Israel (1956). He spent most of his political career in the Jewish Agency. For a short time, 1969–70, he served as a minister without portfolio.

Eban, Abba (1915–2002): member of Israel's foreign policy-making elite from 1948 to 1974. Eban was deputy prime minister, 1963–66, and foreign minister, 1966–74. From 1950 to 1959 he served as ambassador to the United States and as chief Israeli delegate to the United Nations. He was a member of Mapai and then of the Labor Party.

Ehrlich, Simhah (1915–1983): leader of the Liberal Party and later of Gahal, especially of the centrist Liberal faction within Gahal and, later, the Likud. In 1977, with the election victory of the Likud, Ehrlich became minister of finance. He was influenced by the American economist Milton Friedman in his economic policies, and he attempted to change the structure of Israel's economy by allowing market forces a greater role, promoting private enterprise in all spheres, removing controls on foreign exchange, and severely reducing or eliminating government subsidies on basic foodstuffs and fuel.

Eisenhower, Dwight D. (1890–1969): president of the United States, 1953–61.

Eitan, Rafael (Raful) (1929–2004): Israeli chief of staff, 1978–83. Eitan began his military career as an officer in the Palmach and held high-ranking positions in the Paratroop Brigade, was operations commander of the Northern Area, 1974–77, and chief of the General Staff Branch, 1977–78. In April 1983 Eitan was succeeded by Moshe Levy.

Eshkol, Levi (Shkolnik) (1895–1969): Israeli prime minister. Eshkol was a Socialist Zionist since his youth in Russia and a founder of both Mapai and the Histadrut, the trade union federation. He served as minister of agriculture, 1951–52; minister of finance, 1952–63; minister of housing, 1965–66; prime minister and defense minister beginning in June 1963. The events of June 1967 forced him to give up the defense portfolio. He remained prime minister until his death in March 1969.

Etzel (acronym for Irgun Zvai Leumi, National Military Organization; also referred to as the Irgun and IZL): military arm of the Revisionist movement, the political and ideological opponent of the dominant trends of Zionism. Etzel was formed in April 1937 when its precursor, the Haganah Bet, split from the Haganah and the Jewish Agency over the issue of independence. Members of Etzel asserted the right to retaliate against Arab attacks on Jews, which were increasing in the late 1930s. In 1944 Etzel began to use terrorist tactics, usually directed against British military installations, in order to force the British out of Palestine. Etzel's activities on behalf of the Revisionist program brought it into conflict with the Haganah. Etzel also came into conflict with the Jewish Agency, and after May 14, even the State of Israel itself. David Ben-Gurion insisted that Etzel disband and join the Israel Defense Forces, while Menahem Begin and Etzel desired to retain at least a certain measure of autonomy.

Evron, Efraim (b. 1921): leading member of the Israeli foreign service for many years. In 1954–55 Evron was head of the Defense Minister's Office. Later, after the Likud came to power, he became ambassador to the United States, succeeding Simha Dinitz in 1978. He stepped down from this post in January 1982 and was succeeded by Moshe Arens.

Eytan, Walter (1910–2001): leading member of Israel's foreign service. Eytan was a member of the Israeli delegation to the Rhodes armistice negotiations. He was director general of the Ministry of Foreign Affairs, 1948–59, and ambassador to France, 1960–70.

Farouk (1920–1965): king of Egypt, 1936–52. Farouk was forced to abdicate in July 1952 after the successful Egyptian Officers' Revolt led by Gamal Abdul Nasser.

Fatah, al- (reverse acronym for Harakat Tahrir Filastin, Palestine Liberation Movement; the acronym also forms the Arabic word for "Conquest"): oldest and largest political and military organization of Palestinians, formed in the late 1950s. Since 1969 al-Fatah has been the dominant member of the Palestine Liberation Organization. Yasir Arafat served as its chairman from 1969 until his death in 2004. After the Oslo Accords Fatah became the mainstay of the Palestinian Authority. In 2006 it lost out in parliamentary elections to Hamas.

Ford, Gerald R. (1913–2006): president of the United States, 1974–76. Ford, who had spent a generation in the U.S. House of Representatives, became vice president when Spiro T. Agnew was forced to resign in 1973. He then became president when Richard M. Nixon resigned in August 1974.

Gahal (acronym for Gush Herut-Liberalim, Herut-Liberal bloc): 1965 coalition of the Liberal party and Herut. Gahal later incorporated several very small parties to form the Likud, which came to power in 1977.

Galili, Israel (1911–1986): deputy minister of defense in the Israeli Provisional Government. Galili began his political career at age fourteen when he founded Hanoar Haoved, a Labor youth movement, and its first agricultural settlement. Later he became a leading member of Ahdut Haavodah, the Socialist Zionist Party, and deputy commander in chief of the Haganah. After the establishment of the State of Israel he served in several governments.

Goldmann, Nahum (1895–1982): Zionist leader, co-founder (1936) and president, 1953–77, of the World Jewish Congress. The Polish-born and German-raised Goldmann emigrated to the United States at the outbreak of World War II. In 1935 he had been stripped of his German citizenship and eventually settled in the United States. In 1962 he left the United States for Israel, where he became a citizen. In 1968 he moved to Switzerland. Goldmann was instrumental in establishing contact with West German chancellor Konrad Adenauer and led the negotiations that culminated in the Luxembourg Agreement establishing the German reparations program.

Gordon, Aharon David (1856–1922): early leader of the Labor Zionist movement who advocated labor as a means of personal self-fulfillment as well as national renaissance. Gordon stressed in particular the importance of "natural" agricultural labor.

Govrin, Akiva (1902–1980): member of Knesset, 1949–65, representing Mapai (later, Hamaarach, current Labor). Govrin served also as minister without portfolio, 1963–64, and minister of tourism, 1964–66.

Gur, Mordechai (Mota) (1930–1995): Israeli military leader who served as a commander of the paratroopers (his brigade fought in Jerusalem in 1967), military attaché to the United States during the Yom Kippur War, and chief of staff, 1974–78. Gur was active in the Labor Party.

Habib, Philip Charles (1920–1992): U.S. diplomat who served as special presidential envoy to the Middle East between 1981 and 1983. Earlier Habib had served as U.S. ambassador to South Korea, 1971–74, and as undersecretary of state for political affairs, 1976–78.

Haganah (Defense): semi-underground military force established in 1920 under the authority of the Jewish Agency and in pre-state years dominated by the Labor movement. With independence the Haganah became the organizational core of the Israel Defense Forces.

Haolam Hazeh–Koah Hadash (This World–New Force): nonsocialist leftist party in Israel led by Uri Avnery, editor of the weekly magazine *Haolam Hazeh.* The party, generally referred to simply as Haolam Hazeh, ran in the 1965 and 1969 elections. In 1973 it split into two factions—Meri (acronym for Mahaneh Radikali; Radical Camp) and the Israel Democrats. Meri, led by Avnery, attracted support from parts of Maki and Siah. The Israel Democrats, led by Shalom Cohen, a longtime assistant to Avnery, gained support from most of the Black Panthers (see doc. 64). In 1977 Meri joined Shelli.

Hamas (est. 1987): Palestinian Islamist organization centered in Gaza, the Palestinian branch of the Muslim Brotherhood. It challenged both Israel and the Fatah, which Hamas saw as less engaged with current issues. In the 2006 elections for the Palestinian Authority, Hamas unexpectedly won a majority of seats.

Hammarskjold, Dag (1905–1961): Swedish diplomat who was secretary general of the United Nations, 1953–61. Hammarskjold won the 1961 Nobel Peace Prize posthumously for his long years of service to the United Nations.

Harari, Yizhar (1908–1978): member of the Knesset, 1949–73. Harari, a lawyer by training, represented the Progressive Party, 1949–61; the Liberal Party, 1961–65; the Independent Liberal Party, 1965–68; and the Labor Party, 1968–73.

Harkabi, Yehoshafat (1921–1995): Israeli general and academic. Harkabi was a member of the delegation to the Rhodes armistice negotiations. He later became head of Israel's military intelligence. In his second career he became a professor of Middle Eastern studies and international relations at the Hebrew University of Jerusalem. His major areas of research included Arab positions regarding Israel and Zionism, and terrorism and guerrilla warfare.

Hazan, Yaakov (Jacob Chasan) (1899–1992): leader of Hashomer Hatzair and Mapam, founder of Hakibbutz Haazi. Hazan served as a member of the Knesset, 1948–73.

Herut (Freedom): political arm and organizational successor to Etzel, formed in June 1948 under Menahem Begin's leadership. Although the Revisionists had refused to accept the legitimacy of the Labor-dominated Jewish Agency Executive, independence forced them to participate in the elections to the First Knesset.

Herzog, Chaim (1918–1997): first military governor of the West Bank, June 1967, and later president of Israel, 1983–93. Herzog's military career included service as chief of staff of the Southern Command, 1957–59; director of military intelligence, 1959–62; and military attaché to the

United States, 1950–54. Subsequently he entered private practice as a lawyer but remained an influential military commentator. He was active in the Labor Party and was Israel's ambassador to the United Nations, 1975–78. He was the son of Rabbi Yizhak Halevi Herzog and the brother of Yaacov Herzog.

Herzog, Yitzhak (Isaac) Halevi (1888–1959): founder of the Religious Zionist Mizrahi movement in England. In 1936 Herzog became the chief rabbi of the Ashkenazi community in Palestine. He is the father of Chaim Herzog (1918–1997), the sixth president of Israel, 1983–93; and Yaacov Herzog (1921–1972) who served as director general of the Israel Foreign and Prime Minister offices.

Hibbat Zion (Love of Zion): movement founded in 1882 as a direct reaction to the widespread pogroms in Russia in 1881, for the purpose of encouraging Jewish settlement in Palestine and achieving a Jewish national revival there. The movement encouraged its members to immigrate to Palestine, and those who did played an important role in founding new agricultural settlements such as Rishon Le'Zion and Zmamrin (current Zichron Yaacov). The movement also played a significant role in the revival of the Hebrew language. But there was tension between its religious and secular wings, and with the emergence of Herzlian Zionism, many members joined the new Zionist organization. Hibbat Zion was formally disbanded by the Soviets in 1919.

Histadrut (Hahistadrut Haklalit Shel Haovdim Beeretz Israel; General Federation of Workers in Eretz Israel; subsequently renamed Histadrut Haovdim Beeretz Israel, Federation of Workers in Israel): workers' organization and trade union federation. In addition to its union activities, it operates a bank, several large industrial enterprises, and a health insurance program (Kupat Holim) covering the majority of Israel's residents.

Hussein (1935–1999): king of Jordan, 1953–99. Hussein was born in Amman and educated in Egypt and England. He assumed the throne after his grandfather, King Abdullah, was assassinated in 1951 and his father, Talal, was subsequently declared mentally unfit to rule.

Hussein, Abdullah Ibn (Abdullah I) (1882–1951): emir and king of Transjordan from 1921 until his assassination in 1951. On behalf of the Hashemite family, Abdullah sought to extend his rule into Syria and eastern Palestine. This aim led to a complex involvement in Palestinian affairs, sometimes in cooperation with the Zionists and sometimes as a catalyst of conflict.

Hussein, Saddam (1937–2006): Iraqi Ba'athist President. Hussein was one of the inner circle that seized power in a 1968 coup. In 1979 he assumed the presidency and soon controlled all aspects of the Iraqi government. He was deposed during the U.S.-led invasion of Iraq in 2003, and tried and executed in 2006.

Jabotinsky, Zeev Yonah (Vladimir Yevgenievich) (1880–1940): leader of the Revisionist movement. Like Theodor Herzl, Jabotinsky regarded the Jewish Question as preeminently the problem of antisemitism and Jewish suffering. Dissatisfied with the accommodation of the World Zionist Organization to the policies of the Palestine Mandatory administration, Jabotinsky resigned from the Zionist Executive in 1923 and founded the World Union of Zionist Revisionists in Paris in 1925.

Jarring, Gunnar (1907–2002): Swedish ambassador to Moscow appointed by U.N. Secretary General U Thant to be his special representative to the Middle East. Jarring's mission began in November 1967. At first Israel opposed the format of his mission because it desired direct negotiations. Eventually, however, Israel accepted his "shuttle diplomacy" (which served as a model for Henry Kissinger's missions after the Yom Kippur War) as a form of indirect negotiations following the precedent set by Ralph Bunche in 1949. Jarring's mission led to temporary cessations of fighting.

Jewish Labor Committee (est. 1934): organization founded by American Socialist Zionist organizations and Jewish trade unions. At first it existed to coordinate efforts to help Jewish labor organizations in Europe. Today it coordinates political activities on issues of mutual concern to its constituent organizational members.

Johnson, Lyndon Baines (1908–1973): president of the United States, 1963–69. As vice president, Johnson assumed the presidency when John Fitzgerald Kennedy was assassinated. He was elected in his own right in 1964 and served during a turbulent period in U.S. history marked by domestic violence, the civil rights struggle, dissent over the Vietnam War, and the Six-Day War.

Johnston, Eric (1896–1963): American businessman sent by President Dwight Eisenhower to seek an Arab-Israeli agreement regarding the distribution and utilization of the waters of the Jordan River. His mission lasted from 1953 to 1955 and successfully laid the groundwork for a de facto agreement between Israel and Jordan.

Joseph (Bernard), Dov (1899–1980): early leader of Mapai. In pre-state years Joseph worked closely with Moshe Sharett in the Jewish Agency's Political Department. Joseph was military governor of Jerusalem, 1948–49, and from March 1949 until January 1966 he held various cabinet positions.

Jumayyil, Bahir (1947–1982): Lebanese Phalange leader elected as president in 1982 but assassinated before his term of office began. Before the election, Jumayyil was president of the Ashrafiyah sector of the Phalange and commander in chief of the United Lebanese forces; he was friendly to Israel. Following his assassination, his brother Amine Jumayyil (b. 1942) became president of Lebanon. Both are sons of Pierre Jumayyil (1905–1984), a founder of the Phalange in 1936.

Kadishai, Yechiel (b. 1923): Menahem Begin's long-time secretary and the prime minister's chief of staff, 1977–83.

Kennedy, John Fitzgerald (1917–1963); president of the United States, 1961–63. Kennedy was assassinated in November 1963.

Kissinger, Henry Alfred (b. 1923): national security adviser to President Richard Nixon, 1969–74, and U.S. secretary of state under presidents Nixon and Gerald Ford, 1973–77. Kissinger was born in Germany to Jewish parents who fled to the United States after the Nazis came to power. Before entering government service he taught international relations at Harvard University. As secretary of state he became particularly concerned with U.S. policy in the Middle East and orchestrated the various policies and diplomatic efforts during and after the Yom Kippur War. His style of conducting foreign relations by personal visits to the principals involved allowed him both to carry out indirect negotiations and to pursue U.S. interests in the area. In 1973 Kissinger won the Nobel Peace Prize for helping to bring an end to the Vietnam War.

Klinghoffer, Hans (1905–1990): renowned legal scholar, a former Austrian diplomat who immigrated to Israel in 1953 and served in the Knesset, 1961–73.

Kol Israel (Voice of Israel): Israeli government broadcasting service. Immediately before independence, Kol Israel was established as the illegal radio station of the Haganah. After independence, control of the broadcasting service was maintained by the Ministry of the Interior and later by the Office of the Prime Minister. In 1965 the independent Israel Broadcasting Authority (IBA) was established by the government to ensure greater freedom in broadcasting. The extent of the IBA's autonomy has become a political issue on several occasions.

Kol, Moshe (1911–1989): leader of the Progressive Party and the Independent Liberal Party. Kol was a member of the Provisional Government and was the Independent Liberal representative in the Labor government, 1965–77.

Kollek, Theodore (Teddy) (1911–2007): mayor of Jerusalem, 1965–93, and formerly director general of the Office of the Prime Minister, 1952–64. Kollek began his career in Mapai, followed David Ben-Gurion to Rafi, and rejoined the Labor party.

Kook, Abraham Isaac (1865–1935): early Religious Zionist leader and the first Ashkenazi chief rabbi of Mandatory Palestine, 1921–35. Kook established his own religious academy, later named Merkaz Harav, which became a training center for Religious Zionist youth movements, especially Bnei Akiva. His son Rabbi Zvi Yehudah Kook (1891–1982) was head of the Yeshivat Merkaz Harav.

Krinitzi, Avraham (1886–1969): one of Israel's longest serving heads of municipalities, Ramat Gan, 1926–69.

Laskov, Haim (1919–1982): leading Israeli military figure and chief of staff, 1958–61. Laskov was a member of the Agranat Commission, which, following the Yom Kippur War, investigated the military's lack of preparedness. He has served for many years as the army's chief ombudsman.

Lavon, Pinhas (1904–1976): defense minister, 1954–55, who resigned due to a conflict with prime minister Moshe Sharett as well as his involvement in the intelligence debacle in Egypt—the Mishap (Haparshah)—in which a group of Egyptian Jews were convicted of spying for Israel. Lavon was general secretary of the Histadrut, 1949–50, 1956–61; member of the Knesset, 1949–61; minister of agriculture, 1950; and minister without portfolio, 1952–54.

Left Poalei Zion: early Marxist Zionist Party that opposed cooperation with "bourgeois Zionism." Based in Eastern Europe, it had a negligible impact on Palestinian affairs. In 1946 it merged with Ahdut Haavodah.

Lehi (acronym for Lohamei Herut Israel, Freedom Fighters of Israel; often referred to as FFI and the Stern Gang): underground military organization formed in 1940 by Avraham Stern, a student at the Hebrew University, after a split in Etzel. Lehi formed the Fighters' list, headed by Natan Friedman-Yellin (Yelin-Mor), during the elections to the First Knesset.

Levin, Nahum (1905–1967): member of the Knesset, 1955–65.

Levy, Moshe (b. 1936): chief of staff of Israel Defense Forces, 1983–87.

Liberal Party: formed in 1961 through a union of the Progressive Party and the General Zionists. The General Zionists appealed primarily to the middle classes and businessmen. Unlike the Revisionists, they had not rejected the World Zionist Organization or the Jewish Agency; unlike the Progressives, they were generally not willing to cooperate with Mapai. In 1965 the Liberal Party joined with Herut to form Gahal, but a significant faction, comprised primarily of former Progressive Party members, seceded to form the Independent Liberal Party (IL), which failed to win a Knesset seat in the 1981 elections. In October 1982 the Independent Liberals joined the Labor alignment as a faction. In 1999 Labor ran under an umbrella party "One Israel" with Meimad and Gesher and in 2001 it ran with Meimad.

Likud (Union): right-wing electoral and parliamentary alliance formed in late 1973 by Gahal with the Free Center (which had earlier split from Gahal), the State list (formed in 1969 by David Ben-Gurion and members of Rafi who refused to join the Labor Party), and a part of the Greater Land of Israel movement. In 1977 the Likud gained a plurality and formed a new government led by Menahem Begin.

Lubrani, Uri (b. 1926): senior official in the Israeli Foreign Ministry and Prime Minister's Office. Lubrani served as head of the Eastern Europe Department; political secretary to the prime minister, 1952–53; adviser on Arab affairs, 1960–63; head of the Prime Minister's Office, 1963–65; ambassador to Ethiopia; and ambassador to Iran, 1973–78.

Maarakh: Labor alignment of Mapai and Ahdut Haavodah formally approved by both parties in 1965 after Prime Minister Levi Eshkol and Ahdut Haavodah leader Israel Galili reached agreement on November 15, 1964. At the same time David Ben-Gurion split from Mapai and formed a new party, Rafi. After the Six-Day War, in January 1968, Mapai, Rafi, and Ahdut Haavodah united to form the Israel Labor Party (ILP; frequently referred to as the Labor Party). In January 1969 the Labor Party reached an agreement with Mapam and formed a new electoral and parliamentary Labor alignment that lasted until 1988. Thus the term Maarakh (Alignment) actually refers to two separate electoral and parliamentary alliances: the alignment of Mapai and Ahdut Haavodah, 1965–68, and the alignment of the Labor Party and Mapam, 1969–88.

Magnes, Judah Leon (1877–1948): important American Jewish leader who helped to found the American Jewish Committee and led the New York Kehillah before immigrating to Palestine in 1922. He was later chancellor and president of the Hebrew University of Jerusalem. Magnes supported a binational Arab-Jewish state in Palestine, a position that brought him into conflict with other Zionists. He also asserted that support for Jewish settlement in Palestine did not necessarily entail a conviction that all Jews should settle there. Rather, he believed in the strength and vitality of the Diaspora and argued that the Jewish National Home should serve as the cultural-spiritual center of modern Jewish life.

Maki (acronym for Miflagah Kommunistit Israelit, Israeli Communist Party): reformation of the Palestine Communist Party (PKP) in 1948. In 1943 Moshe Sneh's Mifleget Hasmol Hasozialisti joined Maki.

In 1919 the Mifleget Poalim Sozialistim (Socialist Workers' Party) was formed by Socialist Zionists who refused to join Ahdut Haavodah. They rapidly moved away from Zionism in order to be granted membership in the Comintern and formed the PKP, which was recognized by the Comintern in 1924 and expelled from the Histadrut. During the 1940s the PKP was plagued with factionalism and schisms, generally over the nationalist issue. In May 1943 many Arabs left the party to form the Arab League of National Liberation; other schisms occurred as well. In 1944 the reduced (and largely Jewish) PKP was reinstated into the Histadrut. In 1948 most of the factions reunited to form Maki.

In 1965 Maki split into two separate parties. One faction, led by Moshe Sneh and Shmuel Mikunis, was primarily Jewish and retained the name Maki. The other faction, led by Meir Vilner and Toufiq Toubi, was primarily Arab and formed Rakah (Reshimah Kommunistit Hadashah, New Communist List). At first both parties were recognized by Moscow, but soon only Rakah had that distinction. In the 1973 elections Maki combined with the Tkhelet Adom (Blue-Red) faction of Siah to form Moked (Focus). In 1977 Maki joined the Shelli coalition.

Makleff, Mordekhai (1920–1978): Israeli chief of staff, 1952–53. Makleff's pre-state military experience was with the Jewish police and in the British army. He was a member of the Israeli delegation to the Rhodes armistice negotiations, indirect talks between the U.N. mediator and the belligerents that led to the 1949 armistice agreements.

Mapai (acronym for Mifleget Paolei Eretz Israel, Israeli Workers' Party): major political party of the Labor movement and the dominant political party in Israel until May 1977. Mapai was formed in 1930 as a merger of Ahdut Haavodah and Hapoel Hatzair. In 1965 David Ben-Gurion led a faction away to form Rafi. In January 1968 these three parties reunited to form the Israel Labor Party. In its early years Mapai was social-democratic; in recent years it has encompassed factions with more liberal-centrist ideological orientations but has remained nominally social-democratic. The party won the elections in 1992 and 1997, but lost again in 2001 and 2005.

Mapam (acronym for Mifleget Hapoalim Hameuhedet, United Workers' Party): Marxist Zionist party with roots in the pioneer Zionist youth movement Hashomer Hatzair (Young Guard). Hashomer Hatzair was formed in Europe during World War I. Beginning in the 1920s its members founded collective settlements, which formed the federation Hakibbutz Haarzi. Eventually the Hashomer Hatzair became a Marxist Zionist party stressing the role of kibbutzim in the building of the national Jewish homeland and in the class struggle of the workers in that new society. Mapam was formed in 1947 and formally established in early 1948 as a merger of Ahdut Haavodah and Hashomer Hatzair. Both groups desired their merger prior to independence in order to challenge Mapai's hegemony over the Labor movement. In 1954 most members of Ahdut Haavodah left to reorganize their party. In January 1969 Mapam joined the Labor Party in an electoral coalition, thus forming the second Maarakh, or Labor alignment.

Marcus, David (1902–1948): American Jewish colonel who was recruited to advise the Israeli army during the War of Independence. Marcus was smuggled into Palestine in January 1948 under the name Michael Stone. Two weeks after independence he became supreme commander of the Jerusalem front. On June 19, 1948, he was accidentally killed by an Israeli watchman.

Mazpen (Compass): publication of the Israeli Socialist organization and the name by which the organization is commonly known. The Israeli Socialist organization originated as a faction of Maki that was expelled in 1962 and became a small anti-Zionist, anti-imperialist faction of the Israeli Left. It criticized Maki for its lack of commitment to revolutionary socialism. Similarly it refused to give its unqualified support to the Palestine Liberation Organization because of its "petit-bourgeois" leadership. Mazpen did not run in national elections; it urged its members and supporters to vote for Rakah (or, in recent years, the Democratic Front for Peace and Equality) as the best alternative.

Meimad (acronym for Jewish State, Democratic State): moderate religious party founded by Rabbi Yehuda Amital, Rabbi Aaron Lichtenstein, Yitzhak Yaeger, and Yishayahu Privas to compete against what they perceived as right-wing supernationalists.

Meir (Myerson), Golda (1898–1979): Israeli prime minister, 1969–74. During the course of her long political career, most of which was as a leader in Mapai, Meir headed the Political Department of the Jewish Agency. She served as minister of labor, 1949–56, and foreign minister, 1956–59. She was also Israel's first ambassador to the Soviet Union, 1948–49. Meir's legacy is blemished by the Yom Kippur War which happened during her tenure as prime minister, and by the debate over her refusal to enter into negotiations with Egypt prior to that war.

Merkaz Hofshi (Free Center): political party and faction that believed Israel should not withdraw from territories conquered in 1967, especially from the West Bank. In early 1967 Shmuel Tamir led a secession of a number of Herut members from Gahal and formed the Free Center, which won two seats in the 1969 elections. In 1973 the party joined the Likud. During the Eighth Knesset the Free Center allied itself with the State list and the Greater Land of Israel movement to form the Laam faction within the Likud. In October 1967 a faction led by Tamir joined the Democratic Movement for Change.

Mossberg, Kurt (1903–1983): pioneering Israeli industrialist in the fields of metals, ceramics, and elevators. Mossberg headed the Israeli-German and Israeli-Japanese trade associations and for many years chaired the board of directors of the Eretz-Israel Museum.

Movement for Greater Israel (also called Greater Land of Israel movement, Greater Israel movement, and Land of Israel movement): organization that emerged after the Six-Day War and was devoted to preventing territorial compromise out of the belief that all of Eretz Israel should be under Israeli sovereignty. Its leaders included Israel Eldad and Eliezer Livneh.

Movement for Peace and Security: organization of liberal and leftist academics who believed that peace could be obtained only by recognizing the Palestinian rights of national self-determination and by territorial compromise on the part of the Israeli government. Established shortly after the Six-Day War, the Movement for Peace and Security seemed to draw on the same network from which the Brit Shalom had drawn earlier and from the Peace List, which ran in the 1969 elections.

Nahal (acronym for Noar Haluzi Lohem, Fighting Pioneer Youth): special corps in the Israel Defense Forces that combines military and agricultural training in order to establish new settlements, usually in border areas.

Namir, Mordechai (1897–1975): general secretary of the Histadrut, 1950–56. Namir later served as minister of labor, 1956–59, and as the mayor of Tel Aviv, 1960–69. He was a member of Knesset, 1951–69, and Israel's second ambassador to the Soviet Union, 1949–50.

Nahmias, Yosef (b. 1912): inspector general in the Israeli police force, 1958–64. Nahmias served as Israeli ambassador to Brazil, 1964–66, and later as a deputy mayor of Tel Aviv, 1969–73.

Nasser, Gamal Abdul (1918–1970): president of Egypt, 1954–70. A key member of the conspiratorial group of officers who overthrew King Farouk in 1952, Nasser soon emerged as the leader of the new regime and generated a new movement—Nasserism—that swept most of the Arab world. He emerged as a leader of the Third World bloc at the 1955 Bandung Conference.

National Religious Front: coalition formed in 1948 of Mizrahi, the Religious Zionist organization, and its Labor wing Hapoel Hamizrahi. In the elections to the First Knesset, the National Religious Front joined with the two other religious parties, Agudat Israel and Poalei Agudat Israel, to form the United Religious Front. Since that time Hamizrahi and Hapoel Hamizrahi have run on their own joint lists. In 1956 the two organizations merged to form the National Religious Party (also called Mafdal, acronym for Miflagah Datit Leumit; in English, NRP). The party and its predecessors have participated in most Israeli governments. In the 1950s and 1960s the NRP was interested primarily in the relationship between religion and state, but in the 1980s and 1990s it made the support for Jewish settlement in the territories one of its major concerns. In 2006 the NRP ran in a joint list with the National Union Party.

Navon, Yitzhak (b. 1921): president of Israel, 1978–83. During the course of his public and political career, Navon served as a diplomat in the Israeli Foreign Ministry, David Ben-Gurion's secretary, a member of the Knesset, and chairman of the Knesset's Committee on Foreign and Security Affairs. Navon joined Rafi when it split from Mapai and rejoined the Labor Party when the factions reunited. In September 1982, following the Phalange massacre of Palestinians in the Sabra and Shatila neighborhoods in that part of Beirut under Israeli occupation, President Navon publicly called for the establishment of an Israeli Commission of Inquiry. Navon was the only

Israeli president who re-entered politics after completing his tenure in the largely symbolic position of president. Navon was reelected to the Knesset, 1984–92, and served as minister of education and deputy prime minister, 1984–90.

Neeman, Yuval (1925–2006): prominent figure in Israeli defense and intelligence establishments, also a well-known physicist and professor. Neeman was deputy commander of the Givati Brigade in 1948. He then became deputy director of the Operations Section of the General Staff and director of the Planning Section. In 1958 he was the military attaché to London. Neeman was an active member of the Likud in the 1970s, but in 1979 he left the Likud and formed a new party, Hatehiyah. In 1982 he reentered the Likud coalition and became minister of science—a position created for him.

Nehru, Jawaharlal (1889–1964): prime minister of India, 1957–64, and a leader of the Bandung Conference. Nehru was a leading advocate of Third World neutralism during the Cold War. As India's minister of defense, 1953–57, he supported the withdrawal of Western troops from Suez in 1956.

Nir (Rafalkes), Nahum Yaakov (1884–1968): leader of the pre-state Socialist Zionist movement and a member of the Provisional State Council. Nir represented Mapam (and later Ahdut Haavodah) in the Knesset.

Nixon, Richard Milhous (1913–1996): president of the United States, 1969–74. Nixon resigned in disgrace in August 1974 following the Watergate scandal. Nixon had served as Dwight D. Eisenhower's vice-president, 1953–61.

Palestine Liberation Organization (PLO): coordinating council for Palestinian organizations. The PLO was founded in 1964 by the First Arab Summit Conference, as an instrument of the Arab states rather than a genuine Palestinian organization, but since its takeover by al-Fatah, headed by Yasir Arafat, in 1969, has been an umbrella organization based on a coalition of constituent organizations but actually dominated by al-Fatah.

For most of its history the PLO maintained that the Palestinian Problem should be solved through the destruction of the State of Israel and the establishment of a Palestinian state. In pursuit of that goal the PLO turned to armed struggle and initiated multiple terrorist attacks against Israeli civilians in the 1970s and 1980s. Initially, the PLO launched these attacks from its headquarters in Jordan, and after 1970 from Lebanon. In 1982 Israel launched a war against the PLO in Lebanon, and as a result the organization's headquarters and personnel relocated to Tunisia.

In the early 1990s the organization changed its course and adopted a more conciliatory policy. This shift was the result of new regional and global realities—the fall of the Soviet Union and the Persian Gulf War (1991)—as well as the organization's inability to achieve its original goals by force. In 1993 the PLO and Israel signed an interim peace agreement that gave the organization limited control in parts of the West Bank and Gaza and was intended to lead to a final status accord.

Despite the establishment of a Palestinian Authority in these territories, the PLO was not disbanded, and many of its operatives assumed positions in the new self-governing authority. The PLO's chairman, Yasir Arafat, headed the Palestinian Authority from its establishment until his death in 2004. With the collapse of the Israeli-Palestinian peace agreement in 2000, many PLO operatives resumed their involvement in the armed struggle and terror activities. With the victory of Hamas over Fatah in the 2006 parliamentary elections, the PLO's position in the Palestinian Authority declined.

Palmach (acronym for Plugot Mahaz, Strike Companies or Shock Force): elite unit of the

Haganah comprised of well-trained soldiers ready to carry out special assignments, including commando operations. Founded in 1941, it was headed by Yigal Allon during the War of Independence and always retained very close relations with the left wing of the Labor movement; it drew its recruits from Hakibbutz Hameuhad. In 1948 David Ben-Gurion disbanded the Palmach and integrated it into the Israel Defense Forces, thereby protecting the new state against the politicization of an important section of its armed forces and protecting Mapai's hegemony over the Labor movement. The left wing of the Labor movement (e.g., Hakibbutz Hameuhad and Mapam) opposed this action.

Peres, Shimon (b. 1923): Israeli president since July 2007. Peres has been an Israeli politician for more than fifty years. Peres has been a member of the Knesset since 1959, and among the many positions he has held are prime minister, 1984–86, and leader of the Labor Party, 1977–90, 1995–97, and 2003. In 1994 he was awarded the Nobel Peace Prize. Like Moshe Dayan, Peres's public and political career developed through his close association with David Ben-Gurion. Considered a superb technocrat, Peres forged the alliance with France and helped shape the defense establishment. After serving as director general of the Defense Ministry, he became deputy minister of defense, 1959–65. Peres's influence declined in the mid-1960s as Ben-Gurion's influence waned. With Ben-Gurion and Moshe Dayan, Peres formed Rafi in 1965. Following the creation of the Labor Party, Peres served as immigrant absorption minister, 1969–70; transportation minister, 1970–74; and defense minister, 1974–77. After Rabin's resignation in 1977, Peres became the leader of the Labor Party until Rabin's victory in the primaries of 1992. Peres became foreign minister in the government formed by Rabin in 1993, and as such was the architect of the Oslo Accords with the Palestinians. After Rabin's assassination in November 1995, Peres became prime minister but lost the parliamentary elections of 1996. In the ensuing years Peres has been at one and the same time the elder statesman of Israeli politics and an active politician. He left the Labor Party in 2006 and joined Ariel Sharon and Ehud Olmert in the Kadima Party.

Phalange (est. 1936): military and political organization rooted in Lebanon's Maronite Christian community.

Progressive Party: small party, formed in 1948, that was antisocialist but willing to cooperate with Mapai and joined some of the early coalition governments. In 1961 the Progressives and General Zionist Party merged to form the Liberal Party. In 1965 the Liberal Party split. The minority, led by Yizhar Harari and coming largely from the former Progressive Party, created the Independent Liberal Party (IL). In 1981 the Independent Liberal Party failed to win enough votes to receive representation in the Knesset and subsequently joined the Israel Labor Party in October 1982.

Qaddafi, Muamar al- (b. 1941): Libyan military and political leader. Qaddafi studied history and military science at Ghazi University and in Britain. In 1969 he participated in the coup in Libya that overthrew the monarchy, and he was promoted to commander in chief of the army. In January 1970 he became prime minister and minister of defense.

Qawuqji (Kaukji), Fawzi al- (1897–1976): Arab political and military leader. Qawuqji served in the Ottoman army and gained fame in the anti-French rebellion of 1925. In August 1936 he was recruited to make a cohesive force out of Arab bands engaged in terror during the Arab Revolt. During the War of Independence he retained a force of troops, loyal to himself, called the Arab Liberation Army. It was defeated in Operation Hiram in October 1948.

Rabin, Yitzhak (1922–1995): Israeli prime minister, 1974–77, and 1992–95. Rabin joined the Palmach in 1941. Just before the War of Independence he took command of the Second Brigade and shortly thereafter of the Palmach force defending Jerusalem. After the war he continued his military career, becoming chief of staff of the Israel Defense Forces, 1964–68. He then entered politics and was ambassador to the United States, 1968–73, and minister of labor, 1974. He became prime minister in 1974 following Golda Meir's resignation. Rabin served as minister of defense in the national unity government, 1984–90, and was re-elected prime minister in 1992. After leading Israel to peace accords with the Palestine Liberation Organization (1993) and Jordan (1994), in 1995 he was assassinated by an Israeli who objected to his vision of peace.

Rafi (acronym for Reshimat Poalei Israel, Israel Workers' List): originally a faction, led by David Ben-Gurion, within Mapai but wishing to submit a separate list for the elections. After faction members were expelled from Mapai, Rafi became a separate party. The leaders were David Ben-Gurion, Shimon Peres, Yosef Almogi, a cabinet member and secretary general of Mapai, 1959–62, and later Moshe Dayan. Most of Rafi united with Mapai (and Ahdut Haavodah) in January 1968 to form the Israel Labor Party, but another faction, the Reshimah Mamlakhtit (State List, or National List) remained independent, only to later join the Likud alignment. The State List, much of the Greater Land of Israel movement, and the faction of the Free Center that had remained in the Likud formed the Laam (For the People) faction within the Likud. The former Rafi members left the Likud January 12, 1981.

Raphael, Gideon (1913–1999): high-ranking Israeli foreign service official. Raphael headed the Political Department of the Jewish Agency, 1943–47. After independence he was a member of Israel's permanent delegation to the United Nations, 1948–53. Raphael rose to become the director general of the Ministry of Foreign Affairs. Subsequently he was the senior political adviser to the foreign minister, 1972–73, and ambassador to the United Kingdom, 1973–78.

Reagan, Ronald Wilson (1911–2004): president of the United States, 1981–89.

Remez, Aharon (1919–1994): first commander of the Israel Air Force. Remez later served in the Ministry of Foreign Affairs, 1960–68, as ambassador to Great Britain, and was chairman of the Ports Authority and of the Airports Authority.

Rimalt, Elimelech (1907–1987): member of the Knesset, 1951–77. Trained as a rabbi, Rimalt was minister of post, 1969–70, and chairman of the Liberal Party, 1971–75.

Rogers, William Pierce (1913–2001): U.S. secretary of state, 1969–73. Rogers was the author of the plan that led to a cease-fire in the War of Attrition.

Rokach, Israel (1896–1959): member of the Knesset, 1949–59. Rokach had been mayor of Tel Aviv, 1936–53.

Rosen, Pinhas (Felix Rosenblueth) (1887–1978): member of the Knesset, 1949–69, minister of justice, 1949–61. A German army officer in World War I, Rosen was an early leader of the German Zionist movement and emigrated to Palestine at the age of thirty-nine. In 1941 he was co-founder of a party that sought to represent German immigrants—Aliyah Hadashah (New Immigration). In 1948 Rosen helped found the centrist Progressive Party. He was a member of the Provisional Government and early cabinets.

Ross, Dennis (b. 1949): American diplomat. Ross served as the point man for the United States in various Israeli-Arab negotiations during the 1990s, first as director of the Policy Planning Staff at the State Department and later as Special Middle East Coordinator for President Bill Clinton.

Rubin, Hanan (1908–1962): member of the Knesset, 1949–62, representing the left-wing Mapam Party. Rubin was an active member of the German Socialist party before immigrating to Palestine in 1933.

Rusk, Dean David (1909–1994): U.S. secretary of state, 1961–69, under Presidents John F. Kennedy and Lyndon Johnson.

Sadat, Muhammed Anwar al- (1919–1981): president of Egypt from September 1970 until he was assassinated on October 6, 1981. Sadat was a co-conspirator with Gamal Abdul Nasser and Mohammad Naguib in the Officers' Revolt that overthrew King Farouk in 1952. In the years following he was in and out of the inner circles around Nasser and was vice-president just before succeeding Nasser. After the Yom Kippur War, Sadat oriented Egyptian foreign policy toward the United States and abandoned Nasser's pan-Arabism—as evidenced, for example, in the change of Egypt's official name from the United Arab Republic to the Arab Republic of Egypt. Following his trip to Jerusalem in 1977 and the Camp David Accords in 1978 (doc. 103), Sadat shared the Nobel Peace Prize with Menahem Begin.

Sadeh, Yitzhak (Landsberg) (1890–1952): founder of the Palmach. Sadeh began his military career in the Russian army during World War I and then, as a company commander, in the Red Army. A Socialist Zionist, he emigrated to Palestine in 1921 and became a leader of the Haganah. Sadeh commanded the Palmach from its beginning in 1941 until 1945. During the War of Independence he commanded the Eighth Armored Brigade. After the war he left the army and assumed a leading role in Mapam.

Sapir, Pinhas (1909–1975): leader of Mapai and the Labor Party. When Levi Eshkol became prime minister in 1963, Sapir inherited Eshkol's position as finance minister and was thus in charge of the country's economic policies. In addition, he dominated Mapai (and subsequently, but to a lesser extent, the Labor Party) either formally as secretary general or by virtue of his actual power. Sapir died in 1975 while serving as head of the Jewish Agency.

Sapir, Yosef (1902–1972): mayor of Petach Tikva, 1940–50, and member of the Knesset, 1949–72. Sapir also served as minister of health, 1952–53; minister of transportation, 1953–55; minister without portfolio, 1967–69; and minister of trade and industry, 1969–70.

Sasson, Eliyahu (1902–1978): a native of Damascus, head of the Arab Department of the Jewish Agency, 1933–48. With the establishment of the State of Israel, Sasson became head of the Middle East Department of the Ministry of Foreign Affairs. He held various ambassadorial and diplomatic positions until 1961, when he joined the cabinet.

Schocken, Gershon (1912–1990): editor and then publisher of the Israeli daily *Haaretz.*

Serlin, Yosef (1906–1974): former private secretary of the Zionist leader Nahum Sokolow and member of the Knesset, 1949–73.

Shaki, Avner (1926–2005): member of the Knesset, most of the time in the NRP.

Shapira, Haim Moshe (1902–1970): early leader of Mizrahi and Hapoel Hamizrahi, the Religious Zionist movement and its Labor wing. Shapira was a member of the pre-state Jewish Agency Executive and early cabinets.

Sharabi, Israel Yeshayahu (1908–1979): member of Knesset, 1949–77, representing Mapai (later Hama'arach, currently Labor). Sharabi served also as minister of post, 1967–69. Sharabi, who was born in Yemen, handled the relationship between the Histadrut (which was controlled by Mapai) and Sephardi Jews early in his career (1934–48).

Sharef, Zeev (1906–1984): cabinet secretary, 1948–57. Later Sharef served as a member of the Knesset, 1965–73; minister of trade and industry, 1966–68, 1969; minister of finance, 1968–69; and minister of housing, 1969–74.

Sharett, Moshe (Shertok) (1894–1965): Israeli prime minister. Sharett was the most important figure in Israel's early foreign relations. Sharett was active in Ahdut Haavodah, the Histadrut, and the Jewish Agency from the early 1920s. From 1930 on he was a member of Mapai. In 1947, as head of the Jewish Agency's Political Department, Sharett was its representative to the United Nations. He then became Israel's first foreign minister, 1948–56. His advocacy of political work and diplomacy, as opposed to reliance on military strength, brought him into conflict with David Ben-Gurion. When Ben-Gurion temporarily resigned, Sharett took over as prime minister, January 1954–November 1955.

Sharon, Ariel (Arik) (b. 1918): Israeli prime minister, prominent Israeli general, and politician. Sharon made his mark as an outstanding and unconventional strategist and field commander. His successes in the Yom Kippur War helped launch his political career. Although he had nominally belonged to Mapai, he left that party when he entered national politics. In 1977 he formed the Shlomzion Party and joined Menahem Begin's government as minister of agriculture. He was placed in charge of the government's controversial settlement policy. In 1981 he ran on the Likud list and became minister. In the aftermath of the 1982 War in Lebanon, the Kahan Commission of Inquiry recommended that he resign his ministerial post (see doc. 109). In 1983 he resigned as defense minister and became minister without portfolio. He then served as minister of trade and industry, 1984–90; minister of housing, 1990–92; minister of national infrastructure, 1996–98; and foreign minister, 1998–99. In 2001 and again in 2003 he was elected prime minister. In 2005 Sharon left the Likud Party and established the Kadima (Onwards) Party. In early 2006 he suffered a severe stroke and was replaced by Ehud Olmert as prime minister.

Shas: religious party established in 1984 that initially represented Sephardi interests.

Shitrit, Behor (1895–1967): Israeli minister of police, 1949–66. Shitrit began his career in the Mandatory police force, becoming head of the Tel Aviv police in 1927 and chief magistrate of Tel Aviv in 1945. He contributed to the building of the Israeli national police force. He was one of the few leaders from the Sephardi community in Mapai.

Shufman, Yosef (1903–1978): member of the Knesset, 1955–69, and Israel's ambassador to Venezuela, 1971–75.

Siah (acronym for Smol Israeli Hadash, Israeli New Left): leftist organization that emerged from two separate, unrelated groups that happened to choose the same name. Shortly after the Six-Day War, a group of students at the Tel Aviv University who were unhappy with Mapam's joining the Labor alignment formed a new organization around the consensus that Israel had to recognize Palestinian national rights and had to be willing to withdraw from all or most of the conquered territories. Most of these students were members of Hakibbutz Haarzi, and they defined themselves as Zionist. Simultaneously, students of the Hebrew University campus in Jerusalem, many of whom had belonged to Mazpen, Maki, or other non-mainstream socialist organizations, also formed a group they called Siah. This organization was unable to reach a consensus regarding whether it was Zionist, anti-Zionist, or a-Zionist. It did, however, reach a consensus regarding its commitment to socialist ideology and to the necessity of Israeli recognition of Palestinian national rights and withdrawal from all the conquered territories. In the summer of 1970 the two groups merged into one national organization.

Throughout the 1970s Siah, like the rest of the Israeli Left, split into factions that reunited in new coalitions. Moken, Shelli, and Shasi received most of Siah's members at various times.

Sisco, Joseph John (1919–2004): U.S. assistant undersecretary of state in charge of the Near East and South Asia, 1969–74, and undersecretary of state for political affairs, 1974–76.

Sneh, Moshe (Kleinbaum) (1909–1972): leader of Maki, the Israeli Communist Party. Sneh began his political career in Europe as a member of the liberal-centrist General Zionists. He was chief of staff of the Haganah, 1940–46. In 1947 he joined the Marxist Mapam Party and was avowedly pro-Soviet. In 1953 he formed a small splinter party, Mifleget Hasmol Hasozialisti (Socialist Left Party), which soon merged with Maki. In 1965 Maki split into two factions. Sneh's faction, which retained the name Maki, became independent and critical of Moscow.

Tabenkin, Yitzhak (1887–1971): ideological leader of Ahdut Haavodah in the 1920s and leader of the Siah Bet faction in the 1930s and 1940s. After the Six-Day War, Tabenkin became one of the leaders of the Greater Land of Israel movement. He served as a member of the Knesset, 1949–51 and 1955–59.

Tamir, Yosef (b. 1915): member of the Knesset, 1965–81. Tamir was a triple gold medalist in the first Maccabi games (the Jewish Olympics) and one of Israel's leading environmental activists.

Tito, Joseph Broz (1892–1980): prime minister of Yugoslavia, 1945–53, and president from 1953 until his death. Although Tito emerged as a leading European communist in the Yugoslavian underground during World War II, he pursued policies independent of Moscow. He was a leader of the Bandung Conference and an advocate of neutralism.

Truman, Harry S (1884–1972): president of the United States, 1945–53. Truman was the U.S. president who recognized the State of Israel within minutes of the declaration of statehood.

U Thant (1909–74): Burmese diplomat who was secretary general of the United Nations, 1961–71.

United Nations Emergency Force (UNEF): U.N. military force established in late 1956 and early 1957 to promote a rapid withdrawal of English, French, and Israeli troops from the Sinai Peninsula and Gaza. The UNEF remained a buffer between Israel and Egypt until Nasser requested its removal in 1967.

United Nations Relief and Works Agency (UNRWA): agency established by the United Nations on December 8, 1949 (U.N. General Assembly Resolution 312 [IV]) to provide assistance and relief to Palestinian refugees and administer refugee camps. UNRWA was not mandated to deal with the political problem per se.

Uzan, Aharon (b. 1924): successor to Aharon Abuhazeira as minister of labor, social affairs, and immigrant absorption. Uzan, who was born in Tunisia, was a member of the Labor Party secretariat and a general secretary of the Tnuat Hamoshavim (Moshav movement). In 1975 he became minister of immigrant absorption before inheriting Abuhazeira's portfolio.

Uziel, Baruch (1901–1977): member of the Knesset, 1961–69. Uziel had been born in Greece and immigrated to Palestine in 1914.

Warhaftig, Zerah (1906–2002): leader of Hapoel Hamizrahi and the National Religious Party. Warhaftig served in many cabinets and was one of the major figures in the Religious Zionist movement in Israel. He retired from the Knesset following the 1981 elections.

Weizmann, Chaim (1874–1952): most prominent figure in the Zionist movement from the end of World War I. Weizmann worked closely with the British Government on preparing the Balfour Declaration. Weizmann was president of the Zionist Organization, 1920–31, 1935–46, and the president of the State of Israel from 1949 until his death.

Women's International Zionist Organization (WIZO): worldwide Zionist service organization established in London in 1920. Its Israeli branch, particularly since the establishment of the State of Israel, has been responsible for administering an extensive range of services and institutions that serve women, their children and families, particularly in development areas. Its candidate, Rachel Kagan, was elected to the First Knesset.

World Jewish Congress (WJC; est. 1936): umbrella organization representing Jewish communal organizations throughout the world. Its greatest achievement is the role it played in bringing about the Luxembourg Agreement.

World Union of Zionist Revisionists: established in Paris in 1925 by Zeev Jabotinsky as a parallel set of institutions to oppose the "official Zionism" of the Zionist Organization and its "organic" approach, advocated by Chaim Weizmann, for slowly building the Jewish national home. Jabotinsky demanded a radical revision of this policy and called upon the Zionist movement to set as its unequivocal objective the immediate establishment of a sovereign "Jewish State within its historic boundaries" and to prepare for the evacuation of the Jewish masses to the state. Etzel and the Herut movement emerged from the Revisionist organizations.

Yadin (Sukenik), Yigael (Yigal) (1917–1984): Israeli chief of operations during the War of Independence and the country's second chief of staff, 1949–52. In 1953 Yadin joined the faculty of the Hebrew University's archaeology department. His work as an archaeologist, particularly on the Dead Sea Scrolls, Hazor, and Masada, sustained his prominence as a national figure. In 1956 he won the Israel Prize for Jewish Studies. In 1977 he formed the Democratic Movement, which merged with the Movement for Change in a successful election campaign. The movement's disintegration was largely caused by Yadin's decision to join Menahem Begin's Likud-led coalition. Yadin became deputy prime minister in Begin's first government, 1977–79.

Yariv, Aharon (1920–1994): leader in the Labor Party and later head of the Center for Strategic Studies at Tel Aviv University. Yariv's military career began in the pre-state years and culminated in his appointment as military attaché to the United States, 1957–60, and director of military intelligence, 1963–72. During the 1970s he served in Labor governments as minister of transportation, 1974, and minister of public affairs, 1974–75. He was a member of the Knesset, 1973–77.

Yehuda, Israel Bar (1895–1965): politician who represented Mapam in the first two Knessets (1949–55), and Ahdut Haavodah in the following three (1955–65). He also served as minister of the interior, 1955–59, and as minister of transportation, 1963–65.

Zimmerman, Zvi (1915–2006): member of the Knesset, 1951–65. Zimmerman was a partisan who fought the Nazis in World War II. He served as Israel's ambassador to New Zealand, 1981–85.

Zisman, Shalom (1914–1967): deputy mayor of Ramat Gan, 1944–67, and member of the Knesset, 1951–55.

Index

Italicized page numbers indicate where major figures, events, and organizations are identified.